GLOBAL CIVIL SOCIETY 2003

Mary Kaldor, Helmut Anheier and Ma[illegible]

OXFORD
UNIVERSITY PRESS

Great Clarendon Street, Oxford OX2 6DP

Oxford University Press is a department of the University of Oxford.
It furthers the University's objective of excellence in research, scholarship,
and education by publishing worldwide in

Oxford New York

Auckland Bangkok Buenos Aires Cape Town Chennai
Dar es Salaam Delhi Hong Kong Istanbul Karachi Kolkata
Kuala Lumpur Madrid Melbourne Mexico City Mumbai Nairobi
São Paulo Shanghai Taipei Tokyo Toronto

Published in the United States
by Oxford University Press Inc., New York

First published 2003

British Library Cataloguing in Publication Data
Data available

Library of Congress Cataloging in Publication Data
Data available

ISBN 019-926655-7 (hbk)
ISBN 019-926656-5 (pbk)

Original design in Rotis
by Hardlines, Charlbury, Oxford
Page layout by
Ben Cracknell Studios
Printed in Great Britain
on acid-free paper
by The Bath Press Ltd, Bath, Avon

Foreword

There are four times as many democratic systems in the world today as there were twenty-five years ago – even taking into account the fact that there are more states in absolute terms. There is a structural reason for this. We are living in something like a global information society: people are no longer passive citizens, they want to be much more active with regard to their own lives.

This is the third of the LSE's yearbooks on global civil society, which analyse and describe the various forms this new activism takes—the ways in which individuals try to participate in and influence global developments. They fill an important gap in research on globalisation.

Global Civil Society 2003 is inevitably coloured by the disagreements over Iraq, especially those across the Atlantic and between politicians and global civil society. This disagreement—this tremendous fissure—came primarily from unresolved problems which we haven't thought through and which are essentially left over from the Cold War period. One might call these the residual problems of 1989. I think we have only gradually come to realise how thoroughly the Cold War defined our institutions.

Global Civil Society 2003 does attempt to illuminate some of these problems and also to explain why we have taken so long to identify them. The conceptual chapters by Martin Shaw and Ulrich Beck argue that, in order to enable people to understand the world today and to further the making of realistic and ethically sound policy decisions, the social sciences need to be revolutionised, shedding their continuing preoccupation with the nation-state. What these authors call 'methodological nationalism' blinds us to the experience of everyday life for many millions of people and prevents us from developing more relevant contemporary interpretations of what is happening.

Many of the themes in *Global Civil Society 2003* offer an alternative way of thinking about the world. One such theme is the rise of what the authors call 'regressive globality'. What they mean by this is the strategy of those groups and governments that favour globalisation only to the extent that it is judged to benefit them. 'Regressive globality' applies to the unilateralism of the Bush Administration, which is neither isolationist nor imperialist; rather, it makes use of global strategies of pre-emption and counter-proliferation in a perceived national interest. 'Regressive globality' also applies to the rise of religious and nationalist groups that are described in Chapter 7. These are the groups that have spawned a new type of geo-political terrorism. Unlike terrorist groups in the past that were largely local or national, these groups may have local, national, or regional goals, but they have to be understood as a response to globalisation, to the impulses that cause individual citizens to be more active. And their methods and strategies depend on the infrastructure of globalisation—global media, Internet, global funding, and so on.

A second theme is the challenge to multilateralism. How do you achieve legitimacy in the international system? I believe it is done quite simply through rules: impersonal rules that are observed by everyone. That is why the WTO is particularly important. It is a rule-bound organisation, and it is extremely important that China and Taiwan have signed up, and that Russia has signalled its wish to do so. Chapter 4, on global trade, describes the dangerous challenges to the WTO that come on the one hand from regressive globality and on the other hand from rejectionists within the anti-capitalist movement who dream of going back to state-bound social-democratic utopias. This combination could undermine global institutions, and might instead lead to a 'wild-west' anarchic trade regime that would in fact give the rich and powerful in the world even more scope to exploit the weak and poor than the present system does.

A similar theme characterises Chapter 5 on chemical and biological weapons. It suggests that multilateral treaties, rather than beefed-up 'homeland defence' or pre-emptive disarmament, are still the best way to combat the threat of biological and chemical weapons. It urges the small and academically inclined civil society community engaged in biological and chemical disarmament to take up campaigning in ways that have much more grassroots and popular appeal.

Despite these disturbing developments, *Global Civil Society 2003* also has an optimistic message. The various data-gathering efforts that have been undertaken show that the infrastructure of global civil society is, after decades of growth, extensive and solid, and that global mobilisation, in the form of the anti-war movement and the social forums, is unprecedented. A similar message emerges from the chapters on violence against women and on peasants' networks. The chapter on violence against women celebrates the way in which women's groups have come together globally on this issue and the successes they have booked at the international level, although it also discusses remaining divisions within the movement and suggests that the movement should now shift from a predominantly legal to a social-policy paradigm. The chapter on transnational peasants' movements challenges the idea that global civil society is primarily an urban middle-class phenomenon. It describes how, especially in the last decade, peasants and small farmers have become active in a plethora of networks to oppose what they perceive to be common threats, such as the European Union's Common Agricultural Policy and the Free Trade Area of the Americas.

Despite all this, civil society, locally and globally, continues to be fragile in the face of government interference and repression. The final chapter discusses the legal environment in which civil society finds itself in different parts of the world, and the international legal framework underpinning the protection of civil society. It outlines the features of a model legal framework that would give civil society legal security but also protect the public interest without constraining civil society.

As was the case in previous years, the Yearbook is the outcome of a process involving seminars, discussion groups and workshops among the authors as well as activists and practitioners. Members of the team have participated in the World Social Forum in Porto Alegre as well as the World Economic Forum in Davos and numerous other events where global debates take place. This year, the project has, in particular, benefited from collaboration with the University of California, Los Angeles, where one of the editors has established a new Center for Civil Society. We hope this collaboration, as well as cooperation with other universities, including Delhi, Witwatersrand, and Cairo, will be extended.

Global Civil Society 2002 was a gripping read. *Global Civil Society 2003* again promises to be stimulating, informative, and authoritative. I am delighted to be able to introduce and recommend this book.

Anthony Giddens

Director, London School of Economics and Political Science
30 May 2003

Acknowledgements

The production of this Yearbook depends on the support, input, and contributions of numerous individuals and organisations. We endeavour to acknowledge them all in these pages. The final publication of course remains the responsibility of the editors.

Editorial Committee

Helmut Anheier, Marlies Glasius (managing editor), Mary Kaldor, Dominick Jenkins, Hagai Katz (map editor), Yahia Said, Hakan Seckinelgin, Sally Stares (data programme editor), Jill Timms.

Consultations

Methodological Nationalism Seminar, 26–27 June 2002: Input on Chapters 2 and 3
Ulrich Beck, Elisabeth Beck-Gernsheim, Nancy Cartwright, Meghnad Desai, Rom Harré, David Held, Daniel Levy, Herminio Martins, Eleonora Montuschi, Mariza Periano, Julian Reiss, Simon Roberts, Emma Rothschild, Saskia Sassen, Jan Aart Scholte, Hakan Seckinelgin, Richard Sennett, Martin Shaw, Sally Stares, Natan Sznaider, Jill Timms, Peter Townsend.

The Dark Side of Civil Society: Fundamentalist and Ultra-Nationalist Movements, Seminar, 28 November 2002: Input on Chapter 7
Eileen Barker, Stephen Bruce, Catherine Fieschi, Montserrat Guibernau, Harry Goulbourne, Jeff Haynes, Christopher Husbands, Mark Juergensmeyer, Denisa Kostovicova, Diego Muro, Anna Prazmowska, Hakan Seckinelgin, Zhand Shakibi, Anthony Smith, Jill Timms.

Other input

Special contributions
Neera Chandhoke (chapter update), James Deane (chapter update), Catherine Fieschi (guest box), Dominick Jenkins (guest boxes), Jarmila Juhasova (tables), Josh Kaldor-Robinson (guest box), Denisa Kostovicova (guest box), José Manuel Mata López (guest box), Melanie Beth Oliviero and Adele Simmons (chapter update), Nadia McLaren (tables), Mario Pianta and Federico Silva (parallel summits), Frances Pinter (chapter update), Saskia Sassen (chapter update), Hakan Seckinelgin (chapter update), Jill Timms (chronology).

Correspondents: Input on chronology
Yeshaiahu Ben Aharon, Mustapha Kamel Al-Sayyid, Mulya Amri, Brian Appelbe, Reine Borja, Joabe Cavalcanti, Hyo-Je Cho, James Deane, Bernard Dreano, Mary Fischer, Louise Fraser, Nihad Gohar, Habib Guiza, Anil Gupta, Vicky Holland, Hagai Katz, Zafarullah Khan, Svetlana Kuts, Silke Lechner, Natalia Leshchenko, Maritza Lopez-Quintana, Maite San Miguel, Nuria Molina, Alejandro Natal, Beatriz Martín Nieto, Mario Pianta, Thomas Ruddy, Yahia Said, Trilochan Sastry, Mukul Sinha, Robert Sommers, Toralf Staud, Elena Tonkacheva, Kate Townsend, Eduard Vallory, Caroline Walker.

Others who provided input or support
Vittorio Agnoletto, Kees Blokland, Anne-France Borgeaud Pierazzi, Mary Blair, Simon Buralls, John Clark, Wendy Cruz, Julie Emond, Arry Fraser, Addy Free, Sharon Heilman, Fiona Hodgson, Dru Oja Jay, Daniel Jennings, Karen Joyce, Rob Kerr, Hetty Kovach, Denisa Kostovicova, Robbie Liben, Vittorio Longhi, Paula Marshall, Doug Miller, Caroline Neligan, Mike Oliver, Tammy Parrish, Suzanne Rosselet-McCauley, Gunther Schönleittner, Mark Smith, Wojtek Sokolowsky, Hilary Wainwright.

Research and editorial assistance
Louise Gaskell, Dominick Jenkins, Marcus Lam, Hagai Katz, Amarjit Singh.

Administrative support
Joanne Hay, Rita Kumar Field, Jane Schiemann, Laurie Spivak.

Design and production
Ben Cracknell Studios, Norwich (page design and make-up), Michael James (copy editor), Gary Hall (indexer).

Photographers
Melanie Conner (front cover), Sidsel Aas, Simone Bruno, Anders Gunnartz, Marcelo Jr, Paul Natkin, Peter Rossett, Purna Sen, Paul Smith, Chris Tordai, Rob van Gelder.

Advisory Board

Financial support

We gratefully acknowledge the financial support of the following organisations:

The Atlantic Philanthropies
BP
John D. and Catherine T. MacArthur Foundation
Rockefeller Brothers Fund
Rockefeller Foundation
University of California, Los Angeles

Contents

Part IV: Records of Global Civil Society

Figures

Maps

Tables

Records
Data Programme

Contributors

Helmut Anheier is Professor at the School of Public Policy and Social Research at the University of California, Los Angeles (UCLA), and Director of the Center for Civil Society at UCLA. He is also a Centennial Visiting Professor at the Department of Social Policy, London School of Economics and Political Science (LSE). His work has focused on civil society, the non-profit sector, organisational studies and policy analysis, and comparative methodology. He is a founding editor of *Voluntas* and author of over 200 publications in several languages. His present research examines the emergence of new organisational forms in global civil society, the role of foundations, and methodological aspects of social science research on globalisation.

Ulrich Beck is Professor of Sociology at University of Munich and Centennial Visiting Professor at the Department of Sociology, LSE. His works include *Risk Society* (1986), *Counterpoison* (1991), *Ecological Enlightenment* (1992), and *Ecological Politics in an Age of Risk* (1994). He is also a regular contributor to the *Frankfurter Allgemeine Zeitung.*

Meghnad Desai has recently retired as Professor of Economics and Director of the Centre for the study of Global Governance at the LSE. He was created Lord Desai of St Clement Danes in 1991, and continues to be active in the House of Lords. His most recent publications include *Money, Macro-economics and Keynes, Essays in Honour of Victoria Chick* (2 vols), edited with P. Arestis and S. Dow (Routledge, 2002) and *Marx's Revenge: The Resurgence of Capitalism and the Death of Statist Socialism* (Verso, 2002). A collection of his writings on India is due to be published by OUP India, and at present he is writing books on the Indian film director, Dilip Kumar, and on the British author, Ezra Pound.

Marc Edelman is Professor of Anthropology at Hunter College and the City University of New York Graduate Center. He has taught at Yale and Princeton, as well as in a community oral history program on New York's Lower East Side. He has done research on agrarian history, rural development, social movements, and the nineteenth- and twentieth-century roots of nationalism and contemporary politics in Latin America. His books include *The Logic of the Latifundio* (Stanford, 1992) and *Peasants Against Globalization* (Stanford, 1999). His present research interests include transnational peasant and small farmer networks in Latin America, the United States and Canada, and Europe.

Daniel Feakes is a Research Fellow at the Science and Technology Policy Research Unit (SPRU) at the University of Sussex, where he works for the Harvard Sussex Program (HSP) on Chemical and Biological Warfare Armament and Arms Limitation. He spent three years as a researcher for HSP in the Organization for the Prohibition of Chemical Weapons (OPCW). His recent publications include book chapters on export controls under the Chemical Weapons Convention and journal articles on its verification system and the collapse of the Biological Weapons Convention Protocol negotiations. He is now beginning a project on the establishment of the OPCW in collaboration with the former Executive Secretary of its Preparatory Commission.

Richard Fries has been a Visiting Fellow at the Centre for Civil Society, LSE, since he retired as head of the Charity Commission, the regulatory body for charities in England and Wales, in 1999. He is chair of the International Center for Not-for-profit Law (ICNL), a Washington-based body promoting enabling civil society laws worldwide. Before becoming Chief Charity Commissioner in 1992 he was a career civil servant in the Home Office, responsible for government policy on charity and the voluntary sector from 1987 to 1991. He is involved in a number of civil society law initiatives in Britain and around the world.

Marlies Glasius is a Research Officer at the Centre for the study of Global Governance, LSE, and managing editor of this Yearbook. In 1999 she published *Foreign Policy on Human Rights: Its Influence on Indonesia under Soeharto* (Intersentia). Forthcoming publications include *The International Criminal Court: A Global Civil Society Achievement* (Routledge, 2004) and *Exploring Civil Society: Political and Cultural Contexts* (Routledge, 2003), co-edited with David Lewis and Hakan Seckinelgin. Her present research interests include global civil society, social forums, the International Criminal Court, and economic and social rights. She is also an organiser of the London Social Forum.

Mary Kaldor is School Professor and Programme Director of the Global Civil Society Programme at the Centre for the study of Global Governance, LSE. Her book *Global Civil Society: An Answer to War* (Polity Press) was published in 2003. Her work *New and Old Wars: Organised Violence in a Global Era* (1999) has been translated into seven languages. She was a founder member of European Nuclear Disarmament (END), founder and Co-Chair on the Helsinki Citizen's Assembly, and a member of the International Independent Commission to investigate the Kosovo Crisis, established by the Swedish Prime Minister and chaired by Richard Goldstone, which published the *Kosovo Report* (Oxford: OUP) in autumn 2000. Her present research interests include global civil society and the changing nature of war.

Hagai Katz is a Research Associate at the UCLA Centre for Civil Society, where he recently co-authored a report on the non-profit sector in LA, and a doctoral student in Social Welfare at UCLA. He is also special reader in the Department of Urban Planning at UCLA, where he teaches Geographic Information Systems (GIS). Previously he was Deputy Director of the Israeli Center for Third-Sector Research (ICTR) at the Ben Gurion University of the Negev, Israel, where he established a national database on non-profit organisations and published extensively on Israel's third sector and civil society.

Diego Muro holds a Lectureship in Spanish and European Politics at the Department of Spanish and Spanish-American Studies of King's College, London. He studied political science at the Autonomous University of Barcelona, holds a Master's degree in European Studies from the University of Sussex and is preparing a doctoral dissertation at the LSE. He has been editor of *Studies in Ethnicity and Nationalism* since 1999 and has published two chapters in John Clark's *Globalizing Civic Engagement* (2003). His research interests include Spanish and Basque nationalism, theories of violence, and global civil society.

Yahia Said is a Research Officer at the Centre for the study of Global Governance at the LSE. His experience combines academic research with private sector work and activism. Prior to joining the LSE he worked as a corporate finance consultant with Ernst & Young in Russia. He also worked as a project coordinator with the Helsinki Citizens Assembly in Prague. Yahia Said specialises in issues of economic transition and security in post-communist societies. His publications include 'The New Anti-Capitalist Movement: Money and Global Civil Society', co-authored with Meghnad Desai, in *Global Civil Society 2001* (Oxford University Press, 2001) and *Building Democracy in Iraq*, co-authored with Yash Ghai and Mark Lattimer (Minority Rights Group, 2003).

Purna Sen is a Lecturer in gender and development at the Development Studies Institute at the LSE and a Visiting Research Fellow at the Centre for the Study of Global Governance, LSE. She has been involved in research as well as NGO work in the field of violence against women in a variety of countries, including India, Jordan, Norway, and the United Kingdom. She manages a worldwide research and advocacy programme on sexual abuse within marriage, and has served on the International Tribunal on Violence against Women. Recent publications include 'Enhancing Women's Choices in Responding to Domestic Violence in Calcutta: A Comparison of Employment and Education', *European Journal of Development Research* (December 1999) and 'Sexual Violence', co-authored with R. Jewkes and C. Garcia-Moreno, in *Global Report on Violence* (World Health Organisation, 2002).

Martin Shaw is Professor of International Relations and Politics at the University of Sussex. A sociologist of war and global politics, his books include *Dialectics of War* (Pluto Press, 1988), *Post-Military Society* (Polity Press, 1991), *Global Society and International Relations* (Polity Press, 1994), *Civil Society and Media in Global Crises* (Pinter, 1996), *Theory of the Global State* (Cambridge University Press, 2000) and *War and Genocide: Organized Killing in Modern Society* (Polity Press, 2003). He is editor of www.theglobalsite.ac.uk.

Part I: Concepts of Global Civil Society

Chapter 1

Global Civil Society in an Era of Regressive Globalisation

Mary Kaldor, Helmut Anheier and Marlies Glasius

The first few months of 2003 witnessed a global popular mobilisation on a scale unprecedented in history. On 15 February 2003, some 11 million people demonstrated in approximately 800 cities all over the world (see Map 1.2). A new generation was politicised with young people walking out of school to demonstrate against the war in Iraq. The *New York Times* was moved to describe global civil society as the 'second superpower' (Tyler 2003), and the *New Yorker* magazine (2003) wondered if the mass mobilisation of people on that day amounted to the largest one-day protest in history.

Yet despite this energy, the anti-war movement was defeated. Within a few weeks, the United States and Britain had gone to war with Iraq. The United Nations was sidelined and all major international institutions were deeply divided. In particular, the European Union has been immobilised by divisions of opinion.

A crisis represents a danger and an opportunity. On the one hand, we face the real possibility of the unravelling of the global institutional framework, painfully built up over the last 50 years, but especially in the last decade. This applies both to the framework of economic institutions that establish rules about trade and investment and to the framework of international law, justice, and human rights. Most troubling is that the prohibition against starting wars, first codified in the Kellogg-Briand pact in 1928 and later fortified by the decisions of the Nuremberg court and by the United Nations Charter, has been seriously undermined. This global institutional framework made possible the growth of global civil society—and global civil society helped constitute global institutions. This synergetic relation is now being challenged by what Martin Shaw in Chapter 2 of this Yearbook calls 'regressive globalism', and which we understand as a form of displaced, latter-day particularist (quasi-imperial, nationalist or fundamentalist) thinking in the context of global capitalism.

On the other hand, the mobilisation of global civil society in the first few months of 2003 was by no means an isolated event that could be easily reversed or neutralised. As we show in this chapter, the 1990s were a period of consolidation of global civil society, a period in which a solid infrastructure was established, based on a broad shift in cultural and social values, especially in developed market economies. Indeed, there are signs that the dramatic development of social forums in the early 2000s, the anti-war movement, and other developments may not only indicate continued expansion of global civil society but may also suggest an evolution in institutional terms.

Of course, we do not know how the present crisis of global governance will be resolved. However, we argue in this chapter that it is possible to outline different directions of change, possible scenarios, which depend both on the positions and strategies of global civil society and on the responses of states and global institutions such as the United Nations or the World Trade Organisation. In order to elaborate this argument, we start with some conceptual themes that run through many of the chapters in this Yearbook. They concern how we think about the complex and conflictual nature of global civil society and its relation to globalisation. We then summarise, in more detail than in previous Yearbooks, what we have learned from our data collection effort that accompanies the production of the Yearbooks and is summarised in our records section. The next section deals with the recent popular mobilisation, the rise of social forums and the anti-war movement. And in the final section, we draw some conclusions and set out what this analysis might imply for possible future directions of change.

Conceptual Themes

In the first edition of this Yearbook, published just days before the tragic events of 11 September 2001, we introduced the concept of global civil society to our readers as a useful and ultimately normative concept for depicting what we saw as an emerging reality of global civic action and connectedness. In our initial understanding, the growing transnational character of civil society seemed to offer a positive response, even counterweight, to narrow notions that linked globalisation to economic processes alone; and the concept also seemed to suggest greater participation and involvement of the world's citizens in shaping a common future. At the same time, we argued, the very notion of a global civil society runs up against the conventional political discourse of a world seemingly dominated by nation-states, and is at odds with the conceptual frameworks and methodological toolboxes of the social sciences (see Chapters 2 and 3).

Aware of the terminological tangle that had developed around the concept of global civil society, we offered a working definition of it as the sphere of ideas, values, organisations, networks, and individuals located primarily outside the institutional complexes of family, market, and state, and beyond the confines of national societies, polities, and economies. At first sight, this working definition might appear rather abstract—or, rather, 'usefully abstract', as we would like to think—but what it suggests is ultimately straightforward: global civil society is about people, organisations, and the values and ideas they represent, but with the major difference that these are, at least in part, located in some transnational arena and not bound or limited by nation-states or local societies.

We are conditioned to believe that nations take stands in international politics en bloc, that governments represent the views of the nation, and that what other people in that country might think is domestic politics

We also emphasised the normative implications of the concept. Global civil society is also about the meaning and practice of human equality in an increasingly unjust world, and about the complex debate on how individual human beings can develop their own capabilities to meet their needs. It is also about searching for, and developing, new forms of civic participation and involvement in a globalising world; it is about finding and giving 'voice' to those affected by old, new, and emerging inequities in the broadest sense, and providing a political and social platform for such voices to be heard. Global civil society is about civic engagement and civic-mindedness in a transnational, potentially global sphere; it is about private action for public benefit however defined. It is an arena for people to express different views, values, and interests, and to agree or disagree about them.

Methodological nationalism

An important theme of this Yearbook is 'methodological nationalism', a term introduced independently by Shaw (2000), Scholte (1999), and Beck (2000). We often read, for example, that Germany and France were against waging war on Iraq, while the British and the Americans were in favour. It is in this reified way that the media explain world politics to us, and it is in this way that we often talk amongst ourselves, wondering whether 'the Italians' might change sides, and what 'Turkey' will do. It seems so natural to equate government positions with the entire country so that, irrespective of the millions of people marching against the war in Britain or Italy, we continued to speak of 'the British' and 'the Italians' on the basis of their government's position. It is hard to even notice that there is something absurd in the complaints of American academics and activists against American (rather than US government) imperialism (see, for instance, Schiller 1998; Mokhiber and Weissman, 2001).

We are conditioned to believe that nations take stands in international politics en bloc, that governments represent the views of the nation, and that what other people in that country might think is domestic politics and irrelevant at the international level. It is conceivable to us that the anti-war mood in Britain might bring down Tony Blair, but we still find it much more difficult to imagine that it might change the dynamics of international decision-making. In our first yearbook, and in reference to Shaw (2000) and Beck (2000), we termed as *methodological nationalism*[1] this deeply entrenched world view that affects everyday language, journalism, and the media as much as it does the social sciences and policy analysis. In this Yearbook, we further refine the concept in essays by Shaw and Beck. Shaw, who compares the old way of doing social science to 'stamp-collecting', pleads for a deep inter-

[1] This nationalism is not a fanatical insistence on the superiority of one nation over another; it means to consider nation-states as the natural and only way to divide up the world. As the 'prime divisor', it takes precedence over all other possible categorisations.

disciplinarity, a global social science in which disciplines are just building blocks. Beck gives us the example of social inequality to show that the myopia of methodological nationalism is not just unhelpful, but ends up being immoral because we can see only small inequalities within nation-states and are blind to global inequalities. Beck insists on a 'methodological cosmopolitanism' to underpin new social science research and teaching.

This is not just an academic discussion but also a matter of great political and practical importance. How scientists do research, what kind of research gets funded, how university professors and secondary-school teachers teach, and what textbooks they use ends up determining how decision-makers, journalists, activists, ordinary people see the world and how they think. It is for this reason that we find it so very difficult to shake the habit of thinking about states as if they were single actors: this is how we have been brought up and taught. The direction of social science therefore determines whether present and future generations will have an analytical toolkit that is appropriate for their decision-making in the twenty-first century context. This is important for policy-makers at all levels, but above all for transnational activists, whose goals and methods simply disappear from view in the methodological nationalist framework.

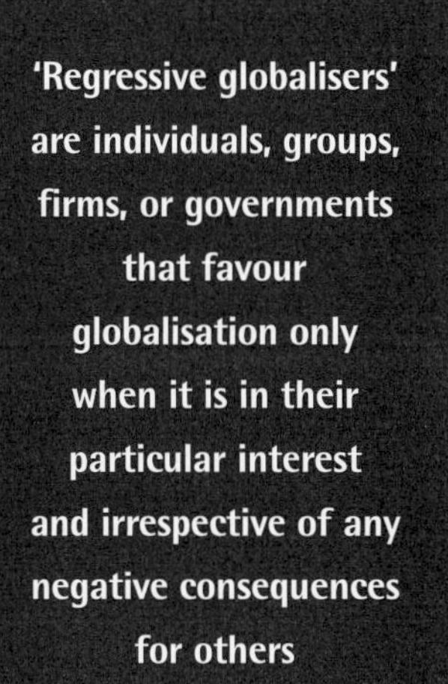
'Regressive globalisers' are individuals, groups, firms, or governments that favour globalisation only when it is in their particular interest and irrespective of any negative consequences for others

In producing the Yearbook, our goal is to engage in the 'global social science' or 'methodological cosmopolitanism' Shaw and Beck call for. Fortunately, we are not alone in this and, as Shaw acknowledges, a transformation of the social sciences is under way. In contrast to standard globalisation research, we emphasise the importance of individual agency in globalisation, and focus on what could be described as 'globalisation from below'. Specifically, the Global Civil Society Yearbooks try to break through conventional social science boundaries by:

- *challenging methodological nationalism.* Both in our choice of subject matter and in our methodology, we try to delineate and illuminate what is both non-governmental and transnational;
- *overcoming disciplinary fragmentation.* Because there is no specific discipline devoted to civil society, nor is any discipline the 'most natural' or dominant one, we experiment with a mix of lenses and methodologies; and
- *building bridges between research, policy, and practice.* Our aim is to create a space for self-reflection and debate about the role of global civil society for practitioners, activists, policy-makers, and researchers alike.

Positions revisited: regressive globalism

While the idea of a global civil society still seems to us as relevant as ever, it is also clear that the global political environment has changed. An important new concept in this respect, proposed by Shaw in Chapter 2, is that of *regressive globalism.* In our first Yearbook, we categorised positions on globalisation in terms of Supporters, Reformers, Alternatives, and Rejectionists—a categorisation close to that of Held et al. (1999: 10). These positions reflect the preferences of actors and organisations in global civil society as well as those of political parties, governments, and individuals. In the course of our research, it has become clear that there are very few 'out and out' Supporters, that is to say, groups or individuals who favour all forms of global connectedness (trade, finance, migration, law, and politics); there are also very few 'out and out' Rejectionists, i.e. people who oppose all forms of connectedness and seek to return to some form of nation-state nirvana however defined.

Rather, the dominant responses to globalisation are mixed. We have therefore revisited the two other positions, and added a new one: *regressive globalisers.* These are individuals, groups, firms, or even governments that favour globalisation when it is in their particular interest and irrespective of any negative consequences for others. Regressive globalisers see the world as a zero-sum game, in which they seek to maximise the benefit of the few, which they represent, at the expense of the welfare of the many, about which they are indifferent at best. What we call Reformers or redistributive

Table 1.1: Positions on globalisation revisited

Globalisation of:	Supporters	Regressives	Reformers	Rejectionists
Economy	*For*: As part of economic liberalism. E.g. *The Economist*; Thomas Friedman	*Mixed*: If beneficial to own country or group and leading stakeholders. E.g. French farmers; British fuel protest; US Administration	*Mixed*: If leading to greater social equity. E.g. ATTAC; Fair trade cooperatives; Novib; Jubilee 2000	*Against*: Greater protection of national economies needed. E.g. 50 Years is Enough; Walden Bello; Ralph Nader
Technology	*For*: As part of of open competition for technological innovation. E.g. gene and plant technologists	*Mixed*: For in economic terms and for military and security purposes, against for social or environmental purposes. E.g. private sector scientists and business associations	*Mixed*: If beneficial to broader groups and the marginalised E.g. Treatment Action Campaign; Copyleft	*Against*: Technology threatens local communities and traditional ways of life. E.g. Friends of the Earth; Aids sceptics; Vandana Shiva
Law	*For*: With emphasis on international commercial law and human rights legislation; role for International Criminal Court	*Against*: For if facilitating private investment and trade but generally against. Emphasis on strengthening national laws on property rights and domestic democracy; no role for International Criminal Court. E.g. anti-Kyoto lobby	*For*: Building global rule of law not solely dependent on sovereign states. Pronounced role for International Criminal Court. E.g. Amnesty; Women's Caucus for Gender Justice	*Against*: Undermines national sovereignty and democracy. E.g Euro-sceptics (left & right); anti-humanitarian intervention(left & right) such as Noam Chomsky, Samuel Huntington
People	*For*: Open border policy, e.g., *The Economist*	*Mixed*: For immigration for economic and domestic needs but against for asylum seekers or people of other cultures and ethnicities	*For*: Open policy. E.g., Genoa Social Forum; European Council on Refugees and Exiles	*Against*: Closed border policy. E.g. European anti-immigrant parties; Australian government

globalisers are groups or individuals who favour 'civilising' or 'humanising' globalisation; in other words, Reformers favour those dimensions of globalisation that benefit the many.

As can be seen from Table 1.1, the Regressive globalisers occupy a somewhat contradictory policy position between Supporters and Rejectionists. In cases where Supporters are generally for the globalisation of the economy, technology, law, and people movements, and Rejectionists against, the Regressive globalisers come out with mixed messages or conditional policy statements. They are for globalisation if it strengthens their national positions and/or if it is likely to benefit key political stakeholders, electoral groups, or particular communities. If, however, globalisation processes could potentially weaken stakeholder institutions and in particular national sovereignty, or otherwise threaten the interests of powerful lobby groups or ethnic or religious groups, Regressive globalisers become very similar to Rejectionists.

Regressive globalisers favour globalisation only if it strengthens their national positions, and if it is likely to benefit key political stakeholders, electoral groups, or particular communities

Regressive globalisation has become much more visible since 11 September and this is why the environment for global civil society has become so much more inhospitable. It has in fact become the new doctrine of a unilateralist Bush White House, a policy position which both Reformers and Supporters regard as a nineteenth-century reaction to twenty-first century problems. The re-emergence of nation-state thinking with pro-market economic policies and minimalist government leads to greater emphasis on international security concerns and assertiveness about domestic values. One important area in which this new policy manifests itself is that of biological and chemical weapons, discussed in Chapter 5. On the one hand, the Bush Administration raises the spectre of biological and chemical terrorism as a justification for increased defence spending and 'pre-emptive strikes', on the other hand it has rejected a new protocol to improve multilateral monitoring of biological weapons capacities.

Regressive globalism also characterises the religious and nationalist groups that are described in Chapter 7. These groups favour nation-state thinking; yet they organise transnationally and indeed are growing both as a reaction to the insecurities generated by globalisation and because they are able to mobilise by making use of the new global media and funding from Diaspora groups. Regressive globalists tend also to promote masculine, aggressive cultures where women have a traditional and passive role to play. In this respect, they also present new challenges for the movement that combats violence against women, described in chapter 6.

At the same time, however, the growth of social forums and the anti-war movement represents what social movements theorists call a 'political opportunity structure' (see McAdam 1996; Diani and McAdam, 2003)—a framework where individuals can participate and engage in global debates. In particular, as we argue, the social forums have become the institutionalisation of the 'newest social movements', from the so-called anti-capitalist movement to environmental concerns and Internet-based forms of activism. The activists who are engaged in these new movements are, in fact, divided between Rejectionists and Reformers. In the anti-war movement, for example, there are those who oppose all forms of state-based humanitarian engagement, believing that this a legitimisation for imperialism. And in the economic field, there are those who oppose free trade and free capital movements. There are also of course those who want to strengthen the capabilities of multilateral institutions to deal with humanitarian emergencies and to contribute to global justice. A big concern in this Yearbook, spelled out in Chapter 4 on trade by Desai and Said, is that the former group, the Rejectionists, might combine with the Regressives to squeeze out the possibilities for a more humane form of globalisation.

Manifestations of global civil society

One of the main characteristics of global civil society, celebrated by some, deplored by others, is its multifaceted nature. We believe it is helpful to think about global civil society not just in terms of the positions it takes but also through the various forms in which it manifests itself. The different manifestations,

Table 1.2: Manifestations of global civil society

Forms	Main actor	Of primary interest to	Example
New Public Management: Civil society organisations as sub-contractors to robust national and IGO policy-making	NGOs and devolved government	Supporters and Reformers	Oxfam, World Vision, Save the Children
Corporatisation: Civil society organisations partnering with companies	NGOs and TNCs	Supporters and Reformers	Nike and GreenPeace; Starbucks and World Wildlife Fund
Social capital or self-organisation: civil society building trust through networking	NGOs and associations; alternatives	Reformers; Rejectionists; Regressives	Community building organisations, faith-based communities
Activism: civil society monitoring and challenging power-holders	Movements, transnational civic networks	Reformers and Rejectionists	Global Witness; Corporate Watch; Social Forums

summarised in Table 1.2, play different roles in the triad of market, governance, and civil society.

The first is the *new public management* manifestation, which is part of the modernisation of welfare states currently under way in most developed market economies, and is, via World Bank, EU, and IMF policy prescriptions, also affecting the rudimentary social welfare systems in developing countries and transition economies. At the international level, new public management is replacing conventional development assistance policies (Deacon, Hulse, and Stubbs 1997; Clark 2003) and seeks to capitalise on what is viewed as the comparative efficiency advantages of non-profit organisations through public-private partnerships, competitive bidding, and contracting under the general heading of privatisation (McLaughlin, Osborne, and Ferlie, 2002).

The main actors, according to this approach, are the professionalised organisational components of global civil society, in other words NGOs and INGOs. Prompted in part by growing doubts about the capacity of the state to cope with its own welfare, developmental, and environmental problems, analysts across the political spectrum have come to see NGOs as strategic components of a middle way between policies that put primacy on 'the market' and those that advocate greater reliance on the state (Giddens 1999). Institutions like the World Bank (Fowler 2000), the United Nations (UNDP 2002) or the European Union (Commission of the European Community 1997) together with bilateral donors and many developing countries are searching for a balance between state-led and market-led approaches to development, and are allocating more responsibility to INGOs. In fact, as shown below, service provision has been the fastest growing area of INGO activities in the 1990s.

With the rise of new public management, the emphasis on NGOs as service providers and instruments of privatisation casts them at the international level essentially in a subcontracting role. NGOs have become instruments of national and international welfare state reform guided by the simple equation of 'less government = less bureaucracy = more flexibility = greater efficiency' (see Kettle 2000). Hence, this approach is typically associated with the Supporters and Reformers of globalisation.

To some, the public management manifestation is associated with co-option (Chandhoke 2002). This takes different forms. In some cases, NGOs are artificially created as a fig-leaf for states unable or unwilling to act, especially in failed states. In other cases, NGOs are supported if not created by international institutions, and then hand-picked for consultation rounds to provide a semblance of democratic legitimacy for the institution (K. Anderson 2000).

Increasing and more frequent *corporate* facets are the second manifestation of global civil society. This has to do with the 'corporatisation' of NGOs as well as the expansion of business into local and global civil society. As Perrow (2001; 2002) argues, corporations use extended social responsibility programmes to provide, jointly with non-profits, services previously in the realm of government (e.g. health care, child care, and pensions, but also community services more widely). On the other hand, NGOs 'professionalise'; under pressure from management gurus they increasingly adopt corporate strategies, as well as being increasingly open to partnerships with business. We suggest that the corporatisation of NGOs will gather momentum, encouraged by a resource-poor international community eager to seek new forms of cooperation, particularly in development assistance and capacity building.

Given that over one third of the world's 100 largest 'economies' are transnational corporations (TNCs), there are growing 'points of contact' between global businesses and global civil society organisations, in particular INGOs like Greenpeace, the World Wildlife Fund, Oxfam, and World Vision—the global brand names of civil society. TNCs and INGOs work together in addressing global problems (e.g., environmental degradation, malnutrition, low skills and education levels) but also many local issues in failed states and areas of civic strife and conflict.

NGOs 'professionalise': under pressure from management gurus they increasingly adopt corporate strategies, as well as being increasingly open to partnerships with business

Yet it is not only in the developing world that global business and INGOs are forging partnerships. In some ways as a backlash to, in other ways as an implication of, neo-liberal policies and 'lean states', public opinion in developed market economies is expecting greater corporate responsibility and 'caring' about the societies in which they operate. Increasingly, as Oliviero and Simmons (2002) point out, this goes beyond adherence to principles of corporate governance and some core of conduct; it implies greater emphasis on service delivery to employees and their communities (e.g., educational programs, child care), addressing negative externalities or 'bads' of business operations (e.g., pollution, resource depletion), and public goods (health, sustainability). Willingly or reluctantly, companies and NGOs team up to divide responsibilities the state is failing to meet. This approach is typically associated with Supporters and Reformers of globalisation.

A third manifestation is *social capital* or self-organisation. Here the emphasis is not so much on management as on building relations of trust and cohesion. The idea is that norms of reciprocity are embodied in transnational networks of civic associations. What is important, according to this approach, is that self-organisation across borders creates social cohesion within transnational communities. In contrast to the basically neo-liberal role NGOs assume in the public management manifestation, they are now linked to the perspective of a 'strong and vibrant civil society characterised by a social infrastructure of dense networks of face-to-face relationships that cross-cut existing social cleavages such as race, ethnicity, class, sexual orientation, and gender that will underpin strong and responsive democratic government' (Edwards, Foley, and Diani 2001:17). Norms of reciprocity, citizenship, and trust are embodied in national and transnational networks of civic associations. Put simply, the essence of this manifestation is: civil society creates social capital, which is good for society and good for economic development.

According to this thinking, NGOs are to create as well as facilitate a sense of trust and social inclusion that is seen as essential for the functioning of modern societies both nationally (e.g. Putnam, 2000; 2002; Anheier and Kendall 2002; Dasgupta and Serageldin 2000; Halpern 1999; Offe and Fuchs 2002) as well as transnationally (Lindenberg and Bryant 2001; see Edwards and Gaventa 2001). The main argument is that participation in voluntary associations, including social movements, creates greater opportunities for repeated 'trust-building' encounters among like-minded individuals, an experience that is subsequently generalised to other situations such as business or politics. Thus, what could be called the neo-Tocquevillian case for NGOs is largely an argument based on the positive and often indirect outcomes of associationalism.

The term 'social capital' is associated with the Supporters of globalisation, who see the creation of transnational social capital as good for political stability and international business. But it is also relevant to the Regressives, who create trust and bonding among transnational religious or ethnic groups, what Putzel (1997) has called the 'dark side of social capital'. And it is relevant for Reformers as well. In our first Yearbook, we included a category of 'Alternatives' in addition to the positions of Reformers, Rejectionists, and Supporters of globalisation. What we meant by this were groups of people who choose to organise their own communities and represent alternative ways of living—local barter schemes, for example, or ecologically responsible communities. The category of 'Alternatives' is more appropriately treated as a form of global civil society organisation than a position. Someone who adopts an alternative lifestyle could be a Reformer (ecological experiment), Rejectionist (protecting the local), or Regressive (orthodox religious communities).

In the activist manifestation of global civil society, social movements, transnational civic networks, and social forums are a source of dissent, challenge, and innovation, a countervailing force to government and the corporate sector

The final form is the *activist manifestation*. Here the main actors are social movements, transnational civic networks, and social forums. They are a source of dissent, challenge, and innovation, a countervailing force to government and the corporate sector (see, for instance, Howell and Pearce 2001; Keane 2001). They serve as a social, cultural, and political watchdog, keeping both market and state in check, and they contribute to and reflect the diversity, pluralism, and dynamism of the modern world. This approach includes Rejectionists and Reformers and, in so far as religious and nationalist militant groups are active, Regressives as well.

The first two approaches—new public management and corporatisation—are more top-down and professional. As we shall show, they dominated global civil society during the last decade, and are important in providing the infrastructure for global civil society. The second two approaches—social capital and activism—are more bottom-up and have again become important in recent years. They tend to provide the mobilising impetus and agenda-setting component of global civil society.

The Contours of Global Civil Society: Portrait and Interpretation

In the context of the dramatically changed geopolitical situation and the rise of regressive globalism since the first edition of the Yearbook, it is important to gain a better understanding of the major contours of global civil society. To this end, we will revisit and expand our initial analysis (Anheier, Glasius, and Kaldor 2001: 4–12) and look closer into the scale, scope, and changing composition of global civil society over time. We will also examine its relationship to other aspects of the globalisation process, in particular economic globalisation and international law. We will summarise our findings under five headings, following our working definition and the notion that global civil society includes an institutional and organisational infrastructure, values and ideas, and individuals willing to participate and contribute to it.

The infrastructure of global civil society

The infrastructure of global civil society includes a vast array of NGOs, voluntary associations, non-profit groups, charities, and interest associations, in addition to more informal or less permanent ways of organising such as Diaspora networks, dot.causes, or social forums. INGOs account for a large part of the formal part of that infrastructure. Quantitative information on the scale of INGO operations is still patchy and limited to very basic indicators such as numbers of organisations and fields of activity. The limitations of organisational counts become clear when we put the number of the some 48,000 NGOs that were included in the Union of International Associations database in 2001 (UIA 2002/3: 3) in relation to the UNCTAD (2001) estimates of over 60,000 TNCs for the same year. Although the respective numbers of organisations seem not far apart, measures of economic scale would obviously dwarf the NGO totals. At the same time, as many have argued, NGO presence, operations, and impact are not primarily about economic measures. Non-economic aspects such as membership base, volunteers, clients served, people mobilised, or indicators of achievements in terms of social and political change would be more in line with the organisational characteristics and *raison d'être* of civil society organisations like NGOs.

Scale. Unfortunately, these data are not available to us at the transnational level in any comprehensive way, and we are limited to examining different facets of the phenomenon. One set of information is provided by the Johns Hopkins Comparative Non-profit Project (Anheier and Salamon 2003; Salamon and Anheier 1996) that attempted to measure basic economic indicators on the size of international non-profits in a broad cross-section of countries. These data allow us to fathom at least some aspects of the scale of INGO activities, albeit from a country-based perspective. For the 28 countries for which such data are available INGOs amount to 1–2 per cent of total non-profit sector employment, or 134,000 full-time equivalent jobs. They also attracted a larger number of volunteers, who represent another 154,000 jobs on a full-time basis (see Record 21).

International INGOs benefit more from volunteer commitment and general mobilisation of the population behind particular causes (e.g., human rights, humanitarian assistance, peace and international understanding) than more conventional non-profits

For some countries, it is possible to examine the growth for the 1990s. Employment in French INGOs grew by 8 per cent between 1990 and 1995 (Archambault et al. 1999: 89), over 10 per cent in Germany (Priller et al. 1999: 115), by over 30 per cent in the UK (Kendall and Almond 1999: 188) during the same period. Even though the data are limited, the resulting pattern is in line with some of the other evidence we present below: international non-profit activities have expanded significantly and, while they continue to represent only a small portion of national non-profit economies, their share has nonetheless increased.

In terms of revenue structure, the international non-profits, as measured by the Johns Hopkins team, receive 29 per cent of their income through fees and charges, including membership dues, 35 per cent from both national and internal governmental organisations in the form of grants and reimbursements, and 36 per cent through individual, foundation, or corporate donations. With volunteer input factored in as monetary equivalent, the donation component increases to 58 per cent of total 'revenue', which makes the international non-profit field the most 'voluntaristic and donative' part of the non-profit sector after religious non-profit (73 per cent) and far more than is the case for domestic service-providing non-profits.

This suggests that INGOs benefit more from volunteer commitment and general mobilisation of the population behind particular causes (e.g., human rights, humanitarian assistance, peace and international understanding) than more conventional non-profits in social services, culture and the arts, or housing, which are increasingly financed by the public sector and commercial revenue sources.

The pronounced donation and volunteer element applies also to INGOs of significant size and with complex organisational structures that increasingly span many countries and continents (Anheier and Themudo 2002; Anheier and Katz in this volume). Examples include Amnesty International with more than 1 million members, subscribers, and regular donors in over 140 countries and territories. The Friends of the Earth federation combines about 5,000 local groups and 1 million members (see Map M2 in methodological chapter). The International Union for the Conservation of Nature brings together 735 NGOs, 35 affiliates, 78 states, 112 government agencies, and some 10,000 scientists and experts from 181 countries in a unique worldwide partnership. Much of the international coordinating work involved is done on a volunteer basis.

As Figure 1.1 shows, the share of NGOs in official aid flows has increased significantly since the 1970s. At that time NGO aid as share of all aid flows from OECD countries to developing countries was 11 per cent. Since then the INGO share has doubled, with most of the gain in the 1990s, a period which coincides with the significant expansion of INGO operations more generally. What is more, INGO contributions increased in both relative and absolute

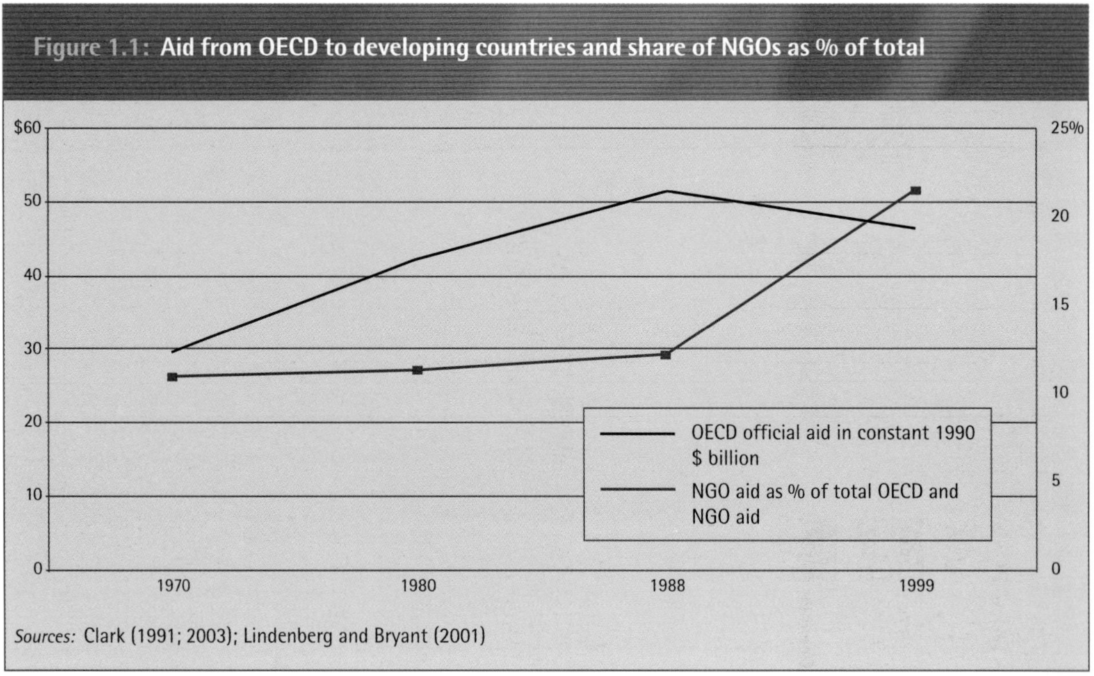

Sources: Clark (1991; 2003); Lindenberg and Bryant (2001)

terms as official aid flows decreased, as Figure 1.1 illustrates.

The change in the economic weight and political importance of INGOs is highlighted even further when we look at the composition of INGO aid flows, using estimates compiled by Clark (2003: 130). Whereas in the 1980s INGOs increasingly become an additional circuit of official development and humanitarian assistance flows, jumping from 44 per cent to 55 per cent of total aid between 1980 and 1988, the 1990s saw a remarkable reversal: official aid flows declined overall, both directly (bilateral and multilateral) and indirectly via INGOs. In 1990 dollars, official grants to INGOs fell from $2.4 billion in 1988 to $1.7 billion in 1999. By contrast, private donations, including individual, foundation, and corporate contributions, more than doubled from $4.5 billion to $10.7 billion. These figures underscore the significant expansion of INGOs in the changing development field of the 1990s, and the major private mobilisation effort they represent.

The infrastructure of global civil society is, of course, broader than that of INGOs in development and humanitarian assistance. The most comprehensive data coverage of INGOs is provided by the UIA in Brussels. Indeed, as we stated in the first edition of this Yearbook (Anheier, Glasius, and Kaldor 2001: 4), the data indicate a sustained rise in the number of NGOs since the 1970s (see also Anheier and Themudo 2002: 194; Keck and Sikkink 1998).

Dispersal. The growth of INGOs and their organisational presence is, of course, not equally spread across the world. Not surprisingly, Europe and North America show the greatest number of INGOs and higher membership densities than other regions of the world (see Map M4 in the methodological chapter). And even though, as we will show, cities in Europe and the United States still serve as the NGO capitals of the world, a long-term diffusion process has decreased the concentration of NGOs so that they are now more evenly distributed around the world than ever before.

There are several ways to illustrate the greater reach of global civil society's infrastructure. Figure 1.2 shows the growth in membership for different world regions. As is to be expected, INGO memberships increased in all regions, but more in some than in others. The highest expansion rates are in central and eastern Europe, including central Asia, followed by East Asia and the Pacific. The growth in central and eastern Europe is clearly linked to the fall of state socialism and the introduction of freedom of association, whereas the growth in Asia is explained by economic expansion and democratic reform in many countries of the region. Figure 1.3 adds a

Figure 1.2: Percentage growth in INGO membership by region, 1990–2000

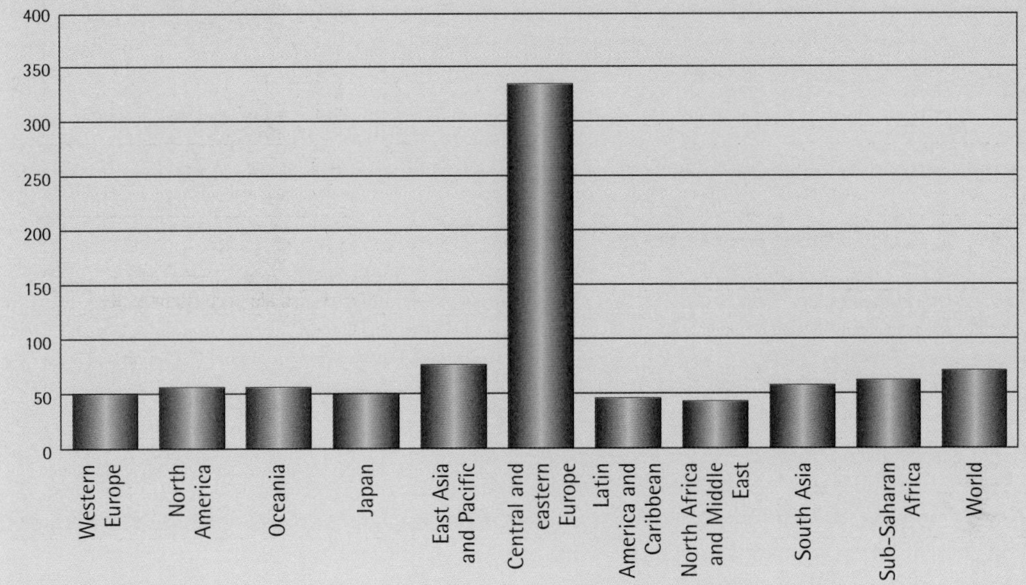

Source: UIA (1990; 2000)

Figure 1.3: Percentage growth in INGO membership by country income group, 1990–2000

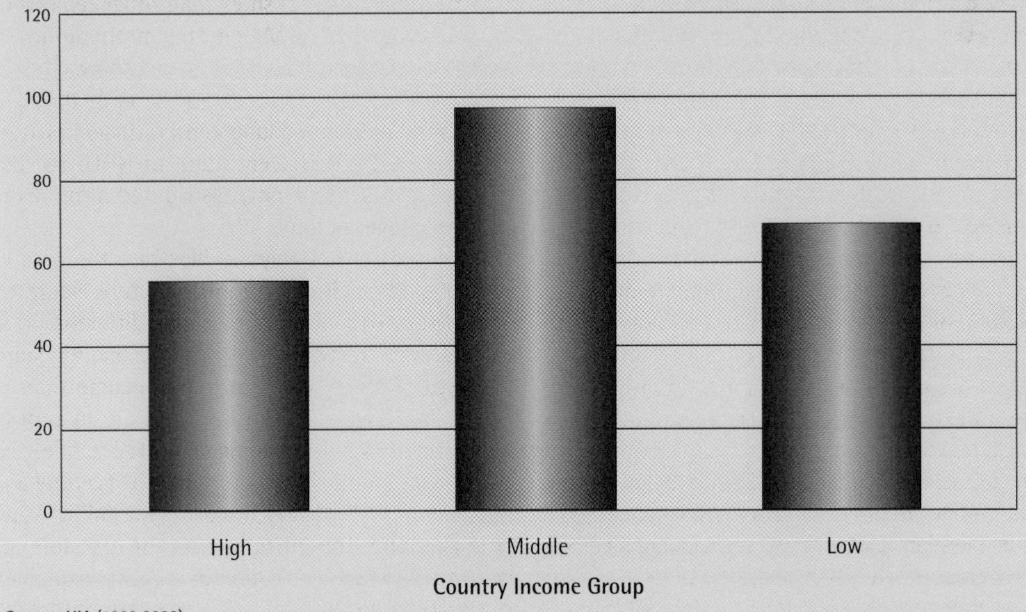

Source: UIA (1990;2000)

different dimension and shows INGO membership growth in relation to economic development. Growth rates throughout the 1990s were higher in middle-income countries (East Asia, central and eastern Europe, parts of Latin America) than in the high-income countries (western Europe, Pacific, and North America). What is more, the expansion rate of INGOs in low-income countries is higher than in richer parts of the world.

Together, these data indicate that the growth of the organisational infrastructure of global civil society does not involve concentration but dispersion, and points to inclusion rather than exclusion. In organisational terms, global civil society today is less a Western-based phenomenon than in the past, and the significant growth rates of recent years enhanced its reach and expansion outside North America and the European Union. In the terms of David Held et al. (1999), the organisational infrastructure of NGOs has attained wider reach (extensity) and higher density (intensity), a finding also supported by Anheier and Katz (Map M4) in the methodological chapter in this volume.

To illustrate the process of dispersion, it is useful to review some basic patterns of NGO locations over time, and to go back briefly to the beginnings of modern NGO development. In 1906, only two of the 169 INGOs had their headquarters outside Europe; by 1938, 36 of the total of 705 INGOs existing at that time were located outside Europe. By 1950, with a significant increase of US-based INGOs and with the establishment of the United Nations, 124 of the 804 existing INGOs were not based in Europe. With the independence movement and the generally favourable economic climate of the 1950s and early 1960s, the number of INGOs increased to 1,768, of which 83 per cent were located in Europe, 10 per cent in the United States, and between 1 per cent and 2 per cent each in Asia, South America, Central America, Africa, Middle East, and Australia (Tew 1963).

By 2001, much of this concentration had given way to a more decentralised pattern around an emerging bipolar structure of INGOs, with two centres: Western Europe and North America (Map M4 in Anheier and Katz). Europe still accounts for the majority of INGO headquarters, followed by the United States, but other regions like Asia and Africa have gained ground, as have seen in Figures 1.2 and 1.3. Nonetheless, among the ten countries hosting the greatest number of intercontinental organisation headquarters in 2001, we find eight European countries (United Kingdom, France, Switzerland, Belgium, Netherlands, Germany, Italy, and Austria), next to the USA and Canada (UIA 2002/3: Vol. 5: 81).

In terms of cities, we find that by 2001 the traditional role of Paris (729), London (807), Brussels (1,392), Geneva (272), and New York (390) has not been diminished in absolute terms. They are, however, less dominant in relative terms: over ten other cities in four continents have more than 100 INGO headquarters and another 35 on five continents over 50 each.

Organisational links. As we have already pointed out in *Global Civil Society 2001*, the infrastructure of global civil society in terms of INGOs has not only become broader in geographical coverage, it also became much more interconnected throughout the 1990s. In 2001, the UIA reported over 90,000 such links among NGOs and 38,000 between INGOs and international governmental organisations. The average number of links jumped from an average of 6.7 in 1990 to 14.1 in 2000: an increase of 110 per cent. The infrastructure of global civil society has not only become bigger and broader, it has also achieved greater density and connectedness.

While these links measure a range of inter-organisational activities from consultations, joint projects, and financing to publication and outreach campaigns, Figure 1.6 focuses on three critical areas of inter-organisational relations from the perspective of institutional development. In each of three cases—participation in founding or creating an INGO, membership interlock, and joint activities—we see substantial increases in recent years, as indicated by the increased thickness of the arrows linking INGOs to INGOs and IGOs. In all of these areas, INGOs have become more interconnected as well as more connected to international institutions like the United Nations or the World Bank.

Composition. Next to scale and connectedness, field of activity or purpose is another important dimension in describing the infrastructure of global civil society. When looking at the purpose or field in which INGOs operate (Figure 1.5), we find that, among the INGOs listed in 2001, two fields dominate in terms of numbers: economic development and economic interest associations (26.1 per cent) and knowledge-based NGOs in the area of research and science (20.5 per cent). At first, the pronounced presence of these activities and purposes among INGOs seems surprising, yet it is in these fields that

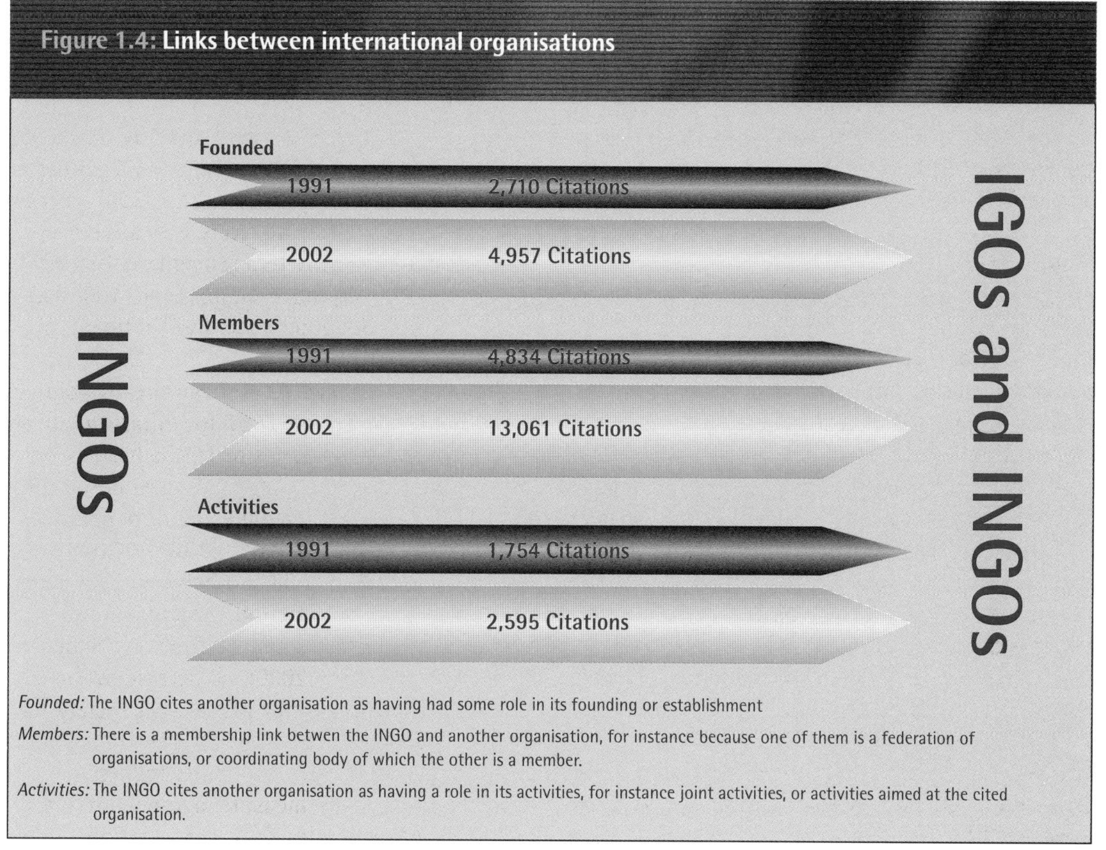

Figure 1.4: Links between international organisations

Founded: The INGO cites another organisation as having had some role in its founding or establishment

Members: There is a membership link betwen the INGO and another organisation, for instance because one of them is a federation of organisations, or coordinating body of which the other is a member.

Activities: The INGO cites another organisation as having a role in its activities, for instance joint activities, or activities aimed at the cited organisation.

the need for some form of international cooperation, exchange of information, recognition and standard-setting has long been felt. There are thousands of scholarly associations and learned societies that span the entire range of academic disciplines and field of human learning. Likewise, there is a rich tradition of business and professional organisations reaching across national borders, such as international chambers of commerce, consumer associations, and professional groups in the fields of law, accounting, trade, engineering, transport, civil service, or health care.

Indeed, the earliest available tabulation of INGOs by purpose lists 639 organisations in 1924, with nearly half in either economic interest associations (172) or learned societies and research organisations (238) (Otlet 1924). Only 55 organisations fell into the category 'political', 28 in sports, 25 in religion, and 14 in arts and culture. In other words, the political, humanitarian, moral, or religious value component to INGOs is a more recent phenomenon. Although some of the oldest humanitarian organisations date back to the nineteenth century, such as the Red Cross or the Anti-Slavery Society, their widespread and prominent presence at a transnational level is a product of the latter part of the twentieth century.

Indeed, as Figure 1.5 shows, today value-based NGOs in the areas of law, policy, and advocacy (12.6 per cent), politics (5.2 per cent), and religion (5.2 per cent) make up the second largest activity component, with a total of 23 per cent of all INGOs. This is followed by a service provisions cluster, in which social services, health, and education together account for 21 per cent of INGO purposes. Smaller fields like culture and the arts (6.6 per cent), the environment (2.9 per cent), and defence and security make up the balance.

Yet next to a greater emphasis on values, the changes in the composition of purposes that took place in the 1990s brought a long-standing yet often overlooked function of INGOs to the forefront: service delivery has become a visible and important part of INGOs. Indeed, the provision of social services as a purpose grew by 79 per cent between 1990 and 2000,

Figure 1.5: Growth in number of INGOs by purpose, 1990–2000

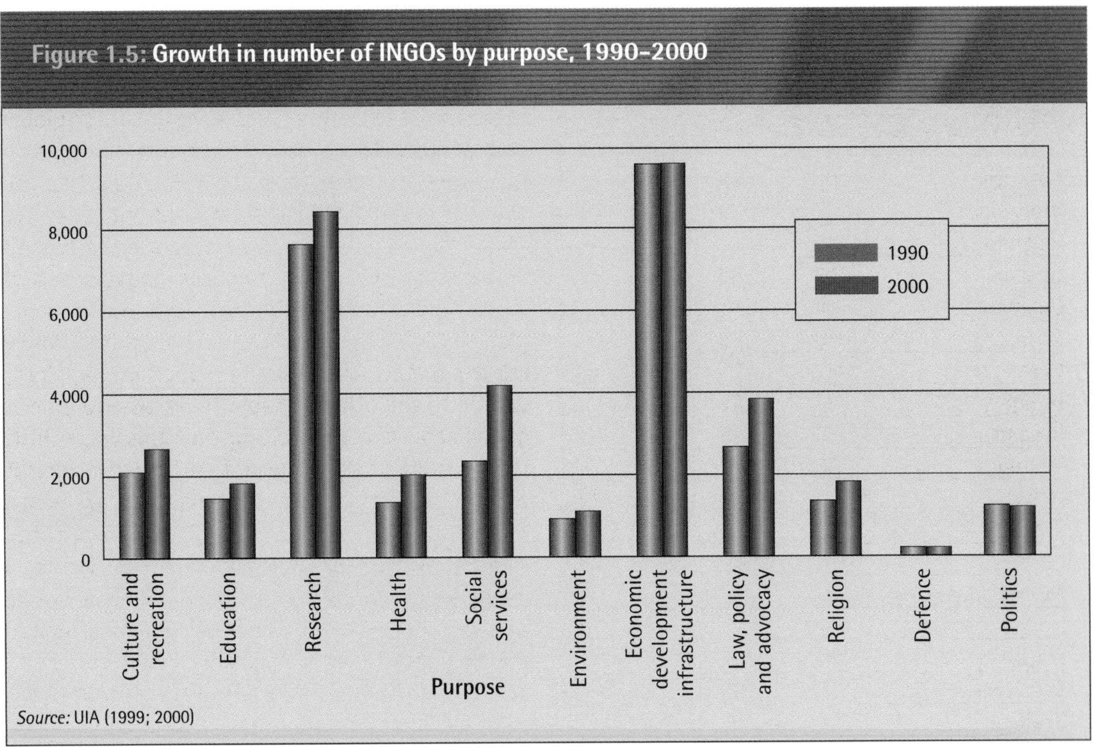

Source: UIA (1999; 2000)

health services by 50 per cent, and education by 24 per cent. This function of INGOs is primarily connected to the public management manifestation of global civil society, which we outlined above.

Although INGOs provide only a partial picture of global civil society, INGO data show that the infrastructure of global civil society has expanded significantly since 1990, in terms of both scale and connectedness. We also saw that the relative focus on these organisations, taken together, shifted more towards value-based activities and service provision. Overall, the expansion of INGOs and the value-activity shift imply both quantitative and qualitative changes in the contour and role of global civil society organisations. Throwing some light on these changes will be the task in the next section, where we examine the relationship between value changes in Western societies from the 1970s onwards, the link to transnationalism, and the rise of civil society in the 1990s.

Values and global civil society

Social, cultural, and political values show significant variation within and across countries and cultures, but the resulting value patterns are relatively stable over time, and typically change more between than within generations (Inglehart 1990). Shifts in basic value pattern are relatively rare, and if they happen they are full of consequences and carry many implications—from social and economic behaviour to politics and the institutions of society at large. However, one such value shift took place in many OECD countries between 1970 and the late 1980s, as social scientists such as Inglehart and Baker (2000), Abramson and Inglehart (1995), Klingemann and Fuchs (1995), Van Deth, and Scarbrough (1995), and others have shown.

Researchers have used several different labels to describe this value shift, and the precise extent and sustainability of the changes involved continues to be debated among experts in the field. While there are many sociological correlates to this value shift and its causation, it is associated with the rise of cosmopolitan values, a preference for democratic forms of governance, and an appreciation of cultural diversity (Inglehart 1990; Van Deth and Scarbrough 1995). In other words, cosmopolitan values such as tolerance, respect for others, emphasis on human rights, and so on have become increasingly important.

Table 1.3 demonstrates the consistent and significant increase of the cosmopolitan value 'Tolerance and respect for others as a quality in children', based

Table 1.3: Tolerance seen as core quality in children, in percent of respondents

Country	1981	1990	2000
Argentina	44	78	70
Belgium	45	67	84
Canada	53	80	82
Denmark	58	81	87
France	59	78	84
Germany	42	76	73
Hungary	31	62	65
Iceland	58	93	84
Ireland	56	76	75
Italy	43	67	75
Japan	41	60	71
Mexico	39	64	72
Netherlands	57	87	90
Norway	32	64	66
South Africa	53	59	74
South Korea	25	55	65
Spain	44	73	82
Sweden	71	91	93
United Kingdom	62	80	83
United States	52	72	80
Average	48	73	78

Source: European Values Surveys (2003); and World Values Survey Study Group (1999–2000; 2003)

on data from the European and World Value Surveys. In all of the 20 countries included for which such data are available across the three waves (1981, 1990, and 2000), 'tolerance and respect for others' becomes a more frequently cited core value; and with very few exceptions this increase took place in the 1980s, with a levelling off in the 1990s at fairly high levels. Across the countries listed in Table 1.3, responses stating that tolerance and respect for others are qualities to be encouraged in children increased from 48 per cent to 75 per cent in the 1980s, and to 78 per cent in the following decade.

This shift in values goes beyond the traditional left-right cleavage in politics. Instead, beginning in the 1960s and more forcefully and widely in the 1970s, many people began to engage in new forms of political activities and to participate in social movements, in particular the women's, environmental, and peace movements. The new social movements provide the institutional connection between the shift in values and the growth of global civil society. These new movements emerged in developed countries from the 1960s onwards: the civil rights and anti-Vietnam war movement of the 1960s, the environmental movement, the women's movement of the 1970s, the peace movement and human rights movement of the 1980, and the anti-globalisation movements of the 1990s, are all closely related to the value shift identified by Inglehart, van Deth, and others. Chapter 6 discusses a crucial global achievement resulting from this value shift: the insertion of language defining violence against women into various international legal instruments.

Importantly, the value set connected with the new social movements had from the beginning a transnational element, and particularly so in Europe (environment, peace, women), Latin America (human rights), and Australia (indigenous rights), but less so in the United States, where the value shift and the changes in social structures could more easily be linked to a renewal of some form of domestic Tocquevillian democracy or the American Way of Life (Anheier 2004; see Edwards, Foley, and Diani 2001; Siriani and Friedland 2000). In Europe, by contrast, the value shift coincided with the development of the European project (from the Common Market to the European Community to the European Union) as the next step in a modernisation process that points to a more peaceful and prosperous future and that necessitates the evolution of nation-states and national societies into a framework of European cooperation and integration.

We have not yet been able to observe how far the rise of regressive globalism, as for example in the case of religious and nationalist militant groups described in Chapter 7, may reverse this value shift. Nor can we assess whether the renewed mobilisation of global civil society will be able to sustain the trend towards cosmopolitan values. The rise of anti-immigrant parties and the entry of 'tough' language on asylum-seekers and integration in Europe and Australia, the pursuit of an 'America first' policy by the US Administration, and the rise of communal politics in many other parts of the world suggest that 'anti-cosmopolitan' values may now be in the ascendant. In these circumstances, it is of particular importance to safeguard and strengthen the legal

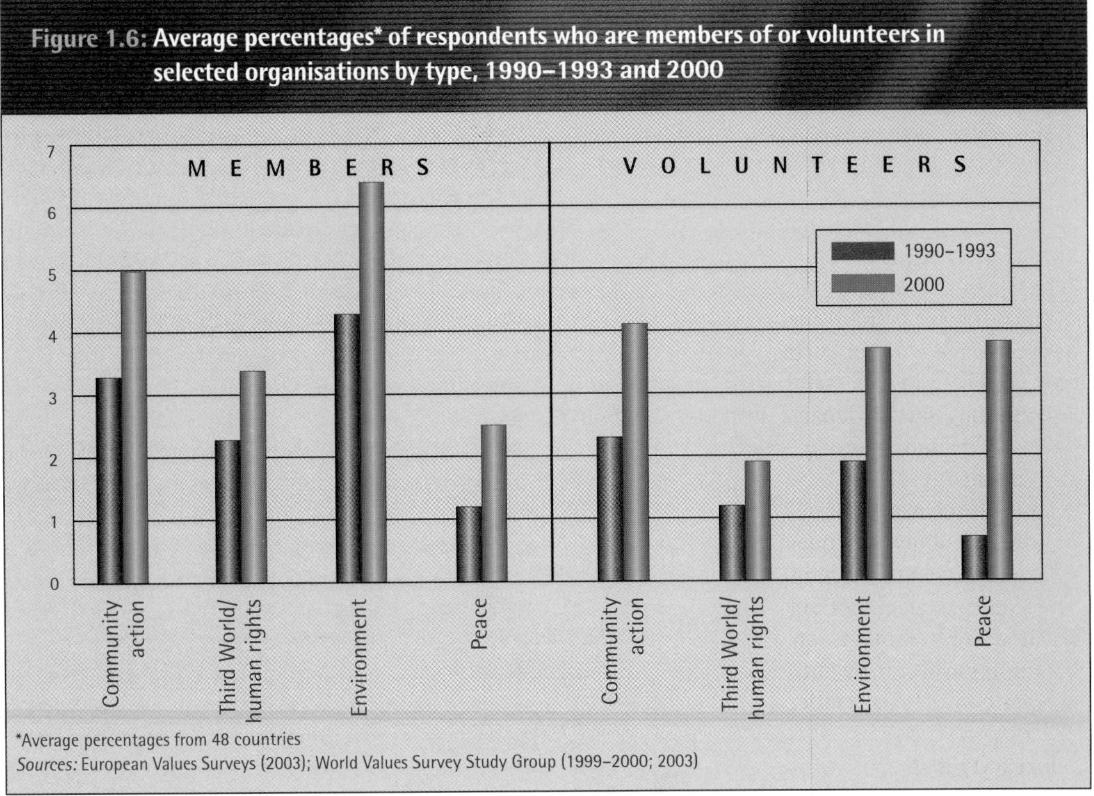

Figure 1.6: Average percentages* of respondents who are members of or volunteers in selected organisations by type, 1990–1993 and 2000

*Average percentages from 48 countries
Sources: European Values Surveys (2003); World Values Survey Study Group (1999–2000; 2003)

security of civil society at the national, regional and global level, as discussed in chapter 9.

Participation in global civil society

Across the western world, the value changes of the latter half of the twentieth century consequently implied a greater mobilisation of society around issues advocated by the new social movements: human rights, gender equality, environmental protection, third world development, peace, and democratisation—issues typically outside the realm of established party politics. By the very nature of the issues involved, these movements implied greater internationalism and linked value changes in the West to developments in Latin America or Africa and vice versa. The new movement of international solidarity was less linked to the workers' movement and the traditional political left. It was far more about human rights and democracy, more about equity than social equality, and more about self-determination of the individual and society than about power politics and the state. Activists for democratisation in Brazil, Chile, and Argentina, or those fighting apartheid and neo-colonialism in Africa, were frequently either part of or linked to the emerging and highly educated post-material middle class of the Western world.

The mobilisation effect of the ideas of 1989, which spread westwards from central Europe, is perhaps the clearest expression of this 'marriage' between changes in value patterns, social movements, and transnationalism (Kaldor 2003). Other are the re-democratisation of many countries in Latin America, the South African resistance to apartheid, the women's and environmental movements, or the human rights movement generally.

Unfortunately, little systematic comparative data exist for membership and participation in the types of associations and groups linked to social movements and transnationalism that would allow us to explore changes for the 1970–2000 period, although very useful case studies exist that show how movements began to cross borders more frequently and more widely than in the past (see Keck and Sikkink 1998; Cohen and Rai 2000). However, with the help of the 1990 and 2000 European and World Value Surveys, it is possible to examine possible changes during the previous decade. Indeed, we find, as Figure 1.6 illustrates, that during the 1990s people were more likely to join voluntary associations in the fields of Third World development, environmental protection, community organising, peace, and human rights than in the past, as both members and volunteers.

The greater participation in NGOs coincided with favourable political opportunity structures throughout the 1990s, with the political opening in central and eastern Europe and the re-democratisation of Latin America as perhaps the best examples. At the same time, many other parts of the world become more open and accessible for transnational organisations, such as Japan, South Korea, or South Africa. Of course, there were exceptions in the Balkans, the Middle East and in Central Asia, but generally it seemed that the world was on a course for greater political openness that welcomed citizen participation and involvement to an extent unknown in the past. It remains an open question, however, to what extent the events of 11 September 2001 and their aftermath changed the opportunity structure for global civil society organisations—an issue to which we will return.

Evidence of growing participation is also suggested by our data on parallel summits and by our annual chronology. Record 28 shows the steady growth of parallel summits during the 1990s and the growth of participation in those summits, particularly in Europe and Latin America. The chronology of global civil society events illustrates the richness of global civil society activities in different parts of the world.

Values change less frequently than political agendas. Yet the new regressive climate that follows the events of 11 September and their aftermath implies a significant challenge to cosmopolitanism

New Trends and Developments

In our overview of the contours of global civil society we have taken a comparative historical perspective and looked at the different dimensions of global civil society, with an emphasis on developments in recent decades. We discussed the trend towards cosmopolitan values associated with the new social movements of the 1970s and 1980s, and the political opening and economic conditions of the 1990s that favoured the institutional expansion of global civil society into a large and growing infrastructure. Of course, the continued development of global civil society is unlikely to stop there and revert to some pre-1990 pattern. The value change that facilitated the growth of global civil society over the last few decades is also the source of its medium- and long-term resilience. Values change less frequently than political agendas. Yet the new regressive climate that follows the events of 11 September and their aftermath implies a significant challenge to cosmopolitanism and the values it represents and builds on.

The explosion of social forums

One way in which global civil society activists have responded is in finding new forms of mobilising and coming together: social forums. In a sense, it could be argued that the social forums represent a new political opportunity structure for a new generation of social movements more concerned with social justice than were the movements of the 1970s and 1980s.

In many ways, these forums are a new way of organising in global civil society; they are an innovation that establishes an intermediary step between traditional ways of mobilisation (INGOs) and dot.cause anonymity. They seem to combine the advantages associated with person-to-person interactions, as with community building and leadership, with the efficiency of web-based organising in terms of information dissemination and management. It is perhaps too early to say whether social forums are the characteristic form of organising in the first decade of this century, just as sit-ins were in the 1960s, demonstrations in the 1970s, the NGO proliferation in the 1980s and early 1990s, and the dot.causes in the brief period between 1999 and 2002. Yet much speaks in favour of this assumption, in particular the low cost of organising and the flexibility and mobility this form allows. At the very least, we expect social forums to evolve as a complementary form of global civil society infrastructure alongside the vast and highly institutionalised network of INGOs described above.

In the 2002 Yearbook we gave an account of the first two World Social Forums (WSF) in Porto Allegre,

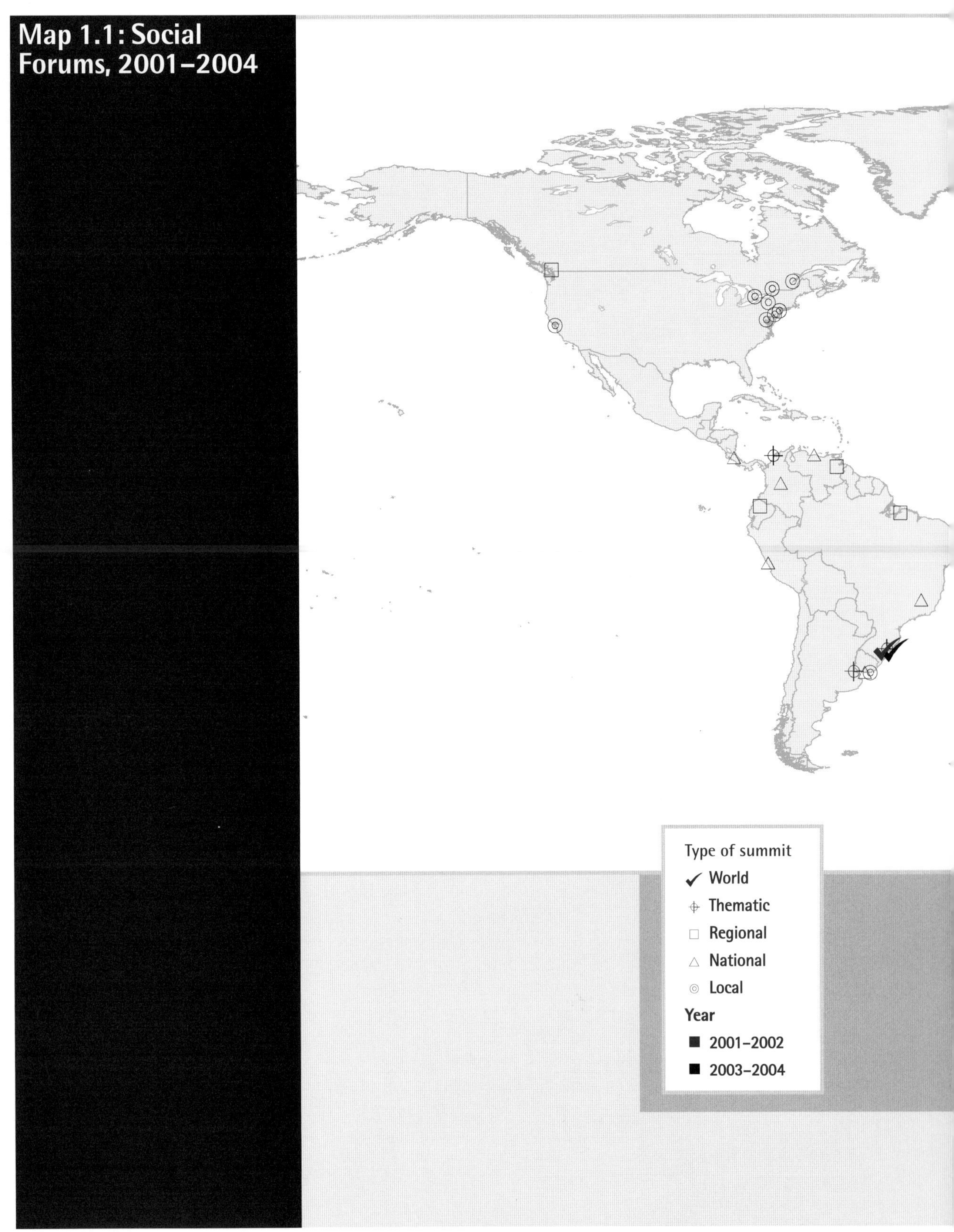
Map 1.1: Social Forums, 2001–2004
Type of summit
World
Thematic
Regional
National
Local
Year
2001–2002
2003–2004

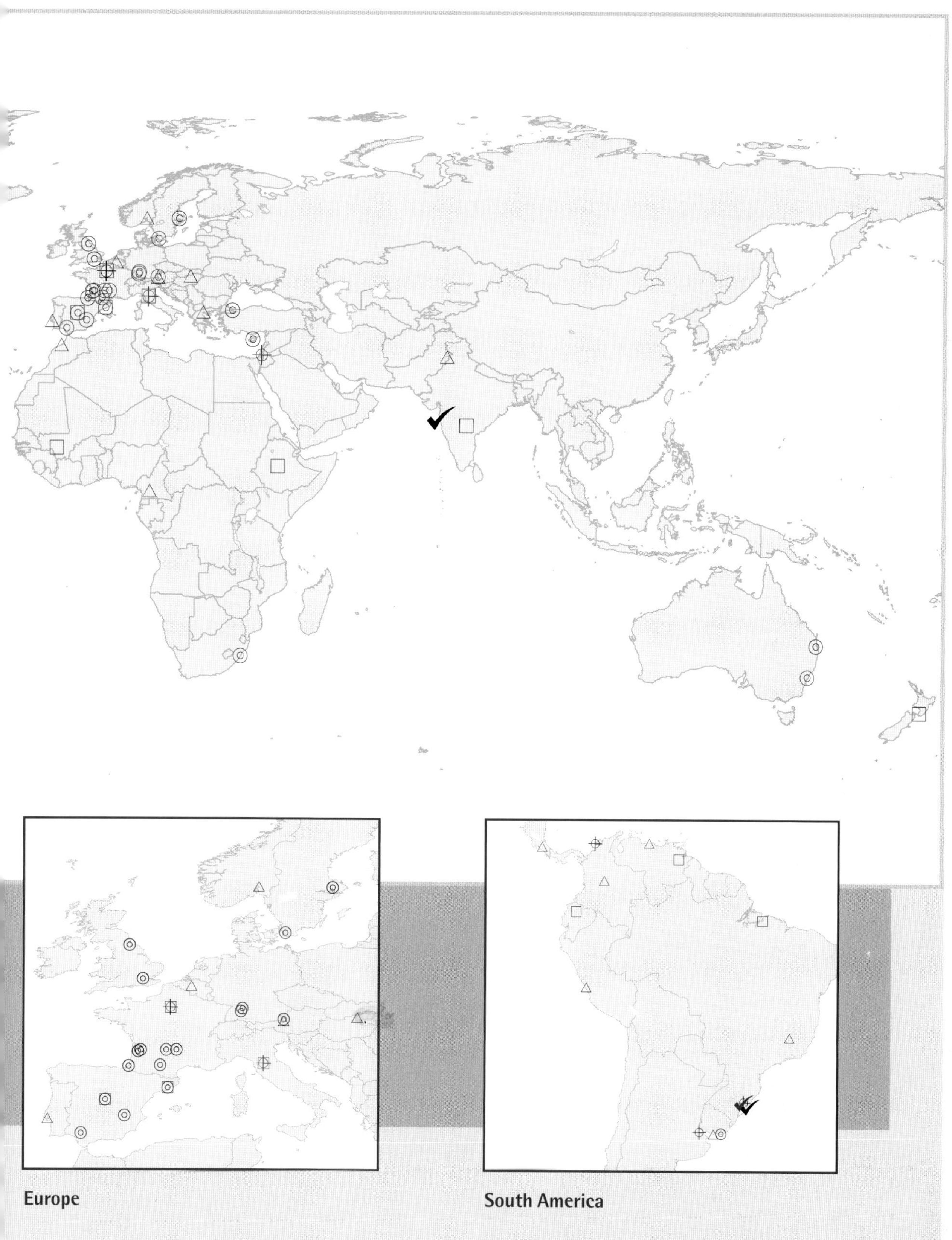
Europe
South America

Table 1.4: List of world, regional, and thematic social forums as of May 2003

Name	Place	Dates	Comments
World social forums			
World SF I http://www.forumsocial mundial.org.br/home.asp	Porto Alegre, Brazil	25–30 Jan. 2001	Born as counter-summit to the Davos World Economic Forum
World SF II http://www.forumsocial mundial.org.br/home.asp	Porto Alegre, Brazil	31 Jan.– 5 Feb. 2002	68,000 participants; incl. 12,000 young people; 5,000 organisations; 3,000 journalists; 800 MPs
World SF III http://www.forumsocial mundial.org.br/home.asp	Porto Alegre, Brazil	23–28 Jan. 2003	100,000 participants from 156 countries; 1,286 workshops, seminars and round tables
World SF IV http://www.wsfindia.org/ event_description.php	Mumbai, India	16–21 Jan. 2004	Preceded by Indian and Asian consultation rounds
Regional social forums			
African SF I	Bamako, Mali	5–9 Jan. 2002	Over 200 people, from 43 countries
African SF II http://www.enda.sn/objectifs.htm	Addis Ababa, Ethiopia	5–9 Jan. 2003	Remains small with c. 200 people.
Americas SF http://www.forosocialamericas.org/	Quito, Ecuador	8-13 March 2004	Postponed by one year to avoid narrow anti- FTAA focus
Asian SF http://www.wsfindia.org/	Hyderabad, India	2–7 Jan. 2003	Transforms from Indian into Asia SF at a late stage. Attracts an unexpected 14,000 participants
European SF http://www.2002.fse-esf.org/	Florence, Italy	6–10 Nov. 2002	Defeats media scare by being peaceful. 40,000 participants; 1 million in closing anti-war march
European SF II http://www.fse-esf.org/	Paris/St Denis, France	12–16 Nov. 2003	
Mediterranean SF http://www.fsmed.info/	Barcelona, Spain	March 2004	
North-American SF http://www.northamerican socialforum.org/	Vancouver, Canada	15–22 Aug. 2003	
Oceania SF http://oceaniasocialforum.org.nz/	Wellington, New Zealand	Oct.–Nov. 2003	Postponed to attract wider participation
Pan-Amazon SF II http://www.fspanamazon ico.com.br/pagina/iiforum.html	Belém, Brazil	16–19 Jan. 2003	Also organising a number of 'meetings without borders' in Amazonian border towns
Pan-Amazon SF III http://www.fspanamazon ico.com.br/	Ciudad Guayana, Venezuela	4–8 Feb. 2004	

Name	Place	Dates	Comments
Transatlantic SF http://www.lahaine.org/global/madrid/programa_fst_eng.htm	Madrid, Spain	9-19 May 2002	Specifically against Spanish neo-imperialism in Latin-America
Thematic social forums			
Argentina Thematic SF http://www.forosocialargentino.org/foro2002.htm	Buenos Aires, Argentina	22–25 Aug. 2002	Focused on debt crisis and IMF policies. Over 20,000 people
Colombia Thematic SF http://www.mamacoca.org/forolegal/fsmt_presentacion_en.htm	Cartagena, Colombia	16–20 June 2003	Theme: Democracy, human rights, wars and crops used for illicit purposes
Health Social Forum II	Porto Alegre, Brazil	20–23 Jan. 2003	First forum started as part of Argentina thematic forum; second convenes separately just before WSF III
Health Social Forum III http://www.cicop.org.ar/forosalud/	Buenos Aires, Argentina	7–9 Nov. 2003	Third health forum returns to Argentina
Palestine Thematic SF http://www.pngo.net/wsf/index.htm	Ramallah, Palestine	27–30 Dec. 2002	250 internationals and 500 locals meet in Arafat's compound; also visit Gaza
Women SF	France	Nov. 2003	To take place just before Paris ESF
World Education Forum II http://www.forummundialdeeducacao.com.br	Porto Allegre, Brazil	19–22 Jan 2003	Just before WSF III, 15,000 teachers from 100 countries
World Education Forum III http://www.forummundialdeeducacao.com.br	Porto Allegre, Brazil	29–31 July 2004	Preceded by regional education forums in Sao Paolo, Brazil; Guadalajara, Mexico; and Barcelona, Spain

This list is based primarily on web searches undertaken between January and May 2003. Inclusion in the list therefore does not guarantee that the social forum in question definitely did, or will, take place on the date in question. For a more comprehensive list, including national and local social forums, consult our web site at <http://www.lse.ac.uk/depts/global/yearbook>.

the number of participants they attracted, and the enthusiasm they inspired. At the second World Social Forum, held in Porto Allegre in early 2002, the decision was taken to disperse the idea of the social forum, organising regional and thematic forums, the ideas and conclusions of which would feed back into the WSF. Even before this decision was taken, there had been a first regional Social Forum in Africa and a national Social Forum in Costa Rica, and an angry counter-meeting of Durban citizens during the World Conference Against Racism decided to call itself Durban Social Forum (Desai 2002). But, especially in Italy, the social forum phenomenon has taken off like nowhere else. When the first WSF decided to postpone regional social forums (national or local social forums do not appear to have been considered), the large group of Italians present, which met frequently as a delegation, decided nevertheless to frame their planned counter-summit to the Genoa G8 meeting as a 'social forum', a format capable of unifying the Italian left (Cannavo 2001; Sullo 2001a; 2001b). More than 200,000 people, mainly Italians, united in Genoa, and many carried away the idea of a social forum. There are now at least 170 (some say many more) local social forums in Italy.[2]

Since the second World Social Forum, Social Forums have mushroomed (see Map 1.1; Table 1.4). While most simply adopt the format of the WSF, organising a one to three day event with workshops, panels, and plenary discussions on a wide number of topics, other organisational forms are also being experimented with: the Brisbane SF operates on an 'open space' principle, which means the agenda is determined by participants on the day of the meeting; the Ottawa SF emphasises that 'this is not a conference' but rather a carnivalesque manifestation, and the Tarnet (France) SF tries to make its web site function as an interactive virtual social forum. Some social forums, including those of Colombia, Madrid, and Limousin (France), have become permanent organisations, while others, such as Tuebingen (Germany) and Philadelphia, have regular events they refer to as 'social forums'. Many of the social forums in Europe are organised to coincide with EU Summits of Heads of State and Government. The European Social Forum in Florence has been the biggest, with 40,000 participants; the Philadelphia SF must be one of the smallest, meeting in a bookshop once a month.

One of the most noteworthy features of social forums is that, while there still are marches and protest actions, they avoid the violence that sparked both media attention and much controversy within the movement

We think that the explosion of social forums can be seen as a new stage in the development of what was initially termed the 'anti-globalisation movement', what Desai and Said (2001; Chapter 4) refer to as the 'anti-capitalist movement', but what is now also increasingly referred to as the 'global justice movement'. The initial phase was one of protest, in Seattle, Prague, Genoa, Quebec, and many other cities. Some of this protest involved direct action, a small proportion of it was violent. There is no doubt that the media's focus on violence, along with the sense that the protesters were expressing a more widely felt sense of unease, helped to put the movement on the map. Apart from the violence, the main criticism levelled at the movement was that it was just 'anti', that it protested but proposed no alternatives. But there are many strands within the social forums. ATTAC groups in 35 countries study proposals to restructure financial markets. The transnational peasants' network Via Campesina in collaboration with NGOs has developed ideas such as 'food sovereignty' in order to confront the corporatisation of farming and food processing (see Chapter 8). Above all, the social forum has emerged as the space for 'reflective thinking, democratic debate of ideas, formulation of proposals, free exchange of experiences and inter-linking for effective action' for global civil society (WSF Charter of Principles 2001).

One of the most noteworthy features of the move to social forums is that, while there still are marches and protest actions, they avoid the violence that sparked both media attention and much controversy within the movement in the earlier demonstrations. Again, this shift is most evident in Italy, where, after the black bloc activities in Genoa in July 2001, the Berlusconi-controlled media had been warning Florentine shopkeepers to board up their shops and flee the city. Instead, the European Social Forum was entirely peaceful; most shops stayed open, did good business, and cheered the march on the last day of the Forum (Longhi 2002).

The decline in violent action might be attributable to three related causes: while initially the non-violent majority would not condemn the violent minority, there was a mounting sense of frustration which culminated in Genoa, where the possibly police-infiltrated black blocs formed the excuse to crack down on peaceful activists. Second, while violence may seem appropriate in direct confrontation with the power-holders, the G8, the World Bank, or the WTO, it has no similar logic in a civil society-only forum, where internal debate is the main item on the menu. Third, as will be described below, many anti-capitalist protestors have focused in recent months on anti-war activities and these have mobilised very large, often non-political, sections of the population who would be deterred by violence.

---

[2] *<http://www.forisociali.org>.*

Another feature of the social forums is that debates are not a means to an end, but the end itself. Social forums discuss proposals and strategies, but they do not produce unified 'final statements'. As Stuart Hodkinson put it, the fact that trade unionists, NGO representatives, and movement activists cannot agree on how to respond to the Free Trade Agreement of the Americas 'seems less important than their willingness to talk openly about the constraints they face' (Hodkinson 2003). This emphasis on debate lends new strength to our suggestion in *Global Civil Society 2001* (Anheier, Glasius, and Kaldor 2001: 10) that 'one way of defining or understanding global civil society is as a debate about the future direction of globalisation and perhaps humankind itself'. The conscious emphasis on debate as a value in itself is particularly important in the post-September 11 world, where Al-Qaeda, other terrorists, and the Bush Administration are successfully promoting violent confrontation instead of debate.

Related to the emphasis on debate is the fact that social forums promote new ways of organising. This does not apply to the plenaries, which are dominated by old-left luminaries like Noam Chomsky, Walden Bello and Susan George. However, the smaller workshops seem to foster the growth of horizontal transnational networks on particular issues, one of the most prominent being water. While the network form predates the social forums, of course, it is still a discovery to members of more traditional organisations, such as trade unions, which have played an important role in many social forums. It remains to be seen how long the debate-for-its-own-sake formula of the social forums can continue to generate the mobilisation and enthusiasm that it does at present. There continues to be a clear split between those we have earlier called 'Reformists', who believe that global capitalism can be harnessed as a force for good but the playing field must be levelled, and those 'Rejectionists' who believe global capitalism itself is the problem, and seek the solution in statist socialism or revolution. At the 2003 WSF, this divide was symbolised by the split between those who applauded the journey of Brazilian President Luis Inacio da Silva ('Lula') from Porto Allegre to Davos and those who condemned it. Indeed, some argue that the social forums have been made possible by the involvement of Third World states like Brazil, and this has tended to strengthen the traditional rejectionist strand of social forum activity.

However, disagreements on global capitalism, and indeed most 'anti-capitalist' activity, have been overshadowed in 2003 by anti-war activism. There appears to have been widespread agreement amongst anti-capitalist activists that, first, the war on terror and the war on Iraq in particular were linked to capitalist interests, and second, that resisting the war was the more urgent matter.

A general feature of the 15 February demonstrations everywhere was that no particular profile of 'the marcher' could be given, they were of all generations, classes, and races, and many had never demonstrated before

The global anti-war movement

While the anti-war movement in 2002 and early 2003 was much wider than the participation in social forums, there is an intimate connection between the two. It was at the European Social Forum in Florence that activists from eleven EU countries agreed to organise protests on the same day, 15 February 2003. As the threat of war continued to linger, activists in North America and elsewhere decided to join in. Eventually, there were demonstrations in almost 800 cities, attracting 11 million people according to one estimate (United for Peace 2003; A. Anderson 2003).

But the influence is deeper than just a decision on a date. The activist networks built at the social forums provide both an organisational base and an ideological alternative to the world view of 'Blair and Bush'. However, that alternative world view is at the same time a problem. In their case against the war on Iraq, the dominant figures in the new global movement tended to lump together corporate capitalism and social inequality, US hegemony, and the plight of the Palestinian people. A declaration of the International Campaign against US Aggression on Iraq, endorsed by the British Stop the War Coalition, for instance, calls the war against Iraq 'part of a U.S. project of global domination and subjugation', and their own opposition 'integral to the internationalist struggle against neo-liberal globalisation'. It goes on to denounce the 'Zionist perpetrators of genocidal crimes against the Palestinians' (Cairo Declaration 2002). Many of the

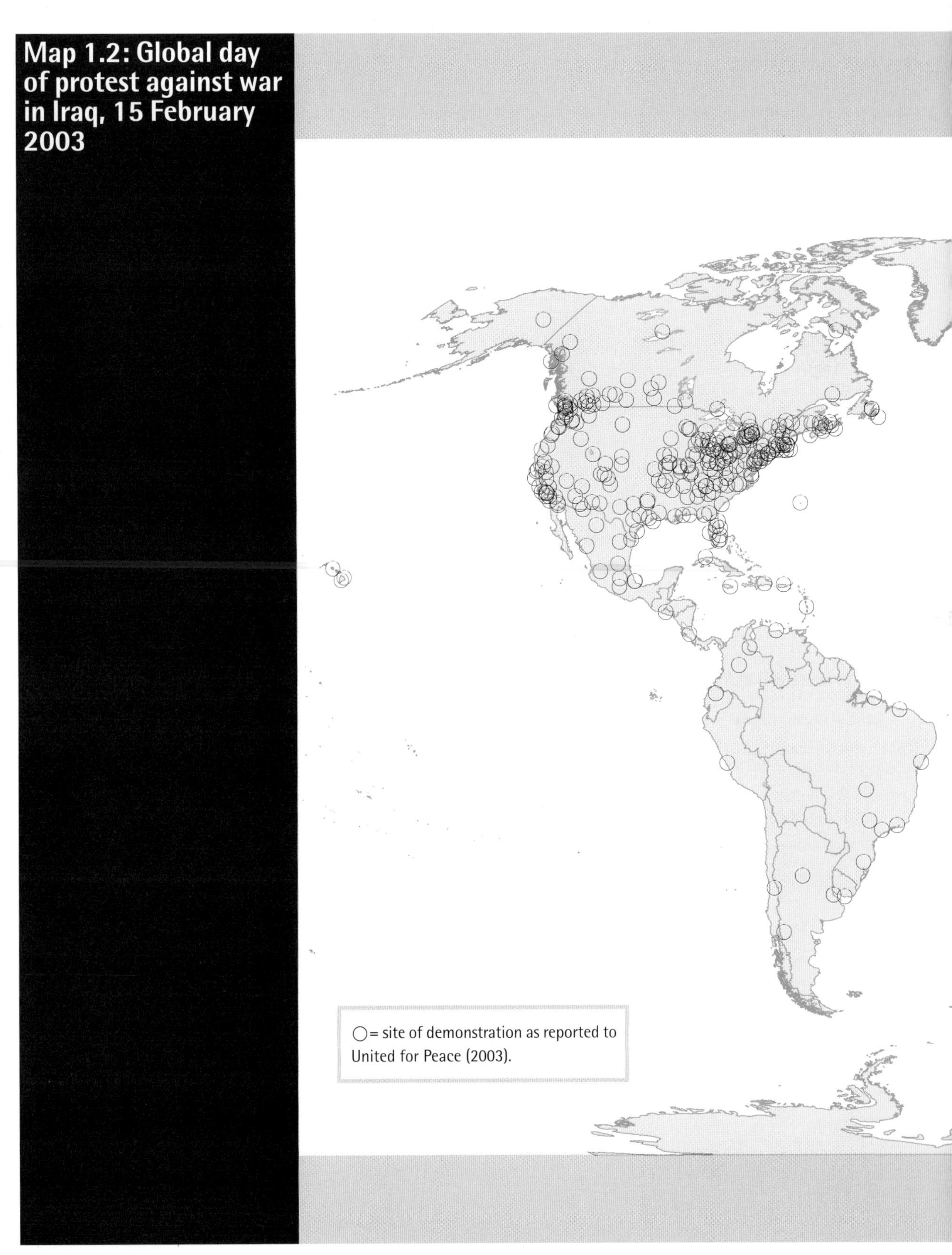

Map 1.2: Global day of protest against war in Iraq, 15 February 2003

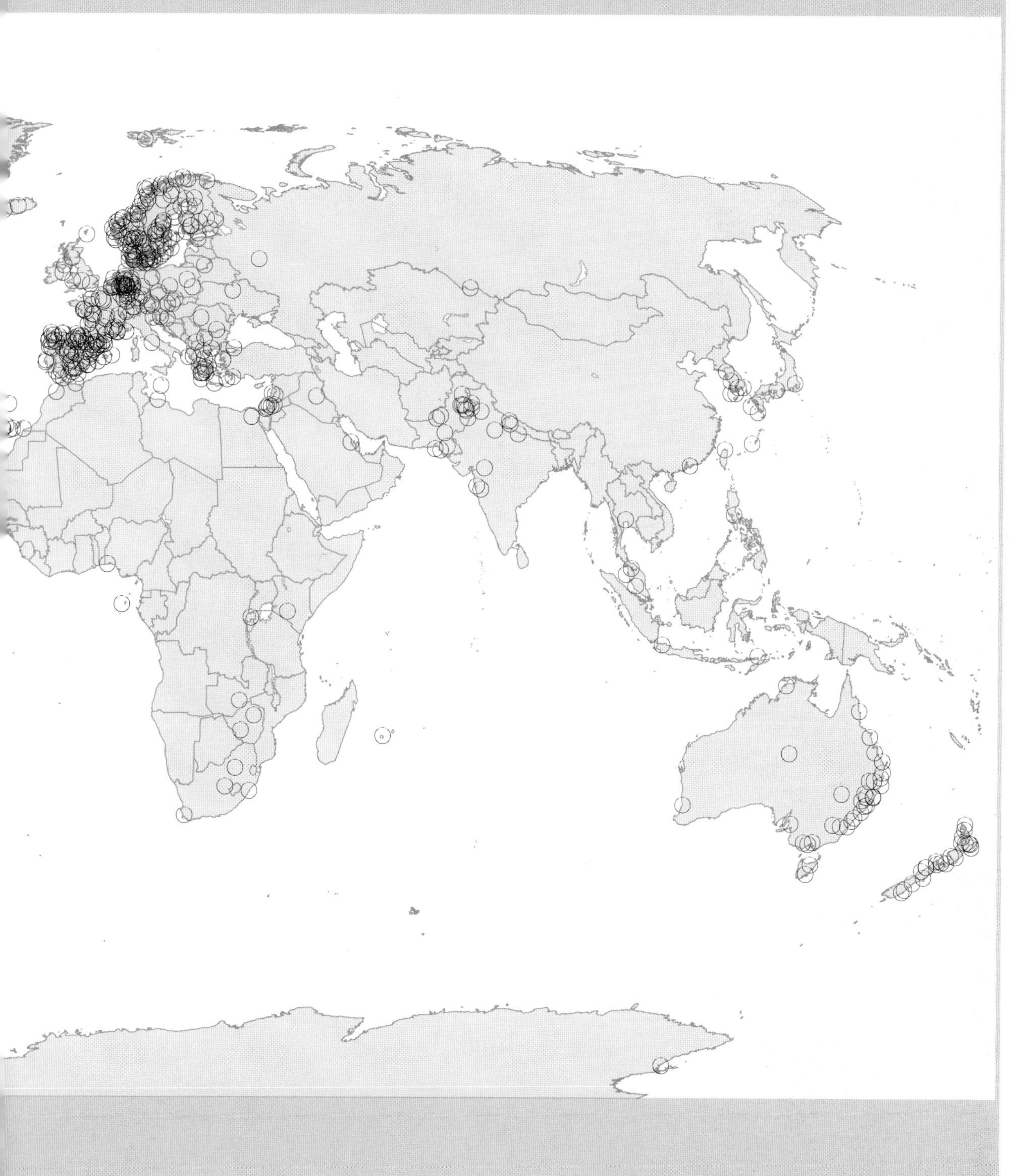

Table 1.5: Changing contours of global civil society

Decade	Infrastructure growth	Composition/ fields	Form innovation	Value changes	Participation
1970s	Medium growth	Economic, research & science	Humanitarian membership-based INGOs	Rise of post-materialism	Slow increase
1980s	Acceleration of growth	Value-based	INGOs linked to international social movements	Cosmopolitan values	Mobilisation
1990s	Medium growth	Value-based; service-provision	Corporate and public management INGOs	Consolidation	Slow increase
2000s	Acceleration of growth	Social justice and opposition to war	Social forums, dot.causes	Resilience	Renewed mobilisation

spokespeople of the anti-war movement appeared to ignore the character of the Iraqi, and indeed Afghan, regimes. Some, such as UK veteran activist Tony Benn, have even gone so far as to visit Saddam Hussein, associating themselves with the genocidal dictator in their campaign against the war.

The anti-war movement is wider, however. Church leaders, including the Pope, the Archbishop of Canterbury and the bishop of Bush's own United Methodist Church, have declared themselves against the war. One of the biggest organisations against the war is the US-based Moveon Peace (URL), founded by 21-year-old Eli Pariser, who collected more than half a million electronic signatures within one week after the 11 September attacks on a petition pleading for a non-violent response. His voice is very different from that of the declaration quoted above: 'We support President Bush's resolve to end terrorism, but not his military agenda for doing it.' More than a hundred Hollywood stars, including Martin Sheen, Matt Damon, Susan Sarandon, and Samuel Jackson have joined in with their 'Win Without War' appeal (which does raise the question: what are they hoping to win?).

A general feature of the 15 February demonstrations everywhere was that no particular profile of 'the marcher' could be given, they were of all generations, classes, and races, and many had never been on a demonstration before. In particular, the anti-war movement brought together North and South, Western and Islamic communities, offering the potential for a new cosmopolitan approach which integrated immigrant and developing-country communities into the global political process for the first time. The biggest demonstrations took place precisely in the places where governments were in favour of the war: London, Rome, Madrid, and New York.

In the post-September 11 world, global civil society does continue to claim space to contest government policies and peacefully debate alternatives. In the marches as in the social forums, the value of this stance is recognised by the people in civil society themselves: the slogan 'Not In My Name', carried in many countries, signals that the expression of dissent matters, even if the war against Iraq could not be stopped. The central role of chemical and biological weapons in the case for war against Iraq suggests that in order to counter the 'Axis of Evil' logic, the anti-war movement ought to pay more attention to these weapons, which are still primarily the preserve of a small group of academic experts (see chapter 5). It is too early to assess whether the new anti-war movement will be a lasting force in global civil society. It may lie dormant, as it did after the war in Afghanistan, until the next US threat to go to war, or it may continue to oppose what it sees as the occupation of Iraq. Even if it can transcend conjunctural upsurges in response to actual warfare, there is still the risk is that the anti-war movement will be dominated by Rejectionists, who oppose the

Table 1.6: Possible future scenarios

	1990s	Scenarios for the 2000s			
		Unilateralist	Bargain	Division	Utopian
Governments	Coalition of Supporters and Reformers	Predominantly Regressive	Alliance of Regressives and Reformers	Division between Regressives, Reformers and Rejectionists	Dominance of Reformers
Global Civil Society	Reformers and Rejectionists	Predominantly Rejectionist	Dominance of Reformers	Contest between Rejectionist and Reformers	Dominance of Reformers

US role in the world but offer no alternative multilateralist mechanism for responding to repression, human rights abuses, or even genocide. Whether the potential of the anti-war movement to provide a new underpinning for the global institutional framework can be realised will depend on whether the reformist cosmopolitan positions within the movement can be heard more loudly.

Conclusion

In this introductory chapter, we have sounded a slightly upbeat if cautionary note about global civil society, a more optimistic note than in the immediate shadows of the September 11 attacks in 2001. We arrived at this view by taking a step back, examining the course of global civil society over the last quarter century, thus taking as much account of what the French historian Ferdinand Braudel called the *longue durée* as the data situation would allow. As summarised in Table 1.5, the development of global civil society over the last three decades has shown a remarkably consistent trajectory. Specifically, we suggest that:

- The growth and expansion of global civil society seems closely associated with a major shift in cultural and social values that took hold in most developed market economies in the 1970s. This shift saw a change in emphasis from material security to concerns about democracy, participation, and meaning, and involved, among other things, a formation towards cosmopolitan values such as tolerance and respect for human rights (see Inglehart 1990).
- These values facilitated the cross-national spread of social movements around common issues that escaped conventional party politics, particularly in Europe and Latin America, and led to a broad-based mobilisation with the women's, peace, democracy, and environmental movements as the best examples of an increasingly international 'movement industry' (Diani and McAdam 2003; McAdam, Tarrow, and Tilly, 2001).
- The 1990s brought a political opening and a broad-based consolidation of unknown proportion and scale (Kaldor 2003), which coincided with the reappraisal of the role of the state in most developed countries, and growing disillusionment with state-led multilateralism in the Third World among counter-elites (Edwards 1999).
- In addition to this broadened political space, favourable economic conditions throughout the 1990s and the vastly reduced costs of communication and greater ease of organising facilitated the institutional expansion of global civil society in organisational terms (Anheier and Themudo 2002; Clark 2003);
- By 2002, the changed geo-political environment and the economic downturn challenged both the (by now) relatively large infrastructure of global civil society organisations and the broad value base of cosmopolitanism in many countries across the world, in particular among the middle classes and elites.
- As a result, new organisational forms and ways of organising and communications have gained in importance, with social forums and Internet-

based mobilisation as prominent examples, as have frictions between 'American' and 'European' visions of the world's future.

In the 1990s, the predominant political force behind globalisation was a coalition between Supporters and Reformers, in transnational corporations as well as in governments and intergovernmental organisations, and in global civil society. The Davos World Economic Forum represented an annual expression of this coalition. It was the combination of Supporters and Reformers that pressed for the globalisation of the rule of law and of technology as well as the economy, although there was disagreement on the globalisation of people. This combination, mainly associated with the corporate and the new public management manifestations of global civil society discussed above, came to be seen by many as depoliticising and co-opting global civil society. However, it also contributed to the growth and solidification of its infrastructure.

We could see the retreat of globalisation in the areas of law and especially people, combined with a lawless and 'unfair' globalisation in the areas of the economy and technology

In the brief era from Seattle to the war on Afghanistan, we saw a huge upsurge in civil society mobilisation, in effect a coalition between Reformers and Rejecters of globalisation. In contrast to the groups that dominated the 1990s, they are more associated with self-organisation and activism. Their protests sent out powerful warning signals, which were just beginning to get picked up in the 'global governance' world where Reformers and Supporters coincided when the Twin Towers came down.

Since September 11, Regressive globalisers have been in the ascendancy. This includes both the unilateralists of the Bush Administration and the growing militant religious and nationalist groups and parties, for instance in the Middle East, India, and many countries in eastern and western Europe. They are Regressive globalisers rather than Rejectionists because they aim to impose their vision on the rest of the world and because of the way in which they make use of the infrastructure of globalisation. At the same time, Rejectionists, generally on the left, have become increasingly powerful within global civil society partly because many activists have not yet come to terms with the rise of regressive globalism and believe they are still fighting against the powerful Supporters of globalisation.

Another factor that we emphasise in this chapter is that forms as well as positions matter. Because the social forums and the anti-war movements have emphasised self-organisation and/or minimal structure, it has been relatively easy for those on the traditional organised left to capture dominant positions and to be allowed to act as spokespeople. Indeed, the anti-war movement was a coming together of individuals whose views were not necessarily reflected by those who acted as their spokespeople. The social forums are meant to be an experiment in democratic form, yet the lack of structure often allowed old left leaders to grab the limelight and give the impression of speaking 'on behalf of'. Hence the form or lack of form submerged genuine debate and alternative thinking. And it is the traditional left that sees the 'pure' globalisers as its main adversary.

Yet 'pure' globalisers, probably always overrated, have been marginalised in recent years. Instead, we fear that a (in many cases unconscious) combination of the Rejecters of globalisation and Regressive globalisers will lead to a polarisation of positions, for instance between Bush and Bin Laden, but also between many of the groups described in Chapter 7, which treat each other as implacable enemies. This is a polarisation, however, that benefits both poles, as they need to sustain fear and hatred as their power base, squeezing the middle. If this combination does come to dominate, we could see the retreat of globalisation in the areas of law and especially people, combined with a lawless and 'unfair' globalisation in the areas of the economy and technology. The apportioning of contracts in Iraq to corporations associated with the Bush Administration is a foretaste of what such globalisation might look like. Precisely because the Regressives propose a radical vision of the world, the Reformers come to be seen as the status quo position and not the progressive position. Thus it is the combination of Regressives and Rejectionists that could lead to the unilateralist scenario we described in the 2002 yearbook, characterised by polarisation and violence.

In the aftermath of September 11, one possibility we envisaged was a bargain between Regressives and Reformers. Tony Blair talked about the need for a new framework of global justice to combat the causes of terrorism. There were some new initiatives: increased development aid promised at the Monterrey Summit, the New Partnership for Africa's Development (NEPAD); increased US funding for the global AIDS fund. But in retrospect these initiatives seem marginal in relation to the scale of the problem and, in the context of the Bush tax cuts, seem very different from the kind of generosity that was offered by the United States to its allies during the Cold War period.

In the period leading up to the war in Iraq, the anti-war movement did find some allies in government. Some of these governments have, at least in rhetorical terms, embraced a Reformist agenda—France and Germany, for example. Others are Regressive or Rejectionist, like Russia, China, Iran, or Egypt, for example. The emergence of new governmental champions of the Reformers, however, at present only leads to division. The British government lost perhaps the most important opportunity of this decade to build a system of global governance by siding with the United States. Had the British and Spanish governments, like the French and the German governments, opposed the war and refused to legitimise American actions, a broad European government coalition could have seized the moment of public mobilisation in favour of multilateral institutions and alternative ways of confronting dictators. It might not have been able to prevent the war but it would have left the European Union united and in a position to greatly strengthen global institutions. Now the division only further weakens multilateral institutions.

Perhaps the most positive conclusion of our chapter is that, by any number of measures, global civil society has been strengthened over the last decade. The most hopeful possibility is that there will continue to be serious space for the reformist strand of activism so that global civil society will be able to offer a radical emancipatory vision that can compete with the Regressives and Rejectionists and eventually have some influence on American politics. Thus it is possible to summarise the scenarios that we described in the 2002 Yearbook in terms of the positions that we have elaborated in this chapter (Table 1.6).

Since we do believe in agency, what happens will depend on choices that are being made now about positions and values as well as forms of organisation. This Yearbook is offered in a reflexive spirit, as a way for readers to help us think about these various possibilities and, by developing new ideas and ways of thinking, we hope this will, in turn, contribute to more constructive choices about the future direction of our globalised world.

References

Abramson, P. and R. Inglehart (1995). *Value Change in Global Perspective*. Ann Arbor: University of Michigan Press.

Anderson, Arthur (2003). 'Global Count of Protestors Hits Eleven Million'. 15 February. <http://www.indymedia.org/archive/features/2003/02/2003-02.html>.

Anderson, Kenneth (2000). 'The Ottawa Convention Banning Landmines, the Role of International Non-governmental Organizations and the Idea of International Civil Society'. *European Journal of International Law*, 11/1: 91–120.

Anheier, Helmut (forthcoming 2004). 'The United States as the "True Expression" of Civil Society'. In Marlies Glasius, David Lewis, and Hakan Seckinelgin (eds), *Exploring Civil Society: Political and Cultural Contexts* London: Routledge.

—, Marlies Glasius, and Mary Kaldor (eds) (2001). 'Introducing Global Civil Society'. In Helmut Anheier, Marlies Glasius, and Mary Kaldor (eds), *Global Civil Society 2001*. Oxford: Oxford University Press.

— and J. Kendall (2002). 'Trust and the Voluntary Sector.' *British Journal of Sociology*, 53: 343–62.

— and L. Salamon (2003). 'The Nonprofit Sector in Comparative Perspective'. In W.W. Powell and R. Steinberg (eds), *The Nonprofit Sector: A Research Handbook*. New Haven: Yale University Press.

— and N. Themudo (2002). 'Organisational Forms of Global Civil Society: Implications of Going Global'. In Marlies Glasius, Mary Kaldor, and Helmut Anheier (eds), *Global Civil Society 2002*. Oxford: Oxford University Press.

Archambault, E., Gariazzo, M., Anheier, H., and Salamon, L. (1999). 'From Jacobin Tradition to Decentralization'. In L. Salamon et al., *Global Civil Society Dimensions of the Nonprofit Sector*. Baltimore, MD: The Johns Hopkins Center for Civil Society Studies.

Beck, Ulrich. (2000). 'The Postnational Society and its Enemies'. Public lecture, London School of Economics and Political Science, 24 February.

Braudel, F. (1980). *On History* (trans. Sarah Matthews). Chicago: University of Chicago Press.

Cairo Declaration Against U.S. Hegemony and War on Iraq and In Solidarity with Palestine (2002). December. <http://www.cairocampaign.com/html/cairo_declaration.html>.

Cannavo, Salvatore (2001). 'Porto Allegre, Un Altra Strada per l'Umanita.' *Carta.* 5 February.

Chandhoke, Neera (2002). 'The Limits of Global Civil Society.' In Marlies Glasius, Mary Kaldor, and Helmut Anheier (eds), *Global Civil Society 2002.* Oxford: Oxford University Press.

Clark, J. (1991). *Democratizing Development: The Role of Voluntary Agencies.* London: Earthscan.

– (2003). *Worlds Apart: Civil Society and the Battle for Ethical Globalization.* London: Earthscan/Kumarian.

Cohen, Robin and S. Rai (eds) (2000). *Global Social Movements.* London: Athlone Press.

Commission of the European Community (1997). *Promoting the Role of Voluntary Organizations and Foundations in Europe.* Luxembourg: Office of Official Publications of the European Communities.

Dasgupta, P. and I. Serageldin. (2000). *Social Capital: A Multifaceted Perspective.* Washington, DC: World Bank.

Deacon, Bob, M. Hulse, and P. Stubbs (1997). *Global Social Policy: International Organisations and the Future of Welfare.* London: Sage.

Desai, Ashwin (2002). *We Are the Poors. Community Struggles in Post-Apartheid South Africa.* New York: Monthly Review Press Books.

Desai, Meghnad and Yahia Said (2001). 'The New Anti-Capitalist Movement: Money and Global Civil Society.' In Helmut Anheier, Marlies Glasius, and Mary Kaldor (eds), *Global Civil Society 2001.* Oxford: Oxford University Press.

Diani, Mario and Doug McAdam (eds) (2003). *Social Movements and Networks.* Oxford: Oxford University Press.

Edwards, B., E. Foley, and M. Diani (eds) (2001). *Beyond Tocqueville: Civil Society and the Social Capital Debate in Comparative Perspective.* Hanover, NH : University Press of New England. .

Edwards, M. (1999). *Future Positive: International Co-operation in the 21st Century.* London: Earthscan.

– and John Gaventa (eds) (2001). *Global Citizen Action.* Boulder, CO: Lynne Riener.

European Values Surveys 1981, 1990, and 2000 *(2003). Cologne, Tilburg: Central Archive for Social Research, University of Cologne (distributor); Tilburg University (coordinator).*

Fowler, Alan (2000). Civil Society, NGOs and Social Development. Geneva: UNRISD.

Giddens, A. (1999). *The Third Way and its Critics.* London: Polity Press.

Halpern, D. (1999). *Social Capital. The New Golden Goose?* London: Nexus/IPPR.

Held, David, Anthony McGrew, David Goldblatt, and Jonathan Perraton (1999). *Global Transformations: Politics, Economics and Culture.* Cambridge: Polity Press.

Hodkinson, Stuart (2003). 'Custard Pies Are Off the Menu.' *Red Pepper.* March: 36–7.

Howell, Jude and Jenny Pearce (2001). *Civil Society and Development: A Critical Exploration.* Boulder, CO and London: Lynne Rienner.

Inglehart, R. (1990). *Culture Shift in Advanced Industrial Society.* Princeton: Princeton University Press.

– and W. Baker (2000). 'Modernization, Cultural Change, and the Persistance of Traditional Values.' *American Sociological Review,* 65: 19–51.

Kaldor, M. (2003). *Global Civil Society: An Answer to War.* Cambridge: Polity Press.

Keane, J. (2001). 'Global Civil Society?' In Helmut Anheier, Marlies Glasius, and Mary Kaldor (eds), *Global Civil Society 2001.* Oxford: Oxford University Press.

Keck, M. and K. Sikkink (1998). *Activists beyond Borders: Advocacy Networks in International Politics.* Ithaca, NY: Cornell University Press.

Kendall, J. and S. Almond (1999). 'United Kingdom.' In L. Salamon et al., *Global Civil Society Dimensions of the Nonprofit Sector.* Baltimore, MD: The Johns Hopkins Center for Civil Society Studies.

Kettl, Donald (2000). *The Global Public Management Revolution: A Report on the Transformation of Governance.* Washington, DC: Brookings Institution Press.

Klingemann, H. and D. Fuchs (eds) (1995). *Citizens and the State.* New York: Oxford University Press.

Lindenberg, M. and C. Bryant (2001). *Going Global: Transforming Relief and Development NGOs.* Bloomfield, CT: Kumerian Press.

Longhi, Vittorio (2002). 'Where Another Europe Seemed Possible.' *Red Pepper.* 15 December.

McAdam, Doug (ed.) (1996). *Opportunities, Mobilization Structures and Framing Processes.* Cambridge: Cambridge University Press.

–, Sydney Tarrow, and Charles Tilly (2001). *Dynamics of Contention.* Cambridge: Cambridge University Press.

McLaughlin, Kate, Stephen Osborne, and Ewan Ferlie (eds) (2002). *New Public Management: Current Trends and Future Prospects.* London: Routledge..

Mokhiber, Russell and Robert Weissman (2001). 'American Imperialism in Latin America'. *San Francisco Bay Guardian*. 2 November.
Moveon Peace <http://peace.moveon.org/peace.php3>.
New Yorker (2003). 'Marches and Parades'. 19 May.
Offe, C. and S. Fuchs (2002). 'A Decline of Social Capital?'. In R. Putnam (ed), *Democracies in Flux*. Oxford: Oxford University Press.
Oliviero, Melanie Beth and Adele Simmons (2002). 'Who's Minding the Store? Global Civil Society and Corporate Responsibility'. In Marlies Glasius, Mary Kaldor, and Helmut Anheier (eds), *Global Civil Society 2002*. Oxford: Oxford University Press.
Otlet, Paul (1924). *Tableau de l'Organisation Internationale. Rapport général à la Conférence des Associations Internationales*. Geneva: Union of International Associations (publication no. 114).
Perrow, C. (2001). 'The Rise of Nonprofits and the Decline of Civil Society'. In H. Anheier (ed.), *Organizational Theory and the Nonprofit Form* (Report No. 2). London: Centre for Civil Society, London School of Economics.
Perrow, Charles (2002). *Organizing America: Wealth, Power, and the Origins of Corporate Capitalism*. Princeton: Princeton University Press. .
Priller, E. et al (1999). 'Germany'. In L. Salamon et al. *Global Civil Society Dimensions of the Nonprofit Sector*. Baltimore, MD: The Johns Hopkins Center for Civil Society Studies.
Putnam, R. (2000). *Bowling Alone: The Collapse and Survival of American Community*. New York: Simon & Schuster.
– (ed.) (2002). *Democracies in Flux*. Oxford: Oxford University Press.
Putzel, James (1997). 'Accounting for the "Dark Side" of Social Capital: Reading Robert Putnam on Democracy'. *Journal of International Development*, 9: 939–49.
Randall, David, Severin Carrell, Andrew Johnson, and Jonathan Thompson. (2003). 'Million Britons Turn Out to Vote with their Feet'. *The Independent on Sunday*. 16 February.
Salamon, L., Sokolowski, S.W., and List, R. (2003). *Global Civil Society: An Overview*. Baltimore, MD: The Johns Hopkins Center for Civil Society Studies.
Salamon, L. and H. Anheier (1996). *The Emerging Nonprofit Sector*. Manchester: Manchester University Press.
Scholte, Jan-Aart (1999). 'Globalisation: Prospects for a Paradigm Shift'. In M. Shaw (ed.), *Politics and Globalisation*. London: Routledge.
Shaw, Martin (2000). *Theory of the Global State: Global Reality as an Unfinished Revolution*. Cambridge: Cambridge University Press.
Siriani, C. and L. Friedland (2000). *Civic Innovation in America: Community Empowerment, Public Policy, and the Movement for Civic Renewal*. Berkeley: University of California Press.
Schiller, Herbert I. (1998). 'Towards a New Century of American Imperialism'. *Le Monde Diplo*. September.
Sullo, Pierluigi (2001a). 'Allegri Saluti, Cartoline dal Nuovo Mondo'. *Manifesto*. 31 January.
– (2001b). 'Note Allegre Dopo Il Forum'. *Manifesto*. 4 February.
Tew, E. (1963). 'Location of International Organizations'. *International Organizations*, 8: 492–93.
Tyler, Patrick (2003). 'Threats And Responses: News Analysis; A New Power In The Streets'. *New York Times*. 17 February.
UIA (Union of International Associations) (1990). *Yearbook of International Associations*. Brussels: Union of International Associations.
– (2000) *Yearbook of International Associations. Guide to Global Civil Society Networks*. Brussels: Union of International Associations.
– (2002/3). *Yearbook of International Associations. Guide to Global Civil Society Networks*. Munich: Saur.
UNCTAD (United Nations Conference on Trade and Development) (2001). *World Investment Report* <http://www.unctad.org/wir/pdfs/wir_tnc_top100.en.pdf>.
UNDP (United Nations Development Program) (2002). *Human Development Report 2002*. New York: Oxford University Press.
United for Peace (2003).'Feb. 15 Protests Around the World' <http://unitedforpeace.org/article.php?id=725>.
Van Deth, J. and E. Scarbrough (eds) (1995). *The Impact of Values*. Oxford, New York: Oxford University Press.
World Values Survey Study Group (1999–2000).*World Values Survey, 1981–1984, 1990–1993, and 1995–97*. CD Rom, cumulative file for the first 3 waves. Ann Arbor: Institute for Social Research (producer); Inter-university Consortium for Political and Social Research (distributor).
– (2003). 'World Values Survey 2000'. Unpublished, by permission.
WSF (World Social Forum) Charter of Principles (2001) <http://www.forumsocialmundial.org.br/>

Chapter 2

THE GLOBAL TRANSFORMATION OF THE SOCIAL SCIENCES

Martin Shaw

Regressive Globalism and the Structure of Globality

The beginning of the twenty-first century has seen a decisive change in world politics compared with the first post-Cold War decade in which 'global' ideas first became enormously influential. The military reassertion of American nationalism by the George W. Bush administration, following the terrorist massacre of 11 September 2001, has widely been seen as marking an end to the liberal globalism of the previous decade. And if 'globalisation' was the buzzword of the 1990s, it now seems distinctly less fashionable. Some critics have gone so far as to argue that it was little more than a passing intellectual fancy that masked underlying realities of class and military power. Certainly globalisation-speak is no longer so prominent among world elites: in Gramsci's terms, there has been a shift within the hegemonic international bloc symbolised by the departure of former US President Bill Clinton and the marginalising of the 'third way'.[1] Correspondingly, some radical activists have shifted from seeing globalisation as the problem ('anti-globalisation' is no longer a label of choice) and have re-branded their movement under a 'global justice' logo.

These shifts in the political discourse surrounding 'global' change represent important challenges to the emergent global civil society. They also offer an opportunity to separate the *conjunctional* features of the first global decade from the *structural* features of globality. The decline in the fashion for naive globalisation-thought enables us to see what is more fundamental and durable in global development. At the same time it helps us to see globality, not as a single set of ideas, but as a complex field of competing forces in which even self-proclaimed 'anti-globalists', whether of the right or of the left, must also recognise some crucial elements of global reality.

In an attempt to understand the development of 'new' intellectual paradigms in the last quarter-century, I have argued that the historical sequence in which they emerged (first 'postmodernity', then 'post-Cold War', and finally 'globalisation') reflects the development of the crisis of the Cold War system (Shaw 2000: ch. 1). When ideas of postmodernity emerged in the 1980s, predominantly in the cultural sciences, they reflected a general sense of emergent crisis that had not reached the stage of decisive political change. Ideas of 'post-Cold War' emerged at the beginning of the 1990s, during the period of political crisis itself, and were centred on political and international thought. Ideas of 'globalisation' became dominant in the mid-1990s, as the crisis was resolved and new world power relations, centred it seemed in economics and communications, became apparent. Whereas 'post-' narratives reflected the sense of transformation of old relations, the idea of the 'global' suggested the positive content of the new.

But in the spread of 'global' ideas, exactly what this term meant was often far from clear. The main idea was that identified by Anthony Giddens (1990), namely, the intensified interconnectedness and the worldwide stretching of social relations. Behind this, of course, lay the core meaning of 'globe' as a planetary sphere, and considerable impetus to globality flowed from the greater recognition of our common physical environment. However, commonality in a deeper and broader sense was also entailed by globality. By 'global' we meant not just transformed conceptions of time and space but the new social meaning that worldwide relations involved. This could be understood as the development of a common *consciousness* of human society on a world scale, with an increasing awareness of the totality of human social relations as the largest constitutive *framework* of all relations. Global civil society represented attempts to give this consciousness the form of purposive action and

[1] *Antonio Gramsci (1972) argued that the dominance of (national) ruling groups was maintained through 'historic blocs' of shifting combinations of social forces, centred on sets of beliefs that were constantly developed and renewed. Applying this idea at the global level is complicated, but the approach has gained ground in the discipline of international relations.*

organisation with an explicit normative agenda; but this kind of awareness was present in all the kinds of social action that globalisation theory embraced, including—as I have suggested—in 'anti-global' thought.

The late 1990s had already seen important shifts in globalisation debates. More sophisticated work was outgrowing the antinomies of the 'undermining' of nation-states by the market (Ohmae 1990) and the reassertion of the centrality of the state (Hirst and Thompson 1996; Weiss 1998). As David Held *et al.* (1999) rather neatly summed it up, an intellectual third way was open that stressed the changing character of the state and broadened the conception of *global transformation* (rather than globalisation) to give equal weight to political and military processes. Corresponding to these intellectual changes, the political third way, briefly supreme as the Clinton-Blair axis of 1997–2000 coincided with wider social-democratic predominance in Europe, headlined a normative global agenda even if its practice didn't live up to its finer ambitions. Increasingly embedded in the institutional agendas of many global international organisations, this partially incorporated the impetus of the still relatively weak global civil society. Given this apparent embrace of globalisation on the centre-left, it is no wonder then that far-left 'anti-capitalists' initially configured themselves as 'anti-globalisers' too.

The decline in the fashion for naïve globalisation-thought enables us to see what is more fundamental and durable in global development

Post-9/11 developments represent significantly new crystallisations of global relations. The uneasy coalescence of global civil society and global state leadership was already falling apart as the new Bush administration abandoned the Kyoto climate change accord, the International Criminal Court, and other globalist projects. Bin Laden's contribution was to turn the US from disengagement towards its own new but regressive global project. The 'war on terrorism' forged a new American global alliance, downgrading the old West at its core and centred on an axis of repressive authoritarian power linking Washington with Moscow, Beijing, Islamabad, and New Delhi. Never before had all the major non-Western powers been so strongly caught up in an American military campaign, nor (since 1989 at least) had the US given so much legitimacy to authoritarian and semi-authoritarian rulers worldwide. In early 2003, the determination of the US to impose its own global order through war against Iraq threatened the stability of the transatlantic Western bloc and the viability of the UN as well as this larger global alliance with major non-Western states.

In these circumstances of *regressive globalism*, the democratic and human rights-oriented globalism of civil society is necessarily more fundamentally critical of established power. The political conjunction fits the opposition of 'humane' and 'inhumane' global governance outlined some years ago by Richard Falk (1995). In line with these new circumstances, a revamped 'global justice' campaign recognises the underlying reality of globality and advocates a progressive version of it. Nevertheless, the contradictions of global power remain very evident, with the progressive agendas of UN control of weapons and global democratisation paradoxically entwined in Bush's narrower project of an 'anti-terrorist' global alliance.

The Political Core of Globality

It is clear from these fast-changing contexts of global politics that the 'global' is more than any one trend. Globality represents a fundamental integrative tendency in world politics, culture, economy, and society. Moreover, while modernity and capitalism in general have promoted these kinds of development over a longer period, they have reached a decisively new maturity in post-Cold War conditions. Contemporary globality cannot be reduced to the underlying structures of capitalist relations, which after all have not been fundamentally changed. Pre-existing trends towards the commodification of social life have been enhanced, but it is political changes that have made this possible. Thus, the specific quality of a global world does not lie in market trends but in the fundamental singularity of social space, however stratified and fragmented, that *political* and even *military* changes have brought about.

There are two main sides to this political infrastructure of globality. On the one hand, the results of the Second World War, the Cold War, and now the 'war on terrorism' have aligned states into more and more integrated *global networks of state power*, regulating the complex political-military as well as political-economic relations of a global world. The worldwide intelligence-sharing in the hunt for Al-Qaeda epitomises this interconnectedness. On the other hand, the emergence of *global civil society* reflects the new awareness in society at large of a common global framework and the interest of social actors in common world agendas and networks to guide, organise, and legitimise their actions. Civil society responds not just to economic, cultural, and technical sides of globalisation, but also to state-level integration.

Thus, it is in politics, and around the tensions of these two sides, that globality crystallises. If globality is the development of a common consciousness of human society on a world scale, with an increasing awareness of the totality of human social relations as the largest constitutive framework, then global political organisation—both state and civil society—is crucial to the *recognition* of globality. I shall argue, therefore, that politics is the main axis around which the changing responses of the social sciences to global change have revolved. Thus the challenges of global social science parallel, and often clearly intersect with, those of global civil society, and civil society needs the theoretical clarification to underpin its own development. In this chapter I shall explore the manifold ways in which the social sciences have articulated and responded to global change and how these developments have affected disciplinary and interdisciplinary structures of knowledge.

The challenges of global social science parallel, and often clearly intersect with, those of global civil society, and civil society needs the theoretical clarification to underpin its own development

Social Science's Ancien Régime

Intimations of globality have fundamentally challenged old ways of doing things in the social sciences (Shaw 2000: ch. 3). It is not far-fetched to liken the world view on which a great deal of mainstream social science was formerly based to that of the stamp collector. As a youthful philatclist in the mid-twentieth century, I sorted my stamps by political jurisdiction. I directed my attention to the national forms—technical and symbolic—through which both intra-national and international communication took place. I was not so concerned with the manifold social relations—personal, commercial, professional, and so on—which these forms concealed, although these were much more important, almost certainly more interesting, and less constituted by the apparatus of statehood.

Much social science of the period sorted social relations in the same way, simply assuming the coincidence of social boundaries with state boundaries and that social action occurred primarily within, and secondarily across, these divisions. Social relations were represented by the national societies that were assumed to frame them. Just as I collected the various ephemera of national postal systems, social scientists collected distinctive national social forms. Japanese industrial relations, German national character, the American constitution, the British class system—not to mention the more exotic institutions of tribal societies—were the currency of social research.

Of course the social sciences had long contained, but in a double sense, the challenge of the global. On the one hand, the master ideas of social thought, developed from the late eighteenth to the early twentieth centuries, centred on concepts of universal, implicitly global significance: civil society, capitalism, industrialism, modernity. On the other hand, the twentieth-century institutionalisation of the social sciences in academic disciplines, research, and teaching practice have largely nationalised—and internationalised—these concepts. Theory and analysis have come to refer, implicitly if not always explicitly, to the national and international frameworks of state and society that dominated social relations in the mid-twentieth century heyday of the imperial nation-state.

The core disciplines of the social sciences, whose intellectual traditions are reference points for each other and for other fields, were therefore largely *domesticated*, in the sense of being preoccupied not with Western and world civilisation as wholes but with the 'domestic' forms of particular national societies. Many writers (including Ulrich Beck in this Yearbook) have called this tendency 'methodological nationalism'. What it involved, above all, was a slippage from the general to the particular without bringing into the open the problematic abstraction involved in isolating the national case.

The particular was often assumed to be representative of the general. In sociology and political science, for example, American or British society, state, and capitalism with all their idiosyncrasies were often held to typify society, state, or capitalism as such. This tendency was not confined to conservative theorists like Talcott Parsons (1952). C. Wright Mills's (1956) radical critique of the 'power elite' was often presented as an alternative model of power in modern society without acknowledging the American specificity that he put at the heart of his account. Marxists could write about class in Britain as though it was a typical rather than a very peculiar case of a capitalist society.

In the domesticated core social sciences, when the general pattern of social relations on a world scale came to be represented by more than a single case, it was not usually by global, transnational, or even international relations but by the *comparative* method. Comparing different particular social forms came to substitute for understanding the relations between them and the general structures within which these comparisons might be explained. National and comparative sociology and politics increasingly dominated the core disciplines in practice.

Intimations of globality have fundamentally challenged old ways of doing things in the social sciences

The discipline of international relations conformed to this pattern as the exception that proved the rule. In the early post-war decades, when international realism was codified, world order could be conceived only in terms of the international. In a world of nation-states, *internationality* represented the relations between units and actors under this single, simple rubric. Inter-national, of course, meant inter-state, since states were mostly assumed, by definition, to represent 'their' nations. The relationship between state and nation was unproblematic.

The division of labour between the domesticated disciplines and international relations reflected a central paradox of the Cold War West. Although Western nation-states were casting off the military rivalries of centuries to create a common network of power, with an increasing number of bloc-wide and world institutions, national forms remained dominant. Western integration was first of all cooperation between the nation-states and, reflecting them, national societies that had emerged from the era of total war. Commonality presented itself first as the *alliance* and *similarity* of what continued to be seen as distinct units.

No wonder, then, that the comparative method became so influential in Western social science and that, instead of global knowledge, international research generated comparative studies. The genre gained new life, indeed, at the end of the twentieth century with the increasing dependence of European social research on European Union funding with its inbuilt balancing of national interests. The post-Cold War incorporation of many central and east European nation-states within the Western social science orbit has only accentuated this trend. Increasingly, however, the comparative method seems anachronistic, as simultaneously not just the Western world and its European sub-unit but world society as a whole begin to see themselves as integrated wholes. Within these larger frameworks, relations between individuals, firms, social groups, and cultures are not necessarily, simply, or even primarily mediated by nationality-internationality.

Crises and Transformation in Social Science Disciplines

It is difficult for any one scholar to know, and therefore to understand, fully what is happening in any one field or even sub-field, let alone in the social sciences as a whole. This section constitutes, therefore, a set of hypotheses about how and why the various social sciences have changed in response to the crisis of old national-and-international ways of social science. It is driven by my argument that global change is profoundly political in character. I contend, therefore, that the diversity of experience of transformation in the social sciences is explained, in part at least, by relationships to political transformation, and reflects the nature of the underlying connections of the disciplines to political forms.

My first hypothesis is that the disciplines of social anthropology and geography have shown greater openness to global understanding than economics, politics, and sociology, the historically defining fields of social science. Interestingly, the former are fields in which, historically, the national-international nexus was formerly not just a methodological bias but more or less *explicitly* constitutive, through nineteenth and early twentieth-century colonialist and nationalist constructions of the subjects. The openness of both social anthropology and geography to globalisation debates follows their abandonment of these historic legacies. These subjects underwent profound theoretical and ideological transformations earlier in the post-war period, which have prepared the way for the recognition of globalisation.

Thus the old colonial-inspired traditions of social anthropology disintegrated with the independence movements of the 1960s (Asad 1971), which required new ways of conceiving spatially differentiated relations. The discipline's bias towards the study of less formal social relations facilitated an interest in relations defined in non-territorial and non-national ways—within and across rather than limited by state borders. The subject was thus transnationally oriented and implicitly globalist before global debates seriously developed. In particular, anthropologists have explored the transformation of culture in plural and hybrid forms (Hannerz 1996; Kahn1995).

Social anthropology and geography have shown greater openness to global understanding than economics, politics, and sociology, the historically defining fields of social science

In geography, similarly, the old geo-political foundations of the subject have long since eroded, rendered anachronistic by the collapse of empire. In geography's case, however, space remains a master concept and, even before global debates became widespread, geographers mapped economic and social relations in transnational terms. Not only have geographers been in the forefront of analysing the economics of globalisation, but the concept of space has also been peculiarly problematised, and geographers have absorbed debates on time, space, and modernity from social theory. The result, however, appears to have been the decline of a distinctive disciplinary sense as the boundaries between geography, political economy, international relations, and sociological thought have become more and more fluid.

Critical geographers have embraced this new fluidity and redefined the role of geography within it. Thus, Peter Taylor sees geography as 'marginalised' in the old 'state-centric orthodoxy' of the social sciences. 'The mainstream social science trilogy of sociology, economics, and political science', he argues, 'neglected questions of space and place because they failed to problematise the embedded statism in which they developed.' 'New spaces' are opened up in theory, however, by the 'new heterodoxy consequent upon globalisation' in which 'the new subtleties of social space are integral' (Taylor 1996: 1921). Taylor sees geography as particularly equipped for a social science that is discarding 'embedded statism' (by which he means something similar to 'methodological nationalism').

How true is it that Taylor's 'mainstream social science trilogy' of constitutive disciplines has failed to globalise, remaining within domesticated concepts? I know least about economics. However, despite the growth of international economics, there seems to be a real paradox in that economic relations are universally acknowledged to be important in globalisation but professional economists are hardly in the forefront of theorising that phenomenon. The degree of abstraction of much academic economic thought from concrete political-economic contexts has meant that, while much economics shows relatively little trace of methodological nationalism, it is equally oblivious of globalising tendencies. It is symptomatic that the economic relations of globalisation are picked up more in geography, sociology, and (especially) the burgeoning field of international political economy (IPE) which has emerged from international relations.

There is conflicting evidence on how sociology as a disciplinary subject has reconstituted itself in global terms. Social theorists like Michael Mann have made us aware of the historic global-national tension in their subject. Writing of the nineteenth century he points out, 'Throughout this period the nation-state and a broader transnational Western civilisation competed as basic membership units. Sociology's master-concept, "society", kept metamorphosing between the two' (Mann 1993: 9). Later, sociology was organised around the twin concepts of industrial and capitalist society. Both of these clearly held a potential for global understanding, but in the mid-twentieth century they were overwhelmingly operationalised as national categories. Even the new Marxism of the 1970s—with exceptions such as 'world-systems' theory that had their own characteristic weaknesses—largely adapted itself to the national contexts of existing social science. Since the Marxist revival petered out, there was if anything a further domestication of sociology, pragmatically integrating it in national and sub-national contexts.

The discipline of international relations, much more than the core social sciences, was a Cold War product: it represented the bifurcation of superpowers and blocs rather than the burgeoning global relations that underlay them

Of course, some strands of social theory have been central to the global revolution in thought; but the work of thinkers like Giddens and Beck has impinged only slowly on the institutionalised intellectual context of the discipline. Sociologists like Martin Albrow (1996) have produced some of the most radical outlines of globality, but global ideas have also met considerable resistance. Barry Smart, for example, explicitly opposes the idea of a 'global sociology', 'with its connotations of a universalising, indivisible discipline', preferring the notion of 'a sociology of globalisation, or better still, sociological analyses of processes of globalisation'. For him, the idea of a 'global sociology', implying that 'there already exists a worldwide culture', is mistaken. Elevating the notion of 'society' to a global level suggests that 'the peoples of the world are incorporated 'into a single world society, global society', and this will not do (Smart 1993: 135). Moreover, where 'global' sociology has developed the global has been largely conceived in socio-cultural terms, and the relationship to political change is weakly represented (see the review of global sociology texts in Shaw 2002).

If sociology still has its difficulties with the global, political science has been even more disabled by its inherited methodological nationalism. Certainly, normative work in political theory has recognised that globalisation has led to a new problematisation of the division of international and domestic politics. What is at stake, as David Held (1995) argued, is nothing less than a fundamental recasting of political theory as it has developed *within* the liberal-democratic nation-state. Democracy and other political values have to be reconstituted in global—or as Held, Kaldor, and others prefer, 'cosmopolitan'—terms. However, in empirical political science the standard demarcation of national and international remains restrictive. Comparative politics suffers from much the same weaknesses as comparative sociology, but politics has the vices as well as the virtues of the more explicitly national focus involved in studying states and party systems. Political studies adapt by analysing politics as process at the expense of grasping the transformation of content. Thus the European Union or the United Nations can be seen as offering new contexts in which to explore the mechanics of political life and institution-building rather than challenges of historical change. What is true of politics may be even truer of law. Despite the growth of international law, which parallels the expansion of international relations, legal studies remain closely attached to bodies of legal practice that are still largely embedded in national legislation, courts, and legal traditions.

The Special Role and Contradictions of International Relations

International relations plays a particular role in the development of global social science. It is the field that superficially most resembles an arena for new global understanding. It has the unique advantage for the purposes of global debate that, while it assumes the national, it was at least constituted *above* the national level. However, the historical forms of the field have reflected pre-global forms in which worldwide relations were conceived. In the Cold War era of institutionalised internationalism, the international encapsulated the dominant form of the emergent global order. It was possible for international relations to theorise world-level problems, but only as matters of international cooperation. In doing so, however, international relationists gave little more attention than any other social scientists to the specificity of the global. Instead they often encouraged a seamless elision of global with international politics.

Indeed, the discipline of international relations, much more than the core social sciences, was a Cold War product: it represented the bifurcation of superpowers and blocs rather than the burgeoning global relations that underlay them. Nevertheless, the erosion of the historic statist core of the field can be traced at least to the period of détente in the 1970s. Rather as geography and social anthropology were transformed in the aftermath of empire, so the ending of the Cold War has led to an accelerated renewal of international relations, making disciplinary definitions of the subject increasingly problematic.

If only at the level of theoretical debate, and outside the United States, the dominant realism has imploded since 1989. The field of international relations is currently one of the most highly theorised of the social sciences, its intellectual ferment testifying to serious issues at stake. A wide range of critical approaches jostles for dominance with new versions of realism and neo-realism. This has opened up the subject (in some eyes at least) as an interdisciplinary field for specialised global studies: global political economy, global environmental politics, global gender studies, and so forth.

The transformation of international relations is, however, very problematic. The international and the global are not two ways of expressing more or less the same idea. Certainly, global relations depend in practice on international, including inter-state relations. This aspect is a source of much confusion. But the two concepts are of fundamentally different kinds. There is a core contradiction between them. Globality involves the unification of the social world and the relativisation of difference within it. The international represents the division of social relations by national (historically state, now increasingly cultural) boundaries and the definition of particular kinds of difference as constitutive. The global incorporates manifold spatial relations: the international defines certain relations as central.

Global understanding can help explain the international (including its defining contradiction and confusion between inter*national* and inter*state*). International theory cannot understand the global, except in the limited sense of one spatial level of inter- or trans-state relations, or as their negation: the undermining of states, interstate relations, and the international. These ways of comprehending the global are profoundly limited: first, because the global is much more than a spatial level and, second, because global transformations involve the reconstitution rather than the simple undermining or overcoming of state forms and interstate relations.

International studies offer both empirical space for many fields of global enquiry and tantalising prospects of theoretical reformation. Ultimately, however, the disciplinary definition of the international is as limiting as the nation-centred operationalisation of universal categories in the core disciplines. Most of the attempts to resolve this problem in international theory have remained ad hoc: greater emphases on non-state actors, supplementing strategy with political economy, cultural theory, feminism, and so on. However, even the most tightly focused global theory that has emerged from international relations has had considerable difficulty in encapsulating globality, as I explored in my book (Shaw 2000: ch 3).

Interdisciplinary Fields, Interdisciplinarisation of the Disciplines

In such transformations of disciplinary relations, an increasingly important role is played by interdisciplinary fields—such as environmental, communications, and cultural studies as well as IPE—which have often seen the most radical posing of global transformation. An early example, of course, was development studies: in the post-colonial era, this was a principal arena for issues of world political economy and world sociology. But development studies also embody some of the contradictions of a social science that is emerging from the national-international framework. Paradigms dominated by national-international conceptions have dominated the field, from the simple Western-sponsored stages-of-development model to the more radical promise of autonomous *national* development that issued from the critique of imperialism. Some development studies have, as a result, a curiously old-fashioned flavour at the

Interdisciplinary fields – such as environmental, communications and cultural studies as well as international political economy – have often seen the most radical posing of global transformation

beginning of the twenty-first century. When it makes the nation-state its premise, development studies, too, is challenged by contemporary global change.

Other interdisciplinary fields have been more obviously congruent with emergent globalism but have also exemplified its difficulties. Communications and media studies have had an empirical importance because of the centrality of communications developments to globality. And yet the communications literature, in stressing the technological mechanisms of worldwide linkages, still leaves us with the question of how to understand their content. Critical political economy approaches, which emphasise the dominance of Western media corporations, are in danger of missing the novelty of contemporary global communications. Media roles crystallise in contrasting ways, in critical tension with as well as supportive of globally dominant interests.

In cultural studies, issues of global content have been more explicitly addressed. The field housed the first extensive debates (for example, Featherstone 1990; King 1990) that were influential in introducing globalisation issues into sociology and, more recently, international relations. Nevertheless, it is difficult to encapsulate globality primarily in terms of culture, as there is the danger of missing the political ruptures that have been the largest markers of change. Alongside economic process and cultural transformation we need to put the conscious practices of political revolution that have defined the beginnings of the global epoch.

If it is difficult to represent the global transformation of social relations in terms of changes within historic disciplines, it is also only partially adequate to see interdisciplinary *fields* as the answer to the global challenge. *Interdisciplinarisation* is a phenomenon of the social sciences as a whole, and involves a radical relativisation not only of historic disciplines but also of established interdisciplinary fields. Interdisciplinarisation is not a new phenomenon: the tendency for disciplines to cross-fertilise is as old as disciplines themselves. It is rather like internationalisation, which has always accompanied apparently entrenched nationality. Both reflect underlying unities of knowledge and human society that are denied by more rigid definitions of disciplines; in the case of knowledge, of course, these were embodied in the very idea of the 'university'. Historically, the tendency towards disciplinary formation, like that towards national autonomy, deepened from the mid-nineteenth to the mid-twentieth century. However, this tendency was always balanced by forms of interdisciplinarity. These were often informed by intellectual trends, like Marxism, that spread across the various fields and, directly or indirectly, challenged narrow disciplinary conceptions of knowledge.

The practice of interdisciplinarity represents more than the ad hoc collaboration of scholars across boundaries: borrowing, cross-reference and constant interplay of ideas have become normal

In the late twentieth century, as internationalisation increased so did interdisciplinarisation. Successive waves of ideas fanned out across the social sciences: the new Marxism of the late 1960s, the feminism of the 1970s, and the postmodernism and environmentalism of the 1980s all preceded the globalism of the 1990s. Because these trends were first instantiated in one or more disciplines or interdisciplinary fields—particularly in sociology—interdisciplinarisation often took the form of 'influence' of one field on another and the importation or borrowing of authors and ideas from one field into another. The most important authors, like Giddens or Jacques Derrida, were widely cited across almost all fields; others' work was taken up across a more modest range.

Thus the practice of interdisciplinarity, at the end of the twentieth century, represented more than the ad hoc collaboration of scholars across boundaries that had always taken place in the disciplinary world. Interdisciplinarisation had become a more thoroughgoing, self-reproducing set of processes in which borrowing, cross-reference, and constant interplay of ideas had become normal. The association of interdisciplinarisation with internationalisation was not accidental: the tendencies towards integration of society and knowledge naturally accompanied each other. Just as internationalisation was a political reflection of the integration of the world, so interdisciplinarisation reflected this integration in the structure of academic knowledge.

Re-imagining the Conceptual Framework of the Social Sciences

The question that arises is whether global thought is just another universal intellectual trend, alongside feminism, postmodernism, and so on. It seems to me that globalisation theory itself can be plausibly represented in this light; it is a particular instantiation of ideas, powerful in its appeal, but very definitely of a particular time. However, globality, as Albrow (1996) suggests, offers scope for a broad historic reconfiguration of social knowledge. Its emergence is the point at which the historic potential of universal, secular, scientific knowledge ceases to be radically opposed to a social, political, and spatial world that can be grasped concretely only in terms of division.

In the global epoch, the world begins be conceived practically as a single community. Globality is a political-spatial representation of the moral cosmopolitanism that was first conceived by Immanuel Kant at the beginning of the modern era, but was inevitably opposed to the empirical forms of an imperially divided world society. Global social science thus offers a new possibility of reunifying social science, just as global politics, and especially global civil society, offer the practical possibility of unifying the social world.

Global social science offers possibilities not only of theoretical clarification but also of worldwide networks of knowledge practitioners who in themselves constitute an important element of global civil society

Of course, disciplines and interdisciplinary fields will continue to exist, rather like nations and international organisations, and will be a large part of the infrastructure through which global social science is developed. Social knowledge, like the social world of which it is a part, is so vast and complex that it cannot be adequately developed within a single unitary framework without many structural differentiations. But global social science, like global civil society, can recognise its internal differences as representations of specificity within unity and convenient building blocks of the larger picture. It should not see them as more absolute divisions of the kind that have sometimes been assumed in representations of discipline as well as national community.

The new transparency of global relations, with the end of the Cold War, has therefore brought with it a conceptual crisis in the social sciences. Since the very meanings of core concepts change in a period of transition, we need to redefine them for a global age. Globality challenges the disciplines to move beyond the ways of thinking which have predominated in their historic development. The possibility of global knowledge released by the end of the Cold War involves the simultaneous transformation both of concepts of nationality and of the ways in which integrationary, internationalist tendencies have been understood. The links between people can no longer be squeezed into a national-international strait-jacket, even if this is still very much one of the dimensions which define them. This is as true of social relations 'within' states as it as of those 'across' their borders.

Instead, social relations are increasingly grasped in their genuine complexity, as interpersonal, familial, industrial, commercial, professional, local, regional, transnational, world-regional, global—as well as national and international. In this variety of terms in which social relations are now understood, some are intrinsically spatial (local, regional, national, transnational, international, world-regional) while others (interpersonal, familial, commercial, professional, lifestyle, movement) do not assume a particular spatial content. 'Global' has an obvious spatial reference but, as I argued above, its significance goes far beyond this. The global is the largest and most inclusive spatial framework of social relations and—interplanetary exploration apart—the maximum possible framework. Its development represents the partial overcoming of the major divisions of the world, cultural as well as territorial. Precisely for these reasons, globality includes both the spatially and the non-spatially defined differentiations of the world.

It is not accidental, therefore, that global categories have emerged as main forms of the new theoretical discourse of the social sciences and that the global has a different significance from the other terms. Those who oppose regional or transnational to global change therefore underestimate the significance of current transformations and misunderstand the debate on the global. To talk of global transformations does not mean that all relations are of a spatially worldwide or trans-regional kind. Rather, global transformation, involving fundamental changes in both the spatial and the non-spatial dimensions of social relations, includes the regional, transnational, and so forth—whereas none of these terms can include the global. Global social science represents, therefore, an important new stage in the development of the social sciences in which disciplines and interdisciplinary fields face common challenges of fundamental theoretical development.

Conclusion: Global Social Science and Global Civil Society

Global social science can make an important contribution to clarifying the potential of global civil society. Civil society itself is a pre-global concept that is now being transposed into global terms. Historically it epitomised the tension of universal values and national social forms, so the general problems of globally reconstructing social knowledge are particularly evident with the idea of civil society. Globalising civil society involves more than moving to a different level; it means understanding civil society as an active project, a contribution towards consolidating global society, and the critical 'other' of global state networks.

Global civil society has already benefited from the ideas about its possibilities that social scientists, in many fields, have developed. One of the differences from earlier national forms of civil society is precisely the contribution that academic understanding, for example in this yearbook, can make to practical activity. Global social science offers possibilities not only of theoretical clarification but also of worldwide networks of knowledge practitioners who in themselves constitute an important element of global civil society.

References

Albrow, M. (1996). *The Global Age*. Cambridge: Polity Press.

Asad, T. (ed.) (1971). *Anthropology and the Colonial Encounter*. London: Ithaca.

Falk, R. (1995). *On Humane Governance: Towards a New Global Politics*. Cambridge: Polity Press.

Featherstone, M. (ed.) (1990). *Global Culture: Nationalism, Globalization and Modernity*. London: Sage.

Giddens, A. (1990). *The Consequences of Modernity*. Cambridge: Polity Press.

Gramsci, A. (1972). *Selections From the Prison Notebooks of Antonio Gramsci* (ed. Q. Hoare and G. N. Smith). London: Lawrence and Wishart.

Hannerz, U. (1996). *Transcultural Connections: Culture, People, Places*. London: Routledge.

Held, D. (1995). *Democracy and Global Order*. Cambridge: Polity Press.

–, McGrew, A., Goldblatt, D., and Perraton, J. (1999). *Global Transformations*. Cambridge: Polity Press.

Hirst, P. Q. and Thompson, G. (1996). *Globalization in Question*. Cambridge: Polity Press.

Kahn, J. (1995). *Culture, Multiculture, Postculture*. London: Sage.

King, A. D. (ed.) (1990). *Culture, Globalization and the World-system*. London: Macmillan.

Mann, M. (1993). *The Sources of Social Power, Vol. II*. Cambridge: Cambridge University Press.

Mills, C. W. (1956). *The Power Elite*. New York: Oxford University Press.

Ohmae, K. (1990). *The Borderless World*. London: Collins.

Parsons, T. (1952). *The Social System*. London: Tavistock.

Shaw, M. (2000). *Theory of the Global State: Globality as Unfinished Revolution*. Cambridge: Cambridge University Press.

– (2002). 'Teaching Global Sociology'. *Sociology*, 36/1: 195–9.

Smart, B. (1993). *Postmodernity*. London: Routledge.

Taylor, P. I. (1996). 'Embedded Statism and the Social Sciences: Opening Up to New Spaces', *Environment and Planning*, 28: 1917–28.

Weiss, L. (1998). *The Myth of the Powerless State*. Cambridge: Polity Press.

Chapter 3

The Analysis of Global Inequality: from National to Cosmopolitan Perspective

Ulrich Beck

In order to analyse the dynamics of global civil society (global politics, global capital, global culture, global inequalities), we need a methodological shift from the dominant national perspective to a cosmopolitan perspective. A cosmopolitan frame of reference calls into question one of the most powerful beliefs of our time concerning society and politics. This belief is the notion that 'modern society' and 'modern politics' are to be understood as nation state organised society and nation state organised politics; in other words, the concept of society is identified with the national imagination of society. When this belief is held by social actors, I call it 'national perspective'; when it is held by scientific observers, I call it 'methodological nationalism'. This distinction between the perspective of a social actor and that of the social scientist is important because there is *no* logical connection between the two, only a common origin.

The Principles of Methodological Nationalism

Methodological nationalism equates societies with nation-states societies and sees states and their governments as the cornerstones of social science analysis. It assumes that humanity is naturally divided into a limited number of nations which organise themselves internally as nation-states and set external boundaries to distinguish themselves from other nation-states. It goes even further: this outer delimitation as well as the competition between nation-states represents the most fundamental category of political organisation. Much social science assumes the coincidence of social boundaries with state boundaries, thus presupposing that social action occurs primarily within, and secondarily across, these divisions.

From a social science perspective, the cosmopolitan question is not primarily normative; that is to say, it is not what a 'cosmopolitan society', 'cosmopolitan democracy', 'cosmopolitan state' or regime ought to be. Rather it is whether there is a clear sociological alternative to the national mystification of societies and political order. Is there an *actually existing* cosmopolitanism, a reality of (re)attachment, multiple belongings or belonging from a distance? In fact, to belong or not to belong: that *is* the cosmopolitan question (Favell 1999; Beck 2002). Is global civil society part of this reality?

A sharp distinction should be made between *methodological* nationalism and *normative* nationalism. The former is linked to the perspective of the social sciences observer whereas the latter refers to the perspective of political actors. Normative nationalism holds that every nation has the right to determine itself within the frame of its cultural distinctiveness. Methodological nationalism assumes this normative claim as a given and simultaneously defines the conflicts and institutions of society and politics in these terms. These basic tenets have become the main grid through which social scientists see the world.

Indeed the social scientist's stance is rooted in the concept of the nation state, his or her sociological imagination dominated by a nation-state outlook on society, politics, law, justice and history. Social scientists are, to a large degree, prisoners of the nation-state.

These premises also structure empirical research; for example, statistical indicators are almost always exclusively national. A refutation of methodological nationalism from a strictly empirical viewpoint is therefore difficult, indeed nigh impossible, because many statistical categories and processes of investigation are based upon it.

Comparative analyses of societies, international relations, political theory, a significant part of history, and jurisprudence are all essentially based on methodological nationalism. Indeed, most positions in the contemporary social and political science debate over globalisation can arguably be systematically interpreted as trans-disciplinary reflexes linked to methodological nationalism. It is therefore very important for the future development of social science that methodological nationalism, as well as the associated categories of perception and institutional discipline, be theoretically, empirically, and organisationally dissected and reassessed.

Methodological nationalism includes the following principles:

1 the *subordination* of society to the state; which implies
2 that there is no singular but only the *plural* of societ*ies*, in contrast to Niklas Luhmann's (2002) argument that there is only *one* society, that is 'world society';
3 a *territorial* notion of societies with state-constructed *boundaries*, that is, the territorial state as container of society;
4 the principle of reciprocal *determination* between state and society: the territorial nation-state is both creator and guarantor of individual citizenship rights, and citizens organise themselves to influence and legitimise state actions;
5 both states and societies are imagined and located within the *dichotomy-between the national and the international*, which up to now has been the foundation of the dominant ontology of politics and political theory;
6 the state as the guarantor of the social order provides the instruments and units for the collection of *statistics* about social and economic processes that empirical social science requires; indeed, the categories of the state census have come to be the main operational categories of empirical social science, and this is true even for most 'global' data, which are based on nation-state statistics and exclude transnational 'networks', 'flows', and 'scapes';
7 in membership and statistical representation methodological nationalism operates on the either-or principle, excluding the as-well-as principle: either 'us' or 'them', either 'in' or 'out'.

There is, however, a problem with the term 'methodological nationalism'. It can be thought of as a sort of prejudice, a 'belief', an 'attitude', and therefore something that can be eliminated from modern enlightened thought in the same way that we eliminate other attitudes such as racism, sexism, or religious bigotry. But the crucial point of methodological nationalism is that it is not a matter of values and prejudices, but rather of science and scholarship and informed expert opinion. To be precise, methodological nationalism refers to a set of beliefs that are statements about empirical reality, statements that mainstream social scientists, using highly sophisticated empirical research methods, accept as true, as propositions supported by 'the facts'. Methodological nationalism is therefore very difficult to understand. We have to ask on what grounds we reflect upon and criticise methodological nationalism. And is there an alternative? Why should one accept it?

The Cosmopolitan Perspective

The critique of methodological nationalism should not be mistaken for the thesis about the end of the nation-state. Nor is it necessarily the case that in criticising methodological nationalism one is promoting the elimination of the nation. Nation-states (as all investigations have shown) will continue to thrive or will be transformed into transnational states. What, then, is the main point of the critique of methodological nationalism? The decisive point is that *national organisation as a structuring principle of societal and political action can no longer serve as a premise for the social science observer.* In order to understand even the re-nationalisation or re-ethnification trend in the USA or in western or eastern Europe one needs a cosmopolitan perspective. How to move away from this underlying methodological bias in the social sciences is primarily an analytical and empirical problem, but it is also a normative and political issue. In this sense, social science can react to the challenge of a global civil society only if it manages to overcome methodological nationalism and to raise empirically and theoretically fundamental questions within specialised fields of research so as to elaborate the foundations of a *cosmopolitan* social and political science.

This paradigmatic reconstruction and redefinition of social science from a national to a cosmopolitan perspective can be understood and explained as a 'positive problem shift' (Lakatos 1970) in the sense of a broadening of horizons for social science research:

> *When politics and society are de-bounded, the consequence is that the labels 'national' and 'international' can no longer be separated. Considering the fact that to an increasing extent governing takes place in de-bounded spaces, the*

increasingly problematic distinction, but which is typical of the field- between 'domestic' and 'foreign' politics, as 'national governmental politics' and 'international relations' becomes definitely obsolete. Thus it is not only a matter of integrating national explanation factors in the analysis of international political processes, or of re-evaluating the international determinants of national political processes, as was pursued in numerous approaches over the past years. Rather, it is a matter of questioning the very separation between 'inside' and 'outside'. (Grande and Risse 2000)

To sum up, traditional conceptualisations of terms and construction of borders between 'national' and 'international,' domestic and foreign politics, and society and state are less and less appropriate for tackling the challenges linked to the global age.

One implication is that the national and the cosmopolitan perspectives understand sovereignty differently. In the national perspective we find it easiest to think about globalisation as a simple alternative to or negation of the modern state or the system of modern states. This framing is often articulated as an opposition between *political realism* as a celebration of the necessity of state interests and a *political idealism* that celebrates the potentiality of some kind of universality, some global or human community. But the cosmopolitan perspective is not concerned with the fall (or rise) of the nation-state in the global age in the same way as the national perspective. The cosmopolitan perspective offers a way of analysing the whole global power game in which states are redefined as one class of actor among others. The either/or of realism and idealism does not make sense in a cosmopolitan perspective. In this either/or game, either the state exists, albeit only as an essential core, or it does not exist at all; either there is national sovereignty—that is, a zero-sum game between national and international competence—or there is no sovereignty at all. In the cosmopolitan perspective, 'realism' is a kind of political *non*-realism because it neglects the second great transformation of the whole global power game. A concept of cosmopolitan *Realpolitik* is necessary in order to understand the positive-sum game of pooled sovereignties. In an era of global crisis, national problems can be solved only by transnational-national cooperation and state networks (Beck 2002).

The horizon opened up by the distinction between methodological nationalist and cosmopolitan perspectives reveals a new configuration of the world. Previously, the national cosmos could be clearly decomposed into 'inside' and 'outside'. The nation-state-governed order was established between the two. In the inner experiential space, the central themes of work, politics, law, social inequality, justice, and cultural identity were negotiated against the background of the nation, which was the guarantor of a collective unity of action. In the international realm, that is, in the outer experiential field, the corresponding concept of 'multiculturalism' developed. Multiculturalism, by delimiting and excluding the foreign, mirrored and crystallised the national self-image. Thus, the national/international distinction always represented more than a distinction; it actually functioned as a permanent self-fulfilling prophecy.

Against the background of cosmopolitan social science it becomes suddenly obvious that it is possible neither to clearly distinguish between the national and the international nor, in a similar way, to convincingly contrast homogeneous units. National spaces have become denationalised so that the national is no longer national, just as the international is no longer international. New realities are arising, a new mapping of space and time, new coordinates for the social and the political which have to be theoretically and empirically researched and elaborated. (This is the research agenda of the 'Reflexive Modernization' Research Centre at Munich University; see Beck, Bonß, and Lau 2003.) What we are talking about is a paradigmatic shift as illustrated in Table 3.1.

The paradigmatic opposition between (inter)-nationalism and cosmopolitanism does not establish a logical or temporal exclusivity but an ambivalent transitional coexistence, a new concurrence of phenomena that are not concurrent.

Institutions and organisations focusing on a form of cosmopolitan social science research have a long history and have competed with the 'self-confirmation circle' of nation-state data and knowledge production. First of all, it is the scientific

A concept of cosmopolitan Realpolitik is necessary in order to understand the positive-sum game of pooled sovereignties

Table 3.1: Paradigmatic change from a national perspective to a cosmopolitan social science

		Political action	
		National perspective	Cosmopolitan perspective
Political science	Methodological nationalism	Nation-state-centred understanding of society and politics in both political practice and political science.	Globalisation seen from within the nation-state: under which conditions do actors change from a national to a cosmopolitan perspective? Actually existing cosmopolitanism.
	Methodological cosmopolitanism	Opening up of the nation-state-centred society and politics, sociology and political science: new critical theory with a cosmopolitan intent; redefinition of basic notions and frames of references from a cosmopolitan perspective.	The cosmopolitan society and its enemies: what does a cosmopolitan society, state, and regime mean?

ethos that bases itself on the higher quality of nation-state data. In parallel, one witnesses, along with the feared 'cosmopolitan turn', the return of either metaphysics or the non-scientific, and often both of them, to the centre of academic social science. Furthermore, methodological nationalism acquires its superiority from the prevalent conviction of philosophy and political theory that Western values—democracy, the rule of law, social justice—are possible only in the shapes and contexts provided by the nation-state. This leads to the conclusion that the cosmopolitan opening betrays and endangers the democratic ethos.

In both these scenarios the major mistake is based on two oversights. On the one hand the interpretation of the classical researchers and their nation-state premises has been a-historicised and set as an absolute. Whoever lauds the classical researchers masks her or his mental sterility, and forces herself or himself to assume the existence of a copyist, a fact which has already been the case for some time. On the other hand one reproduces the mistake according to the old principle of 'es darf nicht sein, was nicht sein soll' ('it cannot be, what ought not to be') of sacrificing curiosity about reality to institutionalised convictions about values. Even the most demanding of data from the methodological point of view can be blind and lead to us being surprised and overwhelmed by the return of the suppressed cosmopolitan reality.

Global civil society actors can be understood as the agents of a cosmopolitan perspective, even though the phenomenon of global civil society encompasses a diversity of cross-cutting beliefs, prejudices, and assumptions. To put it another way, global civil society could be represented as one element of actually existing cosmopolitanism. To grasp the meaning of global civil society, social science must be re-established as a transnational science of the reality of denationalisation, transnationalisation, and 're-ethnification' in a global age—and this on the levels of concepts, theories, and methodologies as well as organisationally. The fundamental concepts of 'modern society' must be re-examined. Household, family, class, social inequality, democracy, power, state, commerce, public, community, justice, law, history and politics must be released from the fetters of methodological nationalism and re-conceptualised and empirically established within the framework of a cosmopolitan social and political science which remains to be developed. This is quite a list of understatements. But nevertheless it has to be handled and managed if the social sciences are to avoid becoming a museum of antiquated ideas.

The Invisibility of Global Inequalities

In the second part of this chapter I would like to address a theme, as well as a research area, which has remained central but has until now received little attention from the cosmopolitan perspective. I focus on the sociology of social inequalities in order to both test and illustrate the relevance of a new critical theory and its empirical claims by using a concrete example. The World Bank's (2002) report on the financial situation of developing countries can be read like a an official written accusation from child rights organisation Terre des Hommes against the ignorance of wealthy countries. The falling prices of raw materials on the world market, the commercial protectionism and the economic slump in industrialised states, and the decline of worldwide tourism after 11 September 2001 have all dramatically increased the destitution of the world's poorest regions. The world has become a dangerously unequal place—and this is true even for the rich in Western metropolises. Through debt repayment alone, $US200 billion dollars is transferred annually from the South to the North. In parallel, private capital investment flows to the South have shrunk for the fifth successive year and have now stabilised at less than their 1997 value. While 1.2 billion people, almost a fifth of the world's population, must make do with less than a dollar a day, state development aid has decreased by 20 per cent since 1990 (World Bank 2002: 1, 11). How can one explain the contradiction between the growing poverty of ever-increasing sections of the population and the growing ignorance about this problem?

The world has become a dangerously unequal place—and this is true even for the rich in Western metropolises. Through debt repayment alone, $US200 billion is transferred annually from South to North

In Germany, many members of the Bundestag belong to the generation which 30 years ago pledged a form of 'international solidarity', were active in Third-World initiatives, or fought against poverty during ecclesiastical action days, and stood for the needs of 'One World'. Now it appears that the policies of this generation have transformed Germany into one of the laggards of development politics. Can this be adequately explained by the impotence of politicians? Or is the fading out of global injustices structurally conditioned? Is there a principle that can account for the contradiction whereby global inequalities grow while from the sociological point of view they are legitimised? There is now a growing global justice movement, sometimes known as the anti-globalisation or anti-capitalist movement, that tries to draw attention to these inequalities. This movement, described in Chapter 4, is probably the most active component of global civil society at the moment. Yet its voices do not translate into concrete policies or generalised public concern. Why not?

There are at least two possible answers to the question of what legitimises social inequality: the merit system and the nation-state principle. The first has been carefully elaborated and criticised, since it derives from the self-understanding of the national perspective and is related to internal, intra-state inequalities. The second can be derived from the cosmopolitan perspective and is related to the 'legitimisation' of social inequalities. The bigger blind spots—and sources of error—of methodological nationalism linked to research on inequality can be revealed only by means of a systematic switch from the national to the cosmopolitan perspective. A new critical theory of social inequalities is needed which provides a scientific expression of the cosmopolitan perspective already held by parts of global civil society. Only on the basis of such a theory can the fundamental asymmetry of inequality, which is reinforced by a perception trapped in the national viewpoint as well as in the social and social science perspective, be unravelled. Such a theory would demonstrate that the 'legitimisation system' of the nation-state rests on the fact that attention is exclusively focused on the inside, thereby excluding global inequalities from the field of vision of the (relatively) privileged.

From a purely spatial point of view, it is possible to distinguish between *big* inequalities (which can further be divided into transnational, supranational, international, and global inequalities) and *small* inequalities. Small inequalities are those found within the nation-state. They appear big to the people or groups concerned and this for the most obvious reasons, but from a cosmopolitan perspective they are small. The merit system both explains and legitimises intra-state inequalities. The appropriate metaphor

Table 3.2: Sociology of social inequalities: national and cosmopolitan perspectives

		Matrix of social positions	
		Large (global) inequalities	Small (nation-state level) inequalities
Legitimisation	National perspective	Irrelevant, non-existent	Merit system
	Cosmopolitan perspective	The nation-state principle excludes the excluded and makes global inequalities invisible	The nation-state principle can only explain inequalities within the nation-state.

for this phenomenon is the exam: all enter as equals but come out unequals (with different positions in the hierarchy of needs). Under the merit system, incomes, for example, can be characterised as both unequal and legitimate. When we say that the nation-state principle 'legitimises' social inequalities, we mean that the lens through which the nation-state observes national inequalities blocks out global inequalities. Big inequalities are thus removed from the national perspective, and can therefore both grow and be 'legitimised' within a form of institutionalised irrelevance and non-reality. How is this possible? It is because the national perspective functions like a microscope. By focusing on small internal inequalities it leaves out the bigger, global ones. In other words, the preoccupation with small national inequalities legitimises big inequalities.

The 'law' of nation-state exclusion of global inequalities is obviously a case in point. The national particularism of the state does not necessarily exclude universal principles and perceptions. Nevertheless, it does appear that the nation-state perspective provides a 'liberation' from the misery of the world. It functions according to the model of *double exclusion*: it excludes the excluded. Global inequalities have grown: 'the average income in the richest 20 countries is now 37 times that in the poorest 20. This ratio has doubled in the past 40 years' (World Bank 2003: 7). It is surprising how the big inequalities which are suffered by humanity can be continuously legitimised through a silent complicity between the state authority and the state-obsessed social sciences by means of a form of organised non-perception.

Principles of the Construction of Non-reality

While the merit system provides a *positive* legitimisation of small inequalities, the nation-state principle produces a *negative* 'legitimisation' of big inequalities. 'Positive' legitimisation means that the merit system validates a reflexive and reciprocal legitimisation, that is, social inequalities can in principle be tolerated by the underprivileged. In contrast, the legitimisation of the nation-state principle is 'negative' because it is characterised by *non*-reflexivity and *non*-reciprocity, meaning that it cannot be tolerated by the underprivileged and the excluded. The nation-state principle is based on non-reflection, not on reflection, as in the case of the merit system. Thus, negative legitimisation through institutionalised silence or blindness precludes acceptance by those whose acceptance is most needed, that is, the poor, the humiliated, and the excluded. The nation-state evidently does *not* legitimise global inequalities. Rather, the *non*-legitimised global inequalities are hidden from view and thereby stabilised. Historically, this means that the European nation-state represents the institutionalised forgetting of colonialism and imperialism, both of which fostered its development.

In elaborating this 'legitimisation through silence', I should like to identify four principles of nation-state irrelevance and non-reality construction.

1. *The fragmentation of the world into nation-states removes accountability for global inequalities.* As long as there is no global jurisdiction or monitoring institution to survey global inequalities, these will

remain disaggregated into a motley pattern of nation-state inequalities. Because there are approximately 200 states, there are approximately 200 different frames of relevance and observation for small social inequalities. But the sum of these recorded inner, single-state inequalities does not correspond to the larger global inequalities, because the logic of the national perspective is not the same as that of the cosmopolitan perspective. In particular, national self-ascription and the endogenous causal suppositions linked to it contradict the cosmopolitan viewpoint, which stresses the fact that transnational interdependences, power relations, and causalities also contribute to the explanation of 'intra-nation-state' inequalities.

In the South Commission (1990: 2) report it is argued that: 'if humanity were a single nation state, the current North-South split would transform it into a politically explosive, semi-feudal unit, the stability of which is threatened by internal conflicts.' This is both right and wrong: it does not recognise that the nation-state world order structurally ignores and therefore 'legitimises' global inequalities.

Big inequalities are removed from the national perspective, and can therefore both grow and be 'legitimised' within a form of institutionalised irrelevance

The nation-state principle explains why the connection between globalisation and poverty has been so seldom researched. As long as the national perspective reigns in both political action and in social science analysis, poverty and wealth will continue to be localised in the national context as a matter of course. Even the mere possibility that the problematic consequences of globalisation materialise in various historical contexts—in the shape of growing inequalities, eroding incomes, the over-exploitation of natural resources, and the undermining of democracy—remains *analytically* excluded. Thus, as far as social science inequality research is concerned, the principle of nation-state fragmentation is linked to a major source of error: the danger of a *misguided 'nation-state-oriented' conclusion.* Global or transnational interdependences, processes, power relations, causalities easily fade away or are misinterpreted within the closed circle of a national perspective. The crucial point is that this big mistake can be neither unravelled nor avoided using a national perspective; only a cosmopolitan outlook can provide a way out of the deadlock.

2. *The perception of social inequalities presupposes equality norms.* Within the nation-state perspective, the stability with which major inequalities can be excluded rests on the validity of national equality norms, whether they be culturally, ethnically, legally, or politically defined. The objectivity of global social inequalities is politically irrelevant as long as these inequalities remain in the shadow of institutionalised equality norms. Within the national paradigm, at least in Westernised welfare states, equality norms rest on the formal equality of the citizen: income differences between men and women, places of residence, and so on, do not justify a differentiated citizen status. All individuals within a nation have the same rights and duties. In this context, a differentiated citizenship status is therefore unacceptable. This legally sanctioned citizen equality corresponds to the nation-state guiding principle of cultural homogeneity (same language, history, cultural traditions). The national principles of inclusion and exclusion thus determine and stabilise the boundaries of the perception of social inequalities. This leads to:

3. *The impossibility of comparing social inequalities between nation-states.* The national perspective and the 'functional capacity' of the nation-state to legitimise global inequalities rests on the fact that politically relevant comparisons can be completed only *intra*nationally and not *inter*nationally. Delegitimising comparisons again presuppose national equality norms. In that sense, income differences between, for example, Nigerians and Germans, South Americans and Finns, Russians and Chinese, Turks and Koreans—even where they have similar qualifications and functions—can be very important. But the delegitimising potential of these comparisons is felt only if they take place within a common framework of perception of institutionalised equality. This can be achieved through belonging to a particular nation or to a globally active corporation. To some extent, it also begins to be achieved through global civil society: international NGOs, for example, or Diaspora links.

This raises the interesting question of how far one can and will be able to legitimise the international wage differences within the European Union by means of the principle of non-comparability. As European self-consciousness grows along with the institutionalisation of European self-observation, will inequalities which were previously ignored because they were international also be perceived as *intra*national inequalities, and will new equality norms have to be developed? To the extent that barriers enforcing the international non-comparability of inequalities dissolve (for whatever reason), the states of the European Union—even when facing so-called 'fixed' inequality relations—will probably experience considerable turbulence.

Nevertheless, the role of the nation-state is not confined solely to a so-called legitimisation function within the system of global inequalities.

4. *The 'fading out phenomenon' legitimises inaction*, or rather it legitimises those actions which increase big inequalities because so-called 'external' effects, from the national perspective, are precipitated into a form of pre-determined non-reality or political irrelevance. The exclusiveness with which social inequalities are thematised as inner inequalities thus facilitates a global redistribution politics whereby risks are externalised, that is, they are imposed upon weaker developing or emerging countries, while profits are maximised within the rich countries of the 'West'.

As long as the national perspective reigns both in political action and in social science analysis, poverty and wealth will continue to be localised in the national, not the global context

While western politicians were busy extolling the fact that we had reached a decade of unexpected peace and wealth, a growing number of countries were becoming engulfed in debts, unemployment, and the decline of health and social services as well as urgently needed infrastructures. What has proved profitable for Western corporations in terms of the strict enforcement of deregulation, privatisation, and flexibilisation in developing countries often turns out to be a disaster for ordinary people in these countries. To take just one example: the World Bank, in its role as implementation agent for the G-7 states, supported contracts with private energy suppliers both in Indonesia and in other countries. 'These contracts obliged the public sector to buy great quantities of electricity at very high prices' (Stiglitz 2002: 71). The international corporations pocketed the profits while the risks were imposed on the 'anyway already' poor states.

> *The U.S. Department of Finance and the World Bank became renowned for precisely this type of private commercial activity. That is already bad enough. But when the corrupt governments of these emerging economies were overthrown (cf. e.g. Suharto (Indonesia) in 1998 ...), the U.S. administration put pressure on the new governments to honour the contracts, instead of releasing them from their obligation to pay or at least re-negotiating conditions. Indeed, there is a long list of unfair contracts, the honouring of which western governments achieved by exerting pressure through oppression. (Stiglitz 2002: 71)*

To sum up these principles: the nation-state world order fragments global inequalities, national equality norms exclude global inequalities, and intranational comparability of inequalities ensures international non-comparability. The predetermined irrelevance of big inequalities enables powerful and wealthy nation-states to burden poor states with risks that flow from their policies. Additionally, these policies are confirmed and strengthened by the methodological nationalism of the social sciences in rich countries. Inequality research based on this perspective greatly reinforces national myopia; it also depicts both itself and its object of research within the framework of a nation-state science which endlessly gives birth to itself. What is normally seen as problematic from a scientific point of view, that is, research which reinforces the researchers' own premises, is extolled here as a methodological principle. At best, this form of national autism is extended into an international comparative autism. But this comparative methodological nationalism remains bound by methodological nationalism. The nation-state is a state of mind. Walls hindering perception are erected and fostered, and are justified and cemented by the knowledge generated by a social science that bases itself on methodological nationalism. However, this social and social-science creation, that is, the non-reality of growing global inequalities, is proving increasingly problematic.

Cosmopolitan Realities Intrude

Nevertheless, there is a growing awareness of the mistakes and contradictions of the national perspective, for several reasons.

First of all, boundaries have become permeable, and interdependences which transcend all borders are growing exponentially. Take for example the obvious contradictions in which restrictive immigration policies are trapped. On the one hand, the rich Northern countries are currently plagued by a spectacular demographic regression, with ageing populations that threaten to overwhelm pension and health systems and reinforce political conservatism. On the other hand, these very countries are busy building ramparts to ward off both the feared and the real immigration flows from the poorer South. In parallel, military, economic, and political interdependences are growing worldwide, leading to new flows of migrants and refugees. Every measure in this field is damned: it leads to side effects that can be anticipated and often proves utterly counterproductive. Thus, in the aftermath of the terrorist attacks of 11 September 2001, the political desire to control migration flows, especially in the US but also in European countries, has been strengthened and sharpened. But it is precisely this repressive impulse that undermines the necessary readiness to authorise more immigration, which could counter falling demographic curves and rejuvenate the population.

The repressive impulse undermines the necessary readiness to authorise more immigration, which would rejuvenate the population

A second reason has to do with the processes of inner globalisation of nation-state experiential spaces. Several developments play a role in this evolution. Human rights are increasingly detached from citizenship status and are no longer bound by national contexts. Examples of this trend include international education curricula, the growing number of bi-national marriages and families, as well as increasing transnational work and private life connections. The national perspective is also imperilled by the growing mobility of communication, information, cash flows, risks, products, and services. Even indigenous groups that have remained immobile are being transnationalised within their experiential capacities through mass communication, publicity, and so on (Held 1999: 374). Moreover, supranational institutions such as the World Bank, UNESCO, or various NGOs systematically provide data which publicise big inequalities worldwide, thus questioning the mechanisms of the national non-reality-making process.

Third, new methods and patterns of differentiating between inclusion and exclusion have gained considerable significance. Increasingly, mechanisms of inclusion and exclusion no longer follow the classification of inequality into strata which end at the national border: a feature typical of the nation-state. New central patterns of inclusion and exclusion are being developed along the lines of, for instance, (1) supranational trade agreements (European Union, NAFTA, and so on), (2) Diaspora cultures which follow ascriptive characteristics: for example, 'Black Atlantic' (Gilroy 1993), or (3) the conditions of everyday life in global cities (Sassen 2001; 2002; Castells 1997; Albrow 1996; Eade 1996; 2000).

Garret Hardin, in 'Living on a Lifeboat' (1977), provided an early and famous defence of the national perspective and a critique of the cosmopolitan outlook. He compared nation-states with diversely equipped lifeboats in which the survivors of a shipwreck find refuge. Hardin argued that every one of these boats is free to offer a seat to the many survivors who are struggling against the wild sea. But this possibility cannot be transformed into a duty since the taking on of castaways disregards the very security regulations of the lifeboat, thus endangering all the passengers on board.

This 'lifeboat ethics' ('the-boat-is-full') argument, which is still very effective today, is especially inappropriate because the nation-state lifeboats suggested by the national perspective have become fewer and fewer. This is no longer a moral issue but an empirical argument. The real current post- and transnational inequality situations, forms, and causalities are being misinterpreted. It is uncovering the misdiagnosis of the national perspective, not a moral critique of it, which constitutes the essence of the cosmopolitan outlook and substantiates its superiority.

Fourth, the distinction between big and small inequalities—or, put differently, between the cosmopolitan and national perspectives—has itself become questionable. We are increasingly confronted with an *internationalisation of national models of inequality*. Competition within and between national spaces increases along with the permeability of national boundaries. Correspondingly, it entails a distribution of globalisation winners and losers according to production sectors that are either shielded from the market or exposed to it. Last but not least, the nebulous concept of 'globalisation' is often used in the *struggle between national and transnational elites*, who fight over positions and resources *within* national power spaces.

Finally, the view-obstructing walls are also disintegrating in relation to the international situation. At least since the terrorist attacks it has become more difficult to exclude the excluded: the increasing poverty of the world population is also perceived as a problem inherent in the wealthy Western countries, but its practical consequences remain to be defined. On the one hand, the danger of terrorism, which defies national borders, undermines the nation-state vision boundaries behind which global inequalities continue to grow menacingly. On the other hand, the emergence of global movements opposed to war and linked to the global justice movement introduces a cosmopolitan perspective on inequality.

The silence of social science concepts on the subject of global inequality is a scandal

There is no doubt that these developments overstrain nation states. They have not developed the capacity to intervene to redress large inequalities. Indeed, they do not even possess the capacity to survey or monitor large inequalities, let alone do anything about them. This is the explanation of the central paradox of a new cosmopolitan orientation. To the extent that the boundaries between big and small inequalities become more permeable and no longer correspond to national borders, the mental wall—that is, the institutionalised non-perception of big inequalities—does not lose its significance; on the contrary, it is further buttressed. Why? Because it is only thus that the growing asymmetry between demands for intervention addressed to states and the actual capacity of these states to intervene can be bridged.

Conversely it can be inferred that, if the nation state 'legitimises' global inequalities according to the Brechtian principle that 'we don't see those who are in the dark', this legitimisation breaks down with the 'cosmopolitisation' of the state. The cosmopolitan state which (however selectively) integrates cultural Others lets loose—even in the most optimal case of stable inequalities—an avalanche of legitimisation problems as a side effect. Why? For the simple reason that it abolishes the boundaries of the non-comparability of social inequalities. In other words, cosmopolitisation actually increases the seductive potential of re-ethnification and re-nationalisation of both society and politics. Precisely because boundaries are no longer fixed, the mental wall which hinders perception is cemented anew.

Can one or must one say now whether the nation-state principle is a trap? Whatever the answer, it is clear that the non-reflective unity between both the state's and the social sciences' capacities to make global inequalities invisible affects political and scientific actors in contrasting ways. Whether or not the national perspective can be attributed to 'functional performance' of the nation-state, it perverts the social sciences. These are gradually trapped into an increasingly obvious contradiction with their scientific reality mission and ethics. Indeed, they base themselves (often imperceptibly and unintentionally) on the generation of non-reality within reality. The silence of social science concepts on the subject of global inequalities is a scandal.

A New Critical Theory

In this new era, a new critical theory with a cosmopolitan intent has a crucial task. It must breach the fixed walls of category systems and research routines of the methodological nationalism used by the social sciences in order to, for example, bring big equalities back into the field of vision. The established *intra*national maps of social inequalities are elegant, depicted in detail, and thought to be generally sufficient to manage politically the more privileged part of the world population. But the dragons of the large, unknown, completely inadequately researched worlds of global inequalities are no longer just simple decorative motifs adorning the borders. The nation-state belief, the national narratives, which dominate both public commentaries and academic research certainly cannot be overlooked or ignored. At least since the 11 September terrorist attacks it has become clear to many people that the view through the wall that separates small inequalities from bigger ones goes straight down the barrel of a gun.

The new critical theory is also a self-critical theory. Its main claim is that, first of all, the cosmopolitan viewpoint, linked to various realities, detects the *chasms* that threaten the beginning of the twenty-first century. Critical theory investigates the *contradictions, dilemmas, and the unseen and unwanted (unintentional) side effects* of a modernity which is becoming increasingly cosmopolitan and draws its critical definition power from the tension between political self-description and the observation that social sciences make of it. The main thesis is then that *the cosmopolitan perspective opens up negotiation spaces and strategies which the national viewpoint precludes*. The cosmopolitan contradicts the argument, often accepted by national political actors and social scientists, that there are no alternatives.

In the debate on globalisation the main point does not revolve around the meaning of the nation-state and how its sovereignty has been subordinated. Rather, the new cosmopolitan perspective of the global power field pushes new actors and actor networks, the power potentials, strategies, and organisation forms of de-bounded politics, or in other words global civil society, into the field of vision. This is why the cosmopolitan critique of nation-state-centred and nation-state-buttressed politics and political science is empirically and politically crucial.

References

Albrow, M. (1996). *The Global Age*. Cambridge: Polity Press.

Beck, Ulrich (2002). 'The Cosmopolitan Society and its Enemies'. *Theory, Culture & Society*, 19/1–2: 17–44.

— Bonß, W., and Lau, C. (2003). 'The Theory of Reflexive Modernization'. *Theory, Culture & Society*, 20/2.

Castells, M. (1997). *Local and Global: The Management of Cities in the Information Age*. London: Earthscan.

Eade, J. (1996). *Living in the Global City: Globalisation as Local Process*. London: Routledge.

— (2000). *Placing London: From Imperial Capital to Global City*. New York: Berghahn.

Favell, A. (1999). *European Integration, Immigration and the Nation State: Institutionalising Transnational Political Actions*. Florence: European University.

Featherstone, M. (2000). 'Technologies of Post-human Development and Potential for Global Citizenship', in J. N. Pieterse (ed.), *Global Futures–Shaping Globalization*. London: Zed.

Gilroy, B. (1993). *Black Atlantic: Modernity and Double Consciousness*. London: Verso.

Grande, E. and Risse, T. (2000). 'Bridging the Gap. Konzeptionelle Anforderungen an die Politikwissenschaftliche Analyse von Globalisierungsprozessen'. *Zeitschrift für Internationale Beziehungen*, 2: 235–67.

Hardin, G. (1977). 'Living on a Lifeboat', in G. Hardin (ed.), *Managing the Commons*. San Francisco: W. H. Freeman.

Held, D. et al. (ed.) (1999). *Global Transformations: Politics, Economics and Culture*. Cambridge: Polity Press.

Lakatos, I. (1970). 'Falsification and the Methodology of Scientific Research Programmes', in I. Lakatos and A. Musgrave (eds), *Criticism and the Growth of Knowledge*. Cambridge: Cambridge University Press.

Luhmann, N. (2002). *Theories of Distinction: Redescribing the Descriptions of Modernity*. Stanford: Stanford University Press.

Sassen, S. (2001). *The Global City: New York, London and Tokyo*. Princeton: Princeton University Press.

— (2002). *Global Networks, Linked Cities*. London: Routledge.

South Commission (1990). *The Challenge to the South*. Oxford: Oxford University Press.

Stiglitz, J. (2002). *Globalization and its Discontents*. London: Allen Lane.

World Bank (2002). *Poverty Reduction and the World Bank: Progress in Operationalizing the WDR 2000/2001*. Washington, DC: World Bank.

— (2003). *World Development Report*. Washington, DC: World Bank.

Part II: Issues in Global Civil Society

Chapter 4

Trade and Global Civil Society: The Anti-Capitalist Movement Revisited

Yahia Said and Meghnad Desai

Introduction

Thousands of people attended the rally which marked the launch of the Third World Social Forum (WSF) in Porto Alegre, Brazil on 22 January 2003. It was the same crowd that has perfected the art of turning desperation into hope, fear into cheer, and chaos into purpose at anti-capitalist riots throughout the world. However, we suggest in this chapter that something was amiss in Porto Alegre, that the 'movement of movements' is in danger of losing its dynamism and taking a dogmatic and ultimately self-defeating turn.

The formidable-looking Brazilian paramilitary policemen and women were on the side of the demonstrators—eager to assist and protect at every step. There was no chance of tear-gas and clubs. Brazilian authorities and businesses, including the state-owned oil multinational Petrobras, did not limit their support to words. They also footed much of the estimated US$3.5 million bill (Osava 2003). Klaus Schwab, founder and President of the World Economic Forum, had 'just one word for Porto Alegre: We are the same' (Mekay 2003).

Why were there no signs of resistance from 'the system' to this event, which is meant to represent the climactic expression of a movement out to destroy it? Why is the political and business establishment so keen on supporting the 'rabble'? (Temel-Kuran 2003)

In this chapter we will argue that three developments have been taking place in the anti-capitalist movement, especially the part of it that focuses on the global trade regime: success, institutionalisation, and radicalisation.

After a moment of hesitation following the September 11 attacks in the US, the Global Justice and Solidarity Movement (GJ&SM), as some of its followers like to call it, continued its meteoric rise. Millions around the globe took part in anti-capitalist protests and social forums. National and coordinated international campaigns succeeded in reversing privatisation plans in Peru and El Salvador. The movement also claimed a success when South Africa won the battle with multinational pharmaceuticals over the compulsory licensing of AIDS drugs. Most importantly, however, the movement succeeded in undermining the legitimacy of the Washington consensus: the neo-liberal economic orthodoxy which captured national and multilateral policy-making throughout the 1980s and much of the 1990s.

Part of the movement's success stems from the adoption of some of its rhetoric, if not spirit, by nationalist leaders and business elites on both sides of the North-South divide. Chavez and Chirac, Mugabe and Mahathir[1] have tried to attach themselves to the movement, with various degrees of success. Their goal is to leverage the movement's power and legitimacy in their struggle with domestic and foreign opponents.

Some in the movement are ready to accept these new allies. The newly elected Brazilian President Luis Inacio da Silva (Lula) and Hugo Chavez were leading attractions at the WSF, which also featured three ministers from Chirac's Gaullist government. Some Asian activists spoke warmly of Mahathir's tough rhetoric, downplaying his authoritarian tendencies. 'How on earth', wonders Naomi Klein (2003), commenting on the reception accorded to Chavez at the WSF, 'did a gathering that was supposed to be a showcase for new grassroots movements become a celebration of men with a penchant for three-hour speeches about smashing the oligarchy?'

The coming together of anti-capitalist activists and nationalist capital and politicians is in part a sign of the movement's radicalisation: a predictable reaction to the advent of the Bush administration in the US and its policies, especially since the September 11 attacks. Susan George (2003*a*), vice-president of ATTAC France, speaking at the WSF states that the 'rich and powerful have apparently concluded . . . that hundreds of millions of people

[1] *Hugo Chavez, President of Venezuela; Jacques Chirac, President of France; Robert Mugabe, President of Zimbabwe; and Mahathir Muhammed, Prime Minister of Malaysia.*

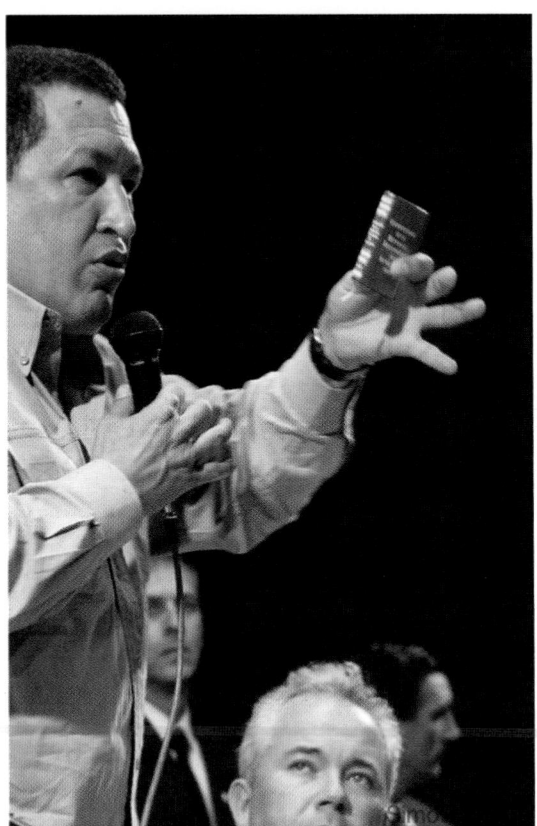

Venezuelan President Hugo Chavez, speaking at the margins of the WSF in Porto Alegre January 25, 2003, waves the 'little blue book' around. © Simone Bruno

in the world today are superfluous'. Samir Amin (2003), one of the main organisers of the WSF, speaks of 'Washington neo-Nazis' who need to be confronted before 'September 1939'.

Along with the acceptance/collusion with national capital/nationalism, there seems to be a general sense of resignation among activists to the impossibility of reform. As Argentina's Mothers of the May Plaza put it: 'Another world is possible, only with revolution and socialism' (Cockroft 2003). In Porto Alegre and elsewhere, activists repeatedly stated that they have given up hope of transforming the international trade regime and its main institution, the World Trade Organization (WTO). Efforts to make the WTO more transparent and accountable, work towards improving market access for Southern products, and campaigns aimed at injecting environmental, social, and labour considerations into the trade regime are giving way to an agenda centred around rolling back international treaties and organisations and returning power to the nation-state.

By seeking to 'Derail the WTO', the activists seem to have misinterpreted the major changes in the international arena resulting from the ascent of the a neoconservatives in the US and the September 11 attacks. The activists seem still bent on fighting a Washington consensus which no longer exists. The US administration has no particular commitment to the WTO or any multilateral institution. Globalisation and global institutions are tolerated only if they serve the interests of US and mature industry corporations associated with the Republican Party. If it is impossible or difficult to agree on rules that benefit the US, then it is better for them not to have any.

A trade regime without rules is unlikely to be more just than one governed by the WTO. Indeed, in the absence of a global set of rules economic superpowers will seek to carve up captive markets by constructing regional trade blocs. Indeed, the US administration is already pursuing such a strategy in the Free Trade Area of the Americas (FTAA) and bilateral negotiations with Chile, Singapore, Jordan, and Australia. Activists are aware of this strategy but do not seem to draw the logical conclusions from it regarding their WTO strategy. Most activists calling for the abolition of the WTO suggest that a new organisation should be built from the ground up to replace it. We have yet, however, to see a detailed proposal for such an alternative or a convincing explanation why that would be more effective than a reformed WTO. Advocates of the abolition of the WTO seem implicitly opposed to global trade in principle: a position few activists would care to embrace.

Civil society movements have not always taken an uncompromising stance on international trade; , indeed historically many have been pro-trade. The next section will address some theoretical and historical aspects of civil society movements on trade. It will be followed by an outline of the various positions on trade issues today. These positions will then be illustrated with the examples of the WTO and FTAA. We will also explore strategies and methods employed by the various strands in the movement in specific campaigns and activities. We will conclude by addressing the challenges and opportunities facing the movement today.

What are 50,000 activists looking at?

... one finger (Brazilian President Luiz Inacio Lula da Silva addresses the WSF in Porto Alegre January 24, 2003 .
© Marcelo Jr/Agencia Brasil

Trade and Civil Society: Theoretical and Historical Aspects

Trade has been a major plank of the global social justice movement. The WTO is seen by many as the driving force of globalisation, and free trade is blamed for many ills: environmental damage, commodification of subsistence crops and consequent food insecurity, falling commodity prices, inequality and inequity in the global distribution of income, and so forth. There are demands for fair trade, for special treatment of the least developed countries, especially in help with negotiations at WTO meetings. But, unlike in the case of money and finance, which we surveyed in *Global Civil Society 2001* (Desai and Said 2001), there are few religious objections to trade. While there are some 'anti-trade fundamentalists' (Hines 2000), even they are only against international trade, that is, trade across national boundaries.[2] This is because some sort of exchange, whether based on money or barter, is endemic to all societies. It is also more or less axiomatic that trade benefits all parties. The dispute arises about the distribution of the gains from trade; the inequality of gains from trade is often blamed for the inequalities of income and wealth in the world today.

Trade and comparative advantage

The counter-argument from the days of the classical economists has always been that, far from being a cause of inequality, trade is 'an engine of growth' and

2 There is an age-old objection to movement of food grains far from their place of origin. Famines were blamed in pre-modern and early modern days on inter-regional movements of food grains. The Physiocrats in the eighteenth century were the first to argue for the unimpeded, toll-free movement of food grain across France; hence the expression 'laisser-passer.' See for an insight into this Rothschild (2001). The idea of 'food miles' indicates that resistance persists in some to food trade even within countries.

Box 4.1: Actors in international trade: classes and interests

The conflict that trade generates within a country, as in the corn law agitation in nineteenth-century Britain, or across countries, as in contemporary movements, can be analysed in a schematic way by delineating the principal actors and how their interests may combine or clash. In the original Anti-Corn Law League debate, the 'actors' were:

(a) manufacturers/capitalists/shopkeepers;
(b) industrial/urban workers;
(c) landlords;
(d) farm/rural workers;
(e) consumers;
(f) civil society.

The story is that (a) and (b) combined to defeat (c). The (d) element was not enfranchised and played little part in the debate. The then government consisted of MPs elected by (a) and (c). Usually it is only (a) and (c) that feature in the argument but governments are also part of the action as signatories to treaties such as the WTO. In neoclassical economists' interpretations of the free trade argument, consumers (e) are the most important group as against industrial producers, (a) and (b) together with agricultural producers (c) and (d). In the neoclassical story free trade benefits (e) by providing cheaper goods and hurts (a) and (b) or (c) and (d) in the short run due to competition; but the long-run effects are beneficial to all by improving resource allocation and allowing higher levels and perhaps a higher growth rate of output and income. Of course, consumers can also be seen as civil society, but to keep the notation clear we label civil society separately as (f).

Under Friedrich List's analysis we have to add the foreign counterparts to the six actors above. Label them (A) to (F). In what follows the rich country is denoted by lower-case letters and the poor country by upper-case letters. Thus (A) would be the local (poor country) manufacturer and (a) the English (rich country) manufacturer. List saw the battle as between (a) and (A). From the two sets of interest groups (a) to (e) and (A) to (E), we can map the location of various protest groups as identified with one or other cluster. Thus the anti-colonial struggle for tariffs took the interests of (A) and (B) to be pitted against those of (a) and perhaps (b). During his visit to England for the Round Table Conference of 1930, Gandhi tried to win over the Lancashire mill workers who had been

that economies which are open and trade in a free environment thrive, as demonstrated by the experience of the rich developed countries. At issue is the theory of comparative advantage, which was the linchpin for Ricardo's argument for free trade and the reason for the triumph of classical economics in the nineteenth century.

Classical economics started as a reaction against the mercantilist system, in which politics dominated markets and national interest was supreme. Adam Smith in his *Wealth of Nations* (Smith 1776/1993) questioned the efficiency of the mercantilist system. Ricardo in his *Principles of Political Economy and Taxation* (Ricardo 1821/1992) made resource efficiency (though he did not call it that) an objective in place of the national interest. Here indeed is the first separation in economic theory between the interests of the state and those of its citizens, even of civil society.

This theory of comparative advantage holds that if two countries—England and Portugal, in Ricardo's much cited example—are capable of producing two commodities—wine and cloth—then each should specialise in producing, and exporting to the other country, that commodity which it can produce more cheaply, *even if it could produce both commodities more cheaply than the other country.* By that specialisation, both countries will benefit from the optimal use of resources. Later neoclassical economists added that consumer welfare will be enhanced in both countries as goods will be cheaper if countries specialised along the lines of comparative advantage.

A history of trade activism

What converted an abstract and unrealistic theory into practical politics was civil society agitation in the nineteenth century on behalf of free trade and

adversely affected by his insistence that Indians bought only Indian cloth. Thus he was aware of the harm to the interests of (b) but sought international solidarity between (b) and (B).

Today we have to add a further dimension: capital is mobile and 'foreign' capital could be hiring domestic workers. In this case the interests of (a) and (B) combine to harm (b) as well as possibly (A). Thus, in attacking foreign direct investment for employing cheap labour and taking jobs away from the home country (as argued by some AFL-CIO groups in Seattle), the interests of (b) are pitted against (B) but blamed on the tendency of (a) to compete with or even align with (A). Farm subsidies by the US or the EU help (d) in these areas but hurt (e) and, via dumping, (D). (Chapter 8 elaborates on tensions versus solidarity between (d) and (D)). In denouncing multinational corporations, protesters identify the villains as (a) foreign capital; but often (A) domestic/poor country capital is no better than foreign capital, say in health and safety risks, environmental damage, or gender discrimination.

Another new element resulting from globalisation is the capacity of civil society movements to forge international or indeed global alliances. In this respect alliances of rich-country and poor-country anti-trade groups do have some confusing clashes of interests which if not resolved can lead to contradictions between anti-trade movements in theory as well as in practice. If we characterise the Anti-Corn Law League as a combination of (a), (b), and (f) against (c) and (d), today we have the possibility of combinations of (f) and (F) championing individual or groups of countries against others i.e. aligning with any permutation of (a) to (e) and (A) to (E).

Thus from the simple alliances of (a) and (b) versus (c) and (d), or even (a) and (b) versus (A) and (B), we have (a) and some (B) versus (b) and some (A) and some (B). We have antagonism of (c) and (d) towards (C) and (D). The anti-trade movement may then represent an alliance of (f) and (F) or some sections thereof against workers in poor countries (B) and in favour of workers in rich countries (b) just because they don't like the rich-country capitalists (a). The movement against trade in food may hurt poor-country farmers (D); but silence on trade distortions such as EU and US farm subsidies benefits rich-country farmers (c) and workers (d) but hurts (C) and (D). Being anti-trade is no longer simply being anti-rich and pro-poor.

against the corn laws, which imposed a tax on food grain imports into Britain. Ricardo's theory became a weapon in the hands of the Anti-Corn Law League, which succeeded in having the corn laws repealed and British agriculture 'globalised'. It was a classic redistributive struggle in which the workers and capitalists challenged the power of the landed aristocracy. In the particular English context of the 1840s, consumers were largely the urban workers and their families, so this movement also acquired a class character, which is why Marx supported free trade against protection.(Desai 2002). The Anti-Corn Law League raised money and set up machinery across England and Wales to increase voter registration, which then enabled it to get MPs elected who would vote down the corn laws. Established in 1839, it succeeded within seven years and the corn laws were abolished in 1846. The Anti-Corn Law League represents the first civil society movement on a trade issue, though pro-free trade.

Despite its triumph in Britain, Ricardo's theory had several features which have made it controversial ever since it was first propounded. First, in theory, free trade operates between countries, but the politics of international relations is absent. Thus, many critics point out that when Ricardo wrote about trade between England and Portugal the Methuen Treaty between the two countries had already relegated Portugal to a subordinate status. Also, by specialising in an industrial commodity—cloth—England could reap the advantages of dynamic increasing returns to scale, while Portugal would be confined to a commodity in which there were diminishing returns and few innovations. Of course, in that case cloth would become cheap over time but not wine; thus, the terms of trade—the ratio of the price of wine to that of cloth would move against England and in favour of Portugal. But later, a terms-of-trade pessimism developed among economists, and the Singer-Prebisch thesis held that over time the country producing the agricultural commodity would see its terms of trade decline (Prebisch 1950) This was because the demand for the primary commodity was income-inelastic as well as price-inelastic (that is, the price of primary commodities and the level of income have little or no impact on the demand for that commodity). Thus, with growing world incomes the demand for primary commodities did not keep pace. Moreover, the markets for primary commodities were competitive; and so, as output increased due to the introduction of new land or better techniques, the price of the primary commodity declined; but this decline in price did not lead to higher demand. Manufactures, on the other hand, it was averred, were produced under oligopolistic conditions and their prices were determined on a cost-plus mark-up basis. Hence, the price of the manufacture would not fall but stay constant or rise while that of the primary commodity would fall. Thus trade would heighten the inequalities between the two rather than narrow them. (The Singer-Prebisch thesis did not go unchallenged. See Spraos 1983 for a response.)

Free trade theory was denounced as an English ideological plant to harm continental economies. Friedrich List began the anti-free trade movement by giving it a developmentalist edge

Second, in theory goods move but factors do not. Trade imposes restructuring on the domestic economy—for example, complete as opposed to partial specialisation—but the theory takes no account of the short-run human costs while emphasising the long-run welfare gains. When one industry has to be shut down while another expands, then workers bear the burden of unemployment and the costs of re-skilling. Politicians are concerned with immediate or short-run losses and not willing to sacrifice their voters for the sake of long-run gains. Thus, tariffs and protection have always had much more political support than free trade. Even in England, the classic free trade country, there was a move against free trade in the early twentieth century after the franchise had been extended.

Free trade in fact operates through the inter-state (so-called international) system. Free markets filter through the power system. The theory of comparative advantage sets out the limits of specialisation on theoretical grounds, but power relations between states define the actual limits. In practice, the international trading system has been an uneasy compromise between mercantilism and free trade. When there has been a hegemon—Great Britain in the nineteenth century and the USA post-1945—championing free trade, then the balance between mercantilism and free trade has edged towards the latter. But even here there has always been a gap between the hegemon's rhetoric and the practice. Thus, Great Britain's shipping acts in the nineteenth century stipulated that British exports should be transported exclusively in British ships, and the USA today protects its agriculture and other sectors.

Free trade theory was denounced as an English ideological plant to harm continental economies. Friedrich List (1837/1966) as well as many American economists of the mid-nineteenth century argued that free trade might be suitable for rich and developed England, but Germany and America needed protection. The *Zollverein*, established in 1833, was a customs union comprising Prussia and other German states. It combined free internal trade with tariff barriers against imports, rather like the European Union today. List began the anti-free trade movement by giving it a developmentalist edge.

This also helped to radicalise the anti-colonial struggles in India, where nationalists saw free trade as part of an imperialist strategy to keep India de-industrialised. A distinction was drawn between the interests of domestic capital/state and foreign capital/state, which turned the discourse against free trade. Classical economic theory had contrasted the interest of the civil society (consumer) with that of the state in attacking mercantilism. With List the contrast was between the rich/developed/metropolitan state and the poor/underdeveloped/colonial state. The interests of civil society in the poor/colonial state were to be identified with those of the state.

There are problems of trade in manufactured goods where production is determined by the status quo in comparative advantage. Until the middle of the twentieth century, most manufacturing industries were located in OECD countries and exported to developing countries. Developing countries as they started industrialising by import substitution methods encountered the criticism that they were ignoring comparative advantage. Nationalists in developing countries dealt with this criticism in Listian fashion by championing the interests of domestic against foreign capitalists regardless of any harm done to the interests of consumers (Box 4.1).

For many years the General Agreement on Tariffs and Trade (GATT), set up after the Second World War, tolerated this deviation from free trade as long as the offending countries were poor and not exporting their goods to rich country markets. But with the Uruguay Round concluded in 1993 things changed. Developing countries which had successfully acquired industries that could compete in export markets wanted greater access to rich country markets. Rich countries in their turn were eyeing the newly emerging markets where there were potential consumers of their products. Thus, the context of international trade negotiations began to change and a long series of negotiations resulted in the Marrakech Agreement and the upgrading of GATT to the WTO.

But with freer movement of capital the old comparative advantage is changing. New developments in Internet, transport, and communications technology are making the dispersal and fragmentation of the production process not only possible but profitable, and industries are relocating from North to South. This leads to the charge that capital is footloose and that it is employing/exploiting cheap labour, that American wages are being determined in Beijing, and so on. It is in this context that the WTO is suddenly emerging as the villain of the piece since these developments in global production relocation coincide with the establishment of the WTO. Of course, not all developing countries have experienced successful industrialisation or acquired an ability to export manufactures. Thus, within the old solid South there are divisions between those whose interests lie in greater access to foreign direct investment and OECD markets, and those who are left outside this process. The latter, mostly in Sub-Saharan Africa, are exporters of primary products and suffer from the inequities of agricultural export subsidies in OECD countries, which in turn dump their surplus primary products on the developing countries. These countries have a genuine complaint about the tardiness of the WTO in tackling this distortion in the world trading system. They also receive little foreign direct investment and hence do not benefit from the globalisation of world manufacturing.

Thus, there are several strands to the modern anti-trade movements and some of them are mutually contradictory. There is resentment of developed-country domination in industrial markets but also fear of footloose capital employing cheap foreign labour and hurting rich-country workers. There is concern about the falling prices of primary commodities of the Third World but also support for farm subsidies in rich countries. There is a sentiment against the environmental consequences of global growth led by free trade, which could deny the poor

Table 4.1: The new layout

	Globalisation is	Position on globalisation	Position on global trade
Supporters	Capitalism minus the state	Should be defended at all costs. The alternative is fascism	Good even if unequal. The problem is in the inter-state system. Support the WTO
Regressives	Capitalism plus the state	On our terms or de-globalisation	Good if on our terms. Same for WTO
Isolationists	Capitalism minus the state	De-globalisation	Inherently bad. Re-empower the state. Abolish the WTO
Reformers	Capitalism plus transformed state	Should be humanised	Can and must be made more equitable. WTO reform, national and international redistributive policies
Alternatives	Less capitalism and less state	Space for alternatives to compete and coexist	Neutral, the problem is with states and corporations

countries the capacity to export and enrich themselves in exactly the ways that rich countries have done until now. In some cases the interests of the different elements in the anti-capitalist coalition are inconsistent with one another.

Positions on Global Trade

In Desai and Said (2001) we divided civil society responses to global capitalism into Supporters, Reformers, Isolationists, and Alternatives. Both Isolationists and Supporters believe that globalisation and global capitalism are one and the same and that they are reversible. They believe that globalisation entails the gradual erosion of the nation-state and the expansion of the rule of the market into every sphere of life. Isolationists think that globalisation should therefore be resisted and reversed. In its place they promote values of self-sufficiency and self-reliance and seek a return to the national liberation states. Supporters believe that globalisation and global capitalism are the only way to combat poverty and totalitarianism and should therefore be embraced wholeheartedly by all and sundry. Reformers believe that there is more to globalisation than capitalism. The state, according to Reformers, is not eroded but transformed, working under new constraints of 'overlapping sovereignties'. They do not believe that globalisation could or should be reversed; instead, they call for it to be humanised. Alternatives reject the entire conceptual framework and are more concerned with carving out spaces where alternative paradigms can coexist. Over the past three years, due to the resurgence of the new group we call the Regressives (see below) and the weakening of Reformers, many activists are being pushed into Isolationist positions.

Today, in contrast to Seattle in 1999, there is a near (if not always declared) consensus within the movement on an agenda of abolishing the WTO and most other international trade initiatives. In this chapter we use a revised classification of civil society positions on trade to reflect these changes (see also Tables 4.1, 4. 2, and 4.3).

Supporters advocate a strict interpretation of trade theories. This group, comprised mainly of academics and officials at international organisations, believe that even without equity or redistributive mechanisms trade liberalisation will benefit everyone by improving productivity. An example of the supporters' argument is a recent call by Nicholas Stern, the World Bank's chief economist, for developing countries to open their markets, even if this was not reciprocated by the developed countries, since liberalisation benefits the liberaliser (Luce 2002). What's good for business is good for everyone.

Supporters, who also include industrial lobbies, especially those associated with new industries, in addition to some of the main liberal media such as the *Economist* and the *Wall Street Journal*, are a declining minority today. 'Even the staunchest partisans of free trade suspect it is an idea whose time has not just come but gone' (Caldwell 2003).

The Supporters' ranks have been dwindling due to defections to the *Regressives*, who claim to adhere to the same orthodoxy but make an exception for their, usually rich-country, governments and corporations. According to this group, globalisation can work only under the leadership of hegemonic superpower(s). Since the well-being of the world community is dependent on the well-being of the superpower(s), they should be allowed to break the rules of free trade when those clash with their national interests. What is good for the superpower(s) is good for everyone.

Civil society Regressives are exemplified by some of the think tanks and mature industry lobbyists associated with the current US Administration. Some of them are ardent supporters of market liberalisation and free trade. As such, it would be hard for them to openly attack the WTO. Nonetheless they occasionally bemoan the organisation's unwieldy nature, which they attribute to its consensus mechanism and the resulting 'disproportionate' influence of Third World nations (Wolf 2002). Yet it is revealing that most of their strategic advice to the Administration is focused on bilateral treaties and negotiations. In the extreme case, the Heritage Foundation completely ignores the WTO in its trade strategy advice to the administration (O'Driscoll and Fitzgerald 2002).

Indeed, the US Administration's policy towards the WTO is similar to that towards other multilateral initiatives. While Trade Representative Robert Zoellick is pursuing a 'positive agenda' at the organisation, the rest of the Administration and Congress are busy sabotaging it.[3] The introduction of 30 per cent steel tariffs in 2001 and the US Farm Bill which substantially increases farm subsidies are recent examples of new trade barriers erected by the Administration. The US recently backtracked on commitments made during the WTO Ministerial Meeting in Doha in 2001 on allowing developing countries to import unlicensed medicines to protect public health. These commitments were critical in obtaining developing country governments' agreement for the launch of a new round of negotiations. Such acts significantly undermine the prospect for the new round. In recent years the EU has won five cases against the US at the WTO. The US is, however, refusing to implement the WTO judgments, thus further undermining the system (Lamy 2003). On the other side of the Atlantic, France and Germany are engaged in similar tactics of pushing for WTO expansion while stonewalling on the Common Agricultural Policy (CAP). CAP subsidies amount to $50 billion annually. If they are left unchanged until 2016, as suggested by a recent Franco-German agreement, they will further undermine the prospect of success at the current Doha Round of trade negotiations. Regressive politics (on both sides of the Atlantic) have more to do with industrial lobbying than with demands by farming communities and labour to which they are sometimes attributed.

The critical plank of the Isolationists' argument is that it is almost impossible to make global trade work for the poor. They view trade as a Trojan Horse through which multinationals spread their power

The implicit double standard of this approach and the fact that its proponents are now in power not only in the US but also in many European counties is behind the radicalisation of activists on the other side of the trade debate. Even reformers are beginning to embrace *Isolationist* positions. The critical plank of the Isolationists argument is that it is almost impossible to make global trade work for the poor. They view trade as a Trojan Horse through which multinationals and their political representatives spread their power. The results are a loss of jobs in the North, poverty and loss of sovereignty in the South, and environmental degradation all round. What is good for the corporation is bad for everyone.

> *Once upon a time, empires were built through direct conquest. Armies plundered their way across continents, claiming lands and resources for king and country, justifying their acts as 'bringing the light of civilisation to the savages of dark*

[3] *US Trade Representative Robert Zoellick is one of few multilateralists within the current US Administration. He could be described as a Supporter under our framework. As such his positions are often at odds with the general policy thrust of the Administration and the Republican majority in Congress.*

> *continents.' These days such invasion has lost its primary appeal, but the equivalent gains are routinely achieved through different, and more efficient, means, which those in power prefer to call not open theft but 'open markets.' (Mittal 2003)*

Many Isolationist groups are united in the Our World is Not For Sale (OWINFS) network, which brings together such groups as Public Citizen, Focus on the Global South, Friends Of the Earth (FOE) International, and Food First. Isolationists call explicitly or implicitly for the abolition of the WTO and other international trade initiatives. As Lori Wallach of Public Citizen explained at the WSF, the goal is to 'Derail the WTO'. Ronnie Hall, Trade Program Manager at FOE, says that it is her 'personal' opinion (though not that of the organisation) that the WTO should be abolished. Kevin Danaher of Global Exchange calls himself an abolitionist (WSF 2003). Aye Aye Win of Dignity International was critical of this approach, describing the mood at the WSF in these terms:

> *If you want a big cheer from the crowd, it's clear what the speakers should do: smash neo-liberalism to pieces, condemn foreign debt, demonize the enemy, the TNCs, the IFIs, and to round it off call for their abolition. A deafening applause is guaranteed. That's exactly what we are witnessing at the big conferences and seminars here. (Win 2003)*

The Isolationists promote two alternatives to the current trade regime: the re-empowerment of the nation-state and the development of an alternative global regime from the bottom up. The alternative regime they call for, however, is defined in quite broad terms for the time being. Examples include *Another World is Possible: Popular Alternatives to Globalization at the World Social Forum* (Fisher and Ponniah 2003) or the new International Forum on Globalization report *Alternatives to Economic Globalization: A Better World is Possible* (IFG 2002). Following is an excerpt from the editors' synopsis of the report:

> *Written by a premier group of thinkers from around the world, Alternatives to Economic Globalization is the defining document of the antiglobalization movement. The culmination of a three-year project by the International Forum on Globalization, whose members include Ralph Nader, David Korten, John Cavanagh, Lori Wallach, and Jerry Mander, it presents both a sober critique of globalization as well as practical, thoughtful alternatives. The authors assert ten core requirements for democratic societies, including equality, basic human rights, local decision making, and ecological sustainability, and demonstrate how globalization undermines each. Offering specific strategies for reining in corporate domination, they address alternative systems for energy, agriculture, transportation, and manufacturing; ideas for weakening or dismantling the WTO, World Bank, and IMF; and rebuilding economies that are responsive to human needs.*

The Reformers are now squeezed between superpowers that would rather see no rules than inhibit their freedom of action and activists who seem to have given up on the reform/institution-building agenda

The main themes of these proposals are state control over food, water and public services, localisation and subsidiarity, re-regulation and 'weakening or dismantling' of multilateral economic institutions, and establishment of new structures which put people before profits.

The *Reformers*, once the broadest camp, embracing not only activists but also many mainstream politicians and representatives of new industries, are in the retreat, squeezed between superpowers that would rather see no rules than any which may inhibit their freedom of action and activists who also seem to have given up on the reform/institution-building agenda at the global level. The main claim of the Reformers is that international trade can, as the theory predicts, bring broad benefits to everyone provided mechanisms and rules are put in place at regional, national, and international levels to ensure optimal and equitable outcomes. Conversely the lack of such rules would not only entail deepening inequality but also may threaten globalisation as such.

The main reformist groups are represented in the Trade Justice Movement (TJM), a coalition which involves groups like Oxfam International, Action Aid, The World Development Movement (WDM), War on Want, and others. Box 4.2 illustrates the debate between reformers and isolationists.

Box 4.2: The 'Rigged Rules and Double Standards' debate

When Oxfam decided to discontinue its Fair Trade business on pro bono advice from management consultants McKenzie and Co., it replaced it by a two-pronged strategy. On the one hand it continued to provide technical assistance to small developing-country exporters in accessing Northern markets. On the other it started an ambitious advocacy campaign on trade issues. The campaign is based at the MakeTradeFair.com web site. It includes education, advocacy, and lobbying. The campaign's flagship document, Oxfam's first major foray into the area of trade advocacy, met a maelstrom of criticism from the Isolationist camp.

The debate, which centred around Oxfam's 'Rigged Rules and Double Standards' report (Oxfam 2002a) began at the Second World Social Forum in Porto Alegre in 2002 between Oxfam on the one hand and a number of groups and individuals including Colin Hines, Focus on the Global South, and Food First on the other. It highlights the differences between the Reformers and the Isolationists. The debate was quite animated and continued in the media and online long after the publication of Oxfam's report. By the time of the Third Forum, however, there was no debate at all, since the great majority of participants including many Oxfam people sided with the Isolationists on most points (WSF 2003).

The Oxfam report, which exemplifies Reformist thinking on the issue of trade, is centred around the proposition that international trade can be beneficial to the poor. Indeed, it argues that trade, as in the example of East Asia, has already lifted as many as 400 million people out of poverty. The problem, however, is that international trade rules today are 'rigged' for the benefit of rich countries and their corporations. Moreover, rich-country governments preach free trade to the developing countries but do not practise it themselves. Finally, even when developing countries are benefiting from trade, the benefits are skewed towards large suppliers and intermediaries at the expense of the poor as a result of inadequate policies pursued by these countries' governments and the multilateral organisations. The report proposes access for poor-country products into rich-country markets: agriculture and textiles in particular should be a major thrust of the campaign for a fairer international trade regime. The report does not promote market access as a panacea and stresses that it should be coupled with domestic policies to ensure an efficient and equitable distribution of the gains from trade. Oxfam also believes that focusing on market access is a useful strategy aimed at exposing the hypocrisy of developed-country leaders who do not practise what they preach.

> *International trade can work for the poor or against the poor. Just as in any national economy, economic integration in the global economy can be a source of shared prosperity and poverty reduction, or a source of increasing inequality and exclusion. Managed well, the international trading system can lift millions out of poverty. Managed badly, it will leave whole economies even more marginalized. (Hobbes 2002)*

Opponents of the report attack it on several fronts. First, they argue that market access, far from providing benefits to the poor in the South, aggravates commodity export dependency. According to this argument, underdeveloped countries get locked into a pattern of exporting low value added products to rich countries and importing expensive manufactured goods and services. Growing efficiency and productivity means that the relative value of poor-country exports is constantly declining, thus condemning these countries to immiserisation in the long term no matter how much they succeed in expanding their exports (Prebisch 1950). Variations of this theory cover agricultural and natural commodity exports as well as exports of labour-intensive products, a phenomenon known as the fallacy of composition (UNDP 2003).

Second, opponents of the report believe that by negotiating for market access Third World governments will be forced to make concessions in other areas. Finally, they argue that focusing on market access is a dangerous diversion from the efforts which should focus on derailing the WTO.

Box 4.3: The fair trade movement

In the aftermath of the Second World War some church organisations marketed handicrafts made by refugees as a way of helping them gain economic independence. Many fair trade groups trace the beginnings of the movement to that period. Alternative Trade Organisations (ATO) spread in the 1960s to market handicrafts and agricultural commodities purchased in the Third World at 'fair' prices.

The ATOs' main argument is that many poor country producers and especially small farmers and cooperatives are not getting a fair price for their products due to the difficulties they face in gaining access to rich-country markets and to finance. The big difference between the retail price in the developed world and the income that these producers receive for the fruits of their labour is, ATOs argue, unfairly appropriated by various intermediaries in both rich and poor countries.

ATOs set out to correct this imbalance by direct trading: purchasing products at higher prices and selling them in rich-country markets, thus circumventing the traditional distribution channels. Many of these organisations combine direct trading with the provision of technical assistance to their suppliers in everything from management to production techniques and market access. They also campaign on all matters related to fair trade. As such ATOs are a unique hybrid of for-profit organisations and NGOs.

Oxfam was a pioneer of fair trade in the UK in the 1960s. In the US the first ATOs included 10,000 villages and Equal Exchange. Many ATOs are based in Third World countries working to protect the rights of disadvantaged producers.

With the growth of the fair trade movement and increased awareness of the issues involved, especially among rich-country consumers in the 1980s and 1990s, many of the twentieth century fair trade groups began to coordinate efforts across borders and work towards establishing common and certifiable fair trade standards. In 1989 the International Federation of Alternative Trade (IFAT) was established, which claims to represent 160 groups in 50 countries of which two-thirds are based in the Third World. The various local groups also coalesced into national organisations which in turn established the International Fairtrade Labeling Organization (IFLO) in 1997 (IFLO URL).

The IFLO is an umbrella organisation which issues the 'Fairtrade' label to qualifying products based on a set of standards applied to both producers and traders. Compliance is monitored by a network of inspectors and an auditing process. There are different sets of requirements for traders and producers. Traders must:

- *pay a price to producers that covers the costs of sustainable production and living;*
- *pay a premium that producers can invest in development;*
- *partially pay in advance when producers ask for it;*
- *sign contracts that allow for long-term planning and sustainable production practices. (IFLO URL)*

There is some overlap between the Isolationists and Reformers; they are united in their opposition to the expansion of the WTO into the new areas such as investment. However, even here Reformers see an opportunity to address outstanding issues at the WTO and other global forums while Isolationists view it as part of a strategy to derail the WTO and return power to the nation state.

> *For the movement against corporate-driven globalization, derailing the 5th Ministerial or preventing agreement on the launching of a new comprehensive round would mean not only fighting the WTO and free trade to a standstill. It would mean creating momentum for a rollback of free trade and a reduction of the power of the WTO. This is well understood by, among others, the* Economist, *which warned its corporate readers 'globalization is reversible'. (Bello 2002)*

Another plank of the Reformist framework is the incorporation of labour and environmental standards in the trade regime:

For producers, the requirements are different for smallholders and cooperatives and for organisations dependent on hired labour. There are minimum progress requirements and specific standards for the various products. The requirements cover social, economic, organisational, labour, and environmental issues.

Most products covered by IFLO are food commodities such as coffee, sugar, and cocoa; but the organisation is beginning to address manufactured products starting with footballs. The member organisations cover a much wider selection of products.

Coffee is one of the main fair trade commodities and shows both the success and limitations of the movement. Despite rapid growth since 1973, when the first batch of fair trade coffee was imported into the Netherlands, it accounts for only 2 per cent of the total coffee market (Oxfam 2002b). Even some of its most avid proponents admit that fair trade coffee can be targeted only at the top end of the market. Moreover, by paying a premium price the fair traders may be sending the wrong signal to a market which is already suffering from excess supply. On the other hand, fair trade buyers are lending a helping hand to some of the most disadvantaged communities in the world in a context where little effort is being made by national governments or multilateral organisations to address the issue of over-supply and the need to shift to other crops. Finally, the example of the fair trade movement is creating an incentive for large coffee buyers to address the issues at hand.

FAIRTRADE
Guarantees
a better deal
for Third World
Producers

The key issue we are addressing here is the worker's human rights, which are clearly defined, such as the right to organize and bargain, and freedom and protection from forced labor, child labor and discrimination . . . The problem we have had with the WTO in recent years, is that they are saying 'these issues have nothing to do with us', that workers' rights are not trade issues. (Seneviratne 2003)

Such demands are not only difficult to pursue at the WTO, but some Southern activists view them either as a way to legitimise the WTO or as another attempt to discriminate against Southern producers. Moreover, the radicalisation of the movement means that, instead of the painstaking work needed to bridge such differences, compromise is being achieved on the basis of the lowest common denominator of deglobalisation.

The polarisation of the debate and the retreat to comfortable old dogmas means that less space is available for the *Alternatives*. The Alternatives are the foot soldiers of the global justice and solidarity movement. Young and with a keen eye for popular culture and new technology they speak globalisation's language. In the tradition of the 1960s radicals, the Alternatives have a deep distrust of authority, be it political or economic. They are not likely to be found in traditional organisations and NGOs. At the WSF they did not even have the particular passes necessary to attend most of the 1,400 workshops. The Alternatives not only account for the bulk of the participants at riots, demonstrations, and social forums but they are also responsible for the most creative ideas at these events: guerrilla gardening (digging up tarmac to plant trees), Marcus's mask (hiding one's face to identify with the faceless victims of global capitalism), white overalls (heavily padded protesters who can withstand police truncheons), critical mass (cyclists who obstruct automobile traffic by riding in large numbers), the pink march (which succeeded in penetrating the heavily fortified World Bank/IMF meeting venue in Prague by looking unthreatening) and the controversial black block (anarchists who do not shy away from using stones and occasionally fire-bombs to attack riot police).

The Alternatives not only account for the bulk of the participants at riots, demonstrations, and social forums but they are also responsible for the most creative ideas at these events

The Alternatives are also the driving force behind 'submerged networks' which surface around certain campaigns, such as SalAMI, which organised the riots against the Summit of the Americas in Quebec in 2001. SalAMI is a direct action network. Its first activities coincided with the Multilateral Agreement on Investments. It is also known for its non-violent blockade of the Montreal Conference on Economic Globalisation in May 1998.

Other submerged networks exercise resistance through the promotion of a particular lifestyle such as the Fair Trade movement (Box 4.3). The network in this case comprises of consumers who choose to pay premium prices for fair trade products (or boycott those viewed to be in violation of ethical trade norms) in addition to those who are involved in organising Fair Trade schemes.

Instead of aiming to transform or reform global capitalism, the Alternatives are concerned with reclaiming 'things' from the encroaching market and creating space for alternatives. They are concerned with the political and cultural consequences of capitalism as much as with its economic and environmental costs. They perceive the encroachment of the market into the public space as a threat to freedom, which takes the form of 'corporate censorship' in the North and human rights abuses in the South (Desai and Said 2001).

Alternatives do not represent a distinct set of positions on the issues of trade. They could thus be viewed, as pointed out in Chapter 1, as a particular form of global civil society, rather than a particular take on globalisation. That said, in a debate where one is expected to take sides between Western governments and corporations on the one hand and Third World leaders and industries on the other, the Alternatives have no favourite. This may explain why some of them felt so uncomfortable with certain aspects of the World Social Forum in Porto Alegre.

> *For some, the hijacking of the World Social Forum by political parties and powerful men is proof that the movements against corporate globalization are finally maturing and 'getting serious'. But is it really so mature, amidst the graveyard of failed left political projects, to believe that change will come by casting your ballot for the latest charismatic leader, then crossing your fingers and hoping for the best? Get serious. (Klein 2003)*

In the following sections we address issues which illustrate the civil society position on trade described above.

The World Trade Organization (WTO)

The WTO is at the heart of most civil society campaigns on trade issues. Established in 1995, it is one of the youngest multilateral organisations. It is simultaneously one of the smallest in terms of staff and bureaucracy yet one of the most influential in terms of impact on peoples' lives worldwide.

For its staunchest opponents, the WTO embodies everything that is wrong with global capitalism and superpower hegemony: a one-size-fits-all tool aimed at prising open Third World markets for the benefit of rich-country-based corporations. One of the organisation's most loathed features is the finality of its mandate: once a market is open it can not be closed again.

For its proponents, the WTO is the most democratic of the multilateral organisations, including the UN. It is, they argue, the only place where Costa Rica can lodge a complaint against the US and win, as was the case with underwear import restrictions (WTO Appellate Body, 1997). WTO proponents view the irrevocable nature of market opening as a strength, imparting certainty to global markets by removing the threat of ad hoc government intervention.

The debate about the WTO focuses on two main issues: governance and mandate.

Governance

On governance, the WTO's opponents argue that, despite the one nation-one vote and consensus systems, the so-called Quad countries (US, EU, Canada, and Japan) and their corporations dominate the WTO agenda:

- The so called 'Green Room' negotiations involving the Quad countries and a selected group of others are where consensus is forged in secret, with the remaining countries left to join the consensus.
- Mini-Ministerials are often organised involving the Quad countries and a selected list of invitees. These meetings are unofficial and are therefore unreported.
- The Quad countries use their political and economic muscle to force concessions from Third World leaders. This was the case with the US using the 'war on terrorism' rhetoric at the Doha Fourth Ministerial meeting in November 2001 (TWN URL).
- The negotiations are packaged in rounds: bundles of issues specifically for the purpose of horse-trading between the various issues. Some activists argue that this makes for further pressure on poorer nations (WDM URL).
- The influence of corporations and the coordination between Quad governments and multinationals is seen by many, including the WTO's new director Dr Supachai, as problematic (WDM URL).
- The WTO has built-in mechanisms which are aimed at rendering the process of market liberalisation irreversible. Once agreement is reached there is very little room for individual countries to revisit certain issues or reinstate barriers, regardless of circumstances. Even existing exemptions, on grounds of health and safety for example, are quite difficult to exercise, as was revealed during the dispute over generic AIDS drugs.
- The WTO's dispute-settlement mechanism, which adjudicates on violations of signed agreements, is specifically designed as an enforcement rather than an arbitration mechanism. The panel's decisions can be reversed only by consensus, rendering them virtually impossible to appeal. However, even detractors of the system admit that it is the right mechanism if the goal is the promotion of market liberalisation (US Senate Finance Committee 2000).

There are other, more prosaic reasons why Third World leaders cannot exercise their full rights within the WTO. Many cannot afford having a full-time representative in Geneva. Some lack the qualified staff and the resources to field representatives to several simultaneous meetings.

WTO proponents concede some of these charges and call for increased 'technical assistance and capacity building [for developing country governments] to be better equipped to participate in the multilateral trading system'. The WTO head considers this one of 'four pillars' which would help successfully conclude the current round of WTO negotiations (Panitchpakdi 2002). Other shortcomings are attributed to the imbalances in the inter-state system rather than the organisation itself.

Developing-country governments, especially India, Brazil, and South Africa, are displaying ever more skill in using WTO mechanisms to defend their interests. There are several Third World blocs within the organisation aimed at pooling resources and coordinating negotiating positions, including the 30 country-strong African Bloc, the Like-Minded Group which includes almost all Third World countries, and the Cairns Group which includes both poor and rich agricultural commodity exporters. Third World governments are leveraging divisions in the Quad group as well as support and pressure from civil society to pursue their goals (see below). The Doha Fourth Ministerial (the first after the failed meeting in Seattle) was a demonstration of this new-found confidence, although it resulted in only limited achievements for developing countries in the shape of a commitment to address the issues deemed critical by these countries before embarking on a new round of negotiations at the upcoming Fifth Ministerial in Cancun. Although no progress has been made so far on any of these issues, governments and activists both seem to have identified elements in WTO procedure from which they can attack the organisation:

> *If derailing the drive for free trade at the 5th Ministerial is indeed the goal, then the main tactical focus of the strategy becomes clear: Consensus decision-making is the Achilles heel of the WTO, and it is the emergence of consensus that we must prevent at all costs from emerging. (Bello 2002)*

Mandate

Campaigns around the Agreement on Agriculture (AoA), The General Agreement on Trade in Services (GATS), Trade-Related Aspects of Intellectual Property Rights (TRIPS), and the new areas of investment, government procurement, trade facilitation, and competition policy provide an illustration of the ongoing debate over the WTO's mandate.

Trade in sectors where developing countries are most competitive—agriculture and textiles in particular—is not being liberalised by the rich

According to activists, by limiting the nation-states 'policy space' the WTO denies developing countries essential tools of development. These countries claim to need preferential treatment to be able to catch up, while the WTO rules are not even equal. Trade in sectors where developing countries are most competitive—agriculture and textiles in particular – is not being liberalised by the rich. At the same time, developed countries press for liberalisation in sectors where trade mostly flows from North to South, such as intellectual property, services, and investment. The WTO also limits governments' freedom to protect small producers, to the benefit of large multinationals which are also predominantly based in the North. The activists use data showing poor countries losing anything from $100 billion to $300 billion a year due to imbalances in the global trade regime (Oxfam 2002a).

WTO defenders argue in response that, if developed countries are dragging out liberalisation in certain markets like agriculture and textiles, it is their consumers who will be the primary losers from such protectionism. They point out that discretionary policy tools such as import substitution and the promotion of infant industries, which were used by many developing countries under GATT, at best were ineffective and at worst promoted patronage and corruption. The main rejoinder from WTO proponents, however, is that the question is not whether the poor are losing out under the current trade regime but whether they would be losing more without the WTO (Bello and Legrain 2000–1). The debate over the impact of the WTO on development is ongoing and has fuelled demands to conduct an economic impact assessment before any further trade negotiations rounds are launched (Martin Khor speaking at WSF 2003).

The Fourth Doha Ministerial Meeting of the WTO in 2001 launched a new round of negotiations, dubbed the Doha Development Round, to replace the Millennium Round, which failed to materialise at the Seattle 1999 Ministerial. Doha is a compromise whereby developing countries agree to the expansion of the WTO mandate into new areas in exchange for redress of their concern over issues from previous rounds.

Outstanding Issues

Agreement on Agriculture (AoA)

Developing countries are demanding the elimination of agricultural subsidies by developed countries, including the $50 billion dispensed annually by the EU Common Agricultural Policy (CAP). They are specifically concerned with export subsidies which have direct bearing on their domestic markets as well as tariffs which prevent access for their products. The US supports this approach (in words if not in deeds, in view of the recent adoption of the Farm Bill) and is proposing across-the-board reductions in its own tariffs and subsidies. The EU, however, is baulking at compromise due especially to resistance from France. Recent agreement between the German and French governments to postpone any changes to CAP until 2016 has been met with indignation across the board. The deadline set at Doha for reaching an agreement on these issues was missed.

Isolationists dismiss the AoA and demand that agriculture and food in particular be taken out of the

Christian Aid's campaign for fairer trade rules. © Christian Aid

WTO remit. According to the isolationists, free trade in agriculture inevitably leads to the promotion of export crops at the expense of subsistence agriculture, which amounts to discrimination against small farmers and leads to environmental degradation and hunger (OWINFS URL; Food First URL). Reformers are campaigning for the elimination of developed-country subsidies and other barriers while allowing developing countries some leeway to ensure food security and the protection for small farmers and indigenous people (see below).

Implementation

Rich countries which were supposed to eliminate tariffs and quotas on textiles over ten years by 2005 have left most of them in place until the last minute. Developing countries are demanding that the rich start reducing tariffs in this area immediately. The US, as part of its 'positive engagement' policy, is proposing drastic reductions not only in textiles but in industrial tariffs across the board. The deadline for reaching agreement on implementation issues has not been met. Reformers support the developing country position in this respect. The Isolationists dismiss this approach as a gimmick designed to allow the developed countries to present their fulfilment of their long-standing obligations as a concession and give the Reformers a sense of achievement (Bello 2002).

Special and deferential treatment

The WTO offers a number of avenues to take special consideration of the development needs of its poorer members. Those include longer implementation periods and technical assistance both during negotiations and at the implementation stage. Agreements usually have mechanisms whereby developing countries can negotiate certain exceptions to satisfy their policies. The developing countries are demanding more flexibility in designing policies which they deem essential for development. The US and the EU are willing to consider such flexibility provided developing countries agree on 'graduation' criteria (Korea, an OECD member, is still benefiting from developing-country exceptions). No agreement was reached on these issues within the deadline set at Doha.

Both Isolationists and Reformers agree that developing countries should be allowed freedom in choosing development strategies and certain forms of protectionism which were employed successfully by developed countries, including late developers in East Asia (Oxfam 2002a).

Trade Related Aspects of Intellectual Property Rights (TRIPS) and public health

One of the few tangible achievements of the Doha meeting for developing countries was the agreement in the final declaration 'that it is important to implement and interpret the TRIPS Agreement in a way that supports public health— by promoting both access to existing medicines and the creation of new medicines'. This is done either by allowing countries to manufacture needed drugs without having to obtain a licence (compulsory licensing) or by importing generic unlicensed drugs from third countries (parallel importing) (WTO 2001). Negotiations were supposed to take place to clarify the modalities for making use of this exception especially by countries that did not have their own pharmaceutical industry. The negotiations broke down when the US backtracked on the principles agreed at Doha and sought to limit the number of diseases to which the exception would apply. Pharmaceutical companies that are behind the US trade representative's change of heart claim, not without some justification, that a blanket exception could be open to abuse by manufacturers of generic drugs, including those based in South Africa and India (Alfeld and Hofheinz 2003). The deadline was missed in this case as well. Activists of all persuasions have no love for TRIPS, especially when it comes to medicine.

New Areas

While there are disagreements among activists on the outstanding issues, there is an almost unanimous rejection of proposals for WTO expansion into new areas. Apart from previously mentioned strategies of reforming or abolishing the WTO, opposition to expansion is based on the activists notion of the market limits and the optimal level of policy space which should reside at the nation-state level.

Market limits are based on an understanding of what is tradable. Can public goods be left to the market or should they remain fully under state control? Should these goods, in principle, also be tradable internationally? Even if there is no principled objection to either, should they be subject to international trade under the present system?

The tradability of utilities and public services is a thorny issue since these usually include social costs and benefits which are not reflected in their market value. Markets for such services have therefore a higher risk of failure, the consequences of which can be more devastating than in other sectors of the economy. A collapsing health-care system is more dangerous than a collapsing automotive industry.

Beyond the issue of market failures and externalities, however, public services and utilities tend to have emotional, cultural, and political dimensions which sit uneasily with market relations, let alone foreign control. 'Services are the public tangible manifestation and expression of our shared values as citizens. How we choose to heal our sick, teach our kids, protect our water, connect to one another through transport and communication are expressions of our collective vision for society' (Klein 2000). 'Water', as a banner in Porto Alegre exclaimed, 'is Life. It can not be bought and sold' (WSF 2003). Finally, poor countries and poor people depend on the free or nearly free provision of these services for their survival, much more than their more fortunate counterparts.

One of the main complaints about the WTO compared with its predecessor, the GATT, is its impact on domestic *policy space* – an issue which arises from its targeting of non-tariff barriers. Environmental and safety regulations and other domestic policies have often been successfully contested through the WTO as trade-restricting. The famous image of protesters dressed in turtle suits in Seattle is related to one example of the WTO reaching into environmental regulations. The activists were protesting a WTO ruling in favour of Asian shrimp exporters who successfully contested a US environmental regulation which prohibits the import of shrimp farmed in ways which harm sea turtles (WTO 1998). There are many other examples of such rulings, including the well-known case when Europe was penalised for banning the import of US hormone-treated beef (WTO 1997).

The expansion of the WTO remit into new areas of services, investment, government procurement competition policy, and trade facilitation will further limit the scope of domestic policy. This is one of the main reasons why many in the Third World view the WTO as a new form of colonialism (Romapu 2003). The New Areas are at the heart of most WTO campaigns. These are not strictly trade issues, but any coverage of the WTO that did not address these issues would be incomplete. The discussion of the Multilateral Investment Framework also provides an update on the Multilateral Agreement on Investment campaign covered in *Global Civil Society 2001* (Desai and Said 2001).

The Multilateral Investment Framework (MIF)

Objections to the MIF are not dissimilar to those raised against its defeated predecessor, the Multilateral Agreement on Investment MAI (Desai and Said 2001). It reduces government's regulatory discretion and grants foreign investors unprecedented legal rights. Activists question the agreement's capacity to increase foreign direct investment. Some even question the link between investment and development (TWN URL). Activists would like to see an agreement which improved regulatory control over multinationals, but believe that such an agreement is unlikely to emerge within the WTO framework. The agreement, according to its detractors, would establish a false equality between the developed and the underdeveloped, which is inconsistent with affirmative action principles. Finally, unlike trade, investment flows only from North to South, which means that the agreement will largely benefit the developed countries and their corporations.

A workshop on the 'WTO Investment Issue' was organised in Geneva on 18-21 March 2003 by the Third World Network, Oxfam International, WWF, Public Services International, Center for International Environmental Law, and Institute for Agriculture and Trade Policy. The workshop issued a statement signed by 50 groups calling on governments to drop investment from the agenda for the upcoming WTO ministerial in Cancun (Khor and Yen 2003).

The defenders of the MIF argue that the agreement will not necessarily restrict regulatory space but make it more transparent. Rules and transparency will promote investment and lead to development (WTO URL).

General Agreement on Trade in Services (GATS)

The GATS has been in effect since the establishment of the WTO in 1995. It is a rolling agreement which aims to open up ever more areas of services, a market estimated at $5 trillion, to WTO rules. GATS in theory should cover 'everything that you cannot drop on your foot' (WDM 2002) with the exception of services associated with the direct exercise of government. This exception is, however, circumscribed by the proviso that these services are not offered on a commercial basis.[4] As Susan George (2003b) puts it in *Red Pepper*, 'All human activities are to become, in the fullness of time, profit-oriented commodities that can be invested in and traded'.

Its proponents argue that GATS covers only sectors which governments agree to include; moreover, governments are entitled to place exemptions on sectors which they offer for opening. For example, India has opened its tourism sector but maintained certain restrictions including the requirement that foreign operators act through local subsidiaries. Malaysia opened up its insurance sectors but maintained a 51 per cent limit on foreign ownership (Lal Das 2003).

GATS is currently undergoing a request-offer round which was supposed to end in April 2003. Countries are exchanging lists of sectors which they want included in GATS. There are also demands to lift previously established restrictions such as the ones listed above. Once a country offers the opening of a sector or a lifting of restrictions to any WTO member, it is obliged to open it to all under most favoured nations (MFN) rules.

Unlike goods, services can cross border in a variety of ways. GATS also covers four modes of delivery of services:

1) cross-border supply, such as banking via wire transfer;
2) consumption abroad, for example studying in a foreign country;
3) commercial presence, for example the establishment of a hotel as part of an international chain; and
4) presence of natural persons such as a construction crew travelling to another country to participate in a project.

Of most interest to many developing countries is Mode 4, which covers provision of services through the movement of physical persons. Developed countries have, however, diluted the potential of Mode 4 by invoking exceptions on grounds of security. Mode 3, on the other hand, is more interesting for developed countries. It covers the provision of services through movement of legal persons and could offer a back-door introduction of the MIF.

The sectors most targeted for inclusion into GATS or further liberalisation are utilities, transport, tourism, and financial services. Thanks to an energetic bipartisan (reformist-isolationist) campaign against it, GATS expansion does not seem to be justifying the activists' worst fears. To judge from the sectors offered for opening by the EU, health, education, and water will remain outside reach of GATS as far as Europe is concerned (OWINFS URL).

Bypassing the WTO: From NAFTA to FTAA

Corporations and the neo-conservatives who serve them are not waiting for the WTO to pursue the opening of new markets. There is a cascade of multilateral, regional, and bilateral

[4] *For example, a government's right to exclude government-owned postal services from the GATS remit is limited if those services are provided on a commercial basis.*

arrangements through which liberalisation is being pursued in ways which are more radical than ever envisaged under the WTO.

While the GATS negotiators debate whether trade in water itself should be liberalised or whether it is 'environmental services' such as water treatment and supply which should be opened to competition, the World Bank has already succeeded in privatising water and utilities in several Third World countries. Trade officials who reject linking the liberalisation of services with privatisation of health and education (WTO URL) have been pre-empted with the introduction of fees for education and health care under the Bank's conditionality, a process which is correctly viewed as a first step towards privatisation.

The FTAA includes radical versions of GATS and the other new agreements on investment and government procurement.

> *Our objective with FTAA is to guarantee North American companies the control of a territory that goes from the Arctic Pole all the way to Antarctica, free access to the whole hemisphere without difficulties or obstacles for our products, services, technology, and capital. (US Secretary of State Colin Powell, quoted in Mittal 2003)*

Finally, bilateral treaties such as the one between the US and Chile or British Petroleum (BP) and Turkey go even further than the FTAA in placing multinational corporations above the law. These treaties lack even the few monitoring and control mechanisms that are available in a multilateral framework like the WTO. For example, the agreement between the Turkish government and the Baku-Tbilisi-Ceyhan Pipeline Consortium led by BP exempts the pipeline from obligations under any current or future Turkish law that may threaten the project's profits, including environmental, social, and human rights legislation. The only Turkish law not superseded by the agreement is the Constitution (Baku Ceyhan Campaign 2002).

Negotiations for the establishment of FTAA were launched at the first Summit of the Americas in 1994. It was then conceived as a trade alliance encompassing all 'democratic' states in the hemisphere, that is, excluding Cuba. The FTAA seeks to expand to the entire continent the model of the North American Free Trade Agreement (NAFTA), which brought together the US, Canada, and Mexico in 1993. The FTAA is seeking a mandate almost identical to that of the WTO, including the new areas of government procurement, competition policy, trade facilitation, and investment. FTAA by design is meant to 'improve upon these [WTO] rules and disciplines wherever possible and appropriate' (FTAA URL). FTAA, like NAFTA but unlike the WTO, is likely to incorporate some labour and environmental provisions.

> *Essentially, what the FTAA negotiators have done, urged on by the big business community in every country, is to take the most ambitious elements of every global trade and investment agreement—existing or proposed—and put them all together in this openly ambitious hemispheric pact.*
> *(Barlow 2001)*

Like the WTO Doha Round, FTAA negotiations are supposed to be completed by 2005. Like the WTO, they have been bogged down in the face of fierce resistance by civil society and, to a lesser degree, governments in most Latin American countries. Like the WTO, the FTAA requires consensus to be approved, which is inspiring optimism among its opponents about its chances of success.

The FTAA seems to attract more vociferous opposition and from a broader set of actors than the WTO. Few of the treaty's opponents seek to improve it, focusing instead on preventing it from ever coming into force. One reason may be the NAFTA track record and the damage attributed to the treaty in the US and Canada but especially in Mexico. Unlike the WTO, NAFTA is directly associated by its opponents with the loss of manufacturing jobs in the US and Canada and the devastation to small-scale agriculture and indigenous livelihoods in Mexico. Global Exchange attributes the loss of 766,000 jobs in the US to NAFTA (Global Exchange NAFTA FAQ URL) while Food First claims that 600 Mexican farmers are forced off their lands every day due to the treaty (Mittal 2003; see also Chapter 8). Moreover the maquiladora jobs created by NAFTA along the US-Mexico border are notoriously unstable and underpaid. Flagrant labour and environmental abuses are attributed to the operators of factories established specifically to service the US and Canadian markets. Environmental degradation along the US-Mexico borders attributed to NAFTA has prompted the establishment of 'Border XXI', a binational border environmental plan to address air and water problems (US Trade Representative URL). Another explanation for the vociferous

Table 4.2: Positions on trade agreements

	Isolationists (e.g. Bello, Hines, Wallach)	Reformers (e.g. Oxfam, WDM, Greens, most Third World governments)	Supporters (e.g. academics, USTR Zoellick, European Commission)	Regressives (e.g. The Heritage Foundation, the rest of the US Administration, France, Italy)
Agreement on Agriculture (AoA)	Take food out of the WTO	Scrap Western subsidies and barriers. Allow poor countries to erect barriers when necessary	Eliminate all barriers	Keep barriers when in the our national Interest
New areas (investment, government procurement, competitions, trade facilitation)	No expansion to new areas	No expansion before addressing outstanding issues	Expand while dealing with outstanding issues	Expand with no restrictions as long as it is to the benefit of our companies
TRIPS (intellectual property and health)	Abolish	Should allow for preferential treatment of poor countries and national emergencies	Should have allowances only for emergencies such as health (both production and import)	Full global protection of intellectual property rights with the exception of our national emergencies
GATS (services)	Abolish	Should not extend to critical public services and public goods	Expand short of ill- defined areas necessary for the exercise of government	Expand as long as it is to our benefit
FTAA	Abolish	Abolish/amend	Support but not at the expense of WTO	Promote as alternative to WTO
Fair trade	Too little too late	At least something	May be trade-distorting	Trade is fair

opposition to the FTAA is fear of being overwhelmed by the USA. More than any of the other regional and international alliances, the FTAA will be dominated by the USA, which accounts for 75 per cent of the hemisphere's GDP.

The campaign against the FTAA has evolved since 1997 into the focal point of anti-capitalist and, over the past year, anti-war activities in the hemisphere. Hundreds of groups have joined forces in a myriad of activities, predominantly trades unions in the US and Canada and peasants organisations in Latin America (see Chapter 8). The organisation which best represents the movement is the Hemispheric Social Alliance (HSA). A network of networks, the HSA involves multi-sectoral national and regional networks such as the Common Frontiers (Canada), the Quebec Network on Hemispheric Integration, the Alliance for Responsible Trade (United States), the Mexican Action Network on Free Trade, the Chilean Alliance for Just and Responsible Trade, and the Brazilian Network for Peoples Integration. It also involves sectoral networks such as the hemispheric coordinators of the labour sector (ORIT) and the peasant sector (CLOC).

The HSA claims to unite groups representing more than 45 million members.

The HSA organised among others the first Peoples' Summit in Santiago, Chile, in April 1998 parallel to the second official Summit of heads of state of the Americas. It has been a visible presence in almost every major activity targeted at NAFTA/FTAA and the WTO in the Americas. The HSA elaborates and updates its own alternative agenda to the FTAA, *Alternatives for the Americas*. The latest version of the document was drafted in December 2002. *Alternatives for the Americas* covers topics on the official agenda, such as investment, finance, intellectual property rights, agriculture, market access, services, and dispute resolution. It also addresses issues of human rights, sustainability, environment, labour, immigration, the role of the state, and gender, which are either ignored or addressed inadequately at the negotiations. The main guiding principle of the document is set out in these terms:

> *Trade and investment should not be ends in themselves, but rather the instruments for achieving just and sustainable development. Citizens must have the right to participate in the formulation, implementation, and evaluation of hemispheric social and economic policies. Central goals of these policies should be to promote economic sovereignty, social welfare, and reduced inequality at all levels. (HSA 2002)*

Strategy

Most civil society groups involved in trade issues pursue a mix of strategies in varying proportions. Most seek to multiply their impact by being involved in overlapping regional, thematic, and international networks.

Inform and educate

The movement on trade issues has developed by leaps and bounds since Seattle. The various groups have almost real-time access to the minutiae of trade negotiations: secret or public, within the WTO or the other treaties. Secret documents are regularly leaked by sympathetic government negotiators and trade bureaucrats. Information is extracted skilfully through parliaments and freedom of information tools. One recent leak in this context is an EU document listing the services which the EU would request for opening under GATS from various countries (WDM URL).

Groups have their own experienced cadre of trade experts and lawyers. They also draw on resources from academia, the civil service, and international organisations, especially the UN. They provide almost real-time analysis of the available information, evaluate negotiating positions and scenarios, and recommend counter-measures.

Outcomes are passed on to the public, parliaments, and friendly negotiators in digestible, actionable, and campaignable form through web sites like Global Trade Watch (Public Citizen), Trade Observatory (Institute for Agriculture and Trade Policy), The Third World Network Information Service on the WTO, and MakeTradeFree.com (Oxfam).

Special tools and information packages are produced for the various audiences including briefs, step-by-step talking points, frequently asked question lists and guides for MPs, their constituents, trade negotiators, and government officials. Some groups produce and commission in-depth research papers, reports, and monographs and conduct workshops for activist policy-makers and experts, and organise speaking tours.

Lobby

Groups target multiple levels in their lobbying including parliament, government, negotiators, and international organisations. Groups have become adept at using fissures among the various establishment actors: MPs, trade officials in the capitals, trade negotiators, ambassadors, and WTO employees. Activists are also quick to exploit tensions between the various actors: EU, US, Japan, Like Minded Group, and Cairns Group.

Movement-Third World government cooperation

There are numerous examples of cooperation between NGOs, think tanks, and UN agencies on the one hand and Southern governments on the other. Cooperation includes designing both negotiating strategies and domestic policies aimed at maximising benefits or reducing adverse effects of trade liberalisation, and improving the bargaining position of the South at the WTO.

One organisation active in this field is Martin Khor's Third World Network (TWN). An example of

Table 4.3: Civil society responses to global trade

● PREDOMINANT
◐ SIGNIFICANT
○ TO SOME DEGREE

	Organisation					Activity					Position				
	Individual	NGO/group	Movement/network	Think tank/academia	Media/website	Inform/educate	Lobby	Mobilise	Serve	Riot/celebrate	Supportive	Regressive	Isolationist	Reformative	Alternative
Action Aid		●				○	◐	●						●	
American Enterprise Institute				●		●		◐			●	◐			
ATTAC			●	◐		○	◐	●					◐	●	
Bello, Walden	●					●		◐					●		
Christian Aid		●				○	◐	◐	●					●	
Corporate Europe Observatory			●			●	◐	○					●	◐	
Economist					●	●	◐				●			◐	
Emergency Committee for American Trade		●					●	◐			●				
Financial Times					●	●	◐				●			◐	
Focus on Global South				●		●		◐					●	◐	
Food First		◐		●		●	○	◐					●	◐	
Friends of the Earth		◐	●				◐	●					●	◐	
GATS Watch					●	●		●					●	◐	
Global Trade Watch (at Public Citizen)					●	●		●					●		
Hemispheric Social Alliance			●					●					◐	●	○
Heritage Foundation				●		●	◐				●	◐			
Institute for Agriculture and Trade Policy				●		●							●	◐	
International Chamber of Commerce			●				●				●				
International Confederation of Trades Unions (ICFTU)			●			○	●	◐						●	
International Federation for Alternative Trade			●			○	◐	●						●	◐
International Forum on Globalization			◐	●		●		◐					●	◐	
International Gender and Trade Network			●			●	○	◐					●	◐	
Klein, Naomi	●					●		◐							●
OneWorld.net					●	●			◐				◐	●	○
Our World Is Not For Sale			●				◐	●					●		
Oxfam		●				○	◐		●					●	
Peoples Global Action			●				●				●				
Polaris Institute				●		●		◐					◐	●	
Public Citizen		●				○	◐	●					●		
Rand Corporation				●		●	◐				●	◐			
SalAMI		●						◐		●			◐		●
Terraviva (of Inter Press Service)					●	●		◐					◐	●	○
Third World Network		●	◐			◐		●					◐	●	
Trade Justice Movement			●					●						●	
Trade Observatory (previously WTO Watch)					●	●		●	●				◐	●	
Trans Atlantic Business Dialogue			●				●				●				
Transnational Institute				●		●	◐	◐					◐	●	
Via Campesina			●			○	◐	●					◐	●	
Wall Street Journal					●	●	◐				●	◐			
World Development Movement		●				◐	○	●						●	

Noam Chomsky and Arundhati Roy address the closing session of the WSF in Porto Alegre, January 26, 2003 . © Simone Bruno

TWN's projects is the Asia Pacific regional consultation which was organised in Colombo, Sri Lanka, on 17–19 April 2003. The consultation dedicated to the WTO/TRIPS Agreement and Access to Medicines was attended by about 70 government officials, health-related NGO representatives, health professionals, and international trade and intellectual property rights experts. It was organised jointly by the Health Action International-Asia Pacific, Sri Lanka Ministry of Health, and the World Health Organisation (South East Asia Regional Office). The main conclusion of the meeting was that TRIPS, despite its adverse impact, does provide flexibilities for governments to safeguard public health. Governments were advised on policies to utilise these flexibilities based on, among other things, the experience of the North.

TWN closely monitors WTO developments and issues regular research and strategy papers for the benefit of Southern delegations and NGOs. Most recently it issued a guide to Southern countries' delegations on handling GATS negotiations (Lal Das 2003). The guide author, Lal Das, is a former Indian representative at GATT.

The Southern and Eastern African Trade Negotiations Institute (SEATINI) is another organisation providing support to Southern governments at the WTO, with a specific focus on Africa. SEATINI is 'dedicated to strengthen Africa's capacity to take a more effective part in the emerging global trading system and to better manage the process of Globalization'. It is an affiliate of the International Southern Group Network (ISGN). It draws on academic, NGO, legal, and trade negotiations resources from governments, UN agencies, academia, and the WTO itself. SEATINI organises regular meetings and advises African policy-makers on negotiating positions and trade policies. It conducts research on trade-related issues and runs an Advisory Clinic which provides ad hoc online assistance to African trade negotiators (SEATINI URL).

Conclusions

The anti-capitalist movement has racked up some impressive advances over the past four years. No longer a ragtag army of romantic activists, the movement has evolved into a well-informed and organised political force to be reckoned with. It has chalked up impressive victories, reversing some privatisation and liberalisation policies in Latin America and restraining the fervour of free traders in Europe. Most importantly, it dealt a severe blow to its main target: the Washington consensus.

The movement may yet fall victim to its own success. Its meteoric rise has attracted some nasty fellow-travellers in the guise of nationalist leaders, Third World multinationals, and old left gurus. They are threatening to hijack the movement and blot out its most attractive features—openness, cosmopolitanism, informality, and popular appeal.

The movement is also at risk of falling into the old trap of investing too much stock in the ability of great national leaders to deliver the goods of justice and equality. Historically these leaders did not justify this trust. They turned into tyrants, or sold out, or provided convenient targets for the forces of global capitalism.

While boosting the positions of Southern leaders and multinationals may contribute to levelling the global economic playing field, these actors are no more committed to global justice than their opponents. Indian and South African pharmaceutical companies produce generic drugs for profit and not out of concern for those dying of AIDS and malaria. More ominously, however, the exclusivist nationalism which comes with some of the newly found allies is threatening to contaminate the movement: 'The Forum's place as a focus for what I would call the new global solidarity is being put in question by those who seek to not only give it national but nationalist character' (Waterman 2003).

A catastrophic success scenario may materialise if the nationalists succeed in using the movement to 'derail the WTO'. At a time when multilateralism is under siege, destroying the only international organisation which has the potential to hold superpower(s) to account is not what one would expect from a global justice and solidarity movement.

Dismantling the WTO won't solve the problems of injustice in the global trading system. Quite the opposite: it may lead to an even less equitable and more hegemonic globalisation. It will hand an easy victory to the movement's worst enemies: unilateralist neo-conservatives, rusty old industries, and politicians who are trying go back in time. Without the constraints of the WTO they will be free to muscle their way into any market through bilateral and regional agreements like the much maligned NAFTA. It will be a Pyrrhic victory like the one chalked up by the music industry when it shut down Napster, only to push music swapping into distributed networks with no single reference point.

Global justice needs global solutions which national leaders, no matter how enlightened, cannot deliver. Present tensions between the negotiators of North and South on how to safeguard the environment and protect labour without jeopardising development will be swept aside. If the painstaking work needed to built a just global trade system is abandoned as futile, unity can be based only on a lowest common denominator agenda of de-globalisation.

The progressive answer to one-size-fits all, elitist institutions which serve corporate interests is democratic multilateral institutions that serve the causes of development and equity, in addition to a robust movement that holds governments, businesses, and international organisations to account. Given the sophistication of the tools at the movement's disposal and its growing political clout, it is no longer sufficient for it be engaged in a purely negative purpose. Drawing up utopian plans to return to the anti-colonial state or, further back, to the state of nature does not amount to building an alternative future.

The movement has matured to the point where it has both the ability and the obligation to get down to the painstaking business of institution (re)building. Fixing GATS or the MIF so that they put people before profits, hold the rich and powerful to account, and protect nature is neither easy nor glamorous but it has to be done.

Delivering an hour-long litany of worn conspiracy theories at the end of the World Social Forum, Noam Chomsky almost managed the incredible feat of putting a full stadium of jubilant young people to sleep. Mercifully, he was followed by his exact opposite: Arundhati Roy was quiet, powerful, cryptic, and accessible. She spoke of the twin evils of liberalisation and nationalism. She called on activists to lay siege to the empire, mocking it with their culture and joy instead of confrontation. By the end of the speech the crowd was ecstatic. Despite its young age this is a sophisticated movement, which we hope will not be content with tired old slogans and idols. Activists are seeking sophisticated answers to the issues of globalisation. They should be prepared to do the hard work necessary to find them.

References

Alfeld, Haiko and Hofheinz, Paul (2003). 'End the Squabble'. *Wall Street Journal*, 14 March.

Amin, Samir (2003). 'Confronting the Empire'. Contribution to WSF. 22–7 January <http://www.forumsocialmundial.org.br/dinamic.asp?pagina=conf_samir_amin_ing>.

Baku Ceyhan Campaign (2002). 'Oil Companies Colonise Turkey: MAI by the Back Door?' Press Release. 30 August.

Barlow, Maude (2001). 'The FTAA and the Threat to Social Programs, Environmental Sustainability and Social

Justice in Canada and the Americas' <http//www.stopftaa.org>.
Bello, Walden (2002). *The Oxfam Debate: From Controversy to Common Strategy* <http//www.maketradefair.com>.
– and Legrain, P. (2000–1). 'Should the WTO be Abolished?'. *The Ecologist*, 30/9.
Caldwell, Christopher (2003). 'Free Trade is Running Out of Time'. *Financial Times*, 1 April.
Cockroft, James (2003). 'Report on Porto Alegre 2003', 25 March. <http://www.forumsocialmundial.org.br/dinamic.asp?pagina=bal_cockcroft_ing>.
Desai, Meghnad (2002). *Marx's Revenge: The Resurgence of Capitalism and the Death of Statist Socialism.* London, New York: Verso.
– and Said, Yahia (2001). 'The New Anti-Capitalist Movement: Money and Global Civil Society'. In Helmut Anheier, Marlies Glasius, and Mary Kaldor (eds), *Global Civil Society 2001*. Oxford: Oxford University Press.
Fisher, William F. and Thomas Ponniah (eds) (2003). *Another World is Possible: Alternatives to Globalization at the World Social Forum.* Basingstoke: Palgrave Macmillan.
Food First <http://www.foodfirst.org>.
FTAA (Free Trade Area of the Americas) <http://www.ftaa-alca.org>.
George, Susan (2003a). 'Corporations Domain and Crisis in the International Financial System'. Contribution to WSF. 22–27 January <http://www.forumsocialmundial.org.br/dinamic.asp?pagina=conf_susan_george_in>.
– (2003b). 'How GATS Could Affect Your Life'. *Red Pepper.* January.
Global Exchange. NAFTA FAQ <http://www.globalexchange.org/ftaa/faq.html>.
Hines, Colin (2000). *Localization: A Global Manifesto.* London: Earthscan.
Hobbes, Jeremy (2002). Speech at WTO Symposium. April.
HSA (Hemispheric Social Alliance) (2002). *Alternative for the Americas.* Ottawa: HSA.
IFG (International Forum on Globalization) (2002). *Alternatives to Economic Globalization: A Better World is Possible.* San Francisco: Berrett-Koehler .
IFLO (International Fairtrade Labeling Organization) <http://www.fairtrade.net>.
Khor, Martin and Yen, Goh Chien (2003). 'NGOs Call on Governments to Drop Investment Issues at WTO Cancun Meeting'. *TWN Information Service on WTO Issues.* March.
Klein, Naomi (2000). Speech at WDM's GATS campaign launch, November. <http://www.wmd.org.uk>.
– (2003). 'Cut the Strings'. *The Guardian*, 1 February.
Lal Das, Bhagirath (2003). 'Services Negotiations in the WTO: Requests And Offers'. *TWN Information Service on WTO Issues*, 25 February.
Lamy, Pascal (2003). 'Come on America, Play by the Rules!'. *Wall Street Journal*, 3 March.
List, Friedrich (1837/1966). *The National System of Political Economy.* New York: Kelly.
Luce, Edward (2002). 'Poor Nations Urged to End Trade Barriers'. *Financial Times*, 29 November.
Mekay, Emad (2003). 'Interview with Klaus Schwab'. *TerraViva*, 27 January.
Mittal, Anuradha (2003). 'Open Markets or Open Plunder'. *TerraViva*, 27 January.
O'Driscoll, Jr, Gerald P. and Fitzgerald, Sara J. (2002). *Trade Promotes Prosperity and Security.* Washington, DC: Heritage Foundation.
Osava, Mario (2003). *TerraViva* (official newsletter of the WSF), 22 January.
OWINFS (Our World is Not For Sale) <http://www.ourworldisnotforsale.org>.
Oxfam (2002a). *Rigged Rules and Double Standards: Trade Globalization and the Fight Against Poverty.* London: Oxfam.
– (2002b). Coffee Report. <http://www.maketradefair.com>.
Panitchpakdi, Supachai (2002). 'From Doha to Cancun and Beyond'. Speech at the General Assembly of the Swiss Bankers Association, 22 September.
Prebisch, Rudiger (1950). *The Economic Development of Latin America and its Principal Problems.* New York: United Nations.
Ricardo, David (1821/1992). *The Principles of Political Economy and Taxation* (ed. Donald Winch). London: Dent.
Romapu, Mina (2003). TWN activist speaking at WSF.
Rothschild, Emma (2001). *Economic Sentiments: Adam Smith, Condorcet, and the Enlightenment.* Cambridge, MA: Harvard University Press.
SEATINI (Southern and Eastern African Trade Negotiations Institute) <http://www.seatini.org>.
Seneviratne, Kalinga (2003). 'Interview with Guy Ryder, Head of the International Confederation of Trades Unions (ICFTU)'. *TerraViva*, 24 January.
Smith, Adam (1776/1993). *An Inquiry into the Nature and Causes of the Wealth Of Nations.* Savage, MD: Rowman & Littlefield.
Spraos, John (1983). *Inequalising Trade? A Study of Traditional North/South Specialisation in the Context of Terms of Trade.* Oxford: Clarendon Press in cooperation with UNCTAD.

Temel-Kuran, E. (2003) 'Report from Porto Alegre'. *Milliet*, 24 January.

TWN (Third World Network) <http://www.twnside.org.sg>.

UNDP (United Nations Development Programme) (2003). *Making Global Trade Work for People*. London: Earthscan.

United States Senate Finance Committee, Subcommittee on International Trade (2000). *Testimony of Lori Wallach Regarding the WTO Dispute Settlement System: Powerful Enforcement of Unbalanced, Extensive Regulations Without Basic Due Process Protections*, 20 June.

United States Trade Representative FTAA <http://www.ustr.gov/regions/whemisphere/ftaa.shtml>.

Waterman, Peter (2003). 'Reflections' <http://www.forumsocialmundial.org.br/dinamic.asp?pagina=balan_waterman2003in>.

WDM (World Development Movement) (2002). *Trade in Services: MP Briefing*.

– <http//:www.wdm.org.uk>.

Win, Aye Aye (2003). 'Righting Global Wrongs: No Simple Solutions'. *TerraViva*, 27 January.

Wolf, Charles (2002). 'The WTO Controversy: Exaggerated Fears and Unrealistic Hopes'. *Straddling Economics and Politics: Cross-Cutting Issues in Asia, the United States, and the Global Economy*. Arlington, VA: Rand Corporation.

WSF (World Social Forum) (2003). Notes from WSF proceedings by Yahia Said who attended the Third WSF in Porto Alegre, Brazil, 22–7 January.

WTO (World Trade Organization) <http://www.wto.org>.

– (1997). *EC Measures Concerning Meat and Meat Products (Hormones) Panel Report*.18 August. Geneva: WTO.

– (1998). *United States – Import Prohibition of Certain Shrimp and Shrimp Products: Report of the Panel* (WT/DS58/R). Geneva: WTO.

– (2001). *Final Declaration: Fourth Ministerial Meeting*. Doha. November.

WTO Appellate Body (1997). *United States - Restrictions on Imports of Cotton and Man-made Fibre Underwear*. 10 February. WTO.

Chapter 5

GLOBAL CIVIL SOCIETY AND BIOLOGICAL AND CHEMICAL WEAPONS

Daniel Feakes

Chemical and biological warfare is the use of poison and disease for hostile purposes. Until the late nineteenth century, the distinction between poison and infectious disease was not a clear one. ''Disease' was used to refer to ailments whether caused by poison or pathogen, toxic agent or microbe. Indeed, many toxins, 'biological agents [which] owe their pathogenicity to toxic substances that they themselves generate' (WHO 2001: 3), can be classed as both chemical and biological weapons. A recent report by the World Health Organization (WHO) defined biological weapons as 'those that achieve their intended target effects through the infectivity of disease-causing microorganisms and other replicative entities, including viruses, infectious nucleic acids and prions', and chemical weapons as 'those that are effective because of their toxicity, i.e. their chemical action on life processes capable of causing death, temporary incapacitation or permanent harm' (WHO 2001: 3).

Chemical and biological (CB) weapons have often been considered together—in law, in military organization, in political debate, and in the public mind. One of the best explanations of this approach dates from a 1965 conference:

> *The dangers to world security posed by all classes of biological and chemical weapons are closely inter-related. Both in public opinion and in military practice it does not appear possible to maintain any lasting distinction between incapacitating and lethal weapons, or between biological and chemical warfare. The great variety of possible agents forms a continuous spectrum, starting from those that are temporarily incapacitating and ending with highly lethal ones. If the restraints on the practice of any kind of biological or chemical warfare are broken down, the entire spectrum of these weapons may come into use. (Rotblat 1972: 242)*

The spectre of chemical and biological warfare is not new. Chemical weapons have been used on the battlefield since the First World War and, as weapons of terror and sabotage, CB weapons have been around for many centuries. The massive use of chemical weapons in the First World War brought CB warfare to the attention of a general public which, by and large, found it repugnant and contrary to the laws of war. Scientific advances in the 1940s opened up the potential for using biological agents not only for sabotage but also as tactical and even strategic weapons. After the Second World War, CB weapons were classed together with nuclear weapons as 'weapons of mass destruction'. However, they were initially overshadowed by their new, more destructive cousin, returning to the international political agenda only in the late 1960s.

Subsequent decades witnessed a number of international negotiations resulting in treaties consolidating what had previously been a fragmented and weak international regime against CB warfare. The heart of this strengthened regime consists of two disarmament treaties—the 1972 Biological Weapons Convention (BWC) and the 1993 Chemical Weapons Convention (CWC)—which reaffirm the prohibition on the use of CB weapons, prohibit their development, production, and stockpiling, and require all member states to destroy any stockpiles. The regime is much stronger for chemical than for biological weapons, since the more recent CWC includes an international verification system of unprecedented intrusiveness whereas no such system was included when the BWC was negotiated. A verification protocol to strengthen the BWC was rejected by the US in 2001. The prospects for further consolidation of the international regime against CB warfare currently look bleak. Indeed, the primary current concern is to ensure that the existing regime is sustained and is not undermined.

As suggested in the 2001 edition of this Yearbook, global civil society is 'a fuzzy and contested concept' (Anheier, Glasius, and Kaldor 2001: 11). In some people's minds, global civil society means activist groups with large constituencies like Greenpeace or grass-roots networks such as the anti-globalisation movement. However, there are few, if any, such

Box 5.1: Chemical and biological agents stockpiled or weaponised since 1946[1]

Tear gases, other sensory irritants, and other disabling chemicals:
- 10-chloro-5,10-dihydrophenarsazine (adamsite, or DM)
- ?-chloroacetophenone (CN)
- ?-bromophenylacetonitrile (larmine, BBC or CA)
- 2-chlorobenzalmalononitrile (CS)
- dibenzoxazepine (CR)
- oleoresin capsicum (OC)
- 3-quinuclidinyl benzilate (BZ)

Choking agents (lung irritants):
- phosgene
- chloropicrin

Blood gases:
- hydrogen cyanide

Vesicants (blister gases):
- bis(2-chloroethyl) sulfide (mustard gas)
- 2-chlorovinyldichloroarsine (lewisite)
- bis(2-chloroethylthioethyl) ether (agent T)
- tris(2-chloroethyl)amine (a nitrogen mustard)

Nerve gases:
- ethyl N,N-dimethylphosphoramidocyanidate (tabun, or GA)
- O-isopropyl methylphosphonofluoridate (sarin, or GB)
- O-1,2,2-trimethylpropyl methylphosphonofluoridate (soman, or GD)
- O-cyclohexyl methylphosphonofluoridate (cyclosarin, or GF)
- O-ethyl S-2-diisopropylaminoethyl methylphosphonothiolate (VX)
- O-ethyl S-2-dimethylaminoethyl methylphosphonothiolate (medemo)
- O-isobutyl S-2-diethylaminoethyl methylphosphonothiolate (VR)

Further toxins
- Ricin
- Saxitoxin
- Clostridium botulinum toxin
- Staphylococcal enterotoxin
- Aflatoxin

Bacteria and rickettsiae
- Bacillus anthracis (anthrax)
- Francisella tularensis (tularaemia)
- Brucella suis (brucellosis)
- Burkholderia mallei (glanders)
- Burkholderia pseudomallei (melioidosis)
- Yersinia pestis (plague)
- Rickettsia prowazeki (typhus fever)
- Coxiella burnetii (Q fever)

Viruses
- Venezuelan equine encephalitis virus

Source: (WHO 2001)

[1] *Toxic and infective antipersonnel agents stockpiled or otherwise weaponised for state forces since 1946 according to official documents of possessor states*

organisations or movements active in CB disarmament. Applying this definition to the organisations and individuals that are involved could lead to the following conclusion: 'Global civil society has not been active in the CBW arena. A small group of specialized NGOs almost exclusively in the North have been. Whether or not you call this largely academic group civil society depends on your definition; but it's worth noting the restricted base' (Hammond 2003).

While not ignoring these facts, in this chapter I use the broad definition of 'global civil society' provided in the 2001 edition of this Yearbook: '[T]he sphere of ideas, values, institutions, organizations, networks and individuals located *between* the family, the state, and the market, and operating *beyond* the confines of national societies, polities, and economies.' (Anheier, Glasius, and Kaldor 2001: 17). Therefore, this chapter assumes that the academics and researchers who follow CB disarmament are a part,

Box 5.2: Chemical and biological warfare programmes since 1946

Chemical weapons	Biological weapons
Albania*	Canada§
Bosnia-Herzegovina*‡	France§
China*	Iraq†
France*	Russia§
India*	United Kingdom§
Iran*	United States§
Iraq†	
Japan*+	
South Korea*	
Russia*	
United Kingdom*	
United States*	
Yugoslavia*‡	

* Countries declaring past or present chemical weapons programmes under the CWC.

§ Countries declaring past or present biological weapons programmes under the BWC confidence-building measures.

† Iraq declared chemical and biological weapons programmes under United Nations Security Council Resolution 687.

‡ Bosnia-Herzegovina and Yugoslavia declared the same site, a former chemical weapons production facility near Mostar in Bosnia-Herzegovina.

\+ In 1997 Japan declared the (now destroyed) chemical weapons production facility used by the Aum Shinrikyo cult as it was under government jurisdiction at the time.

albeit a small and highly specialised part, of global civil society. Similar organisations and individuals can be found in related issue-areas such as nuclear disarmament or landmines; but they are generally one element of a larger network which includes activist and advocacy organisations (Short 1999; Johnson 2000). For a number of reasons, this combination has so far not materialised in relation to CB disarmament.

This chapter will attempt to answer two main questions: why has civil society involvement in CB disarmament been so restrained when compared with, for example, its involvement in nuclear disarmament? And do recent developments both within CB disarmament and within global civil society more generally mean that this characterisation may be losing its accuracy?

The first section explains the development and use of CB weapons. The second section outlines the three principal ways in which CB weapons have been framed by governments and civil society. The third and fourth sections set the scene for the fifth and sixth by describing the civil society organisations involved in CB disarmament and external factors which influence their composition and activities. In so doing, these two sections aim to answer the first of the questions posed above. The fifth section summarises the international political response to CB weapons, including the contribution of civil society where appropriate. The sixth section describes the methods by which civil society has sought to exert its influence on CB disarmament. Together, these two sections are designed to provide preliminary answers to the second of the questions posed above. The chapter concludes by considering what has been and what remains to be achieved in CB disarmament and by proposing an alternative frame within which further progress could be made.

The Development and Use of Chemical and Biological Weapons

Early developments

CB warfare as currently understood has existed since the early twentieth century. However, as the existence of ancient bans on the use of poison in warfare and historical accounts of battles testify, the use of chemical and biological agents for hostile purposes has a much longer history. Through the centuries, clouds of poisonous smoke have been used to overcome fortifications and to reduce resistance within besieged cities, sometimes successfully but often unsuccessfully (SIPRI 1971b: 125–6). During the siege of the Crimean city of Caffa in 1346, the attacking Tatar forces used catapults to throw their plague victims into the Genoese city, whereupon the subsequent outbreak forced the defenders to flee (Wheelis 2002a).

During the nineteenth century, as synthetic chemicals became more readily available, there were numerous proposals for the military use of chemicals. But it was only with the later industrialisation of chemistry that large-scale use of chemical weapons became possible. Germany was first to use lethal CW in the First World War but the other belligerents soon followed suit. The inter-war period saw chemical weapons used during the Russian civil war (1919–21), by British forces in the Middle East and Afghanistan in the early 1920s, and in colonial wars by Spain in Morocco (1921–7), by Italy in Libya (1930), by the USSR in Sinkiang (1934), by Italy in Abyssinia (1935–6), and by Japan in China (1937–45). In the 1940s, Japan also used relatively primitive biological weapons in China; but until the 1940s biological warfare on a large scale was not technologically feasible and was primarily seen as a weapon of sabotage (SIPRI 1971b: 111).

A number of reasons have been given as to why chemical weapons were not used militarily during the Second World War, including the deterrent value of either side's stockpiles, the availability of protective equipment, and Hitler's personal aversion to chemical weapons after being exposed to them in the First World War. However, toxic chemicals were of course used to kill millions of Jews and others in extermination camps.

A quantum leap in the development of chemical weapons occurred with the discovery by German scientists of the nerve agents sarin and tabun, which were much more aggressive than earlier weapons. In biology, new developments during the 1940s, particularly in the field of aerobiology, opened up the possibility of the tactical or even strategic use of biological weapons (SIPRI 1971b: 123). In the 1950s, the first of a family of more toxic nerve agents, the V-agents, was produced.

During the 1990s, the use of CB weapons by non-state actors became a major concern, particularly in the West. A defining event was the 1995 sarin attack in Tokyo by Aum Shinrikyo

CB programmes after the Second World War

After the Second World War, a number of states retained an interest in CB warfare. The US, UK, and Canada agreed a division of labour on the research, testing, and production of CB weapons, formalised through a trilateral agreement. The UK and Canada abandoned their offensive CB warfare programmes in the 1950s and 1960s but continued defensive work. The USSR also continued its CB warfare programmes, eventually establishing the world's largest stockpile of chemical weapons. A number of other European and Asian countries have also operated CB warfare programmes since the Second World War (see Box 5.1). While these countries have admitted past or present CB warfare programmes, a number of other countries are suspected of possessing CB weapons but have made no public admission.

During the 1950s and 1960s, the US carried out a series of large sea and land trials of CB weapons to assess the effectiveness of CB weapons and its vulnerability to them. In 1969, the US unilaterally renounced possession of lethal and incapacitating biological weapons and declared its support for a global ban. At the time, the renunciation was justified by claims that biological weapons were ineffective and unreliable. However, it later transpired that the US renounced biological weapons and pushed for a global ban for precisely the opposite reason. The trials of the 1950s and 1960s had demonstrated that biological weapons posed a potential threat to cities: 'It was therefore important to discourage the development and production of these weapons by additional countries and to maintain US strategic deterrence based on other weapon systems' (Tucker 2002: 128).

Chemical weapons have been used in at least three conflicts in the mid- to late twentieth century, once again all in the developing world. In Vietnam, the US used tear gas and herbicides despite widespread international criticism, in the Yemeni civil war Egypt used chemical weapons against the Royalist forces (1963–7), and Iraq used chemical weapons against Iran and its own Kurdish civilians (1983–8). In contrast, biological weapons have not verifiably been used in combat since the end of the Second World War.

The USSR had a biological weapons programme and believed the US renunciation to be a deception. While joining the global ban on biological weapons, the USSR accelerated its programme by concealing activities within a seemingly legitimate civilian concern (Alibek and Handelman 1999). US and UK suspicions about this programme were confirmed only later by Soviet defectors.

Chemical and biological weapons have never played a central role in military strategy. They have remained on the periphery of war-fighting doctrine and capability

Proliferation and use in developing countries

By the 1980s, both East and West no longer regarded chemical weapons as an essential part of their arsenals and decided to negotiate their stockpiles away. In addition, all BWC members had undertaken to continue negotiations on a chemical weapons ban. Fear of each other's weapons was replaced by fear of proliferation of CB weapons to developing countries. These fears were confirmed by the use of chemical weapons by Iraq against Iran and its own civilians in the 1980s, by the revelation of an apparent Libyan chemical weapons programme, and further disclosures about Iraq's CB warfare programmes by United Nations weapons inspectors in the 1990s. In the developing world, CB weapons were seen as force-equalisers—the 'poor man's atom bomb'—either against regional adversaries or against the US (Robinson, Stock, and Sutherland 1994: 711).

A number of countries, especially in the Middle East, are suspected of possessing CB weapons. The US Central Intelligence Agency mentions Iran, Iraq, Libya, North Korea, Syria, and Sudan as possessing or developing CB capabilities, while State Department officials have listed the same countries but also add Cuba. Some of these countries are not members of the CWC or BWC and these allegations cannot therefore be subjected to international verification.

However, Iran and Cuba are members of both the CWC and BWC, and Iraq, Libya, and North Korea are BWC members; but the US has chosen not to make use of the mechanisms provided for in each treaty for investigating violations. In addition, it is widely assumed that Israel, a member of neither the CWC nor the BWC, possesses stockpiles of CB weapons, in addition to its nuclear arsenal (Cohen 2001).

During the 1990s, the use of CB weapons by non-state actors became a major concern, particularly in the West. A defining event was the 1995 sarin attack in Tokyo by Aum Shinrikyo and the subsequent discovery that the cult had previously launched 19 attacks with CB weapons, most of which had failed (Smithson and Levy 2000: 103). Although fears that Aum's activities would set a precedent for other terrorists to follow have not been realised, a great deal of government attention and resources has been committed to preventing CB terrorism, especially in the US.

This was evident before the 2001 anthrax letters in the US, but American anti-CB terrorism programmes have been enhanced massively since then, although there is no proven link between the anthrax letters and international terrorism. While many allegations have been made about the CB capabilities of al-Qaeda, there is no publicly available evidence that the organisation has developed a sophisticated CB capability.

Iraq's alleged possession of CB weapons was a primary justification for the 2003 US-UK invasion. Between 1991 and 1998, United Nations weapons inspectors uncovered a large chemical weapons programme and oversaw the destruction of many chemical weapons. The inspectors also discovered a biological weapons programme but their further investigation was hampered by Iraqi non-cooperation. When the inspectors were withdrawn in 1998, much of the infrastructure of Iraq's CB programmes had been destroyed but many questions remained unanswered.

When the inspectors returned in 2002, they encountered a lack of substantive cooperation in addressing the unresolved issues but also did not find any significant stocks of undeclared CB weapons before they were withdrawn again in 2003. American and British military forces are now searching for hidden CB weapons in Iraq but, at the time of writing, had yet to find anything despite extensive intelligence data, information from pre-war defectors, and now information from people within Iraq.

Despite this history of the development and use of CB weapons, they have never played a central role in military strategy. They have instead remained on the periphery of war-fighting doctrine and capability, with even militaries being reluctant to adopt CB weapons, preferring instead the reliability of high explosives. Developed countries have largely abandoned their CB warfare programmes but have maintained protective programmes for their armed forces, leaving today's CB weapons in the hands of a small number of developing countries unable to afford similar protection against CB weapons. While the chances of CB weapons being used in a major international conflict have thus decreased, the likelihood that such weapons will be used in so-called 'New Wars' has increased (Kaldor 1999). The use of CB weapons in 'New Wars' is likely to see a return to the age-old practice of poison and disease being used to intimidate and terrorise civilians rather than between armies on a battlefield.

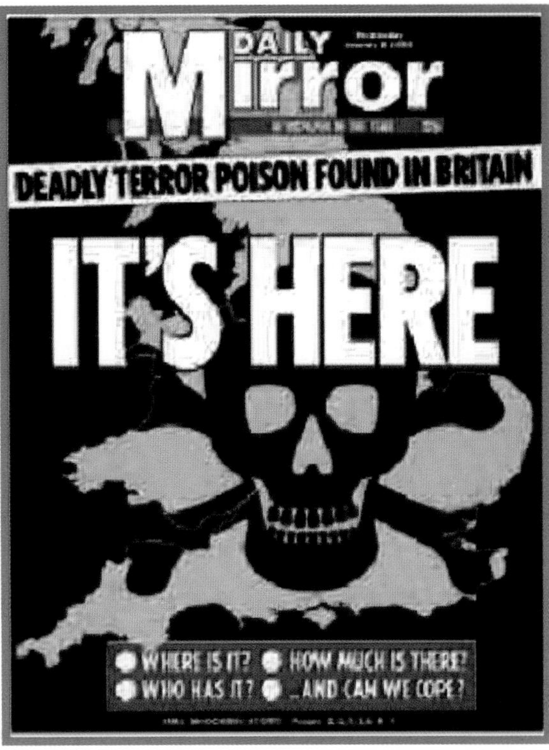

Front cover of the British *Daily Mirror* tabloid, 8 January 2003

Current technological developments

Scientific and technological progress will influence the future development and use of CB weapons. Current advances in biotechnology and pharmacology hold out the potential for significant gains but also run the risk of being misused for hostile purposes (Wheelis 2002b). The Harvard geneticist Matthew Meselson (2000: 16) asks: 'Every major technology—metallurgy, explosives, internal combustion, aviation, electronics, nuclear energy—has been intensively exploited, not only for peaceful purposes but also for hostile ones. Must this also happen with biotechnology, certain to be a dominant technology of the twenty-first century?'

If so, the prospects are frightening:

> *During the century ahead, as our ability to modify fundamental life processes continues its rapid advance, we will be able not only to devise additional ways to destroy life but will also become able to manipulate it—including the processes of cognition, development, reproduction, and inheritance. A world in which these capabilities are widely employed for hostile purposes would be a world in which the very nature of conflict had radically changed. Therein could lie unprecedented opportunities for violence, coercion, repression, or subjugation. (Meselson 2000: 16)*

Developing countries do not possess the resources and capabilities to misuse biotechnology in this way. Instead, it is the actions of major developed countries which should be of concern. Commenting on revelations about secret US biodefence research, Wheelis and Dando (2002: 6) argue:

> *The likelihood that the US programme goes well beyond the projects so far revealed further suggests that the US may be embarking on an exploration of the military applications of biotechnology—actively exploiting it to develop an offensive 'non-lethal' chemical weapons capability; beginning to use it to explore possible offensive bioweapons development strategies as part of threat assessment; and eager to*

use it to develop antimateriel BW. We fear that this is pioneering very dangerous ground.

Although at first glance so-called 'non-lethal' CB weapons might seem more acceptable than lethal ones, the introduction of 'non-lethal' CB agents onto the battlefield undermines the existing taboo against the use of any poison or disease for hostile purposes and brings with it the risk of escalation to lethal CB agents. In addition, the description 'non-lethal' is a clear misnomer as in certain situations such weapons can have a similar lethality to conventional weapons, as demonstrated when Russian special forces used a derivative of the chemical fentanyl to end the siege of a Moscow theatre in October 2002 (Klotz, Furmanski, and Wheelis 2003). This incident, and reports that the United States transported riot control agents and incapacitating chemicals to the forces which invaded Iraq (Lean and Carrell 2003), has raised awareness of the potential that novel weapons, even 'non-lethal' ones, based on biotech research have for undermining the international regime against CB warfare (Dando 2003).

The taboo against the use of poison in warfare has ancient and cross-cultural roots. There is a particular odium and fear associated with CB weapons in the popular imagination

Framing Chemical and Biological Weapons

How an issue is framed influences the way civil society addresses it and the resonance the issue has with the general public (Keck and Sikkink 1998). Three distinct but related frames can be identified as having been applied to CB weapons often concurrently, namely, the 'taboo' frame, the 'WMD' frame, and the 'CB terrorism' frame.

The first of these frames still very much applies to CB weapons today and the other two frames depend upon it. The taboo against the use of poison in warfare has ancient and cross-cultural roots. References to toxic warfare can be found in the Indian epics *Ramayana* and *Mahabharata* and in later Chinese and Greek sources. From the Sanskrit Laws of Manu which forbade the use of poison weapons 'a line of ancestry can be drawn for the 1925 Geneva Protocol, and therefore for the 1993 [Chemical Weapons Convention] as well. It is a culturally diverse ancestry, reaching back not only through Hague and Roman law via Grotius, but also through the warfare regulations which the Saracens derived from the Koran' (Robinson 1998: 17). For many centuries, 'any use of poison, even against soldiers, has come to be understood as an unacceptable practice of warfare. The use of poison has come to be stigmatized as immoral in and of itself' (Price 1997: 26).

Just why CB warfare has been delegitimised to such an extent is disputed. A 1973 study refers to a 'deep psychological aversion among the majority of people, including the military, who become aware of CB weapons ... Poison and disease can unnerve people to an extent which other dangers cannot; and the outbreaks of mass hysteria and the superstitions which they have provoked in the past are well recorded' (SIPRI 1973a: 118). The number of popular films and novels about escaping viruses testifies to this. Another explanation is that the aversion to CB warfare is deeply rooted in human nature, 'perhaps in human chromosomes themselves' (Mandelbaum 1981: 39).

Whatever the rationale, it cannot be denied that there is a particular odium and fear associated with CB weapons in the popular imagination. This is one reason why the international community has been relatively successful in negotiating disarmament treaties for CB weapons. The main products of the 'taboo' frame include major elements of the present-day international regime against CB warfare such as the 1899 and 1907 Hague Conventions and Declaration and the 1925 Geneva Protocol.

Despite their widespread delegitimisation, CB weapons, like other weapons systems, are considered within the 'state security discourse'. This discourse is based upon 'an essentialized notion of state sovereignty' in which the state possesses a monopoly on the use of force as 'necessary' to the preservation of the state, and the possibility of their removal from national arsenals is seen as a threat to the state. The 'state security discourse' thus 'effectively forecloses the capacity of civil society to contest or to question the weapons of war that secure its existence' (de

Box 5.3: The politics of fear: historical precedents

Since late 2001 the idea that terrorists could use chemical, biological, or nuclear weapons has dominated the news. States have used this to justify curtailing civil liberties at home and pursuing aggressive foreign policies. Most notably it has been used to justify America and Britain breaking the UN Charter's prohibition of pre-emptive war. The use of the spectre of chemical and biological weapons by a government to instil fear in its own population, in order to advocate a particular policy, has historical precedents.

The first example is from the United States (Jenkins 2002). After the First World War, American chemists, chemical warfare officers, and chemical manufacturers launched a campaign with two goals. The first was to secure wartime investments in the new American artificial dye industry by getting a high tariff imposed on foreign dye imports. The second was to stop the army establishment closing down the giant chemical warfare programme America had developed during the First World War. America had been preparing to produce and use more poison gas in 1919 than Britain, France, and Germany combined. The campaign's strategy was to convince Americans that German aeroplanes and airships would soon be able to cross the Atlantic and drop new poison gases on American cities. It was argued that the only way to prevent such an attack was to deter Germany by developing the world's greatest chemical warfare capability.

The problem the campaign faced was that Americans believed that the vast reaches of the Atlantic Ocean made such an attack impossible, and many military experts believed that the actual use of chemical weapons in the First World War had shown they had real limitations as it was difficult for artillery to build up the large concentration of gas needed to kill; gas masks, clothing, and shelters provided a defence; and it was not clear that gas was more effective than high explosives.

To overcome these difficulties, the leaders of the chemical campaign described bomber aircraft and poison gas as being in their 'infant stage'. This meant that their use in the First World War was no guide to their future potential. This transformed them into blank screens for popular fantasies. Americans could imagine aircraft crossing the Atlantic and annihilating the entire population of New York, Washington, Chicago, and other cities in a single air raid.

There was no such German threat. Germany's wartime government had been replaced by a Social Democratic administration hostile to a new war. After years of war the German people would not initially support a new war. Even as late as 1929, the historian A. J. P. Taylor (1981: 59) reports, 'the most popular cry in Germany was "No More War" not "Down with the Slave Treaty"'. The annihilation of American cities by a transatlantic attack was also impossible. The shape of buildings, wind conditions, and the necessity of either accurate bombing or the laying of a gas plume by precise level flying close to the ground all make it difficult to build up a lethal concentration of gas over the whole of a large city. These difficulties are multiplied if the city is defended by either aircraft or anti-aircraft guns, and if the civilian population is equipped with gas masks. The problems become intractable when the bombers must cross the Atlantic Ocean.

My second example is from Germany (Fritzsche 1993). The 1930s saw the emergence of a coalition between German veteran air pilots, air strategists, aviation engineers, and Nazi Party ideologists. They sought to overcome what they identified as the cause of German defeat in the First World War: the collapse of civilian morale in November 1918. Their success in this would enable Germany to pursue an aggressive expansionist foreign policy. They argued that, instead of seeing themselves as civilians whose defence against air attack should be left up to technical experts (fire wardens, police, the Red Cross, civil-defence officials), German men and women should see themselves as soldiers on the home front whose task was to keep the nation working so that German armies could win the war. The goal of civil defence was accomplished when 'the individual thinks, feels, and acts as a fighter' and 'is as disciplined as a soldier'. All citizens must become bound into 'one unbreakable national community'. Or, as one air-defence poster's slogan summed it up, 'One People, One Danger, One Defence'.

Like the American chemical campaign, the coalition played on German fantasies about air power and poison gas. This was achieved through a strategy of saturating Germany with images and writings showing Germans' total vulnerability to the air threat and by getting Germans to experience the threat as a lived reality by participating in air defence.

The strategy included (1) exhibitions showing aerial photographs. These sought to show that big cities, and the nation as a whole, formed a giant system which could be fatally disrupted by air attack. (2) German cities were subjected to simulated air attacks to demonstrate their vulnerability. On 24 June 1933, 'unknown foreign' aeroplanes bombed Berlin with leaflets. The journal *Flugsport* warned that the next time it might be 'gas or incendiaries'. (3) Across Germany the Reich Air Defence League installed eight-foot high dummy bombs, marked with a vivid yellow stripe. In city squares aerial explosives dangled from street lamps and streetcar wires. (4) The German Airsports League, founded in 1933, and heavily subsidised by the Nazis, provided another vehicle for educating Germans about the aerial danger and, more importantly, through its glider clubs, in persuading civilians that they should be actively involved in defending the nation. (5) In physics classes students learnt about the mechanics of flight, in chemistry they studied poison gas, in literature they read the memoirs of air aces, and in history they studied the development of aviation and how Allied restrictions during the 1920s on aviation had left Germany vulnerable to air attack. (6) Teachers also discussed the theories of air strategists, showed students how to wear gas masks, and drilled students in how to remain calm during air raids. School rooms became centres of air-mindedness: model aeroplanes hung from the ceiling, posters showing bomber attacks hung on the walls, and aeroplane books sat on the shelves. (7) An Air Defence League was set up. Every apartment building was asked to elect a house warden. They in turn assigned a fire detail, a hose crew, medical aides, and a dispatcher from among the residents. They formed the bottom of a pyramid linking house wardens to block wardens, district leaders, city-wide air raid officials, and so on up to Air Minister Goering. By January 1936 there were over 7,000 branches of the League with a total of over 8 million members.

These two examples show how a real thing—deadly gases—can be described so as to transform it into a blank screen for popular fantasies by emphasising its unprecedented nature, and this can form the basis for persuading people to support the extension of state power at the expense of their own civil liberties. How can we respond to these dangers? Alexis de Tocqueville warned that, in a modern liberal democracy in which each citizen finds themselves an atom in a sea of millions of other atoms, there is a strong tendency to identify with the state in times of danger. He argued that it is only through being a member of a civic association that citizens have the strength to call into question the state's use of real dangers to extend its powers and to assemble the scientific, legal, and other forms of expertise necessary to call into question the state's claims (Tocqueville 1968: 657–70, 872; Hirst 1994: 1–14).

Take Secretary for Defense William Cohen's claim, intended to gain American support for possible military action on Iraq. Appearing on ABC television's *This Week* in November 1997, Cohen held up a five-pound bag of sugar and stated, 'this amount of anthrax could be spread over a city, say, Washington, it could destroy half the population'. The ordinary American, or indeed world citizen, has no way of knowing how to assess Cohen's claim. Through joining a civic association, however, she can have access to biologists whom she trusts who can tell her, for example, that while it is relatively easy to produce anthrax it is very difficult to infect a large population (WHO 2001: s. 2.4), and to historians who can tell her that even a large state like Britain was not sure it had produced an effective biological weapon of mass destruction after a decade of trying (Balmer 2001: 128–30).

Thus, the saturation of the global space with the fear of terrorism to justify imperial expansion abroad and the rolling back of civil liberties at home can be challenged only through the creation of global civil society organisations and networks which can operate in many national spaces at once.

Dominick Jenkins, London School of Economics

Larrinaga and Turenne Sjolander 1998: 370). The international consideration of CB disarmament takes place within 'a world view where states are perceived to be the primary agent for analysis and action' (Carroll 2002: 23). As will be shown below, this environment impacts greatly upon civil society and its activities in CB disarmament.

Since the mid-1940s, CB weapons—along with nuclear weapons—have been framed as 'weapons of mass destruction' (WMD) by governments, international organisations, and civil society. The term originated with attempts within the United Nations to devise a 'system for the regulation of armaments' under Article 26 of the UN Charter. However, as noted above, major elements of the international regime against CB warfare pre-date the definition of CB weapons as WMD. The definition of WMD adopted by the United Nations mentions only 'lethal chemical and biological weapons', thus legitimising by default the range of CB weapons sometimes termed 'non-lethal' but which some regard as the bigger threat to international security.

By equating CB weapons with nuclear weapons, they are conceptualised as a threat to the very survival of the state and therefore as an issue in which only states can legitimately be involved

The association of CB weapons with nuclear weapons has proved useful to Western states seeking to justify their continued possession of nuclear weapons (as a deterrent against the use of CB weapons by 'rogue states') and now to rationalise preventive action, and has also proved useful to legitimise the possession of CB weapons by states in the South as a deterrent against the nuclear powers or, in the case of the Middle East, as a counter to Israel's nuclear arsenal (Price 1995: 99–100; Croddy 2002: 46).

By equating CB weapons with nuclear weapons, the WMD discourse conceptualises them as a threat to the very survival of the state and therefore as an issue in which only states can legitimately be involved. Over the years, states have developed a generic approach to dealing with WMD based, in part, on concepts such as arms control and verification. This approach emphasises consensus-based multilateral treaty negotiation, oversight by an international organisation, and referral of violators to the United Nations Security Council. A distinct field of international law has been developed in which one international agreement borrows elements from another so that treaty provisions are similar whether dealing with nuclear, biological, or chemical weapons.

Another characteristic of the WMD frame is that it is a product of the developed world; it lacks resonance with developing countries and their populations and with large sections of global civil society. For example: 'African civil society has not been active in the CBW arena at all. While there is interest in the issue, civil society organizations have naturally focused on more pressing and immediate issues including small arms proliferation and use, HIV/AIDS and food crises' (Gould 2003). At the state level, this is reflected in the fact that Africa has the lowest membership of any region in the CWC and BWC despite the fact that chemical weapons have been used in a number of African countries and others are suspected of possessing either chemical or biological weapons. By not joining the CWC and BWC countries also limit their access to technology and to assistance if attacked or threatened with attack by CB weapons.

More recently, and particularly in the West, a third frame has been applied to CB weapons: CB terrorism. Although the threat of CB terrorism emanates from non-state actors possibly with state sponsorship, once again it is the state which has responded and which has set the agenda. In many ways, the rise of CB terrorism is not a new framing of CB weapons; rather; it is a return to the ancient use of chemical or biological agents to terrorise, intimidate, and sabotage. The 2001 anthrax letters in the US caused a worldwide panic and national hysteria within the US but killed only five people.

In assessing the real threat posed by CB terrorism, it is worth recalling the resources expended by the US and USSR to develop effective biological weapons and that Aum Shinrikyo in Japan spent $30 million on its chemical weapons programme (Smithson and Levy 2000: 80). Few terrorist organisations have such resources available. In addition, the ease of production and dissemination of CB weapons is frequently overstated by both the media and politicians. It is likely that terrorists will continue to prefer weapons with high levels of effectiveness and reliability, such as high explosives and small arms, rather than CB weapons which are difficult both to produce and to use. While international activity under the WMD frame has been based on multilateral solutions and international cooperation, the response to CB terrorism has been largely national and couched in terms of 'homeland security'. This is despite the threat posed by state-sponsored terrorism which may still require reliance upon more traditional solutions directed at states rather than non-state actors.

Since 11 September 2001, the response to CB weapons has been further re-framed, particularly in the US and UK, by the combination of the WMD and CB terrorism threats to produce a new 'nexus of proliferation and terrorism' (Ellis 2003: 117). Thus re-framed, responses to the issue of CB weapons are now as likely to involve military force as traditional diplomacy. In his 2002 State of the Union address, US President Bush spoke of an 'axis of evil' consisting of Iran, Iraq, North Korea, and 'their terrorist allies', and said: 'The United States of America will not permit the world's most dangerous regimes to threaten us with the world's most destructive weapons.' The clearest expression to date of this policy has been the recent US-UK invasion of Iraq, which was initially justified on the basis of disarming Iraq of its WMD. Both the US and UK governments made strenuous efforts to convince their populations of the threat posed by Iraq's alleged WMD stockpiles, a threat which, after the invasion, appears to have been overstated.

It is likely that terrorists will continue to prefer weapons with high levels of effectiveness and reliability, such as high explosives and small arms, rather than CB weapons

In dealing with CB warfare threats this view emphasises the national above the international, the military above the diplomatic, and unilateral action above multilateral consultations: 'The Bush administration's new national security strategy, aimed at refocusing US efforts to deal with proliferant states and nonstate actors, essentially replaces the traditional state-centered US nonproliferation approach with one that—for the first time—privileges counterproliferation and explicitly acknowledges prospective requirements for preemption' (Ellis 2003: 115).

Civil Society Involvement in Chemical and Biological Disarmament

The civil society involvement in CB disarmament provides a good example of an 'epistemic community', defined by Haas (1992: 3) as 'a network of professionals with recognized expertise and competence in a particular domain and an authoritative claim to policy-relevant knowledge within that domain or issue-area'. Epistemic communities are common in other areas of civil society. A study of civil society involvement in the negotiation of the 1996 Comprehensive Test Ban Treaty highlights the role of 'elite, principally non-governmental experts, academics and professionals' (Johnson 2000: 52), while a 'relatively small' epistemic community was initially involved in the tropical forest issue (Keck and Sikkink 1998: 134).

The difference between these two issue-areas and CB disarmament is that in both cases the epistemic community forms but a part of a broader civil society involvement in the issue made up of, in the case of the Comprehensive Test Ban Treaty negotiations, 'public movement campaigns' and 'non-violent direct action'. In contrast, civil society involvement in CB disarmament is largely limited to the members of the epistemic community. According to one observer of the BWC protocol negotiations: 'This was predominantly academic, research and policy analysis based nongovernmental participation; there was little of the traditional, grass roots NGO advocacy' (Rissanen 2002: 33). Using a definition applied to civil society organisations following corporate social responsibility, civil society in CB disarmament has many 'insiders' but few 'outsiders' (Oliviero and Simmons 2002: 82).

Civil society involvement in CB disarmament has a number of more specific defining characteristics which have a direct bearing on what activities are undertaken and how. The majority of the most active civil society organisations are based in the West, principally in North America and Western Europe, but there are of course some exceptions. They are overwhelmingly based within academia and, even among those not in academia, academic qualifications are highly regarded. In very general terms, three main types of civil society organisation are most actively involved in CB disarmament: academic centres and programmes; scientific networks; and research and policy centres. There are of course overlaps between these three categories, and other organisations are involved in a more ad hoc fashion. While most of these organisations are national rather than international, they network and collaborate extensively with one another across borders.

Academic centres and programmes active within CB disarmament include the Harvard Sussex Program on CBW Armament and Arms Limitation (URL), the Department of Peace Studies at the University of Bradford (URL), and the Center for Nonproliferation Studies at the Monterey Institute for International Studies (URL). One observer has noted that the preponderance of academics within the community means that it includes 'people who don't know if they want to document or change the world' (Hammond 2003).

Three main types of civil society organisation are most actively involved in chemical and biological disarmament: academic centres and programmes, scientific networks, and research and policy centres

Reflecting the origins of civil society involvement in CB disarmament and the technical nature of the issue, there are many natural scientists, specifically chemists and biologists. The Pugwash Conferences on Science and World Affairs (URL) has been active in CB disarmament since the 1950s (see Box 5.4). Other scientific networks include the Federation of American Scientists (URL) and the International Network of Engineers and Scientists for Global Responsibility (URL).

Research and policy institutes include the Stockholm International Peace Research Institute (URL), the Chemical and Biological Arms Control Institute and the Verification Research, Training and Information Centre (URL). Green Cross International (URL) has done a lot to empower and bring together local communities in both the United States and Russia which are situated close to chemical weapons storage facilities.

Outside of this core group of civil society organisations are a number of organisations with a more irregular or less active involvement in CB disarmament. Among them are religious groups such as the Quakers, humanitarian groups such as Amnesty International and Human Rights Watch, and environmental groups such as Greenpeace.

Mention should also be made of civil society organisations, particularly in the United States, which oppose elements of the international regime against CB warfare. For example, in 1991 the Heritage Foundation proposed the reversal of the US decision to renounce chemical weapons production and US retention of a modest biological weapons stockpile, while in 1997 the Center for Security Policy opposed US ratification of the CWC.

The interrelationship between CB weapons and the WMD frame imposed by governments upon them means that the community's boundaries can be easily discerned as few of its members participate in other issue-areas, even in nuclear disarmament. While this allows for subject specialisation, it also means that the community is somewhat insular and immune from developments in other issue-areas. All of these characteristics contribute to a community which is both discrete in its activities and restrained in its policy proposals. In this, it is similar to the epistemic community in nuclear disarmament which promotes 'limited, practical, incremental demands and policy initiatives that are perceived by governments as pragmatic steps that can be realized in the short to medium term' (Johnson 2000: 50).

At the individual level, there is a remarkable degree of continuity among the community's members, with some participants having been involved in CB disarmament for over four decades. While this level of continuity bring great advantages in terms of subject-matter expertise and institutional memory, it can also make it more difficult for the community to renew itself through the recruitment of new members. The community is also a rather small one, similar to the 'handful of people' within the tropical forest epistemic community (Keck and Sikkink 1998: 134). According to the originators of the concept, an epistemic community typically has under 35 members and sometimes much fewer (Adler and Haas 1992: 380). It would not be surprising to find that the number

Box 5.4: The Pugwash movement and chemical and biological warfare

No account of the role of global civil society in CB disarmament would be complete without reference to the Pugwash Conferences on Science and World Affairs (Moore 1997). Pugwash grew out of the 1955 *Russell-Einstein Manifesto* and is so named because its first meeting was held in the village of Pugwash, Nova Scotia. Pugwash first held an international conference on CB warfare in 1959 and has been involved ever since. One account of Pugwash's work in this area says of the 1959 meeting: 'The meeting had no precedent; it was the first clear marker on the route towards the new international anti-CBW regime that exists today' (Robinson 1999: 230).

Pugwash's involvement in CB disarmament was subsequently taken forward by the BW Study Group and its successors. The various study groups have all had three elements: a steering committee, workshops, and policy research projects. Their meetings, of which there have been over 50 since 1964, are the primary forum for the presentation of new research, for airing new topics, and for increasing awareness of new developments. But perhaps their main function has been 'bringing policymakers and other governmental officials into continuing working contact with the Study Group' (Robinson 1999: 236).

The workshops have also served as a meeting place for global civil society allowing scientists, researchers, analysts, and NGO staff to build up relationships, discuss issues, and share ideas. All participants take part in the workshops as individuals rather than as representatives of their governments or organisations, thus providing for more informal, and frequently more revealing, discussions.

At various times in its history, the Study Group has conducted, or been closely associated with, policy research projects. These have often occurred at times of low governmental activity on CB disarmament. In the mid-1960s, the Study Group, in collaboration with the Stockholm International Peace Research Institute (SIPRI), itself largely a creation, through the Swedish parliament, of Pugwash, undertook a project to assess the feasibility of international inspections to biological laboratories. Although the BWC as opened for signature in 1972 did not include any serious verification measures, the work done by SIPRI did feed into later intergovernmental negotiations.

In the 1970s, the Study Group did work on the philosophy and design of on-site inspections in the civil chemical industry, including a number of trial inspection visits. Through this work, Pugwash facilitated contacts between the diplomats in Geneva and the civil chemical industry, which were essential to the eventual success of the CWC negotiations. This approach was emulated by governments with the use of national trial inspections during both the CWC and BWC protocol negotiations.

The story of Pugwash involvement in CB disarmament is also the story of the involvement of particular individuals, some for many decades. Chief among them is Martin Kaplan, who was the instigator of the 1959 meeting and has played a leadership role in Pugwash work in this area ever since (Robinson 1999: 230). In the early 1950s, Kaplan was a WHO microbiologist already concerned about CB weapons. He attended a Pugwash conference in 1958 and was then involved in planning the 1959 meeting. Kaplan went on to become Secretary-General of Pugwash from 1976 to 1988 (Kaplan 1999). Alongside Kaplan, Matthew Meselson from Harvard University and Julian Perry Robinson from the University of Sussex have been closely involved in the Study Group since the 1960s. Indeed, Meselson, through his Harvard colleague Henry Kissinger, then President Nixon's National Security Adviser, had much to do with the US renunciation of biological weapons in 1969–70 (Kaplan 1999: 151).

Assessing the influence of Pugwash in CB disarmament is not easy due primarily to a lack of documentation. It chiefly resides in the continuity of its involvement, the informal nature of its workshops, and the originality of its policy research . Between 1959 and 1998, 645 people from 46 countries had participated in Pugwash activity in this field: a 'remarkable community of interest', as one account describes it (Robinson 1999: 245). This same account concludes that 'perhaps the greatest achievement of Pugwash [at the level of government] has been its role in gradually securing respectability for the goal of an international treaty on chemical weapons. This was a goal which, in the late 1960s, government officials in the more prominent Western countries would often simply mock'.

of individuals actively involved in CB disarmament is somewhat similar.

In terms of organisations involved, the most recent CWC and BWC meetings were attended by, respectively, only 6 and 16 civil society organisations, compared with the 62 which attended the 2002 Non-Proliferation Treaty Preparatory Committee. One advantage of this small size is the ease of communication and collaboration among the community. Members are in frequent contact by e-mail and telephone and meetings such as those organised by Pugwash often involve a large proportion of the community.

The community is also well-connected in terms of its relationship with governments and international organisations. The long-term involvement of some community members means that they have developed strong personal contacts with government officials. Additionally, some individuals now active for civil society in CB disarmament were previously responsible for the issue-area as government officials or diplomats, thus further strengthening the contacts between global civil society and policy-makers. While this may provide civil society with a better understanding of how decisions are made, it also contributes to the discrete and restrained character of civil society involvement in CB disarmament and it further reinforces the process-minded, state-centric approach to CB disarmament.

Throughout the 1990s, the community changed little, it remained highly specialised and academic, operating mainly through technical publications and discrete communications with government officials and diplomats

Since the early 1990s, there have been remarkable developments in civil society both in terms of the number and diversity of organisations and individuals involved and in terms of the activities undertaken. Even in the disarmament field, civil society has demonstrated that it can undermine the 'state security discourse' and make a role for itself, as it did most successfully in the negotiations for the 1997 Mine Ban Convention.

It might be expected that these developments would have impacted on civil society in CB disarmament but, until recently, there had been little evidence of 'spillover'. Throughout the 1990s, the community changed little, it remained highly specialised and academic, operating mainly through technical publications and discrete communications with government officials and diplomats. However, there are recent indications that developments elsewhere in global civil society are beginning to filter through.

A relative newcomer to CB disarmament, the Sunshine Project (URL), has been instrumental in introducing new thinking to the existing civil society actors. In contrast to the individuals traditionally involved in CB disarmament, the Project's staff have backgrounds in public advocacy and grass-roots networking. While utilising traditional civil society tools, such as the resolution supporting the BWC protocol handed to the ad hoc group chairman in April 2001, the Sunshine Project has also attempted to re-frame CB disarmament so that it resonates more widely. In particular, the Project has emphasised the relevance of biodiversity and biosafety, areas of great civil society activity, to CB disarmament. In so doing, it has brought the issue to a whole new audience, thus broadening the traditional CB disarmament community.

The collapse of the BWC protocol negotiations and the success of *Landmine Monitor* encouraged the establishment of the BioWeapons Prevention Project (URL) to undertake a similar global monitoring role for the BWC. The Project was launched in November 2002 and is currently still in its start-up phase. Funds have been pledged by a number of sympathetic governments and two have already contributed. The Project aims to improve global monitoring of BWC compliance by empowering civil society nationally, raising public awareness, and publishing an annual *BioWeapons Monitor* which it hopes will emulate the success of *Landmine Monitor* in monitoring national compliance with the 1997 Mine Ban Convention. The Project is specifically intended to create a network encompassing sections of global civil society which have not previously been active in CB disarmament. The network already includes civil society organisations from Europe, North America, and Africa.

External Factors: Access and Funding

The main external factor influencing civil society in CB disarmament is the 'state security discourse' and the framing of CB weapons as WMD and as potential terrorist weapons. This shapes the environment in which civil society operates in CB disarmament and influences its character and activities. However, at least two other factors also matter, namely, the degree of access granted to CB disarmament processes and the availability of funding for activities; while a third, the indirect influence of developments in other sections of global civil society, may be becoming more important.

One study has found that the formal access of civil society in international disarmament forums is 'almost invariably at the lower end of the spectrum' (Carroll 2002: 21). Access matters because without it civil society is less aware of the issues at stake in a conference or negotiation and has to rely on other sources of information, invariably the participating diplomats themselves who do not always have an interest in providing a balanced account. Without access, civil society is little more than a disenfranchised observer able to listen to bland political statements but kept away from the real debate. Of course, access is not all-important: '[A]n exclusive focus on the question of the relative lack of formal NGO "access" to multilateral disarmament badly distorts the reality of the many important roles that NGOs can and do play in disarmament affairs' (Atwood 2002: 9).

The formal access of civil society in international disarmament forums is almost invariably at the lower end of the spectrum

Accredited civil society organisations have access only to the opening and closing plenary sessions of the annual CWC conferences, the BWC ad hoc group, and the respective review conferences. They cannot attend sessions of the subsidiary bodies where the main debates occur. Documentation available does not include draft decisions or working papers, and documents submitted by civil society are not distributed as official documents. They are also provided with no or very minimal office facilities. Civil society organizations were allowed to address informal sessions of the fourth and fifth BWC Review Conferences and a half-day 'Open Forum' took place parallel to the first CWC Review Conference.

However, this level of access compares poorly to that now granted to civil society in other areas, particularly human rights and the environment, but even in nuclear disarmament. At the Nuclear Non-Proliferation Treaty Preparatory Committee in 2002, civil society presentations were heard during a formal session for the first time. In contrast, during the Preparatory Committee for the fifth BWC Review Conference, Mexico's proposal, that 'in order to keep pace with practice regarding NGOs in other multilateral fora' civil society be allowed to submit material orally and in writing, was not adopted (Pearson 2001: 18). Those civil society organisations present submitted a note to the chairman which included the following: '[W]e would like to be present as observers in all sessions as we would thereby become much more aware of the real issues—rather than just the fixes in Plenary. We are, however, realists and recognize that evolutionary progress is the way forward.' However, there was no 'evolutionary progress' at the conference and, in retrospect, the note looks timid and reactive. In the future, civil society will have to cooperate proactively with sympathetic states like Mexico in order to gain greater access.

Civil society compensates for its lack of formal access to meetings in CB disarmament through its good connections with diplomats, whether at the meetings or nationally. Some states actually go out of their way to keep civil society informed and involved in ways other than observing meetings, ways which are sometimes of more mutual benefit. For example, under an initiative begun by the French presidency of the European Union in 2000, successive presidencies hosted lunchtime meetings between European Union diplomats and civil society organisations during sessions of the BWC ad hoc group.

A practice which has only rarely been transferred to CB disarmament is the inclusion of non-governmental experts on state delegations, although it is common practice among some Non-Proliferation Treaty states parties. Proposals for improved access in nuclear disarmament apply equally to CB disarmament: 'Effectiveness could be enhanced by opening working sessions of negotiations to NGOs, and in particular allowing NGOs not only to observe from a distance but to work with diplomats on the floor, making NGO access comparable to that enjoyed in the human rights and environmental fields' (Burroughs and Cabasso 1999: 476).

The large bulk of funding for civil society in CB disarmament comes from a small number of mainly American private foundations including the MacArthur Foundation, the Ford Foundation, the Carnegie Corporation, and the Ploughshares Fund, as well as, in the UK, the Joseph Rowntree Charitable Trust, which have long supported progressive thinking on international security. As with all sections of civil society, the actors concerned with CB disarmament have long struggled for funds and survived on an insecure financial footing.

In the 1990s, three factors made this situation even worse. The end of the Cold War and the dissolution of the USSR encouraged some foundations to 'declare victory' and reorient their funding priorities away from security issues towards issues more 'relevant' in the post-Cold War world (Bernauer 2001: 631). Another consequence of the Cold War's end was the increased complexity of the international security field, now incorporating a plethora of new groups seeking funding on topics such as small arms, landmines, conflict resolution, and peacekeeping. Also during the 1990s, the successful negotiation of treaties such as the CWC and the Comprehensive Test Ban Treaty and the indefinite extension of the Non-Proliferation Treaty convinced other foundations that the important work had been done. Taken together, these three factors contributed to a huge reduction in the number of foundations making grants in international security. From more than 75 foundations making grants in the international security field in 1984, the number dropped to 25 by 1994 (Wallerstein 2002: 86).

In 1918, the International Committee of the Red Cross protested against the use of chemical weapons, describing it as 'criminal'

Organisations working in CB disarmament fared particularly badly because, according to one foundation official, 'there has been a natural reluctance to abandon or reduce the scope of [work on nuclear reductions] in order to divert resources to other, more contemporary threats, such as biological weapons' (Wallerstein 2002: 85). Funding constraints limit the activities which civil society can undertake and also restrict the entry of new talent into CB disarmament, precisely at a time of generational change when new entrants are much needed.

The International Response to Chemical and Biological Weapons

The international community identified CB weapons as being separate from other weapons at an early stage. A United Nations (1969: 1) report states: 'No form of warfare has been more condemned than has the use of this category of weapons.' Much effort, particularly from the mid-1960s, has been made to develop rules and practices among states which reinforce the notion that the use of CB weapons should be limited, if not banned entirely. Over the years, CB disarmament has developed an architecture of principles, norms, rules, and procedures which can aptly be described as an international regime (Krasner 1983: 2).

The 1900s: The Hague Peace Conferences

The codification of the norm into international law actually began over a century before the negotiation of the first major CB disarmament treaty. The 1874 *International Declaration Concerning the Laws and Customs of War* especially forbids the 'employment of poison or poisoned weapons'. Although the 1874 declaration never entered into force, its prohibition of poison or poisoned weapons was taken up in the 1899 *Regulations Respecting the Laws and Customs of War on Land* signed in The Hague along with Declaration IV.2 under which the contracting parties agreed to 'abstain from the use of projectiles the object of which is the diffusion of asphyxiating or deleterious gases'. Study of the papers of the 1874 conference shows that the reference to poison and poisoned weapons in the declaration included the spreading of disease, an interpretation which was adopted without discussion in The Hague (SIPRI 1973b: 96).

The 1910s and 1920s: The First World War and the Geneva Protocol

Although chemical weapons were massively used during the First World War, it was widely accepted that these prohibitions had entered international customary law. All belligerents went to great efforts to deny that their own actions were in contravention of the treaties while at the same time demonising their opponents for their use of chemical weapons. In 1918, the International Committee of the Red Cross protested against the use of chemical weapons, describing it as 'criminal' (ICRC 1918).

After the war, the next significant milestone in the development of the international regime against CB warfare was the 1925 Geneva Protocol, which acknowledged the existing norm against the use of chemical weapons: 'Whereas the use in war of asphyxiating, poisonous or other gases, and of all analogous liquids, materials or devices, *has been* justly condemned by the general opinion of the civilised world . . .' (emphasis added). The Protocol also codified the extension of the prohibition to include biological weapons.

The negotiation of the Geneva Protocol took place in an atmosphere of intense public opposition to chemical weapons created in part by counterproductive claims from chemical weapons proponents about supposed new 'super' weapons. (See Box 5.4). According to one account: 'From their initial mobilization at the hands of publicists and lobbyists, popular attitudes towards CBW throughout much of Europe and America were concerted in their hostility. As they gathered strength in the early 1920s, they had the effect of stimulating and sustaining international efforts to abolish CBW' (SIPRI 1971b: 263).

In 1972, the Biological Weapons Convention was the first treaty to outlaw an entire class of weapons of mass destruction

The 1960s: The Vietnam War and the Biological Weapons Convention

CB weapons returned to the international political agenda only in the mid-1960s, prompted by the use of chemical weapons in the Yemeni civil war, by concerns expressed publicly by eminent scientists, but mostly by the use of toxic chemicals by the US in Vietnam. The situation in Vietnam and the public attention it was attracting inspired the United Nations General Assembly to adopt a resolution on CB warfare in 1966 which led to the inclusion of CB weapons in the agenda of the Geneva disarmament conference.

Public attention to CB weapons was heightened by two authoritative reports: one, by a group of experts appointed by the United Nations Secretary-General, induced the other, by a World Health Organization group of consultants. The authors of the UN report hoped it would 'contribute to public awareness of the profoundly dangerous results if these weapons were ever used and that an aroused public will demand and receive assurances that Governments are working for the earliest effective elimination of chemical and bacteriological (biological) weapons' (United Nations 1969: 88).

By 1968, the prohibition of CB warfare was 'generally considered one of the most urgent measures to be taken up following the conclusion of the Treaty on the Non-Proliferation of Nuclear Weapons' (SIPRI 1971a: 253). In the US, 22 prominent scientists and doctors (including 7 Nobel laureates), supported by 5,000 scientists, sent a petition to President Johnson. In other countries, revelations by journalists and protests by students also raised popular awareness (Sigmund 1980). In the UK, one of the main activists identified 'the need for a grass-roots movement' (Sigmund 1980: 7). Gradually, many states also came to the conclusion that the international regime against CB warfare was in need of strengthening. CB weapons were under consideration together by the Geneva disarmament conference but a ban on chemical weapons seemed far off.

In 1968, the UK therefore proposed that the issues be separated and introduced a draft convention on biological weapons. Many states initially opposed the separation, but political momentum was provided in 1969 when President Nixon announced the US renunciation of biological weapons (also partly inspired by opposition to the Vietnam war) and its support for the UK draft, and in 1971 when the USSR and its allies reversed their earlier opposition to separation. The subsequent negotiations led to the 1972 BWC prohibiting the development, production, and stockpiling of biological weapons and requiring the destruction of any existing stocks. The BWC was thus the first international disarmament treaty to outlaw an entire class of WMD. One of the authors of the WHO report wrote later that it and the report by the Secretary-General's expert group 'were influential in achieving the Biological Weapons Convention of 1972' (Kaplan 1999: 151).

Article IX of the BWC required that states parties undertake 'to continue negotiations in good faith with

Signing ceremony for the Chemical Weapons Convention. © Organisation for the Prohibition of Chemical Weapons.

a view to reaching early agreement on effective measures' for the prohibition of chemical weapons. However, the issue remained on the agenda for another 20 years until an even more comprehensive agreement prohibiting the development, production, stockpiling, and use of chemical weapons was eventually finalised.

The 1980s: The Iran–Iraq war and the Chemical Weapons Convention

During the 1980s, there was 'a widespread sense that the existing regime of international law and custom which inhibited resort to toxic warfare was coming under increasing threat, and that it might well prove to be in the best interests of all states if the regime, symbolised by the Geneva Protocol of 1925, were somehow strengthened' (Robinson 1993: 37). In Western Europe, scientists and peace activists joined together to protest against the possibility of new US 'binary' chemical weapons being deployed. In the UK, over 2,000 scientists signed a petition in 1981 against the new weapons (Murphy, Hay, and Rose 1984: ix). The UK Scientists' Campaign and its associated Working Party on Chemical and Biological Warfare was intended to emulate civil society opposition to the stationing of new US nuclear missiles in Europe led by European Nuclear Disarmament (Murphy, Hay, and Rose 1984: 107).

Political and public interest in the CWC negotiations increased when Iraqi use of chemical weapons was confirmed by the United Nations in 1984 and in subsequent years (see Box 5.5). Press reports of the attacks and the transfer of some of the victims to hospitals in Western Europe increased public awareness of chemical weapons, although political condemnation of Iraq was less forthcoming as major Western countries were supporting Iraq in the ongoing war. The 1989 Paris Conference on the Prohibition of Chemical Weapons referred only to 'recent violations' of the 1925 Geneva Protocol without mentioning Iraq by name.

Key political events in the negotiation of the CWC during the 1980s included the introduction in 1984 of a new US draft chemical weapons convention, the acceptance by the USSR in 1987 of the intrusive verification provisions proposed by the US, and the announcement in 1989 of a more flexible US negotiating position. A number of factors contributed to the finalisation of the 1993 CWC:

> *First, the end of the cold war increased mutual trust and confidence among states. Other positive factors included changes in the US negotiating position, the*

Box 5.5: Halabja: The chemical weapons campaign against the Kurds

The Iran-Iraq war of 1980–8 was the most recent war to see the widespread use of lethal chemical weapons. It appears that Iraqi forces had begun to use chemical weapons against Iranian troops by 1983 or even earlier. In 1984, a UN investigation team confirmed the use of mustard gas and the nerve agent tabun in the war, without stating which side had used them. In 1986, however, another investigation stated specifically that 'on many occasions, Iraqi forces have used chemical weapons against Iranian forces'. In 1987, a further investigation reported that 'a new dimension is that civilians in Iran have also been injured by chemical weapons'. According to Iranian figures, an estimated 100,000 military personnel and civilians were exposed to chemical weapons during the war, of whom 3,500 died during the war. Even now, many years after the end of the war, over 34,000 victims are still being treated for the long-term effects of exposure to mustard gas.

The attack on the Iranian city of Sardasht in June 1987 set a precedent for the widespread use of chemical weapons against civilians by Iraq as part of its campaign against its own Kurdish population. Human Rights Watch (1995) has described the Iraqi Anfal campaign against the Kurds as genocide and has published a detailed account of events. The use of chemical weapons against Kurdish villages appears to have begun in 1987 but intensified in 1988. The most well-known incident was the attack on the border town of Halabja, but Human Rights Watch records attacks on over 60 villages.

During the afternoon of 16 March 1988, Iraqi aircraft dropped mustard gas and nerve agents on Halabja. Based on interviews with survivors, Human Rights Watch describes the scene as follows:

> *In the shelters, there was immediate panic and claustrophobia. Some tried to plug the cracks around the entrance with damp towels, or pressed wet cloths to their faces, or set fires. But in the end they had no alternative but to emerge into the streets. It was growing dark and there were no streetlights; the power had been knocked out the day before by artillery fire. In the dim light, the people of Halabja could see nightmarish scenes. Dead bodies—human and animal—littered the streets, huddled in doorways, slumped over the steering wheels of their cars. Survivors stumbled around, laughing hysterically, before collapsing. Iranian soldiers flitted through the darkened streets, dressed in protective clothing, their faces concealed by gas masks. Those who fled could barely see, and felt a sensation 'like needles in the eyes.' Their urine was streaked with blood.*

Refugees from Halabja fled to Iran where survivors of the attack were treated. A few days after the attacks, Iran allowed journalists to visit the town. The pictures which they took were seen around the world and clearly showed that most of the dead had been Kurdish civilians. The number of dead has been estimated at around 5,500 but could have been much higher. Every year on 16 March Halabja Day is marked in Iraqi Kurdistan and in countries around the world with remembrance ceremonies, political statements and appeals for more assistance for the victims.

In the years since the attack on Halabja, the victims have received little in the way of international attention. What assistance they have received has been due in large measure to academics and researchers in the West collaborating with Kurdish doctors in Iraq. The Washington Kurdish Institute has organised a series of international meetings in recent years to raise awareness of the suffering of the people of Halabja.

A postgraduate medical institute has been established in Halabja with international assistance. Staff of the institute have carried out a medical survey of Iraqi Kurdistan which has found that rates of congenital abnormalities are four to five times those suffered by victims of the atomic bomb attack on Hiroshima and that cancer rates are four times the Middle East average. The researchers have also identified 281 sites throughout northern Iraq where Iraqi forces used chemical weapons.

collapse of the Soviet Union, the outcome of the 1991 Persian Gulf War (which clearly demonstrated that chemical weapons are no longer politically desirable), and not least the clear political will of the majority of states to totally prohibit chemical weapons. (Robinson, Stock, and Sutherland 1994: 705)

The negotiation of the CWC, particularly as it entered its end-game, attracted high-level political attention from the likes of Australian Foreign Minister Gareth Evans and US Vice-President George H. W. Bush. Thanks in part to the efforts of civil society, the chemical industry actively followed the negotiations and was largely supportive of the CWC.

The CWC represents a significant consolidation of the international regime against CB warfare with the creation of a verification system of unprecedented intrusiveness overseen by a new international organisation. The CWC has already served as a model for the 1996 Comprehensive Test Ban Treaty and the failed BWC Protocol (see Box 5.5) and will doubtless act as a precedent for future developments within international law.

Few civil society actors in CB disarmament paid much attention to the negotiation of the ICC Statute, and an opportunity to further codify the norm against CB warfare was missed

The 1990s and 2000s: The ICC Statute and the BWC Protocol

The negotiation of the 1998 Statute of the International Criminal Court (ICC) represented a missed opportunity for strengthening the international regime against CB warfare. The draft statute included four options for defining what weapons were to be criminalised, two of which expressly prohibited both chemical and biological weapons. In negotiating the Statute, states agreed that the war crimes over which jurisdiction was to be established should go no further than existing customary international law. With respect to CB warfare, this meant that they should reflect the Hague Conventions and the Geneva Protocol but not the more recent BWC and CWC, which are not regarded as having entered customary law. However, other parts of the Statute are more progressive about what constitutes customary law, above all the gender provisions.

As the result of political horse-trading in the closing days of the negotiations, the Statute criminalises the use of 'asphyxiating, poisonous or other gases and all analogous liquids, materials or devices' and the employment of 'poison or poisoned weapons' (Burroughs and Cabasso 1999: 471–2). So, while the use of chemical weapons is criminalised, no direct reference to biological weapons is made. Some have argued that the Statute could be interpreted as also applying to biological weapons (Burroughs and Cabasso 1999: 472), but the UK government recently stated: 'The use of biological weapons in not specifically a crime under the ICC Statute at present' (United Kingdom 2002: Ev. 24).

The explicit reference to biological weapons in earlier drafts was dropped under pressure from Arab states: 'Some states argued that, if nuclear weapons were not expressly included, then biological and chemical weapons, "poor man's weapons", ought not to be included either' (Glasius 2002: 158).

It is also not clear whether the Statute criminalises the use of 'non-lethal' chemical weapons in warfare. However, later elaboration of the Elements of Crimes saw the inclusion of a footnote stating: 'Nothing in this element shall be interpreted as limiting or prejudicing in any way existing or developing rules of international law with respect to development, production, stockpiling and use of chemical weapons' (United Nations 1999: 25). The reference to 'existing or developing rules of international law' implies recognition of the provisions of the Geneva Protocol and the CWC relating to 'non-lethal' chemical weapons. In fact, this footnote was the result of discrete pressure from civil society.

Few if any of the civil society actors in CB disarmament paid much attention to the negotiation of the ICC Statute and none were in Rome for the final negotiations. The disarmament organisations present in Rome were overwhelming concerned with nuclear weapons; as they had not been sensitised to the importance of the explicit inclusion of biological weapons, they did not lobby on the issue. However, the Statute as adopted is a lot more ambiguous on this point than if biological weapons had been expressly included, and an opportunity to further codify the norm against CB warfare was missed.

The 1999 Hague Appeal for Peace gathering to celebrate the centenary of the Hague peace conference represented an opportunity for raising civil society awareness of CB weapons. However, alongside the many panels on nuclear disarmament and small arms, only two were devoted to CB weapons. The resultant *Hague Agenda for Peace and Justice* included just one paragraph on CB weapons. Similarly, the peace, security, and disarmament strand of the Millennium Forum in 2000 made no mention of chemical weapons and lumped discussion of biological weapons in with a number of other issues. While this might be the result of ignorance on the part of the event organisers, it probably also reflects the isolation of civil society in CB disarmament from other sections of global civil society.

The 25th anniversary of the entry into force of the BWC and the 75th anniversary of the adoption of the Geneva Protocol both fell in 2000 and the events could have been used to draw much-deserved attention to the treaties. In the event, the BWC anniversary was marked by specialist workshops in New York and Geneva and the Geneva Protocol anniversary by written statements from Presidents Clinton and Putin. Lacking, however, was any attempt by civil society to sensitise a wider audience to the significance of these treaties or indeed to launch a coordinated campaign to encourage states to ratify them.

Unlike in other areas of global civil society activity, in CB disarmament there has been little space for any actors other than governments to play a role in agenda-setting

The end-game of the negotiations to draft a supplemental protocol to strengthen the BWC took place in 2001 (see Box 5.6). From 1995, civil society had focused on influencing the negotiations through publications and meetings but had failed to promote the importance of the protocol to wider global civil society, had not sensitised the media to the issue, and was unable to mobilise the general public. One assessment of civil society's role describes it as 'successful in shaping the verification protocol and prodding it along, yet unable to engender sufficiently broad civil society interest when the rubber hit the road and intense politics were in order' (Hammond 2003).

Global Civil Society Activities in Chemical and Biological Disarmament

Given the characteristics of civil society involvement in CB disarmament and the 'state security discourse' within which it operates, the range of activities undertaken is limited compared with other issue-areas and takes as its target audience state representatives. One study of civil society activity in international negotiations has identified seven types of activity: problem definition, agenda setting and goal setting; enforcement of principles and norms; provision of information and expertise; public advocacy and mobilisation; lobbying; direct participation in the formulation of international agreements; and monitoring and other assistance with compliance (Albin 1999: 378).

Problem definition, agenda setting, and goal setting

Unlike other areas of global civil society activity, in CB disarmament there has been little space for any actors other than governments to play a role in agenda-setting. Whereas the International Coalition to Ban Landmines was able to re-frame antipersonnel landmines from a purely military to a wider humanitarian and societal issue (Short 1999: 496), in CB disarmament global civil society has to operate within the 'state security discourse' and has largely had to react to an agenda set by governments, specifically an agenda dominated by WMD and lately by CB terrorism. 'Compared with agenda-setting processes in international trade, human rights, or environmental policy, nongovernmental actors have been only very indirectly involved in identifying and framing problems and possible solutions' (Bernauer 2001: 630).

The 'state security discourse' means that governments do 'not like having civil society involved in national security issues' (Johnson 2000: 49). One way in which governments operationalise this dislike is by allowing civil society little or no access to the agenda-setting process in CB disarmament when compared with other issue-areas. In the 1960s, civil society in the shape of Pugwash did achieve a degree

Box 5.6: The Biological Weapons Convention Verification Protocol

The BWC which was eventually approved by the Geneva disarmament conference in 1971 was a much diluted version of the original UK draft treaty introduced three years earlier (Sims 2001: 24). Most significantly, it lacked any of the functional substitutes for verification included in the UK draft. From its very birth, therefore, some felt that the BWC was in need of strengthening. At each of the subsequent five-yearly review conferences, various states parties have spoken in favour of strengthening the BWC, with verification having been discussed since 1986 (Sims 2001: 83).

The 1991 review conference established an ad hoc group of governmental experts 'to identify and examine potential verification measures from a scientific and technical standpoint'. A special conference in 1994 created an ad hoc group 'to consider appropriate measures, including possible verification measures, and draft proposals to strengthen the Convention, to be included, as appropriate, in a legally binding instrument'. Between 1995 and 2001, the ad hoc group drafted a detailed 'verification protocol' intended to supplement, but not replace, the original BWC.

This protocol, like the CWC upon which it was largely modelled, was built upon three verification 'pillars', namely, national declarations, visits by international inspectors to declared facilities, and investigations in cases of suspected violations. Implementation of the protocol would have been overseen by a new international organisation (Feakes 2001). The negotiations proceeded slowly with deadlines for completion being set and then missed. The European Union and others such as Australia, Canada, and South Africa were strongly supportive of the protocol. While many non-aligned countries did not participate actively in the negotiations, a group including Pakistan, Iran, India, and Cuba actively opposed further restrictions on technology transfers, setting them in opposition to Western countries keen to strengthen export controls.

A largely unknown quantity in the negotiations was the US. The Clinton Administration's acceptance of the ad hoc group process was a reversal of previous US policy, which had considered the BWC to be 'unverifiable' but did not represent a whole-hearted commitment to verification (Sims 2001: 108). However, throughout the negotiations the US was a relatively passive participant, many officials from the previous administration remained in post, and President Clinton never gave much-needed political direction to the lower-level officials.

Civil society was represented by a small number of academics and researchers who followed the negotiations as best they could given their limited access to the meetings. They produced reports of the negotiations for a wider audience and also technical reports aimed at the diplomats participating in the negotiations (Rissanen 2002: 33).

The chairman of the negotiations released his draft of the verification protocol in March 2001, a few months after President Bush assumed office. While he urged civil society to support the protocol and pressure governments to do likewise, the issue lacked profile and the small group of academics and researchers who had been following the negotiations lacked the means and constituency to organise a large campaign. In addition, there were splits among this group with some arguing that the draft protocol did not go far enough but most that it was 'better than

of success in shaping the international agenda on CB warfare, but this was before the agenda became dominated by concerns of WMD and CB terrorism.

Enforcement of principles and norms

Civil society has been more active in CB disarmament with regard to the normative area aided by the fact that the taboo against CB warfare is so long-standing and widely accepted and that disarmament treaties are in force. These treaties 'establish standards against which transnational civil society can, and does, loudly and publicly compare the actual behavior of states and corporations' (Florini 2000: 225). One example of this is the role played by civil society in upholding the broad definitions of CB weapons used in the CWC and BWC, otherwise known as the 'general purpose criteria' (Tuerlings and Robinson 1999). Given the

nothing'. During early 2001, the Bush Administration conducted an internal review of the protocol. This was the time of greatest (but still limited) non-governmental pressure within the US joined also by diplomatic pressure from Washington's European allies. However, leaks to the press made it very clear that the protocol lacked strong supporters within the new administration (Feakes and Littlewood 2002).

With the November 2001 deadline for completion of the protocol negotiations fast approaching, BWC states parties met in July in Geneva to give their opinions on the protocol. On the first two days, over 50 states spoke in support of the chairman's efforts. However, in its statement the US announced not only its rejection of the protocol as drafted, but also its rejection of the entire approach taken by the ad hoc group since 1995 (Chevrier 2001). Unlike in other treaty negotiations the idea of continuing without the US was never seriously considered by the ad hoc group despite being mentioned by some delegates and non-governmental experts. A number of different reasons have since been given. The ad hoc group always operated on the basis of consensus and the US could have blocked adoption of the protocol. Without the US, the protocol would not apply to the world's largest biotech and pharmaceutical industry, thus disadvantaging competitors in countries which did join. It was also argued that the absence of the US would create a domino effect, with other countries also deciding to stay out.

Paradoxically, it was only with the rejection of the protocol by the US that the issue achieved a higher public profile and many of the academics and researchers who had been following the negotiations were interviewed on television news programmes and in newspapers. The issue was also raised by parliamentarians in a number of countries. Despite the early warnings, there was little that could be done to prevent the US rejection of the protocol or to pressure other governments to continue without the US. After the US announced its rejection, '[t]he NGOs came together and launched a "counter-offensive", trying to rally public and governmental support for the Protocol. They contacted members of their respective parliaments and wrote op-eds and letters to the editor in newspapers and magazines, trying to enhance greater domestic interest in and support for the Protocol' (Rissanen 2002). However, this reactive approach was really too little too late, and it ultimately failed.

However, the protocol soon faded from public attention and is remembered now, if at all, in the wider world as just one in a series of international treaties rejected by the new Bush Administration.

The US rejection of the BWC protocol had already soured the atmosphere prior to the November 2001 review conference. However, the situation worsened further when the US tabled a last-minute proposal to terminate the mandate of the ad hoc group. No other country could accept this and the conference was therefore suspended for a one-year cooling-off period. As states parties reconvened in Geneva in November 2002, expectations of a successful outcome were low. In the end, a minimal action plan for the period up until the 2006 review conference was adopted involving annual meetings on specific topics. With the first meeting scheduled for August 2003, the value of this so-called new process cannot yet be ascertained.

preponderance of scientists within the CB disarmament community, much attention has been paid to the ethics of chemical, and particularly biological, research.

As in other areas of international humanitarian law, the International Committee of the Red Cross has played its traditional normative role in CB disarmament. In 2002, it launched an appeal on *Biotechnology, Weapons and Humanity*, which called on 'all political and military authorities to strengthen their commitment to the international humanitarian law norms which prohibit the hostile uses of biological agents and to work together to subject potentially dangerous biotechnology to effective controls' and also on 'the scientific and medical communities, industry and civil society in general to ensure that potentially dangerous biological knowledge and agents be subject to effective controls' (ICRC 2002).

Provision of information and expertise

The primary activity for civil society in CB disarmament is the provision of information and expertise. This reflects the academic backgrounds of many of the individuals involved. For them, written publications and the provision of expertise are more highly valued than participation in public advocacy or mobilisation. There are four target audiences: policy-makers and diplomats; other global civil society actors; the media; and the general public.

The vast majority of the civil society actors in CB disarmament see policy-makers in national capitals and diplomats involved in negotiations as their primary audience. During the BWC protocol negotiations, the University of Bradford Department of Peace Studies produced a series of 33 briefing papers and 22 evaluation papers for the diplomats involved (Pearson 2002: 3). One diplomat wrote later that the negotiations 'received an important political and substantive impetus by discussions in and publications emanating from academic and scientific circles and the NGO-community' (Kervers 2002: 278). Civil society also provides information and expertise to governments through service on advisory bodies such as the CWC National Authority Advisory Committee in the UK and the Biological and Chemical Defence Review Committee in Canada.

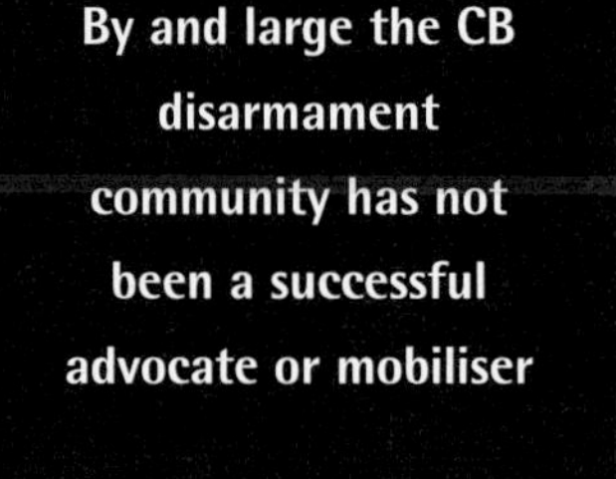
By and large the CB
disarmament
community has not
been a successful
advocate or mobiliser

Other publications provide information to fellow civil society actors in CB disarmament. For example, the quarterly *CBW Conventions Bulletin* contains the only publicly available account of developments within the Organization for the Prohibition of Chemical Weapons in addition to a chronology of recent CB warfare-related events and a bibliography of relevant publications. While undertaking and publishing its own research, the Sunshine Project has also established an on-line clearing house of official US documents declassified under the Freedom of Information Act, thereby allowing others to use them in their own research (Sunshine Project 2003). In addition, professional or membership-based organisations such as the World Medical Association or the British Medical Association have disseminated information to their members, drawing their attention to CB disarmament issues.

While the media are some of the primary consumers of CB disarmament information and expertise, the relationship is a relatively reactive one from the point of view of the experts. Civil society actors in CB disarmament do not spend a lot of time proactively sensitising the media to particular issues, but they do spend time responding to questions from journalists and reacting to events. The passive approach was illustrated recently when, although many experts doubted that Iraq possessed a stockpile of CB weapons worth going to war for, few of them proactively sought opportunities to promote their opinion. An example of a proactive approach from civil society was the briefing packs prepared for the media on the BWC protocol by the International Security Information Service (URL) in the UK.

Occasionally, civil society actors involved in CB disarmament write for a wider audience, particularly in an attempt to explain a complex issue and to play down the often exaggerated threat portrayed by the media (Murphy, Hay, and Rose 1984: ; Croddy 2002). In 2001, the British American Security Information Council published a guide to BW intended for non-specialists (Crowley 2001) and a shorter information pamphlet. The pamphlet summarised the main concerns about BW and advocated the completion of the BWC protocol negotiations.

Public advocacy and mobilisation

It is with public advocacy and mobilisation that civil society has had most difficulties in CB disarmament. There are exceptions, but by and large the CB disarmament community has not been a successful advocate or mobiliser. In the words of one community member: 'We have excellent subject matter experts; but don't know how to do outreach.' (Hammond 2003). This can be explained by at least four factors: the types of civil society actors involved; the complexity of the subject matter; the difficulty of engaging the public generally on disarmament issues; and the fact that the CWC and BWC give the impression that CB disarmament has been achieved.

An interesting contrast is provided by the public campaign mobilised in March 2002 against the US decision to call for the removal of the director-general of the Organization for the Prohibition of

Chemical Weapons, the Brazilian diplomat Jose Bustani. The campaign did not originate with the civil society actors in CB disarmament (some of whom shared the US concerns about Bustani's leadership), but with peace activists in the MoveOn.org (URL) organisation. However, it gained widespread press attention in the UK, an Internet petition, and a letter to *The Guardian* signed by figures from popular culture, and forced the UK government to explain its support for the US in Parliament. The issue was a transient one as Bustani was soon removed nonetheless, but it did demonstrate what could be achieved.

Lobbying

The CB disarmament community has had some success in lobbying but, as with public advocacy and mobilisation, lobbying is not an activity which comes naturally to those involved. In addition, lobbying in CB disarmament is an activity which takes place mainly at a national rather than an international level.

Governments have allowed no scope for civil society to directly participate in the formulation of international agreements relating to CB disarmament

The US ratification of the CWC, for example, was helped considerably by US civil society. When the CWC was first considered by the Senate in September 1996, opponents of the CWC made all the running, led by Republican senators assisted by some civil society organisations opposed to the treaty. When it was reintroduced early in 1997, the treaty's supporters in the White House, Congress, and civil society were better prepared. Although the ratification process was handled badly by the Clinton Administration, the US eventually ratified with a few days to spare (Smithson 1997). According to an account of the campaign, civil society contributed to the national debate in four ways. They

> *elevated the intensity of public debate on the Convention and the problems posed by the proliferation of chemical weapons ... [I]mproved coordination and communication among themselves, with the executive and legislative branches of government, and with the news media ... [H]elped to focus members of the Clinton administration on the task at hand in the months prior to active presidential engagement, while providing encouragement to supportive Senators ... [W]ere able to make unique contributions to the national debate that can only be made by outside, independent actors. (Parachini 1997: 37)*

Direct participation in the formulation of international agreements

Governments have allowed no scope for civil society to directly participate in the formulation of international agreements relating to CB disarmament. The closest which civil society comes to such a role is the opportunity for transmitting policy ideas indirectly within the Pugwash CB warfare study group, which has both governmental and non-governmental membership, including industry participation. As Adler (1992: 105) notes: '[T]he political influence of transnational epistemic communities, such as the Pugwash group in the security field, is most likely to rest on the transfer from the international to the domestic scene of the ideas that *national* scientists and experts raise at their transnational meetings.' Workshops of the Pugwash study group on CB warfare are nowadays timed and located so as to coincide with international conferences relating to CB disarmament, thus ensuring a high level of attendance by both civil society and governmental representatives.

Monitoring and other assistance with compliance

Opportunities for civil society to monitor compliance in CB disarmament do exist and have been exploited to a limited degree. However, once again the influence of the 'state security discourse' means that the role of civil society is limited and that what few activities have taken place have done so at a national rather than a global level. An example of national monitoring is the work of the Sunshine Project in detailing the extent of the biodefence programmes of the German military (van Aken 2001) and its investigation into the US Joint Non Lethal Weapons Directorate (Sunshine Project 2002a).

The Sunshine Project, in a tactic borrowed from civil society groups working on environmental problems, has also taken this monitoring role a stage further by filing a legal suit against the Directorate for violating the national law which implements the BWC in the US (Sunshine Project 2002b). Tuerlings and Robinson (1999), in their elaboration of a 'tri-sectoral network' involving the public (governments), the private (industry), and the civil (non-government) sectors, highlight the role of the civil sector, particularly academic and research scientists, in monitoring new developments within biology and chemistry and thus contributing to upholding the relevance of the CWC and BWC in the face of scientific and technological advances.

Conclusions

The current situation is one in which, in contrast to nuclear weapons, the use, production, development, and stockpiling of CB weapons has been banned under international law. The international regime against CB warfare has many adherents: the BWC has 146 states parties; the CWC has 151 states parties; and the Geneva Protocol has 132 states parties. In many ways this is an immensely encouraging situation but it also works against the international regime. With regard to nuclear weapons, disarmament and delegitimisation have not yet taken place, meaning that a lot of political and public attention is still paid to achieving or obstructing these goals.

CB disarmament treaties have been successfully negotiated, meaning that CB disarmament appears to have been done

In contrast, CB disarmament treaties have been successfully negotiated and are now in force, meaning that CB disarmament is no longer a significant political issue as it appears to have been 'done'. It is common for international treaties to lose political and public profile once they have entered the phase of routine implementation and the international regime against CB warfare is no exception (Flowerree 1990).

While many governments and civil society organisations were involved in campaigns for CWC ratification at the national level, many of them did not maintain their involvement once the campaign had succeeded. Key issues in this post-negotiation phase include: how to ensure that the BWC and CWC keep pace with developments in science and technology, how to uphold restrictions on non-lethal CB weapons, how to ensure effective national implementation of both treaties, and, perhaps most importantly, how to address non-compliance with treaty obligations and enforce treaty prohibitions. Failure to address these implementation challenges can be just as damaging to the international regime against CB warfare as failure to further consolidate the regime.

The involvement of civil society in CB disarmament is now in a phase of transformation. There are four primary driving forces at work: the apparent end of multilateral treaty-making as exemplified by the collapse of the BWC protocol negotiations; a heightened public awareness of CB weapons, particularly of proliferation and terrorism; developments in other sections of global civil society; and the creation of an alternative frame for CB weapons. Not all of these phenomena are new; CB weapons rated high in the public consciousness in the late 1960s and again in the 1980s, and there have been other periods when treaty-making seems to have been at an end. What makes the current situation unique is the combination of all of these factors and the interplay between them.

The collapse of the BWC protocol negotiations made some civil society actors in CB disarmament seek out new, more radical approaches, which they readily found in other areas of global civil society. Increased public awareness has provided an opportunity and a requirement for CB disarmament to be re-framed away from the state-centric, abstract, and technically complex focus on WMD and towards a more inclusive and resonant alternative.

For a number of reasons, the way in which CB weapons are currently framed is neither useful nor accurate. WMD is in many ways a spurious concept because CB weapons have much more in common with each other than either have with nuclear weapons: 'Only nuclear weapons are completely indiscriminate by their explosive power, heat radiation and radioactivity, and only they should therefore be called a weapon of mass destruction' (Harigel 2001). CB weapons differ from nuclear weapons in their potential lethality and destructive power, feasibility of protection, and defences, potential mission, and legal constraints on use and possession (Panofsky 1998).

The current public concern about CB terrorism overestimates the ease with which CB weapons can be produced and disseminated, as a closer study of the Japanese cult Aum Shinrikyo demonstrates. According to the US Department of Defense in 1996: 'The ability to create mass casualties by using chemical and biological weapons depends on many factors. Finding the right agent, weaponizing the agent, delivering the agent in an effective manner, and waiting for the optimal meteorological conditions would be a challenge to any terrorist group. We just need to keep in perspective the reality of recent and potential events' (Swain 1996).

In addition, the current framing of CB weapons lacks resonance for global civil society. While participation in and attention to other areas of international law by civil society are increasing, its involvement in CB disarmament has remained static. This matters because, as other areas of global civil society have shown, when international agreements or regimes are under threat, public pressure and civil society action can be effective in reducing the threat. The small epistemic community currently following CB disarmament can only sit and watch when, for example, the BWC protocol collapses.

If an alternative frame for CB weapons is to be realised, the existing civil society actors will have to change their mindset and habits

An alternative frame for CB weapons would encourage the evolution of a what Keck and Sikkink (1998) describe as a 'transnational advocacy network' consisting not only of an epistemic community but also of public movement campaigns and non-violent direct action, all cooperating with each other. This is already the case in nuclear disarmament: 'The track record shows that civil society was most successful when it worked at both the elite and public movement levels ... The very different strategies of prominent public activism and quiet, behind-the-scenes partnerships with policy makers can reinforce each other' (Johnson 2000: 75).

An alternative frame would incorporate numerous elements. The state-centric focus of the WMD frame would be replaced by an emphasis on the threat which CB weapons pose to global security and a return to the taboo against the use of poison and disease in warfare: 'Indeed, perhaps we must now start looking at that ancient taboo against CBW and at the BWC it has generated, not so much as a contribution to our national security, but as essential underpinning for the welfare and even the survival of our species'(Poste and Robinson 2000: 9). After all, infectious disease knows no boundaries and West Nile Virus or Severe Acute Respiratory Syndrome demonstrate that our globalising world actually facilitates the spread of disease, primarily through air transport. One eminent biologist writes that: '[T]he problem of biological weapons rises above the security interests of individual states and poses an unprecedented challenge to all' (Meselson 2000: 19).

As the issue of landmines was 'humanitarianized' (de Larrinaga and Turenne Sjolander 1998), the new frame for CB weapons would have to incorporate CB weapons into the emerging concept of 'human security'. Few other weapons are as indiscriminate as CB weapons and almost none affects only humans (and plants and animals), leaving property and infrastructure untouched. A more inclusive frame for CB weapons would build on the linkages between CB disarmament on the one hand and public health and biodiversity on the other.

The current frame has failed to resonate with governments or civil society in the developing world, so an approach which emphasises the linkages with public health and biodiversity should be more successful. Another element in this alternative frame, again reflecting developments in other areas, would be the concept of individual responsibility. The current treaties against CB warfare are directed mainly to the actions of states, not individuals. Recently, it has been proposed to make acts prohibited to states crimes under international law. The International Criminal Court Statute does not criminalise the specific prohibitions of the CWC and BWC, so a draft treaty to do so has been prepared by the Harvard Sussex Program (Meselson and Robinson 1998). By extending universal jurisdiction to violations of the CWC and BWC, the draft treaty would make violators *hostes humani generi* ('enemies of all humanity').

However, it is by no means certain that the issue can be re-framed satisfactorily. The negotiation of the Mine Ban Convention provides some food for thought: 'One of the great turning points in the efforts to ban [anti-personnel landmines] involved changing the terms of the debate from a military to a humanitarian issue ... The Ottawa Process certainly benefited from a media-friendly, morally unambiguous issue. Unfortunately, it may also suggest that the scope for such initiatives may be limited to certain topics' (Short 1999: 496). Comparisons with landmines are not necessarily useful. CB weapons have already been banned by international law and treaties are being implemented, thus removing the potential for a simple and direct 'ban CB weapons' campaign.

A campaign based on 'implement the CWC and BWC as negotiated' is not nearly as memorable. In addition, landmines are a tangible item intended for a single use. CB weapons, in contrast, are largely intangible items and the chemical and biological agents which are their key components are dual-use, with many legitimate purposes which cannot be hindered. Symbolism is also important. The landmines campaign, like other civil society campaigns, used powerful images and testimony from witnesses and victims, often women and children. While there are, of course, victims of CB weapons—for example, Iraqis who survived the Halabja massacre and those who were infected with anthrax from contaminated letters in the US—they are not nearly so numerous.

If an alternative frame for CB weapons is to be realised, the existing civil society actors in CB disarmament will have to change their mindset and habits. More emphasis needs to be placed on public advocacy and mobilisation, activities which the current academically oriented community is too ill-equipped and under-resourced to carry out. In particular, partnerships need to be established with other sections of global civil society so that, as in nuclear disarmament, the different actors can conduct joint campaigns involving policy research, public movements, and direct action, with all actors playing to their own strengths.

The creation of the BioWeapons Prevention Project could indicate that moves in this direction are under way; but the Project's prolonged birth is also a sign that this approach is not unanimously accepted. The current civil society actors in CB disarmament need to become better communicators so that their ideas and policy proposals reach beyond the present narrow target audience. As in other civil society campaigns, more use ought to be made of political opportunity structures, such as the anniversary of particular treaties and other international conferences and events like the anthrax letters and the war against Iraq, to educate or interest the public. The introduction of biological weapons issues into biodiversity and biosafety negotiations is one such example, but other opportunities exist.

I would like to thank Julian Perry Robinson, Mary Kaldor and Marlies Glasius for their comments on earlier drafts of this chapter, and Edward Hammond and Chandre Gould for their insights via e-mail.

References

Adler, E. (1992). 'The Emergence of Cooperation: National Epistemic Communities and the International Evolution of the Idea of Nuclear Arms Control'. *International Organization*, 46: 101–45.

– and Haas, P. M (1992). 'Conclusion: Epistemic Communities, World Order, and the Creation of a Reflective Research Program'. *International Organization* 46: 367–90.

Albin, C. (1999). 'Can NGOs Enhance the Effectiveness of International Negotiation?' *International Negotiation*, 43: 371–87.

Alibek, K. and Handelman, S. (1999). *Biohazard: The Chilling True Story of the Largest Covert Biological Weapons Program in the World—Told From Inside by the Man Who Ran It.* London: Hutchinson.

Anheier, H., Glasius, M., and Kaldor, M. (2001). 'Introducing Global Civil Society'. In H. Anheier, M. Glasius, and M. Kaldor (eds), *Global Civil Society 2001.* Oxford: Oxford University Press.

Atwood, D. C. (2002). 'NGOs and Disarmament: Views from the Coal Face'. *Disarmament Forum*, 1: 5–14.

Balmer, B. (2001). *Britain and Biological Warfare: Expert Advice and Science Policy 1930–1965.* London: Palgrave.

Bernauer, T. (2001). 'Warfare: Nuclear, Biological, and Chemical Weapons'. In P. Simmons and C. de Jonge Oudraat (eds), *Managing Global Issues: Lessons Learned.* Washington, DC: Carnegie Endowment for International Peace.

BioWeapons Prevention Project <http://www.bwpp.org/>.

Burroughs, J. and Cabasso, J. (1999). 'Confronting the Nuclear-Armed States in International Negotiating Forums: Lessons for NGOs'. *International Negotiation*, 4: 459–82.

Carroll, S. (2002). 'NGO Access to Multilateral Fora: Does Disarmament Lag Behind?' *Disarmament Forum*, 1: 15–26.

Center for Nonproliferation Studies at the Monterey Institute for International Studies <http://cns.miis.edu/>.

Chemical and Biological Arms Control Institute <http://www.cbaci.org/>.

Chevrier, M. (2001). 'The Biological Weapons Convention: The Protocol That Almost Was'. In T. Findlay and O. Meier (eds), *Verification Yearbook 2001*. London: VERTIC.

Cohen, A. (2001). 'Israel and Chemical/Biological Weapons: History, Deterrence, and Arms Control'. *The Nonproliferation Review*, 8/3: 27–53.

Croddy, E. (2002). *Chemical and Biological Warfare: A Comprehensive Survey for the Concerned Citizen*. New York: Copernicus Books.

Crowley, M. (2001). *Disease by Design: De-Mystifying the Biological Weapons Debate*. London and Washington, DC: British American Security Information Council.

Dando, M. (2003). 'The Danger to the Chemical Weapons Convention from Incapacitating Chemicals'. G. Pearson and M. Dando (eds), *Strengthening the Chemical Weapons Convention*. Bradford: Department of Peace Studies, University of Bradford.

de Larrinaga, M. and C. Turenne Sjolander (1998). '(Re)presenting Landmines from Protector to Enemy: The Discursive Framing of a New Multilateralism'. In M. Cameron, R. Lawson and B. Tomlin (eds), *To Walk Without Fear: The Global Movement to Ban Landmines*. Oxford: Oxford University Press.

Department of Peace Studies at the University of Bradford <http://www.brad.ac.uk/acad/sbtwc/>.

Ellis, J. (2003). 'The Best Defense: Counterproliferation and US National Security'. *The Washington Quarterly*, 26/2: 115–33.

Feakes, D. (2001). 'The BWC Protocol: dissecting the Composite Text'. Briefing Paper 01/0. London: VERTIC.

– and Littlewood, J. (2002). 'Hope and Ambition Turn to Dismay and Neglect: The Biological and Toxin Weapons Convention in 2001'. *Medicine, Conflict and Survival*, 18/2: 161–74.

Federation of American Scientists <http://www.fas.org/bwc/index.html>.

Florini, A. (2000). 'Lessons Learned'. In A. Florini (ed.) *The Third Force: The Rise of Transnational Civil Society*. Washington, DC: Carnegie Endowment for International Peace.

Flowerree, C. (1990). 'On Tending Arms Control Agreements'. *The Washington Quarterly*, 13/1: 199–214.

Fritzsche, P. (1993). 'Machine Dreams: Airmindedness and the Reinvention of Germany'. *The American Historical Review*, 98: 685–709.

Glasius, M. (2002). 'Expertise in the Cause of Justice: Global Civil Society Influence on the Statute for an International Criminal Court'. In M. Glasius, M. Kaldor and H. Anheier (eds), *Global Civil Society 2002*. Oxford: Oxford University Press.

Green Cross International <http://www.gci.ch>.

Haas, P. M. (1992). 'Introduction: Epistemic Communities and International Policy Coordination'. *International Organization*, 46: 1–36.

Harigel, G. (2001). 'The Concepts of WMDs: Chemical and Biological weapons, Use in warfare, Impact on Society and Environment'. In M. Martellini (ed.), *Biosecurity and Bioterrorism*. Proceedings of conference held at the Istituto Diplomatico Mario Toscano, Villa Madama, Rome, Italy, 18–19 September 2000. Como: Landau Network Centro Volta, with the support of the Italian Ministry for Foreign Affairs.

Harvard Sussex Program on CBW Armament and Arms Limitation <http://fas-www.harvard.edu/~hsp/>.

Hirst, P. (1994). *Associative Democracy: New Forms of Economic and Social Governance*. Cambridge: Polity Press.

Human Rights Watch (1995). *Iraq's Crime of Genocide: The Anfal Campaign against the Kurds*. New Haven, London: Yale University Press.

ICRC (International Committee of the Red Cross) (1918). *Appeal of the ICRC to the Belligerents Against the Use of Poisonous Gases* <http://www.icrc.org/Web/Eng/siteeng0.nsf/iwpList513/1C92114513290AD92C1256B66005AB669>.

– (2002). *Appeal on Biotechnology, Weapons and Humanity* <http://www.icrc.org/Web/Eng/siteeng0.nsf/iwpList515/274D02080643296C3E005C2338>.

International Network of Engineers and Scientists for Global Responsibility <http://www.inesglobal.org/>.

International Security Information Service in the UK <http://www.isisuk.demon.co.uk/0811/isis/uk/bwproject/contents.html>.

Jenkins, D. (2002). *The Final Frontier: America, Science and Terror*. London: Verso.

Johnson, R. (2000). 'Advocates and Activists: Conflicting Approaches on Nonproliferation and the Test Ban Treaty'. In A. Florini (ed.), *The Third Force: The Rise of Transnational Civil Society*. Washington, DC: Carnegie Endowment for International Peace.

Kaldor, M. (1999). *New and Old Wars: Organized Violence in a Global Era*. Cambridge: Polity Press.

Kaplan, M. (1999). 'The Efforts of WHO and Pugwash to Eliminate Chemical and Biological Weapons—A Memoir'. *Bulletin of the World Health Organization*, 77/2: 149–54.

Keck, M. and K. Sikkink (1998). *Activists Beyond Borders: Advocacy Networks in International Politics*. Ithaca: Cornell University Press.

Kervers, O. (2002). 'Strengthening Compliance with the Biological Weapons Convention: The Protocol

Negotiations'. *Journal of Conflict and Security Law*, 7: 275–92.

Klotz, L., Furmanski, M., and Wheelis, M. (2003). 'Beware the Siren's Song: Why "Non-Lethal" Incapacitating Chemical Agents are Lethal'. Federation of American Scientists Working Group on Biological Weapons <http://www.fas.org/bwc/papers/sirens_song.pdf>.

Krasner, S. D. (1983). 'Structural Causes and Regime Consequences: Regimes as Intervening Variables'. In S. D. Krasner (ed.), *International Regimes*. Ithaca: Cornell University Press.

Lean, G. and Carrell, S. (2003). 'US Prepares to Use Toxic Gases in Iraq'. *The Independent*. London.

MacKenzie, D. (1998). 'Tacit Knowledge and the Uninvention of Nuclear Weapons'. In Donald MacKenzie, *Knowing Machines: Essays on Technological Change*. Cambridge, MA: MIT Press.

Mandelbaum, M. (1981). *The Nuclear Revolution: International Politics Before and After Hiroshima*. Cambridge: Cambridge University Press.

Meselson, M. (2000). 'Averting the Hostile Exploitation of Biotechnology'. *The CBW Conventions Bulletin*, 48: 16–19.

– and Robinson, J. P. (1998). 'A Draft Convention to Prohibit Biological and Chemical Weapons Under International Law'. *The CBW Conventions Bulletin*, 42: 1–5.

Moore, M. (1997). 'Forty Years of Pugwash'. *Bulletin of the Atomic Scientists*, 53/6: 40–5.

MoveOn.org <http://www.moveon.org/>.

Murphy, S., Hay, A., and Rose, S. (1984). *No Fire, No Thunder: The Threat of Chemical and Biological Weapons*. London: Pluto Press.

Oliviero, M. B. and Simmons, A. (2002). 'Who's Minding the Store? Global Civil Society and Corporate Responsibility'. In M. Glasius, M. Kaldor, and H. Anheier (eds), *Global Civil Society 2002*. Oxford: Oxford University Press.

Panofsky, W. K. H. (1998). 'Dismantling the Concept of "Weapons of Mass Destruction"'. *Arms Control Today*, 28/3: 3–8.

Parachini, J. (1997). 'NGOs: Force Multipliers in the CWC Ratification Debate'. In M. Krepon, A. Smithson, and J. Parachini (eds), *The Battle to Obtain US Ratification of the Chemical Weapons Convention*. Washington, DC: Henry L Stimson Center.

Pearson, G. (2001). 'Progress in Geneva: 15th Quarterly Review'. *The CBW Conventions Bulletin*, 52: 15–30.

– (2002). 'Contributions from Non-Governmental Organizations: The Contributions of the Department of Peace Studies of the University of Bradford to Strengthening the BTWC Regime'. In: G. Pearson and Dando, M. *Strengthening the Chemical Weapons Convention*. Bradford: Department of Peace Studies, University of Bradford.

Poste, G. and Robinson, J. P. (2000). 'Appendix 2: International Control Measures: The Biological Weapons Convention and its Projected Protocol'. *Measures for Controlling the Threat from Biological Weapons*. London: Royal Society.

Price, R. (1995). 'A Genealogy of the Chemical Weapons Taboo'. *International Organization*, 49: 73–103.

– (1997). *The Chemical Weapons Taboo*. Ithaca: Cornell University Press.

Pugwash Conferences on Science and World Affairs <http://www.pugwash.org>.

Rissanen, J. (2002). 'NGO Perspectives: NGOs at Geneva Negotiations'. *Disarmament Forum*, 1: 31–5.

Robinson, J. P. (1993). 'Origins of the Chemical Weapons Convention'. In B. Morel and K. Olson (eds), *Shadows and Substance: The Chemical Weapons Convention*. Boulder, CO: Westview Press.

– (1998). 'The Negotiations on the Chemical Weapons Convention: A Historical Overview'. In M. Bothe, N. Ronzitti, and A. Rosas (eds), *The New Chemical Weapons Convention–Implementation and Prospects*. The Hague: Kluwer Law International.

– (1999). 'The Impact of Pugwash on the Debates over Chemical and Biological Weapons'. In A. Cerreno and A. Keynan (eds), *Scientific Cooperation, State Conflict: The Roles of Scientists in Mitigating International Discord*. Annals of the New York Academy of Sciences. New York: New York Academy of Sciences.

– , Stock, T., and Sutherland, R. (1994). 'The Chemical Weapons Convention: The Success of Chemical Disarmament Negotiations'. *SIPRI Yearbook 1993: World Armaments and Disarmament*. Stockholm: Oxford University Press.

Rotblat, J. (1972). *Scientists in the Quest for Peace: A History of the Pugwash Conferences*. Cambridge, MA: MIT Press.

Short, N. (1999). 'The Role of NGOs in the Ottawa Process to Ban Landmines'. *International Negotiation*, 43: 483–502.

Sigmund, E. (1980). *Rage Against the Dying: Campaign Against Chemical and Biological Warfare*. London: Pluto Press.

Sims, N. (2001). *The Evolution of Biological Disarmament*. Oxford: Oxford University Press.

Stockholm International Peace Research Institute (SIPRI) <http://projects.sipri.se/cbw/>.

SIPRI (Stockholm International Peace Research Institute) (1971a). *CB Disarmament Negotiations, 1920–1970.* Stockholm: Almqvist and Wiksell.

– (1971b). *The Rise of CB Weapons.* Stockholm: Almqvist and Wiksell.

– (1973a). *CB Weapons Today.* Stockholm: Almqvist and Wiksell.

– (1973b). *CBW and the Law of War.* Stockholm: Almqvist and Wiksell.

Smithson, A. (1997). 'Bungling a No-Brainer: How Washington Barely Ratified the Chemical Weapons Convention'. In M. Krepon, A. Smithson, and J. Parachini (eds), *The Battle to Obtain US Ratification of the Chemical Weapons Convention.* Washington, DC: Henry L Stimson Center.

– and Levy, L. (2000). *Ataxia: The Chemical and Biological Terrorism Threat and the US Response.* Washington, DC: The Henry L. Stimson Center.

Sunshine Project <http://www.sunshine-project.org/>.

Sunshine Project (2002a). *US Military Operating a Secret Chemical Weapons Program: Sunshine Project Provides Evidence for US Violation of International Law.* Austin and Hamburg: The Sunshine Project.

– (2002b). *US Department of Justice Receives 'Non-Lethal' Biological Weapons Documents.* Austin and Hamburg: The Sunshine Project.

– (2003). 'US "Non Lethal" Chemical (and Biochemical) Weapons Research: A Collection of Documents Detailing a Dangerous Program' <http://www.sunshine-project.org/incapacitants/jnlwdpdf/>.

Swain T. (1996). [Deputy Assistant Secretary of Defense for Policy and Missions]. Prepared Statement before the House National Security Subcommittee on Military Research and Development, 12 March.

Taylor, A. J. P. (1981). *The Origins of the Second World War.* London: Hamish.

Tocqueville, A. (1968). *Democracy in America*, vol. 2. London: Fontana.

Tucker, J. (2002). 'A Farewell to Germs: The US Renunciation of Biological and Toxin Warfare, 1969–70'. *International Security*, 27: 107–48.

Tuerlings, E. and Robinson, J. P. (1999). 'A Trisectoral Analysis of the Chemical Weapons Convention'. In W. Reinicke and F. Deng (eds), *Critical Choices: The United Nations, Networks and the Future of Global Governance.* Ottawa: International Development Research Centre.

United Kingdom (2002). Foreign Affairs Committee, House of Commons. *The Biological Weapons Green Paper.* London: The Stationery Office.

United Nations (1969). *Chemical and Bacteriological (Biological) Weapons and the Effects of Their Possible Use.* New York: United Nations Department of Political and Security Council Affairs.

– (1999). 'Annex III: Elements of Crimes, Preparatory Commission for the International Criminal Court'. UN document PCNICC/2000/INF/3/Add.2 dated 6 July 2000.

van Aken, J. (2001). *Biologische Waffen: Forschungsprojekte der Bundeswehr.* Hamburg: Sunshine Project.

Verification Research, Training and Information Centre <http://www.vertic.org/>.

Wallerstein, M. B. (2002). 'Wither the Role of Private Foundations in Support of International Security Policy?' *Nonproliferation Review*, 9/1: 83–91.

Wheelis, M. (2002a). 'Biological Warfare at the 1346 Siege of Caffa'. *Emerging Infectious Diseases*, 8: 971–5.

– (2002b). 'Biotechnology and Biochemical Weapons'. *The Nonproliferation Review*, 9/1: 48–53.

– and Dando, M. (2002). 'On the Brink: Biodefence, Biotechnology and the Future of Weapons Control'. *The CBW Conventions Bulletin*, 58: 3–7.

WHO (World Health Organization) (2001). *Public Health Response to Biological and Chemical Weapons: WHO Guidance* (2nd Edition—Prepublication Issue). Geneva: WHO <http://www.who.int>.

E-mail interviews

Gould, Chandre (2003). Centre for Conflict Resolution, South Africa

Hammond, Edward (2003). Sunshine Project, United States

Chapter 6

Successes and Challenges: Understanding the Global Movement to End Violence Against Women

Purna Sen

Women everywhere live with the danger of violence, whether experienced or feared. Awareness of potential violence can restrict women's options and movements, the experience of rape can mar a woman's life or bring her an unwanted pregnancy, child abuse or harassment can set the contours of her adult life, political or armed conflict may mean she is a preferred target for any type of violence. Some forms of violence can be specific to particular contexts, but the fact that women all over the world are targeted by men in broadly similar ways sets a common framework for women's lives. Despite contextual differences and political variations, the last 25 years of the twentieth century saw the coming together of an effective and well-organised international movement to challenge violence against women (for example, Sinha, Guy, and Woollacott 1999; Ang-Lygate, Corrin, and Henry 1997; Kerr 1993; Corrin 1996; Davies 1994; Brasileiro 1997). This collective effort amounts to a broadly coherent movement to challenge, resist, and end violence.

In this chapter I set out some of the knowledge we now have about violence against women, highlight key developments in the coming together of the international movement as well as profiling key players, consider some conceptual developments on the international stage, and highlight central debates and challenges for the movement.

Changing Myths and Increasing Understanding of Violence

Until the early 1970s there was little public discussion about violence against women. What there was highlighted the extraordinariness of some of its forms, especially if it was viewed as primitive or backward as a result of colonial encounters (for example, suttee in India). During and since that time information about women's experiences has burgeoned, and in some countries the public has slowly, perhaps reluctantly, come to accept that violence against women constitutes a social and public policy concern. The true nature and meaning of women's experiences of violence is not uniformly accepted, however, and the persistence of certain myths in many parts of the world testifies to their strength and to the public's slowness to accept unpalatable facts.

Information about violence against women emerged in the 1970s with the growth and advocacy of women's organisations that began to work with women on issues of violence. Initially such groups drew solely on the experiences of women with whom they worked. One result of their advocacy was that research and government initiatives began to improve data collection. This in turn strengthened women's groups' information base and arguments.

Popular perceptions of women's experiences of violence are common across many parts of the world. They include the beliefs that violence against women is:

- unusual;
- committed by strangers;
- committed by men who have psychological or personality abnormalities;
- prompted by some action, inaction, or appearance of women ('she asked for it');
- accepted by women;
- not 'real' violence;
- inevitable;
- culturally acceptable; and
- caused by poverty, alcohol, or drug use or abuse.

A number of these beliefs are undermined by research evidence on the prevalence of violence (see Table 6.1). The high rates provide counter-evidence to the claims that violence is rare, that violent men are abnormal (unless great swathes of the male population have psychological disorders), that the danger springs from unknown men ('stranger danger'), and that violence is specific to certain regions, cultures, or classes. The fact that violence against women is predominantly committed by men, that it is gendered,

Table 6.1: Selected research findings on the prevalence of violence against women

Country	Incidence of violence	Data source
	Violence in the home/by intimates	
Barbados	30% of women had never experienced physical or sexual assault by a partner	Heise, Elsberg, and Gottemoeller (1999)
India	Every 4 minutes a crime of violence is committed against a woman	NCRB (1999)
UK	Two women are killed by their husbands/partners/boyfriends every week. 635,000 incidents of domestic violence in England and Wales. 81% of the victims were women and 19% were men.	UK, Home Office (1999; 2002).
	Women experiencing sexual assault from an intimate partner	
Mexico	23%	WHO (2002)
Switzerland	12%	
UK	23%	
	Women reporting physical abuse from husband/partner	
Egypt	34% of women reported physical abuse from husband/partner	WHO (2002)
Papua New Guinea	67% of women reported physical abuse from husband/partner	WHO (2002)
USA	22% of women reported physical abuse from husband/partner	WHO (2002)
Canada	29% of women report being assaulted by a husband/partner	Johnson (1996)
Egypt	47% of victims of femicide were killed by a relative after being raped	Mercy et al. (1993)

has slowly come to be recognised (though in a few quarters this is still contested).

Prior to the successes of the women's movement against violence, in many countries women would not seek protection from, or redress for, violence suffered at the hands of men known to them. Agencies with mandates to uphold the peace and enforce the rule of law (lawyers, the police, and the criminal justice system) would not take such reports seriously and women were often blamed for the violence they suffered (see, for example, Human Rights Watch 1995; 2000). Victim-blaming might take the form of judging women's dress, behaviours, movements, or friendships to be 'inappropriate' and thereby 'prompting' the violence.

The law itself commonly offered women little protection, despite nominally outlawing interpersonal violence. For example, legal prohibitions on bodily harm, killing, or assault tended to be little used to protect women, especially from men known to them, and particularly from men with whom they had prior or ongoing relationships. Rape provisions tended to be

	Violence associated with political conflict	
Rwanda	Approximately 500,000 women were raped during the 1994 genocide	IWTC (2002)
Bosnia	An estimated 20-50,000 women were raped during five months of conflict in 1992	IWTC (2002)
	Violence in the community	
South Africa	37,556 rapes were reported to the police in 2000	South Africa, Police Service (2001)
India	One rape every 34 minutes, every four minutes a woman is kidnapped or abducted	India, Ministry of Woman and Child Development (1998)
	Other forms of violence	
Bangladesh:	327 women were murdered in 2001, 130 suffered acid attacks, 146 died 'unnatural' deaths	The Independent (Dhaka) (URL)
Czech Republic	Police statistics for 1994–9 show 1,100–1,400 cases of child sexual abuse each year	European Intelligence Wire, 040602
Nepal	An estimated 500–700 Nepalese girls are trafficked to India for prostitution each year, 20% of them under the age of 16; 60–70% of those returning to Nepal carry HIV or have AIDS	Maiti Nepal (1997)
Pakistan	Reports of 196 cases of honour killings in 1998 and more than 300 in 1999 in the province of Sindh. Every year more than 1,000 women are killed in the name of honour in Pakistan alone	The Special Task Force for Sindh of the Human Rights Commission
Palestine	A suspected 70 per cent of all murders in Gaza and the West Bank were honour killings. They are usually attributed to natural causes.	Statement, Khaled Al-Qudra, Attorney General. Palestinian National Authority (1997)
Switzerland	20% of girls aged 13–17 experienced contact forms of sexual assault	
Turkey	200 women killed each year for reasons of 'honour'	Amnesty International (2002)
World	4 million people are trafficked internationally each year. The 'trade' is valued at \$5bn–\$7bn a year	UNGA (1998)

limited to penile-vaginal penetration and contained marital exemptions, while judicial processes tended to require marks and injuries to prove that a man used force and the woman resisted (Women, Law and Development International 1998). Rape and sexual abuse of women in war was not recognised, sexual harassment was not taken seriously, and women were ridiculed for complaining about domestic violence. I write here in the past tense; but, sadly, some of this remains true today. What *has* changed shows where the movement has been effective.

The Global Movement: History and Key Players

Women's efforts to challenge and stop male violence are not new. There is a history of women individually (El Saadawi 1999; Jayawardena 1995) and collectively contesting abuse in many countries, which goes back to the early twentieth century and is often linked intrinsically with broader struggles for women's rights (Kumar 1993; Badran 1995). While many of these were

Box 6.1: A thriving national movement in India

The history of women's opposition to violence is long and varied and to be found in many countries. One example of a strong and well-established national movement is to be found in India, where the effectiveness of NGO organisation, political work, and legal change are demonstrated (Basu 2003; Butalia 1998).

Since at least the nineteenth century, it has been recognised in India that certain practices abuse women and girls and should be eliminated (Kumar 1993; Jayawardena 1995). Some of this awareness was fuelled by indignant reactions to violence committed by colonial forces, such as rapes of Indian women by British soldiers, but was also gradually able to take in the more dramatic and public types of violence which were not characterised as imperialist aggression during British rule, such as suttee (widow-burning). More recently, many forms of violence have been highlighted by the women's movement: rape in custody, marital rape, sexual harassment, trafficking and prostitution, labelling and harassing women named as 'witches', domestic violence, dowry-related violence (including killings), and caste-based violence against women, including public parading of stripped women (often associated with gang and mass rapes) (Jayawardena and De Alwis 1997; Datar 1993; Manushi, various).

The Indian movement against violence has a long and active history. Early attempts to highlight violence were associated, sometimes positively, at other times confrontationally, with colonial forces. Post-independence, many of the women's groups agitating against violence were allied to leftist political groups, which meant that their ability, or willingness, to deal with private violence (in which some of their comrades might be implicated) was compromised. It was therefore autonomous women's groups that led on these issues. The links between the women's movement against violence and left political groups remains and perhaps explains the continuing importance attached to violence which lends itself to class-based explanations. The independent feminist movement is, however, also strong and includes Sanlaap (working against prostitution and trafficking), Forum Against the Oppression of Women (formerly the Forum Against Rape), Women's Lawyers Collective, All India Women's Conference, Sanhita (resource centre), and Swayam. The National Commission on Women has held public hearings on violence, state commissions have investigated violence against women, and feminist groups have pushed for recognition in law of issues that affect all socio-economic groups of women, such as marital rape.

The movement has agitated through many avenues, including public efforts, the law, conferences, meetings, and arts performance. The women's movement has used demonstrations to bring public attention to the issue, including lengthy walks that might take days, such as a 1980 youth march against violence from Rajasthan to Delhi. Demonstrations may be more targeted too, taking place outside police stations where officers have been accused of rape or outside homes of perpetrators of violence against women. Such public shaming tactics have sought to shift the public tolerance of violence, and have included painting on the walls of houses to alert locals to violence—for example, 'burnt her' on a house where a dowry death has taken place. The Indian movement has been extremely effective at combining small- and large-scale actions such as these, showing the larger, social patterns of woman abuse and the specific cases that are the manifestation and reflection of these.

The women's movement has expended a huge amount of effort on campaigning against rape, naming many types of rape as existing and requiring attention, including landlord rape, rape in the workplace, custodial rape, police rape, army rape, caste rape, marital rape, and rape of minors and of women in prostitution (Kumar 1993).

Levels of literacy among women in India are poor, except in a few regions, and non-written means are needed for effective mass communication. Street theatre, a long-established tradition of left political groups, has been widely used in the campaigns against violence and have covered areas such as dowry, domestic violence, and the rights of women. This method can travel well and thereby reach women, and men, in areas and among groups who might not otherwise be reached through press and other media coverage of campaigns. The movement has sought not only to raise the awareness of, and improve responses to, violence, but also to change the law and enable women to use the provisions more widely through legal literacy and rights awareness training. Some such efforts are through formal training programmes while others are less formal and include art performance and discussions.

In the 1980s, disparate campaigns against rape in various parts of the country converged into a national initiative, sparked by the Mathura rape case, in which a teenage girl was raped by police who were acquitted at the final stage of appeal by the Supreme Court on the grounds that, because Mathura had had a boyfriend, she was of unsound virtue and therefore could not be raped. The Bombay-based Forum Against Rape made this case a rallying call for women's organisations across India and called on groups to demonstrate on 8 March (International Women's Day) for a retrial. The problems of coordination and convergence of ideas and strategies across such a vast and densely populated country were difficult to overcome, however, and a national movement proved hard to maintain. Nevertheless, the issues of women's rights and violence against women in particular grew in importance on the public stage during this period, and were taken up by a growing range of political organisations beyond the socialist and Communist groups.

The women's movement campaigned against suttee and dowry deaths, using the language of women's rights and bodily integrity. Gains were made through changes in the law. These include the requirement in the Indian Penal Code (Government of India 1993) that any death of a wife within seven years of her marriage should be investigated by police, a response to the alertness that has now developed to dowry-related violence and killings.

However, feminist language and intentions have also been usurped and used to promote violence against women. Women's wings of Hindu religious fundamentalist political parties have claimed that it is a woman's right to commit suttee, promoting the notion that women voluntarily enter the funeral pyre of their deceased husbands.

The Indian movement is well-connected with the global movement, where it is regarded as both well-organised and effective. Indian groups consistently promote issues such as dowry deaths and custodial rape. These forms of violence are not specific to India but in much of the international movement there is a tendency to focus on specific forms of violence (especially domestic violence, trafficking, and rape in war). Women's organisations from certain countries have drawn attention to other forms of violence, including dowry death and custodial rape in the Indian case.

Crime category	Number of incidents reported to the police
Rape	16,496
Kidnapping and abduction	15,023
Dowry death	6,995
Torture	45,778
Molestation	32,940
Sexual harassment	11,024
Importation of girls	64
Sati Prevention Act	0
Immoral Traffic (P) Act	9,515
Indecent Rep. of Women (P) Act	662
Dowry Prohibition Act	2,876
TOTAL	141,373

Source: Government of India (2000)

national efforts, some had international dimensions and were often associated with imperialist relationships;[1] these movements have left an important legacy. It is, however, only since the 1970s that national and international movements have seen a marked increase in networking, organising, and effectiveness. In order to complement the mainly international focus of this chapter, Box 6.1 sets out an example of a national movement against violence against women, the movement in India.

Global power relationships between governments have meant that attention to, and condemnation of, violence against women has often been from the West to poorer countries. In the NGO movement this relationship has been effectively challenged, with strong voices and organisations emanating from Africa, Asia, and Latin America, which have also been able to turn the gaze of the movement onto the West. One example is a 'call to action' in support of US NGOs, issued by the NGO network Women Living Under Muslim Laws (WLUML) against the practice of polygamy in the USA (WLUML 2002).

The International Tribunal on Crimes Against Women, held in Brussels in 1976, was the first to gather activitst internationally in order to name, understand and combat violence against women

Key meetings

A series of international meetings and networks facilitated and strengthened the international movement. Several inter-governmental meetings, often under the auspices of the UN, brought together women's NGOs from across the world, enabling international dialogues between them. These events have been catalysts for the growing cooperation and strength of the international movement. A pivotal juncture in this development is an NGO/independent event at which violence against women was the key concern and where for the first time women came together under their own direction to name violence against women and begin to mobilise collectively across countries. That event was the International Tribunal on Crimes Against Women.

The International Tribunal on Crimes Against Women

In 1976 the first international and independent gathering of women's organisations addressing violence against women was held in Brussels. The Tribunal sought to gather activists together in order to name, understand, and organise against violence against women (Russell and Van de Ven 1976).

Over 2,000 women from 40[2] countries participated in this first Tribunal on crimes against women. The event grew out of an International Feminist Conference in 1974 and was a response to the UN International Women's Year. Organised by an eight-woman coordinating committee, this was not a Tribunal structured along legal lines: 'there was no panel of judges . . . we were all our own judges' (Russell and Van de Ven 1976: xv). It was a meeting and a way of thinking that was rooted in feminist thought in many countries, full of challenge and confrontation and rejection of 'the patriarchal order'. The Tribunal rejected established notions of crime, which they identified as being defined by men, preferring instead a woman-centred approach: 'the women present completely rejected patriarchal definitions of crimes; all man-made forms of women's oppression were seen as crimes' (Russell and Van de Ven 1976: xv). Personal testimony was the method used the Tribunal, understood as the appropriate means by which individual experiences could be politicised and thereby translated into collective struggle. The methods of speak-outs and testimonies were to be used again and again in women's movements against violence across the world.

The Tribunal sought to take individual and national struggles successfully into an international context. Like many international gatherings before and since then, it was the wealthier countries that dominated in numbers (see Table 6.2) although the registration fee was a mere $3.75.[3] As with all such meetings, travel to a Western country and the cost of staying

[1] *In the sense that they involved not only Western women who had travelled to the colonies as wives of colonial officers etc. but also those who were allied to nationalist, anti-imperialist causes.*

[2] *Russell and Van de Veer (1976) report that 40 countries were represented, but a list that appears later in the book, however, names only 39. The list provides the basis for the information in Table 6.2.*

[3] *$11.87 in 2002 dollars: still a remarkably low fee for an international conference.*

Table 6.2: The 1976 International Tribunal on Crimes Against Women: Topics and speakers' countries

Topic	Speakers' countries
Rape	France, Denmark, Portugal, Netherlands and Norway
Battering	Scotland, England and Netherlands
Forced incarceration in mental hospitals and marriage	Ireland
Assault	Belgium
Femicide	USA and Lebanon
Castration of females: clitoridectomy,	
excisions and infibulation	Guinea
Violent repression of non-conforming girls	France
Torture of women for political ends	Korea
Violent treatment of women in prison	Iran, Chile, India, Spain, Greece, USSR, Northern Ireland, Switzerland, Argentina
Violence against women in general	Australia, Italy, USA
Prostitution	Japan, Korea, USA
Pornography	Denmark

there would have been prohibitively expensive for many would-be participants. There appears to have been no funding available for participants to attend from poorer countries. Testimonies on violence were given predominantly by women from Western countries (see Table 6.3).

The Tribunal was part of a series of women's events focusing on violence against women. Important among these were the four World Conferences on Women that were held by the UN, as well as the decade for women (1976–85). The Conferences were held in Mexico (1975), Copenhagen (1980), Nairobi (1985), and Beijing (1995) and provided important spaces and catalysts for women from different parts of the world to meet, discover a shared and strong commitment to ending violence against women, and increase cooperation between them. International networking in the NGO sector was given considerable impetus by these meetings.

Brighton Conference on Violence, Abuse and Women's Citizenship

Before moving on to the UN meetings, we should mention a second international NGO conference: the Conference on Violence, Abuse and Women's Citizenship, held in Brighton, UK, in 1996 (Violence Abuse and Women's Citizenship, 1996). This was organised by a group of NGOs and academics in the UK; unlike many similar events, it also enjoyed some commercial support, from the Body Shop and Scottish Widows. Over 2,000 delegates attended from all over the world. Unlike the Brussels Tribunal, this was not a meeting only of activists or NGOs. It attracted participants from governmental agencies, such as various police forces, and from international governmental organisations too, including the World Health Organisation (WHO). There was a huge representation from civil society, which took a leading role in organising and managing the conference. This mixed attendance profile reflects the changes in working practices that had occurred in the intervening twenty years, with increasing linkages and cooperation between the voluntary groups, government agencies, and academics. This non-isolationist positioning of the NGO world also illustrates the way in which engagement has taken place at the policy level and the degree of respect and credibility the NGO world has won among policy-makers, who attended in good numbers.

Key organisations and networks

The international movement against violence against women is made up of several key networks and many sub-national, national, and regional NGOs. Many of these are led by legal activists or professionals and

Table 6.3: Participation in the 1976 Tribunal, Beijing Plus Five, and the first ten years of the 16 Days Campaign

Country	International Tribunal on Crimes Against Women (1976) attended	Number of Organisations: Beijing Plus 5 (2000)	Number of Organisations: 16 days Campaign against Violence Against Women (1991–2001)
Africa			
Angola	✓	2	2
Botswana		1	0
Cameroon		3	4
Chad		1	0
Congo		2	1
Côte D'Ivoire		1	2
Ethiopia		2	0
Gabon		1	0
Gambia		2	0
Ghana		4	3
Guinea	✓	2	0
Kenya		14	7
Mali		3	1
Mauritius		1	3
Morocco		15	0
Mozambique	✓	0	3
Namibia		3	0
Niger		4	0
Nigeria		14	19
Rwanda		0	1
Senegal		4	0
Somalia		1	0
South Africa	✓	6	37
Sudan		8	0
Tanzania		1	3
Togo		0	1
Tunisia		9	1
Uganda		8	5
Zambia		4	2
Zimbabwe		5	5
Total Africa		121	100
Europe			
Albania		2	0
Armenia		1	1
Austria	✓	7	19
Belgium	✓ (100+)	22	1
Bulgaria		3	5
Croatia		0	12
Cyprus		1	1
Czech republic		1	1
Denmark	✓	9	0
Finland		4	2
France	✓ (40)	23	3
Georgia		1	5
Germany	✓ (300)	5	5
Greece	✓	3	0
Iceland	✓	0	0
Ireland	✓	7	5
Israel	✓	8	8
Italy	✓	19	3
Liechtenstein		1	0
Lithuania		3	0
Luxembourg	✓	0	0
Macedonia		1	0
Moldova		1	0
Netherlands	✓	23	5
Norway	✓	11	10
Poland		2	2
Portugal	✓	1	0
Romania		4	2
Russian Federation		7	5
Serbia		0	3
Slovakia		2	0
Spain	✓ (60)	49	12
Sweden	✓	15	0
Switzerland	✓ (30)	17	3
Turkey		11	0
Ukraine		3	5
United Kingdom	✓(Eng–40)	44	15
Total Europe		311	130

Latin-America			
Argentina		18	18
Barbados		1	3
Bolivia		3	10
Brazil	✓	11	11
British Virgin Islands		0	2
Cayman Islands		0	1
Chile	✓	8	15
Colombia		2	9
Costa Rica		3	40
Cuba		1	0
Dominican republic		3	8
Ecuador		5	21
El Salvador		2	35
Guatemala		4	3
Guyana		5	0
Haiti		1	3
Honduras		1	1
Jamaica		2	1
Mexico	✓	10	39
Dutch Antilles	✓	1	0
Nicaragua		4	8
Panama		2	2
Peru		10	27
Puerto Rica	✓	1	0
Suriname		2	3
Trinidad and Tobago		3	2
Uruguay		5	1
Venezuela		2	11
Total Latin America and Caribbean		110	271
Asia-Pacific			
Australia	✓	18	21
Azerbaijan		1	0
Bangladesh		10	5
Cambodia		2	5
China		9	0
East Timor		0	22
Fiji		2	3
Hong Kong		1	1
India	✓	29	49
Indonesia		4	10
Japan	✓	25	6
Kazakhstan		2	0
Kyrgyzstan		0	18
Korea	✓	7	14
Malaysia		8	6
Marshall Islands		0	1
Mongolia		4	0
Nepal		15	9
New Zealand		2	6
Pakistan		8	11
Philippines	✓	23	8
Singapore		2	0
Sri Lanka		7	3
Taiwan	✓	0	0
Thailand		8	5
Tajikistan		0	2
Tibet		0	1
Uzbekistan		1	0
Vanuatu		0	1
Vietnam	✓	0	0
Total Asia - Pacific		188	207
Middle-East			
Egypt	✓	8	0
Iraq		1	0
Iran	✓	4	0
Jordan		2	1
Kuwait		5	0
Lebanon		2	0
Palestine		1	0
Saudi Arabia		1	0
Yemen	✓	2	0
Total Middle East		26	1
North America			
Canada	✓	43	23
USA	✓ (50)	229	140
Total North America		272	163
TOTAL		1,028	872

Sources: Russell and Van de Ven (1976); List of ECOSOC/Beijing (URL) and CWGL 16 Days (URL)

several locate their work within a broader framework of the promotion of women's human rights. Table 6.4 indicates the number of organisations active in this field; a small number of key actors are described here.

Women in Law and Development in Africa (WiLDAF)
WiLDAF is an African network of women concerned with women's rights, including issues of violence against women.

Established as a result of a conference held in Harare in 1990, WiLDAF brings together organisations and individuals using a variety of tools, including law, to promote a culture promoting the exercise of and respect for women's rights in Africa. WiLDAF is primarily concerned with promoting and strengthening action strategies that empower women and improve their status in Africa. WiLDAF's overall goal is to promote the effective use of a variety of strategies, including law, by women in Africa for self-, community, national, sub-regional, and regional development. The WiLDAF Secretariat is based in Harare, Zimbabwe. WiLDAF has a board of management, with sixteen members drawn from Ghana, Botswana, Cameroon, Mali, Uganda, Tanzania, Lesotho, Nigeria, Mozambique, Swaziland, Mauritius, Sudan, Zambia, Zimbabwe, and Senegal.

WiLDAF networks in a variety of ways, including especially information sharing among member groups to build solidarity and coalitions, and publishing documents that assist in this aim. Activities and events in the region are publicised, workshops and meetings are organised, and WILDAF also acts as the link between African women's organisations and networks operating beyond the region. WiLDAF's newsletter is a multilingual publication, available in English, French and Portuguese, reflecting the complexity of working across this region. The network has also produced a directory of women's resources, posters for training and education work, and information brochures on women's rights.

CLADEM
CLADEM (Comite de America Latina y el Caribe para la Defensa de los Derechos de la Mujer—Caribbean and Latin American Committee for the Defence of Women's Human Rights URL) is a network of women and women's organisations that seeks to defend the human rights of women in the Caribbean and Latin America. The network undertakes a range of activities, including: formulating legislative proposals, research, training, litigation, university teaching, sharing information, and undertaking solidarity actions.

CLADEM initially formed through the coming together of a number of lawyers who met at the Nairobi Women's conference (1985). It was formally established in 1987 and has since given a high profile to legal approaches to dealing with violence against women. The network liaises and cooperates closely with other international organisations, with whom it shares lobbying and advocacy activities. At the national level, CLADEM has pressed for systems and tools for monitoring governments' activities in furtherance of commitments they make to women's human rights.

The network has given significant attention to the experiences of ethnic and racial groups in the region, including in the main thematic areas of work: economic, social, and cultural rights and globalisation; citizenship and participation; sexual rights and reproductive rights; and the right to a life free from violence.

CLADEM is organised through national and thematic work, as well as being highly visible and vocal at international levels, both regional and global. CLADEM has groups or organisers in Argentina, Bolivia, Brazil, Chile, El Salvador, Ecuador, Guatemala, Honduras, Mexico, Nicaragua, Panama, Peru, Puerto Rico, and Uruguay. In additional there is a regional coordinator and office and thematic coordinators working on

- sexual reproductive health;
- economic, social, and cultural rights and globalisation; and
- violence against women.

CLADEM has a major project on violence, for which the United Nations Development Fund (UNIFEM) has provided support. This work has included bringing together judges from supreme and constitutional courts to consider domestic violence (2002), exploring the nature and membership of alliances against violence in the region (2002), holding meetings in Porto Alegre in 2003 on violence against women of African descent and against rural women, and developing focused work with indigenous women in the region.

CLADEM is internationally respected for its members' energy and success in raising awareness and changing laws and its effective organisation around violence against women. Its contribution to a model piece of legislation on violence is also extremely well-regarded, indeed envied and considered a positive example by many other women's groups around the world. The Americas is the only region which has adopted international legislation to promote the eradication of violence against women: the 1994 Inter-American Convention on the Prevention, Punishment and Eradication of Violence Against Women defines, and commits states to a number of actions towards the eradication of violence against women.

Asia Pacific Forum on Women Law and Development (APWLD)

Like CLADEM, this network grew out of the meeting of women at the 1985 Kenya conference on women. The initial group included lawyers, social scientists, and activists who in 1988 formally established the regional forum, with a secretariat in Kuala Lumpur, Malaysia, which in 1997 was moved to Chiangmai, Thailand.

The Forum seeks to enable women in the region to use law as an instrument of change for empowerment in their struggle for justice, peace, equality, and development, and to promote basic concepts of human rights in the region as enshrined in the Universal Declaration of Human Rights, the UN Convention on the Rights of the Child, the Convention on the Elimination of All Forms of Discriminations Against Women (UNGA 1979), and other relevant international human rights instruments. APWLD understands violence against women as an abuse of women's human rights and a form of discrimination against women under international law. The Forum organises its work through working groups on labour and migration, rural and indigenous women, violence against women, women and the environment, women's human rights, and women's political participation.

The primary objective of the violence against women (VAW) programme is to develop feminist-oriented, regional-level strategies to address violence against women and prevent the further discrimination and abuse of women's human rights through gender violence. The VAW working group holds an annual meeting of regional experts to review and plan this area of work.

A major current initiative on violence against women is the cooperation between the Forum and the Shan Women's Action Network in Burma to research, document, publicise, and oppose systematic sexual and other violence perpetrated by the military in Burma against Shan and other ethnic minority women. This campaign, 'Stop Licence to Rape', is led by the Shan women's group and the Shan Human Rights Foundation, while the APWLD has facilitated the publicity and advocacy of the campaign internationally. This includes advocacy at the Asian Social Forum (2003), Hyderabad, India and at the UN Commission on the Status of Women, and the Commission on Human Rights.

The APWLD also undertakes documentation and resource collection. One project is the collation of all regional laws on domestic violence to provide a resource base for groups seeking legal reform on this issue. The Forum has also worked on violence against young women in the region.

APWLD brings together organisations from across the Asia-Pacific region, with a structure consisting of a regional council, a steering committee, and a secretariat.

Women Against Violence in Europe (WAVE)

WAVE is a European network of non-governmental women's organisations that work to end violence against women and children. It was set up in 1994 and launched at the Beijing Conference in 1995, and has tended to stress work against violence in interpersonal relationships.

The network aims to provide a central point for the region where information can be collated and shared through which links between work in different parts of Europe can be strengthened, and to build feminist analyses and facilitate common activities. WAVE also provides a channel for member groups to influence European and international policies and other initiatives relevant to violence against women.

The network comprises of around 1,000 members, including shelter providers, telephone help-line services, and training organisations. The main office is located in Vienna, Austria, and there are 50 focal points through which information is gathered and disseminated. The steering group has eight members from various countries.

WAVE has held a series of conferences on violence, beginning in 1998. The organisation houses a database on organisations in Europe, produces period reports and a regular newsletter, and is a regularly heard in international advocacy and debates on violence against women.

CWGL/16 days campaign

Women activists worldwide have participated in a series of leadership programmes run by the Centre for Women's Global Leadership (CWGL) in the USA. The

Launch of book by Kiranjit Ahkuwala and Rahila Gupta, London 1999. The former killed her abusive husband and was eventually released from prison after a campaign led by Southall Black Sisters and other women's groups. © Purna Sen.

CWGL works within a human rights framework to promote feminist approaches to decision-making and policy shaping, focusing on violence against women, sexual and reproductive health, and socio-economic well-being. Institutes run by the Centre have shaped the thinking of women activists all over the world.

A key action coordinated by the centre is what has become known as the '16 days campaign'. This has been held every year since 1991, runs between 25 November and 10 December, and provides a focus for a period of intense activity on violence against women. 25 November [4] is the International Day of Action Against Violence Against Women, and 10 December is International Human Rights Day; the 16 days provide a clear link between the two not only in actions but also in concepts and work. This period takes in World AIDS day on 1 December and the anniversary of the Montreal massacre on 6 December, when 14 women were killed by a gunman at Montreal's École Polytechnique in 1989 and whose letter of explanation blamed feminists for ruining his life .

Each year organisations across the world separately and collectively engage in a range of activities, advised supported and coordinated by the CWGL. They are supported through an Action Kit which contains information on the campaign, including a list of suggested activities and an online posting of all previous International Calendars of Campaign Activities. The CWGL also makes available to those participating in the campaign contact details of others, thereby facilitating international networking on specific activities, outcomes, and strategies.

In principle, the purposes of the 16 days campaign are to:

- raise awareness about gender-based violence as a human rights issue at the local, national, regional, and international levels;
- strengthen local work around violence against women;
- make a clear link between local and international work to end violence against women;
- create a method to share and develop new and effective strategies;
- show the solidarity of women around the world organising against violence against women; and

[4] *The date commemorates the brutal 1961 assassination of the three Mirabal sisters, political activists in the Dominican Republic, on orders of Dominican ruler Rafael Trujillo.*

- create tools to pressure governments to implement promises made to eliminate violence against women.

A theme is selected each year for the campaign, around which activities are organised. Over the first ten years these included Violence Against Women Violates Human Rights, in 1991; Awareness, Accountability, Action: Violence Against Women Violates Human Rights, in 1994; and Fulfilling the Promise of Freedom from Violence, in 1999).

The campaign is extremely successful in linking up women and organisations from all over the world. A survey of names of those participating over the first ten years shows that 872 organisations from 89 countries have been involved (see Table 6.2).

Women's Caucus for Gender Justice

Another more recent extremely successful international networking and advocacy organisation is the Women's Caucus for Gender Justice (WCGJ) (URL), a network that has successfully brought gender concerns to the heart of the International Criminal Court (ICC). The Caucus had four central aims: to work towards the establishment of the ICC and ensure its responsiveness to the principles of gender justice; to participate in the campaign for ratification of the ICC; to monitor and assist the court fairly and effectively in prosecuting cases of gender violence; and to promote awareness of the ICC.

An executive group made up of members from across world regions—Philippines, USA, Latin America, Kenya, and India—manages the caucus. The Caucus brought together 300 organisations from many parts of the world to specify and pursue three main goals:

1. to ensure a worldwide participation by women's human rights advocates in the negotiations on the ICC treaty to lobby for an effective and independent court;
2. to take advantage of the opportunity to educate governments' delegations and mainstream human rights NGOs in their commitments to women and the need to integrate a gender perspective into the UN; and
3. to use the establishment of the ICC as a basis for popular education on women's human rights and to raise public awareness of the nature of crimes committed against women

The Caucus has organised international representation at the negotiating sessions for the ICC from women's groups worldwide. They have successfully set up training and briefing sessions for participants who work under their umbrella. This has enabled women activists to be updated on the most recent developments and to be well prepared for advocacy and lobbying work with governmental delegations. It is unusual for a network in this field to have been so very well organised and to have mobilised sufficient funding to facilitate such widespread participation and to prepare participants so well. In April 2003 the Caucus announced its closure, judging that its original objectives had been achieved. Several features of the Caucus's work have helped achieve its extremely successful record: a clear and specific mandate, planning effective participation from partners (legal specialists and others) across the world, funding their involvement and providing them training, and ongoing and widespread channels of communication facilitating successful lobbying and advocacy.

The Caucus has a remit that is broader than simply promoting awareness and recognition of effective responses to violence against women; however, this subject has been central in its work. Two important indications of its success have been the inclusion of sexual and gender violence within the remit of the ICC and the incorporation of experts on sexual and gender violence in the staffing of the Court. (Glasius 2002; Steains 1999; Axel, Marrow, and Martinez 1997). This was recognised by the UNHCHR:

> *I would like to pay tribute to the women of the Women's Caucus for Gender Justice who have taken the experiences of women in war, identified strategies for dealing with violations and, overcoming intense opposition from many representatives at the International Criminal Court negotiations, managed to ensure that rape, sexual slavery, forced pregnancy and other forms of gender-based and sexual violence are included in the statute of the ICC. (Mary Robinson [URL], UN High Commissioner for Human Rights on the occasion of International Women's Day, 8 March 2000)*

For an institution (the ICC) not originally set up to deal with violence against women, this is indeed a significant achievement for the movement.

Table 6.4: Selected organisations and networks active in challenging violence against women

Country	Organisation
Bangladesh	Ain O Sailish Kendra Bangladesh Mahila Parishad Naripokko
Bosnia-Herzegovina	Medica-Zenica
Brazil	Centro de Mulheres 8 de Marco
Bulgaria	Animus Association
Canada	Immigrant and Visible Minority Women Against Abuse
Chile	National Network on Domestic and Sexual Violence Against Women Centro de Estudios Sociales
Costa Rica	Central American Human Rights Commission (CODEHUCA)
Croatia	Be Active Be Emancipated (BABE)
East Timor	East Timor Action Network
El Salvador	Network Against Gender Violence
Fiji	Fiji Women's Crisis Centre
India	Association for Advocacy and Legal Initiatives Chitrakoot Sanhita Gender Resource Centre
Indonesia	Indonesian Women's Association for Justice
Italy	Filipino Women's Council
Japan	Abused Women's Centre Asian Centre for Women's Human Rights
Jordan	Jordanian Women's Union
Kenya	Kenya Women's Medical Association
Korea	Korean Sexual Violence Relief Centre
Kyrgystan	Committee of Soldiers' Mothers Coalition on Violence Against Women (COVAW)
Mali	Association pour le Progres et la defense des Droits (AIDF)
Mauritius	SOS Femmes
Mexico	Asociacion Mexicana contra la Violencia a las Mujeres

The role of 'leaders'

As with any movement, there are some key individuals who are influential, charismatic, and vocal. Their importance on the international stage cannot be ignored, they are in effect the spokeswomen for the movement and act as links between parts of the movement and between the movement and governments. At Beijing Plus 5, a list of thousands of women's names was publicised in order to honour activists who had fought for the rights of women (Walker 2002). Although that list goes beyond violence against women, it includes some women who have been particularly active in this field.

The way in which such women are viewed by the movement is mixed. There is genuine respect for some; however, career advancement, a high profile, and power motivate some of these leaders, as is the case in any movement. A failure to consult, to hear, encourage or acknowledge other women, their views, or their ways of working inevitably engenders their distrust and resentment. Where women behave in these ways there are bound to be whispers, critical or malicious, that mar the otherwise cohesive nature of the movement. There is a tradition in the women's movement in many countries of taking great care over what, if any, disagreements or debates can be allowed to become public. The fear of appearing

Country	Organisation
Nepal	Alliance against Trafficking Maiti
Nigeria	BAOBAB
Norway	Feminist Group Ottar
Pakistan/Afghanistan	Revolutionary Association of Women of Afghanistan
Pakistan	Shirkat Gah
Philippines	Gabriela Network
Russia	Moscow Sexual Assault Recovery Centre 'Girlfriend' Centre
South Africa	People Opposing Woman Abuse (POWA) Masimanyane Women's Support Centre
Spain	Asociacion de Mujeres para la Salud
Sri Lanka	Centre for Women's Research (CENWOR) Campaign Against Gender Violence
Suriname	Women's Rights Centre
Thailand	National Council of Women of Thailand
Tibet	Tibetan Women's Association
Togo	Les Organisations Non-Gouvernementales Contre la Violence au Foyer
Turkey	Women for Women's Human Rights
UK	Zero Tolerance
Uganda	Uganda Women's Network (UWONET)
USA	Clearinghouse on Femicide International Reproductive Rights Research and Action Group Human Rights Watch/Women's Rights Project Equality Now
Europe (Brussels)	European Women's Lobby
USA/UK/International	International Planned Parenthood Federation
International	Women in Black
Chile, Kenya, Philippines	ISIS network

disunited is inhibiting and cohesive at the same time and in this case has meant that there is little discussion of the repeated patterns of domination and self-aggrandisement that undoubtedly exist. There are whispers and looks, there is reluctance to work with certain people or organisations, and there is also some degree of open hostility. There has also been some masking of personal differences and difficulties behind a politicisation of issues. It is perhaps the case that, with the increasing successes and strength of the movement there is also an increasing ability to acknowledge problems, though perhaps not yet constructive ways in which to deal with such issues.

Conceptual Shifts and Institutional Gains

The movement has been successful in raising a public profile for women's experiences of violence and for pressing for state actions to combat this. There are institutional gains that have been won as well as important shifts in the way such violence has come to be understood.

Institutional gains at the international level

Major successes have been secured at the institutional level, including at the UN and other intergovernmental forums. These include, as a result of the Vienna conference in 1993, the creation and appointment of a Special Rapporteur to the UN on Violence Against Women, Its Causes and Consequences. Other such posts had direct relevance to the movement; for example, the Special Rapporteur on Extra-Judicial Killings brought attention to the issue of 'honour' killings; likewise, the Special Rapporteur on Human Rights Defenders has a concern with violence against women which informs her work.[5] While neither of these posts can be claimed as a success of the VAW movement, the personal and political histories of both women appointed to these positions enhanced the international attention paid to VAW.

International agreements and laws have begun to name, and to seek government actions against, violence against women. Recent years have also seen an increasing recognition of the need to address and hold accountable non-state actors who perpetrate violence against women.

The UN has been a key arena in which there have been both gains and challenges for the international movement. In the 1970s the UN began to name violence against women as problematic, predominantly through a focus on the family; three decades later, the language has shifted to a concern with women being enabled to enjoy their human rights fully and an understanding that this is hindered by their experiences of violence. Documents and statements arising from the four UN world conferences on women are significant staging posts for this development. The entry point was a concern with dignity, security, and equality in the 1970s (Plan of Action from First World Conference on Women, Mexico 1975); then the UN moved on to recognise 'battered women' in 1980 (1980 Copenhagen Conference). This showed a simple and narrow recognition of the problems faced by women experiencing violence; but a more complex and sophisticated analysis began to emerge at the Nairobi conference, where the NGO sector began to be especially well-organised. The Nairobi conference of 1985 produced the Forward Looking Strategies for the Advancement of Women, in which the achievement of peace was tied to the eradication of violence against women in the private and public spheres. This in itself was a significant step, though at this stage such thinking was still confined to the 'women's sector'. The Fourth World Conference on Women, in Beijing in 1995, once again saw an extremely well-attended and well-organised NGO meeting, articulating women's experiences of violence, demanding that such violence be seen as an area of state responsibility and pressing for commitments to actions to address the violence. The Beijing Platform of Action, as the outcome document is popularly known, has since become a benchmark and a point of leverage for government action against violence against women.

The Beijing Platform of Action has become a benchmark and a point of leverage for government action against violence against women

Finally, at a special session of the UN General Assembly on women ('Beijing Plus 5' 2000) there was again a well-organised lobby on violence. The outcome document here was essentially a restatement of the principles established in the Beijing Platform. Although this did not represent great progress, it was an achievement given the prevailing climate and the nature of the NGO profile at that meeting. Opposition to progress on the rights of women, in particular any gains on sexual and reproductive rights, was strong and located primarily in religiously defined NGOs and religious states (see Box 6.2).

Other successes at the United Nations

The early 1990s saw a number of other developments influenced by the international movement. The UN was sufficiently aware of the need to address violence against women to respond positively to NGO pressure for a specific initiative. In 1993 the UN adopted the Declaration on Violence against Women (UNGA 1993), which defined and stressed the need for actions to address such violence.

International law on women had seen a key treaty adopted by the UN in 1979—the Convention on the Elimination of all forms of Discrimination Against Women (CEDAW)—which enjoyed wide ratification from member states. CEDAW failed to mention VAW

[5] *One case of 'honour' killing directly involved both these Special Rapporteurs as it took place in their office. In April, 1999, Ms Samia Sarwar was murdered in the legal offices in Lahore, Pakistan, shared by the Rapporteurs, both of whom were involved in advising the victim in a case against her family concerning divorce. Human Rights Watch (1999); Sisterhood is Global Institute (1999).*

Box 6.2: The 'opposition'

Of great concern to the feminist movement against violence in the 1990s in particular has been the growth of the so-called pro-life and pro-family lobbies and their well-organised and well-funded opposition to sexual and reproductive rights. These lobbies have found an extremely powerful ally in the US Bush administration, which has introduced measures in domestic and foreign policy that sit comfortably with the aims of the 'pro-family' lobbies (Detroit Free Press 2003). Important to the international movement is the 'global gag' rule, which prevents US aid funding being used by organisations that give abortion-related advice even if that advice is funded from non-US governmental sources (CRLP URL).

The Beijing Plus 5 event in New York event saw a considerable representation from the pro-life and pro-family lobbies, which could afford to send many representatives to the meetings, where they consistently clashed with the anti-violence activists. The North American religious (Christian) and anti-abortion NGOs were particularly numerous and allied with their colleagues from other parts of the world. They also had allies in certain government delegations such as Sudan, Guatemala, and the Holy See (Vatican). Multi-faith coalitions have formed around opposition to the promotion of women's rights.

The women's movement was initially caught unawares by the support for and organisational strength of this opposition. However, its experience in cooperation, liaison, and coordination has borne fruit in renewed successes at recent key events. The 5th Asian and Pacific Population Conference (APPC Bangkok, 11–17 December 2002), for instance, saw the right-wing groups organise in cooperation with the US government delegation and the Holy See. This coalition not only opposed abortion, which has been its consistent position, but also took up some of the Holy See's other arguments, such as opposition to condoms and other modern methods of birth control, proposing 'natural' methods instead (Sen 2003). The anti-violence movement and the reproductive rights lobbies were able to repel these moves in this instance, succeeding in getting language on unsafe abortions inserted which reaffirms commitments made at the Cairo conference on population and development, in the final Plan of Action. This was possible due to the breadth of and preparedness within alliances that included women's groups, some international governmental organisations, such as UN Population Fund (UNFPA), and members of government delegations and drafting committees in which health ministry representatives were aware of the consequences of denying women access to reproductive control.

The 'pro-family' lobby is gaining strength, has a cross-religious nature and has found several allies in government, including, importantly, the single global superpower. It remains a challenge to the anti-violence women's movement. However, its tactics and arguments are now known, and resistance to them is not only strong but increasingly strategic and effective.

(except for a clause on trafficking, though this does not use the language of violence) but the Committee monitoring this treaty was influenced by and responsive to the shift in international thinking that during this period came to make violence a matter of public concern. This Committee issued an interpretive statement of the Convention in 1992 (General Recommendation Number 19; UN Committee on the Elimination of the Discrimination Against Women URL), which explained gender-based violence against women as a form of discrimination, thereby bringing such violence under the auspices of the Committee and the Convention. This offered a considerable strengthening of other international monitoring systems, allowing states to be held accountable to a body of the UN on actions to remove gender-based violence—a new interpretation of states' obligations to remove discrimination against women.

Language similar to that of the Nairobi strategies was adopted at the 1993 Vienna World Conference on Human Rights. The Vienna declaration named certain forms of violence against women, such as in armed conflict, as violations of human rights and reaffirmed the private sphere as an arena of concern

A demonstration outside the United Nations in New York, at the Beijing Plus 5 Conference, June 2000, calling for the UN to pay more attention to violence against women. © Sidsel Aas/FOKUS.

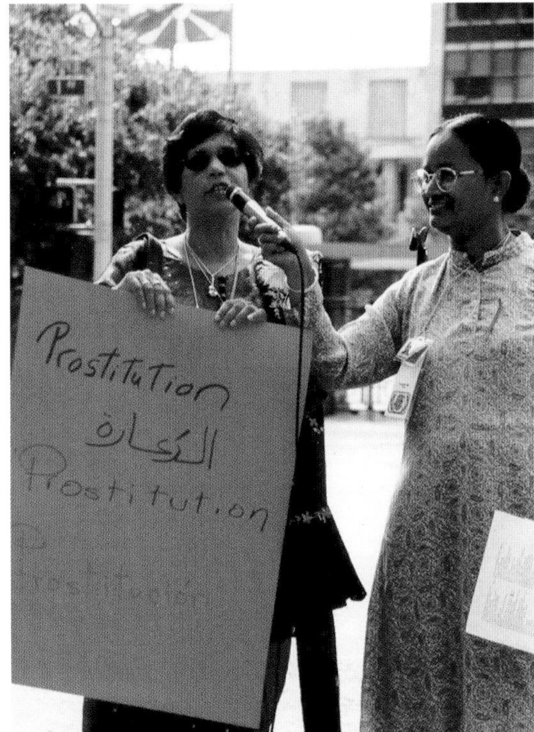

Rada Gungaloo of SOS Femmes, Mauritius, draws attention to prostitution as a form of violence against women. © Sidsel Aas/FOKUS.

for the human rights community. In 1994 the UN appointed the Special Rapporteur on Violence Against Women, Its Causes and Consequences. She has investigated and reported on domestic violence, rape and sexual abuse, custodial violence, trafficking, culture and violence, and violence condoned or perpetrated by the state. Her final report to the UN in 2003 (Coomaraswamy 2003) provided an impressive country-by-country review of the current status of actions addressing violence against women.

While these developments arise from and speak primarily to developments specifically concerning women, other sectoral and general developments picked up the theme of violence against women. The Vienna Conference of Human Rights in 1993 responded to concerns on violence raised by the NGO sector. The 1994 Cairo International Conference on Population and Development sought to have women's reproductive control protected, understanding this to be threatened by violence and meshing with arguments being put elsewhere under the VAW agenda.

Conceptual shifts: definitions

Violence against women

In addition to institutional changes there has been major progress in terms of moving towards explicit and agreed common understandings of what constitutes violence against women, and how it is to be understood. In the 1970s few countries recognised or dealt with domestic violence, definitions of rape tended to focus on penile-vaginal penetration and to exclude marriage, violence was limited to physical abuse evidenced by physical injury, and perpetrators were considered in large part to be strangers to their victims. Knowledge about violence against women described in the introduction was very much at odds with such perceptions. In the decades since the 1976 Tribunal the effectiveness of the movement in gaining recognition of its understanding is evidenced by some key outcomes. Notable are the definitions adopted by governments and inter-governmental organisations as they provide the markers for *international* agreement.

Recognising that many women's experiences of violence are gendered, the UN has adopted the following definition of gender-based violence:

> *The term 'violence against women' means any act of gender-based violence that results in, or is likely to result in, physical, sexual or psychological harm or suffering to women, including threats of such acts, coercion or arbitrary deprivation of liberty, whether occurring in public or private life. Accordingly, violence against women encompasses but is not limited to the following:*
>
> *(a) Physical, sexual and psychological violence occurring in the family, including battering, sexual abuse of female children in the household, dowry-related violence, marital rape, female genital mutilation and other traditional practices harmful to women, non-spousal violence and violence related to exploitation;*
>
> *(b) Physical, sexual and psychological violence occurring within the general community, including rape, sexual abuse, sexual harassment and intimidation at work, in educational institutions and elsewhere, trafficking in women and forced prostitution;*
>
> *(c) Physical, sexual and psychological violence perpetrated or condoned by the State, wherever it occurs.*

This definition appears in the Declaration on Violence Against Women 1993 and in the 1993 Committee on the Elimination of Discrimination Against Women Recommendation No. 19 (UN, CEDAW URL) and the Beijing Platform for Action 1995 (UN 2001). It has become the most widely accepted conceptualisation of violence against women and therefore a benchmark definition.

Notable elements here reflect the influence of civil society concerns and demands. These include: that the family, the community and the state are named as perpetrators or enabling agents of violence; forms of violence recognised include marital rape, exploitation, traditional practices, and trafficking; and in addressing the state the definition is not limited to actions but extended also to inaction or acquiescence in violence committed anywhere. This provides a route by which states can be held accountable for failure to act to prevent, investigate, or punish violence against women, even if the state itself has not committed these acts. In this sense, the state is responsible for violence perpetrated by private actors unless measures were taken that could be seen to have reasonably prevented such actions.

Rape

A second key shift in conceptualising violence against women draws heavily on the nature of arguments put by the movement and experiences for which it has sought recognition. This concerns the first definition of rape in international law, provided by the International Criminal Tribunal on Rwanda:

> *In the opinion of the Chamber, rape is a form of aggression the central elements of which cannot be captured in a mechanical description of objects and body parts. The Chamber also notes the cultural sensitivities involved in public discussion of intimate matters and recalls the painful reluctance and inability of witnesses to disclose graphic anatomical details of the sexual violence they endured. The Chamber defines rape as a physical invasion of a sexual nature, committed on a person under circumstances which are coercive. Sexual violence, including rape, is not limited to physical invasion of the human body and may include acts which do not involve penetration or even physical contact. The*

Chamber notes in this context that coercive circumstances need not be evidenced by a show of physical force. Threats, intimidation, extortion and other forms of duress which prey on fear or desperation may constitute coercion.[6]

This definition is a watershed. It is the first time that international law has defined rape; it is not limited to penile-vaginal penetration, does not limit evidence of rape to physical injury, and does not contain exclusions by relationship (such as marriage). All of these elements reflect concerns raised by activists in many countries and channelled especially though NGOs and lawyers who participated in these hearings to provide expert, impartial evidence on sexual violence as amici curiae (friends of the court).

The definitions of gender-based violence and of rape are broadly in keeping with an international consensus found in the global movement against violence against women.

Trafficking

A third definition illustrates both the influence of the movement and the strength of one element of a debate within that movement, discussed below. The definition of trafficking in persons as set out in the UN Trafficking (UNGA 2001) is as follows:

> *For the purposes of this Protocol,*
>
> *(a) 'Trafficking in persons' shall mean the recruitment, transportation, transfer, harbouring or receipt of persons by means of the threat or use of force or other forms of coercion, of abduction, of fraud, of deception, of the abuse of power or of a position of vulnerability*
> *or*
> *of the giving or receiving of payments or benefits to achieve the consent of a person having control over another person, for the purpose of exploitation. Exploitation shall include, at a minimum, the exploitation of the prostitution of others or other forms of sexual exploitation, forced labour or services, slavery or practices similar to slavery, servitude or the removal of organs.*
>
> *(a bis) The consent of a victim of trafficking in persons to the intended exploitation set forth in subparagraph (a) shall be irrelevant where any of the means set forth in subparagraph (a) have been used.*
> *(b) The recruitment, transportation, transfer, harbouring or receipt of a child for the purpose of exploitation shall be considered 'trafficking in persons' even if this does not involve any of the means set forth in subparagraph (a) of this article.*
> *(c) 'Child' shall mean any person under eighteen years of age.*

This definition was the most contested part of the treaty, with agreement being reached only on the last day of two years of negotiations. Important features include the fact that there is no need to demonstrate force but coercion, deception, or abuse of power are all recognised as being potential means of trafficking and that consent can be won in unscrupulous ways. The presence of consent is not understood as a defining feature in trafficking; rather, the means used for transport, harbouring, and so on are prioritised. The definition names prostitution, among other practices, as a form of exploitation.

Divisions within the Movement

The stories told so far have concentrated on the ways in which the movement has networked and organised successfully over a period of 25 years. Personality differences are not the only point on which activists have fallen out; issues of definition, politics, and strategy have also split the movement. The language of particularity, or debates over the specificity of meaning, have fostered divisions within the movement. It is also true that a significant variety of interpretations and understandings of cultural, religious, or contextual situations have complicated or curtailed conversations between women at a global level.

Sex industry

There is a growing consensus in many agencies and parts of the world that the sex industry—prostitution, 'lap-dancing', and other activities built around the selling of sex or sexual arousal—is growing in both size and monetary value (Mameli URL; McNulty 1999). A

6 From Summary of the Judgement in Jean-Paul Akayesu Case, International Criminal Court of Rwanda (ICTR-96-4-T). Delivered on 2 September 1998; emphasis added.

considerable proportion of this industry draws upon the trafficking of women and girls across borders. Women's movements against violence tend to be united in opposition to trafficking but divide vehemently over whether engagement in the sex industry is to be understood as a legitimate area of employment or a site of exploitation and violence. The division operates not only at a conceptual level—how to understand the area—but also plays out in consequent policy and intervention approaches. The fissure is almost absolute, with the camps having little contact with each other.

The first group considers the sex industry to be part of an opening up of sexuality and sexual behaviour for women, an opportunity for self-expression. They argue that paid sexual activity can be a positive earning opportunity or means of expression and empowerment. Women in the industry should not be stigmatised; and the way to ensure this is by state support for the industry, and recognition of 'sex work' as a legitimate choice in the face of poverty; the state should provide a regulatory framework as a means for upholding the health and welfare of women engaged therein. This lobby refers to engagement in the industry as 'sex work'. In order best to protect the women who have chosen to enter this work, prostitution and other parts of the sex industry should be legalised. It is argued that this would remove the stigma and danger faced by women and girls and allow them to organise and benefit from health and safety requirements relevant to all businesses. Brothels would thereby become legalised and businesses in which women sell sex could operate openly, trade shares, and be listed on stock exchanges.

Women's movements against violence divide vehemently over whether engagement in the sex industry is to be understood as a legitimate area of employment or a site of exploitation and violence

The Global Alliance Against Trafficking in Women (GAATW URL) is in the vanguard of this argument. Agencies locating themselves on this side of the debate include NGOs and IGOs. The Human Rights Caucus brings together a range of NGOs sharing this position. Anti-Slavery International, which in earlier times treated prostitution and trafficking as forms of slavery, is now more equivocal and has begun to refer to women's engagement in the industry as 'sex work'. The International Labour Organisation has done the same; and in parts of the UN the language of, and restriction of the problem to, forced prostitution reflects the thinking that prostitution is, at least in part, the outcome of 'free' choices made by women. This approach underlines policy initiatives in Australia and the Netherlands, where prostitution and brothels are legalised. This lobby is predominantly located in North America, some countries in Western Europe, and Australia.

The converse argument rests upon an understanding of the sex industry, and women's place within it, as inescapably exploitative and marked by violence, abuse, and even death. There is clearly an intellectual and political inheritance from the abolitionist cause. This lobby also points to evidence that a considerable proportion of the women in this area have a history of violence or abuse in either childhood or adult life and that their journey into this sector is marked by a variety of actions that deny human rights and women's ability to make choices. It is argued that trafficking may be the route of entry and rape may be the initiation rite; and confiscation of identity or travel documents, as well as earnings, frequently happen. Rather than seeing the industry as something which women have the right to enter, this view understands it as an abuse of human rights by men who buy women as well as those who control the industry. Rather than a focus on changing the situation for women, there is a clear stress on the men who are the buyers of services in this industry: women are located in the sex industry because (mostly) men provide the demand. The purchasing of women as sexual-service providers itself is problematised, with one appropriate policy response being to criminalise the buyers, as is the case in Sweden, rather than those who are abused in the industry. Sweden has initiated this approach and it is currently under consideration in Finland and Norway, promoted in Europe by European Women's Lobby.

The UN Trafficking Protocol will see a range of countries consider domestic legislation in line with the newly agreed definition of trafficking, which was supported by many countries in the South. Article 10 of the Protocol calls on states to discourage the demand that fosters trafficking and may find countries looking to the Swedish model.

Box 6.3: Debates on women's engagement in the sex industry

Sex industry as work	Sex industry as exploitation/violence
• Women have the right to choose the work in which they will engage. • The sex industry allows women expression of their sexuality. • Work in this industry can be a site of power for women. • Women in this industry should benefit from the rights and protections enjoyed by other workers, such as trade unions, health and safety protections, advertising, sound management practices, and so on. • Legalisation of prostitution is therefore the way to deal with this area of work.	• The sex industry is unavoidably exploitative of women, who form the majority of prostitutes, 'dancers', etc. • Significant proportions of women in this industry have a background of abuse and are therefore vulnerable • 'Choices' to enter this industry are an exemplar of the discrimination and marginalisation experienced by poor or abused women. • Prostitution and related activities are not 'work' as normally understood but disproportionately marked by violence, danger, and death. • Women (and girls) in this industry are vulnerable to violence; they should not be penalised for being in this industry; men should not be supported in purchasing women for sex; demand should be named as the problem and addressed as such. • Criminalisation of the buyers is therefore an appropriate response.

This lobby recognises that many women enter the industry without being literally forced, but rather are recruited as a result of deception or the abuse of power or authority. It is the absence of real alternatives that compromises the interpretation of women's entry into the industry as 'choice'. Women need to have better protection from violence and effective routes through which to exit the industry. The criminalisation of men buying women in prostitution is a policy with increasing support amongst both NGOs and governments in the South, as is the view that the sex industry is a form of violence and unlike other business or commercial ventures. This lobby has been strong and effective, despite the political power of the opposition to it. While the distinction between 'forced' and 'free' entry into prostitution has found its way into some international documents, this lobby won a major victory in the UN Trafficking Protocol of 2001. The definition of trafficking in this Protocol reflects the arguments of this lobby, with no distinction between forced and free entry and without reliance upon the victim of trafficking having to demonstrate that she had been forced. This new definition sets the baseline of international consensus for the foreseeable future. The lobby may therefore be in the ascendancy.

Organisations that oppose all aspects of the sex industry include Coalition Against Trafficking in Women (CATW 2002; 2003) and the International Human Rights Network which consists of over 140 NGOs, Equality Now, and Movement for the Abolition of Prostitution and Pornography. This position and its proponents have influenced anti-sex industry measures in the Philippines, Venezuela, Bangladesh, and Japan.

Culture as the divisor: female genital cutting and 'honour' crimes

Both the practice of female genital cutting (FGC; also known as mutilation, FGM, or circumcision) and violence associated with crimes of 'honour' have been the subject of debate and sharp disagreements within the movement, concerning whether or to what extent such traditional practices are appropriate for external scrutiny and, if not, who might legitimately criticise practices rooted in culture and belief.

Female genital mutilation/cutting

FGM/C is a rite of passage for females, a procedure that marks the transition from girlhood into womanhood (Dorkenoo and Elworthy 1992). It involves cutting of the girls' genitals by women, based on the belief that it removes the possibility of sexual pleasure and thereby curbs sexual activity, or promiscuous behaviour, among girls/women/wives, thereby ensuring their chastity before marriage and fidelity after.

There are three forms of cutting—clitoris only, clitoris plus inner labia, and clitoris plus all labia and stitching up of the remaining opening. The small opening is intended to allow for the passing of urine and menstrual flow. Health complications can follow, including impeded menstrual flow, painful periods, poor urine flow, childbirth complications, pelvic infection, and even death. In many countries the cutting is carried out in unhygienic conditions with unclean implements, such as a piece of glass or a razor blade, resulting in infections that can be severe. Sexual activity becomes something feared and extremely painful, and can involve either being torn or cut open for penile penetration. Post-childbirth stitching is sometimes used to restore the closure of the vagina and can take place following each delivery. FGM/C is practised in many countries in sub-Saharan Africa, in some Middle Eastern countries, and in South Asia. Migrants or refugees from countries which observe this tradition have carried the practice with them to new locations, continuing the practice either through local cutters or by returning girls to their original countries at the chosen age for cutting. Increasingly states are outlawing this practice, in both African countries and Western countries receiving migrants from the practising states, such as France (see Winter 1994 for discussion of this debate in France) and the UK.

It was less common in the last decade of the twentieth century than previously to hear widespread and explicit defences of FGM/C. Considered an inherent part of ethnic or cultural identity and essential to the construction of womanhood, FGM/C has been seen as pivotal to the continuation of a group's very existence; there is a belief that 'the abolition of the surgical element in this custom means to the Gikuyu the abolition of the whole institution' (Kenyatta 1938/1979:133).[7] Kenyatta wrote that opponents of the practice, especially Europeans, criticised the tradition from a position of ignorance and prejudice; it was important to understand the context in which the surgery takes place and the significance it has in the cultural practices of the tribe. Education, he argued, was the way forward but 'the best way was to leave the people concerned free to choose what custom was best suited to their changing conditions' (Kenyatta 1938/1979:132). Kenyatta was writing in the 1930s but the issues he identified continue to shape the nature of more recent differences of approach: is FGM/C a cultural tradition to be understood and determined by those who practise it or a violation that must be stopped? Is FGM/C a problem to be outlawed or an essential aspect of a group's identity that should remain intact or be approached with great caution?

At the Copenhagen conference in 1985 FGM/C was brought up as an issue by Western feminists. Some African women's groups responded angrily to what they saw as a critique of African customs by Western, white women. These African women felt compelled to defend their culture, and felt that the Western women had not acted in solidarity with them but had simply judged their traditions. This led to a stalemate in which public and international debate was notable by its absence. However, by the time of the Beijing conference in 1995 African women's groups and the Inter-African Committee on Traditional Practices Affecting the Health of Women and Children (IAC) (Ras-Work 1998) were active in advocating against FGM/C.

There is little debate in contemporary times as to whether FGM/C should continue. At the international level it is commonly referred to as a 'harmful traditional practice' (by the UN, WHO, etc) and therefore something which should be eradicated. More recent debates have tended to focus on the legitimacy and credibility of various actors in challenging the practice. Of note is the fact that one of the most significant actors against FGM/C—the IAC—hails from Africa. With member committees in 26 African countries, the IAC is prominent in conducting training, running educational campaigns in the media and in schools, and providing alternative employment for traditional cutters. The Committee has also encouraged legislators to introduce appropriate legislation and has advocated inclusions of FGM/C into regional agreements, such as the Addis Ababa Declaration on the Rights of Women.

[7] *He appears to refer here both to the initiation ritual and to the very tribal identity itself.*

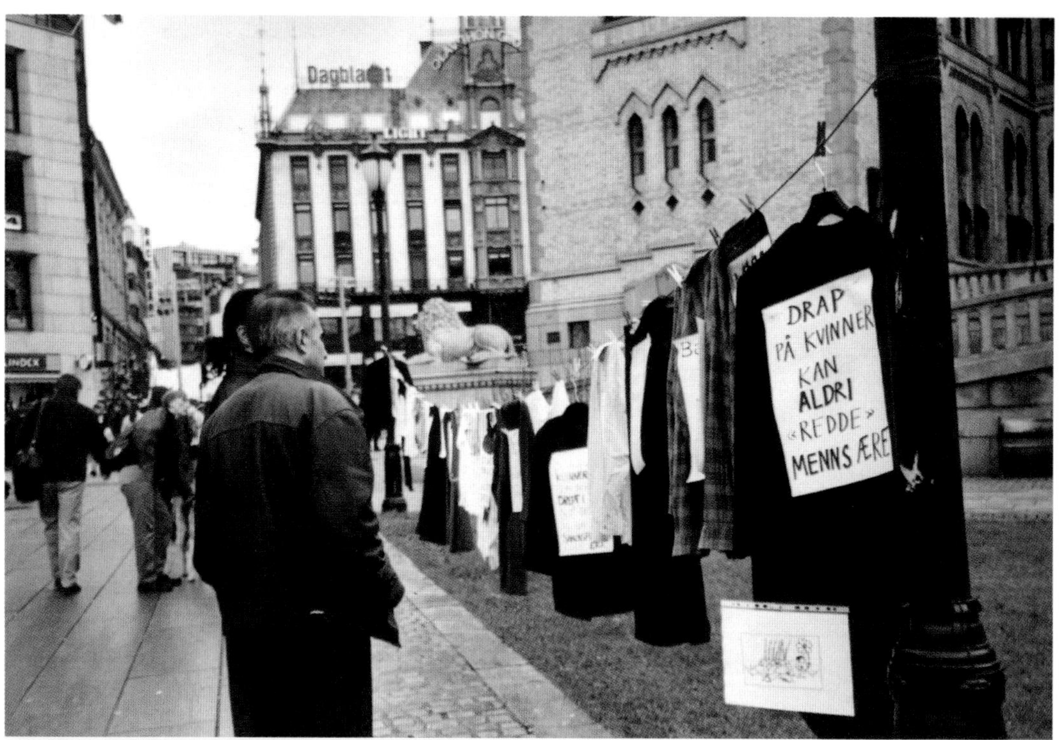

This manifestation outside the Norwegian parliament aimed to bring public attention to the 'dirty laundry' of violence against women. The poster on the first dress says 'Killing women can never save the honour of men'. © Purna Sen.

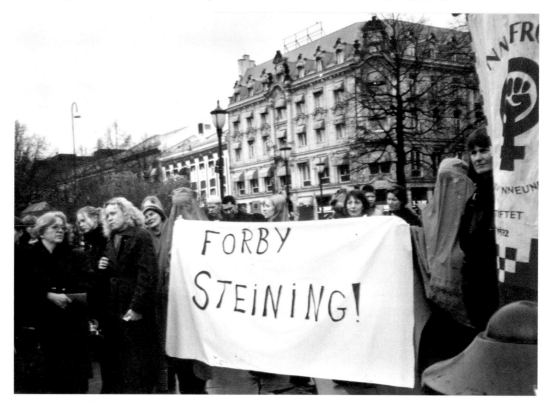

Demonstration in Oslo as part of the 'dirty laundry' campaign. The banner says 'Forbid Stoning'. © Purna Sen.

FGM/C has become accepted as a health issue, with the WHO having major programmes on this area of work. Fifteen years after the divisions at Copenhagen the organisations leading the movement against FGM are either African-based or, if Western, tend to be headed by African women. Some of the active NGOs include the Foundation for Women's Health Research and Development (FORWARD), International Planned Parenthood Federation (IPPF), Amnesty International, Equality Now, Research Action and Information Network for the Bodily Integrity of Women (RAINBOW), and the international FGM Networking Project.

The defence of the practice is no longer absolute, though it can be found in muted forms in arguments about cultural integrity and traditions that have to be *understood*, not necessary left intact. Under debate at the start of the twenty-first century is the variety of approaches used to tackle FGM/C, who should be involved, and whether each has been successful. Is the appropriate intervention public education on the harmful results, criminalisation of the cutters, or the development of alternative initiation rites? The present focus is upon evaluating the many intervention projects that have been undertaken.

There is considerable defensiveness and anger in some states and organisations that Islam is considered to provide the justification for a practice they consider un-Islamic but traditional

'Honour' crimes

The term 'crimes of honour' is predominantly used to refer to actions in which lost family, or tribe, or clan honour is reclaimed through curtailing the actions, or life, of someone who has brought dishonour. These are found in societies where an honour code operates and is a major organising principle of social life. Significant elements of the honour code are played out through the bodies and behaviours of women and girls, through limits on their friendships, movements, and sexual lives. Mixing in the 'wrong' company, spending time with a male outside the family, and so on can be enough to dishonour a girl or woman's family and can result in her being confined to the home, being married off, or being killed as the means of restoring that honour. It is men's actions that restore honour. In countries where these codes operate, legal provisions reflect these values, often containing recognition that 'honour' is a motive behind what is otherwise a crime and permitting a reduction of sentence where the honour principle is shown.

Such countries are often predominantly Muslim; in Western eyes 'honour' crimes have become conflated with Islam. But scholars of Islam (Abdullahi An-Na'im, Centre of Islamic and Middle Eastern Laws, CIMEL) and religious leaders have in many instances stated that Islam does not authorise such killings. Honour crimes came to the attention of Western countries and activists late in the twentieth century, at a time when other dynamics hostile to Islam have also grown in strength. A documentary on 'crimes of honour' shown on US television in 2000 opened with an image of a mosque and the sound of the call to prayer. Such simple equations between religion and violence against women in this context have done considerable damage both to indigenous struggles against 'crimes of honour' (which can be strong, as in Jordan and Pakistan) and to international coalitions that seek to address this issue.

There is considerable defensiveness and anger in some states and organisations that Islam is considered to provide the justification for a practice they consider un-Islamic but traditional. However, much of this view is located within the governmental or religious sectors rather than within the anti-violence movement. In the movement, there is more of a consensus that 'honour' crimes and killings are forms of violence that cannot be tolerated and that legal provisions which recognise 'honour' as a mitigating defence should be ended (for example, Women for Women's Human Rights—Turkey, Women Living Under Muslim Laws—international network, Kurdish Women Action against Honour Killings, Lebanese Council to Resist Violence Against Women, National Jordanian Campaign to Eliminate 'Honour Crimes'). Within the movement against violence there is a debate about the transferability of the concept of 'honour' crimes to non-Islamic contexts where similar defences for killing can be found in legal provisions, as is the case in several South American countries. This debate is being explored in cross-country and cross-cultural dialogues, such as that facilitated by the international Project on Strategies to Address 'Crimes of Honour' (CIMEL and Interights URL).

Even fewer voices than is the case with FGM/C today defend the practice of 'honour' killings. If the phases through which resistance to violence travels involve explicit defence of violence, challenge to this view, and then an end to the public acceptability, then discourse on 'honour' killings seems to have moved into the last of those phases. This is less true of other crimes of 'honour', such as forced marriage, control of movement and friendships, and so on. However, unlike the case of FGM/C, today there is a considerable degree of sensitivity to intervention in (predominantly Islamic) cultures by the West. This interest in and condemnation of what has been interpreted as an Islamic cultural practice has come at the same time as the rise in Islamophobia in the 1990s and the 'war on terror' in the 2000s. Some of the interest from the West has been extremely clumsy and has undoubtedly equated the tradition with Islam, in ignorance or rejection of Islamic scholars who have demonstrated that there is no religious basis to this tradition. Polarisation and stalemate have set into the debate; for example, the Commission on the Status of Women in March 2003 failed to reach an agreed resolution on violence against women because of intractable disagreements over the use of culture as a barrier to addressing violence (Freeburg 2003).

It is not clear at this time how this debate will progress. The women's movement is strong and unequivocal in condemning 'honour' killings and seeking legal and social changes to reflect an intolerance of such practices. Some governments, on the other hand, although not defending the practice, are strongly resisting pressures to change.

Some important themes run through these cleavages and emerge in other areas of work within the movement. One concerns dialogues across cultures—whether and how these can respect tradition and heritage rather than slipping into cultural imperialism. Another concerns how violence is to be understood. Both themes will continue to need attention and will have to be worked through within the movement.

Remaining Challenges

An overview of the work of the movement in challenging violence against women reveals stories of considerable successes. Elements of the struggle are waged at national and regional levels and some at a global level. The last are of special interest as they pose the greatest challenge for working cohesively, yet also provide some of the most remarkable achievements. Highly organised lobby groups, agendas, and networks have effectively taken women's experiences, clarified the responses considered appropriate, and taken these strategies forward to governmental audiences. Although governmental initiatives have built upon and in turn enabled international networking, NGO events have been critical in the development of effective international organising within this movement.

The international movement to end violence against women continues to experience internal challenges, as well as ongoing battles with governments to effect real change, beyond rhetorical commitments, in the lives of women. Considerable successes have been achieved, with national governments and at the global level. Challenges do remain.

The story of the international movement to end violence against women is undoubtedly one of success but it has not been without opposition. Naming acts and behaviours as violence can itself invite controversy, as to do so will require those actions to be condemned—few will publicly defend actions that are considered violent. Governments have often been resistant to pressure from the movement to specify time frames for action plans to eradicate violence. The language used in the strategy sections of agreements has consistently been watered down by official delegations. The movement lobbies hard to have governments commit to taking actions, reviewing policies and laws, providing training and so on; but resistance is strong and the final draft tends to be 'states will consider...'. The movement will need to turn these weaknesses into *real* changes in order to make a difference in the lives of women.

The movement against violence is vast in scale and in the range of issues it seeks to address. Indeed, to describe it as one movement may suggest greater cohesion than exists. The commonality that unites is an absolute shared commitment to ending women's experiences of violence—in war, at home, at work, in community and public life, by the state, and so on. There is a broad agreement on what these forms of violence are—but some divisions appear to be intractable. This is not unexpected, nor is it essential to overcome every disagreement that exists. Debate and disagreement can be productive.

But they can also become vitriolic. Where debate has become division, as in the case of the sex industry, contact between various positions can end. The sex industry polarisation seems to me to be the most fundamental divide in the movement, which on other issues still engages in discussion. The sex industry divide will continue, with little contact and with one side or the other having ascendancy in policy and legal influence—perhaps alternating over time and place. Currently the abolitionist argument appears to be on the rise. With the testimonies of women abused in the industry receiving increasing public attention across the world, this trend may continue for some time.

Debate and disagreement within the movement can be productive. But they can also become vitriolic. Where debate has become division, as in the case of the sex industry, contact between various positions ends

The debates over cultural differences have a slightly different character. The discontinuities and lack of cross-cultural learning possibilities posited by some do risk closing down dialogue. However, this does not seem to be taking place. The arguments for cultural closure are more influential among those opposing the adoption of human rights principles (as in the 'Asian values' view) than they are among those who want to end violence. So those who most strongly promote the cultural divisions argument are not allied to those who want to end the violence. This may help to ensure that dialogues across cultures continue to seek shared understandings, collective and solidarity approaches to the common agenda of ending violence.

Religion-based oppositions to the human rights of women remain a significant challenge, not simply because they exist but because they are gaining in strength and finding increasing numbers of allies in governments. This makes them increasingly powerful (see Chapter 7). The anti-violence movement will continue to contest their politics and actions and will certainly be united in doing so. The agenda of these groups privileges an attack on women but does not limit itself to this; the Christian right, for example, promotes the teaching of creationist history in schools. This means that alliances between the women's movement and others who are in opposition to these groups is possible. Indeed, they may be necessary to defeat this lobby.

Finally, a considerable challenge remains for the movement and at all levels of work to address violence: the domination of the field by lawyers and legal thinking. Two important factors have contributed to this situation. First of all, a major demand from activists in many countries has been for violence against women to be named and treated as crimes at the national level. How this should be done, what shape judicial procedures should take, and the drafting of laws has been the preserve of lawyers, inside and outside the movement. Second, the international agitation on violence has been allied with human rights discourse and frameworks. At the international level human rights are seen as a question of law: what protections should exist, how documents should be worded, what redress is possible, and so on. Again, lawyers take a leading role in these discussions and render much of the debate legal-technical—with a tendency to exclude or marginalise non-lawyers.

The progress made in legal domains has in some places been considerable and in others less so (Women, Law and Development International 1996; 1998). However, for substantive changes in women's lives such that violence is reduced and eliminated, a raft of policy domains beyond the law need to be engaged. These include safe housing, community intolerance of violence, enforceable codes of practice at places of employment and study, adequate welfare systems, prevention work, and awareness raising. These are social policy considerations and such measures should complement the appropriate legal structures that have been the primary consideration to date. In order for the movement to be even more successful, this particular challenge will need to be grasped and will require a shift not only in the nature of the debates but also in the expertise of those involved in international and national struggle. The task, therefore, is to take back the agenda from lawyers and locate it within a social policy arena. This will involve a major shift both in concepts and in institutional arrangements and the dynamics of the movement in which lawyers continue to play a major role. Such a shift in personnel and expertise will no doubt cause friction. However, this could be a democratising process and allow spaces for a less exclusive set of conversations.

References

Amnesty International (2002). *Annual Report*. London: Amnesty International.

Ang-Lygate, M., Corrin, C., and Henry, M. (eds) (1997). *Desperately Seeking Sisterhood*. Basingstoke: Taylor and Francis Ltd.

Axel, D., Marrow, M., and Hall-Martinez, K. (1997). 'Women's Caucus on International Cooperation'. *The International Criminal Court Monitor (Special Edition)*. December: 8 <http://www.iccnow.org/publications/monitor/06se/monitor06se.199712.pdf>.

Badran, M. (1995). *Feminists, Islam, and Nation: Gender and the Making of modern Egypt*. Princeton, NJ: Princeton University Press.

Basu, A. (2003). *Women's Struggle: A history of the All India Women's Conference, 1927–2002*. Delhi: Manohar.

Brasileiro, A. (ed.) (1997). *Women Against Violence–Breaking the Silence*. New York: UNIFEM.

Butalia, U. (1998). 'The Women's Movement in India: Action and Reflection' <http://www.twnside.org.sg/title/india1-cn.htm>.

CATW (Coalition Against Trafficking in Women) (2002). *CATW Report 2001* North Amherst, MA: CATW.

– (2003). *CATW Report 2002*. North Amherst, MA: CATW.

CIMEL (Centre of Islamic and Middle Eastern Laws) and Interights. 'Combating "crimes of honour" through data, documentation, networking and development' <http://www2.soas.ac.uk/honourcrimes/>.

CLADEM (Latin American and Caribbean Committee for the Defence of Women's Rights) <http://www.cladem.org/english/>.

Coomaraswamy, R. (2003). *Integration of the Human Rights of Women and the Gender Perspective. Violence Against Women* (Report of the Special Rapporteur on Violence Against Women). UN Economic and Social Council. E/CN.4/2003/75 of 6 January.

Corrin, C. (ed.) (1996*). Women in a Violent World: Feminist Analysis and Resistance Across 'Europe'*. Edinburgh: Edinburgh University Press.

CRLP (Centre for Reproductive Law and Policy). 'Global Gag Rule: Endangering Women's Health and Democracy' <http://www.reproductiverights.org/hill_int_ggr.html>.

CWGL (Centre for Women's Global Leadership) 16 days <http://www.cwgl.rutgers.edu/16_days_pages/16_days_home.html>.

Datar, C. (ed.) (1993). *The Struggle Against Violence*. Calcutta: Stree.

Davies, M. (ed.) (1994). *Women and Violence: Realities and Responses Worldwide*. London: Zed Books.

Dorkenoo, E. and Elworthy, S. (1992). *Female Genital Mutilation: Proposals for Change*. London: Minority Rights Group.

Freeburg, E. (2003). 'UN Pact Sinks on Issue of Violence Against Women'. Women's ENews 24 March <http://www.womensenews.org/article.cfm?aid=1304>.

GAATW (Global Alliance Against Trafficking in Women) <http://www.thai.net/gaatw/>.

Glasius, M. (2002). 'Expertise in the Cause of Justice: Global Civil Society Influence on the Statute for the an International Criminal Court'. In Marlies Glasius, Mary Kaldor, and Helmut Anheier (eds), *Global Civil Society 2002*. Oxford: Oxford University Press.

Government of India (1993). *Indian Penal Code, 1860 (Act No 45 of 1860)*. New Delhi: Orient Law House.

– (2000). *Crime in India 2000*. New Delhi: National Crime Records Bureau.

Heise, L., Elsberg, M., and Gottemoeller, M.(1999). *Ending Violence Against Women*. Baltimore, MD: Centre for Communications Programmes Johns Hopkins University School of Public Health.

Human Rights Watch (1995). *Violence against Women in South Africa*. New York: Humans Rights Watch.

– (1999). 'UN Executions Envoy Threatened With Death'. Press Release. 14 April. <http://www.hrw.org/press/1999/apr/pak1404.htm>

– (2000). *Seeking Protection*. New York: Human Rights Watch.

The Independent (Dhaka) <http://www.independent-bangladesh.com/news/oct/28/28102002cr>.

Jayawardena, K. (1995). *The White Woman's Other Burden: Western Women and South Asia during British Colonial Rule*. New York: Routledge.

– and De Alwis, M. (eds) (1997). *Embodied Violence: Communalising Women's Sexuality in South Asia*. London: Zed Books.

Johnson, H. (1996). *Dangerous Domains: Violence Against Women in Canada*. Scarborough, Ontario: Nelson Canada.

Kenyatta, J. (1938/1979). *Facing Mount Kenya: The Tribal Life of the Kikuyu*. London: Heinemann.

Kerr, J. (ed.) (1993). *Ours by Right*. London: Zed Books.

Kumar, R. (1993). *The History of Doing: An Illustrated Account of Movements for Women's Rights and Feminism in India, 1800–1990*. New Delhi: Kali for Women.

List of ECOSOC/Beijing and New Accredited NGOs that Attended the Special Session of the General Assembly'Women 2000: Gender Equality, Development and Peace for the Twenty-first Century'. <http://www.un.org/womenwatch/daw/followup/b5ngo.htm>.

McNulty, J. (1999). 'Activist to Discuss Sex Trafficking of Children'. <http://www.ucsc.edu/oncampus/currents/98-99/02-22/traffic.htm>.

Mameli, P. *Interpol, Europol and the Transnational Sex Industry.* <http://www.aqpv.ca/diffusion/textes/mnopqr_t/Mameli_pa.pdf>

Maiti Nepal (1997). *Report on Cross Border Workshop on Girl Trafficking.* Birtamod, Jhapa, Nepal, 8–10 April <http://www.maitinepal.org/report2.htm>

Manushi: A Journal About Women and Society (Delhi) <http://free.freespeech.org/manushi/>.

Mercy, J. et al. (1993). 'International Injuries'. In A. Mashaly, P. Graitcer, and Z. Youssef (eds). *Injury in Egypt: An Analysis of Injuries as a Health Problem.* Cairo: Rose el Youssef New Press.

NCRB (National Crime Records Bureau) 1999. *Crime in India.* Ministry of Home Affairs.

Ras-Work, B. (1998). *FGM: A Holistic and Realistic Approach, Proceedings of the Expert Meeting on Female Genital Mutilation.* Ghent, November.

Robinson, M. <http://www.iccwomen.org/>.

Russell, D. and Van de Ven, N. (eds) (1976). *Crimes Against Women: Proceedings of the International Tribunal on crimes against Women.* Millbrae, CA: Les Femmes.

Sen, G. (2003). 'Abortion at the APPC, or How the Right Wing Fell on its Face!' *DAWN Supplement for the World Social Forum*, January <http://www.dawn.org.fj/global/health/gitasenjan03.html>.

Sinha, M., Guy, D., and Woollacott, A. (1999). *Feminisms and Internationalism.* Oxford: Blackwell.

Sisterhood Is Global Institute (1999). 'Human Rights Advocates Threatened in Pakistan'. 15 April. <http://www.sigi.org/Alert/pak0499.htm>.

South Africa. Police Service (2001). 'Rape and Attempted Rape in the RSA for the Period January to September 1994 to 2001'. <http://www.saps.gov.za/8_crimeinfo/200112/crime/rape.htm>.

Steains, C. (1999). 'Gender Issues'. In R. Lee (ed.), *The International Criminal Court: The Making of the Rome Statute – Issues, Negotiations, Results.* The Hague: Kluwer Law International.

United Kingdom. Home Office (1999). *Criminal Statistics England & Wales 1999.* <http://www.archive.official-documents.co.uk/menu/byhoff.htm>.

– (2002). *British Crime Survey*, July. <http://www.homeoffice.gov.uk/rds/pdfs2/hosb702.pdf>

UNGA (United Nations General Assembly) (1979). *Convention on the Elimination of All Forms of Discrimination against Women.* A/RES34/180 of 18 December 1979.

– (1993). *Declaration on the Elimination of Violence against Women.* A/RES/48/104 of 20 December 1993.

– (1998). *Advancement of Women: Trafficking in Women and Girls: Report of the Secretary-General.* 53rd Session. Agenda Item 103. September.

– (2001). *Protocol to Prevent, Suppress and Punish Trafficking in Persons, especially Women and Children, Supplementing the United Nations Convention against Transnational Organized Crime.* A/RES/55/25 of 15 November 2000.

UNWire (2003). 'Magazine Cites Advances By Anti-Abortion Groups' . 14 January <http://www.unfoundation.org/unwire/util/display_stories.asp?objid=31393>.

United Nations (2001). *Beijing Declaration and the Platform for Action 1995.* New York: Dept. of Public Information, UN.

– CEDAW (Committee on the Elimination of the Discrimination Against Women) <http://www1.umn.edu/humanrts/gencomm/generl19.htm>.

Walker, A. (2002). *Initiatives and Activities of Women Worldwide.* IWTC Women's Globalnet #212, 23 October <http://www.iwtc.org/212.html>.

WCGJ (Women's Caucus for Gender Justice) <http://www.iccwomen.org>.

WHO (World Health Organisation) (2002). *World Report and Violence and Health.* Geneva: WHO.

Winter, B. (1994). 'Women the Law and Cultural Relativism in France: The Case of Excision'. *SIGNS: A Journal of Women, Culture and Society*, 19: 939–74.

WLUML (Women Living Under Muslim Laws) (2002). 'USA: Call For Action - Polygamy-Related Abuses in Utah, 15 February' <http://www.wluml.org/english/alerts/2002/usa/polygamy-utah.htm>.

Women, Law and Development International (1996). *State Responses to Domestic Violence: Current Status and Needed Improvements.* Washington, DC: The Institute for Women, Law and Development

– (1998). *State Responses to Rape.* Washington, DC: The Institute for Women, Law and Development.

Part III: Infrastructure of Global Civil Society

Chapter 7

Religious and Nationalist Militant Groups

Mary Kaldor and Diego Muro

Is Al Qaeda or the Mafia part of global civil society? Can a movement that uses violence and extortion be put in the same box as Amnesty International, Friends of the Earth, or the World Social Forum? And what about those groups that use violence but claim that they are aiming at a greater good or acting in self-defence? What about movements such as the Mexican Zapatistas from Chiapas or the Kosovar Liberation Army (KLA)? Should they be rejected on the same grounds as Al Qaeda or the Mafia? In other words, can we establish a clear criterion to decide which groups are part of global civil society and which are not? And, most importantly, can we find a definition that does not heavily rely on subjective opinion?

In our first Yearbook, we defined global civil society for operational purposes as 'the sphere of ideas, values, institutions, organisations, networks, and individuals located *between* the family, the state and the market, and operating *beyond* the confines of national societies, polities, and economies' (Anheier, Glasius, and Kaldor 2001: 17). According to this definition, surely we have to include groups like Al Qaeda, what we might call the 'dark' side of global civil society. Yet the concept of global civil society also has a normative content. Historically, civil society has been about minimising violence in everyday relations, about finding ways to debate and negotiate about public affairs, and to agree on rules, making use of reason in place of fear and superstition. Moreover, the concept was based on an assumption of human equality. Most scholars, like John Keane for example, would exclude violent or intolerant groups from the definition of global civil society (Keane 2001: 39). Others, like Richard Falk (1998), argue that the role of global civil society is to democratise the public sphere; his distinction between 'globalisation from above' and 'globalisation from below' refers to state power and citizens' power respectively. If we accept the normative content of global civil society, should we not exclude anti-democratic groups?

In earlier times, when the boundaries of civil society were territorial, it was easier to distinguish between peaceful societies in, for example, north-western Europe, where violence was more or less excluded from domestic public affairs, and uncivil coercive societies in other parts of the world. Even so, what Jeffrey Alexander (2000: 100) calls 'actually existing civil society' was always intertwined with war, 'the ultimate expression of relationships of an uncivil kind'. Nowadays, when civil societies operate beyond borders, it is even harder to draw a distinction between what is civil and what is uncivil. Are groups that use violence in self-defence uncivil? Are groups that advocate exclusion themselves to be excluded from the democratic discourse? Are groups that claim that sacred law overrides scientific reason necessarily 'uncivil'? Should we tolerate the intolerant?

In this chapter, we take the view that these questions have to be discussed but cannot be definitively answered. However, a Yearbook about global civil society has to describe and analyse those groups that are at least on the margin of a normative definition of global civil society. We are particularly interested in religious and nationalist militant groups that operate beyond borders or have transnational links and that do appear to have increased over the last decade. The destruction of the World Trade Towers on 11 September 2001 drew global attention to a new transnational terrorist phenomenon. Yet Al Qaeda and other groups that use violence need to be seen as part of a wider political phenomenon that has generated violence and exclusion in many parts of the world as well as mobilising large numbers of people. Some of these groups are clearly 'uncivil'; others less so. Since it is difficult to make an arbitrary distinction between the civil and the uncivil, this chapter addresses the broader phenomenon of religious and nationalist militant groups.

Of particular interest for a Yearbook like *Global Civil Society 2003* is the relationship of these groups to globalisation. To what extent is the growth of these groups a reaction to globalisation? Do they gain or lose from globalisation? To use the categories of Chapter 1, are they rejectionists? Or are they regressive or redistributive globalisers? In what follows, we outline the development of these groups over the last two decades and some of their key characteristics, with the aim of clarifying at least some of these questions.

Analysing Religious and Nationalist Militant Groups

Before describing some of the main characteristics of religious and nationalist movements, it is useful to take into account some analytical and definitional considerations. By religious and nationalist militant groups, we mean groups that are politically active in support of religious or nationalist goals. For nationalists, this is self-evident; to be a nationalist is to claim political power for the nation. For religious groups, it is less obvious. Many religious groups are non-political—the Amish, for example—and many are active politically in causes that they share with other religions or with secular groups. The groups we cover may be concerned about democracy or development but only as a secondary issue; their primary preoccupation is the political promotion of a particular religious or nationalist ideology.

Some argue that there is no such thing as a moderate nationalist or religious militant and indeed that all ideologies contain the potential for extremism in specific contexts. It is obviously the case that nationalist and religious ideologies tend to be based on certainties that override the use of reason in some cases, on assumptions of spirituality that may not always conform to secular logic and run counter to the assumptions of the Enlightenment that rationality would eventually triumph over religion. It is also the case, however, that it is possible to point to liberal, tolerant, or emancipatory versions of religious and nationalist militancy. Nationalism, for example, provided the base for French revolutionaries to overthrow the *ancien régime*. It also provided the African and Asian decolonisation struggles of the 1960s and 1970s with the necessary ideology to fight for independence. In established nation-states, it is argued that nationalism provides citizens with a sense of national identity, which increases societies' cohesiveness. In those cases, nationalism is often described as patriotism. Even for liberals like Will Kymlicka (1995) or David Miller (1996) the nation can be the building block on which a multicultural society can be constructed.

Similar examples of progressive religious groups can also be identified. In *Global Civil Society 2002* Abdullahi An-Na'im (2002) analysed the role of religion in global civil society. He referred to religious ideas like liberation theology, Gandhianism, or liberal Islam, which are militant about emancipatory secular causes like poverty, non-violence, or human rights. There are many religious groups that are engaged, for example, in humanitarian issues or, like the Quakers, in advocacy for peace or democracy. Most religions preach doing good and being moral in order to gain internal peace; and this usually implies helping others even from different religions and ethnic groups.

Characteristics of extreme militant groups

We take it as given that not all nationalist and religious militant groups are extremist. But our focus in this chapter is on such groups, often located at the margins of society.

By 'extreme', we mean:

1. groups that use violent means. These range from terrorism, violent incidents against civilians, and communal riots, to full-scale armed conflict;
2. groups that are exclusive: that is, they exclude other nationalities or religions in ways that range from discrimination to ethnic cleansing and, in the worst instance, to genocide. Exclusion is typical of ethnic nationalists, who claim the right to citizenship on the sole basis of ethnicity; and
3. groups that are 'fundamentalist'. By 'fundamentalist' we mean groups that are inflexible about their doctrines and try to impose these doctrines on others. Normally, fundamentalism refers to religion, but it can also apply to nationalism or, indeed, to other secular ideologies like Stalinism or extreme forms of neo-liberalism.

Not all the groups we study meet all three of these criteria. On the contrary, it is possible to identify tensions and dichotomies among these criteria that distinguish different groups. One dichotomy is between identity politics and missionary politics. For some groups, the goal is political power on the basis of 'label'. This is what is meant by 'identity politics'. Such groups are campaigning for political power in the name of a particular group, whether nationalist

Man at prayer in a synagogue on a settlement in the West Bank. © Chris Tordai/Panos Pictures

or religious. The militants argue that they have a right to power because they are Serb, Muslim, Buddhist, or whatever; they use the language of self-determination and collective rights. They are not interested in converting others to their beliefs or in implementing particular policies related to ethnicity or religion. Bosnian Muslims, for example, tend to be secular; the term 'Muslim' refers to their group identity, not to their beliefs. For other groups, those who could be described as conforming to 'missionary politics', the aim is to introduce religious or national practices—for example, shariah law, anti-abortion laws, or the use of particular national languages. In practice, this distinction is not necessarily clear-cut. Those who are, first and foremost, interested in power on the basis of labels may need to adopt certain policies and practices to justify their claim to power. Those who are more inclined to a missionary position must seek power in order to implement their policies.

A second dichotomy is between fundamentalists and fanatics. Fundamentalists, as defined above, are those who take their doctrines seriously. The term originated in the United States in the 1920s among Protestants who wanted to revive Christian faith in the face of growing secularism, in a series of pamphlets entitled *The Fundamentals of the Faith* (see, for example Marty and Appleby 1994). It is perfectly possible to be a fundamentalist and to oppose all forms of violence or reject all forms of political power. Fanatics, on the other hand, are those who are most militant, who pursue their causes with great zeal. Those who act fanatically and who use violence are often not the most fundamentalist. A good example of the distinction between fundamentalists and fanatics is that between Gush Emunim and the Haredim. Gush Emunim is a militant settler group; the aim is to recreate Biblical Israel, and members of Gush Emunim use violence to pursue that aim. It was they who attacked the Cave of the Patriarchs in Hebron, thought to be the burial ground of Abraham, Isaac and Jacob and their wives, but now a mosque. And it was they who planned to blow up the Dome of the Rock. In contrast, the Haredim, ultra-orthodox Jews in Jerusalem and abroad, oppose Zionism and the use of violence. They want to preserve their privileges in Jerusalem and not expand into the West Bank. Rabbi Hirsch, one of the Haredim scholars, has attacked Zionism as a 'folly of human arrogance': 'Notwithstanding the fact that they are religious and devout and uphold the commandments, the people of

Gush Emunim seem to be impatient with God's "incompetence" to ingather the exiles and therefore they have taken things into their own hands. According to Jewish theology, however, taking divine things into martial hands can only be catastrophic' (quoted in Marty and Appleby 1992: 96). Hirsch describes himself as a 'Palestinian who is fighting [the state of] Israel'. He has advised the Palestinian delegation to the peace talks and hopes to be Minister of Jewish affairs in a future Palestinian state (quoted in Marty and Appleby 1992: 97).

Yet another distinction is between particularist and universalist aspirations. Are these groups, particularly religious groups, aiming at the universal spread of their religion? Or are they concerned about access to power for particular groups as opposed to others? Nationalism tends to be particularist, although the notion that the world has to be divided into ethnically pure nations is a universalist aspiration. Religious ideologies appear to be more universalist—political Islam, for example—yet often religious groups are concerned with rights for their own groups rather than with the spread of their philosophy.

Contrary to the assumption of the enlightenment, that modernity ultimately will displace religion, organised religion continues to grow

Why study religious and nationalist militants together?

On the face of it, religious and nationalist ideologies appear to be very different. While religion tends to be cosmic and is about the 'other world', nationalism tends to be about this world. What is then the point of having them both in this chapter? There are three main reasons. First, it can be argued that both nationalism and religion perform similar functions, a point that has been made by Carlton Hayes (1960) and what we may call the Durkheimian School. For them, nationalism is a political religion, a secularised religion. Also of this view was Elie Kedourie (1960), who argued that nationalist movements often use religious elements to mobilise the masses in a similar way to religion. Nationalists, then, are secular parishioners who want to build a nationalist heaven on earth. In a different tone, Anthony D. Smith (2000) has also established the similarities between the two ideologies by pointing out the 'sacred' dimension of nationalism. Nationalism like religion arouses passion and emotion that goes beyond rational argument.

Second, there are considerable overlaps among nationalist and religious groups. Is Hindu nationalism a religious or a nationalist movement? Are Protestants and Catholics in Northern Ireland religious militants or nationalists of differing hues? And what about the different nationalisms that could be found in the former Yugoslavia? Most of them define themselves in religious terms: Serbs are Christian Orthodox; Croatians are Catholic, and Bosniaks are Muslim. In *The Origins of Totalitarianism*, Hannah Arendt (1968) describes how Jews were transformed from a religious minority into an ethnic group as part of the nineteenth-century European process of constructing nations. Something very similar happened to the Muslims of Bosnia Herzegovina, to Catholics and Protestants in Northern Ireland, or to Hindus and Muslims in South Asia.

Third, religious and nationalist militant groups have to be understood as counter-constructions of modernity. As many scholars have pointed out, these groups are not relics or throwbacks to the past. On the contrary, they are as much a part of modernity as the liberal secular projects that they tend to oppose. Religious and nationalist counter projects—'enemies of the Enlightenment'—are part of the story of modernity. In the context of revolutionary France, Darrin M. McMahon (2001) has explored the Catholic Counter-Enlightenment from the mid-eighteenth century to the beginning of the nineteenth century. Some of these authors, McMahon points out, warned well before the excesses of the French Revolution that the Enlightenment 'augured regicide, anarchy, and the annihilation of religion'. Much of the history of nineteenth century Europe could be described as the confrontation between liberalism and absolutism, with the latter defending religion and the traditional way of life. In the twentieth century many of these religious movements came to be called 'fundamentalist'.

Contrary to the assumption of the Enlightenment that modernity ultimately will displace religion, organised religion continues to grow. Over the last one hundred years, the share of the world's population that professes to one of the four major religions (Christianity, Islam, Hinduism, and Buddhism) has risen from 68 per cent to 74 per cent of the world's population. In particular the share of the world's population that is Muslim has risen from 12.5 per cent to 20 per cent. The Christian share of the world's population has remained roughly constant. Church membership has risen in America, dramatically over the last two hundred years although not in recent decades, but has declined in Europe.

Ernest Gellner (1994) has argued that nationalism and Islam, and also Soviet Marxism, are all alternative routes to modernity. Western forms of civil society are by no means an inevitable outcome of modernity; on the contrary, they were constructed through happy chance, and Gellner is sceptical about whether the Western model can be reproduced elsewhere. While we agree that these ideologies are alternative routes to modernity, it is difficult to argue, as Gellner does, that these are separate and distinct. Nationalism and religion, in particular, have to be understood in relation to the Western liberal and consumerist model. It is this mutual dependence of the modern and the anti-modern that is described by Benjamin Barber in *Jihad vs. McWorld* (1995). For Barber, religious and tribal fundamentalism (Jihad) and consumerist capitalism (McWorld) are interdependent and need each other in order to survive.

What is new in the current period about counter-enlightenment projects is globalisation. Both civil society and the extremist groups we describe now cross borders and compete in global space

What is new in the current period about what might be called counter-Enlightenment projects is globalisation. Whereas liberalism and absolutism tended to be geographically distinct, now both civil society and the extremist groups we describe cross borders and compete in global space.

The Rise of Religious and Nationalist Movements

As we have shown in previous Yearbooks, the last two decades have witnessed a tremendous growth of civil society organisations (CSOs). According to Anheier and Themudo (2002: 194), the number of international organisation increased from 13,000 in 1981 to over 47,000 in 2001. This exponential growth has been possible due to globalisation and to people's need to express themselves beyond traditional channels. These new opportunities globalisation offers have been taken by organisations like Greenpeace, Jubilee, and the World Social Forum, but also by Hamas, ETA, or the Liberation Tigers of Tamil Eelam (LTTE). What may be called 'the dark side of global civil society' has also taken the opportunities of globalisation in order to have a say in domestic and international politics. In particular, we have seen the rise of religious violent groups such as Al Qaeda, Kahane Chai, Jemaah Islamiah, or the Abu Sayaf Group.

Table 7.1 provides a selective account of nationalist and religious militant groups. It is not possible to provide a comprehensive list; the aim of the table is to provide an indication of the kind of groups that we describe in this chapter. According to several scholars, the number of religious and ethnic nationalist armed groups has increased in the last twenty years (Coker 2002; Hoffman 2001; Mayer 2001). Certainly most of the groups shown in the table were formed after 1970, although many had their origins in earlier organisations, many of which were formed in the 1920s and 1930s. Thus, the Hindu nationalist family of organisations traces its origins to the founding of the Rastryiya Swayemsevak Sangh (RSS) in 1925. The Muslim Brotherhood founded in Egypt in 1928 is often considered the source of most contemporary Islamist groups. And the nationalist parties in central Europe and the Balkans often reproduce the symbols and language of the pre-war nationalist parties. But these groups seem to have been quiescent during the immediate post Second World War period, and it is only in the last two decades that they have acquired an increased political presence. Nationalist parties captured power in the Balkans, for example, and in India. Islamic parties are ruling in Iran and Turkey and have done well in elections in Pakistan and Algeria, where electoral victory led to a military coup. In western Europe, right-wing anti-immigrant parties have increased their share of the vote and in the United States Christian fundamentalist and Zionist groups are increasingly influential in the Republican Party. Dramatic examples include the French presidential elections of 2002, when Jean Marie Le Pen

Table 7.1: Selected religious and nationalist militant groups

Name/organisation	Type	Primary area(s) of operation	Leader	Goals
Africa				
Civic United Front, CUF	PP	Tanzania	Ibrahim Lipumba	Islamic autonomous Zanzibar
Groupe Islamique Armé, GIA	AG	Algeria	Abdel Rahman al-Zaytouni	Algerian Islamic stat
Interahamwe	AG	Rwanda		Hutu State
Lords Resistance Army, LRA	AG	Uganda (North)	Joseph Kony	Millenniarianism
al-Nahda (Revival)	PP	Tunisia	Sheikh al-Ghannushi	Islamic civil society
Sudan People's Liberation Army, SPLA	AG	Sudan	John Garang	Autonomy for Southern Sudan
Americas				
Christian Coalition	LG	US	Roberta Combs	Christian America
Colonia Dignidad	AG	Chile	Paul Schäfer	Millenarian anti-Semitic & anti-Communist
Asia				
Aleph (formerly Aum Shinrikyo)	S	Japan		Apocalypse
Jamaat-e-Islami Party	N	India, Pakistan, Bangladesh		Muslim unity
Jemaah Islamiyah, JI	AN	Indonesia, Malaysia, Philippines, Singapore	Abu Bakar Ba'asyir; Abdullah Sungkar	Islamic Asian state
Liberation Tigers of Tamil Eelam, LTTE	AG	Sri Lanka	Velupillai Prabhakaran	Tamil homeland
Parti Islam SeMalaysia, PAS	PP	Malaysia (Kelantan, Terengganu)	Abdul Hadi Awang; (leader) Nik Aziz Nik Mat (spiritual leader)	Malaysian Islamic state
Patani United Liberation Organisation, PULO	AG	Thailand (South)	Tunku Bilor Kortor Nilor	Islamic autonomous state
Rashtryia Swayamsevak Sangh, RSS	SM	India		Hindu nationalism
Shiromani Akali Dal, SAD	PP	India (Punjab)		Sikh state

Abbreviations of types: AG: armed group; AN: armed network; LG: lobby group; N: network; PP: political party; SM : social movement: S:

Source: Global Civil Society Programme database. For comments and suggestions e-mail: kaldor_muro@postmaster.co.uk.

Strategy	Members/ supporters	Founded	Global links	Web page
Protest		1992		www.cuftz.org
Terrorism	200	1992	Al Qaeda	
Genocide; guerilla tactics	Several thousand	1988	Support from Congo	
Extreme violence	7,000		Support from Sudan	
Win votes	Unknown, few		London-based TV station El Zeitouna	
Armed struggle	Tens of thousands	1983	US support through Uganda	
Political support to Republican right; education; broadcasting	Claims 2 million; approx. 300,000 more likely	1989	Likud	www.cc.org
Defends armed colony	300, mostly German	1961	Nazi groups Argentina, Brazil	
Education; terrorism	1,500-2,000	1987		www.aum-shinrikyo.org/
Support Islamic groups	2.2 million	1941		www.jamaat.org
Terrorism	Few hundred	1995	Alleged links to Al Qaeda	http://jemaahislamiah. newstrove.com/
Ethnic violence	8,000-10,000	1972	Tamil Diaspora	www.eelam.com & www.eelamweb.com
Win votes and introduce Islamic law	800,000	1951		www.parti-pas.org/
Ethnic/religious violence		1968		www.pulo.org/
Violence; grass-roots mobilisation		1925		www.rss.org
Parliamentary politics		1920		www.shiromani akalidalmann.org/

Table 7.1: continued

Name/organisation	Type	Primary area(s) of operation	Leader	Goals
Europe				
Democratic Unionist Party, DUP	PP	Northern Ireland	Reverend Ian Paisley	Union with UK
Euzkadi Ta Askatasuna, ETA	AG	Spain, France	Changing leadership	Independent Basque state
Front National, FN	PP	France	Jean Marie Le Pen	Anti-Immigrant
Greater Romanian Party	PP	Romania	Corneliu Vadim Tudor	Greater Romania; anti-Roma; anti-Semitic
Hungarian Justice and Life Party	PP	Hungary	Istvan Csurka	Greater Hungary; anti-Roma
Liberal Democratic Party of Russia	PP	Russia	Zhirinovski	Restore Russia's greatness
Lega Nord	PP	Northern Italy	Umberto Bossi	North Italian autonomy
Real IRA, RIRA	AG	Ireland, UK (Northern Ireland + mainland)	Changing leadership	Union with Ireland
True Slovak National Party	PP	Slovakia	Jan Slota	Anti-Hungarian; anti-Roma; anti-Semitic
Serbian Radical Party	PP	Serbia	Vojislav Seselj, facing charges in The Hague	Greater Serbia
Middle East				
Gush Emunin	SM	Israel	Rabbi Moshe Levinger	Biblical Israel
Hamas	AN	Palestine; Jordan	Sheik Ahmed Yassin	Islamic Palestine state
Hizbollah	AN	Lebanon		Islamic Lebanon
Islamic Jihad	AG	Egypt, Palestine	Mohammed Abdel-Salam Faraq	Pan-Islam
al-Jamaa al-Islamiyya	AN	Egypt	Sheikh Omar Abdel-Rahman	
National Union Israel Beteina	PP	Israel	Avigdor Liberman	Biblical Israel
Kurdish Freedom and Democracy Congress (KADEK), formerly Kurdistan Workers Party, PKK	AG	Turkey	Group leadership, with direction from imprisoned Abdullah Öcalan	Kurdish nationalism
Al Qaeda	AN	International	Osama Bin Laden	Muslim caliphate

Abbreviations of types: AG: armed group; AN: armed network; LG: lobby group; N: network; PP: political party; SM : social movement: S: s

Source: Global Civil Society Programme database. For comments, suggestions, and further information, e-mail: kaldor_muro@postmaster.

Strategy	Members/ supporters	Founded	Global links	Web page
Win votes		1971		www.dup.org.uk
Terrorism	200-500 + supporters	1959		www.basque-red.net
Win votes		1976		www.front-national.com
Win votes	155,000 votes	1991	Front National	
Win votes		1993		www.miep.hu
Win votes				www.ldpr.ru/
Win votes	125,000	1991		www.leganord.org
Terrorism	100-200	1998		
Win votes		1990		www.prava.sns.sk
Win votes; violence	840,000 votes	1991		www.srs.org.yu
Settlements	20,000?	1973	Jewish Diaspora	
Terrorism; grass-roots mobilisation	Unknown members 10,000s sympathisers.	1987	Palestinian Diaspora; Saudi Arabia	www.palestine- info. org/hamas/index.htm
Paramilitary; social services; win votes	Membership 100s; Supporters 1,000s	1982	Worldwide network; support from Syria and Iran	www.hizbollah.org/
Terrorism	Several hundred	1970s	Iran	
Terror; social services	Members 1,000s; sympathisers 1,000s	Late 1970s	Part of Al Qaeda	www.ummah.org.uk/ ikhwan/index.html
Win votes			Jewish Diaspora	
Armed struggle renounced	4,000-5,000	1974	Kurdish Diaspora	www.pkk.org/
Terrorism	Several thousand	Late 1980s	Worldwide network	

unexpectedly passed to the second round with President Jacques Chirac, and the victory of the Lijst Pim Fortuyn in the 2002 Dutch elections, after its leader was assassinated.

As well as electoral influence, religious and nationalist groups are increasingly engaged in major episodes of violence. Western governments emphasise the terrorist threat. But in terms of the scale of violence even more important are the involvement of such groups in communal clashes, wars, and genocide. Table 7.2 shows the scale of deaths in major episodes of violence—wars, communal clashes, and so on—as well as the scale of casualties (dead and wounded) in terrorist incidents. The figures are conservative. Nevertheless, they show that the risks of armed conflict are much greater than the risks of terrorism. Thus, during the last decade, some 8,000 men and boys were massacred by extreme Serb nationalists in Srebrenica in 1995, between 500,000 and 1 million Tutsis were killed by Hutu paramilitary groups in Rwanda in 1994, and some 2,000 Muslims were killed by Hindu extremists in Gujarat in 2002.

There has been shift from ideological causes to religious and nationalist causes. In Europe, for example, 'red terrorism' has almost disappeared

It is difficult to argue that terrorist incidents or major episodes of violence have actually increased in the last two decades. In the whole post-war period, some 5 million people have been killed every decade in wars. But it does seem to be the case that both the actors and the character of the violence have changed. In recent decades, it has become more difficult to distinguish between state and non-state actors. More and more violence spills over borders. And there has been a shift from ideological causes to religious and nationalist causes. In Europe, for example, 'red terrorism' has almost disappeared (see Box 7.1) Nowadays, the overwhelming majority of terrorist or other violent episodes are perpetrated by nationalist and/or religious groups. Moreover, more and more violence is directed against civilians as opposed to enemy forces.

Another change has been the increase in cross-border violence and the geographical dispersal of violence. Because of Diaspora networks, the spread of transnational crime, and the pressures of migration, it is becoming harder to insulate parts of the world, as happened during the Cold War period. This is exemplified in the case of the US, a country that was hardly touched in its own territory by acts of international terrorism but which now feels under threat from outside (Al Qaeda, Axis of Evil, and so on). But the importance of interconnectedness for violence is even greater the other way round. The dramatic growth in support from Diaspora groups in the United States or other industrialised areas for nationalist and religious movements through money and skills and through the use of the new media for mobilisation has undoubtedly had a disproportionate effect on the scale and intensity of violence in their countries of origin. Moreover, the growth of such groups is a more or less a worldwide phenomenon; the United States faces its own home-grown sources of terrorism, like the 'militia movement', the anti-abortion militants, or individuals like Timothy McVeigh, the 'Oklahoma bomber' who blew up a federal government building in 1995.

An exception to this trend is Latin America and the Caribbean. In this region, there has been a steady decline of war and violence since the Second World War. The horrendous 1970s military dictatorships of Chile and Argentina or the civil wars of El Salvador, Nicaragua, and Guatemala in the 1980s are long gone. Non-state violence has also declined, Peru being the best example. The government of the now exiled Alberto Fujimori gave a final coup to the Maoist terrorist group Shining Path by imprisoning its leader Abimael Guzmán in 1992 and heavily weakened the Tupac Amaru Guerrilla after the storming of the Japanese embassy in 1996. Data from RAND (1968–97) and the US Department of State (URL) show there may have been a decline in terrorism in Latin America and the Caribbean during the 1990s. Moreover, it is difficult to find examples of nationalist and religious extremists. There are, of course, still violent episodes like the invasion of Panama in 1989, the civil war in Haiti during the early 1990s, or the continuing fighting in Colombia, which accounts for most of the terrorist incidents in the region in recent years; but they do not tend to involve religion or extreme ethnic nationalism. There are also populists like Chavez in Venezuela; but their ideology is secular and leftist rather than anti-modernist.

In most of the world, however, religious and nationalist militancy does seem to have grown over the last two decades. What are the factors that have

Box 7.1: The decline of 'red terrorism' in western Europe

The decline of socialism as an ideology started in the 1970s and intensified with the collapse of the Soviet Union. Since then, the number of organisations that define themselves as socialist has declined dramatically. In western Europe the decline of socialism has caused the disappearance of the so-called Red Terrorist groups, which threatened numerous government from the 1960s to the 1990s. These groups were found predominantly in industrialised countries and were small urban armed groups guided by Marxism-Leninism. In their view, capitalism and imperialism were the root of all the problems of the proletariat and their role as 'revolutionary vanguard' was to awaken the working class. Their preferred method was the 'armed struggle' as it helped to expose the latent fascism of Western regimes. The ultimate objective of these groups was to overthrow the democratic regimes in their countries of origin and replace them with a vaguely defined 'proletarian dictatorship' (Alexander and Pluchinsky 1992).

The main reason for their decline should be sought in their lack of appeal beyond highly ideological Marxists. These organisations were characterised by their extremely low membership and its concentration in urban areas. It is believed that the German RAF, the Italian *Brigate Rosse*, or the Greek 17N never had more than 40 or 50 hard-core members each. The fact that their strength lay in large cities also made them easier to infiltrate. Hence, the anti-terrorist measures of several Western governments were effective in eliminating these organisations since they had no social support. To date, none of these Red armed groups accomplished their goals and almost all of them have disappeared. Only the Spanish GRAPO and the Greek 17N remain active.

Table 7.2: Red terrorist groups in western Europe

Organisation	Country	Active period	Situation
Rote Armee Fraktion, RAF (Red Army Faction)	Germany	1970–98	Disbanded
Cellules Communistes Combattantes, CCC (Fighting Communist Cells)	Belgium	1984–5	Disbanded
Action Directe, AD (Direct Action)	France	1979–87	Disbanded
Brigate Rosse, BR (Red Brigades)	Italy	1970–88	Disbanded
Forças Populares 25 Abril, FP-25 (Popular Forces of 25 April)	Portugal	1980–86	Disbanded
Grupo Revolucionario Anti-Fascista Primero de Octubre, GRAPO (First of October Anti-Fascist Resistance Groups)	Spain	1975–	Active
Epanastaiki Organosi 17 Noemvri, 17N (Revolutionary Organisation 17 November)	Greece	1975–	Active

contributed to this rise? It is not possible to provide a comprehensive causal explanation but it is possible to point to some common trends. First and perhaps most important is the decline in secular left ideologies, particularly socialism and post-colonial nationalism. For millions of people, disillusion with these ideologies set in long before the end of the Cold War because of authoritarianism, corruption, and the failure to deliver on promises of development. The new militancy developed in response both 'from above' and 'from below'. Political leaders use nationalist and religious appeals when other tools of political mobilisation have failed. Often it was secular leaders who opened the space for these ideologies. Thus the Congress Party in India began to use Hindu rhetoric long before the rise of the Bharatiya Janata Party (BJP). In the former Yugoslavia and Soviet Union, nationalism grew within the administrative confines of the centrally planned

Table 7.3: Major episodes of political violence (MEPVs) 1990–1999 and terrorist incidents 1991–2001

	1990	1991	1992	1993	1994
Africa					
MEPVs	11	16	14	15	16
Deaths	115,000	122,000	118,000	136,000	632,000
Terrorist incidents		5	12	7	25
Deaths and injuries		3	29	1,013	55
Asia					
MEPVs	13	13	9	8	8
Deaths	29,000	22,000	13,000	12,000	12,000
Terrorist incidents		48	13	37	24
Deaths and injuries		150	25	135	71
Middle East					
MEPVs	4	3	2	3	3
Deaths	103,000	53,000	3,000	3,000	4,000
Terrorist incidents		78	79	100	116
Deaths and injuries		33	236	178	256
Europe					
MEPVs	2	3	5	6	5
Deaths	1,000	10,000	61,000	61,000	51,000
Terrorist incidents		199	113	185	88
Deaths and injuries		56	65	117	126
Eurasia					
MEPVs	2	3	3	2	3
Deaths	6,000	7,000	9,000	8,000	24,000
Terrorist incidents		6	3	5	11
Deaths and injuries		7	0	1	151
Latin America					
MEPVs	5	4	4	4	5
Deaths	16,000	11,000	11,000	11,000	24,000
Terrorist incidents		229	143	97	58
Deaths and injuries		68	374	66	329
North America					
Terrorist incidents	0	0	2	1	0
Deaths and injuries	0	0	1	1,006	0
WORLD					
MEPVs	37	42	37	38	40
Deaths	270,000	224,500	214,500	298,000	746,500
Terrorist incidents	375	437	565	363	431
Deaths and injuries		317	730	2,516	988

Source: These figures are calculated from the Major Episodes of Political Violence Database at the Center for Systemic Peace, University of Maryland (URL). The casualty figures are conservative since the database uses a mean of different sources to estimate the numbers of deaths. In this table, the number of casualties for each episode is further averaged over the duration of each episode. The figures on terrorist incidents are taken from the US Department of State (URL). No MEPV figures are available for 2000, 2001.

1995	1996	1997	1998	1999	2000	2001
15	14	15	10	11		
127,000	152,000	154,000	148,000	148,000		
10	11	24	21	53	55	33
8	80	35	5,379	185	102	150
9	10	9	10	10		
16,000	16,000	15,000	16,000	16,000		
16	11	21	49	72	98	33
5,639	1,507	344	635	690	898	651
4	4	5	4	4		
4,000	4,000	4,000	4,000	4,000		
45	45	37	31	26	20	29
445	1,006	480	68	31	78	513
5	3	4	4	5		
51,000	1,000	11,000	8,000	9,000		
272	121	52	48	85	30	17
287	513	17	405	16	4	20
2	2	1	2	3		
17,000	17,000	4,000	5,000	155,000		
5	24	42	14	35	31	3
29	20	27	12	8	103	0
6	5	4	3	3		
25,000	24,000	6,000	3,000	3,000		
92	84	128	111	122	192	194
46	16	18	11	195	20	16
0	0	13	0	2	0	4
0	0	7	0	0	0	3,315
41	38	38	33	36		
239,500	211,500	193,000	173,500	334,500		
322	440	296	304	274	426	348
6,454	3,132	928	6,510	1,125	1,205	4,205

system because other forms of ideological competition were excluded. In Africa, patrimonial leaders used tribal networks as a way of rationing scarce governmental resources. And as disillusion set in, new political parties were able to exploit apathy and loss of public trust to make electoral gains. Hence Le Pen capitalised on the loss of support for the left parties in France, while the BJP has made inroads into the Congress Party's traditional bases.

A second factor is insecurity. The last two decades have been a period of dramatic structural change, with declines in state provision and public employment, rapid urbanisation, the growth of an informal criminalised economy, and large-scale migration from countryside to town and from poor countries to the industrialised West. Nationalist and religious movements offer a sense of certainty in uncertain times, security in times of insecurity, and a narrative that provides psychological comfort when material comfort is missing. Many scholars emphasise the importance of marginalisation and exclusion as an explanation for the growth of these movements. This is particularly important in cities, where nationalist and religious groups have their strongholds. Typical recruits to these movements are restless young men, often educated for roles that no longer exist because of the decline of the state or of the industrial sector, often unable to marry because they lack income, and sometimes needing to legitimise semi-criminal activities in which they can find their only source of income. Membership in nationalist or religious groups offers meaning, a sense of historical relevance, and also adventure.

And related to the sense of insecurity is the encounter with globalisation, that is to say, with growing interconnectedness, and the sense of impotence that arises when crucial decisions that affect everyday life are taken further and further away. The young men that committed suicide on September 11 were all educated in the West. This is typical of many religious militants, especially Muslims, who are often migrants, either from countryside to town or from South to North, who have experienced the loss of ties to their places of origin and yet do not feel integrated in their new homes.

For militants in Western Europe or the United States, growing marginalisation is linked to the loss of national sovereignty and to multiculturalism. In western Europe the enemy is 'Europe', while in the United States the patriotic Christian Right demonises anything that is linked to the word 'global'.

Ideology: A Modern Political Agenda with Anti-Modern Symbols

Summarising the ideology of nationalist and religious groups present in five continents and operating in distinct domestic environments is an ambitious and probably impossible task. However, we can identify a set of characteristics common to all these groups.

1. They seek political power—generally, control of the state

All the groups in Table 7.1 seek political power. Nationalist groups seek one of the following goals.

- Territorial expansion to include historic lands or lands inhabited by the ethnic nations, especially in Europe, where nationalist parties of Serbs, Croats, Hungarians, or Romanians all espouse irredentist policies. Thus Hungarians claim Transylvania, parts of Slovakia, and Vojvodina in northern Serbia where large numbers of Hungarians still live. Romanians want to reunite Romania and Moldova. Gush Emunim and other extreme Zionist groups want the expansion of territory to include the biblical lands of Israel.
- Secession for minority groups who want their own state. This is the case for the Moros in the Phillipines, the Acehnese in Indonesia, the Sikhs in India (Khalistan), the Tamils in Sri Lanka, Corsicans in France, the Uighurs in China, or the northern Italians (Padania). The Basques argue both for secession and for expansion since they want to unite the lands where Basque people live. The same is true of Kurdish nationalist groups, who for the moment argue for secession or autonomy within Turkey and Iraq. The Catholics in Northern Ireland want the province to unite with Ireland.
- Ethnically pure states and a strengthening of sovereignty. This is the case for Hindu nationalists who want to preserve Hindu culture in India and downgrade or eliminate Christians and Muslims. A similar goal characterises the new right anti-immigrant parties in Western Europe and Australia.

The nationalist groups argue that the liberal state fails to respect the principle of self-determination. For them, self-determination tends to be seen as an ethnic principle—that is to say, the nations is composed of people who share a common culture, language, or origin—rather than the civic principle, under which the nation is composed of people who live in a particular territory. Nowadays, there are hardly any nation-states in an ethnic sense; most states are multi-national, and all of them are multi-ethnic.

Religious groups often share the same goals but they emphasise the importance of using state power to introduce religious practices. Thus the Algerian Armed Islamic Group (GIA) aims to overthrow the secular Algerian regime and replace it with an Islamic state. The same goal is shared by groups like the Islamic Group and the Islamic Jihad in Egypt, Hizbollah in Lebanon, and the Islamic Movement of Uzbekistan (IMU). Likewise in America, the Christian right wants to build a Christian America that applies its version of Christian doctrine. Many of the nationalist groups described above are also religious groups. The Uighurs in China, the Moros in the Philippines, or the Acehnese in Indonesia all want secession in order to build an Islamic state. The Sikhs see Khalistan as a way of preserving the Sikh religion. Hamas, which means 'zeal' or 'enthusiasm', wants not just an independent Palestine but an Islamic Palestine.

Among Islamic groups, however, there are also those who see themselves as multi-ethnic and want to create a state that is the expression of Muslim unity. According to the Ayatollah Khomeini, the leader of the Iranian Islamic revolution:

> *'As far as Islam is concerned there is no question of Kurds, Turks, Fars, Baluchi, Arab, or Lor, or Turcomen. Islam embraces everyone and the Islamic Republic observes the right of all groups under Islamic justice . . . Everyone shall enjoy the protection of Islam' (quoted in Bruce 2000: 62).*

Thus Al Qaeda favours a Muslim caliphate for the whole of the Middle East, while Jemaah Islamiya, a network spread across Indonesia, Malaysia, the Philippines, and Singapore favours an Asian Muslim caliphate (Jones and Smith 2002: 352). The South Asian organisation Jamaat-e-Islami similarly wants to unite Muslims. It is other religions and religious practices they exclude rather than ethnicities.

It should be emphasised that all these groups have what might be described as a modernist view of the state. They still believe in state sovereignty and reject the conditionality that has accompanied globalisation. They believe that borders can be restored and religions and ethnicities can somehow be kept within borders.

2. They see themselves as opposed to modernity

In his book on fundamentalism, Steve Bruce mentions four ways in which religious fundamentalist groups object to modernity (some of which also apply to nationalist groups). First, they object to the concept of human equality. 'For most of human history the idea that the godly and the ungodly, the righteous and the sinner should be equally favoured would have been abhorrent' (Bruce 2000: 33). Thus, while Khomeini was able to talk about uniting ethnicities, he employed very different language and behaviour towards people of other religions, especially Jews and Baha'is. Extreme nationalists also tend to think that people of a different ethnicity do not count as equals. Often they use animal terms to describe other groups; thus the Hutus of Rwanda described the Tutsis as cockroaches, while the Serbs described Kosovars as rabbits or eels (supposedly a reference to their breeding proclivities).

Second, they object to the division between public and private, the idea that belief is somehow relegated to the private sphere. Public secularism is seen to have emptied the lives of many people, as, in the case of nationalists, has the commitment to multiculturalism.

Third, they object to what they see as both the relativism of modernity and the claim that human reason is superior to other forms of human knowledge. They object to the scepticism and questioning that characterise modern society. They insist that sacred knowledge is the superior form of knowledge, that there is a 'correct' God-given interpretation of events which cannot be contradicted by human reason. Many nationalists also insist that their beliefs are God-given, but even for secular nationalists, at least extreme secularists, the assumption is that there is one model for society that has to be applied, whatever the obstacles. It is this emphasis on certainty and the unique character of divine knowledge that explains how so many fundamentalist groups can hold extraordinary beliefs. Fundamentalist groups, say Marty and Appleby (1992: 24), want to 'scandalise':

They catch the attention of the rest of us by scandalising (or amusing) us with preposterous claims about virgin births or hidden Imams or personified books. But the 'show' carries a lesson: there is another way of imagining the world, of understanding human destiny, of tapping the enthusiasms, hopes and talents of modern individuals.

Finally, they object to changed gender relations that have accompanied modernity. Nearly all religious and nationalist groups insist on traditional family values. Christian groups take militant positions on abortion (see Box 7.2). Islamic groups insist that women wear burkhas and, in some cases—the most well-known being Afghanistan (the Taliban) and Saudi Arabia—they introduce what is essentially a form of gender apartheid. Most groups are also homophobic, although an interesting exception was Pim Fortuyn, the openly gay leader of the Dutch far-right party.

The notion of struggle may be the most important shared characteristic of religious and nationalist ideologies. The notion of 'us' and 'them' is deeply embedded in the ideologies of such movements

3. Emphasis is placed on the need to regenerate and unify a corrupt society.

The myth of decline is common to many social movements and acts as a powerful justification for their existence. Whether nationalist or religious, such groups are often backward-looking, nostalgic for a 'pure' past where religion was practised widely and according to ritual and/or where the nation was 'unpolluted' by foreigners, minorities, or mixed groups. Islamists, for example, propose a return to Islam's founding period 1,400 years ago and judge any state deviation from that golden age as *jahiliyya*, or pre-Islamic ignorance. For these groups, says Ibrahim A. Karawan, 'Islam encompasses the three –'Ds'—*din* (religion), *dunya* (life) and *wa dawla* (state)- and has to be implemented in its entirety' (Karawan 1997: 14). Bin Laden is a good example of this since he wants to purge Islamic countries of Western influences and aims at uniting all Muslims under the rule of the Caliphs. In the 1998 'Declaration of the World Islamic Front Statement urging Jihad Against Jews and Crusaders', Bin Laden declared that his goals were to stop the Western invasion of the Arabian Peninsula, overthrow the Saudi regime, liberate Islam's holy sites of Mecca and Medina, and support revolutionary groups around the globe (Bin Laden 1998). Radical Protestant sects, on the other hand, see themselves as returning to the Arcadia of the early Christian Church.

In effect these groups reinvent a past, based on a particular time and place, ignoring more recent history or, indeed, what historians have discovered about the period they pick that does not fit their preconceptions. For all fundamentalist and nationalists, places and dates are of critical importance. The Serbs claim that Kosovo is their holy land, like Jerusalem for the Jews, and they celebrate (actually only since the nineteenth century) the date in June 1389 when, in the famous Battle of Kosovo, the Serbs were defeated by the Turks. The Albanians are equated with the Turks despite the fact that, in the actual battle, Albanians were fighting on the same side as the Serbs (Malcolm 1998). 'Fundamentalists', say Marty and Appleby (1992: 184), 'idealise sacred lands, "freezing" them at one time and place and lifting them out of their complex and changing historical context to serve as emblems of communal identity and as the raison d'etre of political movements.'

These groups are both traditional and anti-traditional. They insist on the reinvention of tradition, on reintroducing past rituals and practices even if these 'traditions' are quite at odds with those of everyday life. Hence Ulster Unionists insist on translation into Ulster Scots—a dialect reinvented as a language to compete with the Catholic insistence on Gaelic.

4. They believe they are part of a great struggle or war against an 'other'

Nostalgia is often linked to notions of struggle that are endemic in the ideologies of both religious and nationalist groups. Indeed, the notion of struggle may be the most important shared characteristic of religious and nationalist ideologies. Islamist groups insist on the importance of jihad and refer to the United States as the 'Great Satan'. Christian right groups talk about

Box 7.2: Where have all the children gone? The global anti-abortion movement

Abortion laws are mainly contested by conservative and religious groups. In the US the anti-abortion lobby has been active since the 1970s as a reaction to two US Supreme Court rulings—*Roe v. Wade* and *Doe v. Bolton*—that established the constitutional right to abortion. In the 1990s, the media focused on the anti-abortion movement because some of its members emphasised the need for 'direct action' as a means to save the 'unborn'. According to the National Abortion Federation (NAF) (URL), during the 1990–2002 period the number of violent attacks against abortion providers in the US and Canada was 3,293. That is an average of 274 incidents a year; and seven people were killed. Other actions included confrontation of female patients at clinic entrances, harassment of clinic staff, and general disruption of clinics. Nowadays, private guards, bomb checks, and escorts for patients are common at many facilities throughout the US. In recent years, however, the use of physical violence, harassment, and vandalism has declined due to effective counter-offensive initiatives from clinic defence groups and as a result of lawsuits.

Although the violent elements of the anti-abortion movement seem to be in decline, the movement continues to thrive and has jumped onto the global stage. In their fight against abortion, US organisations have been very active in the international arena. Hence, the 'killing of babies' has stopped being a concern for Americans and has become a problem for Christianity. In other words, abortion does not go against just America's soul but the Christian spirit. The fight against abortion has assumed an unprecedented transnational dimension: US-based pro-life organisations have funded similar groups in other countries such as Poland, Russia, Guatemala, and Zambia.

The second major player in the global anti-abortion debate has been the Roman Catholic Church. One of the major transnational actors in the world, the Catholic Church's official position has been voiced by Pope John Paul II, who believes the Vatican needs to defend the right to life of the foetus, the 'unborn', and to strongly oppose abortion. A summary of this position can be found in the papal encyclical of 1968, *Humanae Vitae*. The Catholic Church has also provided organisational assistance and direction to pro-life groups, sometimes through organisations like Opus Dei and the Knights of Malta (Kulczycki 1999). However, since the Catholic Church is not a unified and monolithic organisation, a variety of views on the issue can be detected in different countries.

a 'civil war' in America, 'a war of allegiances, whose God and whose laws are going to prevail in this culture' (anti-abortion activist Randall Terry, quoted in Marty and Appleby 1992: 1). RAHOWA stands for 'racial holy war', which is the greeting and rallying cry in the World Church of the Creator, an American group which undertook targeted racial killings in Illinois and Indiana in 1999 (Juergensmeyer 2000). This emphasis on war is also characteristic of nationalist groups. Almost always, their narratives contain stories of great battles lost or won or even merely symptomatic of disorder (Kosovo, the Battle of the Boyne, the Mahabharat, for example).

The notion of 'us' and 'them' is deeply embedded in the ideologies of such movements. The contrast with the 'other' becomes part of the definition of the group, whether it is another nationality or religion or, in the contemporary period, secularity and/or cosmopolitanism. Religious leaders see their struggle as a cosmic war against evil and promote the idea that every follower has to participate in that struggle. By doing so, their political causes are given sacred legitimacy and their members are given a sense of participation in something larger than everyday life. Likewise, nationalist groups often claim to be avenging historic injustices. In the Basque case, for example, ETA has skilfully used the myth that Basques were an eternally independent nation in order to mobilise its supporters. For the ETA nationalists, the Basques have resisted for centuries foreign invasion (from the Romans to Charlemagne) but only the Spaniards have managed to 'conquer' them. It is, then, for Basques to

Box 7.3: The rise of far-right populist parties in western Europe

Though referred to in a variety of ways (far right, extreme right, right-wing populist), movements of the populist far right, characterised by strident nationalism and an anti-immigrant stance, began to experience a resurgence in western Europe in the early 1980s. From their relative absence in the 1950s and 1960s to their modest renewal throughout the 1970s and 1980s, these parties achieved significant electoral success in the 1990s and the early years of the twenty-first century: some lead coalition governments (such as the Austrian Freedom Party), others enter government in coalition (such as the Italian Alleanza Nazionale) and a few periodically undermine the legitimacy of the political systems in which they thrive by their high electoral scores and permanent media presence (such as the Front National in France).

While inevitably shaped by the contexts within which they emerge, these parties share an abhorrence of what they refer to as the 'socialist liberal order', which they see as responsible for the chaotic handling of ethnic and immigration issues, the surrendering of state sovereignty to the hated European Union (EU), and the decline of law and order. The parties' anti-immigration stance and deep mistrust of the EU are two of their most characteristic features: European institutions and the multicultural and multi-ethnic societies resulting from immigration trends are perceived and depicted as the consequences of the globalising cosmopolitan trends which traditional parties have either failed to stem or, worse, actively encouraged. Taken in conjunction with the parties' nationalism, their respective attitudes towards immigration and Europe are evidence that they may be, in part, a consequence of some voters' unease with increasingly globalised polities.

The parties' anti-Europeanism is particularly pronounced in France and in the Scandinavia, while much less salient in Italy; attacks on corruption and accusations of 'foul play' are, predictably, far more prevalent in Italy and France than in the other countries. An anti-immigration stance is a consistent feature across parties.

While some of the parties have connections to the fascism of the 1920s and 1930s (chief amongst them

Table 7.4: Electorally relevant far-right parties in western Europe

Organisation	Country	Active since	Recent results
Freiheitliche Partei Osterreichs, FPO (Austrian Freedom Party)	Austria	1956	1999: 26%; 2002, 10%
Vlaams Blok, VB (Flemish Block)	Belgium	1977	2003: 12%, 18 seats
Dansk Folkeparti, DF (Danish People's Party)	Denmark	1995	2001: 12%, 22 seats
Front National, FN (National Front)	France	1972	April 2002 (presidentials): 16% May 2002 (legislatives):11%, no seats
Alleanza Nazionale, AN (National Alliance)	Italy	Formally 1994—but AN is an electoral umbrella bringing together parties dating from the 1920s	2001: 12.%, 24 seats (in coalition government with Berlusconi)
Lijst Pim Fortuyn, LPF	Netherlands	2002	2002: 17%, 26 seats; 2003: 5.7%, 8 seats
Fremskrittspartiet, FrP	Norway	1973	2001: 14,7%, 26 seats

the Italian Alleanza Nazionale, which took over in 1994 the 'post-fascist' electoral platform of the formerly Fascist MSI—whose hard-core members formed a small breakaway Fascist party), most of them have, publicly at least, renounced violence and embraced the rules of the democratic game. Their weapon of choice is a robust populist stance that is critical of the ruling political elites, who are perceived as overly intellectual, corrupt, inefficient, and therefore illegitimate (see Canovan 1999).

These parties fare especially well in polities characterised by overwhelming political consensus and a perceived decline of the left-right cleavage. It is not uncommon for their platforms to include, alongside a nationalist appeal, a call for 'real politics', a politics for the 'common people', with 'clear-cut solutions' rather than speculative programmes. All of this betrays a sense of fatigue with and alienation from the political realm itself viewed as a space of compromise and blurred values. Even in polities such as France, traditionally home to a polarised party system encompassing an extreme right and an extreme left, parties such as Le Pen's Front National have found a comfortable electoral niche, capitalising on the terminal decline of the French Communist Party and the mainstream parties' consensus on, in particular, the question of European integration. The impression of overwhelming consensus at the expense of the 'common people' was epitomised, in the French case, by five years of 'cohabitation' government which were duly capitalised upon by the Front National.

It is difficult to judge whether these parties should be seen as a permanent feature of the west European political landscape. Although many have been in existence for several decades, recent events in Austria and in the Netherlands suggest that they generally fare badly once in government and may be condemned to remaining an outlet for a fluctuating and unstable protest vote.

Catherine Fieschi, University of Nottingham

expel Spaniards through all necessary means in order to return to the path of independence that the Basque nation should have never abandoned.

The notion of martyrdom is closely linked to the idea of cosmic war. Suicide bombers, even if not religious, like the Fatah suicide bombers or the kamikaze in the Second World War, see themselves as making the highest possible sacrifice for their cause. The distinction between murderers and heroes, so important in the justification of war, acquires a sacred meaning. Of course, those who undertake such missions may be terrorised or alternatively seduced by promises of virgins in heaven, or they may believe that it is a way to help their families, who often receive large sums of money. Nevertheless, these acts substantiate the deeply held notion of struggle.

War implies certainty, the impossibility of compromise or co-existence—indeed, the more blood that is shed, the more the cause is sanctified. According to Juergensmeyer (2000: 149),

> *A warring attitude implies that its holder no longer thinks compromise is possible or—just as likely—did not want an accommodating solution to the conflict in the first place. In fact, if one's goal is not harmony but the empowerment that comes with using violence, it is in one's interest to be in a state of war.*

Methods, Tactics, and Strategy

Religious and nationalist activists have opted for different strategies according to the domestic and international political situation in which they operate. Broadly speaking, we can distinguish three main modes of operation that are not necessarily mutually exclusive: competing in elections, other legal forms of protest, and violence. By and large, the more democratic and open the environment in which they operate, the more likely these groups are to adopt more peaceful, moderate methods; but there are many exceptions to this rule.

Competing in elections

As can be seen from Table 7.1, many of the groups we describe are organised as political parties and try to gain power through winning votes. In the US, for example, the Christian Right is now an integral part of the Republican Party and mobilises to support candidates who share its views; President Bush himself has become a born-again Christian. The BJP in India has managed to become the biggest party in India. The leader of the Great Romanian Party, Corneliu Vadim Tudor, was a contestant in the run-off for Romania's presidential elections in 2000. The Islamic Action Front (IAF) in Jordan and the Islamic Constitutional Movement (ICM) in Kuwait aim to islamicise the state through political means, accepting the supreme authority of their hereditary monarchies (Karawan 1997: 20–1). The adaptability of political parties has also caught the attention of armed groups who often develop a political wing of their own. This is the case for old separatist movements in western Europe (IRA and ETA) and Islamic movements like Hizbollah. In Israel the pro-settler group Gush Emunin, the National-Religious Party, and the Kach Party present their non-conciliatory views about the occupied territories through the formal political institutions. Last but not least, in western Europe fascist, extreme-right, populist, and ultra-nationalist parties have risen since the 1970s while maintaining anti-system attitudes (see Box 7.3).

The political party route, however, should not be understood as an alternative to violence. Most of these parties exploit fear and insecurity to gain votes. West European far-right parties exploit fears about immigrants, crime, or Aids. The Australian right exaggerates the risks of asylum seekers. Most of these parties try to whip up prejudices against Jews, Muslims, Roma, and so on. Some parties exploit external fears. Thus the BJP emphasises the threat from Pakistan and has tried to use nuclear competition as a way of gaining popularity. The American right, formerly preoccupied with the Evil Empire (the Soviet Union), now stresses global terrorism and the Axis of Evil.

The political party route should not be understood as an alternative to violence. Most of these parties exploit fear and insecurity to gain votes

But it is not only through ideology that these parties mobilise fear. In many cases, violence is actually used to create the insecurity and fear on which these parties capitalise. One of the most dramatic examples was the massacre in Gujarat in 2002, which was followed by an overwhelming victory for the BJP. In Croatia and Bosnia, extreme nationalist Serbs and Croats deliberately and successfully created ethnically pure territories, which allowed them to win elections.

Many of these parties have paramilitary wings. ETA, the IRA , Hizbollah , and Gush Emunim have already been mentioned. In the Balkans or the former Soviet Union, it is common for extreme nationalist parties to organise themselves through militia. Thus, the Croatian Party of Rights has a black-shirted paramilitary unit, established by the party's leader Dobrosav Paraga, which fought in the Croatian-Serbian conflict. The paramilitaries sported Ustashi (Second World War Croatian fascists) insignia. Likewise, the Serbian Radical Party, led by Vojislav Seselj (currently in the detention unit of the United Nations Criminal Tribunal for Former Yugoslavia following an indictment for crimes against humanity and violations of laws and customs of war), had paramilitary fighters known as Seseljevci or Chetniks (wartime Serbian nationalists), who fought in Croatia, Bosnia and Kosovo.

Legal protest

Many groups engage in classic forms of legal protest: demonstrations, the publication of pamphlets, boycotts, strikes, the use of the law courts, often in addition to other methods. Thus, the Civic United Front in Tanzania, which claims regional autonomy for the Muslims of Zanzibar, has used street protests, hunger strikes of imprisoned members, and a boycott of the Zanzibar parliament in order to gain international attention for its claim that elections in Zanzibar have been rigged by the ruling party; through this strategy, it has succeeded in getting the Commonwealth to act as a mediators between it and the government.

Most fundamentalist groups in the United States use legal methods. For example, the American Family Association organised Christian boycotts of advertisers who support 'morally objectionable' television programmes. In 1992, it filed a lawsuit against the producer of a documentary film on censorship and succeeded in preventing the film from being shown in the US. Some fundamentalists make alliances with other groups—with feminists against pornography, with Roman Catholics against abortion, or with blacks against the drug culture (see Marty and Appleby 1992). In recent years, in the United States, the Christian Right has chosen to ally increasingly with Zionists (see Box 7.4).

Violence

Most of the groups shown in Table 7.1 use violence. But there are many forms of violence, as our figures on terrorism and Major Episodes of Political Violence indicate. One form of violence that is typical of these groups is what Mark Juergensmeyer calls 'symbolic' violence. Juergensmeyer contrasts symbolic violence with strategic violence, which is calculated to achieve a particular goal. Symbolic violence, by contrast, is a form of message, a way of making a statement. Terrorist attacks against civilians are typical of 'symbolic violence'. Violence is 'deliberately exaggerated' and often macabre. The Lord's Resistance Army in Uganda cuts off ears and lips. Hamas suicide bombers put nails in their bombs so as to kill as many people as possible. Juergensmeyer likens 'symbolic violence' to theatre—these are 'performance acts'—'stunning, abnormal and outrageous murders carried out in a way that graphically displays the power of violence—set within grand scenarios of conflict and proclamation' (Juergensmeyer 2000: 122). The targets of such attacks are often important symbols: the World Trade Center, the Federal Building in Oklahoma that symbolised welfare and gun control, the mosque in Ayodhya. These 'rituals of violence' carry with them an other-worldly significance and produce the sense of struggle, of Armageddon or Jihad, or of cosmic war. Those who took part in the nerve-gas attack on a Tokyo subway, for example, in 1995 believed that this was the start of the world catastrophe predicted by Shoko Ashara, the spiritual leader of Aum Shinrikyo (the extreme Buddhist sect).

Violence is not merely symbolic. In many of the recent armed conflicts, the aim has been deliberate elimination or indeed extermination of the 'other'

The theatrical character of much violence is illustrated by the way many of the perpetrators dress up for killing as though it is not they themselves who perform the acts. The notorious Frenki's Boys, who were responsible for atrocities in Bosnia and Kosovo, wore cowboy hats over ski masks and painted Indian stripes on their faces. Their trademark was the sign of the Serbian Chetniks and a silhouette of a destroyed city with the words 'City Breakers' in English. Joseph Kony, the leader of the Lord's Resistance Army, wears aviator sunglasses and dresses his hair in beaded braids hanging to his neck; sometimes he wears women's clothes.

But violence is not merely symbolic, not just 'letters to Israel', as one Hamas activist described the suicide bombers. In many of the recent armed conflicts, the aim has been deliberate elimination or indeed extermination of the 'other'. The Hutus in Rwanda wanted to get rid of the Tutsis, just as Hitler wanted to get rid of the Jews. The goal of the wars in the former Yugoslavia or the South Caucasus was to create ethnically pure territories. In these cases, exaggerated violence was aimed at making people hate their homes. Systematic rape, for example, was widespread in the former Yugoslavia. This was rape, not as a side effect of war, but as a deliberate weapon of war with the aim of making women, particularly Muslim women, feel ashamed and defiled so that they would not want to return to their homes. Likewise, violence against symbolic targets was aimed at removing any trace of the culture of the 'other'. In Banja Luka during the Bosnian war, two unique sixteenth-century Ottoman mosques were razed to the ground. They were blown up on a Friday; and on the following Monday the bulldozers grassed over the site so as to eliminate all evidence of their existence.

And in some conflicts classic guerrilla tactics are adopted with very specific strategic goals—for example, attacks on state officials, high-ranking civil servants, or military and security officers. This was a tactic of European groups like the IRA and ETA, and also the GIA in Algeria and LTTE in Sri Lanka. Other groups have preferred to target foreign diplomats and businessmen in order to exert pressure on their governments. Targeting the sources of state revenues has also been a much-used tactic: the oil and gas industry in Algeria, the tourism industry in Egypt and Spain, etc. In other cases, violence has accompanied kidnappings which have ended in demands for the release of prisoners or for ransom. Sometimes the aim is to provoke outside intervention. Thus, the KLA targeted Serb policemen so as to provoke an exaggerated Serb response, which would mobilise international opinion.

The trend, however, is away from these more classic tactics towards both symbolic and strategic violence aimed at the killing of civilians. This is one way that extremist groups succeed in mobilising extremist sentiment. The killings and displacement in

Box 7.4: The emerging Christian-Zionist alliance

Think like Jesus . . . Fight like David . . . Lead like Moses . . . Run like Lincoln.

(Motto of the Christian Coalition)

America's most powerful Christian Right organisation, the Christian Coalition, has led the development of a Christian-Zionist alliance.

Founded by Pat Robertson in 1989, the organisation claims 2 million members ... the real number may be closer to 300,000 (People for the American Way, 2002). It threw its weight behind George W. Bush, and gained him the support of the religious right, which makes up a third of the Republican Party's base.

The Israeli right also contributed to the alliance (Fisk 2002). In 1978 the Likud Party published a plan to encourage fundamentalists to support Israel. By 1980 there was an 'International Christian Embassy' in Jerusalem, and 1985 saw Benjamin Netanyahu at a 'National Prayer Breakfast for Israel'. This led to the National Unity Coalition for Israel becoming the lobbying arm of Christian Zionism. When he visited America, Netanyahu made a point of meeting televangelist Jerry Falwell before meeting President Clinton.

The Israeli right has helped organise trips to Israel on which evangelicals visit biblical sites, meet with Jewish settlers, and talk to political and military leaders. Ehud Olmert, mayor of Tel Aviv, has made Pat Robertson the co-chairman of the 'Jerusalem Prayer Team', whose goal is to secure financial and political support from American evangelicals. May 2002 saw the Israeli embassy bringing together Jerry Falwell, Pat Robertson, and the boards of 'Promise Keepers' and 'The Christian Broadcasting Network' at a prayer breakfast in Washington.

The Coalition has given strong support to Jewish settlements in the West Bank and Gaza. Its leaders have played a double game. In interviews they claim scaling back settlements is contrary to God's grant to Abraham in Genesis 15:18 of all the land from 'the rivers of Egypt' to the Euphrates. At the same time, they have continued to signal to their supporters that they really believe we are living in the biblical 'end times' and support for Israeli expansion is essential if America is to avoid God's wrath (Boyer 1992; 2003).

The system of prophecy the Coalition invokes is known as 'pre-millennial dispensationalism'. According to this account, the present 'Dispensation' will end with 'Rapture'. True believers will be swept up in to the air where they will meet with Christ. This will be followed by the 'Tribulation'. A charismatic figure, the Antichrist, will arise in Europe, seize world power, and impose a universal tyranny. After seven years, Christ and the Saints will return and defeat the Antichrist at Armageddon near Haifa. Christ will then inaugurate the 'Millennium', a thousand-year reign of peace and justice.

This scheme is taken as a guide to current events. During the Cold War interpreters focused on Ezekiel's prophecy that a northern kingdom, Gog, which they claimed was the Soviet Union, would be destroyed. Now the focus has shifted. The new location of evil is the New World Order: the United Nations, the World Trade Organization, and other international bodies, and global media, financial, and manufacturing corporations. This system is taken to be preparing the way for the Antichrist's dictatorship.

The foundation of the Jewish state in 1948, the occupation of all the lands ascribed to the Jews in the Bible, the future rebuilding of the Jewish Temple on Muslim holy sites, the massacre of the Jews by Islam, and the conversion of the survivors to Christianity are all seen as essential steps in the fulfilment of the prophecy. Islam is seen as evil and destined for destruction. Thus, in Hal Lindsey's 1996 prophecy novel, *Blood Moon*, Israel responds to a planned nuclear attack by an Arab extremist by launching a vast thermonuclear attack on the entire Arab world.

It would be a mistake to underestimate the hold of this story within America. The Left Behind series of prophetic novels, of which Lindsey's book is one, have sold no fewer than 50 million copies. A March

2002 Gallup Poll revealed that '46 per cent of Americans describe themselves as "born-again" or evangelical', while a 1999 *Newsweek* poll showed 71 per cent of evangelicals believed the world would end in a battle between Jesus and the Antichrist at 'Armageddon' (Cherry 2002).

The Christian-Zionist alliance is not based on shared ideas. The bridge-builders operate at a more visceral level (Lieven 2002). They draw on shared hatreds of the United Nations and Europe. They focus on each side's attraction to violent military 'solutions'. They indulge each side's sense of itself as victim of history. The Christian right, with its Southern white roots, sees itself as the loser of the Civil War. It believes that since the 1960s it has been under attack by the forces of irreligion and cultural change. And the bridge-builders intensify each side's sense of being the defenders of civilisation against the savages. The Christian right has had to mask its sense of racial superiority and paranoia about Black Americans; now after September 11 it rejoices in a new freedom to vilify and excoriate Arabs and Muslims.

Christian Zionism has divided American Jews. Some support the alliance because 'what counts is support for Israel now'. Author Gershom Gorenberg disagrees: 'They love us as characters in their story, in their play, and that's not who we are. If you listen to the drama they are describing, essentially it's a five-act play in which the Jews disappear in the fourth act' (Engel 2002).

The power of the alliance is considerable. President Bush's chief strategist, born-again Karl Rove, saw Christian right support as a key to Bush's gaining the presidency (Vulliamy 2003). Bush himself is a born-again Christian. While governor of Texas he went on a Christian Zionist pilgrimage to Israel and on returning declared he was a 'changed man'. In casting Saddam Hussein as a demonic figure who threatens to unleash a 'day of horror like none we have known', Bush not only played on recent memories of the September 11 attack, he also sent a message to the millions of Americans who believe that they are living in the end-time that he is one of them (Boyer 2003).

Since September 11 Rove has crafted a foreign policy which fits Christian right depictions of the Middle East. Islam, Rove has argued, 'was one of the world's great empires' which had never been reconciled to 'the loss of power and dominion' (Vulliamy 2003). In response, the United States must be prepared to 'enforce respect' in the region. The Christian right also occupies key positions in Congress. As leader of the Republican majority in the House of Representatives, Evangelical Dick Armey has stressed his belief that the Palestinians should leave the land they now occupy ... in other words, has advocated 'ethnic cleansing' ... while House Majority Chief Whip, Tom Delay, sits beneath a plaque stating 'This could be the day', indicating his belief in pre-millennial prophecy.

Members of the administration have had a more direct role in the Israeli right. Thus, Richard Perle and Douglas Feith, who now occupy key positions in the Pentagon, in 1996 wrote a paper titled 'A Clean Break' for the then leader of Likud, Binyamin Netanyahu. This emphasised the need to break with the Oslo process, and argued that Israel's 'claim to the land (including the West Bank) is legitimate and noble' (K. Smith 2002).

The future significance of Christian Zionism will rest on whether it manages to change the structure of American and world politics. American Jews have traditionally voted for the Democrat Party (Lieven 2002). The Republican Party's low tax agenda, however, has a strong appeal to wealthier Jewish Americans. By presenting itself as the supporter of Zionist expansionist plans, the Republican Party now has a chance to become the natural party of government by depriving its rival of not only a key voting bloc but also of intellectuals and finance.

Dominick Jenkins, London School of Economics.

conflict, as in Yugoslavia, generate the very ideologies that were supposed to have been the cause of the conflict. In the conflict between Armenia and Azerbaijan, for example, the idea that political control could be achieved through expelling those of a different nationality 'spread as the scale and intensity of the conflict increased' and was 'converted into a deadly ideology by fears of pre-emption and memories of past blood shed' (Melander 2001: 65). Indeed, this may be the point of the violence. It is difficult to explain suicide bombing in Israel as a way of achieving a Palestinian state, just as it is difficult to explain the brutal Israeli responses as a way of improving security. But if the goal is to strengthen extremist sentiment—support for Hamas or for the extreme Zionist groups—what is happening is much easier to explain.

Organisation, Media, and Funding

A wide variety of organisational forms characterise the groups described in this chapter. But some general remarks are relevant.

First, many of the groups we describe are part of a family of organisations, as for example shown in Box 7.5 on ETA. It is often the case that nationalist and religious groups organise what might be described as parallel societies, sophisticated organisational infrastructures with political, military, educational, welfare, and publishing components. In recent years the establishment of religious schools, often linked to extremist groups, has been widespread. Christian schools have increased dramatically in the United States; some 20 per cent of enrolments in private schools is now in Christian schools. Madrassahs, particularly in Pakistan and Afghanistan, have also increased, as have Hindu schools, especially in tribal areas.

Some groups even have 'scientific' wings. The Japanese doom cult, Aum Shinrikyo, specifically recruited graduates with scientific and engineering degrees from Japan's leading universities and provided them with state-of-the-art laboratories and lavish budgets with which to fund the group's variegated weapons R&D programmes (Hoffman 2001: 420). The Christian Heritage College in San Diego has an Institute for Creation Research, aimed at disproving evolutionary theory. Humanitarian NGOs also play an important role; especially for Islamic groups, it is these religious NGOs that often provide the only form of welfare for immigrants newly arrived in cities.

Indonesian girl in a pesantren, a Muslim boarding school, reading the Koran. © Anders Gunnartz/Panos Pictures

Second, a highly typical feature of these groups, and something that tends to distinguish them from NGOs, is the importance of charismatic leaders, often surrounded by a hard core of committed activists. Many groups are organised around particular personalities, usually men—Osama Bin Laden of Al Qaeda, Vojislav Seselj of the Serbian Radical Party, Abdullah Öcalan of the PKK, or Joseph Kony of the Lord's Resistance Army. And these movements are greatly weakened once their leaders die or disappear. After the Kurdish leader Abdullah Ocalan was captured, the armed struggle fizzled out, and the PKK has now changed its name. It is worth noting that this is true both of the more traditional hierarchical parties and of those that adopt a more horizontal network form of organisation. These leaders are seen as the personification of a set of beliefs, the polar opposite of the impersonal abstract rationality of modernity.

Third, the increasingly transnational character of these movements has led to a shift from vertical forms of organisation to more horizontal network-like structures. At the moment, only one of our case studies fulfils the definition of a network and that is Al Qaeda (see Glasius and Kaldor 2002). It is not only the distribution of independent cells around the world but the training camps and the complex system of funding that makes Al Qaeda a truly global network. Other movements like Hamas are moving in that direction. The Jamaat-e-Islami party, for example, is present in at least three countries: India, Pakistan, and Bangladesh. According to Bruce Hoffman, a scholar from RAND, this is part of a general trend from the pyramidal structure of terrorist organisations of the 1970s and 1980s to today's flexible network:

> *These movements also tend to operate on a linear rather than hierarchical basis. Hence, instead of the classic cellular structure that was common to previous generations of terrorist organizations, some contemporary groups are more loosely connected or indirectly linked through networks comprised of both professional terrorists and amateurs. (Hoffman 2001: 418)*

All of the groups that we describe make use of the 'new media'—satellite and cable television, Internet, video cassettes. Regardless of their strategy they all want to put their message across. In order to do so, they have combined their traditional ideologies with the opportunities of globalisation (IT, satellite television, air travel, etc). Symbolic violence is important because it often performed before audiences of millions. The mesmerising pictures of the collapse of the World Trade Center towers beamed over and over again on all global television channels was perhaps the most successful media event of all time. In the aftermath of 11 September, Osama Bin Laden carefully staged and distributed his video messages through the television channel from Qatar, Al Jazeera. Many groups have their own television channels. Pat Robertson created his own television channel, the Christian Broadcasting Network, later renamed the Family Channel. The Hindu nationalists benefit from the new Satellite Channel, Star TV (see Deane 2002). Serbian television paid a critical role in the years leading up to the Yugoslav wars in promoting nationalist propaganda, interchanging contemporary events with the Second World War and the 1389 Battle of Kosovo. Television and radio reach out to people who do not have the reading habit. In Africa, the radio is regarded as magic, and it was Milles Collines hate radio that incited the genocide in Rwanda (see Kaldor 1999).

The use of the Internet and e-mail has been particularly important in building transnational networks (see Box 7.6). Since September 11, Rohan Gunaratna (2003: 20) points out, 'sympathetic websites [to Al Qaeda] are proliferating—many of them operationally unconnected but ideologically sympathetic to the group'. The Internet has provided nationalist and religious leaders with cheap and effective means to communicate with their members. Primarily through e-mails, web-cams, and web pages they can provide their supporters with information. But, because of the anonymity and unregulated nature of the Internet, nationalist and religious activists have also been able to go beyond their traditional audiences and post their ideas in cyberspace. The aim of communicating with the Diaspora, some of whose members may no longer speak their language of origin, and perhaps of convincing the 'misinformed' international public is clearly evident from the fact that many of these web pages have an English version. Hence, in the course of our research we have found a large number of groups that have web pages, some of them official and some put up by supporters (see Table 7.1). The sites usually provide information about the organisation's leaders, actions, ideology, and often a detailed account of what it is fighting for. A section on the history of 'the problem' also comes hand in hand with a description of the organisation's goals. In the case of armed groups, almost all sites avoid presenting their violent activities, the exceptions being Hizbollah and Hamas (Tsfati and Weimann 2002).

The organisations that we describe have three main sources of funding. One is the traditional form of donations from supporters. Many groups levy 'taxes' on their supporters. Some groups, like Al Qaeda or the Christian Right, benefit from wealthy individuals. Members of political parties pay membership fees.

A second source of income is illicit commercial activities. Loot and pillage, extortion and kidnapping are the typical forms of funding for armed groups. ETA, for example, collects most of its revenues by kidnapping important businessmen and through the 'revolutionary tax' (in effect, protection money). Small

Box 7.5: The Basque National Liberation Movement (BNLM)

The Basque National Liberation Movement (BNLM) is a network of organisations that actively pursue the independence of the seven Basque provinces (*Euskal Herria*) currently under French and Spanish sovereignty. The central element of the BNLM is the terrorist group *Euskadi Ta Askatasuna* (ETA), created in 1959 and mainly operative in Spain where it is responsible for almost a thousand deaths. The network, however, was founded during the late 1970s and early 1980s. Since 1982, the entire organisational network has been totally dependent on the needs and aims of ETA. Such dependency exists not only in terms of ideology and strategy but also with regard to the internal organization of the network.

The most important characteristics of BNLM members are an expression of this subordination to ETA: the emphasis on the essential role of armed struggle as key to Basque existence; the support given to ETA as the leading organisation (both symbolically and in practice); the perception of ETA prisoners as heroes, since they represent the most visible sign of Basque resistance and victimisation by the Spanish state; the belief that legitimacy is acquired not through elections but through armed struggle against representatives of the Spanish state, with ETA as the vanguard of such a struggle; an attitude of hatred towards the security forces; and the contemporary repulsion towards the Basque and Spanish political and legal systems. For ETA, this group of organisations remains the most important source of new recruits and a complementary means of fighting for independence.

ETA created these political and social organisations during the years of the Spanish transition to democracy (1975–82). The BNLM should be understood as an organisational network that takes advantage of all the opportunities for political participation that a democratic system can provide. The BNLM widens and develops the aims of terrorist organisation in both the social and political spheres while providing ETA with new supporters and sources of legitimacy. In other words, the BNLM is the organisational basis for an alternative society in which being a radical nationalist is a necessary condition. The divide between Basques and Spaniards is not established by ethnicity but by the will to participate in the struggle. The 'real' Basque wants the boundaries of the Basque nation to coincide with a state and works for that goal through his or her participation in the BNLM. On the other end of the spectrum, the Spaniards are those who do not share their objectives, and are hence potential targets for ETA.

Under the leadership of ETA, the BNLM rejects the status quo and shares the aim of building an independent Basque state made up of the territories of the current Basque Autonomous Community and Navarre in Spain, and the Basque territories in France. The Basque language, spoken in all these territories, becomes the defining factor of the community that is entitled to self-determination. Although all the organisations share a common nationalist goal, each group has a specific field of action, with the aim of placing immense confrontational pressure on the Spanish authorities to force them, in the end, to negotiate and/or to agree to the BNLM's demands.

Within this organisational network, the basic collectives (some of which have recently been declared illegal) are: ETA, the top echelon commanding the movement; KAS-Ekin (ideological coordination and design) at the second level; and *Segi* (youth), the main source of ETA members. Among the specialised collectives covering the different domains of society, we find: LAB (trade union), *Askatasuna* (prisoners' families and defence), *Egizan* (women), *Eguzki* (environment), *Ikasle Abertzaleak* (students), and *Askapena* and *Xaki* (international action). The political party Batasuna— whose role has been assumed by *Autodeterminaziorako Bilgunea* (AuB) due to a judicial stay of activities—was conceived as a coalition which acts as a political catalyst in attracting support for BLNM's operational strategy. In the latest elections to the Basque parliament in 2001, support for the radical nationalist party declined, and it became the fourth political force (with 10 per cent of the votes). In addition, there are Basque language teaching groups and anti-military and leisure organisations which are highly influenced by the BNLM.

Bars, or *Herriko Tabernak*, may also serve as meeting points for radical activists. Further, the BNLM runs its own media network that provides much ideological input. Significant publications include the newspaper *Gara*, the magazines *Herria 2000 Eliza* and *Kale Gorria*, as well as bulletins edited by individual satellite organisations and publishing houses, training seminar brochures, web sites, and various local and regional radio stations.

José Manuel Mata López, University of the Basque Country

Figure 7.1: Network structure of the Basque National Liberation Movement (BNLM)

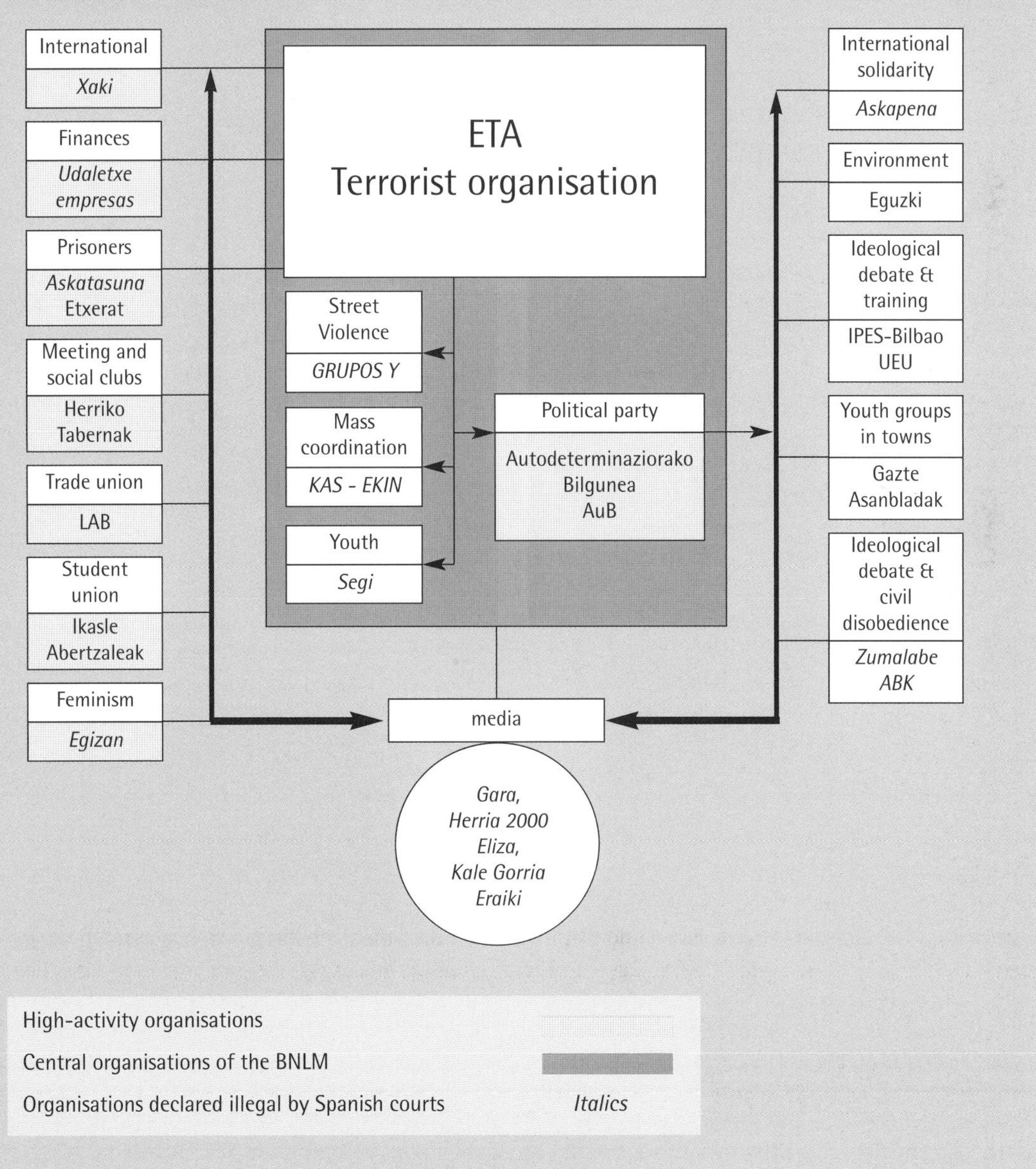

Box 7.6: Nationalism and the Internet

The printing press and the development of a print culture was one of the key factors in the development of modern nationalism, allowing individuals to share in the same imagined community. The development of new forms of media allows new ways to imagine and participate in shared communities. The Internet, more so than other new medium, has the potential to transform the way in which the nation is envisaged. The impact of this on nationalist groupings is only starting to be felt. There are three distinct ways in which this impact can already be seen: on nationalism within existing nation-states, on the operation of militant nationalist groups, and on Diasporic communities.

Nationalism within the nation-state

Within the nation-state, the Internet serves as an extra medium for transmitting ideas about national identity. National institutions transmit information to strengthen a sense of national community. A good example of this is the BBC's recent 'Great Britons' survey, an attempt to find who was considered the 'greatest Briton' (Churchill won), while the BBC broadcast documentaries about each of the candidates. The majority of the 2 million or so votes were cast on-line. At the same time both on the BBC's web site (URL) and on numerous other sites debates and lobbying for favoured candidates took place. In this instance the Internet made possible a far greater degree of participation by members of the nation than would otherwise have been possible. The Internet also allows members of the nation-state far greater opportunities to express solidarity and patriotism, particularly in times of national crisis. A striking feature of the response to the attacks of September 11 was that virtually all American web sites—from businesses to pornography and fan sites—displayed at some point on the front page an image of the American flag and a message of solidarity with the people of New York.

Militant nationalist groups

One of the functions of the Internet is to give like-minded individuals the opportunity to meet one another on-line and form virtual communities. For the most part this means that fans of a particular pop star or television show have a forum to discuss their views, but it also means that militant nationalists can meet one another and share and develop their views. In most states extremist nationalist propaganda is censored to some degree or other through laws against inciting racial hatred and through control of access to traditional media. But the Internet makes such controls easy to circumvent. Thus, web sites such as Stormfront (URL), which describes itself as a 'White Nationalist Resource Page' and claims to have been visited more than 6 million times, start to appear. These web sites give the opportunity to distribute propaganda to a far greater degree and to a wider audience than was previously possible. Each nationalist web site will also contain links to other similar web sites, both nationally and internationally; thus, the British National Party website (URL) contains links not just to other British nationalist web sites but also to extreme nationalist groups around Europe, such as the Front National in France or the Vlaams Blok in Belgium. One organisation that tracks the use and development of extremist sites is Hatewatch (URL).

businesses and individuals receive letters which 'offer' the chance to contribute to the 'liberation of the Basques'. It is estimated that up to 10 per cent of small businesses in the Basque region pay ETA between 30,000 and 60,000 euros a year in order to 'protect' family members from 'reprisals'(Sussman URL) In Northern Ireland, loyalist groups such as the UDA and the UVF funded themselves through involvement in robberies, tax fraud, drinking clubs, smuggling, and drug dealing (Silke 2000). Kidnapping is also used by other groups to fund their activities. This is the case with Hizbollah, or Abu Sayyaf in the Philippines. Some engage in both illegal and legal activities. Hence, we have the case of the Japanese Aum Shinrikyo, which funded itself through a lucrative series of noodle shops, estate agents, computer shops, and pharmaceuticals but also through land fraud and drug trafficking (Muir 1999: 83). In the end, the Japanese sect managed to grow to 60,000 members and open offices in New York, Germany, Australia, Sri Lanka, and Russia with estimated assets of $1 billion (Hoffman 2001: 420).

Militant nationalist groups have also made their presence felt on the Internet through attacking web sites opposed to their cause. For example, during the late 1990s a group of Serb nationalists calling themselves the Black Hand (after the Serbian nationalist group active at the beginning of the century, one of whose members, Gavrilo Princip, assassinated Archduke Ferdinand, triggering the First World War) attacked a number of Croatian and Kosova Albanian web sites, bringing them down and replacing them with messages such as 'Long Live Great Serbia'. It also threatened to bring down the NATO web site in protest against the bombings of Yugoslavia. This type of action has been repeated by a number of different groups against targets including the Palestinian Authority, the Israeli government, and the Indian Army in Kashmir.

Diasporic nationalism

The nationalist groups on which the Internet (and associated new media) has had the greatest impact are the Diasporas. By their very nature, Diasporas have been more cut off from their homelands and national discourse than any other group. A traditional stereotype has been of émigrés gathering in cafes and social clubs anxiously exchanging stories of the homeland, reading old newspapers sent to them, and trying to stay in contact with other members of communities which have been, often forcibly, shattered and dispersed across national boundaries. The Internet has allowed these groups instant access to news from the homeland, and also access to a range of outlets rather than remaining dependent on occasional copies of newspapers from the homeland found in the more cosmopolitan kiosks and newsagents. A corollary to this is that members of Diasporas can also participate in national debates taking place in their homelands, whether through e-mails to concerned individuals and media outlets or through maintaining web sites that put forward a Diasporic viewpoint. The web site of the Serbian Unity Congress (URL) is a fairly typical example.

These web sites also play an important role in generating support within the Diasporas for particular viewpoints as well as performing a useful economic role in exhorting visitors to the web site to buy goods and services from other members of the Diaspora or directly from the homeland, thus often providing links to relevant companies and directories of businesses owned by the Diaspora's community. For example, <http://www.armenian.com> describes itself as a 'yellow pages' for the Armenian community, offering links to all manner of Armenian-owned businesses offering everything from accident reconstruction to yarn. The Internet and related newsgroups and e-mail lists also increase the ability of Diasporas to take part in lobbying the homeland, their adoptive countries, and international institutions and companies through promoting coordinated responses among the community to issues of concern. As Internet usage becomes more and more commonplace, it is clear that its impact on Diasporic nationalism and indeed on the notion of the 'imagined community' can only increase.

Josh Kaldor-Robinson, University of Cambridge

One of the most notorious Serb paramilitary leaders, Arkan, owned a string of pizza parlours that were a cover for the drug trade. The 'right to be the first to loot' was payment for the atrocities committed by his paramilitary groups, the Tigers. In recent years, human trafficking has become an important source of income for Balkan groups.

A third and increasingly significant source of income is Diaspora support. The first and most important diasporic groups were those of the Jews, the Armenians, and the Greeks. Robin Cohen (1996) has described how in recent times the term has been applied to a variety of peoples—expatriates, political refugees, alien residents, immigrants, and ethnic and racial minorities alike—and at least 30 ethnic groups are said to have a Diaspora. Diasporas provide money, ideas, skills, and even volunteers. A feature of the Bosnian war was the weekend fighters who came from Germany to fight. Far away from what they see as their homeland, Diaspora groups are often vulnerable to the appeals of extremist groups and to the imaginary depiction of struggle that is supposed

Box 7.7: Diaspora funding for Hindu nationalism

During the 1990s, funding from abroad for Hindu nationalist organisations has grown exponentially. Figure 7.2 shows the main organisations that promote Hindu ideology (Hindutva) in India and their affiliates abroad. The RSS is the fount of Hindutva. It is organised into cells (*shakha*) and based on volunteers (*swayemsevaks*). It was founded in 1925 and, at that time, its leaders were openly fascist, drawing inspiration from Hitler and Mussolini. Gandhi's assassin had an RSS association and for a time RSS was banned in India. Since then, it has spawned a range of organisations. Particularly important is the political wing, the BJP, which is now the ruling party in India; the VHP, which aggressively promotes Hindu nationalism, including its paramilitary wing, Bajrang Dal; and Sewa Vibhag, the service or welfare wing. All these organisations were involved in the destruction of the sixteenth century Babri Masjid mosque in Ayodhya in 1992, supposedly the site of Ram's birthplace; this was followed by religious riots in which some 3,000 people were killed. More recently, according to Human Rights Watch, members of the VHP and the Bajrang Dal, dressed in shorts and saffron scarves, were actively engaged in the massacre of some 2,000 Muslims in Gujarat after a train carrying 58 Hindu pilgrims was blown up. The chief Minister of Gujarat, Narendra Modi, a member of VHP, condoned the violence, as did the ruling BJP. Further, these groups have also been involved in increasing numbers of attacks against Christians, especially in tribal areas. Since 1998, when the BJP came to power, there have been some 500 reported incidents of attacks against Christians, compared with 50 in 1952–98.

All these organisations have international counterparts, as shown in Figure 7.2. The web site www.Hindu-unity.org, the mouthpiece of the Bajrang Dal, is virulently anti-Muslim. As far as funding is concerned, it is the counterparts to Sewa Vibhag, the service organisation, that are important. In particular, Sewa International, based in the UK, and the India Development and Relief Fund (IDRF), based in Maryland, US, are key conduits for funds. Both are charities and both claim to be non-political. Sewa International is currently under investigation by the UK Charities Commission.

Fund-raising activities are organised around temples and ceremonial occasions. For example, the IDRF brochure states:

> *If you are celebrating a birthday or a wedding anniversary, enjoying a graduation party, solemnising a pooja, rejoicing a festival or commemorating your beloved ones, IDRF is at your service. It offers you a unique opportunity for serving God through selfless humanitarian service and thus enhancing your inner joy.*

Students are encouraged to engage in fund-raising activities. VHP-America has also organised Dharma Samsads, ceremonial gatherings, which suggest rules by which Hindu Americans should live their lives and also function as fund-raising events. (Jamaat and Sikh organisations hold similar camps or conclaves.)

Another method of funding is corporate matching. Some companies match contributions by employees to charities, and Hindu organisations have encouraged this. Since the Gujarat riots, Cisco, Sun Microsystems, and Oracle have all suspended IDRF from their list of eligible charities.

Analyses of the disbursement of funds by IDRF and Sewa International show that the money goes overwhelmingly to Sangh organisations (i.e. organisations linked to RSS). Thus, in 2000, 80 per cent of the $1.7million dispersed by IDRF went to Sangh organisations. In terms of activities, 70 per cent was spent on what could be described as Hinduisation (schools and tribal activities aimed at conversion). Although RSS started as an upper-caste organisation aiming at the 'purity' of the Indian nation, now a major effort is directed at converting scheduled tribes, which account for 25 per cent of the Indian population. It is argued that these groups, indigenous Indian tribes, are really Aryans in disguise and must be integrated into the Hindu nation before they are converted to Christianity. These groups represent an important electoral potential for the BJP and also a source of communal tension on which the Sangh organisations thrive. In recent years, Hindu religious schools similar to Madrassahs have sprung up in various places, especially in tribal areas.

US affiliates of RSS had total assets of almost $11 million in 2001, according to returns filed by the Internal Revenue Service in 2001. In particular, IDRF raised $3.8 million in 2001, of which $1.7million was disbursed. Another organisation, the Hindu Heritage Endowment, is said to have raised $2.6 million since its establishment in 1994. The UK Charities Commission estimates that Sewa International and the HSS raised $4.3million in the UK in 2001. The actual sums are likely to be much larger; they include informal cash transfers through the *hawala* system, funds to religious trusts, which are tax exempt in the US, and funds channelled through various US tax shelters.

Sources: Prashad and Mathew (1999); Chowgule (2002); Luce and Sevastopoulu (2003).

Figure 7.2: International funding for Hindu nationalist organisation Sangh Parivar (Sangh family)

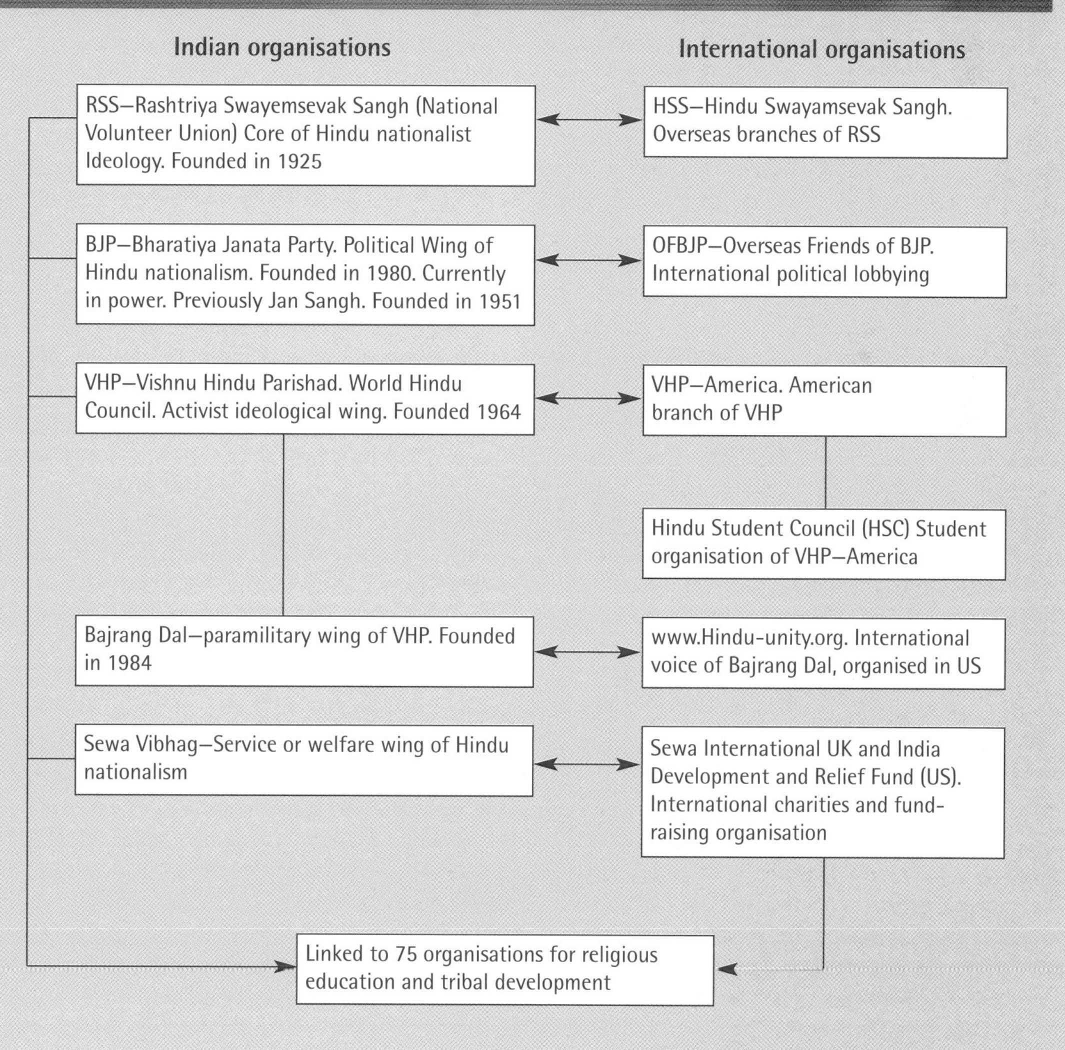
Indian organisations
International organisations
RSS—Rashtriya Swayemsevak Sangh (National Volunteer Union) Core of Hindu nationalist Ideology. Founded in 1925
HSS—Hindu Swayamsevak Sangh. Overseas branches of RSS
BJP—Bharatiya Janata Party. Political Wing of Hindu nationalism. Founded in 1980. Currently in power. Previously Jan Sangh. Founded in 1951
OFBJP—Overseas Friends of BJP. International political lobbying
VHP—Vishnu Hindu Parishad. World Hindu Council. Activist ideological wing. Founded 1964
VHP—America. American branch of VHP
Hindu Student Council (HSC) Student organisation of VHP—America
Bajrang Dal—paramilitary wing of VHP. Founded in 1984
www.Hindu-unity.org. International voice of Bajrang Dal, organised in US
Sewa Vibhag—Service or welfare wing of Hindu nationalism
Sewa International UK and India Development and Relief Fund (US). International charities and fund-raising organisation
Linked to 75 organisations for religious education and tribal development

to be happening at home. Hence Diaspora support is increasingly important for all South Asian groups (see Box 7.7), Serbs, Croats, Kosovar Albanians, as well as Kurds. Many people in the Diaspora support charitable organisations. Whether knowingly or not, funds to extremist groups are often channelled through religious NGOs. Islamic NGOs were one of the first targets of the FBI after September 11 in its efforts to crack down on terrorism.

In some cases, the Diaspora can be profoundly influential. An interesting example is the Sikh Diaspora, which traditionally was not engaged in the political project of defining the Sikh homeland, or Khalistan, which corresponds to the Indian state of Punjab. However, this changed dramatically in 1984 when the Indian army stormed the Golden Temple in Amritsar. After three days of heavy fighting, hundreds were killed and the symbolic centre of Sikhdom was desecrated. The measure angered the 16 million Sikhs worldwide who saw the assault on the temple as a premeditated act of Indian brutality. In the aftermath of the attack the millions of Sikhs who lived in Britain, Canada, and the USA reacted by founding organisations that could defend the 'threatened homeland'. Hence, the already established Sikh organisations were reinforced and new ones were created, such as the North American-based World Sikh Organization, the International Sikh Youth Federation, and the Council of Khalistan (Singh Tatla 1999). In the case of the Kosovar Albanians, a key turning point leading to war was when Kosovar Albanians living abroad decided to switch their funds from support for the non-violent movement led by Ibrahim Rugova to a fund called Homeland Calling, which financed the KLA. The opposite may have been the case in Northern Ireland. American Irish support for the peace process and the decline in American funding for the IRA was probably a key factor leading to the Good Friday agreement in 1998.

The Relationship to Globalisation

The rise of nationalist and religious militant groups in recent decades can be understood in terms of both reacting to and feeding off globalisation. In this chapter, we have tried to show that the growth of these groups can be explained in terms of the insecurities generated by globalisation as well as disillusion with the secular ideologies of the state. At the same time, these groups make use of the opportunities created by globalisation: the new media, especially television and Internet, and increased opportunities for funding from the Diaspora as well as from transnational criminal groups.

But where many of these groups differ from other actors in global civil society is in their focus on the capture of state power, as was the case for earlier territorially based forms of civil society like labour movements or anti-colonial movements. This difference is reflected in both their organisational structure and their tactics and strategy. They tend to combine traditional and contemporary forms of organisation and tactics. Thus many groups are organised as political parties and make use of established strategies like taking part in elections, mass demonstrations, and so on. On the other hand, the political party form is often combined with transnational infrastructure networks and with grass-roots militia. Moreover, traditional tactics are often combined with symbolic protests aimed at media impact, even though, unlike with other global civil society actors, these symbolic protests are often violent.

Whereas other actors of global civil society may aim to 'civilise' globalisation, these groups aim to roll back globalisation while making use of the instruments of globalisation to mobilise feelings of insecurity and cultural loss that result from globalisation, especially among migrants. These groups could be described as regressive globalisers, that is to say, they make use of globalisation in the interests of particular groups, ethnic or religious. They claim to be rejectionists, to want to roll back globalisation, and to establish what they see as old-fashioned states; yet to do so they build on the opportunities offered by globalisation (financial, symbolic, and psychological) to increase the impact of their particular religious or nationalist vision and so extend their power.

If our analysis is correct, these groups are likely to grow both because of growing insecurities and because they are only now beginning to exploit fully the organisational opportunities provided by globalisation. And yet, in the context of globalisation, their political goals are fundamentally contradictory. Absolutist forms of sovereignty cannot be re-established, if they ever were fully established. The goal of achieving ethnically pure or religious states is more elusive than ever. Perhaps these groups do not expect to achieve their stated goals; it is the struggle on which they thrive and the difficulty of achieving their stated goals will make the struggle even more legitimate. Unless other actors in global civil society are able to offer more effective forms of security, alternative ideas that resonate with the marginalised and excluded, and unless they are able to construct a sophisticated infrastructure, with schools and television channels that enable them to reach out beyond the globalised cosmopolitan class, the prognosis is depressing. We are likely to face an increasingly polarised and violent world.

References

Alexander, Jeffrey (2000). 'Contradictions: The Uncivilising Pressures of Time, Space and Function'. *Soundings: A Journal of Politics and Culture*, 16: 96-112.

Alexander, Yonah and Pluchinsky, Dennis A. (eds) (1992). *Europe's Red Terrorists: The Fighting Communist Organizations*. London: Frank Cass.

Anheier, Helmut, Glasius, Marlies, and Kaldor, Mary (eds) (2001). *Global Civil Society 2001*.Oxford: Oxford University Press.

Anheier, Helmut and Themudo, Nuno (2002). 'Organisational Forms of Global Civil Society: Implications of Going Global'. In Helmut Anheier, Marlies Glasius, and Mary Kaldor (eds), *Global Civil Society 2002*. Oxford: Oxford University Press.

An-Na'im, Abdullah (2002). 'Religion and Global Civil Society: Inherent Incompatibility or Synergy and Interdependence?'. In Marlies Glasius, Mary Kaldor, and Helmut Anheier (eds), *Global Civil Society 2002*. Oxford: Oxford University Press.

Arendt, Hannah (1968). *The Origins of Totalitarianism* (New edn). New York: Harcourt, Brace and Jovanovitch.

Barber, Benjamin R. (1995). *Jihad vs. McWorld*. New York: Ballantine Books.

BBC web site <http://www.bbc.co.uk/history/programmes/greatbritons/>.

Bin Laden, Osama (1998). *World Islamic Front Statement urging Jihad Against Jews and Crusaders* <http://www.fas.org/irp/world/para/docs/980223-fatwa.htm>.

Boyer, P. S. (1992). *When Time Shall Be No More: Prophecy Belief in Modern American Culture*. Cambridge, MA: Belknap Press.

– (2003). 'When U.S. Foreign Policy Meets Biblical Prophecy'. *Alternet*, 20 February <http://www.alternet.org/story.html?StoryID=15221>

British National Party website <http://www.bnp.org.uk>.

Bruce, Steve (2000) *Fundamentalism*, Malden, Mass.: Polity Press in association with Blackwell Publishers.

Center for Systemic Peace, University of Maryland <http://members.aol.com//CSPmgm/warlist.htm>.

Canovan, Margaret (1999). 'Trust the People! Populism and the Two Faces of Democracy'. *Political Studies*, 47: 2–16.

Cherry, Matt (2002). 'Apocalypse Now'. *New Humanist*, Autumn.<http://www.newhumanist.org.uk/issues/0209/cherry.htm>.

Chowgule, Ashok (2002). *The Foreign Exchange of Hate: IDRF and American Funding of Hindutva*. Mumbai: Sabrang Communications and Publishing PvT Ltd and South Asians Citizens Web <http://www.mnet.fr>.

Cohen, Robin (1996). 'Diasporas and the Nation-State: From Victims to Challengers'. *International Affairs*, 72: 507–20.

Coker, Christopher (2002). *Globalisation and Insecurity in the Twenty-First Century: NATO and the Management of Risk*. Oxford: Oxford University Press for the International Institute for Strategic Studies.

Deane, James (with Njonjo Mue and Fackson Banda) (2002). The Other Information Revolution: Media and Empowerment in Developing Countries'. In Marlies Glasius, Mary Kaldor, and Helmut Anheier (eds), *Global Civil Society 2002*. Oxford: Oxford University Press.

Engel, M. (2002). 'Meet the New Zionists'. *The Guardian*, 28 October.

Falk, Richard (1998). 'Global Civil Society: Perspectives, Initiatives, Movements', *Oxford Development Studies*, 26: 99–110.

Fisk, R.(2002). 'A Strange Kind of Freedom'. *The Independent*, 9 July.

Gellner, Ernest (1994). *Conditions of Liberty: Civil Society and its Rivals*. London: Hamish Hamilton.

Gunaratna, Rohan (2003). 'Still Threatening'. *The World Today*, 59/1: 18–20.

Hatewatch <http://www.hatewatch.org>.

Hayes, Carlton Joseph Huntley (1960). *Nationalism: A Religion*. New York: Macmillan.

Hoffman, Bruce (2001). 'Change and Continuity in Terrorism', *Studies in Conflict & Terrorism*, 24: 417–28.

Jones, David Martin and Smith, Mike Lawrence (2002). 'From Konfrontasi to Disintegrasi: ASEAN and the Rise of Islamism in Southeast Asia'. *Studies in Conflict and Terrorism*. 25: 343–56.

Juergensmeyer, Mark (2000). *Terror in the Mind of God: The Global Rise of Religious Violence*. Berkeley: University of California Press.

Kaldor, Mary (1999). *New and Old Wars: Organised Violence in a Global Era*. Cambridge: Polity Press.

Karawan, Ibrahim A. (1997). 'The Islamist Impasse'. *Adelphi Paper* 314. London: The International Institute for Strategic Studies.

Keane, John (2001). 'Global Civil Society?'. In Anheier, Helmut, Glasius, Marlies, and Kaldor, Mary (eds), *Global Civil Society 2001*. Oxford: Oxford University Press.

Kedourie, Elie (1960). *Nationalism*. Oxford: Blackwell.

Kulczycki, Andrzej (1999). *The Abortion Debate in the World Arena*. London: Macmillan.

Kymlicka, Will (1995). *Multicultural Citzenship*. Oxford: Oxford University Press.

Lieven, A. (2002) 'The Push for War'. *The London Review of Books*, 3 October.

Luce, Edward and Sevastopoulu, Demetri (2003). 'Blood and Hate'. *Financial Times*, 20 February.

McMahon, Darrin M. (2001). *Enemies of the Enlightenment: The French Counter-Enlightenment and the Making of Modernity*. New York, Oxford: Oxford University Press.

Malcolm, Noel (1998). *Kosovo: A Short History*. London: Macmillan.

Marty, Martin E. and Appleby, R. Scott (1992). *The Glory and the Power: The Fundamentalist Challenge to the Modern World*. Boston: Beacon Press.

— (1994). *Fundamentalisms Observed*. Chicago: Chicago University Press.

Mayer, Jean-François (2001). 'Cults, Violence and Religious Terrorism: An International Perspective'. *Studies in Conflict and Terrorism*. 24: 361–76.

Melander, Erik (2001). 'The Nagorno-Karabakh Conflict Revisited: Was the War Inevitable?' *Journal of Cold War Studies*, 3/2: 48–75.

Miller, David (1996). *On Nationality*. Oxford: Oxford University Press.

Muir, Angus M. (1999). 'Terrorism and Weapons of Mass Destruction: The Case of Aum Shinrikyo'. *Studies in Conflict and Terrorism*, 22: 79–91.

National Abortion Federation <http://www.prochoice.org/>.

People for the American Way (2002). *Right Wing Organisations: The Christian Coalition* <http://www.pfaw.org/pfaw/general/default.aspx?oid=6101>.

Prashad, Vijay and Mathew, Biju (1999). 'Deceit of the Right'. *Himal*, 12/12.

RAND (1968–97). *Terrorism Chronology* <http://db.mipt.org/rand_68_97.cfm>.

Serbian Unity Congress <http://www.suc.org>.

Silke, Andrew (2000). 'Drink, Drugs, and Rock n'Roll: Financing Loyalist Terrorism in Northern Ireland—Part Two'. *Studies in Conflict and Terrorism*, 23: 107–27.

Singh Tatla, Darshan (1999). *The Sikh Diaspora: The Search for Statehood*. London: UCL Press.

Smith, Anthony D. (2000). 'The "Sacred" Dimension of Nationalism'. *Millennium: Journal of International Studies*, 29: 791–814.

Smith, K. (2002). 'Swept up to Heaven: Apocalyptic Fundamentalism and the Crusade for Israel'. *Common Sense*, 17/3 <http://www.nd.edu/~com_sens/v17_n3.html#swept>.

Stormfront <http://www.stormfront.org>.

Sussman, Paul. 'ETA: Feared Separatist Group' <http://www.cnn.com/SPECIALS/2001/basque/stories/background.html>

Tsfati, Yariv and Weimann, Gabriel (2002). 'www.terrorism.com: Terror on the Internet'. *Studies in Conflict and Terrorism*, 25: 317–32.

United States. Department of State. *Patterns of Global Terrorism* <http://www.stste.gov/s/ct/rls/pgtrpt/>

Vulliamy, E. (2003). 'Two Men Driving Bush into War'. *The Observer*, 23 February.

Chapter 8

Transnational Peasant and Farmer Movements and Networks

Marc Edelman

In 1999, thousands of protesters—some dressed as monarch butterflies and sea turtles—disrupted the Seattle meeting of the World Trade Organization and helped to shine a spotlight on controversial global development issues. A less flamboyant and fashionable part of the crowd consisted of organised peasants and small farmers, from dozens of countries, who proclaimed that worldwide economic liberalisation endangered their livelihoods. Sporting green baseball caps and bandannas, these activists have been a significant presence outside post-Seattle meetings of international financial, trade, and governance institutions in Washington, Prague, Cancún, Quebec, Genoa, Barcelona, and elsewhere, as well as in the civil society delegations to the 2001 Food and Agriculture Organisation summit ('Rome+5'), the 2001, 2002, and 2003 Porto Alegre World Social Forums, and the 2002 World Summit on Sustainable Development ('Rio+10'). The voices of small agriculturalists ('peasants and 'farmers', see box 8.1) are having a growing impact in global arenas. Farmers in India were among the first to object to the controversial Trade-Related Intellectual Property Agreement (TRIPS), which empowers the WTO to enforce global rules on patents, copyrights, and trademarks. The French Confédération Paysanne, which grabbed headlines worldwide when its supporters dismantled a half-built McDonald's restaurant, played a key role in having the European Union declare a moratorium on commercial planting of genetically modified (GM) crops. The success of the Brazilian Landless Movement (MST) in pressing for agrarian reform influenced peasant organisations throughout the Americas and as far away as South Africa. Much of this rural effervescence developed from cross-border links that peasant and small farmer organisations from many parts of the world forged with each other and with NGOs concerned with agrarian reform, food security, trade, biotechnology, and environmental and human rights issues.

This chapter first examines early and mid-twentieth-century attempts to link agriculturalists' organisations in different countries. It then analyses how the farm crisis, market openings, and regional integration projects of the 1980s galvanised new cross-border links among farmers in Latin America, North America, Europe, and India. This 'globalisation from below' allowed agriculturalists to develop common agendas and protest repertoires, as well as to have tangible impacts in areas as diverse as trade policy and human rights. In the past two decades, farmers have achieved a prominence in international arenas that they rarely enjoyed in their own countries, where they were often the most economically and culturally marginalised sectors of the population. The networks that make up global civil society, including those of agriculturalists, nonetheless raise delicate questions about representation. Who speaks for the peasant and farmer, and through what political processes are such claims to legitimacy established or contested?

Historical Organisations

Associated Country Women of the World

Transnational networking among small farmer organisations accelerated during the 1980s and 1990s, but its roots lie in the late nineteenth and early twentieth centuries. This suggests that cross-border organising is neither a new phenomenon nor simply an outcome of recent revolutions in communications technology, the emergence of supranational governance institutions, or a weakening of the contemporary state system under globalisation. Early transnational farmers organisations manifested eclectic amalgams of elite-led reformism and *noblesse oblige*, pacifism, Christian missionary zeal, first-wave feminism, and agrarian populism.

The genealogy of Associated Country Women of the World (ACWW) exemplifies these diverse origins. ACWW, 'the largest international organisation for rural women', claims a membership of nine million in 365 participating societies in over 70 countries (ACWW 2002). It developed in the late 1920s through encounters between leaders of the International

Council of Women (ICW)—founded by women's suffrage and temperance activists in Washington in 1888—and the Women's Institutes (WI), which began in Canada in the 1890s as auxiliaries to the Farmers' Institutes extension programme and spread to the United States, England, and many British colonies.

In 1913 Canadian WI activist Madge Watt moved to Britain, where she helped found several hundred local Women's Institutes and interested long-time ICW President Ishbel Gordon Aberdeen in starting an international federation. Watt and Lady Aberdeen, a feminist whose husband had served as British Governor General of Canada, called a meeting in London in 1929 with women from 23 countries who established an ICW committee on rural women (Drage 1961). The committee published a yearbook and circulated leaflets in three languages to recruit new national associations (Meier 1958). In 1933 in Stockholm, it became Associated Country Women of the World.

It was ridiculous to push new varieties when a farmer's biggest problem was not seedlings, but a place to plant them. Military rule had soldiers in every village and land-grabbers fast behind them

In ACWW's early years, women from the English, Belgian, Romanian, German, and Swedish aristocracy played key roles. The Association set up speakers' schools for organisers and researched issues such as midwifery services and nutrition. In the pre-war period it worked with the League of Nations and, following the Second World War, it attained consultative status with several United Nations agencies. More recently, ACWW has supported development and income-generating programmes and advocated in international forums for women's rights. Despite growing participation by women from less developed countries and an increasingly sophisticated approach to gender issues, ACWW never transcended its elite British origins. Its conventions are still held in English without translation services, which limits participation from outside the English-speaking world primarily to educated middle- and upper-class women, most of whom are NGO personnel rather than rural producers.

Agricultural Missions

Agricultural Missions, a multi-denominational Christian organisation founded in 1930 by US religious leaders and deans of agricultural colleges, originally assisted churches in sending missionaries to some 50 countries. Supported by the US National Council of Churches, it emphasised technical assistance and a gospel of rural life. In the 1970s, influenced by liberation theology's 'preferential option for the poor' and by anti-colonial struggles, the organisation established relations with grass-roots movements. In 1979, as Agricultural Missions neared its 50th anniversary, it sponsored a 'consultation' in Jayuya, Puerto Rico, that brought together religious and farmer activists from the Caribbean, Central America, Micronesia, Africa, Korea, and the Philippines, as well as Mexican-, Native-, and African-Americans (Matejka 1979). 'It was useless to speak of mini-tractors, hybrid seeds or breeding techniques with the rural poor', J. Benton Rhoades, the Missions' executive secretary wrote,

> *if those small farmers were unsure of their land ownership, or trapped between tenancy and loan sharks. It was ridiculous to push new varieties when a farmer's biggest problem was not seedlings, but a place to plant them. It was difficult to bring people together when military rule had soldiers in every village and land-grabbers fast behind them. (Matejka 1979: 3)*

This shift in Agricultural Missions' orientation facilitated transnational collaboration by peasant and farmer activists. In 2002, Agricultural Missions organised a three-week 'Education for Rural Justice Tour' in ten US states, which featured peasants from Mexico, Brazil, and Venezuela who spoke on conditions in their countries to audiences of farmers, church members, students, and environmentalists (NCC 2002).

International Federation of Agricultural Producers

The International Federation of Agricultural Producers (IFAP) was founded amidst post-Second World War optimism about global cooperation and fears of impending food shortages and a recurrence of agricultural depression like that of the 1930s. In 1946 the British National Farmers' Union convoked a

Box 8.1: 'Peasant' and 'farmer'—what's in a name?

In the 1960s and 1970s, scholars devoted a great deal of attention to defining the term 'peasant.' Teodor Shanin, dean of the new field of 'peasant studies', suggested that 'peasants' everywhere shared four main characteristics: (1) a livelihood based on subsistence and also perhaps on commodity production, but not usually involving profit maximisation as an objective; (2) a reliance on family labour and on the household as a unit of production, consumption, reproduction, and risk-spreading; (3) political, economic, and cultural subordination to dominant classes and state authorities; and (4) traditional village relations of solidarity and reciprocity (Shanin 1971:14–15). 'Farmers', in contrast, primarily produced for the market, and they did so with advanced technology, hired labour, and formal credit. In the popular imagination, 'farmers' were emblematic of modernity; 'peasants' represented backwardness.

Bounding the 'peasant' category permitted certain kinds of analysis but foreclosed others. Some rural people who considered themselves 'peasants'—agricultural labourers, for example—were not usually included in the definition, even if they acted politically in concert with others who were. Urbanites or members of elites sometimes claimed to be 'peasants' in order to marshal support for revolutionary or clientelistic political programmes. Rigid definitions also tended to obscure the complexity of rural social relations in places where an individual might labour for wages, till a small plot of land for food, produce export crops under contract to a foreign corporation, and engage in a non-agricultural income-producing activity such as fishing or repairing machinery.

Equivalent terms in other languages—*campesino* or *paysan*—had different, usually broader, connotations, often implying simply 'people from the countryside'. And some widely used terms—the Spanish *agricultor*, for example—were scale-neutral, including those who in English would be both 'peasants' and 'farmers'.

By the 1990s, academic specialists had largely discarded 'peasant studies' in favour of 'agrarian change' or 'agrarian studies', a conceptual field that more easily covered relations between the rural poor and a variety of other actors, such as large landowners, banks, and agribusiness corporations, and urban politicians and social movements (Bernstein and Byres 2001). A few scholars maintained that the term 'peasant' was so imprecise or so laden with pejorative meanings and cultural freight that it ought to be discarded (Kearney 1996). This position, however, ignored the efforts of contemporary activists to reappropriate the term 'peasant' and infuse it with new and positive content, including a celebration of peasants as sophisticated bearers of modern values and political projects . This rethinking leads today's rural activists to insist on the commonalities of 'peasants' and 'farmers', and often to use the two words interchangeably—in conversation, in written analyses, and in their movements' names (the European Farmers Coordination and the Coordination Paysanne Européenne, for example, are the same organisation). As Nettie Wiebe, a Vía Campesina activist and past president of the National Farmers Union of Canada, remarked in an interview,

> *If you actually look at what 'peasant' means, it means 'people of the land'. Are we Canadian farmers 'people of the land'? Well, yes, of course. And it's important to take that language back . . . We too are peasants and it's the land and our relationship to the land and food production that distinguishes us . . . We're not part of the industrial machine. We're much more closely linked to the places where we grow food and how we grow food, and what the weather is there . . . The language around this matters. It begins to make us understand that 'people of the land'—peasantry everywhere, the millions of small subsistence peasants with whom we think we have so little in common—identifies them and it identifies us. They're being evicted from their land, and that decimates their identity and their community. And we're also being relocated in our society—it's as undermining for us as it is for them. The language? As long as you keep us in separate categories and we're the highly industrialized farmers who are sort of quasi-business entrepreneurs and they're the subsistence peasants, then we can't see how closely we and all our issues are linked. (Interview 22 November 2002, Saskatoon, Saskatchewan)*

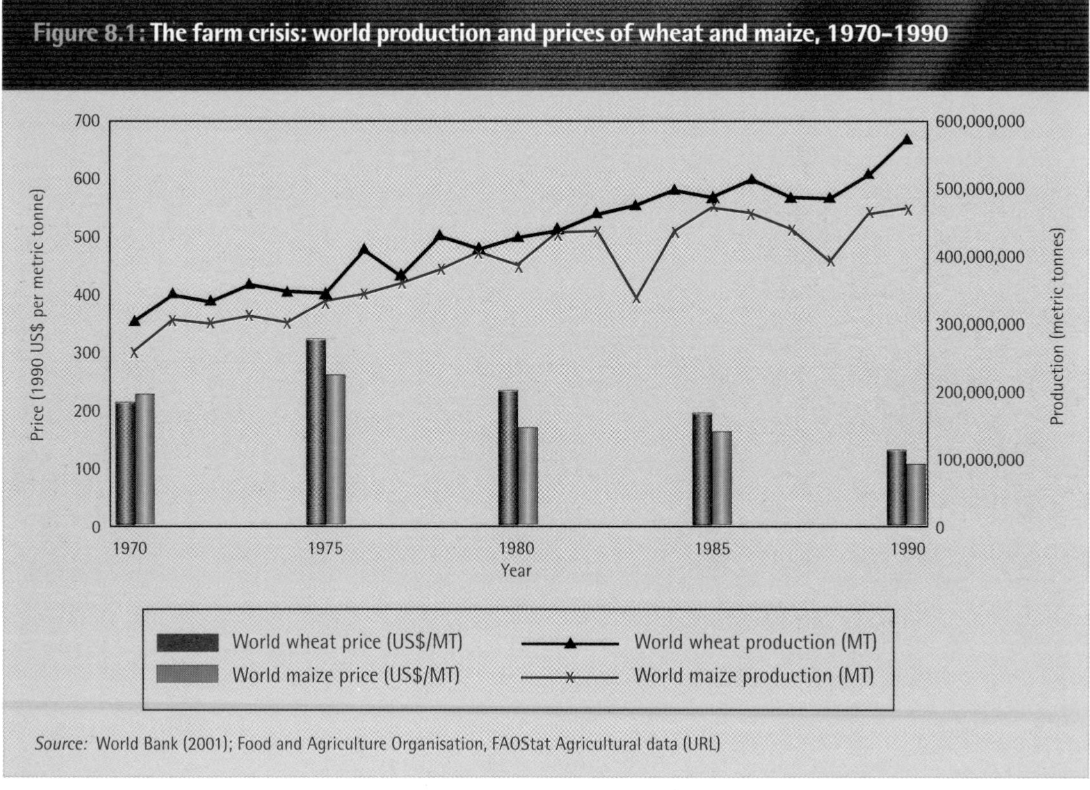

Figure 8.1: The farm crisis: world production and prices of wheat and maize, 1970–1990

Source: World Bank (2001); Food and Agriculture Organisation, FAOStat Agricultural data (URL)

meeting in London of agriculturalists' representatives from 30 countries, with the objective of supporting the newly formed UN Food and Agriculture Organisation (FAO) and overcoming differences between commodity-based interest groups within the agricultural sector (*Times* 1946a; 1946b).

The northern European groups that dominated IFAP already had a decades-long history of international congresses, many involving cooperative societies and Christian farmers' organisations created in the early twentieth century (ICA & IFAP1967; IFAP 1957: 5). Despite a certain ambivalence about market liberalism, these forces often backed centre-right political parties.

The post-war food crisis led IFAP to emphasise increasing production, even though some delegations, such as the Canadians, called for international marketing mechanisms that 'would distribute abundance efficiently and in such a way that surpluses would not spell disaster to the producers' (*Times* 1946b). IFAP leaders served in government delegations to FAO conferences, sometimes exercising substantial influence on FAO policies (IFAP 1952).

The 1980s farm crisis

The upsurge in transnational agriculturalists' movements during the past two decades is a direct result of a worldwide farm crisis. The origins of the crisis in the 1970s included skyrocketing prices for petroleum and fossil fuel-based inputs; sharply higher interest rates, resulting from oil-price shocks and monetary policies intended to slow inflation; and the breakdown of the Bretton Woods system of capital controls and fixed exchange rates, which set the stage for a rapid expansion and liberalisation of global food trade (Greider 2000; McMichael 1998). At the same time, growing concentration among input and machinery suppliers, and in the processing, storage, brokering, and exporting stages of key commodity chains, allowed a handful of giant corporations to garner a rising share of the total value added between field and dinner plate (Kneen 2002).

Since the 1960s, high subsidies in the United States and Europe had generated vast food surpluses. Excess grain had been dumped in the countries of the South, but by the late 1960s huge European markets

Tractors of the Movimento Sem Terra (Landless Peasant Movement), Brazil, plough land after occupying a farm.

opened up for France, the continent's largest agricultural economy, and the Soviets began to purchase enormous quantities of US wheat. In 1970–80, US farm exports jumped 150 per cent and France's doubled (Sheingate 2001). New demand led to shortages and climbing prices. The response was a worldwide credit-based expansion by commercial farmers. By the late 1970s surpluses had returned, a problem which worsened when the United States and Canada cut off grain sales to the Soviets following the invasion of Afghanistan (See figure 8.1). Commodity and land prices plummeted, and interest rates soared (Friedmann 1993). Many US and Canadian producers defaulted on loans and lost their land, spurring militant farmers' movements and reviving anti-foreclosure tactics such as 'farm gate defences' not seen since the 'penny auctions' of the 1930s depression (Mooney and Majka 1995; NFU 1985a; Wilford 1985).

In poorer countries, particularly in Latin America, the debt crisis of the early 1980s, also rooted in part in rising interest rates and oil import bills, brought neo-liberal reforms that devastated small agricultural producers accustomed to guaranteed prices, low-interest loans, and state-sponsored extension services (Edelman 1998). Ironically, these reforms, encouraged by the Bretton Woods institutions, dismantled the same commodities boards and the systems of subsidies for inputs, machinery, fuel, water, and credit that the World Bank had helped to set up in country after country in the 1950s and 1960s in order to make capital-intensive agriculture possible in conditions of poverty (Shiva 2001).

While the main focus of this chapter is on agriculturalists' participation in global civil society, it is important to acknowledge that the farm crisis generated a tremendous range of political responses, from great enthusiasm for transnational solidarity to extreme hostility towards producers in other countries. Economic liberalisation and the growing export orientation of highly subsidised farm sectors in Europe and the United States tended to enlarge markets and force down prices for key internationally traded commodities such as grains, oil seeds, and cotton. Falling commodity prices boosted the profitability of, and encouraged mergers among, giant agribusiness corporations such as Cargill, ConAgra, and Archers Daniel Midland, which dominated input sales, post-harvest processing, and export trade (and, with increased consolidation and vertical integration, they could readily engage in non-competitive pricing practices). Farmers sometimes reacted to intensifying competitive pressures with organised transnational efforts to directly affect the supra-national governance structures that pushed for and administered the newly liberalised global economic system. In some countries, in contrast, they chose to influence supra-national institutions through pressuring national governments that participated in them.

At times, the changed economic environment led farmers to view their counterparts elsewhere as a threat, especially when influxes of inexpensive foreign products collapsed prices. In Europe in 1992–7, for example, farmers' protests which had a transnational dimension were much more likely to have nationalist and protectionist objectives than cooperative ones (Bush and Simi 2001).

More rural and for the most part poorer than the rest of Latin America, the Central American countries were small and had long seen intra-regional migrations of peasants and agricultural labourers

Regional Integration: Latin America

The rise of regional integration and supra-national governance institutions in the 1980s and early 1990s fuelled the cross-border organising that was already occurring in response to the farm crisis. In Latin America, North America, and Europe, in particular, new free trade accords and supra-national governance institutions became the focus of an increasingly internationalist peasant and farmer activism and fostered new alliances between agriculturalists in different countries, and between them and social movements and NGOs from other sectors.

Central American origins

Within Latin America, the Central America region proved especially significant as a fount of innovative transnational peasant organising. More rural and for the most part poorer than the rest of Latin America, the Central American countries were small and had long seen intra-regional migrations of peasants and agricultural labourers. Some peasant movements in the region, notably in Honduras, were historically among the best organised in the hemisphere and had won significant agrarian reforms in the 1970s (Posas 1985), while others, in Costa Rica, were among the first to develop analyses of the impact of neoliberal reforms on small-scale agriculturalists (Edelman 1999). The 1979 Sandinista revolution made Nicaragua a reference point for radical social movements throughout the area, a top priority for European cooperation agencies, and a key champion of new forms of internationalism (Blokland 1995: 161; Freres 1998: 23). In the early 1980s, European governments reacted with alarm to Reagan Administration attempts to overthrow the Sandinistas in Nicaragua and roll back leftist guerrillas in El Salvador and Guatemala. This anxiety—based on fears of a major regional war and an analysis that stressed inequality and injustice rather than communism as causes of the conflicts—brought large increases in European cooperation expenditures and extensive backing for the Contadora peace process, initiated in 1983 by Mexico, Colombia, Venezuela, and Panama (and later for the efforts of Costa Rican President Oscar Arias that led to the 1987 Esquipulas Peace Accords).

In El Salvador, Guatemala, and Nicaragua in the 1980s, peasants joined armed movements and hundreds of thousands became refugees, frequently elsewhere on the isthmus. In Panama, Honduras, and Costa Rica organisations of the rural poor engaged in bitter struggles over structural adjustment programmes which had slashed extension services and credit, reduced price supports and subsidies for loans and inputs, reversed hard-won agrarian reforms, and facilitated the penetration of transnational capital in agriculture (Stein and Arias Peñate 1992). In the late 1980s and early 1990s, governments and business groups moved toward regional integration as the civil wars ended or ebbed. The Central American Integration System, founded in 1991, institutionalised periodic summit meetings and a consultative committee for regionally-organised civil society groups. Also in 1991, a presidents' summit in San Salvador promulgated an 'Action Plan for Central American Agriculture', which had as its main objectives intra-regional free trade in grains and the linking of regional prices to international ones (Segovia 1993).

In 1990 the European-funded Support Committee for the Economic and Social Development of Central America (CADESCA), based in Panama, started a Food Security Training Program directed at government functionaries and peasant leaders. This concern with training movement leaders reflected a view of civil society and democratisation that stressed grass-roots participation in policy-making, a conception which contrasted with the US emphasis on free elections and elite-led reforms (Macdonald 1994). Around the same time, European cooperation strategies shifted and donors began to support projects with a Central

Box 8.2: Central America–the rise and fall of the ASOCODE network

For a half-dozen years in the 1990s, the Association of Central American Peasant Organizations for Cooperation and Development (ASOCODE) achieved an extraordinarily high profile in regional and hemispheric politics, attending numerous presidential and ministerial summits, sending frequent delegations to Europe and North America, publishing numerous position papers and a newsletter in Spanish and English, sponsoring meetings and courses for peasant activists, and attracting a copious flow of cooperation funds that reached an annual peak in 1996 of US$1.5 million, largely from the Dutch agency HIVOS, Ibis-Denmark, Oxfam, and other NGOs in the Copenhagen Initiative for Central America (Biekart 1999: 280). Led initially by a charismatic young Costa Rican, Wilson Campos, ASOCODE spawned several other Central American networks: the Indigenous and Peasant Community Agroforestry Coordinator (CICAFOC); the Central American Indigenous Council (CICA), and the Civil Initiative for Central American Integration (ICIC), an umbrella group for diverse movements aimed at participating in the consultative committee of the Central American Integration System (and, not incidentally, at securing additional funding and employment for ASOCODE leaders).

In 1994–7, according to an internal ASOCODE report, 'cooperation resources were so abundant that they exceeded the capacity of the headquarters' to administer them (ASOCODE 1999: 24). 'Overfunding' contributed to struggles for resources that exacerbated already existing factionalism and ultimately led funding agencies to cut off support (Biekart 1999: 286-93). In 2000, ASOCODE closed its Managua office, and in 2001 representatives of its member coalitions from five countries agreed to reorganise it as a decentralised network of issue-specific working groups that would communicate virtually or meet on an ad hoc basis, with a nominal headquarters in the office of one of the main Honduran peasant confederations (ASOCODE 2001). Most of ASOCODE's network 'offspring' were never able to shake off their image as creations of EU cooperation agencies.

The 'crisis and rupture' (ASOCODE 1999: 25) in ASOCODE raises questions for scholars, supporters, and activists of transnational civil society networks that have only begun to be addressed. Conservative and left-wing theorists (Ronfeldt and Arquilla 2001; Castells 1996) coincide in highlighting the potency and durability of network forms of organisation and in giving scant attention to how civil society networks may rise and fall, much as individual social movements manifest a periodicity linked to broader 'cycles of protest' (Tarrow 1998). Only rarely is the possibility considered that the 'network' may become 'a form that supersedes analysis and reality' and that its '"failure"' is endemic, indeed . . . [an] effect of the Network form' (Riles 2001: 174, 6).

In ASOCODE's case, a top-heavy organisation, a preponderance of activities that responded to donor rather than peasant priorities, and incessant internecine squabbling brought the association to a point where it still exists in name but enjoys little of its earlier support, dynamism, or prestige. Cooperation agencies, having identified similar problems in other Central American regional civil society networks, tempered their enthusiasm for cross-border initiatives, even though several donors that supported ASOCODE have backed other networks—generally leaner and less centralised—which it or its erstwhile activists helped to establish.

American regional, as opposed to a national or local, focus (Biekart 1999: 204–6; Edelman 1998).

The Food Security Training Program brought peasant leaders from Panama, Costa Rica, Nicaragua, Honduras, and El Salvador to two seminars in late 1990 and early 1991 for intensive mini-courses in credit, marketing, land reform, technology, and environmental issues. In the first seminar, several organisation leaders demanded, as a condition of their participation, that the Program provide time so that peasants from different countries could discuss common problems. By the end of the second seminar, the leaders had formed a commission—coordinated by the Costa Rican delegation—with a view to forming a Central America-wide association. The Association of Central American Peasant Organ-

Box 8.3: Latin American peasant movements: expanding cross-border links

1970
Founding in Guatemala of Campesino a Campesino, a peasant-led extension programme that spread to Mexico in the 1970s and Nicaragua in 1986.

1980
Founding of the Confederation of Cooperatives of the Caribbean and Central America (CCC–CA), which came to include many rural producers groups.

1981
Panama: Nicaragua's newly formed National Union of Agriculturalists and Livestock Producers (UNAG) convenes a meeting of a short-lived Continental Coordinating Group of Agricultural Workers and Peasants of Latin America.

1984
Mexico: Latin American Meeting of Peasant Organisations includes delegates from Mexico, Brazil, Nicaragua, Peru, Ecuador, and the Dominican Republic, as well as observers from France.

1985
Brazil: The first congress of the Landless Rural Workers Movement (MST) hosts an international meeting of Latin American peasant organisations.

1986
Ecuador: The National Federation of Peasant Organisations (FENOC) sponsors a meeting of Latin American peasant organisations.

1987
Panama: The Interamerican Cooperative Institute invites 50 women representatives of rural organisations from 14 Latin American and Caribbean countries to a workshop on women and grass-roots development.

1988
Brazil: The Fourth National Meeting of the MST discusses struggles for land with peasant organisation representatives from Chile, Paraguay, and El Salvador.

Colombia: Encounter of Rural and Indigenous Women in Latin America and the Caribbean, with delegations from Brazil, Chile, Colombia, Costa Rica, Honduras, Mexico, Nicaragua, Panama, and Peru. Italian trade union representatives also attend.

Costa Rica: Peasant activists seek funds from the European Economic Community to organise a meeting of agriculturalists from El Salvador, Nicaragua, and Honduras.

1989
Mexico: First International Forum on the Human Rights of Indian Peoples prepares for a campaign against the Columbian quincentenary and for justice for indigenous peoples.

Colombia: Latin American Meeting of Rural and Indigenous Organizations inaugurates campaign titled '500 Years of Popular and Indigenous Resistance'.

1990
Panama: The Support Committee for the Economic and Social Development of Central America (CADESCA) begins a food security research and training program for peasant movement leaders.

Mexico: Coffee producers from Mexico, the Dominican Republic, Honduras, Guatemala, Nicaragua, Costa Rica, and Panama found the Union of Small and Medium-Size Coffee Producers of Central America, Mexico, and the Caribbean to address the crisis caused by the collapse of the supply quota system of the International Coffee Agreement.

Ecuador: The first issue appears of the *Boletín Campesino-Indígena de Intercambio Informativo*, a newsletter that in 1994 becomes an organ of the Latin American Coordinating Group of Rural Organisations (CLOC).

Costa Rican peasant activists participate in the parallel forum that coincides with the annual meeting in Washington of the World Bank and International Monetary Fund.

1991
Guatemala: A meeting of the Continental Campaign for 500 Years of Indigenous, Black and Popular Resistance attracts representatives from 24 countries.

Nicaragua: Founding congress of the Central American Association of Peasant Organisations for Cooperation and Development (ASOCODE), a seven-country coalition.

1992

Nicaragua: The National Union of Agriculturalists and Livestock Producers (UNAG) invites leaders of farm organisations from Central America, North America, and Europe to its congress. They issue 'The Managua Declaration', which becomes the founding document of the Vía Campesina network.

Nicaragua: Participants in a meeting of the Continental Campaign for 500 Years of Indigenous, Black and Popular Resistance agree to hold a founding congress of CLOC. Two hundred women delegates form a Continental Women's Commission to promote women's participation at all levels of the participating movements.

1993

Guatemala: Second Congress of ASOCODE, attended by President Ramiro de León Carpio.

1994

Peru: First congress of CLOC, attended by representatives of 84 organisations from 21 countries.

1996

Mexico: Second International Conference of the Vía Campesina, attended by representatives of 69 organisations from 37 countries. During the event 19 peasants, supporters of the Landless Movement (MST), are massacred by gunmen in Eldorado de Carajás, Brazil.

Mexico: Thousands of foreign activists in diverse social movements attend the Zapatista-sponsored First International Encounter for Humanity and Against Neoliberalism, held in a remote jungle in Chiapas.

1997

Brazil: First Assembly of Latin American Rural Women, attended by 125 delegates from 23 countries, is held in conjunction with the second congress of the CLOC. The CLOC Congress resolves that women will be allocated one-half of all leadership and decision-making positions in its constituent organisations.

1998

El Salvador: Peasant organisations from throughout Latin America, many of them affiliated with ASOCODE, CLOC, and Vía Campesina, participate in the International Forum on Communication and Citizenship held to celebrate the fiftieth anniversary of the Universal Declaration of Human Rights.

1999

Washington, DC: A South-North Encounter to construct alternatives to neo-liberalism is held under the auspices of the Convergence of Movements of Peoples of the Americas (COMPA), with representatives of organised peasants and other sectors from Brazil, Cuba, El Salvador, Haiti, Honduras, Mexico, and Nicaragua.

2000

Nicaragua: Foreign donors end all support for ASOCODE, which closes its regional headquarters.

Honduras: International Landless Meeting sponsored by Vía Campesina's Global Campaign for Agrarian Reform attracts 84 participants from 24 countries in Africa, Asia, Europe, and Latin America.

Mexico: The Second South-North Exchange takes place in Chiapas with 222 representatives of 128 peasant, indigenous, and other civil society organizations from 16 countries of the Americas.

2001

Brazil: Over 1,000 Brazilian peasants from the MST, joined by Vía Campesina activists attending the first World Social Forum, occupy a biotechnology facility and experimental farm owned by Monsanto and uproot genetically modified corn and soybean plants from test plots.

Mexico: More than 500 delegates from 171 organisations in 15 countries gather in Chiapas at the first meeting of the Forum for Biological and Cultural Diversity, which aims to defend native medicinal and crop plant varieties against threats posed by free trade,

Box 8.3: continued

genetic engineering, bio-piracy, and corporate agriculture.

Mexico: The Third Congress of the CLOC is followed by an International Meeting of Social Movements, sponsored by Vía Campesina, Focus on the Global South, ATTAC-France, and the Brazilian labour federation CUT, called to plan participation in the second Porto Alegre Social Forum and other upcoming events.

Cuba: World Forum on Food Sovereignty supported by CLOC, Vía Campesina, APM-Mondial, and various other farm organisation networks and NGOs.

2002

Mexico: Vía Campesina organisations participate in the NGO Forum at the UN International Conference on Financing for Development.

Mexico: The First Mesoamerican Peasant Meeting (ECM) attracts more than 250 delegates from Central America and Mexico who condemn Mexican President Vicente Fox's Plan Puebla-Panamá (PPP) as a 'savage project of colonization that will destroy our lands, our cultures, biodiversity and natural resources'.

New York and Washington, DC, October: Representatives of the Mesoamerican Initiative for Trade, Integration and Sustainable Development (Iniciativa CID) meet with US labour, church, and development organisations to discuss the proposed hemispheric and Central American free trade treaties.

Ecuador: The Continental Campaign against the Free Trade Area of the Americas (FTAA) holds a meeting of 14 networks, including CLOC and the Hemispheric Social Alliance, to plan for a hemispheric referendum on the proposed FTAA. Protestors from CLOC and Vía Campesina organisations, along with other social movements in the Hemispheric Social Alliance, disrupt the FTAA Trade Negotiation Committee and Ministerial Meeting.

isations for Cooperation and Development (ASOCODE), founded in 1991 and headquartered in Nicaragua, came to have member coalitions in all seven countries of the isthmus. During its brief heyday, it was widely viewed in and beyond the Central American region as a quintessentially successful model of transnational small farmer organising (see Box 8.2).

CLOC and Vía Campesina

Although ASOCODE entered into a marked decline several years after its founding, its accomplishments—training a generation of sophisticated activists, attracting funding for cross-border organising, and gaining peasant access to the powerful—contributed to the formation of two wider networks that still have a visible presence. In 1992 in Nicaragua, two years after the Sandinistas' electoral defeat, the National Union of Agriculturalists and Livestock Producers (UNAG), then ASOCODE's Nicaraguan affiliate, invited leaders of farmers' movements from Central America, the Caribbean, Canada, the United States, and Europe to its second congress (Desmarais 2002: 95). The 'Managua Declaration', signed by representatives of Central American, Caribbean, North American, and European organisations, condemned the inclusion of agriculture in the GATT negotiations and the impact of foreign debt on poor countries, demanded direct participation in the upcoming Rio Environmental Conference, and called on 'sister farm organisations from around the world' to join in constructing an alternative development model (Vía Campesina 1996: 67–9). A small Dutch NGO, the Paulo Freire Foundation, coordinated plans for the founding congress of a global network, the Vía Campesina (Peasant Road), which took place in Belgium in 1993 (see below).

In early 1994, in Lima, Peru, representatives of 84 organisations from 21 countries formed the Latin American Coordinator of Rural Organizations (CLOC). The network's proximate origins were in the 1992 continental indigenous campaign against official celebrations of the Columbian quincentenary. CLOC and its affiliates express militant opposition to neoliberalism and to the US embargo on trade with Cuba. Closely allied with Vía Campesina, CLOC campaigns for food sovereignty, agrarian reform, and indigenous rights (CLOC 1997; 2001; Petras 1998; Welch 2000). Almost all Vía Campesina member organisations in Latin America participate in CLOC and many CLOC organisations participate in Vía Campesina. Both contributed to the formation of other Latin American networks, including the Grito de los Excluidos/Cry of the Excluded and the Forum for Biological and Cultural Diversity (Bell 2002).

New forms of communications facilitated the expansion of networks of Latin American peasant and other movements, although adoption of new technologies was slow until the late 1990s, when computer skills had spread and Internet and telephone services became more reliable. As recently as 1997, however, only 26 of the 46 movements attending the second CLOC congress in Brasilia had electronic mail (León, Burch, and Tamayo 2001: 102), and the digital divide between national- and local-level organisations remains significant. The launching in 2000 of a Latin American social movements Internet portal, www.movimientos.org, has solidified information flows and simplified the organisation of protests and meetings.

Willie Nelson with other members of the Farm Aid Board of Directors at Farm Aid 2001, held in Noblesville, Indiana.

Regional Integration: North America

National mobilisation in the 1980s

The farm crisis and the advance of trade liberalisation and regional integration in North America spurred new forms of cross-border collaboration among farmers and between farmers and other sectors. In 1984, the election of Brian Mulroney, whose Conservative Party won the largest number of parliamentary seats in Canadian history, and the re-election of Ronald Reagan in the United States created an opportunity for pro-free trade forces in both countries to advance a common agenda. Until just before the 1993 signing of the NAFTA and GATT, however, farmers in each country expressed opposition to economic integration and liberalisation mainly through national politics, and sometimes looked askance at the possibility of solidarity with counterparts across the border.

Many farmers' movements in the United States espoused right-wing conspiracy theories about the 1980s crisis and championed ultra-nationalist and, at times, violent responses, such as the formation of armed 'militias' (Berlet and Lyons 2000; Diamond 1995). Other movements, such as the US Farmers Association (USFA), included members who had been expelled as communists from the US National Farmers Union during the McCarthy period, as well as more recent migrants to rural areas who had new left, counter-cultural perspectives. Some organisations combined right- and left-wing influences, notably the American Agriculture Movement (AAM), which worked closely with country singer Willie Nelson in producing a series of high-profile 'Farm Aid' concerts to benefit indebted farmers. In 1978 AAM vaulted to prominence with a massive 'tractor-cade' demonstration in Washington for higher price supports (Mooney and Majka 1995).

In Canada, the National Farmers Union (NFU) had conducted an active programme of international exchanges almost since its formation in 1969. An amalgamation of several provincial unions, the founding of the NFU was part of a wave of sectoral coalition building that occurred across Canada during the 1970s as diverse kinds of policy-making increasingly shifted from the provinces to Ottawa (Ayres 1998: 50). Strongly influenced by farmers' historic successes in winning preferential rail freight rates, creating cooperatively owned grain handling pools, and establishing a national wheat board, the NFU and its predecessor organisations were fervent advocates of orderly marketing and supply management policies that permitted producers to receive adequate prices for their harvests (Qualman and Wiebe 2002). Like many other Canadians, small farmers feared that economic integration with the United States would not only worsen the agricultural crisis but dilute an already fragile national identity by undermining the strong, interventionist state and social welfare system (Ayres 1998: 22).

Box 8.4: National Farmers Union of Canada: growing international involvement, 1971–1994

1971
NFU President and Women's President travel to China.

NFU Vice-President attends FAO conference in Rome.

1977
Nine NFU representatives attend the fifteenth Triennial Conference of Associated Country Women of the World.

1978
NFU leader joins representatives of farm organisations from major wheat-exporting countries in London.

1980
Four NFU representatives visit the Eastern Caribbean to participate in the founding convention of the St Vincent National Farmers Union.

1981
NFU delegation visits Cuba and meets with members and officials of ANAP, the association of small agricultural producers.

NFU representative lobbies at FAO conference in Rome in favour of conserving plant genetic resources.

1982
NFU member participates in trade union tour of Nicaragua and meets with representatives of UNAG, the main organization of small farmers and livestock producers.

1983
Farmers from nearly 50 countries attend the First International Farm Crisis Summit in Ottawa, sponsored by the North American Farm Alliance.

NFU President accompanies a government delegation to the Rome FAO Conference and expresses opposition to plant-breeders rights legislation and in favour of continuing public-sector crop research.

1984
NFU Women's President is an official delegate to the World Food Assembly in Rome.

NFU members participate in a Canadian Farmers Technical Brigade to Nicaragua.

NFU and the Windward Islands Farmers Association (WINFA) initiate a Canada-Caribbean farmer exchange, with young agriculturalists from each region spending between four and six weeks in the other region.

1985
NFU Women's President is a delegate to the Women's Conference in Nairobi, Kenya, where she chairs a panel on rural women.

A representative of the recently founded Peasant Movement of the Philippines (KMP) tours Canada, meeting with the NFU and other organisations and denouncing the Marcos dictatorship's repression.

1986
NFU members participate in Oxfam Farmers Brigade Project, which aids Nicaraguan farmers with machinery maintenance and repair.

Farmers from ten countries attend the Second International Farm Crisis Summit in St Louis, Missouri, sponsored by the North American Farm Alliance.

1987
NFU President tours Europe to gain first-hand knowledge of the European Economic Community's Common Agricultural Policy.

NFU representative attends International Conference in Solidarity with the Filipino Peasantry sponsored by the KMP.

1988
NFU representatives participate in GATT counter-conference in Montreal.

1989
NFU initiates campaign to educate Canadians about negative consequences of NAFTA.

NFU representatives meet with three North Dakota farm organisations to discuss binational trade issues.

NFU women's delegation tours Nicaragua.

1990
NFU President, together with Canadian labour leaders, tours *maquiladora* free-trade zone along Mexico's northern border.

Farmers from Jilin, China, and Saskatchewan participate in a lengthy work exchange programme.

1991
Three NFU women visit Nicaragua on a ten-day working tour sponsored by the UNAG women's section. UNAG women later visit Saskatchewan.

Filipino farm leaders tour Canada, seeking international support for their agrarian reform campaign.

1992

NFU Women's President attends conference in Honduras on how free trade and structural adjustment impact rural communities.

NFU delegates to the Associated Country Women of the World convention in the Hague persuade ACWW to take a stand against GATT.

1993

NFU Women's Vice-President joins GATT protests in Geneva, speaks to 5,000 farmers from across Europe.

NFU Youth President travels to Mexico on a labour exchange.

NFU President demands that government use Free Trade Agreement provisions to prohibit US export subsidies aimed at traditional Canadian wheat markets, particularly Mexico.

NFU representative attends founding conference of the Vía Campesina in Belgium.

1994

NFU representative attends congress in Guatemala City of ASOCODE.

ASOCODE leaders make a speaking tour, with NFU support, to four Canadian cities.

NFU leadership meets with Northern Plains Resource Council from US to discuss joint wheat marketing strategies.

NFU President meets in Austin, Texas, with U.S. and Mexican farm and labour organisations.

Representatives of Nicaragua's UNAG visit Saskatchewan to meet with NFU members.

NFU Women's President travels to New York for the Women, Food and Agriculture Working Group, comprising 100 people from 40 countries.

Sources: *Union Farmer* (Saskatoon, Saskatchewan, various issues); Ayres (1998); Ritchie (1996: 495); Wilford (1985).

The Canadians also highlighted women's issues within the emerging transnational farmers' networks, in North America and elsewhere. Many of the provincial groups that coalesced in the National Farmers Union had reserved specific leadership posts for women, a practice rooted in the parallel structure of the early twentieth-century Women's and Farmers' Institutes. The NFU preserved this system, with a women's president and vice-president responsible for defending the interests of farm women within and outside the organisation (Gleave 1991: 121–2).

One early cross-border initiative was the North American Farm Alliance (NAFA), formed in 1983 by activists from 23 US States and two Canadian provinces who convened at a USFA-sponsored assembly in Iowa. NAFA drew members largely from the USFA, the left-wing of the AAM, and a small AAM offshoot called the Canadian Farmers' Survival Association (Mooney and Majka1995; Wilford 1985). In 1983, NAFA hosted the First International Farm Crisis Summit in Ottawa, which attracted peasant, farm worker, and family farm leaders from nearly 50 countries. Delegates from different regions pointed to similar concerns, particularly the push by export-oriented agribusiness corporations to boost international competitiveness at the expense of small farmers (Ritchie 1996; Wilford 1985). NAFA was unusual among 1980s US farm organisations in its advocacy of environmentalism and less capital-intensive agriculture, which some of its spokespeople argued was a form of supply management, a traditional demand of farmers' movements (Mooney and Majka 1995). The Canadian NFU, which had briefly joined NAFA (NFU 1985b; 1985c), withdrew after a few years, as key NAFA member groups, particularly the AAM, took protectionist stances and protested along the border to keep Canadian wheat and meat out of the US market.

Farmers, the US-Canadian Free Trade Treaty, and NAFTA

Prime Minister Mulroney's announcement in 1985 that he intended to negotiate a free trade treaty with the United States galvanised opposition from farmers and other sectors and led to the formation of several Canadian civil society networks, notably the Coalition Against Free Trade, the Council of Canadians, and the Pro-Canada Network. At first, these groups devoted most of their efforts to lobbying, organising, and protesting within Canada.

The Canadian economy depended heavily on export production and the vast majority of exports went to the United States. Pro-free trade groups argued that a free trade treaty would gain Canada greater access to US markets and thwart any US attempts to impose protectionist measures. The protracted treaty negotiations provided an ample period in which both sides could organise and, in 1988, with free trade the principal election issue, Mulroney won re-election. The treaty went into effect in 1989, and the US and Canadian governments announced their intention to broaden it to Mexico. This double setback for free trade opponents in Canada led to a greater willingness to seek allies in the United States and Mexico (Ayres 1998: 121–3).

With the US-Canada Free Trade Treaty a fait accompli, the attention of transnational activists turned to Mexico, and especially to its northern border region. Much of the bilateral and trilateral coalition building of the early 1990s involved joint action around the proposed NAFTA, or sectoral alliances around environmental, occupational safety and health, or other issues. US agricultural workers' unions, with Mexican members, had already established cross-border links and, in the early 1990s, encouraged the American Federation of Labor-Congress of Industrial Organizations (AFL-CIO) to modify its traditionally protectionist position toward foreign labour. In 1987, the Farm Labor Organizing Committee (FLOC) developed joint bargaining strategies with a Mexican counterpart when Campbell Soup threatened to move an Ohio canning plant to Mexico (IRC 1992).

The US-based Rural Coalition began to oppose NAFTA on both sides of the border in 1992 with an assembly in El Paso and Chihuahua, and more than doubled the number of its affiliated organisations in 1993. The Rural Coalition helped sponsor a reception in Washington for new congressional representatives from rural areas, who would soon have to vote on NAFTA, and hosted several who visited northern Mexico. On 16 November 1993, the day before the US House of Representatives was to vote on NAFTA, a US delegation marched to the Santa Fe International Bridge to meet Mexican supporters coming from the south. On their return, the Mexican demonstrators were attacked by police. 'We deeply regret that NAFTA has been passed by the House', peasant leader Víctor Quintana wrote two days later to US Representative Bernard Sanders.

> *But every one of us fought from his trench: you in the House, we in the street or the bridge . . . This battle against NAFTA brought something we hadn't even imagined: the closeness, cooperation, [and] solidarity between the people who love and struggle for democracy on both sides of the border. (Rural Coalition 1994: 21)*

In 1990 a Canada-Mexico meeting of anti-NAFTA labour, farm, environmental, church, and human rights groups led to the formation of the Mexican Action Network on Free Trade (RMALC) (IRC 1992). RMALC became an important source of analysis on trade issues for Mexican peasant movements. These were almost universally opposed to NAFTA, although the official National Peasant Confederation (CNC) argued that 'liberalisation was already a given' and that the important question was that peasants be represented in the negotiations and have access to US markets. Among the many cross-border farmers' exchanges in this period, one of the most significant was the Trinational Meeting on Agriculture, Environment and the Free Trade Treaty in November, 1991, which included the National Union of Autonomous Regional Peasant Organisations (UNORCA), the US Institute for Trade and Development Policy, and the Canadian Centre for Policy Alternatives (Hernández 1992: 257).

The movements of farmers and others around NAFTA reconfigured traditional alliances and oppositions along non-national lines

The movements of farmers and others around NAFTA reconfigured traditional alliances and oppositions along non-national lines. While once US, Canadian, or Mexican actors stood opposed to each other in discussions of trade, environment, or migration, the social cleavages that NAFTA opened blurred domestic and foreign policy concerns in all three countries, generating new forms of contention that required transnational action and that increasingly divided or united people less along national lines than in relation to shared class, issue-based, or sectoral interests. The common preoccupation with continental free trade also opened the way for new kinds of cross-sector collaboration, between agriculturalists and environmentalists, for example, and between NGOs and popular movements. More broadly, it contributed to transcending the parochial, identity-based politics characteristic of the 'new social movements' of the previous two decades.

Mesoamerica: New Zapatistas and peasant organisations in global civil society

The Zapatista uprising in the southern Mexican state of Chiapas began on 1 January 1994, the day NAFTA went into effect, dramatically highlighting the multiple crises affecting rural and indigenous Mexicans and calling attention to the devastating impact on the peasantry of the 1992 constitutional reforms that permitted privatisation of agrarian reform lands and, more generally, of neo-liberalism. As the first post-Cold War peasant and indigenous insurrection in Latin America, the Chiapas rebellion sparked enormous hopes in Mexico and generated tremendous sympathy in much of the rest of the world. Although the Zapatistas initially had no international allies, their dissemination of e-mail communiques and their poetic disdain for the status quo provided a platform for democratising Mexico and for imagining new alliances and alternatives to the dominant economic model. Not surprisingly, the Zapatista-sponsored First International Encounter for Humanity and Against Neoliberalism, which brought thousands of Mexican and foreign activists to a remote Chiapas jungle in 1996, is sometimes considered the 'genesis' of today's global justice movement (Seoane and Taddei 2001: 108; Desai and Said 2001: 70–1). But while the Zapatistas established ties to diverse, largely urban movements in Mexico and abroad, their connections to Mexican and transnational networks of peasant and indigenous organisations remained tenuous. On 1 January 2003, when Mexico lifted tariffs on all agricultural imports from NAFTA countries except corn, beans, and powdered milk, peasants staged widespread demonstrations and hunger strikes under the banner of a coalition called 'the Countryside Can't Take Any More' ('El Campo no Aguanta Más'). Yet the same day, when 20,000 machete-wielding native Mexicans converged on San Cristóbal, Chiapas, to mark the ninth anniversary of the Zapatista uprising, their leaders voiced a range of indigenous and international solidarity concerns but said little about the country's broader agrarian crisis (Bellinghausen 2003).

At the ninth anniversary of the Zapatista uprising, their leaders voiced a range of indigenous and international solidarity concerns but said little about the country's broader agrarian crisis

In northern Latin America, Central America (without Mexico) was the key reference point for regional cross-border peasant organising in the early 1990s. In 2001, however, Mexican President Vicente Fox's unveiled Plan Puebla-Panamá (PPP), a 25-year industrial development and transport infrastructure project, stretching from central Mexico to the Panama Canal, to be funded largely by the Inter-American Development Bank. This expanded the relevant space to Mesoamerica, usually understood to include Mexico and most of Central America. In 2002 the president of an almost moribund ASOCODE joined Mexican peasant organisations in convening conferences of a new Mesoamerican Peasant Meeting (ECM) and remarked that the new network 'was betting on Mesoamerica as a space of convergence' for opponents of Plan Puebla-Panamá (CCS-Chiapas 2002). The new group's Action Plan called for gaining it 'public recognition as Regional Coordinator' of the organised peasantry in Mexico and Central America, a status previously claimed, in the latter zone at least, by ASOCODE.

A second new network, the Mesoamerican Initiative for Trade, Integration and Sustainable Development (Iniciativa CID) takes a less categorically rejectionist stance toward Plan Puebla-Panamá and the proposed Free Trade Treaty of the Americas and US-Central American Free Trade Treaty. Supported in part by Oxfam, Catholic Relief Services, and the AFL-CIO, Iniciativa CID contends that these accords may present opportunities and that it is important to lobby during the negotiations for measures to compensate peasants for low market prices caused in part by the subsidies given US farmers (Iniciativa CID 2002).

Box 8.5: European farmers and new forms of protest and solidarity

1970s
France: Dissidents in the mainstream National Federation of Agricultural Enterprises(FNSEA) and its youth wing organise a minority tendency, Interpaysanne, which leads protests against agricultural taxes, overproduction of commodities, and corporate agribusiness.

1981
France: Founding of the National Confederation of Worker-Peasant Unions (CNSTP) by groups that left the FNSEA.

Austria: The first of four annual meetings that precedes the formal creation of a European peasant coordinating group. Participating organisations come from Germany, Austria, France, the Netherlands, and Switzerland.

1985
Founding of the European Farmers Coordination (EFC).

1986
Madrid: The EFC holds a meeting with representatives of 27 organisations from eleven countries on the theme of 'European Peasants: Competitors or Partners?'

1987
Geneva: Over 50 farm activists from Europe, North America, and Japan meet to discuss the GATT negotiations. A statement of principles, emphasising measures to restore world prices and the necessity of market share negotiations, is drafted for distribution to farm organisations around the world.

1989
Brussels: The EFC opens a headquarters office.

1990
Brussels: Thousands of farmers from around the world protest against the GATT talks. The EFC attributes the GATT adjournment 'primarily' to 'the successful farmers' resistance' and calls 'for public GATT negotiations under UN control'.

France: Elizabeth Lepetitcolin, a veterinarian in the sheep-farming region of Larzac, a centre of Confédération Paysanne support, travels to the Middle East and establishes ties with a group of Palestinians in the occupied territories.

1991
Brussels: The EFC and the US National Family Farm Coalition issue a joint communiqué warning that proposed reforms to the European Common Agricultural Policy (CAP) are modelled on the US Farm Bill that contributed to the demise of one-fifth of all US farms during the 1980s.

1992
France: Protests against reforms to CAP include a FNSEA-led demonstration with over 300 tractors around Euro-Disney, highway blockades, and dumping of manure and rotten vegetables in front of government buildings.

Geneva and Strasbourg: Ten thousand demonstrators from Europe, Japan, South Korea, Latin America, and Canada protest against the GATT talks.

Strasbourg: The FNSEA brings tens of thousands of demonstrators to a protest against the EU-US Oilseeds Agreement (also called the Blair House Agreement), which limits the area eligible for support payments.

1993
France: Farmers protesting against the French government's stance on oil seed production in the GATT talks smear the office of Foreign Minister Alain Juppé (who became Prime Minister in 1995) with yellow paint (the colour of canola seed). Other demonstrators dump manure outside government offices in Normandy and stage a new blockade of Euro-Disney.

Geneva: Farmers from Europe, Canada, the United States, Japan, and India demonstrate against the signing of the GATT.

Mons, Belgium: Representatives of 55 peasant and farmer organisations from 36 countries found a world network called Vía Campesina (Peasant Road).

1994
Austria, Luxembourg, Netherlands: The EFC launches a campaign to continue a ban on the bovine growth hormone manufactured by Monsanto, citing widespread anxiety among consumers, farmers, environmental, and animal welfare organisations.

The EFC asks the European Commission to ban meat flour consumption by ruminants, noting that BSE (mad-cow disease) is an example of 'the shortsightedness to which intensive farming can lead'.

Austrian and Norwegian farm organisations issue a joint declaration charging that their countries' entrance into the EU single market will spell disaster for small grain and dairy farmers and the environment.

France: Larzac region civic associations host a farm visit from two Palestinians, representatives of the Palestinian Agricultural Relief Committee and the International Family Planning Committee.

1995
Netherlands: Farmers dump manure at the entrance to the Ministry of Agriculture in the Hague to protest against EU regulations about processing animal waste.

France: Larzac farm militants travel to French Polynesia and, in collaboration with Greenpeace, protest against French underground nuclear weapons tests.

1996
Rome: Dozens of peasant and farmer activists attend the FAO Food Security Summit.

Greece: Thousands of farmers block the country's main north-south highway for over two weeks to protest against trade liberalisation, cuts in subsidies, and growing indebtedness. They declare that 'Farmers can't go to Brussels to protest. That's the government's job'.

Britain: In March the government reverses its position and reveals that the recent death of a young man was caused by exposure to BSE. British farmers launch beef give-aways and other protests against the EU-imposed international ban on exports of British beef.

The EFC calls on the EU to stand firm in the face of a US complaint in the WTO against the European ban on hormone-treated beef.

1997
The EFC calls on the EU to block US efforts in the Codex Alimentarius to ban trade in raw milk-based cheeses. This would 'impose an industrialised production model and, as a result, rob food of its originality, as has happened in the USA'.

The EFC condemns the marketing of false Roquefort, feta, and parmesan cheeses and suggests that 'the agri-food multinationals now want to plunder the riches that have been preserved in the regions of the "South" [of Europe] and use their images of high-quality local produce to deceive consumers'.

Basel: The EFC protests in front of the offices of Novartis, the agribusiness and pharmaceutical firm, against imports of genetically modified maize. The demonstration is part of an international action week against genetic engineering in agriculture.

1998
The EFC is granted rights to attend the European Commission's advisory committees, which provide a small subsidy to civil society organisations that participate in their deliberations.

France: Confédération Paysanne supporters enter a warehouse belonging to Novartis and spray genetically modified corn seed with fire extinguishers in order to protest against the dangers of GM food. José Bové receives an eight-month suspended sentence.

France: The Confédération Paysanne participates in the founding of ATTAC, an international network that advocates the Tobin tax, a small levy on speculative currency transactions that would be used to 'tame' volatile capital movements and generate funds for development.

1999
The EFC coordinates a multi-country caravan of farmers from India, who came to Europe to protest against corporate control of seeds, particularly by Monsanto, and the WTO's forced liberalisation of agricultural trade.

France: Confédération Paysanne activists and visiting Indian farmers enter a greenhouse in Montpellier and uproot genetically modified rice plants before they could be replanted in a nearby nature preserve. José Bové receives a six-month prison sentence.

France: José Bové and Confédération Paysanne supporters 'symbolically dismantle' a McDonald's restaurant under construction in Millau.

2000
France: Tens of thousands of demonstrators gather in Millau during José Bové's trial for the McDonald's action. Bové receives a sentence of three months in prison for criminal vandalism.

Dresden: The EFC, together with Thai and Filipino peasant groups and Vía Campesina, present a proposal for a new concept of farmer-driven agricultural

Box 8.5: continued

research at a parallel conference to the Global Forum on Agricultural Research, part of the Consultative Group on International Agricultural Research (CGIAR), which coordinates the world's principal centres of crop plant genetic research.

2001

France: José Bové sentenced to 14 months in prison for participation in direct action protests against GM crops.

Rome: Vía Campesina brings approximately 100 supporters to the NGO parallel forum at the FAO World Food Summit (Rome+5). The farm activists constitute about one-sixth of all delegates at the parallel forum. At a University of Rome campus, EFC supporters sheath genetically modified olive trees in plastic as a symbolic prophylactic measure.

2002

Austria, Belgium, France, Netherlands, and *Spain*: On 17 April, the International Day of Peasant Struggles, farmer and environmentalist organisations stage coordinated protest actions against the testing of GM crops. In the Netherlands, visiting farmers from Vía Campesina member groups in Indonesia and Bangladesh join the actions.

Madrid: A meeting in May of women in Vía Campesina organisations resolves that quotas must be established to assure greater representation of women in leadership positions.

Madrid: The Third World Congress of Rural Women is held in October, presided by Queen Sofía. The plenaries and workshops are dominated by government representatives, leaving little space for interventions by grassroots activists.

Ramallah: Two EFC leaders, José Bové and Paul Nicholson, join Vía Campesina activists Doris Gutiérrez (Honduras) and Mario Lill (Brazil) and other members of an international delegation that protests against the Israeli blockade of the city.

European Integration and Anti-GATT Protest

Europe experienced an earlier and more profound process of regional integration than any other part of the world, and this conditioned the character of farmers' organising. In the Americas supranational governance institutions were quite new and transnational activism emerged in response to a growing perception that threats to rural livelihoods were shared or, in some cases, to deter government repression. In Europe, in contrast, regional policy-making bodies had been significant for decades.

The Common Agricultural Policy (CAP), established as part of the 1957 treaty that created the then-six-member European Community, was phased in during the 1960s as the EC customs union went into effect. The CAP provided incentives to farmers that aimed at guaranteeing food supplies, stabilising prices, modernising production, and assuring farmers adequate incomes. In practice, however, CAP subsidies generated huge surpluses of commodities and absorbed a rising share of the EC budget. France—and the large wheat farmers of the Paris Basin, in particular—was the main beneficiary of the CAP, contributing in its first year less than one-quarter of contributions to the Guarantee Fund but receiving over three-quarters of all monies paid out (Sheingate 2001: 175). Within Europe, France was (and still is) the most important national actor in the contentious area of agricultural politics. While less than 8 per cent of the economically active population works in agriculture, the centrality of fresh, artisanal foods and wines in beliefs about quality, local distinctiveness, and national identity has contributed to a strong identification with farmers among urban dwellers (Trubek 2000).

French farmers also have greater representation in the political system than their counterparts in most other developed countries. Nearly one-third of French mayors are farmers, most parliamentarians represent rural districts, and many National Assembly deputies and senators sit on communal and departmental councils (Bush and Simi 2001: 113). Elected local, departmental, and national Chambres d'Agriculture have, since the 1920s, served as forums of consultation between the farm sector and the state, which is also the Chambres' main source of funds. In the 1960s, the Chambres d'Agriculture became the primary extension services provider and a significant source of rural development funds. The importance of the Chambres d'Agriculture in French rural life has made them a barometer of support for different agrarian organisations.

The Chambres d'Agriculture are one element in a corporatist arrangement that links the French state to mainstream agriculturalists' organisations, particularly the National Federation of Agricultural Enterprises (FNSEA). As the FNSEA won control of the Chambres, it gave supporters privileged access to employment and services. FNSEA domination of the Chambres d'Agriculture was also consonant with the French state's emphasis on capital-intensive agriculture (Gorneg 2001; Sheingate 2001: 172–6).

The French state's corporatist pact with the FNSEA mirrored the relation at the European level between the European Commission and the Committee of Professional Agricultural Organisations (COPA) (Roederer-Rynning 2002). FNSEA's and COPA's emphasis on technological modernisation met with scepticism and resistance in mountain and smallholding regions, where greater mechanisation was often not practical. In 1981, farm activists from Austria, France, Germany, the Netherlands, and Switzerland held the first of several annual meetings that led in 1985 to the founding of the European Farmers Coordination (EFC).

In France, the centrality of fresh, artisanal foods and wines in beliefs about quality, local distinctiveness, and national identity has contributed to a strong identification with farmers among urban dwellers

European protests against CAP reform and GATT

The 1986 inauguration of the Uruguay GATT round and the efforts the following year of the EC's Council of Ministers to reform the Common Agricultural Policy brought the discontent of many European farmers into sharp relief. Reform of the CAP was required by budgetary constraints, but also to bring it into compliance with GATT. Farmers' organisations, particularly those in the EFC, called for the CAP to establish a per-farm ceiling on price supports, so that large enterprises would not be the main beneficiaries of CAP subsidies. Improved supply management, they argued, was necessary to prevent the production of huge surpluses, which had to be stored at public expense, as well as to limit over-intensification, ownership concentration, and emigration from rural areas. The EFC further charged that unchecked production of surpluses, together with export subsidies, led to dumping in poor countries that undermined peasant livelihoods. The linkage of CAP reform and GATT also caused concern, especially in France, that European officials were caving in to US pressure to liberalise agricultural trade at farmers' expense (Sheingate 2001: 214–22).

Some accounts of the GATT process, which culminated in 1994 with the establishment of the World Trade Organization (WTO), suggest that elite disagreements over export subsidies and market access accounted for the delay in concluding the Uruguay Round. Pressure from small farmers, however, was also a conspicuous factor. The GATT ministerial session in Brussels in 1990 was supposed to complete the Round, but protests from a multinational coalition of small farmer, consumer, and environmentalist groups helped stall the talks, in part because massive protests made some developing-country GATT delegates feel sufficiently empowered to raise objections to provisions in the draft agreement that would harm their countries' economies. Among the estimated 30,000 farmers who joined the 1990 protests were 100 from North America, 200 from Japan, and others from Korea, Africa, and Latin America (Brecher 1993; Ritchie 1996). These protests–'far bigger than Seattle [1999], but less violent' (Ritchie 2001: 4)– followed on related anti-GATT farmers' demonstrations in the United States and Canada.

The first round of CAP reforms, however, went forward in 1992 in conjunction with the Maastricht Treaty that established the European Union (a second round would occur in 2000 and a third was under discussion in 2003, tied to the planned enlargement of the EU). It provided retirement incentives for older farmers, extended the dairy quota system, and cut livestock and cereal support prices, while providing for compensatory payments contingent on producers' taking some land out of cultivation. Critics in the EFC and other organisations argued that the failure to impose a ceiling on payments did little to address the problem of farm ownership concentration and that the land set-aside provisions, while intended as a conservation measure, would bring intensified production, with detrimental environmental impacts, in areas not left fallow.

Protests became increasingly dramatic in the two years before the signing of the GATT accord in 1993. FNSEA supporters used hundreds of tractors to blockade Euro-Disney, suggesting that US pressure was behind the French government's concessions on oil-seed subsidies in the GATT talks. Elsewhere, protesters sprayed defoliants around the home of European Commissioner Jacques Delors, staged highway blockades, and dumped manure and rotten vegetables in government buildings (see Box 8.5).

India: Farmers Mobilise against GATT and TRIPS

Small farmer opposition to GATT burgeoned in India towards the end of the Uruguay Round (Gupta 1998: 291–2). The lightning rod for peasant anger was the proposed Trade-Related Intellectual Property Agreement (TRIPS), which would empower the WTO to enforce global rules on patents, copyrights, and trademarks. This was a sensitive issue, since W. R. Grace and other companies had acquired US patents for active ingredients in the seeds of the neem tree (*Azadirachta indica*), which South Asians had utilised since ancient times as an insecticide, toothpaste substitute, and medicine (Shiva and Holla-Bhar 1996). With the prospect of a TRIPS agreement in the early 1990s, W. R. Grace sought to begin production of neem-derived products in India, threatening both national manufacturers and local users of the tree. Many peasants viewed the neem 'theft' as a harbinger of future corporate attempts to monopolise crop genetic material that they and their ancestors had developed over generations.

In December 1992 some 75 members of the Karnataka State Farmers Association (KRRS) raided the Bangalore offices of Cargill, the multinational grain giant, smashing furniture and tossing files out the window to a large crowd, which set the papers on fire. The action drew a formal protest from Washington and is widely credited with bringing the proposed TRIPS Agreement to world attention (Gupta 1998: 322). In the following months, giant rallies of several hundred thousand peasants in Bangalore and New Delhi demanded that the Indian government reject the TRIPS draft and that all international agreements be approved by both houses of parliament and at least half the state legislatures.

While this ambitious agenda remained unrealised, the KRRS won new allies by helping to reframe the TRIPS discussion. Critics asserted that TRIPS was a form of protectionism that shielded developed-country seed and pharmaceutical monopolies and that it contradicted the Convention on Biological Diversity developed at the 1992 Rio Earth Summit. Even Columbia University economist and WTO adviser Jagdish Bhagwati, normally an enthusiast of global trade liberalisation, came to argue that protection for intellectual property should not fall within the WTO's purview and that 'the IP leg of the WTO [ought] to be sawn off' (Ramanujam and Sangeetha 2001).

Giant rallies of several hundred thousand peasants in Bangalore and New Delhi demanded that the Indian government reject the TRIPS draft

Vía Campesina/ Peasant Road

Emergence of a radical transnational network

The anti-GATT campaign by farmers in the Americas, Europe, and Asia was the main impetus for founding the Vía Campesina (Peasant Road), a network that sought to coordinate peasant and farmer struggles worldwide. The group's initial nucleus consisted of a small number of Central American, Canadian, and European activists who met at the 1992 congress of the Nicaraguan National Union of Agriculturalists and Livestock Producers (UNAG) (see above). Vía Campesina's founding convention, in Belgium in 1993, occurred as anti-GATT protests were mounting in Europe. From the beginning, Vía Campesina was marked by disagreements between the Paulo Freire Foundation, which had helped to plan the convention, and farm organisation leaders who opposed the participation of conservative groups affiliated with the International Federation of Agricultural Producers (Desmarais 2002). Few IFAP members were in attendance, however. The US National Farmers Union, an IFAP member, had endorsed the 1992 Managua Declaration but did not come to Belgium or affiliate with Vía Campesina. Several other organisations, including Nicaragua's UNAG, which despite its Sandinista roots was an IFAP affiliate, participated in the founding congress but did not stay in Vía Campesina. Nevertheless, the 55 peasant and farmer organisations from 36 countries that joined the network represented an unprecedented unity on a considerable range of political positions and between producers in developed and poor countries (PFS 1993).

Vía Campesina's structure was initially based on an International Coordinating Committee (ICC), with representatives of organisations from different regions, each in charge of its respective area. The Europeans, assigned overall responsibility for the network, chose Basque activist Paul Nicholson Solano as its coordinator. In 1996, an International Operational Secretariat was established to oversee day-to-day functioning of the network and complement the work of the ICC. Because of the Central Americans' experience in cross-border work, the secretariat was entrusted to ASOCODE, which assigned its Honduran coalition responsibility for the Vía Campesina. Rafael Alegría, an energetic peasant activist who had completed a law degree, became executive secretary and installed the Vía Campesina in a small office provided by one of the main Honduran peasant coalitions. Alegría had been a peasant organisation promoter in the Department of Olancho in 1975, when the Honduran military and landowners massacred 14 activists who were planning a hunger march on the capital (Posas 1985: 59–60).

The Vía Campesina first emerged as a significant international actor at the 1995 Global Assembly on Food Security, held in Quebec City. The Canadian National Farmers Union, part of the Assembly's steering committee, succeeded in having numerous Vía Campesina representatives invited as panellists and plenary speakers (Desmarais 2002: 103). In a hastily typed press release faxed to news media and signed by Canadian, Honduran, Brazilian, Spanish, Polish, and Filipino activists, the Vía Campesina condemned 'the coexistence in the world of food surpluses and hunger' and 'the large-scale dislocation of farmers', and called for 'respect for the food sovereignty of every country' and 'the inclusion in the price of foodstuffs of all the real costs of production—social, ecological, and economic' (Vía Campesina 1995).

In 1996, the Vía Campesina held its second congress, in Tlaxcala, Mexico, which was attended by representatives from 37 countries and funded by NGOs from Europe, Canada, and the United States. Many delegates, particularly from Asia and Africa, belonged to organisations that were not officially part of the Vía Campesina; nearly three dozen were denied visas and could not attend. During the congress news arrived that Brazilian military police had massacred 19 peasants in Eldorado dos Carajás, where supporters of the Landless Workers Movement (MST) had blocked a highway to pressure the government to negotiate an agrarian conflict (Vía Campesina 1996: 49; Fernandes 2000: 209). Television reporters stuck in nearby traffic caught the action on film, which created a public uproar (Cadji 2000: 30). In Mexico, the Vía Campesina condemned the murders and declared that 17 April would henceforth be commemorated as an International Day of Peasant Struggles. Later that year, dozens of peasant and farmer organisation leaders attended the Rome World Food Summit, some invited and accredited by the FAO and others by IFAP, Vía Campesina, and the NGOs that sponsored a parallel forum. Vía Campesina supporters advanced the position that the summit's emphasis on 'food security' ought to be replaced with a commitment to 'food sovereignty', reflecting a view of food as a human right rather than primarily a commodity.

Memorial service for the 19 victims of the massacre in Pará. © Paul Smith/Panos Pictures

Media-savvy protests and Vía Campesina's rising profile

In 1999 some 75 Vía Campesina supporters from more than a dozen countries converged on Seattle to join protests at the World Trade Organisation ministerial meeting and to take part in press conferences, workshops, and strategy meetings. Their activities included a symbolic tree planting and visits to a farmers' market. They distributed Roquefort sandwiches to passers-by in front of a McDonald's restaurant in an effort to explain European farmers' opposition to US sanctions imposed on their products in retaliation for the EU's ban on imports of hormone-treated US beef (Vía Campesina 1999a). In the giant demonstrations that ultimately contributed to derailing the Seattle WTO negotiations, Vía Campesina activists adopted a practice employed by the Brazilian MST and its allies (and earlier by the American Agriculture Movement), where the symbolic politics of wearing bandannas and flying movement flags built a mystique among militants and generated media photo opportunities (MAB 2001). Donning green bandannas and baseball caps, and distributing more to sympathisers in the crowd, Vía Campesina supporters attracted considerable attention from other activists and the many journalists covering the protests.

This high-profile participation in international protests and civil society gatherings continues to be a hallmark of Vía Campesina activity. Its supporters played prominent roles at the World Social Forums in Porto Alegre, Brazil and at the 2002 'Rome +5' FAO World Food Summit. Following the violence outside the 2001 G-8 summit in Genoa, *Newsweek* (2001) singled out the Vía Campesina as one of eight 'kinder, gentler globalist' groups behind the anti-G-8 protests.

Much of the Vía Campesina's organising is carried out by its constituent groups, often with funds from European NGOs. The Vía Campesina itself has a tiny staff: the executive secretary, a part-time bilingual 'technical secretary', and a regular secretary in the Operational Secretariat in Honduras; a part-time consultant in Nicaragua who works with the Vía Campesina's Global Agrarian Reform Campaign; and a multilingual technical assistant based in Europe, who handles the network's internal communications and media relations. It relies on Yahoo list serves for distributing position papers and announcements, which circulate in English, Spanish, and occasionally in other languages.

The revival of agrarian reform

In the early 1990s, agrarian reform had largely dropped off policy-makers' agendas. In Latin America,

Peasant demonstration at a day of resistance against the Free Trade Area of the Americas in Quito, Ecuador. © Peter Rossett.

in particular, diverse reform programmes had been stymied by elite intransigence, privatisation measures, and 'counter-reforms', or by failure to provide the complementary resources—credit, titling, irrigation, technical assistance, and transport, processing, and marketing facilities—required for the success of peasant enterprises. At the 1995 FAO conference, several member nations called for eliminating land reform from the programme. However, at the following year's FAO conference, the issue of agrarian reform re-emerged forcefully in discussions over food security and at the insistence of the dozens of peasant and farmer activists present. The same countries which had asked the FAO to cut support for land reform were, within a few years, requesting FAO aid for new reform projects. Citing land invasions in Brazil, Malawi, and Zimbabwe, a FAO specialist acknowledged in 1998 that 'first and foremost land reform is back on the agenda because rural populations have put it there' (Riddell 1998).

In 1999, Vía Campesina and the German-based Food First Information and Action Network (FIAN) launched a Global Campaign on Agrarian Reform intended to take advantage of this growing momentum and to counter the World Bank's promotion of 'market-assisted land reform', in which public- and private-sector credits are provided to beneficiaries who individually negotiate land purchases with willing sellers. Vía Campesina and FIAN believe that the World Bank approach will not solve the problem of access to land for the poorest farmers or for those in places where property ownership is highly skewed and the supply of land is inelastic (FIAN 2000). The campaign briefly brought Vía Campesina into dialogue with the World Bank. Rafael Alegría spoke at a 1999 Bank forum on 'Strengthening Producer Organisations', which was also attended by an IFAP representative (Vía Campesina 1999b). Not long after, Vía Campesina and FIAN presented a petition to Bank officials, arguing that 'land is much more than a commodity' and that state-sponsored agrarian reforms are a human right (FIAN 2000). In early 2001, the Bank's Director of Rural Development responded by changing the programme's name from 'market-assisted' to 'community-managed' and by suggesting that the Bank's approach was complementary to, 'and not a substitute' for, laws enabling governments to expropriate land for distribution to peasants. Alegría and FIAN director Michael Windfuhr wrote another letter to Bank President James Wolfensohn reiterating their concerns, but found few grounds for believing that continued negotiations would be productive (Thomspon 2001; Windfuhr and Alegría 2002).

Three Vía Campesina leaders were among the activists who accompanied Yasir Arafat inside the PLO compound during the Israeli siege of Ramallah

An emergency human rights network and widening political engagement

The 'emergency network' established as part of the Vía Campesina-FIAN agrarian reform campaign has likely had more impact than the discussions with the World Bank. Modelled on the urgent action campaigns of Amnesty International and other human rights organisations, the 'emergency network' seeks to apply rapid pressure to state authorities in situations where peasants have suffered or are threatened with violent repression. When peasants involved in land conflicts were in danger, the network circulated electronic communiqués with instructions about how to contact government officials and peasant organisations. In 2001, Vía Campesina sponsored an 'international seminar on agrarian reform for peace in Colombia' which drew 300 participants from Colombia and beyond, including French activist José Bové, Bolivian parliamentary deputy (and later presidential candidate) Evo Morales, and the president of the European Parliament's Development Commission, Joaquim Miranda (Vía Campesina, ANUC, and FENSUAGRO 2001). Similar missions to the Philippines, Brazil, and Honduras generated media coverage and increased government efforts to resolve agrarian disputes. The Global Campaign for Agrarian Reform also sponsored training seminars in eight countries, as well as radio campaigns and protest actions (Vía Campesina 2000).

Concern with peasants' human rights and increased experience in international protest actions led the Vía Campesina to a dramatic engagement with the Palestinian-Israeli conflict in 2002. Ties between Palestinian peasants and French agriculturalists in the Larzac region, home base of the peripatetic José Bové, dated back to 1990, and had included visits and other intermittent contacts (Alland

Map 8.1 Peasant and farmer networks

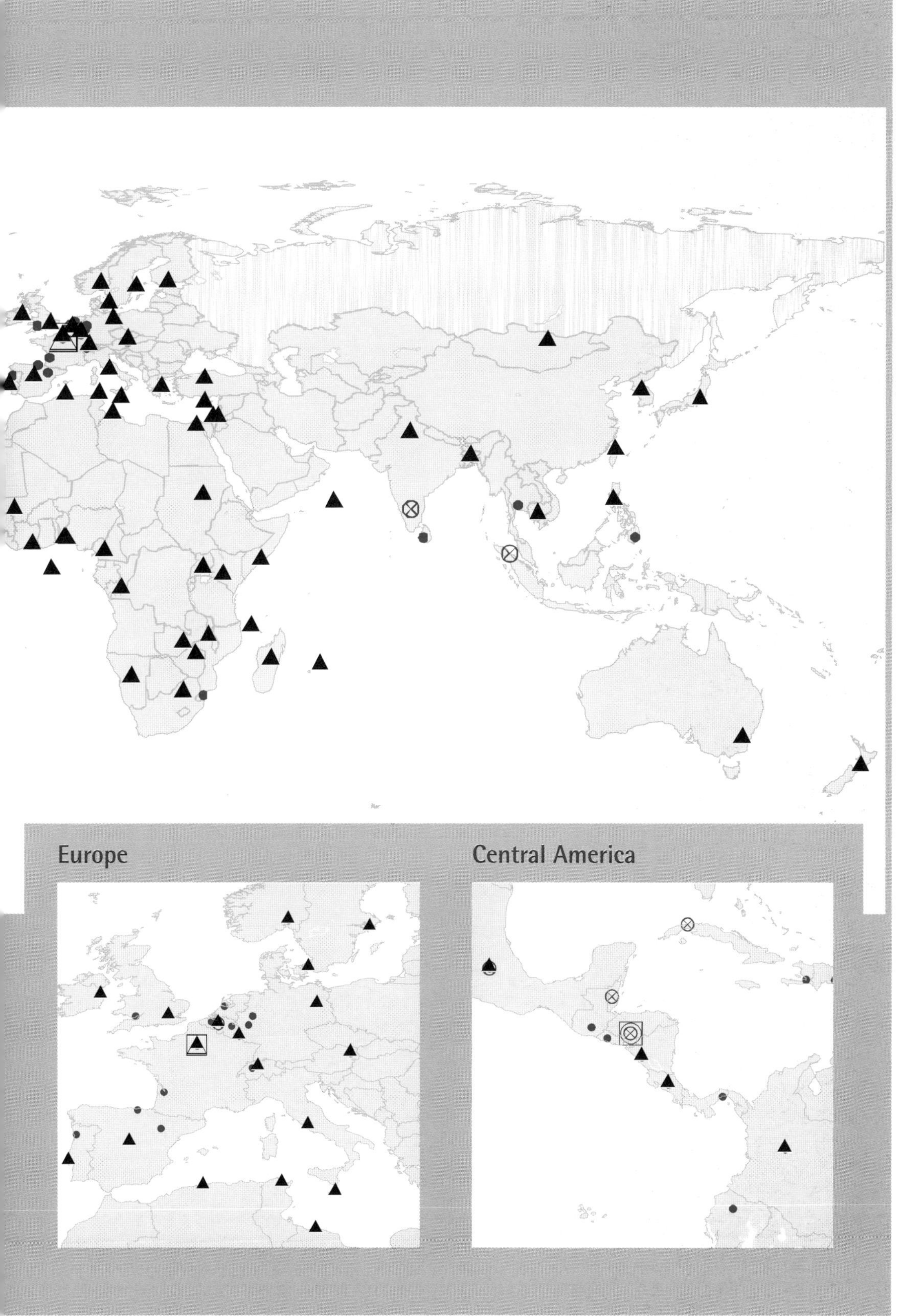
Europe
Central America

Table 8.1: NGO collaboration with peasant and small farmer networks

Organisation	Headquarters and offices
Action Group on Erosion, Technology and Concentration (formerly Rural Advancement Foundation International, RAFI)	Canada
Agriterra (formerly Paulo Freire Foundation, PFS)	Netherlands
Popular Coalition Agrarian Reform Network (ARnet)	Italy
Asia-Pacific Research Network (APRNet)	Philippines
Brot Für die Welt (Bread for the World)	Germany
Food First Information and Action Network (FIAN)	Germany, with sections in 18 other countries
Institut de Recherches de d'Application des Méthodes de Développement (Research Institute on Applied Development Methods, IRAM).	France
Farmers Link	United Kingdom
Focus on the Global South	Thailand, Philippines, Switzerland
Food First/Institute for Food and Development Policy	USA
Genetic Resources Action International (GRAIN)	Spain
Humanistisch Instituut voor Ontwikkelingssamenwerking (Humanist Institute for Development Co-operation, HIVOS)	Netherlands
Institute for Agriculture and Trade Policy	USA, Switzerland
Instituto Brasileiro de Analises Sociais e Economicas (Brazilian Institute of Social and Economic Analysis)	Brazil
Oxfam International	Twelve national organisations, including United Kingdom, Belgium, Canada, Germany, Ireland, United States, Netherlands, and Spain.
Pesticide Action Network	Five regional centres, with several hundred participating NGOs.
Red Interamericana de Agriculturas y Democracia (Interamerican Network on Agricultures and Democracy, RIAD)	Mexico
Servicio, Desarrollo y Paz, A.C. (Service, Development and Peace, SEDEPAC)	Mexico
Solidarités Agroalimentaires (Agro-Food Solidarities, SOLAGRAL)	France

Activities and positions
Mobilises public opinion against patenting of life forms, especially crop genetic material.
Played a key role in founding Vía Campesina. Specialises in agricultural credit and technology issues and works closely with IFAP and with some organisations in Vía Campesina.
Promotes land reform and related initiatives, in areas such as water rights, common property resources, inheritance rights for women, and indigenous rights. Part of the Popular Coalition to Eradicate Hunger and Poverty, a consortium of governmental organisations and NGOs established by the International Fund for Agricultural Development.
Sponsors capacity-building advocacy training and strategy workshops around WTO-related issues. Collaborates with the Pesticide Action Network and Vía Campesina.
Funds meetings and development projects of local-level and transnational farmers organisations.
Advocates agrarian reform, founded an urgent action network to alert participants about land conflicts, human rights violations, and food emergencies.
Supports programmes in agricultural credit and micro-finance, food security, local development, rural organisation, and micro-enterprises.
Promotes awareness of sustainable agriculture, food production and distribution, and rural development issues. Works on fair trade campaigns. Sponsored farmer exchanges between England and Nicaragua, France, Zimbabwe, India, Chile, the United States, and Cuba.
Research and reporting on trade negotiations; accompaniment of small farmer organisations at protests and parallel forums. Very critical of free-trade accords.
Research and analysis on agronomic, trade, and food sovereignty issues; accompaniment of small farmer movements at protests and parallel forums. Strongly opposed to free-trade treaties and biotechnology.
Promotes sustainable management and agricultural biodiversity based on people's control over genetic resources and local knowledge.
Works with organisations of the poor and marginalised in the countries of the South. Facilitates access to fair trade markets and small-scale credit, and supports arts, gender equity, human rights, HIV-AIDS, information access, and sustainable development programmes.
Works on behalf of family farms, rural communities, and ecosystems through research and education, science and technology, and advocacy. Provides analysis to farmers' organisations involved in anti-neo-liberal movements.
Conducts research on social and economic conditions, which it makes available to peasant organisations and other grass-roots sectors.
Supports famine relief, grass-roots development, international farm movement meetings, and public education around food, agriculture, and development issues. Oxfam's 2002 Make Trade Fair campaign, while critical of unfair trade practices, produced scepticism among radical peasant and farmer organisations.
Member groups hold training workshops and protests and campaign against corporate agribusiness and for low-input agriculture.
Provides an information clearing house and source of analysis for peasant organisations and NGOs working on agricultural issues.
Promotes organisational development, labour rights, and sustainable production practices. Co-sponsored international meetings of the Programa Campesino a Campesino in the 1980s and 1990s.
Seeks to support citizens' networks and to influence global trade and environmental policies by strengthening the negotiating capacity of delegates from poor countries to international governance institutions.

The Dutch Union of Rural Women has a longstanding cooperation with rural women's groups in Benin. © Van Gelder/Agriterra.

2002: 176). In January, Palestinian olive farmers came to the Porto Alegre World Social Forum, where they contacted the large Vía Campesina delegation and spoke of the difficulties they faced under Israeli occupation. A few months later, four Vía Campesina leaders travelled to the West Bank, where they visited Bedouins whose olive trees had been sprayed with herbicides by the Israeli military. Three of the four Vía Campesina leaders were among the activists who accompanied Yasser Arafat inside the PLO compound during the Israeli siege of Ramallah. José Bové was deported after a few days, but Paul Nicholson from Spain and Mario Lill from Brazil remained in Arafat's compound for three weeks (Vía Campesina 2002).

The Vía Campesina's involvement with the Palestinian-Israeli conflict is illustrative of how cross-border networking and the increasingly global and complex character of agricultural policy itself have broadened the alliances and concerns of peasant and farmer movements. Trade, phytosanitary measures, intellectual property rights, animal and human health, environment, human rights, biotechnology, gender equity, and food sovereignty have, in everyday political contention, become inextricably bound up with one another. Protest repertoires too have converged, as political campaigns are carried out in transnational contexts and as movements from different sectors and countries exchange experiences.

The multiple foci and theatricality of agriculturalists' public actions in recent years need to be understood in relation to these processes. The much-heralded 1999 symbolic 'dismantling' of a flimsy, half-built McDonald's restaurant by José Bové and his Confédération Paysanne neighbours in Millau was a carnivalesque protest against US tariffs imposed on Roquefort cheese in retaliation for the EU ban on US hormone-treated beef (Bové and Dufour 2001: 3–31; Herman and Boisgontier 2002: 68). More generally, it responded to a series of food safety crises in Europe: dioxin-tainted poultry, and mad-cow and foot-and-mouth diseases. It also tapped fears about GM crops, which farmers' movements saw as part of the economic and ecological logic of intensive agriculture and a US- and corporate-dominated food system that threatened to undermine health, environment, and cultural specificity. The Millau 'McDo' episode could also be read in part as a reprise of the 1996 attack on a Kentucky Fried Chicken outlet in Bangalore, India, by 150 members of the Karnataka State Farmers Association, who accused KFC of selling 'carcinogenic junk food' (Gupta 1998: 331). The 1999 Indian farmers' caravan to Europe, which had brought many of the protagonists in both actions together, ended barely two months before the incident that catapulted Millau to world attention. And the Vía Campesina's third congress—and its first international women's meeting—in Bangalore in 2000 brought them together once more.

A Profusion of Networks

The geographical coverage of the transnational networks is decidedly uneven. Vía Campesina, for example, has significant backing in most of the Spanish-speaking world but virtually no affiliates in Africa, a region where the International Federation of Agricultural Producers (IFAP) has a number of member groups (see Map 8.1). IFAP, in turn, has little presence in Mexico or Chile and counts among its members only a handful of non-elite groups in the rest of Latin America or in Europe. Neither Vía Campesina nor IFAP has a presence in China (perhaps not surprising given the political system), which has the largest number of peasants, despite widespread rural unrest there attributable, in many cases, to market-driven dislocations of the rural population (Walker 2002).

IFAP's close collaboration with governments and multilateral agencies, as well as its big-producer orientation, gives it access to resources and makes it a centrist or even conservative voice within the spectrum of global agriculturalists' movements. Operating primarily behind the scenes as a traditional lobby, however, its public profile has been lower than that of Vía Campesina, even though it includes more participating organisations. Although IFAP affirms its commitment to family farms as the basis of a sustainable agricultural system (PROSI 1996), many of its constituent organisations represent elites and corporate producers. This is particularly evident in Argentina, Brazil, Canada, Colombia, France, the Philippines, and the United States, where IFAP affiliates enrol large farmers and more radical Vía Campesina organisations represent peasant, indigenous, and small family farmers. IFAP leaders, in contrast to those of less conservative groups, are frequently sceptical of, or even hostile to, environmentalists and critics of industrial agriculture. In 2001, some charged that 'lunatic eco-terrorists' might have deliberately caused epidemics of foot-and-mouth disease and swine fever in Britain in order to 'scare' the public and 'destroy meat consumption' (Byrnes 2001).

In 1983 the Swiss-based Charles Léopold Mayer Foundation for Human Progress (FPH) initiated a programme for agriculturalists' organisations in Senegal, Tanzania, and a few other African countries. Within a few years, the FPH decided that the problems peasants faced in Africa—glutted markets, dismantling of state commodity boards, liberalisation of agricultural trade—required an international response.

In 1993, in Cameroon, 20 peasant and NGO activists started a regional network called APM Afrique (Agriculture Peasant and Modernisation Network-Africa). In contrast to Vía Campesina, which favoured pressure tactics and protests, APM-Afrique sought principally to 'rediscover the intellectual capacity' of its peasant participants—largely from francophone Africa—with a view to 'resolving concrete problems' (Berthomé and Mercoiret 1993: 67). By 1995, APM-Afrique had created working groups on the WTO and the coffee and cotton sectors, a magazine, and an 'itinerant' African Peasants' Academy (Université Paysanne Africaine), which offered courses in Senegal and Cameroon. Simultaneously with the creation of APM-Afrique, the FPH initiated a parallel project in Eastern Europe and sponsored international meetings of peasant organisations in the Larzac region of France in 1993, in Cameroon in 1996, in Brazil in 1998, and again in the Larzac in 2000. By 1996, these events had given rise to APM-Mondial, which helped to create the Interamerican Network on Agricultures and Democracy (RIAD) and also maintained links with NGOs close to Vía Campesina, such as the US-based Institute for Trade and Agricultural Policy (APM-Afrique 2001). The APM network's analysis of the WTO is similar to that of the Vía Campesina, and the two networks eventually collaborated on projects such as the 2001 World Forum on Food Sovereignty in Havana.

In 2002, APM-Mondial assembled 130 peasant and indigenous leaders from 36 countries at a World Peasant Meeting in Cameroon. Some of the Asian and Latin American organisations that attended belonged to Vía Campesina, but most of the participating groups were in other networks. The Meeting's Yaoundé Declaration condemned 'the negative impacts of neoliberal globalisation' in terms very similar to those employed by the Vía Campesina and, echoing the slogan of the World Social Forum, declared that 'another world is possible'. APM-Mondial has also had set up an APM network in China (Réseau APM Chine) and convened conferences there, although the individuals and institutions involved are designated by the Chinese government (APM-Mondial 2001; 2002).

To what extent does the proliferation of networks with similar agendas—Vía Campesina and APM-Mondial, among others—represent a force for synergy, a territorial division of labour, or, alternatively, a kind of organisational competition or redundancy? The balance between these possibilities is likely to be constantly shifting and rather delicate, best illustrated perhaps by the networks' activities in Africa. The Vía Campesina tried on a number of occasions to make inroads in Africa, hosting African organisations at its 1996 congress and holding a 1998 coordinating committee meeting in Senegal at the invitation of a convention of African peasant groups (Vía Campesina 1996; 1998). These efforts bore little fruit, however, in terms of building durable ties to what was, as Vía Campesina leader Rafael Alegría put it in an interview in Tegucigalpa on 2 August 2001, a largely 'blank' region. Around the time of the 2002 World Summit on Sustainable Development in Johannesburg, the Vía Campesina joined African organisations in an acerbic exchange of letters about land reform with the World Bank and issued joint statements with the National Land Committee, backing its demands for negotiations with the South African government. But these efforts were hard to sustain once the Summit ended and did not lead to the formal incorporation of African organisations, many of which were part of APM-Afrique, into Vía Campesina (Mngxitama 2002; NLC and LPM 2002). APM and Vía Campesina were, in effect, territorially specialised, but while this helped each by not spreading scarce resources too thinly it also undercut the claims of both networks to truly global reach.

Contradictions and Future Prospects

In little more than a decade of intensive transnational networking and political action, peasant and small farmer movements have contributed to stalling the Uruguay and Millennium rounds of world trade talks, to achieving at least temporary bans in several countries and regions on commercial planting of GM crops promoted by giant agribusiness corporations, and to returning agrarian reform to the global agenda in an era of privatisation and paeans to the magic of the marketplace. They have also attempted to shift the terms of discussion in international arenas towards fundamental development and ethical issues, arguing, for example, that quantitative measures of 'food security' need to be replaced with an understanding of 'food sovereignty' which prioritises a multidimensional commitment to human well-being and which insists that food and land are not simply commodities. Importantly, small farmers have reinforced alliances with, and heightened the legitimacy of, movements around trade, biotechnology, corporate accountability, environment, health, and human rights issues. Participants in the peasant and farmer networks have also come to have a dynamic sense of themselves as political actors, empowered with new knowledge, conceptions of solidarity and tools of struggle, and surprisingly unlike the unsophisticated rustics that urban elites often imagine them to be.

Participants in the peasant and farmer networks have also come to have a dynamic sense of themselves as political actors, empowered with new knowledge, conceptions of solidarity and tools of struggle

These are formidable accomplishments for movements that not long ago often barely knew of one another's existence, but they exist alongside opposing trends that are hardly auspicious. Relations between NGOs and the peasant and farmer networks have frequently been tense. At times this has involved questions of representation—who may speak in the name of the peasantry—and on other occasions accountability to constituencies and to those who provide funds for network activities. The imposition of donor-driven agendas has contributed to the decline or demise of more than one civil society initiative.

Network activists, like other overworked professionals, feel the tug of disparate demands from regional, national, and local organisations in which they take part and, in the case of farmers, from the imperatives of agricultural production, in which they usually must participate to sustain their livelihoods and their legitimacy vis-à-vis supporters and antagonists. Concretely, the same individuals who mobilise for international conferences may also have to assemble a legal team to defend contested property titles, follow up on orders for a cooperative's rubber boots, and harvest a field of cabbages before the rains arrive. Tensions between transnational and national activism may become more acute as democratisation advances in previously authoritarian societies, since possibilities of affecting transnational processes through national action may improve and traditional political forms—parties, unions, and lobbies—may assume many demands initially articulated through transnational civil society initiatives. In Central America, for example, several organisations that pioneered cross-border linkages in the 1980s have largely withdrawn from time-consuming transnational activism.

An added contradiction is what one critic terms network activity's 'dual quality as both a means to an end and an end in itself' (Riles 2001: 51). Networks appear, formally, to link organisations, but they also are based on personal ties between activists (and between activists and funders). These, together with some organisations' 'verticalist' tendencies, may produce instances of exclusion that limit network members' political imagination, effectiveness, and credibility. Network practices of representation—submitting proposals, organising meetings, publishing newsletters or web sites, drafting 'action platforms'—sometimes seek to demonstrate the effectiveness of a network with reference to its own self-description and activities rather than to tangible impacts on targeted constituencies, policies, and institutions. The difficulty is compounded for organisations that participate in various transnational networks of differing geographical scope or purpose. Movements of poor rural people, with few skilled leaders, can usually ill afford the cost in separation from their constituencies that intense transnational activism implies.

The major obstacle facing the peasant and small farmer networks, however, continues to be the sheer force of ongoing worldwide economic liberalisation and ever greater corporate power. No society has ever entirely resolved the tension between agriculture and industry over terms of trade, over fair prices for farmers versus cheap food for urban people or cheap raw materials for food and fibre manufacturers. Many societies in the past, however, did achieve a decent, stable balance between the interests of farmers and those of large and small consumers through political compromises or stalemates. Farmers in many places sought and achieved a degree of vertical integration, through cooperatives and other non-corporate ownership forms, that provided them with more value added and constituted a check on the agribusiness monopolies. These hard-won gains, however, are everywhere disappearing in the face of heightened competition at the farm level and decreased competition and ever larger mergers among the corporations that buy, process, and transport what farms produce. As societies throughout the world urbanise, rural areas and rural people often lose political clout.

The regional and global free-trade pacts targeted by the peasant and farmer networks, such as NAFTA, WTO, and the proposed Free Trade Area of the Americas, generally aim to legislate the behaviour of national governments but only secondarily that of corporations. Today's conflicts over farming and food pit some of the most powerful global institutions against incipient transnational movements of some of the most marginalised and destitute people on earth. The peasants and small farmers of the twenty-first century—still almost half of the world's economically active population—have, in the past decade, risen to the challenge, found new means of struggle, and scored an occasional victory, but it is still too early to call the match.

Many thanks to Brenda Biddle and Alcira Forero-Peña for research assistance, to the US National Science Foundation for fieldwork support, and to Helmut Anheier, Brenda Biddle, John Clark, Annette Desmarais, Marlies Glasius, and Dominick Jenkins for comments on an earlier draft.

References

ACWW (2002). Associated Country Women of the World <http://www.acww.org.uk/>. Accessed 20/11/02.

Alland, Alexander, with Alland, Sonia (2002). *Crisis and Commitment: The Life History of a French Social Movement* (2nd edn). New York: Harwood.

APM-Afrique (2001). 16 March. Université Paysanne Africaine <http://lnweb18.worldbank.org/essd/essdext.nsf/16DocByUnid/0142D977A5E003DA85256B50005F3A74/$FILE/UPAFA0.pdf>. Accessed 5/7/2001.

APM-Mondial (2001). 'Asie'. *Zooide.* <http://www.zooide.com/apm/htm/racti.html>. Accessed 24/10/2002.

— (2002). 11 May. 'Encuentro Mundial Campesino: Declaración de Yaoundé'. <http://www.zooide.com/apm/doc/declarationes2.doc>. Accessed 24/10/2002.

ASOCODE (1999). *Documento para la discusión sobre el 'Proceso de reorganización y reorientación de ASOCODE'.* Managua, January.

— (2001). *Memoria: Encuentro regional de dirigentes campesinos centroamericanos.* Tegucigalpa , 4–5 April.

Ayres, Jeffrey M. (1998). *Defying Conventional Wisdom: Political Movements and Popular Contention against North American Free Trade.* Toronto: University of Toronto Press.

Bell, Beverly (2002). *Social Movements and Regional Integration in the Americas.* <http://www.econjustice.net>.

Bellinghausen, Hermann (2003). 2 January. 'Rompe el silencio la comandancia del EZLN y toma San Cristóbal'. *La Jornada.* <http://www.jornada.unam.mx/2003/ene03/030102/003n1pol.php?origen=index.html>. Accessed 5/1/2003.

Berlet, Chip and Lyons, Matthew N. (2000). *Right-Wing Populism in America: Too Close for Comfort.* New York: Guilford.

Bernstein, Henry and Byres, Terence J. (2001). 'From Peasant Studies to Agrarian Change'. *Journal of Agrarian Change*, 1/1: 1–56.

Berthomé, Jacques and Mercoiret, Marie-Rose (1993). *La Rencontre de M'Balmayo, Cameroun, 26 au 30 Avril 1993.* Cameroun: APM-Afrique.

Biekart, Kees (1999). *The Politics of Civil Society Building: European Private Aid Agencies and Democratic Transitions in Central America.* Amsterdam: International Books.

Blokland, Kees (1995). 'Peasant Alliances and "Concertation" with Society'. *Bulletin of Latin American Research*, 14/2: 159–70.

Bové, José, and François Dufour (2001). *The World is Not For Sale: Farmers Against Junk Food* (interviewed by Gilles Luneau). London: Verso.

Brecher, Jeremy (1993). 'The Hierarchs' New World Order—and Ours'. In Jeremy Brecher, John Childs, and Jill Cutler (eds), *Global Visions: Beyond the New World Order*. Boston: South End Press.

Bush, Evelyn and Simi, Pete (2001). 'European Farmers and Their Protests'. In Doug Imig and Sidney Tarrow (eds), *Contentious Europeans: Protest and Politics in an Emerging Polity*. Lanham, MD: Rowman & Littlefield.

Byrnes, Michael (2001). 'Eco-terrorists May Have Planted FMD Plague-Farmers'. *Reuters*. 15 May. <http://www.earthchangestv.com/2001_secure/Breaking_News/0516eco_terrorists.htm>. Accessed 19/5/2001.

Cadji, Anne-Laure (2000). 'Brazil's Landless Find their Voice'. *NACLA Report on the Americas*, 33/5: 30–5.

Castells, Manuel (1996). *The Rise of the Network Society*. The Information Age: Economy, Society and Culture, 1. Oxford: Blackwell.

CCS-Chiapas (Coordinación de Comunicación Social, Estado de Chiapas) (2002). 5 May. 'Con la participación de la CNPA, UNORCA, CIOAC y CLOC en Tapachula'. <http://www.ccschiapas.gob.mx/pagina_anterior/boletines/2002/mayo/bol1115.htm>. Accessed 1/3/2003.

CLOC (Coordinadora Latinoamericana de Organizaciones del Campo) (1997). *First Latin American Assembly of Rural Women*. São Paulo: CLOC.

— (2001). 31 July. 'III Congreso Coordinadora Latinoamericana de Organizaciones del Campo'. <http://listas.ecuanex.net.ec/pipermail/infodesarrollo/2001-August/000312.html>. Accessed 10/11/2001.

Desai, Meghnad and Said, Yahia (2001). 'The New Anti-Capitalist Movement: Money and Global Civil Society'. In Helmut Anheier, Marlies Glasius, and Mary Kaldor (eds), *Global Civil Society 2001*. Oxford: Oxford University Press.

Desmarais, Annette-Aurélie (2002). 'The Vía Campesina: Consolidating an International Peasant and Farm Movement'. *Journal of Peasant Studies*, 29/2: 91–124.

Diamond, Sara (1995). *Roads to Dominion: Right-Wing Movements and Political Power in the United States*. New York: Guilford.

Drage, Dorothy (1961). *Pennies for Friendship: The Autobiography of an Active octogenarian, a Pioneer of ACWW*. London: Gwenlyn Evans Caernarvon.

Edelman, Marc (1998). 'Transnational Peasant Politics in Central America'. *Latin American Research Review*, 33/3: 49–86.

— (1999). *Peasants Against Globalization: Rural Social Movements in Costa Rica*. Stanford: Stanford University Press.

Fernandes, Bernardo Mançano (2000). *A Formacão do MST no Brasil*. Petrópolis, RJ: Editora Vozes.

FIAN (Food First Information and Action Network) (2000). Land is Much More than a Commodity <http://www.fian.org/english-version/petition-worldbank.htm>. Accessed 19/8/2001.

Food and Agriculture Organisation. FAO Stat Agricultural data, <http://apps.fao.org/page/form?collection>.

Freres, Christian (1998). *La Cooperación de las Sociedades Civiles de la Unión Europea con América Latina*. Madrid: AIETI.

Friedmann, Harriet (1993). 'Distance and Durability: Shaky Foundations of the World Food Economy'. *Third World Quarterly*, 13: 371–83.

Gleave, Alfred P (1991). *United We Stand: Prairie Farmers 1901–1975*. Toronto: Lugus.

Gorneg, Paol (2001). January. 'Un Syndicat Agricole "à la Soviétique": Voyage au Coeur de la FNSEA'. *Le Monde Diplomatique* <http://www.monde-diplomatique.fr/2001/01/GORNEG/14741>. Accessed 3/12/2001.

Greider, William (2000). 'The Last Farm Crisis'. *The Nation*, 271/16 (20 November): 11–18.

Gupta, Akhil (1998). *Postcolonial Developments: Agriculture in the Making of Modern India*. Durham, NC: Duke University Press.

Herman, Patrick and Boisgontier, Christian (2002). *Confédération Paysanne: Changeons de Politique Agricole*. Les Petits Libres, Vol. 40. Paris: Mille et Une Nuits, Librairie Arthème Farard.

Hernández, Luis (1992). 'Las Convulsiones Sociales'. In Carlota Boteyo, Julio Moguel, and Luis Hernández (eds), *Autonomía y Nuevos Sujetos Sociales en el Desarrollo Rural*. Mexico: Siglo Veintiuno Editores.

ICA and IFAP (International Cooperative Alliance and International Federation of Agricultural Producers) (1967). *Cooperation in the European Market Economies*. Bombay: Asia Publishing House.

IFAP (International Federation of Agricultural Producers) (1952). 'FAO Position on International Commodity Problems'. *IFAP News*, 1/1: 6.

— (1957). *The First Ten Years of the International Federation of Agricultural Producers*. Paris and Washington: IFAP.

Iniciativa CID (Iniciativa Mesoamericana de Comercio, Integración y Desarrollo) (2002). Campaña Regional en Torno al Tratado de Libre Comercio entre los Estados Unidos y Centro América. Document provided by the Federación Nacional de Cooperativas, Nicaragua.

IRC (Interhemispheric Resource Center) (1992). Cross-Border Links: Where the Action Is. <http://www.us-mex.org/borderlines/1992/bl1-main.html>. Accessed 12/20/2002.

Kearney, Michael (1996). *Reconceptualizing the Peasantry: Anthropology in Global Perspective*. Boulder, CO: Westview.

Kneen, Brewster (2002). *Invisible Giant: Cargill and its Transnational Strategies* (2nd edn). London: Pluto Press.

León, Osvaldo, Burch, Sally, and Tamayo, Eduardo (2001). *Movimientos sociales en la red.* Quito: ALAI.

MAB (Movimento dos Atingidos por Barragens) (2001). *O Valor dos Nossos Símbolos*. Caderno de Formação, 3. São Paulo: MAB.

Macdonald, Laura (1994). 'Globalising Civil Society: Interpreting International NGOs in Central America'. *Millennium: Journal of International Studies*, 23/2: 267–85.

McMichael, Philip (1998). 'Global Food Politics'. *Monthly Review*, 50/3: 97–111.

Matejka, Michael G. (1979). *The Christian Rural Mission in the 1980's—A Call to Liberation and Development of Peoples*. New York: Agricultural Missions.

Meier, Mariann (1958). *ACWW 1929–1959*. London: ACWW.

Mngxitama, Andile (2002). 9 July. 'The World Bank Must Still Apologise'. <http://southafrica.indymedia.org/print.php?id=1522>. Accessed 16/10/2002.

Mooney, Patrick H. and Majka, Theo J. (1995). *Farmers' and Farm Workers' Movements: Social Protest in American Agriculture*. New York: Twayne.

NCC (National Council of Churches News Service) (2002). 'Agricultural Missions "Education for Rural Justice Tour" is Underway'. <http://nccusa.org/news/02news84.html>. 11/4/2002.

Newsweek (2001). 'The New Face of Protest: A Who's Who'. 30 July: 17.

NFU (National Farmers Union, Canada) (1985a). '1985: A Year of Struggle, Heartache, Victory and Solidarity'. *Union Farmer*, 36/7: 6–7.

— (1985b). 'NFU Becomes a Member of NAFA'. *Union Farmer*, 36/7: 2.

— (1985c). 'NFU Presents Brief to Wheat Board Minister'. *Union Farmer*, 36/3: 5.

— (1988). 'Defending Canada's Rural Communities'. *Union Farmer*, 39/8: 6–7.

— (2001). The National Farmers Union: Fighting for the Family Farm for Over 30 Years. <http://ww.nfu.ca/nfuhistory3.pdf>. 11/3/2002.

NLC (National Land Committee) and LPM (Landless People's Movement) (2002). 24 August. 'Arrested Landless People's Movement Members Released'. <http://www.focusweb.org/publications/press-statements/wssd-2002/arrest-2.html South Africa>. Accessed 13/12/2002.

Petras, James (1998). 'The New Revolutionary Peasantry'. *Z Magazine*. October. <http://www.zmag.org/zmag/articles/petrasoct98.htm>. Accessed 1/3/2000.

PFS (Paulo Freire Stichting) (1993). 'La Vía Campesina' (unpublished paper). Doetinchem, Netherlands: PFS.

Posas, Mario (1985). 'El Movimiento Campesino Hondureño: Un Panorama General'. In Pablo González Casanova (ed.), *Historia Política de los Campesinos Latinoamericanos*, ii. Mexico: Siglo Veintiuno.

PROSI (1996). 'August. Cinquantenaire de la FIPA: Déclaration des agriculteurs du monde'. *PROSI Magazine*, 331 <http://prosi.intnet.mu/FIPA331.htm>. Accessed 1/15/1998.

Qualman, Darrin and Wiebe, Nettie (2002). *The Structural Adjustment of Canadian Agriculture*. Ottawa: Canadian Centre for Policy Alternatives.

Ramanujam, T.C.A., and. Sangeetha, T.C.A (2001). 24 April. 'New IPR regime–Protection for Indian patents'. *The Hindu Business Line*. <http://www.blonnet.com/businessline/2001/04/24/stories/042420ma.htm>. Accessed 26/2/2002.

Riddell, J. (1998). 'Contemporary Thinking on Land Reforms'. <http://www.ifad.org/popularcoalition/immago/re_mon_fao_contemp.htm>. Paper prepared by the staff of the Land Tenure Service, Rural Development Division, FAO, Rome. Accessed 7/2/2001.

Riles, Annelise (2001). *The Network Inside Out*. Ann Arbor: University of Michigan Press.

Ritchie, Mark (1996). 'Cross-Border Organizing'. In Jerry Mander and Edward Goldsmith (eds), *The Case Against the Global Economy and for a Turn toward the Local*. San Francisco: Sierra Club.

— (2001). 'From Seattle to Doha: The Role of Agrarian Movements in Shaping the Post-Bretton Woods World Order'. Paper presented at the Yale Agrarian Studies Seminar, New Haven, CT.

Roederer-Rynning, Christilla (2002). 'Farm Conflict in France and the Europeanisation of Agricultural Policy'. *West European Politics*, 25: 105–25.

Ronfeldt, David and Arquilla, John (2001). 'What Next for Networks and Netwars?' In John Arquilla and David Ronfeldt (eds), *Networks and Netwars: The Future of Terror, Crime, and Militancy*. Santa Monica, California: RAND.

Rural Coalition (1994). *Building the Movement for Community Based Development: Rural Coalition 1994 Annual Assembly*. Arlington, Virginia: Rural Coalition.

Segovia, Alexander (1993). *Mercado de alimentos y sistema de banda de precios en Centroamérica*. San Salvador: CENITEC.

Seoane, José and Taddei, Emilio (eds) (2001). *Resistencias Mundiales: De Seattle a Porto Alegre*. Buenos Aires: CLACSO.

Shanin, Teodor (1971). *Peasants and Peasant Societies*. Harmondsworth: Penguin.

Sheingate, Adam D. (2001). *The Rise of the Agricultural Welfare State: Institution and Interest Group Power in the United States, France, and Japan*. Princeton: Princeton University Press.

Shiva, Vandana (2001). *Yoked to Death: Globalisation and Corporate Control of Agriculture*. New Delhi: Research Foundation for Science, Technology and Ecology.

– and Holla-Bhar, Radha (1996). 'Piracy by Patent: The Case of the Neem Tree'. In Jerry Mander and Edward Goldsmith (eds), *The Case Against the Global Economy and for a Turn toward the Local*. San Francisco: Sierra Club.

Stein, Eduardo and Arias Peñate, Salvador (1992). *Democracia Sin Pobreza: Alternativa de Desarrollo para el Istmo Centroamericano*. San José: DEI.

Tarrow, Sidney (1998). *Power in Movement: Social Movements and Contentious Politics* (2nd edn). Cambridge: Cambridge University Press.

Thomspon [sic], Robert L. (2001). 'Your Petition on Land Reform'. Thomspon to Rafael Alegría. Washington, DC. Photocopy.

The Times (London) (1946a). 'Conference of World Farmers: Supporting the F.A.O'. 20 May: 6.

– (1946b). 'Marketing of Food'. 30 May: 4.

Trubek, Amy B (2000). 'The Taste of Place'. <http://wiscinfo.doit.wisc.edu/eucenter/Conferences/foodweb/foodpapers/paper3.htm>. Paper presented at the conference on Taste, Technology and Terror, European Union Center, University of Wisconsin, Madison. Accessed 1/12/2002.

Vía Campesina (1995). 'Neo-Liberal Food Policies: The Road to Hunger'. Press release from FAO symposium, Quebec City, 11 October.

– (1996). *Proceedings from the II International Conference of the Vía Campesina, Tlaxcala, Mexico, April 18–21, 1996*. Brussels: NCOS Publications.

– (1998). November. 'Dakar Declaration of Vía Campesina'. Accessed 19/1/1999. <cpe@agoranet.be>

– (1999a). 'Mobilization Actions and Incidences Carried Out at Seattle 28th November to 3rd December, 1999'. <http://ns.sdnhon.org.hn/miembros/via/seattle%20incidences.htm>. Accessed 8/30/00.

– (1999b). August. 'Vía Campesina Sets Out Important Positions at World Bank Events'. *Vía Campesina Newsletter*, 4. <http://ns.sdnhon.org.hn/miembros/via/carta4_en.htm>. Accessed 9/27/2000.

(2000). 'Acciones Desarrolladas en el Primer Año de la Campaña'. <http://ns.sdnhon.org/hn/miembros/via/acciones-esp.htm>. Accessed 23/3/2001.

– (2002). 5 April. 'Vía Campesina Demands Respect for the Principle of Food Sovereignty and Right of Palestinian Farmers to Produce and to Remain on their Land' (press release sent from <Viacam-info-palestina@yahoogroups.com>).

–, ANUC (Asociación Nacional de Usuarios Campesinos), and FENSUAGRO (Federación Nacional Sindical Unitaria Agropecuaria) (2001). 'Statement of the International Seminar on Agrarian Reform for Peace in Colombia'. Bogotá, 27 June.

Walker, Kathy Le Mons (2002). '"Gangster Capitalism" and Peasant Politics in China'. Paper presented at the Workshop on Terror and Violence in State and Institutional Context After September 11, Social Science Perspectives, New York Academy of Sciences.

Welch, Cliff (2000). 'Marking Time with the CLOC: International Rural Labor Solidarity in the Americas from World War II to the Third Millennium. Paper presented at the XXII International Congress of the Latin American Studies Association, Miami, 16–19 March.

Wilford, Allen (1985). *Farmgate Defense*. Toronto: New Canada Publications.

Windfuhr, Michael and Alegría, Rafael (2002). Letter from Global Campaign for Agrarian Reform to James D. Wolfensohn, the World Bank. Heidelberg and Tegucigalpa.

World Bank (2001). *World Development Indicators*. http://www.worldbank.org/data/wdi2001/pds/tab6_4.pdf>.

Table 8.2: Abbreviations

AAM	American Agriculture Movement
ACWW	Associated Country Women of the World
AFL-CIO	American Federation of Labor-Congress of Industrial Organizations
ANAP	National Association of Small Agricultural Producers (Asociaciación Nacional de Agricultores Pequeños) (Cuba)
ANUC	National Peasant Association (Asociación Nacional de Usuarios Campesinos) (Colombia)
APM Afrique	Agriculture Peasant and Modernization Network-Africa (Réseau Agricultures Paysannes et Modernisation Afrique)
APM Mondial	Agriculture Peasant and Modernization Network-World (Réseau Agricultures Paysannes et Modernisation Mondial)
APRNet	Asia-Pacific Research Network
ARnet	Agrarian Reform Network
ASOCODE	Association of Central American Peasant Organizations for Cooperation and Development (Asociación Centroamericana de Organizaciones Campesinas para la Cooperación y el Desarrollo)
ATTAC	Association for the Taxation of Financial Transactions to Aid the Citizenry (Association pour la Taxation des Transactions Financières por l'Aide aux Citoyens)
CADESCA	Support Committee for the Economic and Social Development of Central America (Comité de Apoyo al Desarrollo Económico y Social de Centroamérica)
CAP	Common Agricultural Policy (EU)
CCC-CA	Confederation of Cooperatives of the Caribbean and Central America (Confederación de Cooperativas del Caribe y Centro América)
CCS-Chiapas	Social Communication Coordinator, State of Chiapas (Coordinación de Comunicación Social, Estado de Chiapas) (Mexico)
CGIAR	Consultative Group on International Agricultural Research
CICA	Central American Indigenous Council (Consejo Indígena Centroamericano)
CICAFOC	Indigenous and Peasant Community Agroforestry Coordinator (Coordinadora Indígena y Campesina de Agroforestería Comunitaria) (Central America)
CLOC	Latin American Coordinator of Rural Organizations (Coordinadora Latinoamericana de Organizaciones del Campo)
CNC	National Peasant Confederation (Confederación Nacional Campesina) (Mexico)
COMPA	Convergence of Movements of Peoples of the Americas
CNSTP	National Confederation of Worker-Peasant Unions (Confédération Nationale des Syndicats Travailleurs-Paysans) (France)
COPA	Committee of Professional Agricultural Organisations (Comité des Organisations Professionelles Agricoles) (EU)
EC	European Community (after 1993, EU)
ECM	Mesoamerican Peasant Meeting (Encuentro Campesino Mesoamericano)
EFC	European Farmers Coordination
EU	European Union
FAO	Food and Agriculture Organisation (UN)
FENOC	National Federation of Peasant Organisations (Federación Nacional de Organizaciones Campesinas) (Ecuador)
FENSUAGRO	Nacional Unitary Federation of Agricultural Unions (Federación Nacional Sindical Unitaria Agropecuaria) (Colombia)
FIAN	Food First Information and Action Network (Germany)

FLOC	Farm Labor Organizing Committee (US)
FNSEA	National Federation of Agricultural Enterprises (Fédération Nationale de Exploitations Agricoles) (France)
FTAA	Free Trade Area of the Americas
FPH	Charles Léopold Mayer Foundation for Human Progress (Switzerland)
GATT	General Agreement on Tariffs and Trade
GRAIN	Genetic Resources Action International
HIVOS	Humanist Institute for Development Co-operation
ICA	International Cooperative Alliance
ICC	International Coordinating Committee
ICIC	Civil Initiative for Central American Integration (Iniciativa Civil para la Integración Centroamericana)
ICW	International Council of Women
IFAP	International Federation of Agricultural Producers
Iniciativa CID	Mesoamerican Initiative for Trade, Integration and Sustainable Development (Iniciativa Mesoamericana de Comercio, Integración y Desarrollo Sostenible)
IRAM	Research Institute on Applied Development Methods (Institut de Recherches d'Application des Méthodes de Développement) (France)
IRC	Interhemispheric Resource Center (USA)
KMP	Peasant Movement of the Philippines
KRRS	Karnataka State Farmers Association (Karnataka Rajya Ryota Sangha) (India)
LPM	Landless People's Movement (South Africa)
MAB	Movement of People Displaced by Dams (Movimento dos Atingidos por Barragens) (Brazil)
MST	Landless Rural Workers Movement (Movimento dos Trabalhadores Rurais sem Terra) (Brazil)
NAFA	North American Farm Alliance
NAFTA	North American Free Trade Agreement
NCC	National Council of Churches
NFU	National Farmers Union
NLC	National Land Committee (South Africa)
PFS	Paulo Freire Foundation (Paulo Freire Stichting) (Netherlands)
PPP	Plan Puebla-Panamá
RAFI	Rural Advancement Foundation International
RIAD	Interamerican Network on Agricultures and Democracy (Red Interamericana de Agriculturas y Democracia)
RMALC	Mexican Action Network on Free Trade (Red Mexicana de Acción Frente al Libre Comercio)
SEDEPAC	Service, Development and Peace (Servicio, Desarrollo, y Paz, A.C.) (Mexico)
SOLAGRAL	Agro-Food Solidarities (Solidarités Agroalimentaires) (France)
TRIPS	Trade-Related Intellectual Property Agreement (WTO)
UNAG	National Union of Agriculturalists and Livestock Producers (Unión Nacional de Agricultores y Ganaderos) (Nicaragua)
UNORCA	National Union of Autonomous Regional Peasant Organisations (Unión Nacional de Organizaciones Regionales Campesinas Autónomas) (Mexico)
USFA	US Farmers Association
WI	Women's Institutes
WINFA	Windward Islands Farmers Association
WTO	World Trade Organisation

Chapter 9

The Legal Environment of Civil Society

Richard Fries

Introduction

Civil society cannot be reduced to a single definition. It cannot be reduced to legal components. A flourishing civil society depends on the freedom and commitment of individuals pursuing their own chosen ends, whether personal or communal. There is a fundamental tension between civil society and legal systems, perhaps even between civil society activists and lawyers! As the free space between the state and the market, beyond family and the personal (to follow broadly the operational definition employed by the editors of this Yearbook, Anheier, Glasius, and Kaldor 2001: 17), much activity that the concept embraces is informal, not organised into formal structures, and thus is not formed by, or in need of, law. Such activity is of course subject to law in the sense that the law sets bounds to individual action. The state requires its citizens to be law-abiding; civil society does not accept this unconditionally. Acceptance of the law, as an emanation of the state, is conditional, reflecting the defining role of civil society in a healthy democratic society to challenge, as well as cooperate with, the state. A legal framework constrains that freedom and flexibility; yet organisational security depends on a secure legal framework. The aim of this chapter is to unpick the paradox that civil society both needs the law and is threatened by the law. Drawing on worldwide experience, it seeks to demonstrate how an enabling legal environment enhances civil society while a hostile legal environment endangers it.

The threat which law poses for civil society is easy to see. The (oversimplified) notion of civil society as a sphere set apart from the state and holding it to account sets law, a mechanism of the state, against civil society. Legal systems as they apply to civil society take many forms, but registration is a basic element in legal frameworks for civil society organisations. Registration may be with government or the courts—and is thus potentially, and all too often actually, a mechanism of state control. What purports to guarantee rights and freedoms in practice often undermines the independence of civil society and threatens its freedom to act as a check on abuse of state power or corruption. Provisions which create an organisation in legal terms, thereby enabling its members to operate effectively, may be misused as a mechanism to control what they may freely do.

Civil society has been described (by Barbara Young at the launch of the report of the Commission on the Future of the Voluntary Sector 1996), as a 'loose and baggy monster' encompassing a diversity of forms and activities which defy definition. While world-renowned organisations like the Red Cross are large, powerful, structured institutions, the vast majority of civil society organisations are small, local bodies rooted in their communities, such as tenants' associations or childcare groups. These are at least as important to civil society as their better-known counterparts. Arguably, by expressing and meeting the needs of the community, and by reflecting the diversity of human interests and activities, they form the heart of civil society. Their essence is the free expression and pursuit of the legitimate interests of individuals coming together for their common purposes. There is much evidence from the developing world that such small-scale initiatives are highly valuable to local people, yet invisible to the outsider. In Pakistan, for example, *tanzeems* (citizens associations) are the commonest form of organisation on *katchi abadis* (areas of squatters' housing). The *tanzeems* organise water, sewage, employment, social services, and education for residents, yet are not formally recognised by the authorities (Fernandes and Fernandes 1997).

Such organisations may find that observing legal form is a bureaucratic burden and that registering with the authorities undermines their freedom. And indeed civil society can flourish in adverse conditions, for example in Kosovo before the 1999 war. Despite overt oppression by the Serbian government, Kosovans fulfilled 'the anarchists' dream of collective responsibility, self-help, creativity and self-control' (Knight 1999).

Box 9.1: Secret schools in Kosovo: between civic action and legal void(s)

Starting the new school year belatedly in January 1992, Albanian pupils greeted their teachers in living rooms, garages, shops, and cellars throughout Kosovo. That year the school bells rang for only a handful of Serbs and Montenegrins: although comprising a 10 per cent minority, they were now almost sole occupants of classrooms in Serbia's disputed province. The application of ethnically discriminatory education and labour laws by Serbia after its forcible abolition of Kosovo's autonomy in 1989 rendered Albanian pupils schoolless and their teachers and administrators jobless.

The number of places for study in Albanian was disproportionately reduced at all levels of education, leaving learning in Serbian the only option for thousands of Albanian-speaking students. In addition, the Serbs took over control of the school curricula for Albanians. When Albanians attempted to defy the Serb-imposed education laws by returning to the classrooms, they were physically prevented from entering their schools and lecture halls.

The clampdown on the Albanian-language education system was only a part of a comprehensive legal assault on Albanians spearheaded by the Serbian state and backed by its repressive security apparatus. It resulted in the Serbs' total ownership of the state, the economy, and the social and cultural sector, and the Albanians' total disenfranchisement in Kosovo. However, it also galvanised the province's marginalised and humiliated Albanian 90 per cent majority into decisive action, prompting a tide of civic initiatives in the post-autonomy period.

Defined by its resistance to the Serbian state, Albanian civil society in Kosovo resorted to self-organisation: from the provision of health care and humanitarian aid to activities aimed at defence of human rights, development of an independent press, and struggle for gender equality. After recovering from its initial numbness following the ruthless Serbian action, the Albanian community was bustling with action. It was realisation of civic empowerment that triggered the turn-about. Albanian-language education was its showcase.

The cause of learning in the Albanian language mobilised the entire Albanian community in Kosovo as organisers, teachers, parents, students, or home-owners who voluntarily turned their houses into classrooms and schools. The restoration of education in private houses in Kosovo for nearly 400,000 Albanian primary and secondary school pupils and university students, taught by over 20,000 teachers and lecturers, was not just an organisational coup. The education system became a source of Albanian national confidence and pride, but also an embodiment of non-violent Albanian resistance to Serbian oppression in Kosovo.

Albanians' educational efforts thrived on enthusiasm and dedication to civic action, but also on endorsement of the Albanians' national cause over nearly a decade of peaceful struggle in Kosovo in the 1990s. Yet, at the same time, the so-called Albanian parallel education system was being steadily emaciated, to the point where its survival was threatened, by the legal void in which it operated, in relation to both the repressive Serbian state and the Albanian parallel state-in-the-making in Kosovo.

The Serbian state's lack of accountability for human rights violations made Albanian students and classrooms an easy target of violence by Serbian security forces stationed in the province. School lessons were often broken up by Serbian police, students were harassed for carrying school diplomas with the stamp of the self-styled Albanian Kosovo Republic, teachers were beaten and even killed for teaching Albanian national content, and sporting events were interrupted. Random violence made the civil act of education a

Yet legal form gives civil society organisations security through enshrining rights in law; it strengthens their capacity to engage with other organisations and with other spheres, both public and market; and it is the basis for integrity. Civil society manifestations like the *tanzeems*, or Kosovo's parallel system under Serbian rule, have no such security. Thus, while a hostile legal environment constrains, controls, and undermines civil society, an enhancing legal environment underpins civil society by giving it rights and security. What is the basis for an enhancing environment? What are its principles? And how may it be fostered?

daily exercise of national resistance. The sharp decline in the number of young female primary and secondary school pupils and male university students in the Albanian parallel schools and university was a direct outcome of existential insecurity caused by the impunity of the Serbian state.

At the same time, the nascent Albanian state in Kosovo appropriated civil society's feat in the sphere of education, presenting it as a proof of its existence and competence. However, the Albanian-language education system could not rely on its legal infrastructure. It was to be additionally strained by an incomplete regulatory framework in the self-organised Albanian institutions in Kosovo quite apart from the repressive environment created by the Serbian state.

The Albanian parallel state in Kosovo was reduced to the office of the president and a handful of ministries. Efforts to constitute a clandestine parliament failed due to a volatile security situation. Consequently, active Albanian institutions in Kosovo likewise remained unaccountable to the electorate. Being the most important functioning segment of Albanian society in Kosovo, Albanian-language education was affected by the ambiguity inherent in the Albanian national struggle in Kosovo in the 1990s.

The issue of funding the parallel Albanian society and state in Kosovo is illustrative. What was originally envisaged as a voluntary citizens' contribution to the Albanian organisational effort became an obligatory tax on Albanians in Kosovo and abroad. But, without a legislative infrastructure to enforce payment of the tax, the only sanction available to the Albanian authorities in Kosovo was social excommunication. It proved to be a weak deterrent.

Soon after the launch of parallel education in the early 1990s, Albanian teachers stopped receiving any payment for their painstaking effort to provide schooling in the native tongue. The tax collection effort faltered at home not only because of the impoverishment of the population but also because of tax evasion. At the same time, the Albanian diaspora failed to deliver funds following a political rift between the Kosovo-based and the diaspora-based institutions of the Albanian parallel state.

Centralisation of funding of Albanian-language education was in line with the Albanian leadership's ambition to pursue national resistance in Kosovo as a state-building project rather than as a national movement thriving on grass-roots action. Similarly, political interference in the appointment of educational administrators aimed at enhancing the power of the Kosovo Democratic League—the largest Albanian party, headed by national leader Ibrahim Rugova—reflected the state's ambition to strengthen itself through the political control of education.

The Albanian state in Kosovo was never fully constituted and its weakness did not widen the field for citizens' action. Civil society in Kosovo suffered from the inability of the Albanian state to provide a legal framework conducive to its flourishing. However, it also suffered from the parallel state's lack of recognition of the power of civic organisation independent from the state and its quest for ultimate control. Nonetheless, the Albanian parallel education system in Kosovo from 1992 to 1999 remains testimony to the power of civic organisation in the face of the repressive Serbian state, and in spite of the weakness of its own, albeit incomplete, Albanian parallel state.

Denisa Kostovicova, London School of Economics

Human Rights as the Underpinning of Civil Society Law

The basis of civil society is freedom of association, expression, and assembly. The evolution of civil society and its legal basis reflects its changing engagement with the state through history. Throughout history governments have sought to set limits to citizen association; constitutions have set frameworks within which citizen action may or may not take place. Both in theory and in practice citizen organisation is now underpinned by the international instruments which were developed during the twentieth century to protect human rights. Central to these is the UN Universal Declaration on Human Rights enshrining basic freedoms, including, centrally, freedom of expression (art. 19), freedom of assembly, and freedom of association (art. 20). Explicitly or implicitly they guarantee the right to form and operate civil society organisations, and provide an international basis for civil society law. The Universal Declaration of Human Rights has a normative effect as a statement of standards to which member states of the United Nations are expected to adhere. This means that, at the global level, the concept of civil society is reflected in the fundamental legal expressions on which civilised society is based. This in turn means that laws and practices at state level which violate these principles breach international standards and are in that sense against the law. This is of crucial importance in promoting civil society globally. The fact that there is a legal basis for civil society at the international level does not, of course, mean that it is enforceable.

The basis for civil society is freedom of association, expression, and assembly

The Universal Declaration does not have a direct binding legal effect in itself. Many of its provisions are, however, included in the International Covenant on Civil and Political Rights (ICCPR), which does create direct binding obligations on the 143 countries which are party to it (see Record 8 in Part IV of this Yearbook). At the regional level there are human rights conventions, such as the American Convention on Human Rights, drawn up by the Organisation of American States; the African Charter on Human and Peoples Rights (Organisation of African Unity); and the European Convention on Human Rights (Council of Europe), all of which enshrine the rights of association, expression, and assembly. For countries which have ratified the European Convention on Human Rights, these rights are enforceable through the courts of the individual member states and ultimately through the European Court of Human Rights (ECHR) in Strasbourg.

These rights set the principles for informal civil society activity and for organised activity at the local level. Thus, associations of individuals pursuing common interests, whether they be social, mutual support, sport, or some other activity, are protected by the framework of human rights law. Written constitutions often translate these rights from international to national level. Securing these rights does of course depend on their being respected by the authorities and upheld by the courts.

Legal Personality

What human rights do not do, even when expressed in national law, is to give voluntary associations a legal personality distinct from their members. Such a personality is desirable as soon as an association reaches even a modest level of complexity. It is therefore necessary for the law to provide a framework which allows for the establishment of legally distinct organisations. Establishing a civil society institution with a distinct legal personality, whether in the form of an association, foundation, or whatever, should be at the discretion of those responsible for the organisation; but it should be a *right* which they can exercise if they so choose.

Legal personality is basic to formal organisation. Groups of like-minded individuals can operate informally. That indeed is the basis of association. Where such groups lack legal personality, the individual members themselves, individually and collectively, constitute the body for legal purposes. This is not normally an inconvenience for small bodies without significant property, let alone legal transactions. But as soon as an organisation requires a continuing identity of its own, it is important that the organisation becomes a legal entity in its own right. Lack of legal personality makes ownership of property and other resources complex and inconvenient. It also makes it difficult to protect members of the organisation from excessive personal liability. Thus, legal form is a basic necessity for civil society activity beyond the simplest scale.

The right to create a civil society organisation with its own legal personality thus brings the benefits of security and identity—part of the richness and diversity of a free society. It also creates a framework for openness and integrity of civil society organisations and indeed for protecting society from abuse by such organisations.

Formal organisation and process may not be necessary for community organisations operating at local level (like the *tanzeems* referred to above), where the people involved and the reputation of their organisation are personally known within the community. But the anonymity of more complex societies, and above all global society, where reputation cannot easily be checked, requires formal organisation and processes.

The Law and Global Civil Society

Civil society operates at the global level; but we cannot really talk of a global civil society legal framework, even though, as discussed above, international human rights law provides an indispensable basis for civil society. Much global civil society activity is, from a legal point of view, informal. It consists, that is to say, of alliances, networks, and movements which depend on global cooperation and communication but do not have a global or supranational legal framework. One example combining the local with the global is Slum/ Shack Dwellers International (SDI), a network of NGOs and community-based organisations for the urban poor (Patel, Burra, and D'Cruz 2001).

Those parts of organised civil society which operate globally are not founded on international law. This reflects the fact that most law is based on national, or sub-national, jurisdictions.

Those parts of organised civil society which operate globally likewise do not depend, and are not founded, on international law. This reflects the fact that most law is based on national, or indeed sub-national, jurisdictions. Not only are legal systems integral parts of individual countries, court systems, and legislatures; the essence of law is enforceability and, with important exceptions, enforcement is through courts rooted in national or sub-national institutions.

Thus, US not-for-profit organisations have their legal basis at state rather than federal level and, wherever they may be active, basic legal enforcement will be through the courts of their state of incorporation. Even international civil society organisations are based in specific jurisdictions. The Red Cross movement is a characteristic example of global civil society, consisting from the legal point of view (and indeed in practice) of a federation of independent but affiliated national Red Cross and Red Crescent organisations. The British Red Cross, for example, is an English-registered charity. The legal status of the International Committee of the Red Cross and the International Federation of Red Cross and Red Crescent Societies, while guaranteed under the Geneva Conventions, is governed by Article 60 ff. of the Swiss Civil Code. In other cases, international civil society organisations may be registered in one country with powers to act across the world. For example, Worldwide Initiative for Grantmaker Support (WINGS) (URL) was a project of the US Council on Foundations, but it has a rotating secretariat, now based at the European Foundation Centre, registered in Belgium.

Even where national law is subject to a supranational framework, as for example in the European Union, civil society law remains essentially reserved to national legal systems. There are moves to develop a legal framework at EU level for civil society associations and foundations; thus far, they remain proposals. The European Association Statute, which would give legal standing throughout the EU to associations accepted in any EU jurisdiction, has languished in draft form for many years (European Association Statute 1992; 1993). More recently the European Foundation Centre has been developing a model statute for foundations at EU level (European Foundation Centre). However, there are formidable technical as well as political problems to overcome before such initiatives can be realised, even within a political union as close as the European Union. So, for the foreseeable future, we have to approach the subject of global civil society law, paradoxically, through national legal systems.

Whether, in an ideal world, it would be advantageous to have globalised law or more generally supranational laws at the level of operation is a moot point. At first glance there might be attractions of convenience in having, say, a UN-based—and enforceable—code of law under which civil society organisations could operate with legal standing throughout the world. Whether an 'International Court (and Commission) for Civil Society' would in practice make it easier for civil society organisations to operate globally is doubtful, at any rate for the foreseeable future. Perhaps laws, institutions, and society operate best at the level where they customarily interact. Developments within growing political unions like the European Union may test the potential for supranational law. But, for the present, 'civil society of the world' seems as much a metaphor—as opposed to a concrete reality—as 'citizen of the world'.

Balancing Rights and Responsibilities

A framework of law that enhances civil society requires a careful balance between rights and responsibilities; between the entitlement of individuals to come together to pursue their own and the wider community's interests, and the right of society at large to have reasonable reassurance that such organisations are what they say they are, and in particular that they are not covertly abusing their position in ways that go beyond the legitimate exercise of individual freedom.

Balancing rights and responsibilities is an extremely sensitive matter. It has to take account of the nature of the civil society organisation: its sphere of activity; the benefits and reputation its status accords it; the scale of its activities; the power and influence it exercises. Proportionality is a key requirement: the smaller and more personal the organisation, the less the complexity; the larger and more powerful, the more rigorous. Power is of course a relative concept. A body may be extremely influential even though it is small, just because its voice is powerful. It is part of the strength and value of civil society, its contribution to free and diverse societies, that civil society organisations do exert influence. Indeed, some NGOs exert at least as much influence in some international negotiations as small individual states. But this itself creates responsibilities for civil society, in particular to avoid abusing its influence.

The challenge to reform is to obtain respect for the basic freedoms. Where that is lacking civil society may have to operate outside the national law

Accountability is discussed later in this chapter. At this point it is sufficient to say that the balance between power and influence on the one hand and accountability and responsibility on the other is perhaps more complex and sensitive for civil society bodies than it is for public and market sector organisations. In democratic constitutions, public sector bodies are, in theory anyway, subject to some form of electoral accountability, indirectly if not directly; and market organisations may have shareholder accountability. Independence is both an essential characteristic and a responsibility of civil society organisations. This means that their legitimacy must be established in different ways from public and market sector bodies. Depending on the benefits accorded by law and government, the legal and regulatory framework should serve to achieve this; but much weight should be accorded to the standards developed by civil society organisations themselves individually and collectively. 'Self-regulation', especially promoted on a peer-group basis, is a vital component of a credible civil society framework.

The relationship of civil society to society at large and to the governmental structure responsible for its overall well-being is a sensitive issue. The role of civil society as watchdog, checking potential abuse of power by state organs, is a fundamental aspect of its place in both open societies and those that lack freedom. The relationship of civil society to the law is thus conditional, dependent on the respect that the law and its enforcement show to the independence of civil society.

Where necessary civil society operates outside the law: for instance, paving the way for the breakdown of Communism through initiatives like Czechoslovakia's Charter 77 (see Box 9.2), Hungary's Civic Forum, and Poland's Solidarity Union.

Freedom depends on the willingness of individuals and groups to counter abuse of state, and other, power. International instruments provide a frame of reference beyond the state to which individuals and groups may appeal in defence of their action against abuse of power. But it places a greater responsibility on civil society to ensure that it operates within the framework of the well-being of society. It ought to be a responsibility of the state, in maintaining a framework of law to support and encourage an independent civil society sector, to set limits to underpin the integrity of civil society. It is easy to exceed these limits. A representative example is Pakistan. The Constitution of Pakistan 1973, following the two previous constitutions, recognises the right of association, but subject to broad-brush 'reasonable limitations'. Article 17 says: 'Every citizen shall have the right to form associations or unions subject to any reasonable restrictions imposed by law in interests of sovereignty or integrity of Pakistan, public order or morality.'

On the other hand, the idea that the exercise of the basic freedoms is automatically good and enriching to society is naive. The diversity of pluralistic democratic societies may be rich and, for the majority, positive. But that stops short of automatic validation of all exercise of freedom and of the organisations to which freedom gives rise. One can, of course, apply the term 'civil society' normatively, as some authors do, to embrace only organisations which do contribute, directly or indirectly, to the well-being of the community (see Anheier, Glasius, and Kaldor, 2001: 15–16, and Howell and Pearce, 2001: 230–1, for discussions of empirical versus normative conceptions). But that introduces a subjective test, on which agreement will be impossible to achieve and which is therefore difficult to subject to legal determination. More seriously, it oversimplifies the range of relationships between civil society organisations of varying types and the public interest. Many civil society organisations are, by their very nature, concerned with the sectional interests of their members. This may contribute to the public well-being, for example, through the protection of the environment or heritage. But it may equally advance the interests of the members at the expense of the interests of others. Thus, associations formed, perfectly legitimately, to pursue the interests of one group in the community, say in the enjoyment of facilities in their area, may conflict with the interests of others. (The issue of the public interest is discussed below.)

How the law should protect society from terrorism without encroaching on the basic freedoms has received added prominence in the post 9/11 world

The 'dark side' of civil society (discussed in Chapter 7) is an inevitable part of freedom of association. Self-regulation by civil society plays a key role in keeping it committed to the ethos of public well-being; self criticism is an important part of the exercise of freedom of expression. But the law has a role to play in maintaining the integrity of civil society. The freedoms are not absolute. Their exercise at the expense of the freedom of others is unacceptable. Laws giving effect to the freedoms must provide for this. Balancing freedom against constraint in law is of course a delicate matter. For example, the European Convention on Human Rights allows for limitations on a range of specific grounds in the wider public interest; but the European Court on Human Rights has been rigorous in overturning attempts by states to use that discretion too easily.

Article 11.2 of the ECHR provides that

> *no restrictions shall be placed on the exercise of the rights of freedom of expression (Article 10), association (Article 11) and peaceful assembly (Article 11) other than such as are prescribed by law and are necessary in a democratic society in the interests of national security or public safety, for the prevention of disorder or crime, for the protection of health or morals or for the protection of the rights and freedom of others.*

This is manifestly a wide range of exceptions. It may be said that it unpacks the concept of 'reasonable restrictions' contained in the Pakistan constitution cited above. It could of course be abused as the pretext for restricting the exercise of the civil society freedoms. Article 13 of the ECHR itself gives protection against such abuse by entitling civic organisations (as well as individuals) to seek redress for violation of the rights protected by the Convention. As Box 9.3 illustrates, cases heard by the European Court have made it clear that civil society organisations are protected from unjustified interference or restriction by state action and Article 11.2 cannot be used except in extreme cases.

Registration and Legal Form

The role that registration of civil society organisations plays, in principle as well as in practice, is complicated. At its simplest it is no more than a mechanism for according legal personality, enabling a civil society organisation to function in its own right. At that level the process requires minimal scrutiny of the organisation by the registration authorities. All that is needed is to ensure that it does not breach the legal constraints on civil society organisations referred to above. In various jurisdictions registration often plays a more complicated role. It can be the basis for accountability—that is, it can check that the organisation is properly constituted and complies with established reporting requirements—and it can be a route to

Box 9.2: Claiming the higher authority of international law: Charter 77

On 1 January 1977, 230 prominent Czech intellectuals signed and published a manifesto announcing the formation of Charter 77, a 'loose, informal and open association of people' committed to human rights. Signatories included the playwright Vaclav Havel, subsequently the first President of Czechoslovakia after the transition to democracy. The manifesto was published in various Western newspapers on 6 January. The Czech authorities arrested several of the signatories the next day, denounced them, and began cracking down on dissident activities. The United States charged Czechoslovakia with violating the 1975 Helsinki Accords on human rights.

While Charter 77 was illegal from the point of view of the Czechoslovak authorities, spokespeople would protest vehemently against being classified as 'illegal' or 'clandestine', insisting that all their activities were strictly lawful and conducted in public. They made use of the Helsinki Accords to try to remind the Czechoslovak and international public that, on the contrary, it was the regime, not Charter 77, that was operating outside the law.

Manifesto of Charter 77

In the Czechoslovak Register of Laws No. 120 of October 13, 1976, texts were published of the International Covenant on Civil and Political Rights, and of the International Covenant on Economic, Social and Cultural Rights, which were signed on behalf of our republic in 1968, reiterated at Helsinki in 1975 and came into force in our country on March 23, 1976. From that date our citizens have enjoyed the rights, and our state the duties, ensuing from them . . .

We accordingly welcome the Czechoslovak Socialist Republic's accession to those agreements. Their publication, however, serves as a powerful reminder of the extent to which basic human rights in our country exist, regrettably, on paper alone . . .

One instrument for the curtailment or in many cases complete elimination of many civic rights is the system by which all national institutions and organizations are in effect subject to political directives from the machinery of the ruling party and to decisions made by powerful individuals.

The constitution of the republic, its laws and legal norms do not regulate the form or content, the issuing or application of such decisions; they are often only given out verbally, unknown to the public at large and beyond its powers to check; their originators are responsible to no one but themselves and their own hierarchy; yet they have a decisive impact on the decision-making and executive organs of government, justice, trade unions, interest groups and all other organizations, of the other political parties, enterprises, factories, institutions, offices and so on, for whom these instructions have precedence even before the law.

Where organizations or individuals, in the interpretation of their rights and duties, come into conflict with such directives, they cannot have recourse to any non-party authority, since none such exists. This constitutes, of course, a serious limitation of the right ensuing from Articles 21 and 22 of the first-

privileged status with concomitant benefits (limited liability for the organisation's directors or trustees, and in some cases tax privileges reflecting 'public benefit' status).

How the step from informal associational activity to a formal structure with legal personality is achieved varies greatly among legal systems and codes, and especially as between civil and common law systems. (Common law is the Anglo-Saxon form of law based on uncodified principles developed by the courts. This contrasts with the civil law system developed in continental Europe and based on written legal codes.) It may be done by private action. The Swiss Civil Code, for example, states that 'associations which have a political, religious, scientific, artistic, charitable, social or any other than an industrial object, acquire the status of a person as soon as they show by their constitution their intention to have a corporate existence' (Title II, Chapter II. art. 60 (1)). Almost as easy is to have the founding documents 'notarised' by a public notary. Many civil law countries, however, require a more formal legal process of registration, whether with the courts or with a government department.

The potential for mixing the roles of registration is clear. The registration requirement provides the

mentioned covenant, which provides for freedom of association and forbids any restriction on its exercise, from Article 25 on the right to take part in the conduct of public affairs, and from Article 26 stipulating equal protection by the law without discrimination . . .

Responsibility for the maintenance of rights in our country naturally devolves in the first place on the political and state authorities. Yet not only on them: everyone bears his share of responsibility for the conditions that prevail and accordingly also for the observance of legally enshrined agreements, binding upon all individuals as well as upon governments.

It is this sense of co-responsibility, our belief in the importance of its conscious public acceptance and the general need to give it new and more effective expression that led us to the idea of creating Charter 77, whose inception we today publicly announce.

Charter 77 is a loose, informal and open association of people of various shades of opinion, faiths and professions united by the will to strive individually and collectively for the respecting of civic and human rights in our own country and throughout the world—rights accorded to all men by the two mentioned international covenants, by the Final Act of the Helsinki conference and by numerous other international documents opposing war, violence and social or spiritual oppression, and which are comprehensively laid down in the U.N. Universal Charter of Human Rights.

Charter 77 springs from a background of friendship and solidarity among people who share our concern for those ideals that have inspired, and continue to inspire, their lives and their work.

Charter 77 is not an organization; it has no rules, permanent bodies or formal membership. It embraces everyone who agrees with its ideas and participates in its work. It does not form the basis for any oppositional political activity. Like many similar citizen initiatives in various countries, West and East, it seeks to promote the general public interest.

It does not aim, then, to set out its own platform of political or social reform or change, but within its own field of impact to conduct a constructive dialogue with the political and state authorities, particularly by drawing attention to individual cases where human and civic rights are violated, to document such grievances and suggest remedies, to make proposals of a more general character calculated to reinforce such rights and machinery for protecting them, to act as an intermediary in situations of conflict which may lead to violations of rights, and so forth.

By its symbolic name Charter 77 denotes that it has come into being at the start of a year proclaimed as Political Prisoners' Year—a year in which a conference in Belgrade is due to review the implementation of the obligations assumed at Helsinki.

We believe that Charter 77 will help to enable all citizens of Czechoslovakia to work and live as free human beings.

Prague, 1 January 1977

authorities with the opportunity to control civil society improperly. Ensuring that the legal and institutional basis for registration is clear and that it supports the right of civil society associations to a secure existence with a minimum of scrutiny is of fundamental importance. If registration serves accountability and/or status functions it is essential that basic legal form is guaranteed with only the necessary minimum of restrictions and bureaucratic formality.

Legal systems and jurisdictions provide for a variety of forms of civil society organisations. The civil law codes are perhaps (at least in principle) the simplest and most widespread. Common law forms are looser and more complex. Broadly speaking, civil society organisations are divided into two basic types: member-based bodies ('associations') and bodies based on capital without members ('foundations' or 'trusts'). Associations are essentially formed by a group of individuals coming together to pursue a specified purpose or purposes. The focus is thus on the members and their purposes. Foundations, in contrast, are formed by committing resources, generally in the form of a capital sum, to a specified purpose or purposes. Foundations do not have members, but a body of individuals is

Box 9.3: ECHR jurisprudence on legitimate restrictions on freedom of association

The European Court of Human Rights (ECHR) will uphold restrictions on Article 11 (freedom of association and assembly) only if they meet three requirements. First, they must be 'prescribed by law', i.e. not applied without a legal provision to that effect. Second, they must belong to one of four permitted purposes laid down in art. 11.2 ('the interests of national security or public safety, the prevention of disorder or crime, the protection of health or morals or the protection of the rights and freedom of others'). Finally, they must be proportionate in protecting these aims, and hence necessary in a democratic society.

Djavit An, a Turkish Cypriot who was active in the 'Movement for an Independent and Federal Cyprus', which aimed to bring together the two Cypriot communities (Greek and Turkish), was routinely refused permits to cross the 'green line' in order to attend meetings of the Movement. Since there was no basis in law for refusing permits, the restriction on his right to associate was not prescribed by law, and hence constituted a violation of art. 11. (*Djavit An v. Turkey*, 20 February 2003).

One of the most comprehensive considerations of art. 11 by the ECHR is the case of *Sidiripoulos and others v. Greece* (10 July 1998). Sidiripoulos and others had founded an organisation called 'Home of Macedonian Civilisation', which the Greek courts were refusing to register. Greece defended the refusal as necessary for 'the maintenance of national security, the prevention of disorder and the upholding of Greece's cultural traditions and historical and cultural symbols'. The ECHR held that exceptions to freedom of association must be narrowly interpreted and that that the third of the three aims put forward by Greece did not constitute a legitimate ground for a restriction. But it did accept that the interference at issue was 'prescribed by law' and intended to protect national security and prevent disorder. However, the Court argued, in cases concerning restrictions of freedom of association it was not enough that the state had acted 'reasonably, carefully and in good faith'; the Court had to determine whether the restriction was 'proportionate to the legitimate aim pursued' and whether the reasons adduced by the national authorities to justify it were 'relevant and sufficient'.

There was nothing in the case file to suggest that any of the applicants had wished to undermine Greece's territorial integrity, national security, or public order. Mention of the consciousness of belonging to a minority and the preservation and development of a minority's culture could not be said to constitute a threat to 'democratic society'. Hence the refusal to register the

responsible for overseeing the fulfilment of the specified purposes.

Most jurisdictions also allow other forms. In particular, non-profit distributing companies can be set up in jurisdictions which allow civil society organisations to engage in enterprise activities. In the Philippines, civil society organisations are typically organised as non-stock corporations registered under the Corporation Code. Similarly the Czech Republic recognises 'public benefit corporations' as a specialised form of non-membership, service-providing civil society organisation.

Legislating for the Activities of Civil Society Organisations

The legal framework for citizen action through civil society organisations interacts with a country's general legal and institutional framework. Thus, civil society organisations are subject to laws affecting other forms of organisation. The general criminal law is an obvious example: it is no more acceptable for civil society organisations than for profit-making bodies to commit fraud. More sensitive is the line drawn between free expression and free association on the one hand and the legitimate protection of the community as a whole on the other. The question of how the law should protect society from terrorism without encroaching on these freedoms has received added prominence in the post-9/11 world, with many jurisdictions passing

organisation was disproportionate to the aims pursued and violated art. 11.

In a series of cases concerning political parties dissolved by the Turkish authorities, the ECHR has tested whether such dissolutions were 'necessary in a democratic society' mainly by inquiring whether the party in question advocated violence; and invariably it has found against the government *(United Communist Party of Turkey [TBKP] and others v. Turkey*, 30 January 1998; *Socialist Party and others v. Turkey*, 25 May 1998; *Freedom and Democracy Party (ÖZDEP) v. Turkey*, 8 December 1999; *Yazar, Karatas, Aksoy and the People's Labour Party (HEP) v. Turkey*, 9 April 2002; *Dicle on behalf of the Democratic Party (DEP) v. Turkey*, 10 December 2002).

In *Refah Partisi v. Turkey* (31 July 2001; 13 February 2003), however, another element was introduced: the leaders of the Refah Partisi had declared their intention to institute shariah law, characterised by the Court as 'a system of law that was in marked contrast to the values embodied in the Convention', although they had also 'left in doubt their position regarding recourse to force'. The Court therefore decided that the 'state concerned could reasonably prevent the implementation of such a political programme, which was incompatible with Convention norms, before it was given effect through specific acts that might jeopardise civil peace and the country's democratic regime'.

The Court has also interpreted art. 11 as containing a 'negative freedom of association', i.e. the right not to be a member of a particular organisation. In *Young, James and Webster v. United Kingdom* (13 August 1981) it determined that the obligation on British Rail employees to belong to a trade union, on pain of losing their job, constituted a violation of art. 11. But in this case also there may be exceptions under art. 11.2. In *Sigurdur A. Sigurjónsson v. Iceland* (30 June 1993), the Court decided that the obligation on a taxi-driver to belong to the Automobile Association was 'prescribed by law', and aimed at 'protection of the rights and freedoms of others', but the measure was 'disproportionate to the legitimate aim pursued' and hence not 'necessary in a democratic society'. Hence, the law making the granting of a taxi licence conditional on membership of the AA was held to be in violation of art 11.

Marlies Glasius, London School of Economics

Sources: The Netherlands Institute of Human Rights (URL); European Court of Human Rights (URL).

laws to strengthen the security authorities' powers over civil society organisations.

British legislation, for example, going back a number of years but strengthened in the Terrorism Act 2000, enables organisations as such to be proscribed. The current list covers organisations adjudged to be involved in terrorism in all parts of the world. The English charities regulator, the Charity Commission, has recently used its powers to remove an imam from a London mosque as 'an employee responsible for misconduct' (Charities Act 1993, s.18 (2) (i)) for 'using his position within the charity to make inappropriate political statements' (Charity Commission for England and Wales 2003). Another example of recent anti-terrorist initiatives is the Canadian Charities Registration (Security Information) Act 2001, under which the Canadian Customs and Revenue Agency takes account of security information in deciding whether to register charities. The OECD's Financial Action Task Force on Money Laundering launched an initiative on 11 October 2002 to 'combat the abuse of non-profit organisations' for the financing of terrorism (FATF 2002).

In addition to issues of criminal law, civil society law interacts with the legal framework which regulates activity in specific spheres. For example, where civil society organisations provide services relating to children they are rightly subject to the general regulatory requirements relating to children's services. Thus, regulations relating to childcare, fostering, and so on are as applicable to civil society organisations as they are to private or public sector providers. The same applies to all such issues: for example, care for the elderly. But such laws and regulations can develop into yet another avenue for

Box 9.4: Reforming registration laws: Pakistan, China, and Japan

Governments in countries of greatly varying backgrounds are now seeking to encourage voluntary action while often being apprehensive about letting loose an uncontrollable force. Reforming the framework of laws to support the contribution of civil society is part of this process and often reveals the tension between setting civil society free and keeping it under state control.

Pakistan has a confused mix of laws inherited from British rule, especially the Societies Registration Act 1860, and post-independence laws in particular the Voluntary Social Welfare Agencies (Regulation and Control) Ordinance 1961. The Enabling Environment Initiative being led by the Pakistan Centre for Philanthropy has been drawing up recommendations to simplify and enhance the legal framework.

China had some 200,000 'social organisations' registered with the Ministry of Civil Affairs by 1996, when a moratorium on registration was announced while new regulations were developed. A key issue is the requirement that organisations registering with the ministry have a sponsoring department, which has forced many citizen organisations to operate as companies or outside the legal framework altogether.

Japan inherited nineteenth-century laws which required civil society organisations to obtain the consent of the government department in whose sphere of responsibilities they sought to operate. Many such bodies operated outside the legal system as the Japanese civil society sector grew, especially after the Kobe earthquake. The Non-Profit Organisations Law introduced in 1998 made provision for non-profit organisations to be incorporated at prefecture level, and further reforms to give tax privileges to public-benefit organisations are being developed.

controlling civil society organisations as such. Therefore, requirements to safeguard children, for instance, should be applied and enforced on that basis and for that reason, regardless of the constitutional or legal status of the organisation concerned, whether public sector, market sector, or civil society sector.

Apart from the applicability of general laws to civil society, each jurisdiction tends to have specific laws aimed at regulating civil society activities. The range of activities which civil society organisations undertake is an important factor in determining the legal environment necessary to support and encourage legitimate citizen action. The diversity of roles civil society organisations play is an important feature of civil society, crucial to the richness and well-being of society. It embraces the notion of civil society as a sphere outside government, playing a key part in holding government to account on the one hand and cooperating with the public sector in providing services and meeting community needs on the other. The balance between these poles varies with circumstances and indeed within spheres. In societies lacking basic freedoms, civil society has to play a larger role in challenging abuse of state power, if necessary confronting illiberal laws that seek to control civil society itself. But, however liberal the legal framework, civil society still has a vital role as critic of the exercise of state power.

The two basic aspects of the role of civil society, meeting needs and upholding integrity (influencing public policy and redressing inequality), mirror two basic respects in which the state may fail: through inefficiency and corruption; and through abuse of power and oppression. A formal legal and regulatory framework enhances the ability of civil society to fulfil these roles; but the practical process of strengthening the law to underpin civil society's service and advocacy roles has to take account of the realities in each jurisdiction, in particular the political situation. The fundamental freedoms are the starting point. National institutions may incorporate freedoms of association, expression, and assembly, but the problem with oppressive regimes is characteristically abuse of power rather than illiberal constitutions. The challenge is to secure respect for the basic freedoms. Where that is lacking detailed laws for civil society may be misused as a means of oppressive regulation. In these circumstances civil society may have to operate outside the national law.

Alongside the roles of advocacy and service delivery, civil society organisations play a key role in providing independent resources. Civil society organisations rely on a range of forms of fund-raising, grants, and economic activities. The legal framework has to support these. Grant-giving foundations and other civil society organisations which channel funds to civil society activity provide a vital source of support as an alternative to public- and market-sector sources. As Frances Pinter (2001: 214) has noted, governments often view independent funding, especially from foreign sources, with mixed feelings or even suspicion, on the grounds that it threatens their control over the policy agenda for service delivery. The Chronology of Global Civil Society Events (Part IV of this Yearbook) documents two examples in 2002 of governments (Azerbaijan and Egypt) adopting legislation to control the flow of overseas grants to domestic civil society institutions. However, diversity of funding is an important guarantor of the independence of civil society.

Most jurisdictions provide tangible privileges to civil society organisations, notably in the form of fiscal relief

The possibility of commercial activity is also important for organisations in many jurisdictions. Enterprise is, however, a controversial issue. Some jurisdictions place restrictions on trading by civil society organisations or prohibit it altogether. In Macedonia, for example, civil society organisations are precluded from directly pursuing 'economic activities', although they may establish business subsidiaries for this purpose.

However, in many jurisdictions the label 'not-for-profit' is misleading since such organisations often engage in trading activities, either as a subsidiary fund-raising activity or in pursuit of their central function. They aim to make a surplus to plough back into their activities. They are thus more accurately described as 'non-profit distributing'.

Public Benefit

The concept of public benefit is important in the arrangements for civil society. It is increasingly widely acknowledged that there is a 'dark side' to civil society, that is to say, there are organisations which clearly fall within the broad notion of civil society with which this chapter began, but which are equally clearly inimical to the well-being of society.

Apart from such bodies, however, civil society as such has been said, by writers from de Tocqueville (1840/1994) to Putnam (2000), to be of general value because of the diversity and active citizenship which it brings to society as a whole regardless of its specific purpose or scope. There are many social policy controversies surrounding this contention. As noted earlier, a great many civil society organisations pursue the narrow interests of particular groups. Organisations providing health care or social services to a particular group are widespread and important. Communally based organisations may, however, exacerbate tensions within society rather than serving the interests of society at large (see Chapter 7). The case for an enabling legal environment for civil society does not depend upon a strong view of the value of civil society at large. Whatever value associations whose purpose is specifically to pursue member or sectional interests have for the wider society, a significant part of civil society is specifically devoted to the public interest and bases its claim to privileged status on those grounds. How the legal and institutional framework underpins this is therefore an important issue.

Most jurisdictions provide tangible privileges to civil society organisations, notably in the form of fiscal relief. This may be a part of tax law and administration, but it has a wider importance as part of the framework for encouraging public-spirited citizen activity. Whether tax privileges are dependent on a specific test of the public benefit contribution of the organisation concerned varies from jurisdiction to jurisdiction. A common form is a list of qualifying purposes, such as the promotion of health and education.

This fundamental principle is shared by civil law and common law jurisdictions. The common law origins of civil society law are, however, distinctive in having a legal concept of charity. The colloquial notion of charity is pretty well universal. In the common law developed in England charity has acquired a technical legal basis different from, indeed much wider than, the ordinary usage. Some jurisdictions, notably England itself, continue to base their civil society law on a legal concept of charity. In essence this covers independent non-profit distributing bodies with a purpose which specifically serves the public benefit. Being a common law system, charity law is not generally accessible as a

Box 9.5: 'Charitable purposes' according to the Australian Inquiry Report

Probably the most thorough and satisfactory contemporary effort to define charitable purposes within a common law framework is that of the Australian Report of the Inquiry into the Definition of Charities and Related Organisations (Australia 2001). The advice in this report is at present under consideration by the Australian government. It defines charity as follows:

Charitable purposes shall be:

- the advancement* of health, which without limitation includes:
  - the prevention and relief of sickness, disease or of human suffering;
- the advancement* of education;
- the advancement* of social and community welfare, which without limitation includes:
  - the prevention and relief of poverty, distress or disadvantage of individuals or families;
  - the care, support and protection of the aged and people with a disability;
  - the care, support and protection of children and young people;
  - the promotion of community development to enhance social and economic participation; and
  - the care and support of members or former members of the armed forces and the civil defence forces and their families;
- the advancement* of religion;
- the advancement* of culture, which without limitation includes:
  - the promotion and fostering of culture and the care, preservation and protection of the Australian heritage;
- the advancement* of the natural environment; and
- other purposes beneficial to the community, which without limitation include:
  - the promotion and protection of civil and human rights; and
  - the prevention and relief of suffering of animals.

* Advancement is taken to include protection, maintenance, support, research, improvement or enhancement.

legal code (though Barbados is unusual in having a statute defining charity). In most jurisdictions, it is necessary to refer to textbooks, such as Picarda (1999) on charity in England.

Determining public benefit is a difficult issue. It is a matter both of technical law and of public policy. But so long as the legal framework is open to and supportive of civil society at large, and confines its control to prohibiting purposes and activities inimical to the general well-being, the added test of positive public benefit is in a sense less critical. That is to say, the existence of the body as such does not depend on the determination. It is nevertheless important if benefits and recognition depend on this distinction.

Especially in civil law jurisdictions, a list of public benefit purposes characteristically includes such obvious and uncontroversial matters as health, education, social welfare, recreation, environment, heritage, and the like. The common law tradition has relied on the development of the scope of charity or public benefit case by case. The well-known judgment of Lord MacNaghten in the Pemsel case of 1891 classified charity as 'the relief of poverty, the advancement of education, the advancement of religion and other purposes beneficial to the community'. The last ('fourth head') element is characteristic of the open-endedness of the common law approach, eschewing a closed definition of public benefit and allowing the courts (or determining agency, like the English Charity Commission) to develop the scope of charity. The Pemsel classification is manifestly out of date and there are a number of proposals for creating a more modern framework for the concept of charity. An interesting attempt is that of the Australian Inquiry Report (see Box 9.5).

This approach raises a number of questions about the application of such categorisations. Three in particular may be singled out, expressed simply in the following form:

1. What exceptions are made under each category?
2. How is the question of the public benefiting under each category dealt with?
3. What decision-making process is involved?

The first issue reflects the fact that, while broad categories like education and health are not controversial, the way in which provision is made often is. Take health. The essence of civil society is that people should be able to pursue their own interests in their own way. However, whether particular ways of making health provision are genuinely beneficial is often disputed; strong views are held about alternative forms of treatment. Health regulation protects people from harmful forms of treatment, but the issue of where that line is drawn has to allow for experimentation and disagreement. Determining a particular form of provision to be positively of public benefit is a step further than merely permitting it.

A related issue is whether restricting benefits to a part of the community, rather than opening them up to the whole community, is compatible with the concept of public benefit. Of course, much provision is directed at specific—often quite small—groups, such as sufferers from particular diseases. More controversial is restriction to parts of the community defined by other criteria, typically by area or communal group.

This leads to the third issue: which agency decides whether a particular organisation is pursuing the public benefit under any particular head, and on which criteria. There is something paradoxical, even objectionable, in the notion of a government agency—an emanation of the state—determining whether or not a purpose pursued by an independent civil society organisation is in the public interest and whether, therefore, that body should have a privileged status. Yet that is the well-nigh universal position. Sometimes it is a department of government or, worse, the department responsible for government policy in a particular area (health, education, and so on). Most often it is a branch of the tax authorities. While it may plausibly be argued that the government is responsible for safeguarding the use to which taxes are put, in the sense of tax privileges for public benefit organisations, having government agencies determine whether or not a particular approach to an issue is in the public interest threatens the independence of civil society. Arguments of liberty may be reinforced by practical considerations: diversity encourages innovation, and government control is inimical to it.

As a matter of principle, therefore, the agency that determines public benefit status for civil society organisations must be autonomous and answerable in an appropriate way to the courts, independently of government.

As a matter of principle, the determining agency for public benefit status must be autonomous and answerable to the courts independent of government

Accountability

There is, superficially, a paradox in holding independent civil society organisations accountable. Accountability is a complex issue, not least in relation to civil society. At its strongest it involves a relationship in which a body or person is accountable to another ('higher') authority which has the right and power to enforce its judgements. Much accountability is weaker than this, and it is important, particularly in the context of civil society, to be clear about the degree of accountability involved. Accountability may involve enforceable sanctions, for example in relation to breaches of the law; or it may involve a trade-off: compliance in exchange for benefits. The former is characteristic of accountability to the state; particularly in relation to civil society, it should be properly limited, concerned essentially with integrity. The latter is characteristic of donor and stakeholder accountability. Accountability is closely connected to two concepts: legitimacy and credibility. Both are important to civil society, at any rate in its wider role, especially for public benefit organisations (see, for example, Lewis 2001: 143 ff.).

The legitimacy of civil society organisations does depend on a bedrock of proper accountability. But the authority with which civil society organisations act, and in particular raise their voices, depends on wider issues. The legitimacy of NGOs challenging governments of course depends on the accuracy of the facts they present and, even more, on the values they uphold. The right of NGOs to claim to speak for particular groups or interests may be challenged, particularly if they are based outside the area concerned. Accountability to beneficiaries and other stakeholders is relevant—but beyond the law. In the context of the present chapter on civil society's legal framework, accountability is, rightly, interpreted narrowly.

The best basis for accountability is self-regulation. The more standards of governance, management, and financial controls are developed internally, the less need there is for external regulation. In the Philippines, civil society organisations play a vital role and have a recognised status in public policy. A number of NGO networks came together in 1995 to develop an NGO Code of Ethics, which recognises the roles, responsibilities, and obligations of the non-profit sector and donor relationships (Clark forthcoming 2003).

There are internal and external dimensions of accountability. The internal dimension is of general importance, but especially for membership bodies where it is the members themselves to whom the integrity of the organisation is the priority. The importance of the external dimension is proportionate to the public interest involved. Small membership bodies have essentially only their own membership to satisfy, though if they enjoy public benefit status or depend on external funding their accountability will be that much wider. Larger bodies, particularly if they claim to be authorities on issues of public importance, depend on their reputation for credibility. Integrity is therefore of more than internal significance. A higher level of accountability arises with bodies which receive privileges and status, especially those which claim to serve the public interest.

The relationship between law and accountability is complex. Accounting standards and practices need to be developed by professional bodies and may be promoted on a discretionary basis, as recommended good practice. The legal framework may support this but the key is the extent of the public interest. This is connected to the basis for registration and the purpose it serves.

It is of course, in the post-Enron world, necessary to acknowledge the limitations of formal accounting processes. 'Creative accounting' is just as much a threat to the reputation and integrity of civil society organisations as to profit-making (or seeking!) companies. The temptation may be based on different motivations: the need to present the most favourable picture to supporters and donors may be as likely to distort accounting as fraud. But the damage to credibility is great. Accounting practices developed independently of the sector are important.

Strengthening civil society is not a guaranteed way of countering the corruption endemic in some societies. But a civil society with commitment and integrity is a powerful force for counteracting corruption

Civil society is no more inherently free of corruption than other sectors. Its 'halo effect', as Lester Salamon has put it, has to be earned. Strengthening civil society is not therefore a guaranteed way of countering the corruption endemic in some societies. But a civil society with commitment and integrity is a powerful force for counteracting corruption. The credibility of civil society is therefore central. The right system of accountability, leaving civil society free but responsible, is thus of critical importance. The promotion of standards within civil society through self-regulation, balanced by appropriate mechanisms of external regulation, is basic.

The basis of internal accountability is laid down in the constitutions of civil society organisations. This does not depend on their having a legal personality; however simple a membership association may be, there must be rules for determining procedures and handling finances. These may be prescribed in law and regulations, or left to internal procedures. In practice, internal governance arrangements—holding of meetings, the election and accountability of office-holders, and the like—are part of the constitution of a civil society organisation and are the basis for its legal status. The legal framework is important in establishing the basis for accountability and integrity, but it should serve the interests of the organisation and its membership, not as a control mechanism unless there is a public interest, and then only as the means of upholding the public interest.

Where there is a public interest in the accountability of civil society organisations—essentially, where they receive fiscal and other privileges as bodies serving the public benefit—legal requirements for accountability are appropriate. In the first place, appropriate requirements may be laid down for 'transparency'. The public interest is served by ensuring that the activities and finances of bodies serving a public purpose are open to public scrutiny. This is distinct from a control or supervisory mechanism; the reporting requirements which may go with registration are essentially a vehicle for openness. 'Compliance' rather than control is the appropriate mode for the authorities responsible for reporting requirements.

In Hungary, for instance, public benefit organisations must prepare a publicly accessible report that includes a summary of public benefit activities; a financial report; a statement on the use of budgetary support and support received from state/governmental sources; benefits granted to operating offices of the organisations; and other related information (Act CLVI of 1997 on Public Benefit Organisations, s. 9(1)).

More active supervisory arrangements are appropriate only to the extent that there is a public interest in how a civil society organisation is managed. They must ensure that its activities are directed to fulfilling the public purpose from which its status (and associated privileges) derive; and that its resources are used for that purpose and not diverted to private gain. Most systems base the accountability requirements for civil society organisations enjoying privileged status in respect of their public benefit purpose on the tangible benefits, especially of tax, they receive.

Conclusion: Proportionality and Judgement

This chapter has sought to dissolve the apparent paradox of the fluidity and autonomy of civil society and the formality and intrusiveness of law. A number of conclusions emerge. First and perhaps foremost, civil society is nothing if not independent. If the legal framework and/or its application places improper impediments on free exercise of the rights of association, expression, and assembly, civil society has to operate outside the law.

Most often, in the modern world law is intrusive rather than oppressive. The intrusion of state regulation often reflects political and bureaucratic apprehension at the potential power and anarchy of civil society. Confidence that civil society is a potential partner of the state, both responsible and public-spirited, is the basis for enhancing law reform. The ideal framework might be summed up as follows:

- the constitution enshrines the basic freedoms;
- basic laws exist against crime and threats to public well-being (applying generally, and not differentially to civil society);
- free space exists within this framework for civil society activity at large;
- an enabling framework offers organisational structures for civil society organisations (including registration on a discretionary basis not subject to substantive tests);
- a positive framework encourages civil society organisations which seek to meet a public benefit purpose; and
- accountability processes are proportionate to the public (and state) interest, based on transparency and integrity.

These guidelines accord with the following principles. The freedoms of association, assembly, and expression need to be protected as enforceable rights. The necessary limitations to which they are subject must be strictly confined in both principle and practice to what is necessary for the general well-being. These and other limitations, for example of criminal law, should apply even-handedly throughout society, and not be targeted specifically at civil society. Finally, the legal and regulatory framework for civil society should provide, as of right, an effective institutional basis for the operation of complex civil society organisations, with accountability justified according to the status and privileges received, especially by organisations claiming to serve the public interest and not just a private or member interest.

At the national level, the extent to which states meet these ideal guidelines is uneven. At the global, or indeed the supranational, level, there is hardly the beginning of a legal framework. This chapter has referred to problems which arise for border-transcending activities of civil society organisations. The lack of a legal institutional framework which can support civil society organisations operating beyond national boundaries makes them dependent on the law of the country where they have their legal basis. In addition to questions of recognition in other countries in which they operate, practical issues of fundraising and grant-giving across national boundaries arise.

There are some signs of interest on the part of intergovernmental institutions, and it may be that the UN Secretary-General's initiative in setting up a Panel of Eminent Persons on United Nations Relations with Civil Society will offer a forum in which the importance of an enhancing legal environment can be developed (United Nations 2003). However, there are formidable problems in getting acceptance for any effective legal framework at the global or even any supranational level, let alone a framework which reflects the sensitive balance between the principles of freedom and responsibility presented in this chapter.

This chapter has been prepared with the assistance of the International Center for Not-for-profit Law (ICNL), a Washington-based NGO whose mission is to encourage an enabling legal and regulatory environment for civil society around the world. Information about ICNL can be found on its website <http://www.icnl.org>.

References

Anheier, Helmut, Glasius, Marlies, and Kaldor, Mary (2001). 'Introducing Global Civil Society', in Helmut Anheier, Marlies Glasius, and Mary Kaldor (eds), *Global Civil Society 2001*. Oxford: Oxford University Press.

Australia (2001). *Report of the Inquiry into the Definition of Charities and Related Organisations*. Canberra: Commonwealth of Australia.

Charity Commission for England and Wales (2003). 'Charity Commission Confirms its Decision to Remove Abu Hamza'. Press Release. 4 February.

Clark, J. (forthcoming 2003). *Worlds Apart: Civil Society and the Battle for Ethical Globalisation*. London: Earthscan.

Commission on the Future of the Voluntary Sector (1996). *Meeting the Challenge of Change: Voluntary Action into the 21st Century*. London: National Council for Voluntary Organisations.

European Association Statute (1992; 1993). *Official Journal of the European Union*, C99 and C236.

European Court of Human Rights <http://www.echr.coe.int/Eng/Judgments.htm>.

European Foundation Centre. Draft Model Statute for Public Benefit Foundations in Europe. <http://www.efc.be/projects/eu/legal/model_statute.asp>.

FATF (Financial Action Task Force on Money Laundering) (2002). *Combating the Abuse of Non-Profit Organisations—International Best Practices*. Paris: OECD. 11 October.

Fernandes, K. and Fernandes, N. (1997). *How Communities Organise Themselves*. Karachi: City Press.

Howell, J. and Pearce, J. (2001). *Civil Society and Development*. Boulder, London: Lynne Rienner.

ICNL for OSI (1997). *Guideline for Law Affecting Civic Organisations*. New York: Open Society Institute.

Knight, Barry. (1999). 'Towards a Perfect Society'. *Alliance*, 4/2: 26–30.

Lewis, David. (2001). *The Management of Non-governmental Development Organizations: An Introduction*. New York: Routledge.

MacNaghten, Lord (1891). *IR Special Purposes Commissioners v. Pemsel* [1891 AC 531].

The Netherlands Institute of Human Rights <http://sim.law.uu.nl/SIM/Dochome.nsf?Open>

Patel, Sheela, Burra, Sundar, and D'Cruz, Celine (2001). 'Slum/Shack Dwellers International (SDI)–Foundations to Treetops'. *Environment and Urbanisation*, 13/2: 45–59.

Picarda H. (1999). *The Law and Practice Relating to Charities* (3rd edn). London: Butterworths.

Pinter, Frances (2001). 'Funding Global Civil Society Organisations'. In Helmut Anheier, Marlies Glasius, and Mary Kaldor (eds), *Global Civil Society 2001*. Oxford: Oxford University Press.

Putnam, R. D. (2000). *Bowling Alone: The Collapse and Revival of American Community*. New York: Simon and Schuster.

Tocqueville, Alexis de (1840/1994). *Democracy in America*. London: David Campbell.

United Nations (2003). 'Secretary-General Announces Establishment of Panel of Eminent Persons on UN Relations with Civil Society'. Press Release, 13 February. UN Doc. SG/SM/8604 NGO/496.

Worldwide Initiative for Grantmaker Support <http://www.wingsweb.org>.

Part IV: Records of Global Civil Society

Mapping Global Civil Society

Helmut Anheier and Hagai Katz

Purpose

Each edition of the Yearbook includes a methodological chapter that explores and presents different approaches to measuring and analysing global civil society. In 2001, we proposed an operational definition of global civil society in the context of the wider data and information system we hoped to develop over the coming years (Anheier 2001). In 2002, we developed and introduced the Global Civil Society Index to enhance comparative analysis in the field and to offer it as a measure complementing similar indices of economic and human development (Anheier and Stares 2002). In the 2003 methodological chapter we examine spatial aspects of global civil society and look at geographical distributions and emerging patterns of transnational connectedness.

Specifically, the purpose of this chapter is twofold, one primarily methodological in nature, the other more theoretical in its intent. First, we search for initial ways of going beyond the nation-state as the geographical unit of analysis, and try to identify regional and other, non-country units for measuring global civil society. Ideally, we are looking for multi-site units (e.g., networks among international NGOs) for identifying emergent spatial patterns among non-contiguous entities (in contrast to countries). Second, the chapter uses geographical information systems (GIS) to throw additional light on the relationship between global civil society, economic globalisation, and the international rule of law.

Introduction

In the methodological chapter of *Global Civil Society 2001*, we suggested that global civil society, as an emerging reality, remains a fuzzy notion that sits uncomfortably in the conceptual and statistical world of modern social science (Anheier 2001). Perhaps nowhere is the tension between the 'methodological nationalism' (see Beck 2000, and Chapter 3 of this volume) of the social sciences and the social reality of globalisation more visible than in geographical representations of the world's economic and political order. Here, nation-state and 'country' are the dominant 'markers', and the world is portrayed as an assemblage of contiguous, territorial units with well-defined boundaries.

All this is very different from the factual geography of a globalising world, where trade, financial flows, communication, or migration increasingly reach across national borders. In factual geography, maps no longer necessarily coincide with national boundaries, and non-contiguous units emerge that are a product of cross-border transactions of many kinds, be they import and export of goods and services, direct foreign investment, Internet connections, travel patterns, corporate structures among headquarters and subsidiaries, collaborations among scientists, or cultural exchanges. Current atlases, however, are of little use for depicting such transnational patterns. Preoccupied with political boundaries—that is, separation rather than connection—they fail to portray the networked and cross-national nature of contemporary economic and political events. Indeed, entire generations of social scientists and ordinary citizens alike have been instructed in 'nation-based' geography, and may well have the wrong 'mental maps' for visualising the changes in territorial meaning occurring in the world today (Staple and Dixon 1992).

The following examples illustrate how different the dynamic, factual geography of globalisation has become from the static political and economic map of national states.

Global cities are frequently cited as exemplars of the new, emerging global geography (Sassen 2002). The assumption is that such cities are increasingly close to each other: that is, they have more connections than with many domestic cities in their respective countries. Map 1 illustrates the geographical distribution of global cities. For our purposes, we defined 'global city' by the presence of transnational corporations (TNCs) (UNCTAD 2001), and estimated the number of

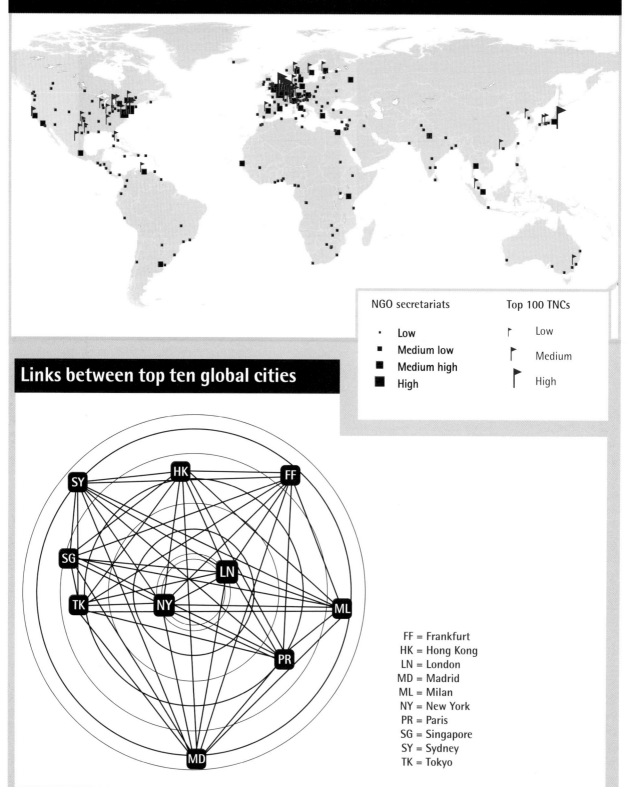

Map 1: Global cities

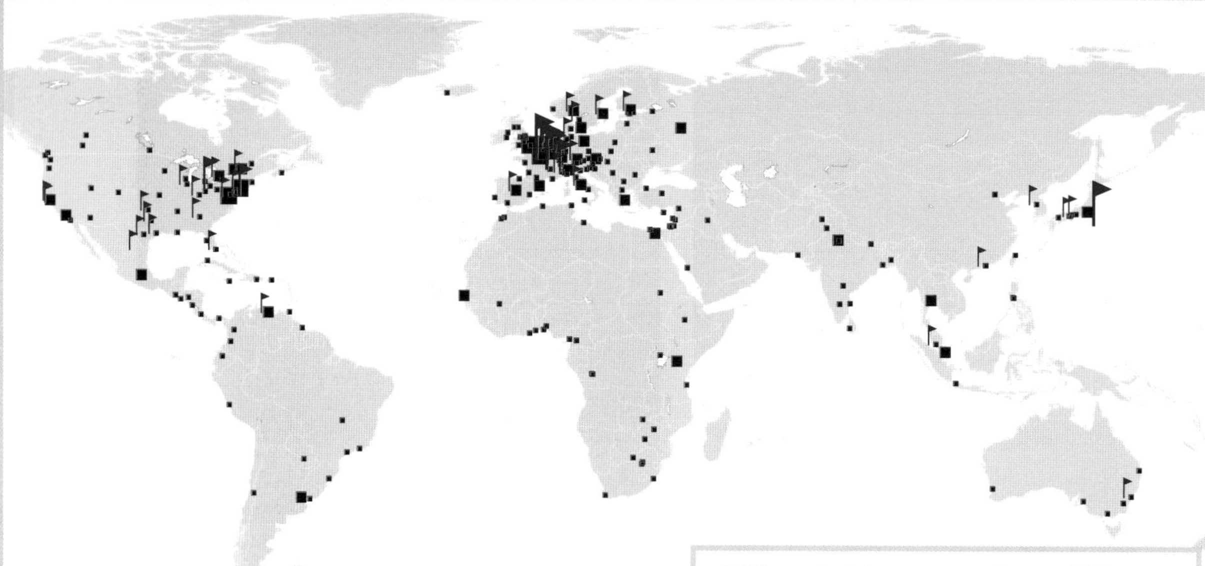

NGO secretariats

- Low
- Medium low
- Medium high
- High

Top 100 TNCs

- Low
- Medium
- High

Links between top ten global cities

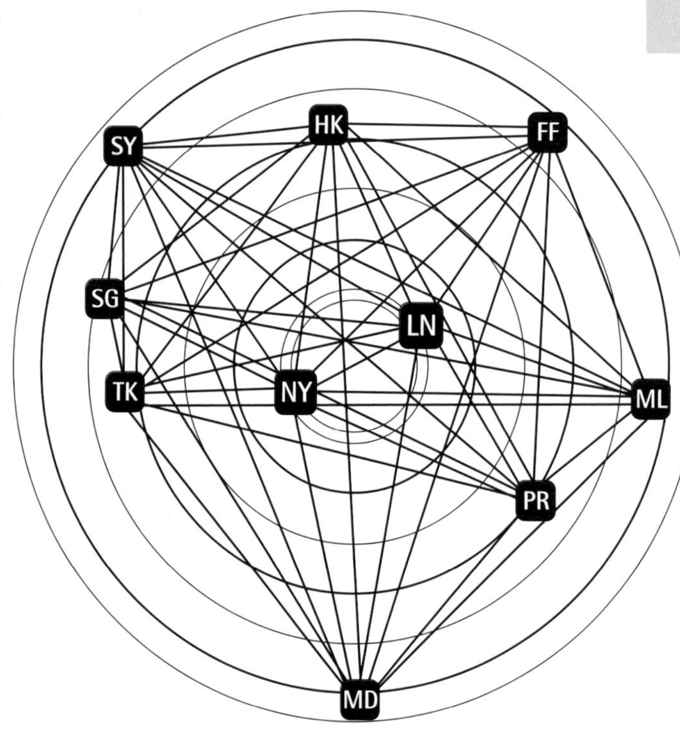

FF = Frankfurt
HK = Hong Kong
LN = London
MD = Madrid
ML = Milan
NY = New York
PR = Paris
SG = Singapore
SY = Sydney
TK = Tokyo

international non-governmental organisations (INGOs) with the help of data provided by the Union of International Associations (which we also used for other maps in this chapter). For both TNCs and INGOs, we counted the number of occurrences per city, and grouped cities into four categories based on distributional properties.[1]

The inset in Map 1 indicates a clear pattern of global city aggregations in western Europe and the eastern United States, followed by Tokyo in Asia. We defined global cities by the presence of multinational business services firms such as finance, insurance, and public relations, with an index for global city links derived from data on interlocking business services branches (see Taylor 2001). As the inset shows, the system of global cities covers a wide geographical range, with London and New York at the centre of global connectedness, followed by Paris, Frankfurt, Milan, and Madrid as the other European global cities, plus Singapore, Hong Kong, and Tokyo in Asia, and Sydney in Australia. These cities form a network of high connectivity and high volume of interactions.

The important point is that these centres do not exist in isolation from each other: they are focal points of centrality, as indicated by the varying strength of the lines in the inset of Map 1. These ties link the major world cities that are part of an emerging system that transcends the boundaries of the nation-state. In other words, in organisational terms the links among the top global cities form the centre of global interconnectedness, as measured by inter-locking TNC business service branches. Significantly, no city in Latin America, Africa, or the Middle East features in this map of world city links so constructed.

Organisational networks. A different way of portraying the non-contiguous character of a globalising world is to look at the geographical spread of INGOs like Amnesty International, the Red Cross and Red Crescent Societies, Caritas, Save the Children, or Greenpeace. These organisations have created global networks of organisational units and membership bases. For example, Map 2 shows the global membership distribution and organisational presence of Friends of the Earth, a federation of environmental NGOs. We see the near global reach of Friends of the Earth in both organisational and membership terms, but also the variation in membership centrality (determined by the number of network-wide functions carried out in each local member organisation), and 'white areas' such as Central Africa as well as Central and East Asia.[2]

But more informal organisational forms have also developed global links, as Chapter 8 on farmers' associations shows (see map 8.1). Here separate farmers' associations developed ties to like-minded organisations across national borders, thereby creating supra-national networks, each with distinct reach and structure. The very fact that farmers' associations in developing countries form trans-national links shows that even rural populations, often thought of as left behind in the globalisation process, are 'globalising'. This finding, in turn, challenges theoretical positions that see cities as the exclusive locus of globalisation and ignore the role of rural areas (for example, Sassen, 2002). The two farmers' association networks shown in map 8.1, International Federation of Agricultural Producers (IFAP) and La Via Campesina (VC), both have global reach but are distinct in the regional emphasis. While IFAP's membership is predominantly in the eastern hemisphere, VC membership is mostly in the Americas. Interestingly, only in very few locations do organisations from these two large networks coincide.

But non-contiguous systems are not only the result of organisational networks. Throughout history, but increasingly so in recent decades, *migrant communities* have created non-contiguous units: Columbians in New York, Armenians in Los Angeles, Irish in Boston, Turks in Germany, Algerians in France, Pakistanis in England, Indians in South Africa, Chinese in south-east Asia, and so on. These communities form Diaspora networks, linking not only migrants to their land of origin but also to each other via a network of migrant organisations (Sassen 2002). The organisation of the Jewish Diaspora is perhaps the best example in this case.

Values. Yet, as we have argued in previous editions of the Yearbook, civil society is not only about organisations. Indeed, the initial operationalisation of global civil society followed a two-pronged approach and viewed global civil society as an infrastructure of organisations and networks (Held et al. 1999; Anheier and Themudo 2002) on

[1] *For INGO secretariats the resulting categories are: low = 0–51; medium low = 52–267; medium high: 268–807; high: 808–1,407. For the top 100 TNCs the size of the 'flag post' is based on the following ranking: low: 1–2; medium: 3–10; high: 11–14.*

[2] *We would like to thank Ann Doherty and Ina Breman for providing the data for this map.*

Map 2: Friends of the Earth International

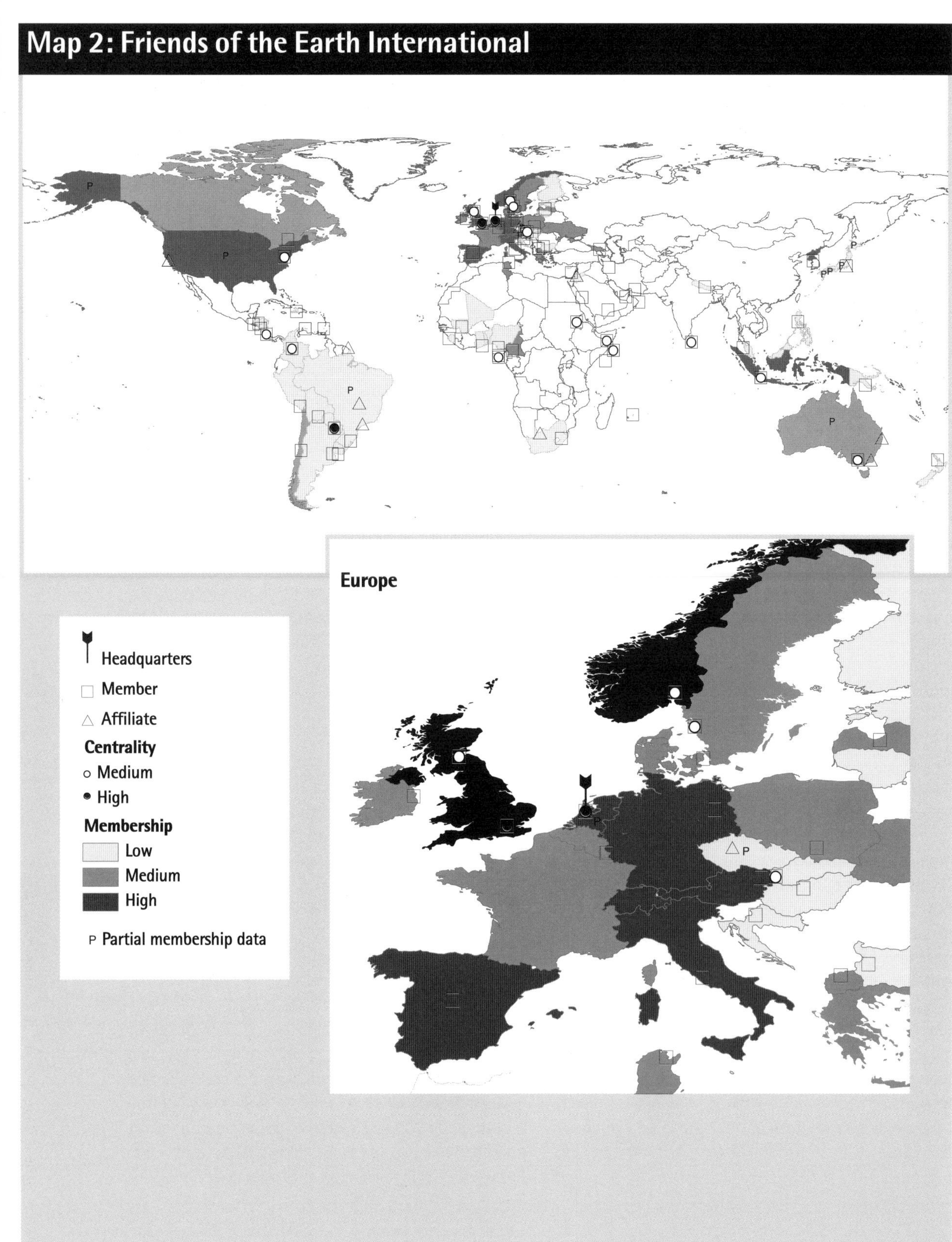

the one hand, and as a set of cosmopolitan values and identities on the other (Anheier, Glasius, and Kaldor 2001). Using a central cosmopolitan value as an example, i.e., the valuation of tolerance and respect for others as an important value to teach children, Map 3 shows significant variation across European countries. With few exceptions such as Portugal and Norway, most European countries rank relatively high on this tolerance measure, with over 70 per cent of respondents affirming that they consider tolerance important. This becomes somewhat less pronounced as we go eastwards, and drops to its lowest level in Romania and Albania, with 55 per cent.

However, the emerging east-west pattern and the imposed uniformity within each geographical unit, that is, nations, also demonstrates the limitations of country-based representations of population surveys, as shown in Map 3. Indeed, within-country variations of cosmopolitan values might easily be more pronounced than between-country differences. For example, cosmopolitan values in the western part of Germany are more manifest and developed than in the eastern parts of the country, and they are different in the industrialised regions of the country from those manifested in global cities like Frankfurt or the rural parts of Bavaria. This would lead us to look for regional differences rather than country differences, with the likely result that a European map of cosmopolitan values not based on country as the unit of analysis would look more 'checkered' and reveal greater differences than the uniformity suggested in Map 3.

In implementing the two-pronged approach to global civil society, we set out to develop measures for both the organisational and the individual level of analysis: as an infrastructure of NGOs and other private, non-profit organizations, groups, and networks of many kinds; and as individual identities, values and norms, and forms of participation. The Global Civil Society Index introduced by Anheier and Stares (2002) took a statistical approach to develop a system that would combine both facets, and tried to measure it at the country level. In this chapter, we take a different though complementary approach to measuring global civil society by looking at the geographical distributions and spatial network patterns that emerge from transnational interconnectedness.

Metaphors, Models, and Maps

Yet the possibility of mapping global civil society and its component parts raises a larger question: why do it in the first place? In other words, what is the analytic added value of using GIS and other techniques for mapping facets of global civil society? The answer is simple yet full of implications, and comes in three parts. First, maps have formative capacities. They ascertain the existence of political and other entities, because maps '*au fond* ... constitute semiological systems (that is, a system of values)' (Wood 1992: 107). Thus, global civil society, like states, if left unmapped carries on a precarious existence, and the difficulty many have with visualising the concept is linked to the absence of a simple and easily communicable map. After all, as the historian Huizinga (1954) and the sociologist Zerubavel (2002) remind us, concepts of reality and their visual representations are closely related.

Second, the literature of globalisation has produced a rich set of metaphors that allude to some facet or another of global geography. Prominent examples include Giddens (1990), who argues in *The Consequences of Modernity* that *time-space distanciations* between local involvements and interactions across distance are much higher and more 'stretched' than they were in the past; Harvey (1989), who suggests that recent decades have experienced an intense *time-space compression* that has had a disorienting and disruptive impact upon political-economic practices, and created a sense of cultural uncertainty as a postmodern condition; Beck (1999), who sees the break up of the *territorial orthodoxy* of the political and the social institutions of the national state along *local-global axes*; and Yergin and Stanislaw (1998), who use the metaphor of the '*woven world*' to suggest global connectedness. Together, these metaphors and descriptors depict a world whose sense of geography has changed and is changing, invoking a new sense of spatiality (Harvey 1989).

Third, several models specifying the contours and structure of globalisation have been proposed in the literature. Dicken's (1998) new *geo-economy* is based on the functional integration of economic production and distribution processes across multiple national borders. Others go beyond the economic sphere. Beck (1999) proposes to examine the scale, density, and stability of regional-global networks and the social spaces they create and the cultural images they carry.

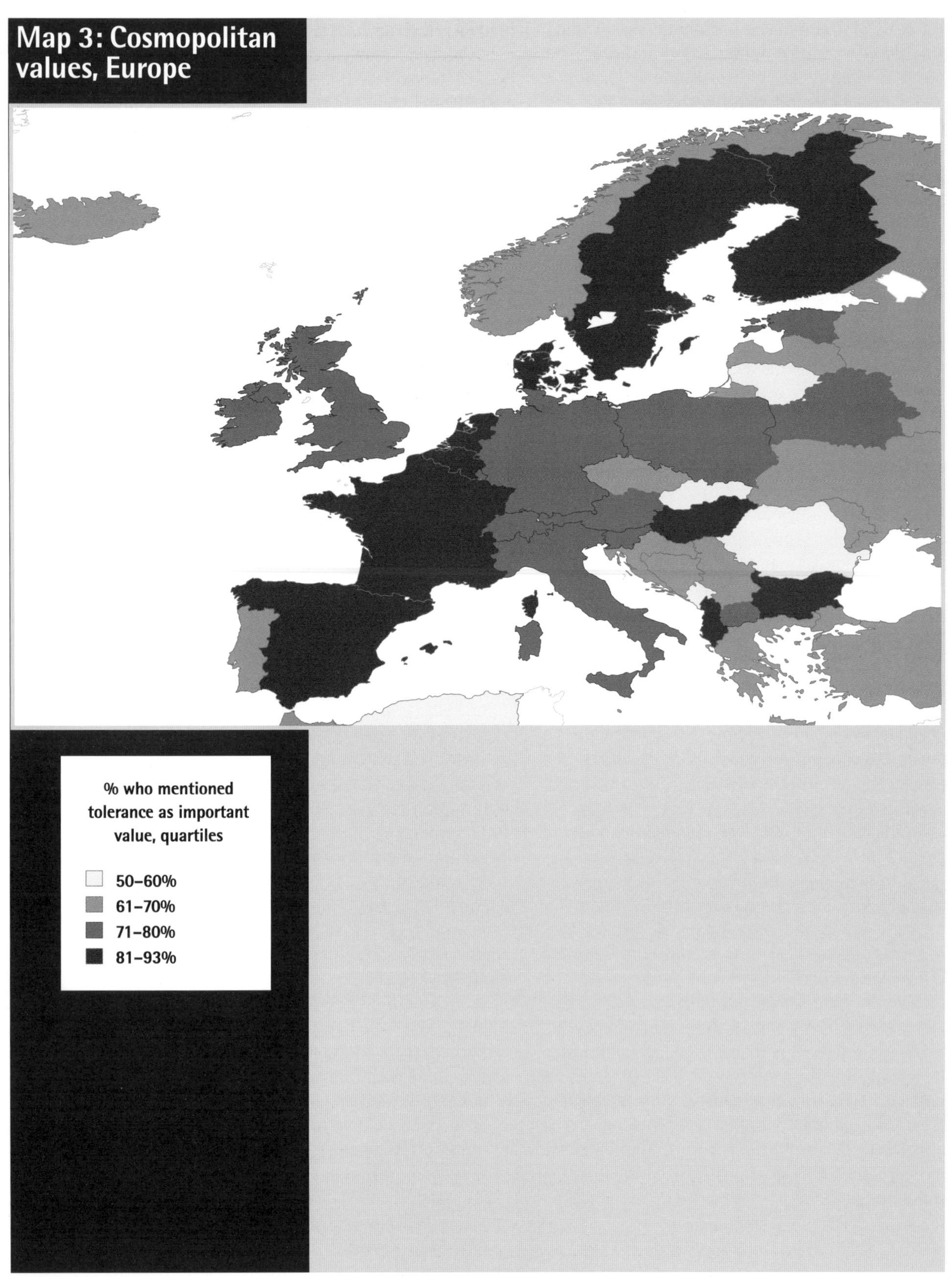
Map 3: Cosmopolitan values, Europe
% who mentioned tolerance as important value, quartiles
50–60%
61–70%
71–80%
81–93%

For Beck, 'globalisation' means world society without a world state and without a world government; it means a *multi-polar world* of continued expansion and contraction along local–global axes. The geographical image of Beck's perception is one of transmission belts (local-global axes) that intersect more frequently in some regions of the world than in others, thereby creating a pattern of varying density and centrality.

Castells (1996) introduces the term '*network society*' to suggest the fundamental shift in power relations in modern societies, where the power of flows (information, goods, finance) takes precedence over the flow of power (government, class relations) that characterised industrial society. The network nodes are the modern loci of power, and they are the more powerful the higher their connectedness in flows of many kinds. For Castells (1996), networks increasingly form meta-networks at the transnational level and create a system of '*decentralised concentration*', where a multiplicity of interconnected tasks takes place in different sites. The spatial image associated with Castell's network society is one of a multi-layered and multi-dimensional network of immense transnational reach.

Of course, the images of Dicken, Beck, Giddens, Harvey, and Castells overlap to some extent, and they all involve significant challenges when it comes to measurement and systematic testing. The most developed in operational terms is the model introduced by Held et al. (1999: 17–27; see also Anheier 2001), who differentiate between *extensity* (the geographical reach of activities), *intensity* (the overall density of the network), and *velocity* (the volume of network flows). Given data availability, it is not possible to measure the velocity of global civil society, nor the impact measures Held et al. (1999) propose. However, with the data provided by the Union of International Associations, it is possible to generate a map for the extensity and intensity of global civil society infrastructure.

Map 4 shows the extensity and intensity of global civil society as measured by the prevalence and density of INGOs by region, and not by country, derived from INGO secretariats geo-referenced by cities (clearly, INGOs do not equal global civil society, but are the best proxy measure available today.) Two centres of the organisational infrastructure of global civil society become apparent in Map 4: Europe, with the highest concentration in Western Europe (see inlet), and North America, with higher concentration along an axis from Montreal to New York and Washington. Other regions of higher INGO prevalence and density are on the US West Coast, in Central America around Mexico City, in South America in the Buenos Aires and Rio de Janeiro areas, New Delhi in India, in south-east Asia the Bangkok and Singapore regions, the Osaka–Tokyo corridor in Japan, and Sydney–Canberra in Australia.

The map also reveals vast regions with low INGO prevalence and density. This is the case for Central Africa, the Middle East, and Central Asia. For these regions, the results in Map 4 suggest an underdevelopment of domestic civil society that corresponds to weak inclusion in the organisational infrastructure of global civil society.

Taking a Different View: Exploring Global Civil Society Relationships

While the first reason for mapping global civil society is methodological and exploratory, the second is theoretical or analytic in nature. As many authors have suggested, the extensity, intensity, and velocity of global civil society, and the values, awareness, and motivations associated with it are not phenomena *sui generis* but the reflection of other processes (see Anheier, Glasius, and Kaldor 2001; Anheier and Stares, 2002; Chapter 1 in this volume). The hypothesis is that global civil society feeds on, and reacts to, globalisation, suggesting a complex relationship between economic globalisation and the thickening in the international rule of law. In other words, we posit that global civil society constitutes one of the three 'drivers' of globalisation.

Using GIS is one way to explore the relationships among these three drivers in a spatial context. Such an analysis would complement the statistical index approach developed by Anheier and Stares (2002: 251), who found that the correlations between the three drivers of globalisation are surprising in their apparent incongruence at the country level (Figure M1): whereas, across the 30 plus countries included in their analysis, the correlation between the Global Civil Society Index and the measure for international rule of law turned out rather low (.24), it was even lower for the relationship between economic globalisation and global civil society (.15). What is more, the correlation between economic globalisation and international rule of law was virtually zero (–.04), suggesting that the relationship among the three drivers may not be linear, and

Map 4: Extensity and intensity of global civil society

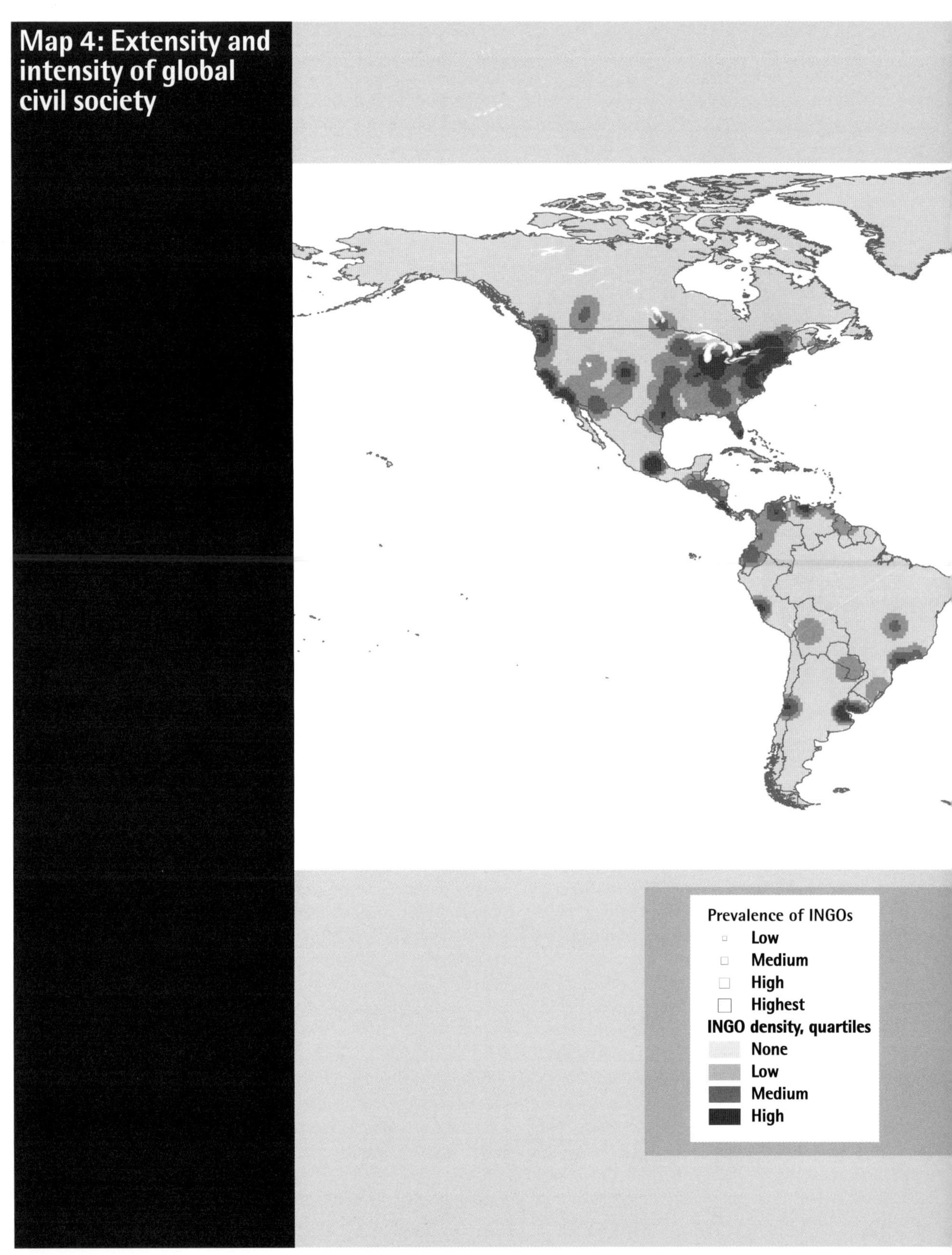

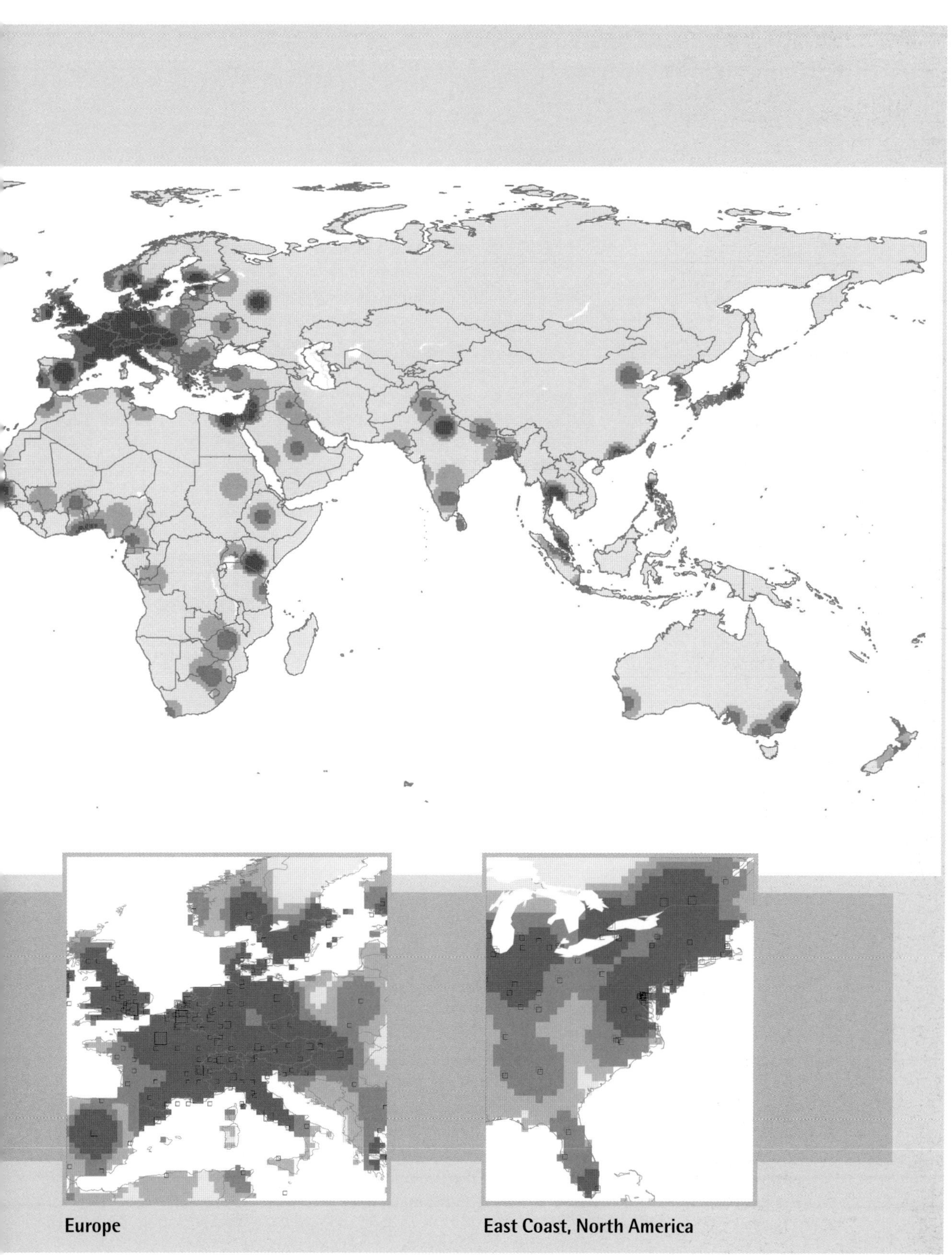
Europe
East Coast, North America

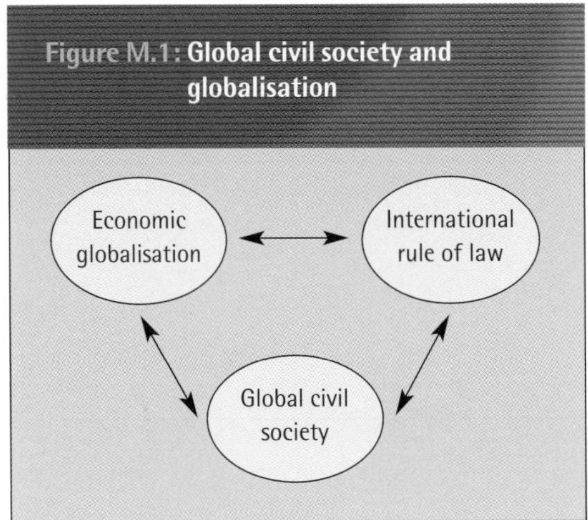

Figure M.1: Global civil society and globalisation

their patterns are certainly less congruent than some globalisation theorists would make us believe, as we will show below. Thus, we want to investigate whether 'mapping' of the globalisation of civil society, economy, and the rule of law can throw some light on the relationships among the drivers of this process.

Map 5 shows economic globalisation based on country as the unit of analysis, and with outbound foreign direct investment as the measure (see Box M1).

North America, western Europe, Australia/New Zealand, southern and parts of western Africa emerge as the centres of economic globalisation, although in terms of dollar volumes the first two regions would account for the bulk of outbound investment flows. Of course, were we to include inbound foreign direct investment (FDI), the map would change somewhat and show higher ratios for China and south-east Asia and lower ratios for Africa as a whole. In either case, the Middle East and Central Asia would remain the 'white spots' in the world map of economic globalisation measured through outbound investment flows.

Map 6 shows the combined spread of the international rule of law, measured in terms of treaty ratifications and the absence of reported human rights violations. The overall country rankings for respect for the international rule of law are based on (1) the inverted average rank in terms of human rights violations reported, combined with (2) the ranked number of international treaties ratified (for data sources see Record R8 and R9). The map indicates that most parts of the world fall in the lower third of the distribution (0–10 = low; 11–13 = medium; 14–17 = high), i.e., countries with fewer treaty ratifications and higher levels of human rights violations. In terms of regional concentration, western Europe, Australia/New Zealand, and Canada, together with parts of Latin America stand out, as does South Africa. The United States ranks lower than other parts of the world due to a lower number of treaty ratifications and higher number of human rights abuses, the latter in particular in terms of relatively high use of the death penalty (the second highest in the world after China) and serious human rights concerns about the treatment of prisoners and captives at US military installations.

From an analytic perspective, the key question is the extent to which economic globalisation, the international rule of law, and global civil society show a pattern of concurrence or divergence. This is what Map 7 attempts to show at the regional level, moving away, to the extent possible, from country as the unit of analysis and using as indicators INGO density, outbound FDI, treaty ratification, and the absence of human rights violations. The combined scores for Map 7 were calculated by overlaying maps 4, 5, and 6, and assigning greater weight to INGO density in score calculations for increased clarity.

If we look in Map 7 at the combined score in terms of quartile rankings (low = 2–7; medium low 8–9; medium high 10–16; higher over 17), two major regional concentrations emerge: Western Europe and the eastern seaboard of North America (Chicago–Toronto–Boston–Washington areas), with the US West Coast, Japan, Australia, and parts of southern Africa coming second. In other words, when economic globalisation, the thickening of the international rule of law, and global civil society are taken together, the structure of globalisation is more bipolar, with two centres, rather than multi-polar, as suggested by Beck (1999), and also more concentrated than Castell's (1996) notion of decentralised concentration would suggest, with most parts of the world showing low to medium patterns of concurrence.

However, the close links between the three aspects of globalisation revealed in Map 7 raise the question just how frequent the congruence along the presence and absence of globalisation drivers might be. Map 8 takes up this analytic question (see maps 4, 5, and 6 on data sources and measures used). Of the 47 countries falling within the high economic globalisation category, 21 also rank high on the other two drivers (see Table M1). With very few exceptions,

Map 5: Economic globalisation

Outbound FDI, % of GDP

- Low
- Medium
- High

Map 6: International rule of law

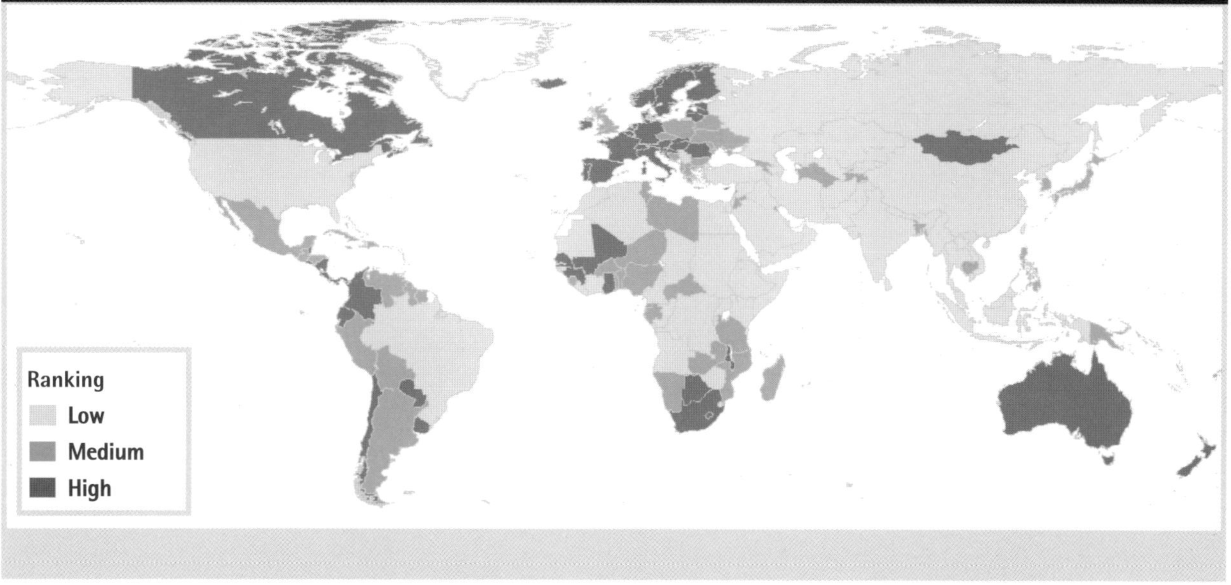

Ranking

- Low
- Medium
- High

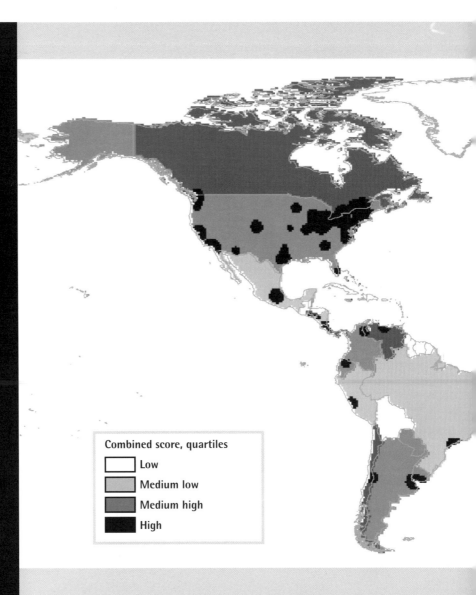

Map 7: Global civil society, economic globalisation and international rule of law

Combined score, quartiles

Low

Medium low

Medium high

High

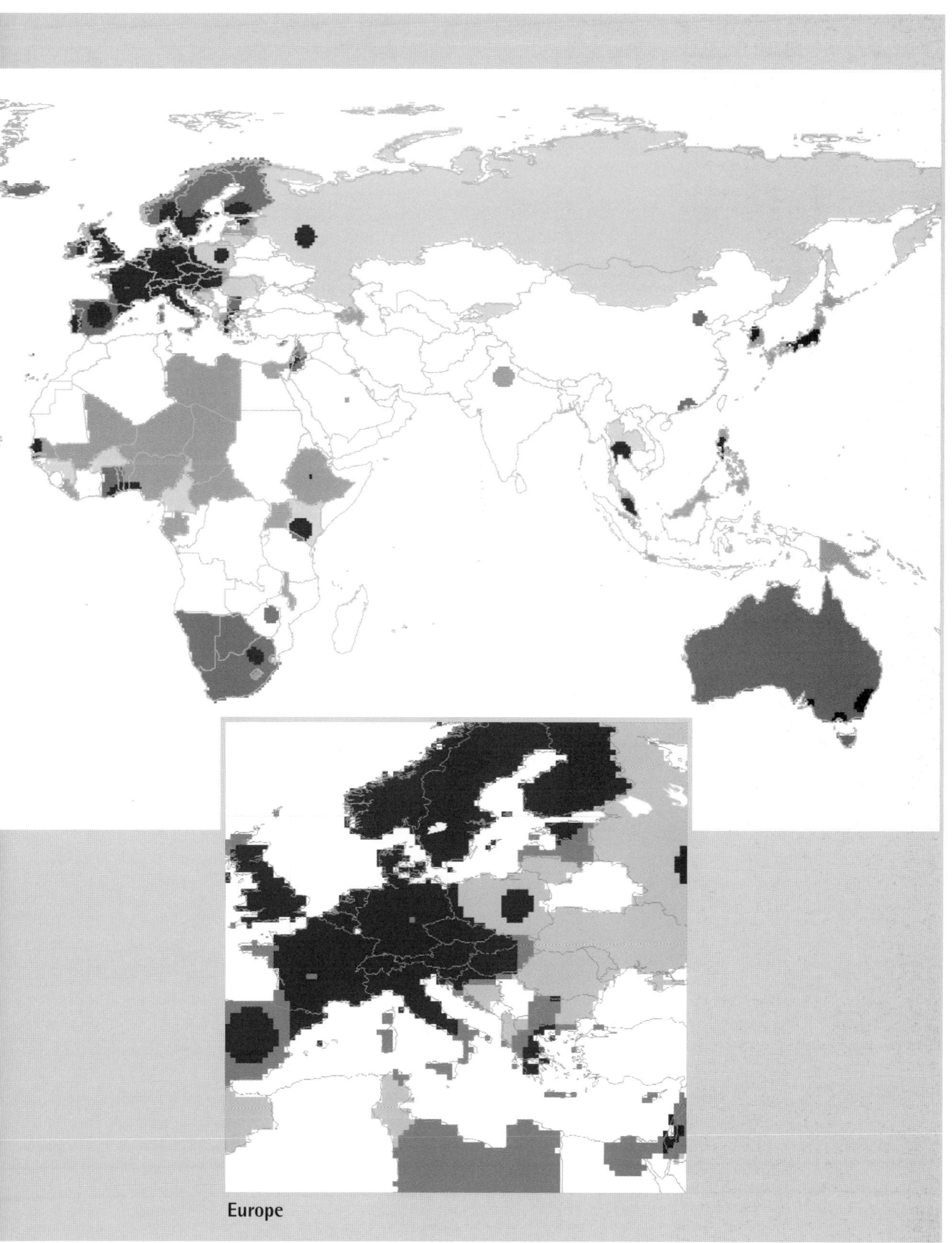
Europe

these 21 countries where economic globalisation, respect for the international rule of law, and high involvement in global civil society coincide are developed democratic market economies such as Australia, Canada, most current EU member states, New Zealand, but also countries such as Chile and Botswana. Western Europe turns out to be the world region with the largest expanse of contiguous countries ranking high in all three aspects of globalisation. Yet, as Map 8 also makes clear, the highly globalised regions of the world take up a smaller share of the world than the less globalised regions. In geographical terms, the highly globalised parts of the world in Map 8 resemble 'islands'.

At the other extreme, we have 28 countries where all three drivers are comparatively low in economic, legal, and civil society terms. Out of the 98 countries with low levels of economic globalisation, 28 also rank low in terms of civil society globalisation and international rule of law. Along them one finds exclusively developing countries such as Eritrea, Haiti, Angola, Burundi, Rwanda, Sudan, Somalia, Yemen, Pakistan, Bhutan, and Uzbekistan: countries typically burdened with authoritarian regimes, extreme poverty, and often prolonged armed conflicts.

Whereas the congruency rate among the three drivers is 46 per cent for highly globalised economies and 31 per cent for non-globalised economies, it is weakest in the middle category with just 7 per cent; here only six countries fall into a pattern where economic globalisation, the international rule of law, and global civil society are at medium level. These findings suggest that it is in these middle-ranking countries, where the relationship among drivers is most incongruent, that our understanding of globalisation generally is perhaps the weakest. They also suggest that the middle part of the globalisation ranking may account for the low correlations among globalisation drivers observed by Anheier and Stares (2002: 251).

As Map 8 illustrates, incongruent relations among the three drivers not only make up the most frequent category among the countries included in this analysis, they also cover the largest areas and most of the world's population, including China, Brazil, Russia, Indonesia, Nigeria, Turkey, and the United States. What these countries have in common are mixed human rights records, but they differ in many other important aspects, including size (which suggests that incongruence is not a 'big country

Box M1: Selecting outbound FDI as a measure of economic globalisation

Trade has been traditionally used as a measure of economic globalisation, typically as a percentage of GDP (Schmitter 1969: 334). Yet there is increasing criticism of its appropriateness due to inconsistent and misleading correlations with measures of cross-national integration (Clark and Welch 1972; Katsiaouni 2001). For example, in terms of trade to GDP ratios African countries appear more 'globalised' than the USA or Japan (since poor African countries are heavily depended on one or few tradable commodities, shares of trade to a lower overall GDP are unusually high).

A country's ability to manage the process of globalisation and to retain its capacity to effect a social and economic policy agenda may be a more appropriate measure of the extent of its integration in the global economy. Katsiaouni (2001) and Quinn and Inclan (1997) have suggested that such integration can best be measured by openness to global financial flows and the ability to exercise 'policy will' or policy choice.

While relevant data are not readily available, some international financial flows such as outbound foreign direct investment (FDI) indicators are second-best approximations in the sense that they incorporate some element of policy control and capacity (Page 1997; Mahler 2002) as well as policy choice. As defined by UNCTAD (2002: 291–2), outbound FDI implies a significant degree of investor influence in host economies.

Although outbound FDI is a better indicator of integration than trade, it can also be an indicator of capital flight. But until more comprehensive data combining flows with economic openness and control become available, outbound FDI remains the second-best approximation.

The data for FDI in Map 5 are derived from UNCTAD (2002: Annex Table B.6). For the purposes of Map 5, outbound FDI was grouped into three categories: low: 0–5% of GDP; medium: 6–15%, and high: 16% and up.

Map 8: Congruency of globalisation drivers

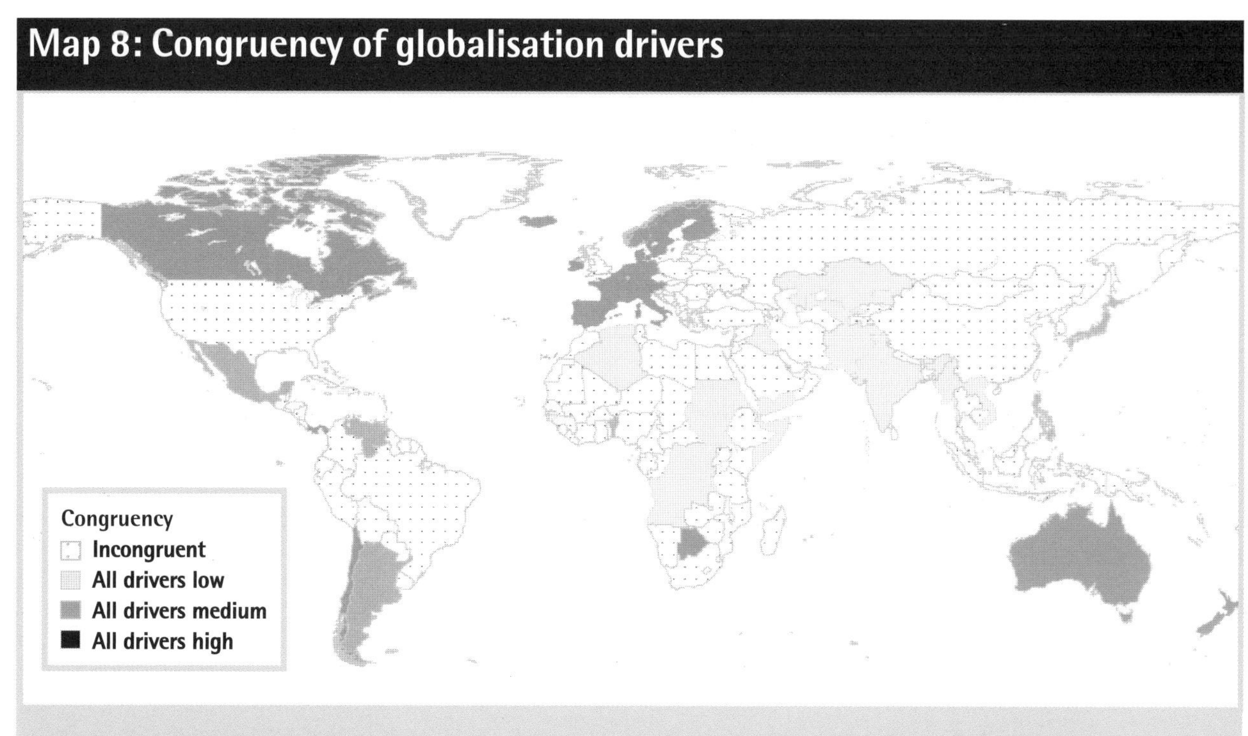

Table M1: Congruency between economic globalisation, international rule of law, and strength of global civil society: count of countries

	Economic globalisation								
	Low			Medium			High		
	Global civil society			Global civil society			Global civil society		
International rule of law	Low	Medium	High	Low	Medium	High	Low	Medium	High
Low	28	10	1	6	9	2	5	4	3
Medium	18	12	7	5	6	3	2	5	6
High	3	6	4	1	6	11		1	21

issue' alone). Indeed, the great diversity among countries with incongruent relations among the three drivers makes it hard to discern underlying effects, and further research will be required to gain more insight on this question.

Looking at the congruency of globalisation drivers from another angle, we reach similar conclusions. Using variables measuring the drivers rather than the countries as unit of analysis, we conducted a series of multivariate analyses. Interested readers can find the detailed statistical results at the Global Civil Society Yearbook website (URL); and in what follows we will limit ourselves to the presentation of the substantive findings that emerge from a correspondence analysis, which basically yields the same results as the other techniques used, namely, factor analysis and multi-dimensional scaling. Correspondence analysis is a tool for simplifying data structures by identifying major dimensions and corresponding characteristics (Greenacre 1993; Greenacre and Balsius 1994). In the present case, we examined the organisational infrastructure of global civil society, measured by the density of INGOs, against other factors measuring different aspects of globalisation:

Economic globalisation
- outbound foreign direct investment (FDI)
- the human development index

Cosmopolitan values and mobilisation
- extent of political participation among population
- acknowledgement among population of tolerance and respect for others as core value

Connectivity
- number of phone lines per 1,000 population
- foreign travel per 1,000 population

International rule of law
- human rights violations
- number of international treaties ratified

In each case, we divided variables into low, middle, and high categories according to the underlying distribution, but typically into an upper and lower quartile, to represent high and low values, and with the inter-quartile range as the middle or medium score.

Our basic question in conducting this analysis was: what characteristics are associated with a high, medium, and low density of global civil society infrastructure, measured, in this case, by INGO presence? The results of the correspondence analysis show one dominant dimension: the distinction between regions with high INGO density versus regions with low INGO density. As Figure M2 shows, this dominant distinction or axis carries nearly 90 per cent of the inertia, or explanatory power, contained in the data pattern. By implication, the difference between high and middle density on the one hand and, on the other, middle and low density of INGOs is less clear.[3]

According to the analysis, the primary characteristics of countries with *high INGO densities* are:

- high levels of outbound foreign direct investment, as an indicator of economic globalisation;
- high human development indicators (income, education, life expectancy);
- high levels of political activity and participation;
- high levels of cosmopolitan values, measured by tolerance and respect for others;
- high communication density (phone lines);
- high international travel volumes;
- low extent of human rights violations; and
- high number of ratifications of international treaties.

By contrast, the primary characteristics of low-density countries are basically the mirror image of the above:

- lack of outbound FDI, i.e., absence of economic globalisation;
- low human development indicators, i.e., low per capita income, lack of education, low life expectancy);
- low level of political activity and participation (though a weaker correspondence);
- low levels of cosmopolitan values, measured by tolerance and respect for others;
- low communication density (phone lines);
- low international travel volumes;
- higher extent of human rights violations; and
- lower number of ratifications of international treaties.

The middle-ranking countries in terms of INGO densities have less clear 'signature profiles' but tend to show:

- medium levels of outbound FDI, i.e. appear somewhat included in the global economic system;
- high or medium levels of political activity and participation;
- medium levels of cosmopolitan values; and
- medium extent of human rights violations.
- Differences in connectivity (travel, phone lines) are not what set them apart, and neither are variations in human development. What seem to make a difference in their status are largely political factors and value patterns.

As in Map 8, congruency between the different drivers of globalisation occurs more in the low and high extremes, while the mid-range poses a more perplexing picture. We find that high INGO density tends to be associated with high levels of economic globalisation and human development, cosmopolitan

[3] There are two interpretations possible for the fact that the dimension involving the middle position of 'medium INGO density' carries only 10% of the model's inertia. First, to some measure, the middle position emerges less clearly in our analysis because these countries are truly in the 'middle' of those characteristics that correspond to either high or low INGO densities; second, it could be argued that we have a better conceptual understanding of high and low positions, but fail to include aspects that measure the peculiar characteristics of the middle rung.

Figure M.2: Correspondence of INGO density and other globalisation drivers

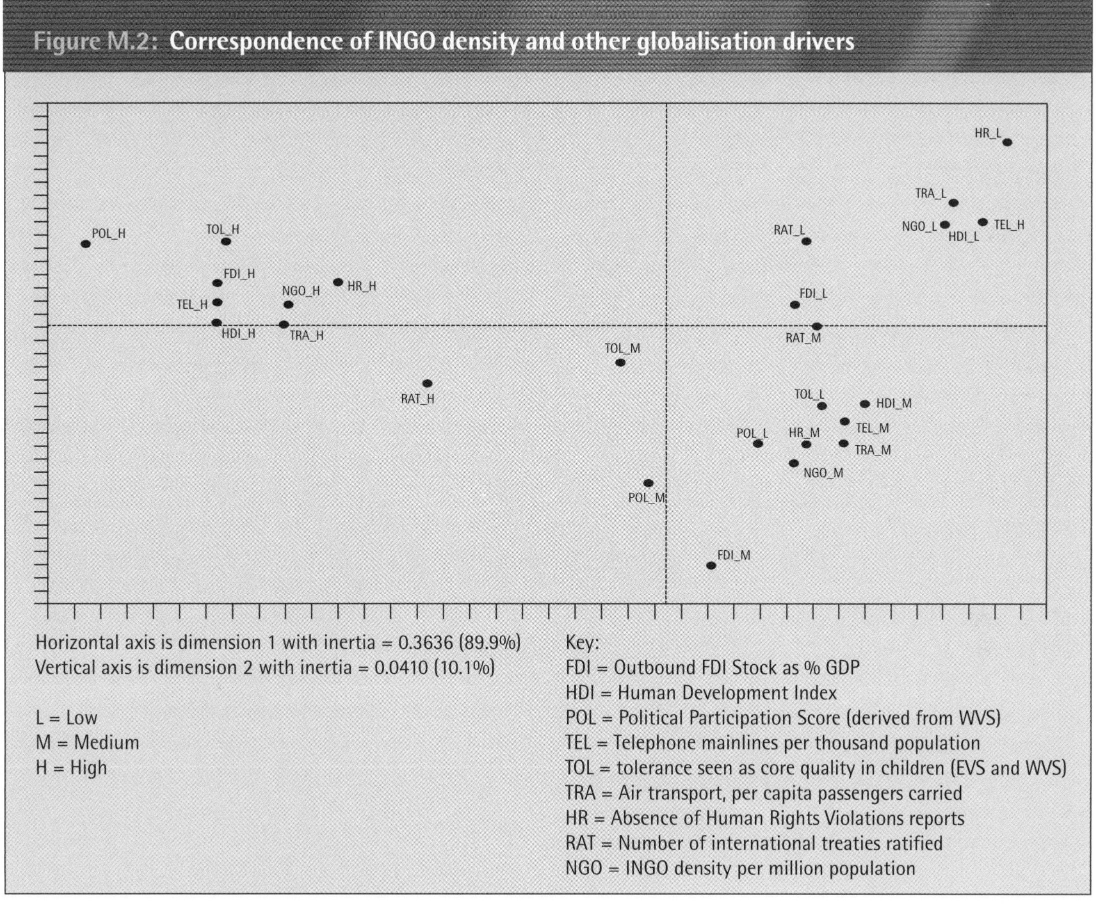

Horizontal axis is dimension 1 with inertia = 0.3636 (89.9%)
Vertical axis is dimension 2 with inertia = 0.0410 (10.1%)

L = Low
M = Medium
H = High

Key:
FDI = Outbound FDI Stock as % GDP
HDI = Human Development Index
POL = Political Participation Score (derived from WVS)
TEL = Telephone mainlines per thousand population
TOL = tolerance seen as core quality in children (EVS and WVS)
TRA = Air transport, per capita passengers carried
HR = Absence of Human Rights Violations reports
RAT = Number of international treaties ratified
NGO = INGO density per million population

values, respect for human rights, political engagement, connectivity, and mobility. Low INGO density tends to correspond to the opposite or the lack of the above characteristics. The mid-level INGO density cannot be significantly attributed to any specific combination among these variables, and further work is needed to explain it.

Conclusion

The purpose of this chapter has been to use geographical mapping techniques to examine spatial aspects of global civil society and discover the distribution and emerging patterns of transnational interconnectedness. Of course, given the exploratory nature of the work presented here, we could do little but scratch the surface of what are undoubtedly complex methodological and analytical problems. Nonetheless, we hope that our attempts to use different units of analysis, to put emphasis on non-contiguous phenomena, and to push spatial metaphors has at least pointed the way for future work in this area. We also hope that we have started the process of developing the imagery for maps needed to represent and understand global civil society and globalisation.

Next steps would include combining the geographical approach taken here with the global civil society index work proposed by Anheier and Stares (2002), and examining emerging patterns over time, in particular inter-organisational networks among INGOs. Other topics not yet explored but potentially useful revolve around global social movements, patterns of leadership in global civil society, and the relationship between civil and uncivil society (crime, terrorists, supremacists, and fundamentalists, and the movements, networks, and organisations they create and operate), and their relationship to other globalisation drivers.

References

Anheier, Helmut K. (2001). 'Measuring Global Civil Society'. In Helmut K Anheier, Marlies Glasius, and Mary Kaldor (eds), *Global Civil Society 2001*. Oxford: Oxford University Press.

–, Marlies Glasius, and Mary Kaldor (eds) (2001). *Global Civil Society 2001*. Oxford: Oxford University Press.

– and Sally R. Stares (2002). 'Introducing the Global Civil Society Index'. In Marlies Glasius, Mary H Kaldor, and Helmut K. Anheier (eds.), *Global Civil Society 2002*. Oxford: Oxford University Press.

– and Nuno Themudo (2002). 'Organisational Forms of Global Civil Society: Implications of Going Global'. In Marlies Glasius, Mary H. Kaldor, and Helmut K Anheier (eds.), *Global Civil Society 2002*. Oxford: Oxford University Press.

Beck, Ulrich (1999). *What is Globalisation?* Cambridge: Polity Press.

– (2000). 'The Postnational Society and its Enemies'. Public lecture, London School of Economics and Political Science, 24 February.

Castells, Manuel (1996). *The Rise of Network Society*. Oxford: Blackwell.

Clark, Cal and Susan Welch (1972). 'Western European Trade as a Measure of Integration: Untangling the Interpretations'. *The Journal of Conflict Resolution*, 16: 363–82.

Dicken, Peter (1998). *Global Shift: Transforming the World Economy*. London: Chapman.

Giddens, Anthony (1990). *The Consequences of Modernity*. Cambridge: Polity Press.

Global Civil Society Yearbook website. www.lse.ac.uk/depts/global/yearbook

Greenacre, Michael (1993). *Correspondence Analysis in Practice*. London: Academic Press.

– and Jörg Blasius (eds) (1994). *Correspondence Analysis in the Social Sciences: Recent Developments and Applications*. London: Academic Press.

Harvey, David (1989). *The Conditions of Postmodernity: An Enquiry into the Origins of Cultural Change*. Oxford: Blackwell.

Held, David, Anthony McGrew, David Goldblatt, and Jonathan Perraton (1999). *Global Transformations*. Cambridge: Polity Press.

Huizinga, Johan (1954). *The Waning of the Middle Ages*. New York: Doubleday.

Katsiaouni, Olympios (2001). *Globalisation and the State: Some Awkward Corners*. New York: Division for Social Policy and Development, United Nations.

Mahler, Vincent A. (2002). 'Economic Globalisation, Domestic Politics, and Income Inequality in the Developed Countries'. Paper presented at the annual meeting of the Southern Political Science Association, Savannah, Georgia, 7–9 November.

Page, Benjamin I. (1997). *Trouble for Workers and the Poor: Economic Globalisation and the Reshaping of American Politics*. Evanston, IL: Institute for Policy Research, Northwestern University (Working Paper 99-06).

Quinn, Dennis P. and Carla Inclan (1997). 'The Origins of Financial Openness: A Study of Current and Capital Account Liberalization'. *American Journal of Political Science*, 41: 771–813.

Sassen, Saskia (2002). 'Global Cities and Diasporic Networks: Microsites in Global Civil Society'. In Marlies Glasius, Mary H. Kaldor, and Helmut K. Anheier (eds), *Global Civil Society 2002*. Oxford: Oxford University Press.

Schmitter, Philippe C. (1969). 'Further Notes on Operationalizing Some Variables Related to Regional Integration'. *International Organization*, 23: 327–36.

Staple, Gregory and Hugo Dixon (1992). 'Telegeography: Mapping the New World Order'. *Whole Earth Review*, 75/Summer: 124-125.

Taylor, Peter J. (2001). 'Specification of the World City Network'. *Geographical Analysis*, 33: 181–94.

UNCTAD (United Nations Conference on Trade and Development) (2001). *The World Investment Report 2001: Promoting Linkages*. New York: UNCTAD.

– (2002). *The World Investment Report 2002: Transnational Corporations and Export Competitiveness*. New York: UNCTAD.

Wood, Dennis (1992). *The Power of Maps*. New York: Guilford Press.

Yergin, Daniel A. and Joseph Stanislav (1998). *The Commanding Heights: The Battle between Government and the Marketplace that is Remaking the Modern World*. New York: Simon and Schuster.

Zerubavel, Eviatar (2002). *Time Maps: Collective Memory and the Social Shape of the Past*. Cambridge, MA: Harvard University Press.

Note on Data

Relation to data programme Global Civil Society 2002

We have updated the information presented in the 2002 edition of the Yearbook wherever possible. Those indicators repeated from the 2002 data programme represent more recent or updated figures. In order to facilitate comparisons, this year's country data are grouped by income and region, using World Bank classifications.

We have added new indicators where we judge them to be valuable, sometimes representing a departure from the indicators presented last year. Such indicators are found in our records on global economy, environment, crime, and leaders of international organisations. This year we include two new records: governance and accountability, and attitudes towards globalisation. Thus we introduce the following new data sources to the Yearbook: the One World Trust <http://www.oneworldtrust.org/>, 2020 Fund <http://www.2020fund.org/>, and Environics International Ltd <http://www.environicsinternational.com/>.

As well as drawing on different sources, we increased our use of graphical formats for presentation of the data. Selected indicators in the tables are illustrated on world maps. In addition, we introduce network diagrams for the records on flows of trade and flows of students between regions. The diagrams should be interpreted by reference to node size and position, and line thickness. Each node in the diagrams represents a (labelled) region, while lines represent flows. Node size is determined by *degree centrality* in the network, which is determined by the sum of its inflows and outflows. The location of nodes in the diagram is determined by *eigenvector centrality*: regions that are more central in the network (transfer more flows to and from them, and are connected to other highly connected regions) are closer to the centre; also, the higher the volume of flows between regions, the closer these regions are to each other. Line width reflects flow volumes: thicker lines indicate greater flows.

For some elements of last year's data programme, we have not been able to obtain updated or equivalent data for this edition of the Yearbook. Thus, we have decided not to reproduce the data on radios, outgoing telephone traffic, environmental sustainability, values data on geographic identity, tolerance towards certain groups of people as neighbours, and willingness to help immigrants, or to publish any data on crime.

All data from previous Yearbooks remain available on our website at <http://www.lse.ac.uk/depts/global/yearbook.htm>.

Sources and explanatory notes

Brief references to sources are found at the end of each record. All major terms used in the records are briefly defined in the Glossary. As will become clear, comparative information is not available for some countries and variables. A blank entry indicates that the data are not available, not comparable, or otherwise of insufficient quality to warrant reporting. To improve readability of the data and to facilitate interpretation, each record is preceded by a brief description of the information presented and points to some of the key findings.

Time periods

Dependent on data availability, data are reported for 1992 and 2002 or the closest years possible. At the request of readers, we have changed the order in which countries appear from alphabetical order to geographic and development groupings, as used by UNDP and the World Bank.

Countries

Countries in these tables are independent states with more than 100,000 inhabitants according to the most recent population estimates. Short or conventional country names are used. It is not the intention of the editors to take a position with regard to the political or diplomatic implications of geographical names or continental groupings used.

China, Hong Kong, Macao, Taiwan, and Tibet
Hong Kong became a Special Administrative Region (SAR) of China in 1997 after formal transfer from the UK. Macao became a SAR of China in 1999 after formal transfer from Portugal. Data for China before these dates do not include Hong Kong and Macao; thereafter they do unless otherwise stated. Tibet was annexed by the People's Republic of China in 1949. Data for Tibet are included in those for China and Tibet. Taiwan became the home of Chinese nationalists fleeing Communist rule on the mainland and claims separate status from the People's Republic of China. No data are given for Taiwan, which is not recognised by the United Nations as an independent country.

Czechoslovakia
Czechoslovakia ceased to exist (in UN terms) on 31 December 1992. Its successor states, the Czech Republic and the Slovak Republic, became UN members in 1993. Figures predating 1993 are given for the Czech Republic and Slovakia separately where possible, or otherwise not at all.

Ethiopia and Eritrea
Eritrea became independent from Ethiopia in 1993. Data for Ethiopia until 1993 include Eritrea, later data do not.

Germany
The Federal Republic of Germany and the German Democratic Republic were unified in 1990. Data for 1990 and 1991 include both unless otherwise indicated.

Indonesia and East Timor
The Indonesian occupation of East Timor ended in late 1999. After a transitional period under the authority of the United Nations, East Timor became independent on 20 May 2002. Data are presented for Indonesia and East Timor together unless otherwise indicated. All data for Indonesia also include West Papua, the status of which has been in dispute since the 1960s.

Israel and the Occupied Territories
Data for Israel generally include both the occupied territories and territories administered by the Palestinian Authority. In Records 16–20 they include territories identified by INGOs as 'Palestine', 'Cisjordania', 'Gaza', 'Jerusalem', and 'West Bank'.

Morocco and the Western Sahara
The Western Sahara (formerly Spanish Sahara) was annexed by Morocco in the 1970s. Unless otherwise stated, data are amalgamated for 'Morocco and the Western Sahara'.

Yugoslavia and Serbia & Montenegro
The Socialist Federal Republic of Yugoslavia dissolved in 1991 into Bosnia and Herzegovina, the Republic of Croatia, the Republic of Slovenia, the former Yugoslav Republic of Macedonia, and the Federal Republic of Yugoslavia. In February 2003 the Federal Republic of Yugoslavia was renamed Serbia and Montenegro, reflecting the implementation of constitutional change to a looser federation of its two republics. For ease of presentation, the name 'Serbia and Montenegro' is used throughout these records, where the 'Federal Republic of Yugoslavia' would have applied pre-2003. Wherever possible, including for 1990, data are given separately for Serbia & Montenegro and the other constituent states of the former Yugoslavia.

USSR
The Union of Soviet Socialist Republics (USSR) dissolved in 1991 into Armenia, Azerbaijan, Belarus, Georgia, Kazakhstan, Kyrgyzstan, Republic of Moldova, Russian Federation, Tajikistan, Turkmenistan, Ukraine, and Uzbekistan. 1990 and 1991 data for the Russian Federation refer only to the Russian Federation, except where they are indicated to refer to the USSR.

Aggregations

Where possible we present data for groups of countries (by region and economy) as well as for individual countries. These groups are generally classified according to World Bank definitions. The aggregations are weighted differently depending on information availability. To give an example, in R1 we present figures for trade as a percentage of GDP. The aggregate figure for South Asia is calculated as the sum of trade for Afghanistan, Bangladesh, Bhutan,

India, Maldives, Nepal, Pakistan and Sri Lanka, divided by the sum of GDP for those countries, and multiplied by 100 to generate a percentage, i.e.

Trade as % GDP for South Asia =

$$\frac{\text{Afghan trade + Bangladeshi trade + ...}}{\text{Afghan GDP + Bangladeshi GDP + ...}} \times 100$$

Most aggregate figures given are calculated in this way. By contrast, in R6 and in the Values Surveys tables, the aggregates we present are simple averages, and are marked as such. For example, with 'main telephone lines per 1,000 people', to calculate the aggregate figure for South Asia we sum the ratios 'mainlines per 1,000 people' in Afghanistan, Bangladesh, Bhutan, India, Maldives, Nepal, Pakistan, and Sri Lanka, and divide this figure by the number of countries in this region (eight), i.e.

Average no. mainlines per 1000 pop. for South Asia =

$$\frac{\text{Mainlines per 1000 pop. in Afghanistan + in Bangladesh + ...}}{\text{Number of countries in South Asia}}$$

Each country's contribution to the regional or world figure is given equal weight under this method of aggregation.

Record 1 Global economy

The first table contains data on the globalisation of domestic economies. Total trade, foreign direct investment (FDI), and receipts of official development aid are presented as a percentage of GDP, and include information on changes over time between 1990 and 2000, using the latest figures available. We try to show the extent to which national economies are parts of an emerging global economy, and where economic growth or contraction has been most pronounced over the last decade in this respect. The table shows significant increases in trade and direct investments between 1990 and 2000 for most countries, and decreases in official development aid for many countries, contrasted to increases in aid in middle- and low-income economies in Europe and Central Asia.

The map illustrates sums of development aid received and comparative levels of outward FDI (the rationale for using outward FDI as an indicator of economic integration is given in Box M1 in the Mapping Global Civil Society chapter).

The second table is taken from the first wave of the 2020 Fund's Global Stakeholder Panel, a survey of 258 leaders of NGOs, governments and companies operating at local to global levels. It shows the average of respondents' perceptions of the overall positive or negative effects of trade, investment and aid, in comparison with other aspects of globalisation.

	Trade			Foreign Direct Investment						Official Development Aid*		
	Total trade in % GDP		% change	Outward FDI stock in % GDP		% change	Inward FDI Stock in % GDP		% change	Aid in % GNI		% change
Country	**1990**	**2000**	**1990-2000**	**1990**	**2000**	**1990-2000**	**1990**	**2000**	**1990-2000**	**1990**	**2000**	**1990-2000**
East Asia & Pacific												
Low income economies												
Cambodia	18.9	87.0	360		0.1		3.4	48.7	1,332	3.7	12.6	236
Indonesia	49.1	69.2	41	0.1	1.5	1,400	34.0	39.6	16	1.6	1.2	-24
Korea, Dem. Rep.							3.4	10.0	194			
Laos		83.9			0.1		1.5	32.2	2,046	17.3	16.8	-3
Mongolia	76.9	147.4	92					18.7			22.8	
Myanmar	7.5	*1.1*	*-85*				11.1	24.7	123			
Papua New Guinea	89.6	*90.0*	1	0.5	14.4	2,780	49.1	53.5	9	13.3	7.5	-43
Solomon Islands	120						33.0	45.7	38			
Vietnam	60						4.0	46.7	1,068	*1.9*	5.4	*186*
Middle income economies												
China**	31.9	49.1	54	0.7	2.4	243	7.0	32.3	361	0.6	0.2	-72
Fiji	129.6	131.6	1	6.3	19.6	211	29.1	50.4	73	3.7	2.0	-45
Malaysia	147.0	229.8	56	6.1	20.8	241	23.4	58.8	151	1.1	0.1	-95
Philippines	60.8	106.5	75	0.3	2.6	767	7.4	16.6	124	2.9	0.7	-75
Samoa		114.7					8.1	22.6	179	29.0	11.6	-60
Thailand	75.8	126.0	66	0.5	2.0	300	9.6	20.0	108	0.9	0.5	-44
Tonga	92.7			0.1	0.8	700	0.7	12.0	1,614			
Vanuatu	123.0						71.8	175.9	145	30.6	20.5	-33
High income economies												
Australia	33.6	*42.2*	26	9.8	20.9	113	23.7	29.2	23			
Brunei					2.9		0.7	74.4	10,529	0.1		
Japan	19.8	*18.4*	*-7*	6.6	5.8	-12	0.3	1.1	267			
Korea, Rep.	59.4	87.2	47	0.9	11.1	1,133	2.3	13.7	496	0.0	0.0	
New Zealand	54.5	*64.7*	*19*	14.7	10.8	-27	18.2	49.4	171			
Singapore	396.7	341.4	-14	21.3	57.5	170	77.9	103.8	33	0.0	0.0	
Europe & Central Asia												
Low income economies												
Armenia	81.3	74.1	-9		1.7			30.0		*0.1*	11.2	*12,481*
Azerbaijan		79.1			9.0			70.9			2.8	
Georgia	85.6	84.1	-2					14.0		*0.0*	5.6	
Kyrgyzstan	78.8	98.7	25		2.5			32.2			17.6	

Record 1 continued	Trade			Foreign Direct Investment						Official Development Aid*		
	Total trade in % GDP		% change	Outward FDI stock in % GDP		% change	Inward FDI Stock in % GDP		% change	Aid in % GNI		% change
Country	1990	2000	1990-2000	1990	2000	1990-2000	1990	2000	1990-2000	1990	2000	1990-2000
Moldova	100.1	126.9	27		1.5			35.7			9.0	
Tajikistan	63.0	165.4	163					14.5			15.2	
Ukraine	56.4	118.4	110		0.3			12.1		0.3	1.8	467
Uzbekistan	76.6	82.8	8					9.1			2.5	
Middle income economies												
Albania	38.1	59.3	56		2.2			15.4		0.5	8.3	1,461
Belarus	89.6	137.2	53		0.2			11.9		*0.5*	0.1	*-74*
Bosnia & Herzegovina		85.0			0.9			8.1			16.0	
Bulgaria	69.8	122.5	75		0.7		0.5	26.4	5,180	0.1	2.7	3,208
Croatia	*163.8*	95.6	*-42*		3.9			27.1			0.4	
Czech Republic	87.8	146.6	67		1.5		3.9	42.6	992		0.9	
Estonia		172.2			5.2		0.0	48.0		*0.3*	1.4	*442*
Hungary	59.7	129.2	116	0.6	4.5	650	1.7	43.4	2,453	0.2	0.6	169
Kazakhstan		106.2			0.1			54.8		*0.4*	1.1	*216*
Latvia	96.7	100.1	3		3.4			29.1		0.0	1.3	3,991
Lithuania	112.8	96.7	-14		0.3			20.6		0.0	0.9	3,232
Macedonia	61.8	107.5	74		0.1			10.9			7.1	
Poland	50.2	61.8	23	0.2	0.6	200	0.2	21.3	10,550	2.4	0.9	-63
Romania	42.9	73.9	72	0.2	0.3	50	2.0	17.7	785	0.6	1.2	88
Russian Federation	36.1	70.7	96		4.7			7.7		0.0	0.7	1,384
Serbia & Montenegro		81.9						15.6			13.4	
Slovakia	62.1	149.6	141		1.9		0.5	24.2	4,740	0.0	0.6	1,261
Slovenia	*157.8*	121.8	*-23*	1.5	4.4	193	3.8	15.5	308		0.3	
Turkey	30.9	55.8	81		1.3		0.9	4.7	422	0.8	0.2	-80
Turkmenistan		*116.4*						20.7			0.7	
High income economies												
Austria	78.0	*90.7*	*16*	2.6	13.2	408	6.1	16.1	164			
Belgium & Luxembourg***	145.1	176.5	22	19.4	154.1	694	27.8	174.0	526			
Cyprus	108.6	*93.0*	*-14*	0.2	6.5	3,150	20.5	23.7	16	0.7	0.6	-7
Denmark	66.6	79.5	19	5.5	39.4	616	6.9	39.6	474			
Finland	47.2	74.8	59	8.2	43.0	424	3.8	20.0	426			
France	43.5	55.9	29	9.9	33.4	237	8.2	19.9	143			
Germany	54.3	66.3	22	8.8	25.2	186	7.1	24.1	239			
Greece	45.9	*48.7*	*6*	3.5	5.1	46	9.4	11.1	18	0.0		
Iceland	66.5	*73.1*	*10*	1.2	7.7	542	2.3	5.7	148			
Ireland	109.3	*161.4*	*48*	5.8	19.4	234	7.2	68.2	847			
Italy	39.4	55.6	41	5.2	16.8	223	5.3	10.5	98			
Netherlands	113.6	*116.4*	*2*	36.3	83.8	131	23.3	65.9	183			
Norway	74.7	77.1	3	9.4	27.3	190	10.7	18.8	76			
Portugal	73.0	74.7	2	1.3	16.7	1,185	14.8	26.5	79			
Spain	35.6	62.2	75	3.0	29.6	887	12.8	25.8	102			
Sweden	59.2	89.5	51	21.3	53.8	153	5.3	36.1	581			
Switzerland	72.0	*79.1*	*10*	28.9	95.1	229	15.0	34.2	128			
United Kingdom	50.6	56.3	11	23.2	63.2	172	20.6	30.5	48			
Latin America & Caribbean												
Low income countries												
Haiti	45.2	39.9	-12		0.1		5.0	5.3	6	5.7	5.1	-10
Nicaragua	71.3				0.3		11.4	57.3	403	33.6		

Record 1 continued

	Trade			Foreign Direct Investment						Official Development Aid*		
	Total trade in % GDP		% change	Outward FDI stock in % GDP		% change	Inward FDI Stock in % GDP		% change	Aid in % GNI		% change
Country	1990	2000	1990-2000	1990	2000	1990-2000	1990	2000	1990-2000	1990	2000	1990-2000
Middle income countries												
Argentina	15.0	22.2	48	4.3	7.3	70	6.4	25.6	300	0.1	0.0	-78
Barbados	100.8	106.7	6	1.3	1.5	15	9.9	11.8	19	0.2	0.0	-94
Belize	125.4	110.7	-12		5.7		18.2	34.6	90	7.6	1.9	-75
Bolivia	46.7	42.6	-9	0.2	0.4	100	21.1	61.0	189	11.8	5.9	-50
Brazil	15.2	23.0	52	0.5	2.2	340	8.0	33.1	314	0.0	0.1	65
Chile	66.0	62.6	-5	0.6	25.9	4,217	33.2	60.9	83	0.4	0.1	-80
Colombia	35.4	42.3	19	1.0	3.7	270	8.7	15.1	74	0.2	0.2	1
Costa Rica	76.0	94.3	24	0.8	0.6	-25	25.3	32.8	30	4.2	0.1	-98
Cuba		33.9						0.3				
Dominican Republic	77.5	69.1	-11		0.3		8.1	26.5	227	1.5	0.3	-78
Ecuador	60.1	73.2	22		2.0		15.2	51.0	236	1.6	1.2	-28
El Salvador	49.8	70.3	41	1.1	0.6	-45	4.4	14.9	239	7.3	1.4	-81
Grenada	105.2	136.2	29	0.1	0.2	100	31.7	83.8	164	6.6	4.4	-33
Guatemala	45.9	47.9	4		0.3		22.7	18.0	-21	2.7	1.4	-47
Guyana	142.6	207.8	46					93.3		61.3	16.4	-73
Honduras	76.1	98.7	30				12.6	25.1	99	15.7	7.8	-51
Jamaica	108.0	99.1	-8	1.0	9.6	860	18.7	43.8	134	7.3	0.1	-98
Mexico	38.3	64.6	69	0.2	1.4	600	8.5	16.9	99	0.1	0.0	-115
Panama	72.2	72.1	0	78.8	40.5	-49	41.4	68.2	65	2.0	0.2	-91
Paraguay	72.7	55.6	-24	2.6	2.8	8	7.6	16.4	116	1.1	1.1	3
Peru	29.6	33.8	14	0.2	0.9	350	5.0	18.5	270	1.6	0.8	-51
St. Lucia	156.7	121.2	-23	0.1	0.1	0	80.2	112.9	41	3.3	1.6	-50
St. Vincent & the Grenadines	142.6	128.9	-10	0.3	0.2	-33	24.3	146.5	503	8.0	2.0	-75
Suriname	55.5	34.7	-38							19.9	4.4	-78
Trinidad & Tobago	74.0	117.8	59	0.4	4.1	925	41.3	95.6	131	0.4	0.0	-106
Uruguay	41.6	40.0	-4	0.3	0.3	0	10.8	10.6	-2	0.6	0.1	-85
Venezuela	59.6	46.4	-22	4.7	22.4	377	4.6	4.8	4	0.2	0.1	-61
High income countries												
Bahamas				19.8	28.7	45	18.9	32.9	74	0.1	0.1	38
Middle East & North Africa												
Low income countries												
Yemen	34.4	91.9	168	0.1	0.1	0	3.7	10.4	181	8.4	3.6	-58
Middle income countries												
Algeria	48.4	64.3	33	0.3	0.6	100	2.2	6.5	195	0.4	0.3	-27
Djibouti		107.4					1.5	6.1	307		12.6	
Egypt	52.8	38.9	-26	0.4	0.7	75	25.6	21.1	-18	12.9	1.3	-90
Iran	45.5	55.5	22		1.3		2.2	2.4	9	0.1	0.1	42
Jordan	154.6	111.0	-28	0.7			15.3	18.1	18	23.3	6.6	-72
Lebanon	117.9	50.8	-57	1.7	0.7	-59	1.9	6.6	247	7.5	1.1	-85
Libya				2.2	4.0	82				0.1		
Malta	184.1	216.7	18		6.0		20.1	84.7	321	0.1	0.6	318
Morocco	58.9	68.6	16	1.9	2.2	16	3.6	18.4	411	4.2	1.3	-69
Oman	83.3			0.1	0.1	0	16.4	12.5	-24	0.6		
Saudi Arabia	82.4	75.3	-9	1.8	1.2	-33	21.5	15.0	-30	0.0	0.0	-50
Syria	56.3	72.6	29				3.0	10.0	233	5.7	1.0	-83
Tunisia	94.2	91.6	-3	0.1	0.2	100	62.0	58.8	-5	3.3	1.2	-64
High income countries												
Bahrain	210.2	145.4	-31	17.0	21.8	28	13.0	71.4	449	3.9	0.6	-83

Record 1 continued	Trade			Foreign Direct Investment						Official Development Aid*		
	Total trade in % GDP		% change	Outward FDI stock in % GDP		% change	Inward FDI Stock in % GDP		% change	Aid in % GNI		% change
Country	1990	2000	1990-2000	1990	2000	1990-2000	1990	2000	1990-2000	1990	2000	1990-2000
Israel & Occupied Territories	80.1	86.9	9	2.2	8.5	286	5.6	19.4	246	2.7	0.8	-72
Kuwait	103.0	88.4	-14	19.9	3.8	-81	0.1	1.4	1,300	0.0	0.0	-71
Qatar					1.1		1.0	13.3	1,230	0.0		
United Arab Emirates	105.8			0.3	0.7	133	2.2	3.8	73	0.0		
North America												
High income countries												
Canada	52.2	*84.5*	*62*	14.7	32.4	120	19.6	28.8	47			
United States	20.6	*24.2*	*17*	7.5	13.2	76	6.9	12.4	80			
South Asia												
Low income countries												
Afghanistan							0.1	0.1	0			
Bangladesh	19.9	33.2	67		0.2		0.5	2.1	320	7.0	2.5	-64
Bhutan	60.5	89.5	48				0.6	0.7	17	16.5	10.7	-35
India	17.2	30.5	77	0.1	0.3	200	0.5	4.1	720	0.4	0.3	-27
Nepal	31.6	55.8	76				0.3	1.8	500	11.5	6.9	-41
Pakistan	38.9	34.6	-11	0.6	0.8	33	4.8	11.2	133	2.9	1.2	-59
Middle income countries												
Maldives	96.1	189.4	97				12.6	21.3	69	17.0	3.7	-78
Sri Lanka	67.2	90.2	34	0.1	0.5	400	8.5	15.0	76	9.3	1.7	-81
Sub-Saharan Africa												
Low income countries												
Angola	59.8	164.4	175				10.0	90.4	804	3.3	6.5	97
Benin	40.6	44.3	9	0.1	4.2	4,100	8.6	28.8	235	14.8	11.1	-25
Burkina Faso	38.4	40.4	5	0.1	1.1	1,000	1.4	6.8	386	12.0	15.5	29
Burundi	35.6	32.6	-9		0.3		2.7	6.9	156	23.6	13.8	-42
Cameroon	37.5	57.6	54	1.3	2.9	123	9.4	14.2	51	4.2	4.6	10
Central African Republic	42.4	29.1	-31	1.2	4.2	250	6.4	11.4	78	17.1	8.0	-53
Chad	42.4	48.6	15	2.7	8.1	200	16.6	30.5	84	18.1	9.4	-48
Comoros	51.4	57.5	12	0.4	0.8	100	6.8	12.1	78	18.2	9.2	-49
Congo, Dem. Rep.	58.7						5.8	10.5	81	10.5		
Congo, Rep.	99.5	120.4	21				20.3	26.6	31	9.4	1.5	-84
Côte d'Ivoire	58.8	85.3	45	0.3	7.4	2,367	9.0	36.6	307	7.5	4.1	-45
Equatorial Guinea	101.7			0.2	0.3	50	19.2	67.0	249	49.2	4.3	-91
Eritrea		101.8						23.3			25.3	
Ethiopia	20.3	46.1	127		6.8		1.8	14.7	717	15.0	10.9	-27
Gambia	131.5	108.9	-17	6.9	10.4	51	49.4	51.2	4	34.0	11.8	-65
Ghana	42.7	118.8	178		6.9		5.4	24.2	348	9.7	12.1	24
Guinea	61.5	57.3	-7		0.3		2.4	9.5	296	11.0	5.2	-53
Guinea-Bissau	47.0	90.0	92				3.3	31.6	858	55.1	39.6	-28
Kenya	57.0	62.1	9	1.2	2.2	83	8.8	9.6	9	14.7	5.0	-66
Lesotho	139.3	116.8	-16				25.0	271.6	986	13.9	3.6	-74
Liberia				36.0	172.5	379	194.9	264.9	36			
Madagascar	43.9	59.4	35		0.1		3.4	8.7	156	13.6	8.5	-38
Malawi	57.2	64.5	13		0.9		9.8	28.9	195	27.4	26.8	-2
Mali	50.9	65.4	29	0.9	5.9	556	1.6	20.8	1,200	20.0	15.9	-21
Mauritania	106.4	97.9	-8	0.3	0.3	0	5.6	11.5	105	22.0	23.3	6
Mozambique	44.2	54.5	23				1.7	29.1	1,612	43.2	24.9	-42

Record 1 continued	Trade			Foreign Direct Investment						Official Development Aid*		
	Total trade in % GDP		% change	Outward FDI stock in % GDP		% change	Inward FDI Stock in % GDP		% change	Aid in % GNI		% change
Country	1990	2000	1990-2000	1990	2000	1990-2000	1990	2000	1990-2000	1990	2000	1990-2000
Niger	37.0	38.6	4	2.2	8.5	286	11.5	23.8	107	16.4	11.7	-29
Nigeria	72.2	78.0	8	9.1	10.6	16	28.3	49.1	73	1.0	0.5	-48
Rwanda	19.7	32.4	64		0.2		8.2	14.1	72	11.3	18.1	60
Sao Tome & Principe	86.9	115.6	33				0.7	8.2	1,071			
Senegal	55.8	70.1	26	0.9	3.2	256	4.5	19.5	333	14.9	9.9	-34
Sierra Leone	49.1	50.7	3					2.6		7.9	29.6	276
Somalia	47.5									59.1		
Sudan		33.0					0.4	12.1	2,925	6.5	2.3	-64
Tanzania	50.1	37.9	-24				2.2	13.1	495	28.8	11.6	-60
Togo	78.8	85.4	8	1.0	11.5	1,050	16.5	43.1	161	16.3	5.8	-64
Uganda	26.6	35.9	35		4.3		0.1	20.3	20,200	15.8	13.3	-16
Zambia	72.5	76.4	5				30.0	79.9	166	16.0	28.5	78
Zimbabwe	45.7	61.0	34	1.0	3.3	230	1.4	14.7	950	4.0	2.5	-38
Middle income countries												
Botswana	105.5	*60.6*	*-43*	11.9	10.3	-13	34.8	36.3	4	4.0	0.6	-85
Cape Verde	56.4	85.0	51	0.4	1.0	150	1.1	28.9	2,527	31.7	17.2	-46
Gabon	76.9	71.8	-7	2.7	8.7	222	20.3	3.9	-81	2.5	0.3	-89
Mauritius	137.7	130.6	-5	0.1	3.0	2,900	6.2	15.5	150	3.4	0.5	-86
Namibia	102.4	*105.2*	*3*	92.6	34.9	-62	106.9	51.9	-51	4.7	4.4	-7
South Africa	43.0	55.1	28	13.4	25.7	92	8.2	34.5	321		0.4	
Swaziland	152.0	146.3	-4	4.5	6.1	36	39.9	29.2	-27	6.1	0.9	-86

	Trade			Official Development Aid		
	Total trade in % GDP		% change	Aid in % GNI		% change
Region	1990	2000	1990-2000	1990	2000	1990-2000
Low income	37.9	54.6	44.1	1.9	2.2	17.4
Middle income	39.9	57.6	44.6	0.7	0.4	-38.6
Low & middle income	39.5	57.2	44.6	1.1	0.8	-28.7
East Asia & Pacific	49.2	77.9	58.4	0.9	0.5	-37.6
Europe & Central Asia	47.0	81.5	73.5	0.2	1.0	390.5
Latin America & Caribbean	26.1	35.6	36.3	0.5	0.3	-37.5
Middle East & North Africa	67.1	65.1	-3.0	2.57	0.9	-66.5
South Asia	22.0	33.4	51.4	1.5	0.7	-51.0
Sub-Saharan Africa	52.7	59.8	13.5	6.4	4.1	-36.4
High income	39.9	*44.3*	11.1	0.0	0.0	0.0
World	**39.8**	***45.8***	**15.0**	**0.3**	**0.2**	**-32.1**

Trade and Official Development Aid: Where data for a particular year are not available, figures are taken from the year before or after as an estimate. These figures, and estimates based on them, are presented in italics.

FDI: Figures for FDI may change as newer data are acquired (data for 1990 may be different in different versions of the WIR).

* Official Development Aid includes both official development assistance and official aid.

** Data for Hong Kong and Macao are not included in this table.

*** FDI data is not supplied for Belgium and Luxembourg individually; figures for trade for Belgium and Luxembourg together are therefore estimates calculated by LSE and are not attributable to the World Bank.

Sources: World Development Indicators 2002, WDI Online, World Bank; UNCTAD, World Investment Report 2002: Transnational Corporations and Export Competitiveness, Annex table B.6. Inward and outward FDI stocks as % of GDP, by region and economy, pp 328-336 <http://r0.unctad.org/wir/pdfs/fullwir02/pp303-346.pdf>

Global stakeholders' views

Is each of the following currently being positive or negative for the future you want by 2020?

Please use a 5-point scale where:
1 means 'major negative influence'
3 means 'neutral / no net influence' and
5 means 'major positive influence'.

Source: 2020 Fund, Towards the Future We Want for our Children: Report of the first survey of the 2020 global stakeholder panel, available at http://www.2020fund.org/downloads/GSP_wave1.pdf

	Mean
International capital markets and currency trading	2.35
The trade of goods and services between nations	3.20
The global exchange of information, culture, and ideas	4.20
Privatization of state-owned enterprises and services	2.67
Official government-to-government aid (Official Development Assistance)	3.34
Development assistance delivered through international charities and non-governmental organizations (NGOs)	4.08
Cancellation of the foreign debt of the poorest countries (debt relief)	3.96
Philanthropy (financial donations to charities/NGOs) by charitable foundations and individuals	3.96
Direct foreign investment by multinational companies	3.09
Socially responsible behavior by companies	4.01
Ways in which international conflict and disagreements are resolved	3.33

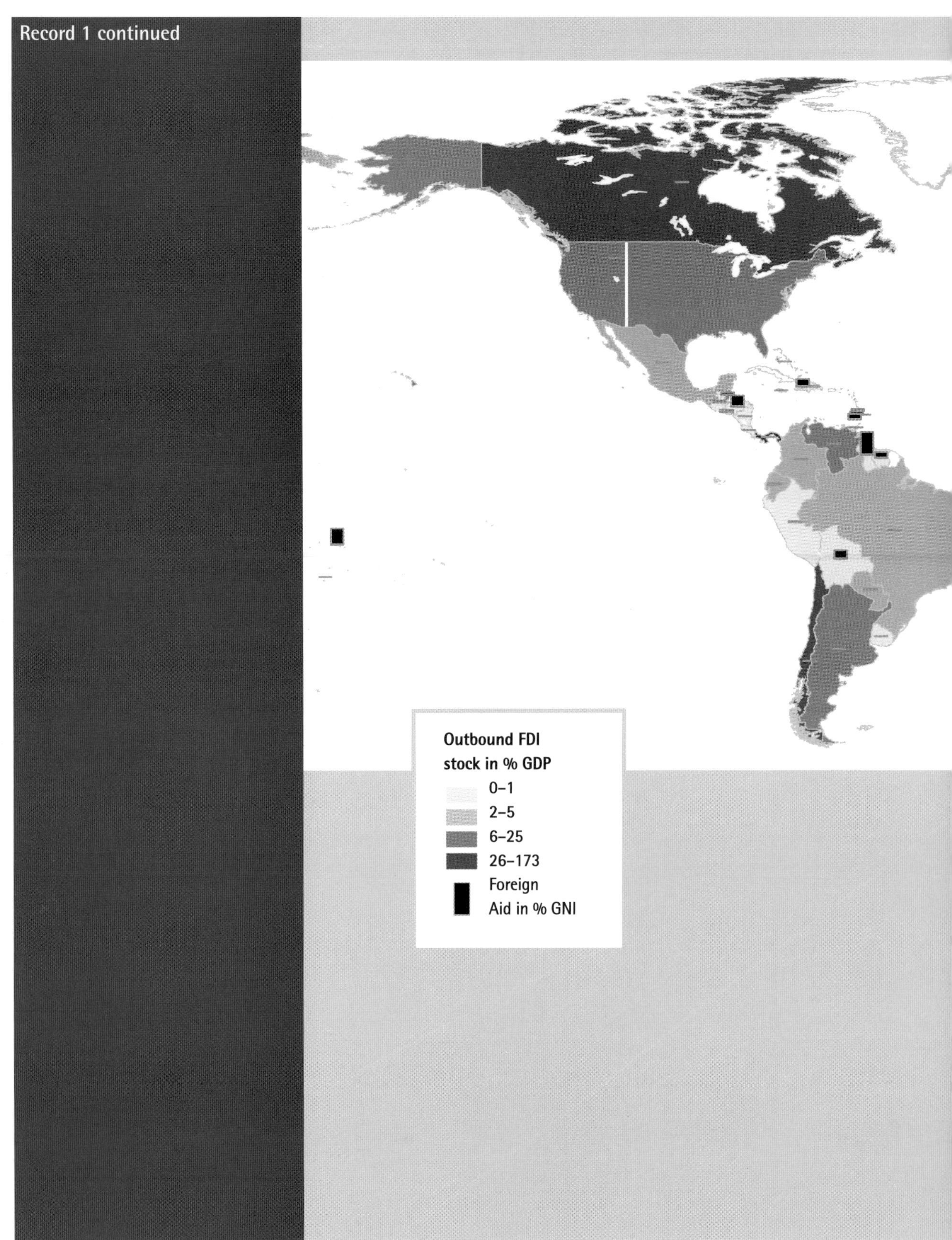
Outbound FDI
stock in % GDP
0–1
2–5
6–25
26–173
Foreign
Aid in % GNI

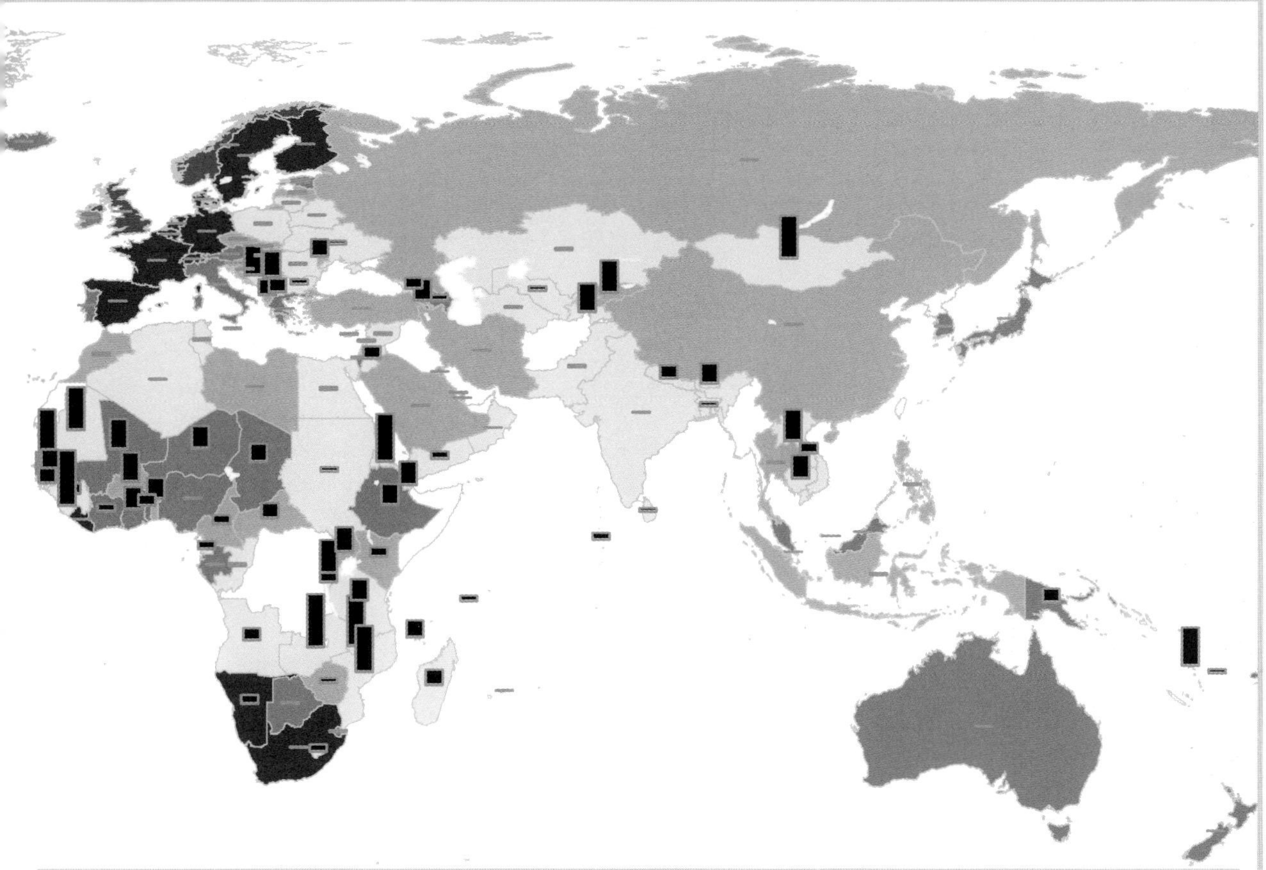

Central Europe

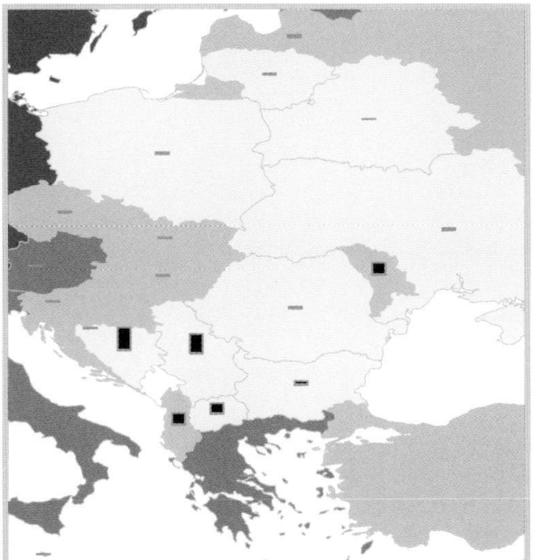

West Africa

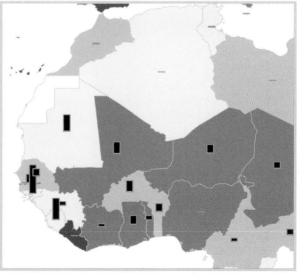

Record 2 Global trade

This network graph offers a simplified and consolidated view of trade flows among major world regions for 2000. It shows the unevenness of economic globalisation as measured by trade flows between three high-income industrial economies (US, Japan, and EU) and six low- or middle-income regions. The graph should be interpreted by reference to the thickness of the lines between regions (indicating volumes of trade) and the position of the regions (spatial centrality reflecting a central position in the trading system). Thus the US, European Union, Japan, and East Asia occupy the most central positions within this network, with the greatest amounts of trade flowing between the EU and the US. The US also trades significantly with Latin America & the Caribbean, but this region remains towards the outer edge of the network due to its comparatively limited trade with other regions.

Direction of flow (export region → import region)	Amount of trade in % world trade
East Asia & Pacific → USA	2.3
East Asia & Pacific → EU	1.7
East Asia & Pacific → Japan	1.7
East Asia & Pacific → Latin America & Caribbean	0.2
East Asia & Pacific → Middle East & North Africa	0.2
East Asia & Pacific → South Asia	0.2
East Asia & Pacific → Europe & Central Asia	0.2
Within East Asia & Pacific	1.6
EU → USA	3.4
EU → Europe & Central Asia	2.5
EU → East Asia & Pacific	1.0
EU → Latin America & Caribbean	0.6
EU → Middle East & North Africa	0.8
EU → Japan	0.6
EU → Sub-Saharan Africa	0.5
EU → South Asia	0.2
Within EU	22.3
Europe & Central Asia → EU	1.7
Europe & Central Asia → USA	0.1
Within Europe & Central Asia	1.3
Japan → USA	2.3
Japan → East Asia & Pacific	1.7
Japan → EU	1.2
Japan → Latin America & Caribbean	0.2
Latin America & Caribbean → USA	3.4
Latin America & Caribbean → EU	0.7
Within Latin America & Caribbean	0.8

Direction of flow (export region → import region)	Amount of trade in % world trade
Middle East & North Africa → EU	1.0
Middle East & North Africa → East Asia & Pacific	0.5
Middle East & North Africa → USA	0.4
Middle East & North Africa → Japan	0.3
Within Middle East & North Africa	0.1
South Asia → EU	0.5
South Asia → USA	0.5
Within South Asia	0.0
Sub-Saharan Africa → EU	0.4
Sub-Saharan Africa → USA	0.3
Within Sub-Saharan Africa	0.2
USA → EU	2.6
USA → Latin America & Caribbean	0.9
USA → East Asia & Pacific	1.1
USA → Japan	1.0
USA → Middle East & North Africa	0.2
USA → Europe & Central Asia	0.2

Record 2 continued

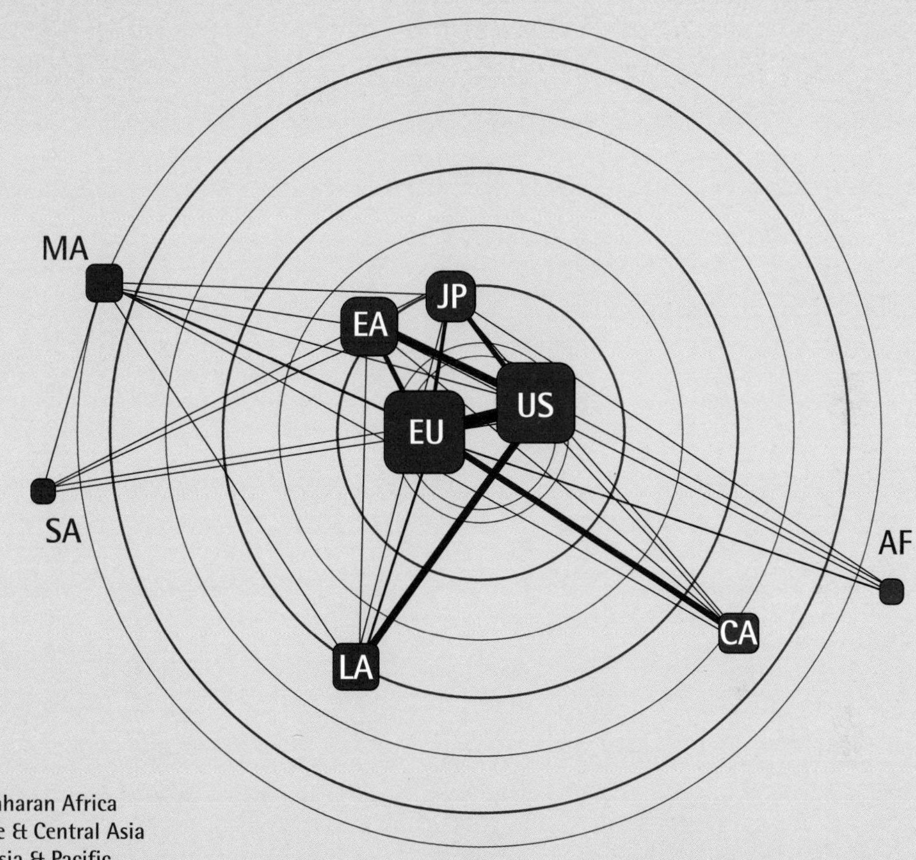

AF = Sub Saharan Africa
CA = Europe & Central Asia
EA = East Asia & Pacific
EU = European Union
JP = Japan
LA = Latin America & Carribean
MA = Middle East & North Africa
SA = South Asia
US = United States

European Union countries: Belgium, Denmark, Germany, Greece, Spain, France, Ireland, Italy, Luxembourg, Netherlands, Austria, Portugal, Finland, Sweden, United Kingdom. All other regions represented in the map comprise the countries listed as in the first table of Record 1 as low or middle income for regions.

Source: World Bank, World Development Indicators 2002, Table 6.2: Direction and growth of merchandise trade.

Record 3 Transnationality of top 100 transnational corporations (TNCs)

This record suggests the importance of TNCs, and the globalised economy they create, as one major reference point for the development of global civil society—from the growing numbers and influence of highly mobile groups of managers and professionals working for TNCs to activists protesting against certain corporate practices and corporate cultures. The names and global headquarter countries for the 100 largest non-financial corporations are listed, alongside figures on their sizes and foreign shares of assets, sales, and employment for 2000. TNCs are listed in order of degree of transnationality, with the most transnational companies at the top, where higher index numbers (and lower rank numbers) indicate an overall greater extent of transnationality.

The map clearly shows that the 100 largest TNCs are mostly located in Europe and the US, and that, of those 100 TNCs, the most globalised in terms of foreign assets are located in the UK, France, Germany, the US, and Japan.

US$ billions and number of employees, 2000

Ranking by: Transnationality Index*			Assets			Sales			Employment			
	Corporation	Country	Foreign	Total	% Foreign	Foreign	Total	% Foreign	Foreign	Total	% Foreign	TNI (%)
1	Rio Tinto Plc	Australia/UK	19.4	19.4	100.0	9.7	10.0	97.0		34,399		98.2
2	Thomson	Canada	15.5	15.7	98.7	6.1	6.5	93.8	33,600	36,000	93.3	95.3
3	ABB	Switzerland	28.6	31.0	92.3	22.5	23.0	97.8	151,340	160,818	94.1	94.9
4	Nestlé	Switzerland	35.3	40.0	88.3	48.9	49.6	98.6	218,112	224,541	97.1	94.7
5	British American Tobacco	United Kindom	23.9	25.1	95.2	16.4	17.6	93.2	82,583	86,805	95.1	94.4
6	Electrolux	Sweden	8.8	9.5	92.6	13.1	13.6	96.3	78,969	87,128	90.6	93.2
7	Interbrew	Belgium	9.3	10.4	89.4	6.7	7.4	90.5	33,000	36,463	90.5	90.2
8	Anglo American	United Kingdom	26.0	30.6	85.0	18.1	20.6	87.9	230,000	249,000	92.4	88.4
9	Astrazeneca	United Kingdom	15.0	18.0	83.3	15.0	15.8	94.9	47,000	57,000	82.5	86.9
10	Philips Electronics	Netherlands	27.9	35.9	77.7	33.3	34.9	95.4	184,200	219,429	83.9	85.7
11	News Corporation	Australia	36.1	39.3	91.9	12.8	14.2	90.1	24,500	33,800	72.5	84.9
12	Akzo Nobel NV	Netherlands	8.6	10.9	78.9	11.9	12.6	94.4	55,600	68,400	81.3	84.9
13	Cadbury-Schweppes Plc	United Kindom	8.8	9.7	90.7	5.4	6.8	79.4	29,648	36,460	81.3	84.1
14	Royal Ahold	Netherlands	14.8	24.0	61.7	33.7	48.0	70.2		248,053		82.5
15	Vodafone	United Kingdom	221.2	222.3	99.5	7.4	11.7	63.2	24,000	29,465	81.5	81.4
16	Michelin	France	12.9	16.0	80.6	12.6	14.3	88.1	96,504	128,122	75.3	81.3
17	Danone Groupe SA	France	10.9	16.2	67.3	9.9	13.4	73.9	88,285	86,657	101.9	81.1
18	Roche Group	Switzerland	23.0	42.5	54.1	17.2	17.5	98.3	56,099	64,758	86.6	79.7
19	Diageo Plc	United Kingdom	26.0	37.6	69.1	15.9	18.5	85.9	59,587	72,474	82.2	79.1
20	L'Air Liquide Groupe	France	9.6	10.7	89.7	5.8	7.5	77.3	20,900	30,300	69.0	78.7
21	WPP Group	United Kingdom	12.1	13.4	90.3	3.7	4.5	82.2		51,195		78.5
22	Stora Enso OYS	Finland	14.7	19.8	74.2	11.3	12.1	93.4	26,697	41,785	63.9	77.3
23	Suez Lyonnaise des Eaux	France	38.5	43.5	88.5	24.1	32.2	74.8	117,280	173,200	67.7	77.1
24	BP	United Kingdom	57.5	75.2	76.5	105.6	148.1	71.3	88,300	107,200	82.4	76.7
25	Pearson	United Kingdom	9.6	13.1	73.3	4.6	5.8	79.3	18,817	24,688	76.2	76.2
26	Alcatel	France	24.5	39.5	62.0	25.3	29.5	85.8		131,598		72.8
27	Coca-Cola	United States	16.6	20.8	79.8	12.7	20.5	62.0	28,200	37,000	76.2	72.7
28	Volvo	Sweden	12.1	21.1	57.3	16.2	17.5	92.6	47,565	72,031	66.0	72.2
29	Alcan	Canada	9.0	18.4	48.9	8.5	9.2	92.4	26,000	37,000	70.3	70.5
30	ExxonMobil	United States	101.7	149.0	68.3	143.0	206.1	69.4	64,000	97,900	65.4	67.7
31	Bayer	Germany	18.2	31.4	58.0	20.3	29.2	69.5	64,100	120,400	53.2	60.2
32	Bridgestone	Japan	9.8	18.9	51.9	10.9	18.6	58.6	89,754	102,615	87.5	65.9
33	Compagnie De Saint-Gobain	France	14.5	29.2	49.7	19.8	26.8	73.9	125,130	171,125	73.1	65.6

Record 3 continued

Ranking by: TNI*			US$ billions and number of employees, 2000									
			Assets			Sales			Employment			
	Corporation	Country	Foreign	Total	% Foreign	Foreign	Total	% Foreign	Foreign	Total	% Foreign	TNI (%)
34	Carnival	United States	9.2	9.8	93.9	0.6	3.8	15.8	27,000	32,000	84.4	64.7
35	Norsk Hydro Asa	Norway	9.4	22.2	42.3	16.1	17.7	91.0	21,901	38,166	57.4	63.5
36	Cable & Wireless	United Kingdom	10.6	34.3	30.9	10.3	14.7	70.1	48,833	54,919	88.9	63.2
37	BASF	Germany	23.2	36.2	64.1	26.3	33.7	78.0	48,917	103,273	47.4	63.2
38	Ericsson	Sweden	12.6	26.4	47.7	23.3	29.8	78.2	62,698	105,129	59.6	61.9
39	McDonald's	United States	12.5	21.7	57.6	8.4	14.2	59.2	250,000	364,000	68.7	61.8
40	Cemex	Mexico	10.9	15.8	69.0	3.0	5.6	53.6	15,448	25,884	59.7	60.9
41	Carrefour	France	17.1	24.1	71.0	28.7	60.3	47.6	209,542	330,247	63.5	60.7
42	Vivendi Universal	France	93.3	141.9	65.8	19.4	39.4	49.2	210,084	327,380	64.2	59.7
43	Honda Motor	Japan	25.6	46.1	55.5	41.9	57.5	72.9	56,200	112,400	50.0	59.5
44	Volkswagen	Germany	42.7	75.9	56.3	57.8	79.6	72.6	160,274	324,402	49.4	59.4
45	Robert Bosch	Germany	11.1	22.8	48.7	21.1	29.4	71.8	108,761	198,666	54.7	58.4
46	Royal Dutch/Shell	Netherlands/ United Kindom	74.8	122.5	61.1	81.1	149.1	54.4	54,337	95,365	57.0	57.5
47	Fiat	Italy	52.8	95.8	55.1	35.9	53.6	67.0	112,224	223,953	50.1	57.4
48	Sony	Japan	30.2	68.1	44.3	42.8	63.7	67.2	109,080	181,800	60.0	57.2
49	Unilever	United Kingdom/ Netherlands	20.4	52.6	38.8	26.1	44.3	58.9	215,000	295,000	72.9	56.8
50	AES	United States	13.7	31.0	44.2	4.2	6.7	62.7		26,606		56.5
51	BMW AG	Germany	31.2	45.9	68.0	26.1	34.6	75.4	23,759	93,624	25.4	56.3
52	Hutchison Whampoa Ltd.	Hong Kong, China	41.9	56.6	74.0	2.8	7.3	38.4	27,165	49,570	54.8	55.9
53	GlaxoSmithKline	United Kindom	12.0	27.4	43.8	18.5	27.0	68.5	58,000	107,517	53.9	55.4
54	Renault	France	7.9	19.7	40.1	24.1	37.4	64.4	98,000	166,114	59.0	54.6
55	Telefónica	Spain	56.0	87.1	64.3	12.9	26.3	49.0	71,292	148,707	47.9	53.8
56	Aventis	France	19.3	38.1	50.7	14.1	20.9	67.5	44,477	102,489	43.4	53.7
57	IBM	United States	43.1	88.3	48.8	51.2	88.4	57.9	170,000	316,303	53.7	53.5
58	Hewlett-Packard	United States		34.0		27.5	48.9	56.2		87,944		53.4
59	Pfizer	United States	19.1	33.5	57.0	10.0	29.4	34.0	56,000	90,000	62.2	51.1
60	Procter & Gamble	United States	17.0	34.2	49.7	19.9	40.0	49.8				48.3
61	Dow Chemical	United States	15.5	36.0	43.1	16.7	29.5	56.6	24,000	53,289	45.0	48.3
62	TotalFinaElf	France	33.1	81.7	40.5	82.5	105.8	78.0	30,020	123,303	24.3	47.6
63	LG Electronics	Korea, Rep.	8.8	17.7	49.7	9.3	18.6	50.0	20,072	46,912	42.8	47.5
64	ChevronTexaco	United States	42.6	77.6	54.9	65.0	117.1	55.5	21,693	69,265	31.3	47.2
65	Usinor	France	8.5	14.3	59.4	5.2	14.8	35.1	24,180	60,521	40.0	44.9
66	Nissan Motor	Japan	23.3	51.6	45.2	28.7	48.7	58.9	39,698	133,833	29.7	44.6
67	Conoco	United States	8.3	15.6	53.2	10.6	31.9	33.2	8,280	17,579	47.1	44.5
68	Peugeot	France	16.3	50.0	32.6	28.5	43.0	66.3	54,500	172,400	31.6	44.2
69	Motorola	United States	14.7	42.3	34.8	21.8	37.6	58.0	58,000	147,000	39.5	44.1
70	Johnson & Johnson	United States	14.4	34.2	42.1	12.1	29.8	40.6	49,338	101,901	48.4	43.7
71	Siemens	Germany		75.2		31.3	71.4	43.8		448,000		41.2
72	Canon	Japan	11.7	24.6	47.6	5.0	24.2	20.7	47,177	86,673	54.4	40.9
73	General Electric	United States	159.2	437.0	36.4	49.5	129.9	38.1	145,000	313,000	46.3	40.3
74	Eni	Italy	20.8	45.7	45.5	19.3	44.6	43.3	21,279	69,969	30.4	39.7
75	Nissho Iwai	Japan	10.7	29.1	36.8	19.5	52.2	37.4	1,951	4,313	45.2	39.7
76	Petróleos de Venezuela	Venezuela	8.0	57.1	14.0	49.8	53.2	93.6	5,458	46,920	11.6	39.7
77	E.On	Germany		115.0		41.8	86.9	48.1	83,338	186,788	44.6	39.4

Record 3 continued

Ranking by: TNI* Corporation	Country	Assets: Foreign	Assets: Total	Assets: % Foreign	Sales: Foreign	Sales: Total	Sales: % Foreign	Employment: Foreign	Employment: Total	Employment: % Foreign	TNI (%)
		US$ billions and number of employees, 2000									
78 Matsushita Industrial Co. Ltd.	Japan	13.7	72.5	18.9	34.0	68.9	49.3	143,773	290,448	49.5	39.3
79 Texas Utilities Company	United States	19.2	43.4	44.2	7.8	22.0	35.5	4,677	16,540	28.3	35.9
80 Toyota Motor	Japan	56.0	154.0	36.4	62.2	125.6	49.5		210,709		35.1
81 Merck & Co.	United States	11.6	40.2	28.9	7.3	40.4	18.1	26,200	49,300	53.1	33.4
82 Petronas	Malaysia	7.7	36.6	21.0	11.8	19.3	61.1	3,808	23,450	16.2	32.8
83 Fujitsu Ltd.	Japan	9.5	41.9	22.7	15.3	44.2	34.6	71,000	187,399	37.9	31.7
84 General Motors	United States	75.2	303.1	24.8	48.2	184.6	26.1	165,300	386,000	42.8	31.2
85 Ford Motor	United States	19.9	283.4	7.0	51.7	170.1	30.4	185,264	350,117	52.9	30.1
86 RWE Group	Germany	13.8	60.0	23.0	16.4	44.6	36.8	45,513	152,132	29.9	29.9
87 Repsol YPF	Spain	31.9	487.8	6.5	15.9	42.6	37.3	16,455	37,387	44.0	29.3
88 Marubeni Corporation	Japan	9.0	52.7	17.1	40.0	96.4	41.5		31,342		28.3
89 Mitsui & Co. Ltd.	Japan	19.1	64.1	29.8	45.9	128.2	35.8	5,659	39,344	14.4	26.7
90 Mitsubishi Motors	Japan	8.2	28.7	28.6	15.1	37.9	39.8	2,091	24,360	8.6	25.6
91 Wal-Mart Stores	United States	25.7	78.1	32.9	32.1	191.3	16.8	300,000	1,300,000	23.1	24.3
92 Sumitomo	Japan	11.7	39.3	29.8	10.1	80.0	12.6	9,153	30,715	29.8	24.1
93 DaimlerChrysler	United States		187.1		48.7	152.4	32.0	83,464	416,501	20.0	24.0
94 Philip Morris	United States	7.4	79.1	9.4	32.1	63.3	50.7		178,000		22.4
95 Hitachi	Japan	14.7	92.8	15.8	22.1	75.5	29.3	67,819	337,911	20.1	21.7
96 Deutsche Post	Germany	13.5	139.4	9.7	9.0	30.7	29.3	51,613	278,705		19.1
97 Japan Tobacco	Japan	10.0	29.2	34.2	3.8	41.2	9.2		41,703		18.7
98 Itochu	Japan	9.9	41.7	23.7	18.7	97.9	19.1		38,867		15.2
99 SBC Communications	United States	14.3	98.7	14.5	6.9	51.4	13.4		220,089		9.3
100 Verizon Communications	United States	14.5	164.7	8.8	2.0	63.4	3.2		263,552		4.0

*TNI = Transnationality Index (average of the ratios of foreign to total assets, sales and employment)

Where data for part of the TNI are unavailable, they are estimated to enable calculation of the TNI (such estimates of assets, sales or employment are not included in this table).

List includes non-financial TNCs only

Definitions of 'foreign' are not straightforward for some TNCs; see notes accompanying this information in World Investment Report for more details.

Source: UNCTAD, World Investment Report 2002: Transnational Corporations and Export Competitiveness, Table IV.1, pp.86-88 (http://www.unctad.org/templates/webflyer.asp?docid=2574&intItemID=2075&lang=1&mode=toc).

Record 3

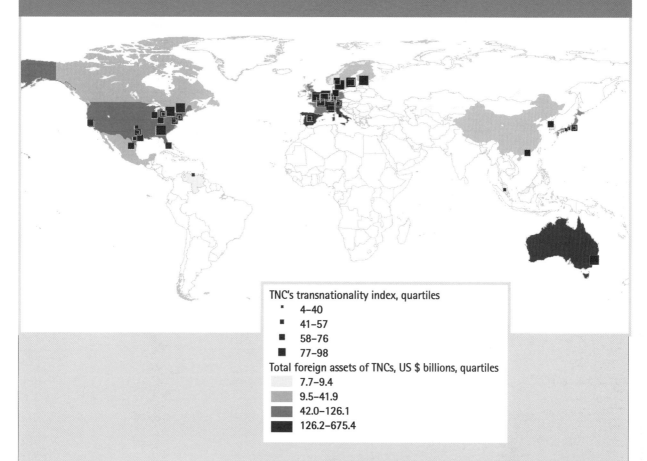

TNC's transnationality index, quartiles

- 4–40
- 41–57
- 58–76
- 77–98

Total foreign assets of TNCs, US $ billions, quartiles

- 7.7–9.4
- 9.5–41.9
- 42.0–126.1
- 126.2–675.4

Western Europe

North America

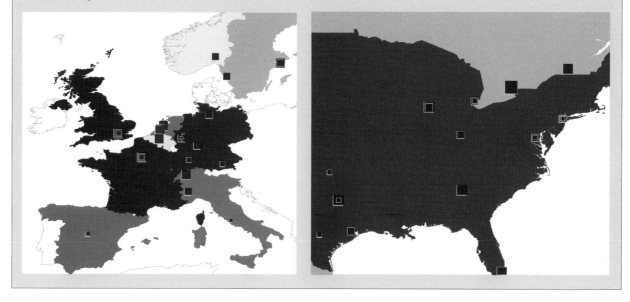

Record 4 Students abroad

Students are major transmitters of knowledge and ideas, and interlocutors among cultures. The growing practice of studying abroad may therefore be *one* a catalyst for the emergence and spread of global civil society.

This network map is constructed in the same way as Record 2, and shows the flows of students between regions for the academic year 2000–1. Information on direction of flow can be read from the tabulated data. The striking feature of the map is the number of students moving from Asia to North America and the EU. Data for this record are collected from hosting countries only (so figures should be interpreted as absolute minimum numbers), and none are available for some major countries known to send significant numbers of students abroad, including China, India, Brazil, Pakistan, Bangladesh, Nigeria, and Egypt.

Direction of flow (region of origin → host region)	Number of students
Africa → Asia	5,673
Africa → Europe*	140,303
Africa → North America	37,841
Africa → Oceania	3,214
Africa → South America	7
Within Africa	22,367
Asia → Africa	2,820
Asia → Europe*	231,088
Asia → North America	308,973
Asia → Oceania	73,422
Asia → South America	139
Within Asia	109,930
Europe → Africa	2,238
Europe → Asia	10,480
Europe → North America	79,386
Europe → Oceania	11,933
Europe → South America	439
Within Europe*	469,697

Direction of flow (region of origin → host region)	Number of students
North America → Africa	262
North America → Asia	2,820
North America → Europe*	40,200
North America → Oceania	4,968
North America → South America	968
Within North America	70,751
Oceania → Africa	102
Oceania → Asia	789
Oceania → Europe*	2,938
Oceania → North America	4,535
Oceania → South America	34
Within Oceania	7,225
South America → Africa	71
South America → Asia	874
South America → Europe*	23,362
South America → North America	31,877
South America → Oceania	906
Within South America	6,588

* *UIS estimate*

Source: UNESCO Institute for Statistics

Record 4 continued

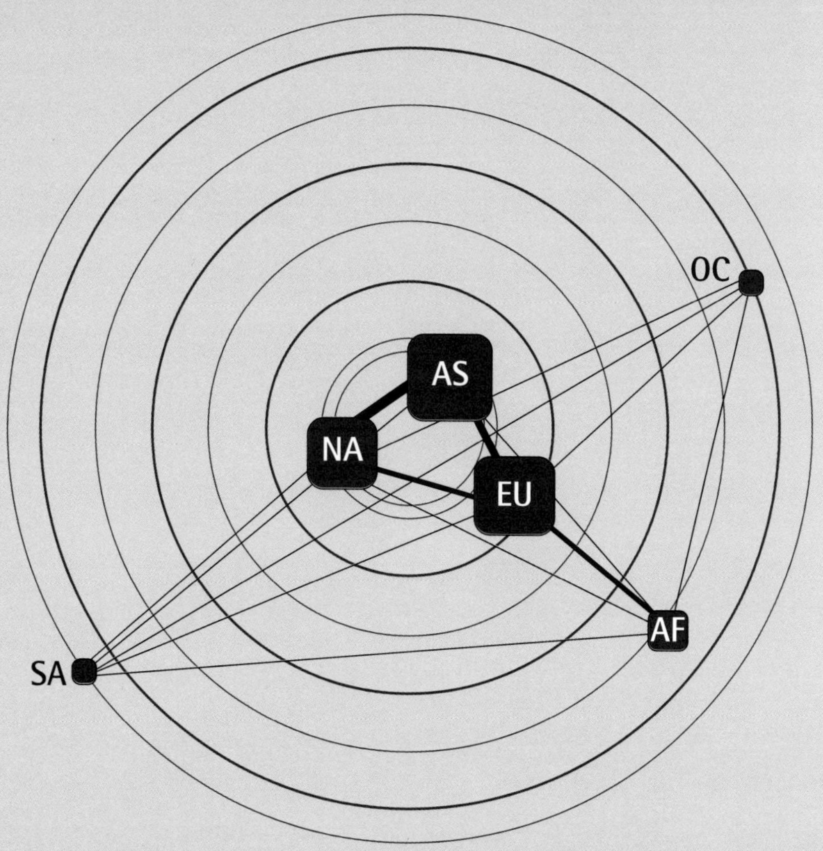

AF = Africa
AS = Asia
EU = Europe
NA = North America
OC = Oceania
SA = South America

Countries included

Africa
Djibouti
Lesotho
Morocco
Rwanda
Tanzania
Tunisia

Asia
Brunei
Cambodia
Georgia
Indonesia
Iran
Japan
Kazakhstan
Korea, Rep.
Laos
Lebanon
Macao
Malaysia
Mongolia
Palestine
Philippines
Qatar
Tajikisatn
Thailand
Turkey
Vietnam

Europe
Albania
Belarus
Belgium
Bulgaria
Croatia
Cyprus
Czech Republic
Denmark
Estonia
Finland
France
Germany
Hungary
Ireland
Italy
Latvia
Lithuania
Macedonia
Moldova
Netherlands
Norway
poland
Romania
Russian Federation
Serbia &
Montenegro
Slovakia
Spain
Switzerland
United Kingdom

North America
Barbados
Cayman Islands
Costa Rica
Cuba
El Salvador
Mexico
Trinidad & Tobago
United States

Oceania
Australia
New Zealand

South America
Argentina
Chile
Uruguay

NB excludes some 72,224 students whose region of origin is not specified in UNESCO records
Source: UNESCO Institute for Statistics

Record 5 Air travel and international tourism

Air travel facilitates global activism and creates economic as well as social ties; international tourism is certainly a measure of globalisation; it can be a point of contact between people from different regions and cultures. The table contains data on air transport and international tourism for 1990 and 2000, including the percentage change for this time period. The map presents per capita air travel figures for 2000 by country, and the inset details relative levels of in-bound and out-bound tourism for European countries. Obviously, any possible decline in air travel after 11 September 2001 is not recorded here.

	Air transport					International tourism									
	Passengers carried					Inbound tourists					Outbound tourists				
	1990		2000			1990		2000			1990		2000		
Country	Total (thousands)	Per capita	Total (thousands)	Per capita	% change in total 1990–2000	Total (thousands)	Per capita	Total (thousands)	Per capita	% change in total 1990–2000	Total (thousands)	Per capita	Total (thousands)	Per capita	% change in total 1990–2000
East Asia & Pacific															
Low income economies															
Cambodia						17	0.00	466	0.04	2,641			*49*	*0.00*	
Indonesia	9,223	0.05	9,485	0.04	17	2,178	0.01	5,064	0.02	45	688	0.00			
Korea, Dem. Rep.	223	0.01	86	0.00	-61	115	0.01								
Laos	115	0.03	211	0.04	83	14	0.00	300	0.06	2,043					
Mongolia	616	0.28	254	0.10	-59	147	0.07	158	0.06	7					
Myanmar	319	0.01	600	0.01	88	21	0.00	208	0.00	890					
Papua New Guinea	931	0.25	1,129	0.23	21	41	0.01	58	0.01	41	66	0.02	106	0.02	61
Solomon Islands	69	0.22	75	0.17	9	9	0.03	*21*	*0.05*	133					
Vietnam	89	0.00	2,881	0.04	3,137	250	0.00	2,140	0.03	756					
Middle income economies															
China	16,596	0.01	61,892	0.05	273	10,484	0.01	31,229	0.02	198	*2,134*	*0.00*	10,473	0.01	391
Fiji	433	0.60	603	0.74	39	279	0.39	294	0.36	5	61	0.08	*89*	*0.11*	*46*
Malaysia	10,242	0.57	16,561	0.75	62	7,446	0.42	10,222	0.46	37	14,920	0.84	*26,067*	*1.17*	*75*
Philippines	5,639	0.09	5,444	0.07	-3	1,025	0.02	*2171*	*0.03*	*112*	1,137	0.02	*1,755*	*0.02*	*54*
Samoa			169	1.06		48	0.30	88	0.55	83					
Thailand	8,201	0.15	17,392	0.28	112	5,299	0.10	9,509	0.15	79	883	[illegible]	[illegible]	0.03	116
Tonga	35	0.35	53	0.53	53	21	0.21	35	0.35	67					
Vanuatu	19	0.12	102	0.52	449	35	0.23	57	0.29	63	6	0.04			
High income economies															
Australia	17,553	1.04	32,223	1.68	84	2,215	0.13	4,946	0.26	123	2,170	0.13	*3,210*	*0.17*	*48*
Brunei	307	1.19	864	2.63	181	377	1.47				*246*	*0.96*			
Korea, Rep.	15,685	0.37	34,331	0.73	119	2,959	0.07	5,322	0.11	80	1,561	0.04	5,508	0.12	253
Japan	76,224	0.62	108,413	0.85	42	3,236	0.03	4,757	0.04	47	10,997	0.09	*16,358*	*0.13*	*49*
New Zealand	5,866	1.75	9,888	2.62	69	976	0.29	1,787	0.47	83	717	0.21	*1,185*	*0.31*	*65*
Singapore	7,046	2.34	16,704	4.16	137	4,842	1.61	*6,258*	*1.56*	*29*	1,237	0.41	*3,971*	*0.99*	*221*
Europe & Central Asia															
Low income economies															
Armenia			298	0.08				30	0.01						
Azerbaijan			546	0.07				681	0.08				*1,204*	*0.15*	
Georgia			118	0.02				*384*	*0.07*				*373*	*0.07*	
Kyrgyztan			243	0.05				*69*	*0.01*						

Record 5 continued	Air transport					International tourism									
	Passengers carried					Inbound tourists					Outbound tourists				
	1990		2000			1990		2000			1990		2000		
Country	Total (thousands)	Per capita	Total (thousands)	Per capita	% change in total 1990–2000	Total (thousands)	Per capita	Total (thousands)	Per capita	% change in total 1990–2000	Total (thousands)	Per capita	Total (thousands)	Per capita	% change in total 1990–2000
Moldova			135	0.03				17	0.00		*49*	*0.01*			
Tajikistan			156	0.03											
Ukraine			963	0.02				*4,232*	*0.09*				*7,399*	*0.15*	
Uzbekistan			1,656	0.07											
Middle income economies															
Albania			149	0.05		30	0.01	*39*	*0.01*	*30*					
Belarus			211	0.02											
Bosnia & Herzegovina			69	0.02				110	0.03						
Bulgaria	1,907	0.22	515	0.06	-73	1,586	0.18	2,785	0.35	76	2,395	0.27			
Croatia	113	0.03	929	0.20	720	7,049	1.56	5,831	1.25	-17					
Czech Republic	1,096	0.11	2,228	0.22	103	7,278	0.71	5,700	0.55	-22	3,510	0.34	*39,977*	*3.89*	*1,039*
Estonia			278	0.20				1,100	0.79				*1,780*	*1.28*	
Hungary	1,363	0.13	2,062	0.21	51	20,510	1.98	15,571	1.56	-24	13,596	1.31	*10,622*	*1.07*	*-22*
Kazakhstan			461	0.03											
Latvia			224	0.09				*490*	*0.20*				*2,256*	*0.93*	
Lithuania			284	0.08				1,226	0.33				*3,482*	*0.94*	
Macedonia			611	0.30				224	0.11						
Poland	1,501	0.04	2,373	0.06	58	3,400	0.09	17,400	0.45	412	22,131	0.58	*55,097*	*1.43*	*149*
Romania	1,322	0.06	1,186	0.05	-10	3,009	0.13	3,274	0.15	9	11,247	0.48	*6,274*	*0.28*	*-44*
Russian Federation	128,761	0.87	17,688	0.12	-86			21,169	0.15		*4,150*	*0.03*	18,371	0.13	343
Serbia & Montenegro	3,668	0.36				1,186	0.12	*152*	*0.01*	*-87*					
Slovakia			116	0.02		822	0.16	1,053	0.20	28	*188*	*0.04*	*343*	*0.06*	*82*
Slovenia			628	0.32		650	0.34	1,090	0.55	68					
Turkey	4,337	0.08	11,513	0.17	165	4,799	0.09	9,587	0.14	100	2,917	0.05	*4,758*	*0.07*	*63*
Turkmenistan			1,284	0.27											
High income economies															
Austria	2,532	0.33	7,263	0.90	187	19,011	2.46	17,982	2.23	-5	8,527	1.10	*3,954*	*0.49*	*-54*
Belgium	3,133	0.31	10,738	1.05	243	5,147	0.52	6,457	0.63	25	3,835	0.38			
Cyprus	814	1.19	1,376	1.76	69	1,561	2.29	2,686	3.43	72	228	0.33	*470*	*0.60*	*106*
Denmark	4,840	0.94	5,923	1.11	22	1,838	0.36	2,088	0.39	14	3,929	0.76	*4,841*	*0.91*	*23*
Finland	4,450	0.89	6,416	1.24	44	1,572	0.32	2,700	0.52	72	1,169	0.23	*5,314*	*1.03*	*355*
France	35,964	0.63	51,927	0.88	44	52,497	0.93	75,500	1.27	44	19,430	0.34	*16,709*	*0.28*	*-14*
Germany	22,147	0.28	59,362	0.72	168	17,045	0.21	18,983	0.23	11	56,261	0.71	*73,400*	*0.89*	*30*
Greece	6,135	0.60	7,099	0.67	16	8,873	0.87	12,500	1.18	41	1,651	0.16			
Iceland	760	2.98	1,426	5.11	88	142	0.56	303	1.09	113	*142*	*0.56*	*257*	*0.92*	*81*
Ireland	4,812	1.37	14,014	3.69	191	3,666	1.04	6,728	1.77	84	1,798	0.51	*3,576*	*0.94*	*99*
Italy	19,750	0.35	30,586	0.53	55	26,679	0.47	41,182	0.72	54	16,152	0.28	*18,962*	*0.33*	*17*
Luxembourg	409	1.07	871	1.99	113	820	2.15	807	1.85	-2					
Netherlands	8,559	0.57	20,794	1.31	143	5,795	0.39	10,200	0.64	76	9,000	0.60	*14,180*	*0.89*	*58*
Norway	8,929	2.11	15,157	3.39	70	1,955	0.46	*4,481*	*1.00*	*129*	2,667	0.63			
Portugal	3,505	0.35	6,563	0.66	87	8,020	0.81	12,037	1.20	50	2,268	0.23			

Record 5 continued

Country	Air transport: Passengers carried 1990 Total (thousands)	1990 Per capita	2000 Total (thousands)	2000 Per capita	% change in total 1990–2000	International tourism: Inbound tourists 1990 Total (thousands)	1990 Per capita	2000 Total (thousands)	2000 Per capita	% change in total 1990–2000	Outbound tourists 1990 Total (thousands)	1990 Per capita	2000 Total (thousands)	2000 Per capita	% change in total 1990–2000
Spain	21,652	0.55	39,559	0.99	83	34,085	0.87	48,201	1.21	41	10,698	0.27			
Sweden	11,403	1.33	13,354	1.51	17	1,900	0.22	2,746	0.31	45	6,232	0.73	*10,500*	*1.19*	*68*
Switzerland	8,603	1.26	17,216	2.40	100	13,200	1.93	11,400	1.59	-14	9,627	1.41	*12,009*	*1.67*	*25*
United Kingdom	47,114	0.82	70,361	1.18	49	18,013	0.31	25,191	0.42	40	31,150	0.54	*53,881*	*0.91*	*73*
Latin America & Caribbean															
Low income countries															
Haiti	0	0.00				144	0.02	*143*	*0.02*	*-1*					
Nicaragua	130	0.03	61	0.01	-53	106	0.03	486	0.10	358	173	0.05	*452*	*0.09*	*161*
Middle income countries															
Argentina	5,369	0.17	9,262	0.25	72	1,930	0.06	2,991	0.08	55	2,398	0.07	*4,786*	*0.13*	*100*
Barbados	0	0.00				432	1.68	556	2.08	29					
Belize						88	0.47	*181*	*0.80*	*106*					
Bolivia	1,238	0.19	1,757	0.21	42	254	0.04	*342*	*0.04*	*35*	242	0.04	196	0.02	-19
Brazil	19,150	0.13	31,845	0.19	66	1,091	0.01	5,313	0.03	387	1,188	0.01	*2,679*	*0.02*	*126*
Chile	1,364	0.10	5,175	0.34	280	943	0.07	1,742	0.11	85	768	0.06	*1,567*	*0.10*	*104*
Colombia	5,267	0.15	8,537	0.20	62	813	0.02	530	0.01	-35	781	0.02	*1,098*	*0.03*	*41*
Costa Rica	467	0.15	861	0.21	84	435	0.14	1,106	0.27	154	191	0.06	*353*	*0.09*	*85*
Cuba	1,138	0.11	1,007	0.09	-11	327	0.03	1,700	0.15	420	12	0.00	*56*	*0.01*	*367*
Dominican Republic	718	0.10	11	0.00	-98	1,305	0.18	2,977	0.36	128	*137*	*0.02*	*364*	*0.04*	*166*
Ecuador	763	0.07	1,181	0.09	55	362	0.04	615	0.05	70	181	0.02	*386*	*0.03*	*113*
El Salvador	525	0.10	1,960	0.31	273	194	0.04	795	0.13	310	525	0.10	*787*	*0.13*	*50*
Guatemala	156	0.02				509	0.06	*823*	*0.07*	*62*	289	0.03			
Guyana	146	0.20	73	0.10	-50	64	0.09	*75*	*0.10*	*17*					
Honduras	610	0.13				202	0.04	408	0.06	102	196	0.04	*235*	*0.04*	*20*
Jamaica	1,004	0.42	1,918	0.74	91	989	0.42	1,323	0.51	34					
Mexico	14,341	0.17	21,001	0.21	46	17,176	0.21	20,643	0.21	20	7,357	0.09	11,081	0.11	51
Panama	266	0.11	1,117	0.39	320	214	0.09	479	0.17	124	151	0.06	*221*	*0.08*	*46*
Paraguay	273	0.06	266	0.05	-3	280	0.07	221	0.04	-21	*264*	*0.06*	*281*	*0.05*	*6*
Peru	1,816	0.08	2,125	0.08	17	317	0.01	1,027	0.04	224	329	0.02	781	0.03	137
St. Lucia						141	1.08	259	1.75	84					
Suriname	133	0.33	233	0.56	76	46	0.11	*57*	*0.14*	*24*	55	0.14			
Trinidad & Tobago	1,285	1.06	1,254	0.97	-2	195	0.16	*336*	*0.26*	*72*	254	0.21			
Uruguay	318	0.10	617	0.18	94	1,267	0.41	1,968	0.59	55			*778*	*0.23*	
Venezuela	6,847	0.35	4,295	0.18	-37	525	0.03	469	0.02	-11	309	0.02	*891*	*0.04*	*188*
High income countries															
Bahamas	1,090	4.27	1,827	6.01	68	1,562	6.13	*1,577*	*5.19*	*1*					
Middle East & North Africa															
Low income countries															
Yemen	671	0.06	844	0.05	26	52	0.00	73	0.00	40					
Middle income countries															
Algeria	3,748	0.15	2,995	0.10	-20	1,137	0.05	866	0.03	-24	3,828	0.15	*903*	*0.03*	*-76*
Djibouti	131	0.26				33	0.07								
Egypt	3,239	0.06	4,522	0.07	40	2,411	0.04	5,116	0.08	112	2,012	0.04	*2,886*	*0.04*	*43*

Record 5 continued

	Air transport					International tourism									
	Passengers carried					Inbound tourists					Outbound tourists				
	1990		2000			1990		2000			1990		2000		
Country	Total (thousands)	Per capita	Total (thousands)	Per capita	% change in total 1990–2000	Total (thousands)	Per capita	Total (thousands)	Per capita	% change in total 1990–2000	Total (thousands)	Per capita	Total (thousands)	Per capita	% change in total 1990–2000
Iran	5,633	0.10	8,830	0.13	57	154	0.00	1,700	0.02	1,004	788	0.01			
Iraq	702	0.04				748	0.04	78	0.00	-90	239	0.01			
Jordan	964	0.30	1,282	0.26	33	572	0.18	1,427	0.29	149	1,143	0.35	*1,560*	*0.32*	*36*
Lebanon	572	0.21	806	0.23	41			742	0.21						
Libya	1,803	0.42	609	0.12	-66	96	0.02	*40*	*0.01*	*-58*	425	0.10			
Malta	598	1.66	1,396	3.58	134	872	2.42	1,216	3.12	39	122	0.34	*179*	*0.46*	*47*
Morocco	1,580	0.06	3,671	0.12	132	4,024	0.16	4,113	0.14	2	1,202	0.05	*1,612*	*0.05*	*34*
Oman	853	0.48	2,120	0.84	149	149	0.08	*502*	*0.20*	*237*					
Saudi Arabia	10,312	0.67	12,567	0.62	22	2,209	0.14								
Syria	613	0.05	750	0.05	22	562	0.05	*916*	*0.06*	*63*	1,041	0.08			
Tunisia	1,313	0.16	1,908	0.20	45	3,204	0.39	5,057	0.53	58	1,727	0.21	*1,480*	*0.16*	*-14*
High income countries															
Bahrain	771	1.57	1,383	2.16	79	1,376	2.81	*1,991*	*3.11*	*45*	147	0.30			
Israel	2,004	0.44	4,073	0.67	103	1,063	0.24	2,400	0.40	126	883	0.20	*3,203*	*0.53*	*263*
Kuwait	966	0.45	2,123	1.11	120	15	0.01				*195*	*0.09*			
Qatar	771	1.70	2,673	4.73	247	136	0.30								
United Arab Emirates	1,686	0.84	6,871	2.64	308	633	0.31	*2,481*	*0.95*	*292*					
North America															
High income countries															
Canada	20,601	1.50	25,778	0.84	25	15,209	1.11	20,423	0.66	34	20,415	1.49	*18,368*	*0.60*	*-10*
United States	464,574	1.82	655,649	2.31	41	39,363	0.15	50,891	0.18	29	44,623	0.18	*58,386*	*0.21*	*31*
South Asia															
Low income countries															
Afghanistan	241	0.02	150	0.01	-38	8	0.00								
Bangladesh	1,044	0.01	1,331	0.01	28	115	0.00	200	0.00	74	388	0.00	*1103*	*0.01*	*184*
Bhutan	8	0.00	34	0.02	330	2	0.00	*7*	*0.00*	*250*					
India	10,862	0.01	17,339	0.02	60	1,707	0.00	2,641	0.00	55	2,281	0.00			
Nepal	679	0.04	643	0.03	-5	255	0.01	451	0.02	77	82	0.00			
Pakistan	5,180	0.05	6,252	0.04	21	424	0.00	543	0.00	28					
Middle income countries															
Maldives	9	0.04	289	0.99	2,969	195	0.90	467	1.60	139	21	0.10	*42*	*0.14*	*100*
Sri Lanka	892	0.05	1,756	0.09	97	298	0.02	400	0.02	34	297	0.02	524	0.03	76
Sub-Saharan Africa															
Low income countries															
Angola	452	0.05	235	0.02	-48	46	0.00	51	0.00	11					
Benin	76	0.02	77	0.01	1	110	0.02				*418*	*0.09*			
Burkina Faso	137	0.02	144	0.01	5	74	0.01	*218*	*0.02*	*195*					
Burundi	8	0.00				109	0.02	30	0.00	-72	24	0.00			
Cameroon	284	0.02	273	0.02	-4	89	0.01								
Central African Republic	130	0.04	77	0.02	-41	6	0.00	*10*	*0.00*	*67*					
Chad	93	0.02	77	0.01	-17	9	0.00	44	0.01	389	24	0.00			

Record 5 continued

	Air transport: Passengers carried					International tourism: Inbound tourists					International tourism: Outbound tourists				
	1990		2000			1990		2000			1990		2000		
Country	Total (thousands)	Per capita	Total (thousands)	Per capita	% change in total 1990–2000	Total (thousands)	Per capita	Total (thousands)	Per capita	% change in total 1990–2000	Total (thousands)	Per capita	Total (thousands)	Per capita	% change in total 1990–2000
Comoros	26	0.05				8	0.02	*24*	*0.03*	*200*					
Congo, Dem. Rep.	207	0.01				55	0.00								
Congo, Rep.	239	0.11	128	0.04	-47	33	0.01	26	0.01	-21					
Côte d'Ivoire	200	0.02	262	0.02	31	196	0.02				2	0.00			
Equatorial Guinea	14	0.04													
Eritrea								70	0.02						
Ethiopia	620	0.01	945	0.02	52	79	0.00	125	0.00	58	89	0.00			
Gambia						100	0.11	*96*	*0.07*	*-4*					
Ghana	188	0.01	314	0.02	67	146	0.01	*373*	*0.02*	*155*					
Guinea	41	0.01	61	0.01	49	*49*	*0.01*	33	0.00	-33					
Guinea-Bissau	21	0.02													
Kenya	794	0.03	1,557	0.05	96	814	0.03	*943*	*0.03*	*16*	210	0.01			
Lesotho	56	0.03	1	0.00	-98	171	0.10	*186*	*0.09*	*9*					
Liberia	34	0.02													
Madagascar	424	0.04	667	0.04	57	53	0.00	160	0.01	202	34	0.00			
Malawi	120	0.01	116	0.01	-4	130	0.01	228	0.02	75					
Mali			77	0.01		44	0.01	91	0.01	107					
Mauritania	223	0.11	185	0.07	-17			*24*	*0.01*						
Mozambique	280	0.02	260	0.01	-7										
Niger	76	0.01	77	0.01	1	21	0.00	50	0.00	138	18	0.00	*10*	*0.00*	*-44*
Nigeria	965	0.01	415	0.00	-57	190	0.00	813	0.01	328	56	0.00			
Rwanda	8	0.00				16	0.00								
Sao Tome & Principe	22	0.19	35	0.25	57	4	0.03								
Senegal	148	0.02	98	0.01	-34	246	0.03	*369*	*0.04*	*50*					
Sierra Leone	30	0.01	18	0.00	-39	98	0.02	10	0.00	-90					
Somalia	88	0.01				46	0.01								
Sudan	454	0.02	408	0.01	-10	33	0.00	50	0.00	52	*203*	*0.01*			
Tanzania	292	0.01	182	0.01	-38	153	0.01	459	0.01	200	301	0.01			
Togo	76	0.02	77	0.02	1	103	0.03	60	0.01	-42					
Uganda	116	0.01	187	0.01	61	69	0.00	151	0.01	119					
Zambia	407	0.05	89	0.01	-78	141	0.02	574	0.06	307					
Zimbabwe	601	0.06	606	0.05	1	605	0.06	1,868	0.15	209	200	0.02	*331*	*0.03*	*66*
Middle income countries															
Botswana	101	0.08	166	0.11	63	543	0.44	*843*	*0.55*	*55*	192	0.15			
Cape Verde	177	0.52	264	0.62	49	24	0.07	143	0.33	496					
Gabon	398	0.43	442	0.36	11	109	0.12	155	0.13	42	161	0.17			
Mauritius	520	0.49	949	0.82	83	292	0.28	656	0.57	125	89	0.08	*154*	*0.13*	*73*
Namibia	455	0.33	245	0.14	-46	*213*	*0.15*								
South Africa	5,365	0.15	8,000	0.18	49	1,029	0.03	6,001	0.14	483	616	0.02			
Swaziland	53	0.07	0	0.00	-99	263	0.34								

International tourism

Country	Inbound tourists: Total (thousands) 1990	Per capita 1990	Total (thousands) 2000	Per capita 2000	% change in total 1990–2000	Outbound tourists: Total (thousands) 2000	Per capita 2000	Total (thousands) 1990	Per capita 1990	% change in total 1990–2000
Low income	12,966	0.01	25,756	0.01	99			11,027	0.52	
Middle income	136,571	0.06	229,502	0.09	68	118,014	0.05	236,011	0.09	100
Low & middle income:										
East Asia & Pacific	30,457	0.02	62,659	0.03	106	23,210	0.01	45,404	0.03	96
Europe & Central Asia	59,439	0.12	97,311	0.21	64	87,991	0.18	176,460	0.37	101
Latin America & Caribbean	33,354	0.08	51,614	0.10	55	17,289	0.04	28,743	0.06	66
Middle East & North Africa	17,932	0.07	27,043	0.09	51	16,180	0.07	8,620	1.06	-47
South Asia	3,004	0.00	4,714	0.00	57	3,503	0.00	1,669	0.18	-52
Sub-Saharan Africa	7,052	0.02	17,455	0.03	148			495	0.16	
High income	308,084	0.41	412,769	0.51	34	274,192	0.37	331,292	0.35	21
World	461,483	0.09	701,855	0.12	52	458,115	0.09	644,804	0.11	41

Data on inbound and outbound tourists refer to numbers of arrivals and departures, not numbers of people.

Where data for a particular year are not available, figures are taken from the year before or after as an estimate. These figures, and estimates based on them, are presented in italics.

Per capita estimates (aggregate and individual country level) are calculated using UN population figures (International Monetary Fund – International Financial Statistics estimates for 1990 population of Tonga and Sao Tome & Principe).

Sources: World Bank, World Development Indicators 2002 (WDI-Online); Population Division of the Department of Economic and Social Affairs of the United Nations Secretariat, World Population Prospects: The 2000 Revision, www.un.org/esa/population/demobase; International Monetary Fund – International Financial Statistics

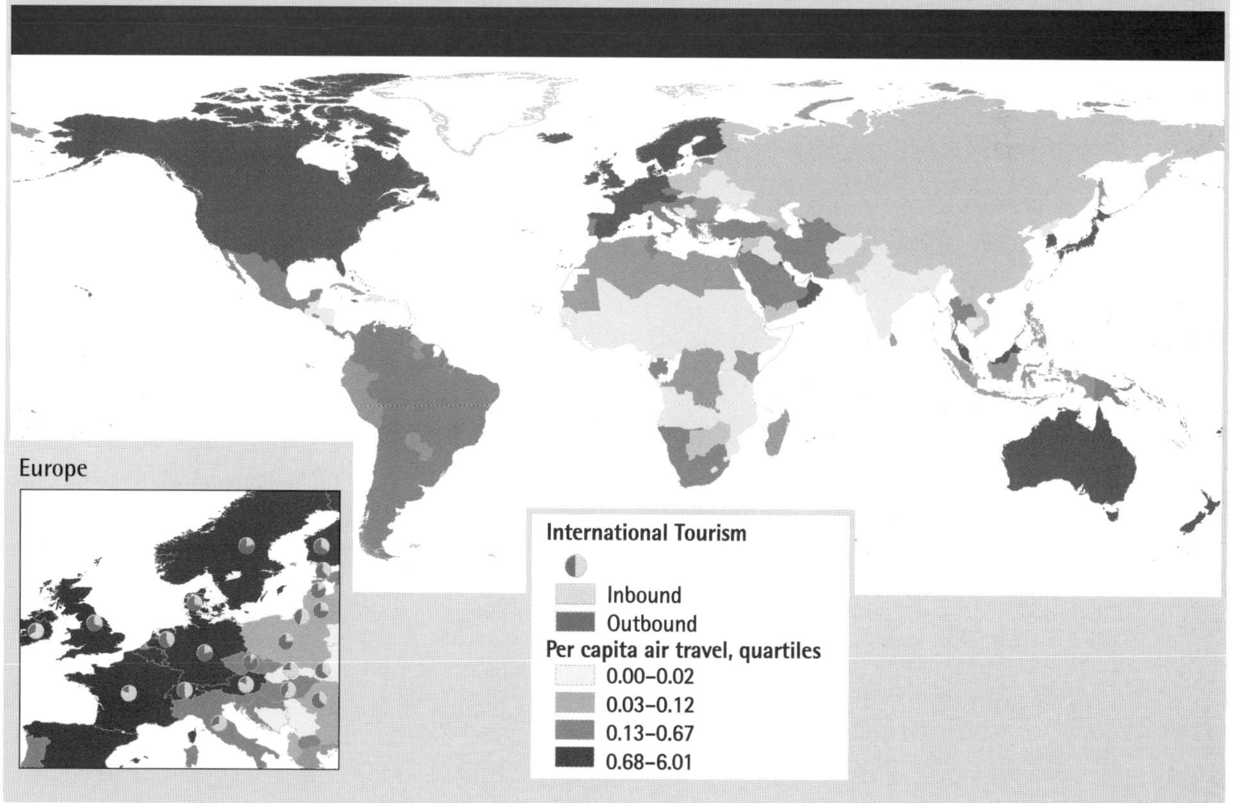

Record 6 Media and communication

This record shows daily newspaper circulation, the numbers of television sets, cable subscribers, main telephone lines, and mobile phones, and estimated Internet use for the latest available year and with a time comparison where feasible. Unfortunately the data do not give any information about the diversity of sources, and ownership, within each medium, but they do give an indication of people's exposure to media and their communication with each other across distances. The map shows clearly the extent to which popular Internet use tends to be concentrated within the higher-income countries.

figures are per thousand of population

	Daily newspapers			Television sets			Cable television subscribers			Main telephone lines			Cellular mobile telephone subscribers			Internet users
Country	1990	1999*	% change 1990–1999	1990	2000	% change 1990–2000	1995	2000	% change 1995–2000	1991	2001	% change 1991–2001	1995	2001	% change 1995–2001	2001 (Estimated)
East Asia & Pacific																
Low income economies																
Cambodia				8	8	-2				0	3	583	1	18	1,201	1
Indonesia	29	*23*	*-21*	61	149	143	*0*			7	37	417	1	31	2,675	19
Korea, Dem. Rep.	244			16	54	234	*0*			39						
Laos	3			6	10	61	*0*			2	10	473	0	5	1,720	2
Mongolia	73			66	65	0	3			33	51	56	*0*	81	*20,028*	17
Myanmar	17	*9*	*-50*	3	7	160	0			2	6	177	0	0	186	0
Papua New Guinea	13			2	17	595				9	12	37	*1*	*2*	*239*	10
Solomon Islands					185		*0*			15	17	16	1	3	363	5
Vietnam	8			39	23	-42	0			2	38	1818	0	16	5,144	13
Middle income economies																
China	42			155	293	89	28	61	115	7	141	1855	3	114	3,826	26
Fiji	37			15	113	660	0			61	110	79	3	98	3,408	18
Malaysia	110			148	168	13	0			99	199	101	50	314	528	273
Philippines	54			49	144	191	6	13	124	10	40	287	7	152	2,010	26
Samoa				39	61	58	1			26	58	127		*19*		0
Thailand	81			108	284	162	4	2	-30	28	98	246	23	123	446	58
Tonga					66		0				96		3	2	-36	28
Vanuatu				9	12	26	*0*			20	34	67	1	1	113	27
High income economies																
Australia	302			520	738	42	0	68		466	519	11	124	576	364	371
Brunei	39			241	640	165	0	*53*		150	233	55	126	397	214	101
Korea, Rep.	280			210	364	74	156			454	477	5	93	610	553	512
Japan	587			609	725	19	87			336	598	78	36	589	1,517	440
New Zealand	291	369	27	442	522	18	0	*4*	*970*	435	476	10	101	594	491	284
Singapore	282			341	304	-11	7	63	817	356	475	33	88	729	727	366
Europe & Central Asia																
Low income economies																
Armenia		8		202	244	21		1		158	139	-12	*0*	6	*6,253*	13
Azerbaijan				195	259	33		0		86	107	24	1	77	9,466	3
Georgia		8		201	474	135	*0*			102	173	69	*0*	59	*14,594*	5
Kyrgystan	7	27	298	18	49	170				75	76	1		5		30
Moldova		*153*		281	297	6	7	12	66	114	158	39	*0*	49	*24,476*	14

Record 6 continued

figures are per thousand of population

Country	Daily newspapers			Television sets			Cable television subscribers			Main telephone lines			Cellular mobile telephone subscribers			Internet users
	1990	1999*	% change 1990–1999	1990	2000	% change 1990–2000	1995	2000	% change 1995–2000	1991	2001	% change 1991–2001	1995	2001	% change 1995–2001	2001 (Estimated)
Tajikistan	47			189	326	73				47	36	-24		0		1
Ukraine	251	122	-51	328	456	39		52		141	400	183	0	45	14,997	12
Uzbekistan				181	276	52		3		70	66	-5	0	3	1,151	6
Middle income economies																
Albania	41			86	123	43				13	57	352	*1*	102	*16,853*	3
Belarus	286	*152*	*-47*	267	342	28		33		163	287	76	1	14	2,207	42
Bosnia & Herzegovina					111					*140*	111	*-21*	*0*	57	*14,266*	11
Bulgaria	466	116	-75	250	449	79		130		246	359	46	3	191	7,532	74
Croatia	49			215	293	36	11	38	246	186	*388*	*108*	7	401	5,314	57
Czech Republic	772				508		46	93	102	166	375	126	5	677	14,300	136
Estonia				344	591	72	13	90	623	212	372	75	21	481	2,245	317
Hungary	237	*465*	*96*	416	437	5	135	158	16	109	366	236	26	488	1,783	145
Kazakhstan				216	241	12				85	124	45	0	39	12,986	7
Latvia	75	145	94	370	789	113		77		244	310	27	6	281	4,655	73
Lithuania	215	34	-84	328	422	29	27	89	231	220	330	50	4	267	6,580	72
Macedonia	29	1597	5424	173	282	63				149	263	76	*1*	109	*21,753*	34
Poland	128	100	-22	265	400	51	70	93	31	93	295	216	2	260	13,584	98
Romania	271			194	381	96	57	158	175	105	183	73	0	172	42,987	45
Russian Federation				365			69		-100	150	246	64	1	38	6,298	30
Serbia & Montenegro	35			176	282	60				172	230	34	*1*	188	*13,306*	56
Slovakia	246	158	-36		407		74	140	88	144	288	100	2	397	17,165	125
Slovenia	152	171	13	275	368	34	111	161	46	229	402	75	14	762	5,462	302
Turkey	71			230	449	95	6	13	108	142	285	101	7	302	4,214	38
Turkmenistan		6		191	196	3				63	73	16		2		2
High income economies																
Austria	350			473	536	13	124	123	-1	429	469	9	48	808	1,594	320
Belgium	201			446	541	21	359	373	4	411	494	20	23	749	3,126	311
Cyprus	115	111	-3	177	179	1	0			446	572	28	69	413	499	197
Denmark	352	294	-17	535	807	51	228			573	726	27	158	740	369	542
Finland	558	451	-19	494	692	40	160			540	548	1	201	780	288	431
France	208			540	628	16	23			511	575	13	23	607	2,598	265
Germany	304	*305*	*0*	526	586	11	193			439	636	45	46	684	1,404	375
Greece	123	22	-82	193	488	153	*0*			408	530	30	26	753	2,785	132
Iceland	510	336	-34	316	509	61	*4*			522	671	29	115	829	619	687
Ireland	169			294	399	35	133			297	485	63	44	730	1,568	233
Italy	106			419	494	18	0			407	473	16	68	844	1,134	284
Luxembourg	374			359	589	64	324	281	-13	492	788	60	65	974	1,398	248
Netherlands	301			480	538	12	377	388	3	476	624	31	35	770	2,114	493
Norway	610	582	-5	422	669	58	155	184	18	514	722	40	225	827	268	597
Portugal	45			186	630	240	6	92	1483	273	430	57	34	780	2,167	244
Spain	89	105	18	388	591	52	10	12	16	341	441	29	24	671	2,683	187

Record 6 continued

Country	Daily newspapers 1990	1999*	% change 1990–1999	Television sets 1990	2000	% change 1990–2000	Cable television subscribers 1995	2000	% change 1995–2000	Main telephone lines 1991	2001	% change 1991–2001	Cellular mobile telephone subscribers 1995	2001	% change 1995–2001	Internet users 2001 (Estimated)
figures are per thousand of population																
Sweden	526	424	-19	466	574	23	213	199	-6	689	740	7	227	792	249	517
Switzerland	456	373	-18	397	548	38	330	358	9	596	719	21	63	725	1,045	308
United Kingdom	388			432	653	51	24	57	134	448	590	32	98	773	689	401
Latin America & Caribbean																
Low income countries																
Haiti	7			5	5	17				7	10	45		*11*		4
Nicaragua	47			65	69	6	23	11	-53	13	30	140	1	30	2,899	10
Middle income countries																
Argentina	123	37	-70	249			135			95	216	128	10	186	1,799	88
Barbados	116			265	310	17				302	462	53	18	198	1,019	56
Belize				143	183	28				112	142	27	7	159	2,103	73
Bolivia	61			113	119	5	3	10	185	30	60	101	1	87	6,621	18
Brazil	43	*43*	*0*	212	343	61	8	14	64	69	217	217	8	167	1,907	46
Chile	103			206	242	17	34	45	32	79	241	203	14	342	2,381	201
Colombia	57			118	282	140	3	14	299	74	170	130	7	76	969	27
Costa Rica	102			221	231	4	17	*19*	*15*	106	243	129	6	80	1,330	99
Cuba	78			206	250	22	0			31	51	63	0	1	261	11
Dominican Republic	32	28	-14	84			16			56	112	100	7	149	1,974	22
Ecuador	80	98	23	85	218	155	4			47	104	122	5	67	1,319	25
El Salvador	53	*28*	*-46*	92	201	119	*5*			25	93	272	2	125	5,109	8
Guatemala	22			53	61	16	18			22	65	193	3	97	3,134	17
Guyana	60	75	24	35	81	131				20	104	424	2	98	6,451	124
Honduras	41			72	96	32	8			18	47	162	*0*	36	*8,934*	6
Jamaica	64			136	194	43	55			56	192	246	18	262	1,349	37
Mexico	135	96	-29	150	283	89	13	23	76	69	139	102	7	219	2,898	37
Panama	98			172	194	13	11			94	148	58	*3*	207	*7,856*	31
Paraguay	39			52	218	319	7	*18*	146	28	*51*	*84*	3	204	6,083	11
Peru	0			96	148	54	2	14	613	25	78	216	3	59	1,810	115
St. Lucia				187	365	96	48			126			7			
Suriname	100	*68*	*-32*	138	253	84	0	3		100	184	84	*4*	207	*4,956*	35
Trinidad & Tobago	78			331	340	3				147	238	62	5	196	3,734	92
Uruguay	232			388	530	37	22	126	474	145	283	95	13	155	1,138	119
Venezuela	144			177	185	5	5	40	768	81	112	39	19	263	1,309	51
High income countries																
Bahamas	137			224	247					301	401	33	15	197	1,242	55
Middle East & North Africa																
Low income countries																
Yemen	17			274	283	3				11	24	114	1	8	1,590	1
Middle income countries																
Algeria	51	27	-47	73	110	50	0			34	61	77	0	3	1,518	2

Record 6 continued

figures are per thousand of population

Country	Daily newspapers 1990	Daily newspapers 1999*	Daily newspapers % change 1990–1999	Television sets 1990	Television sets 2000	Television sets % change 1990–2000	Cable television subscribers 1995	Cable television subscribers 2000	Cable television subscribers % change 1995–2000	Main telephone lines 1991	Main telephone lines 2001	Main telephone lines % change 1991–2001	Cellular mobile telephone subscribers 1995	Cellular mobile telephone subscribers 2001	Cellular mobile telephone subscribers % change 1995–2001	Internet users 2001 (Estimated)
Djibouti				43	71	66	0			12	15	30	*0*	5	*2,228*	5
Egypt	46	31	-32	107	189	76				34	102	205	0	43	42,768	9
Iran	28			66	163	147	0			44	160	264	0	32	10,661	16
Iraq	36			72	83	15				36						
Jordan	71	*75*	*6*	76	84	10	0			60	131	120	2	172	7,384	42
Lebanon	88			349	335	-4	0	*6*	3354		155			169		68
Libya	16			96	137	44	0			50	113	128		9		4
Malta	152			323	556	72	99	212	114	386	530	37	29	354	1,121	253
Morocco	13	25	86	102	166	62	0			20	41	105	1	164	14,770	14
Oman	38			657	563	-14	0			64	96	50	4	132	3,476	49
Saudi Arabia	36	339	840	250	264	6		4		89	151	70	1	118	13,024	14
Syria	17			60	67	11				40	109	172		12		4
Tunisia	42	19	-55	77	198	156				40	*109*	*172*	0	*40*	*9,957*	41
High income countries																
Bahrain	58			424	402	-5		9		198	243	23	48	419	783	196
Israel	258			259	335	29	160			262	487	86	59	827	1,311	283
Kuwait	252			433	486	12				233	231	-1	70	429	517	98
Qatar	165			392	869	122	45	62	37	194	280	44	34	299	793	67
United Arab Emirates	136			91	292	220				221	354	60	55	642	1,062	328
North America																
High income countries																
Canada	209			627			265	259	-2	579	6126	957	88	4139	4,593	435
United States	250			772	854	11	240	252	5	552	72	-87	128	38	-70	503
South Asia																
Low income countries																
Afghanistan	10			8	14	64	0			2						
Bangladesh	6			5	7	42				2	4	75		4		2
Bhutan					20		0			5	17	245				4
India		*60*		32	78	145	17			7	34	402	0	6	6,124	7
Nepal	8			2	7	281	0	*3*		4	13	261		1		3
Pakistan	17	40	139	26	131	406	0			10	24	150	0	6	1,814	4
Middle income countries																
Maldives	14			24	40	65	0			35	96	176	*0*	67	*66,743*	35
Sri Lanka	32			35	111	214	0	0		7	42	477	3	34	1,114	8
Sub-Saharan Africa																
Low income countries																
Angola	12			6	19	207				8	6	-21	0	6	3,101	4
Benin	0	5	2421	5	45	797	0			3	9	197	0	19	9,610	4
Burkina Faso	0			5	12	120				2	5	162		6		2
Burundi	4	*2*	-34	1	30	2,970				2	3	60	0	3	2,783	1
Cameroon	7			23	34	47				4	*7*	*91*	0	20	10,099	3

Record 6 continued

Country	Daily newspapers			Television sets			Cable television subscribers			Main telephone lines			Cellular mobile telephone subscribers			Internet users
figures are per thousand of population	1990	1999*	% change 1990–1999	1990	2000	% change 1990–2000	1995	2000	% change 1995–2000	1991	2001	% change 1991–2001	1995	2000	% change 1995–2000	2001 (Estimated)
Central African Republic	1			4	6	31				2	3	47	*0*	3	*872*	1
Chad	0	*0*	-40	1	1	13	0			1	*1*	*98*		3		1
Comoros				2						8	16	92		0		4
Congo, Dem. Rep.	2			1						1	0	-58	0	3	1,332	0
Congo, Rep.	8			6			*0*			7	7	-4	*0*	48	*11,982*	0
Côte d'Ivoire	8			60	60	0	0			7	18	167	*1*	44	*4,339*	4
Equatorial Guinea	6			9			0			4	15	309	*0*	32	*31,877*	2
Eritrea					26					*4*	8	*95*		0		4
Ethiopia	2	*0*	-81	2	6	138	*0*			3	5	74		0		0
Gambia	2				3					11	26	149	1	41	3,061	13
Ghana	13			16	118	621				3	12	309	0	10	2,358	2
Guinea				7	44	540	0			2	3	77	0	7	7,249	2
Guinea-Bissau	6									6	10	55		0		3
Kenya	14			15	25	62				8	10	24	0	20	19,421	16
Lesotho	12			6	16	178				7	11	56	*1*	16	*2,568*	2
Liberia	14			18	25	39				1						
Madagascar	4			19	24	24				3	4	31	0	9	9,133	2
Malawi	3				3			*0*		3	5	56	*0*	5	*1,223*	2
Mali	1			9	14	51	0			1	4	221	*0*	4	*3,983*	3
Mauritania	0			15						3	7	123		3		3
Mozambique	6	*2*	-57	3	5	89				4	5	34		9		1
Niger	0			11	37	226				1	2	62		0		1
Nigeria	18			36	68	86				3	4	28	0	4	3,750	1
Rwanda	0			0						2	2	30		7		2
Sao Tome & Principe					228					9	36	297		0		60
Senegal	7			36	40	10				7	24	274	*0*	40	*19,901*	10
Sierra Leone	3			10	13	30	0			3	4	38		5		1
Somalia	1			12	14	18				2	0	-100		0		
Sudan	25			73	273	274	0			3	14	472	*0*	3	*3,214*	2
Tanzania	3			2	20	1,175				3	4	49	0	12	12,295	9
Togo	3	2	-20	6	32	420	*0*			3	10	256		20		32
Uganda	2			11	27	156				2	3	64	0	14	14,059	3
Zambia	13			34	134	297				9	8	-11	0	12	5,794	2
Zimbabwe	21			26	30	16	0			12	20	60		26		8
Middle income countries																
Botswana	14			16	25	58				25	93	278		172		31
Cape Verde				3	5	57				26	137	430		69		26
Gabon	21			45	326	626				27	30	9	4	205	5,433	13
Mauritius	76	101	33	170	268	58				60	256	328	11	250	2,285	132
Namibia				22	38	72				40	66	62	2	56	2,326	25
South Africa	38			97	127	30				95	115	21	14	255	1,776	71
Swaziland	14			19	119	529	0			18	30	71		62		13

Record 6 continued (figures are per thousand of population)	Cable television subscribers			Avg. main telephone lines			Avg. cellular mobile telephone subscribers			Avg. estimated Internet users
Region	1995	2000	% change 1995–2000	1991	2001	% change in average	1995	2001	% change in average	2001
Low income	*6*			18	32	80	0	10	4259	6
Middle income	29	50	69	85	153	80	7	130	1792	37
Low & middle income:										
East Asia & Pacific	28	43	57	42	112	168	78	99	27	28
Europe & Central Asia	*35*	35	-1	136	253	85	3	142	4048	42
Latin America & Caribbean	19	15	-20	92	162	77	8	160	1789	50
Middle East & North Africa		1		64	97	53	4	51	1126	12
South Asia	14			9	29	224	0	6	1388	6
Sub-Saharan Africa				13	14	9	1	26	3239	8
High income	145	174	20	416	595	43	70	600	753	410
World	46	69	48	166	169	2	25	151	504	80

Empty cells indicate that data was unavailable. In such instances, where possible, figures are taken from the year before or after as an estimate. These figures, and estimates based on them, are presented in italics.

*Raw figures for newspaper circulation in 1999 are provided by UNESCO but "per 1000 people" and % change calculations are made by LSE and therefore have not been subjected to consistency checks by UNESCO.

Sources: UNESCO, Culture and Communication Statistics Team (2003); World Bank, World Development Indicators 2002 (WDI-Online) International Telecommunications Union (ITU), Yearbook of Statistics; Telecommunications Services, 1991-2000 (Geneva: ITU, 2001); ICT – Free statistics homepage, http://www.itu.int/ITU-D/ict/statistics/

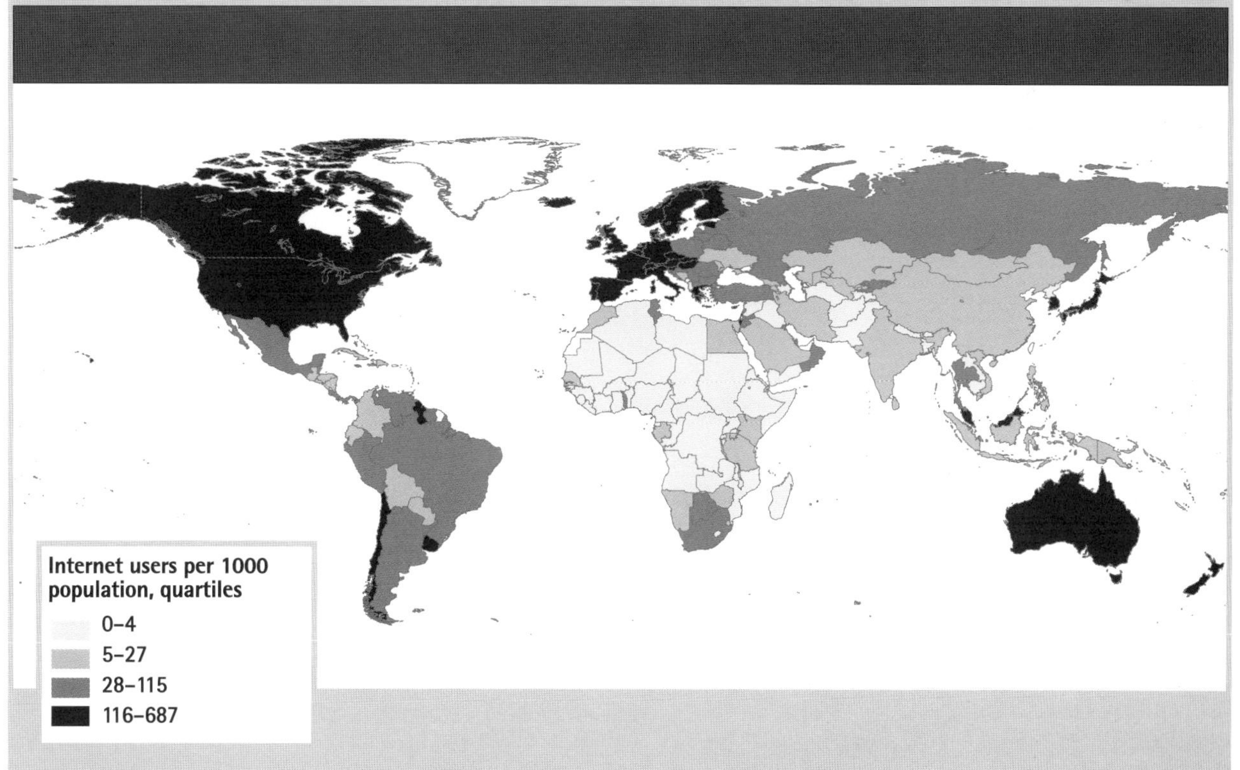

Record 7 Governance and accountability

The first section of this record presents the findings from another part of the 2020 Fund's Global Stakeholder Panel. Here, respondents are asked to state their preferred approaches to achieving accountability. The results are clear: respondents favour reforming existing multilateral and UN organisations rather than disbanding them, and making global institutions accountable to citizens rather than to governments.

The graph presents some results from the One World Trust's Global Accountability Report. The report is the first of its kind to compare the accountability of inter-governmental organisations (IGOs), transnational corporations (TNCs), and international non-governmental organisations (INGOs). Eighteen of the world's most powerful organisations are assessed in this pilot study, along two dimensions of accountability: member control and access to information. The graph gives scores for these two dimensions individually and as additive totals. It also indicates the presence of relevant activities or structures that are not captured by the numerical indicators. A yellow card indicates an accountability gap in the organisation, while a green card indicates that the organisation is developing particular mechanisms for greater accountability not found in the other organisations. Further explanations are given in the full report, which may be viewed at <http://www.oneworldtrust.org/>.

Governance

For each of the following pairs of opposites, please choose the one you believe will best get us to the future you want by the year 2020?	% in agreement
A Reforming existing multilateral agencies like the World Bank, IMF and WTO	61
Disbanding these existing multilateral agencies and building new structures/mechanisms	34
Other	3
B Reforming United Nations organizations like the World Health Organization, the UN Development Program, the UN Environment Program, & the International Labor Org.	81
Disbanding these UN Organizations and building new structures/mechanisms	10
Other	4
C Having global institutions continue to be accountable to national governments	27
Having global institutions accountable directly to citizens	63
Other	6

For the purposes of this survey, "governance" is defined as the way in which society ensures that its values and goals govern the actions of its citizens and organizations. It includes government at all levels, the United Nations system, multilateral agencies like the World Bank and IMF, as well as governance systems within civil society and business.

Source: 2020 Fund, Towards the Future We Want for our Children: Report of the first survey of the 2020 global stakeholder panel, available at http://www.2020fund.org/downloads/GSP_wave1.pdf

Accountability

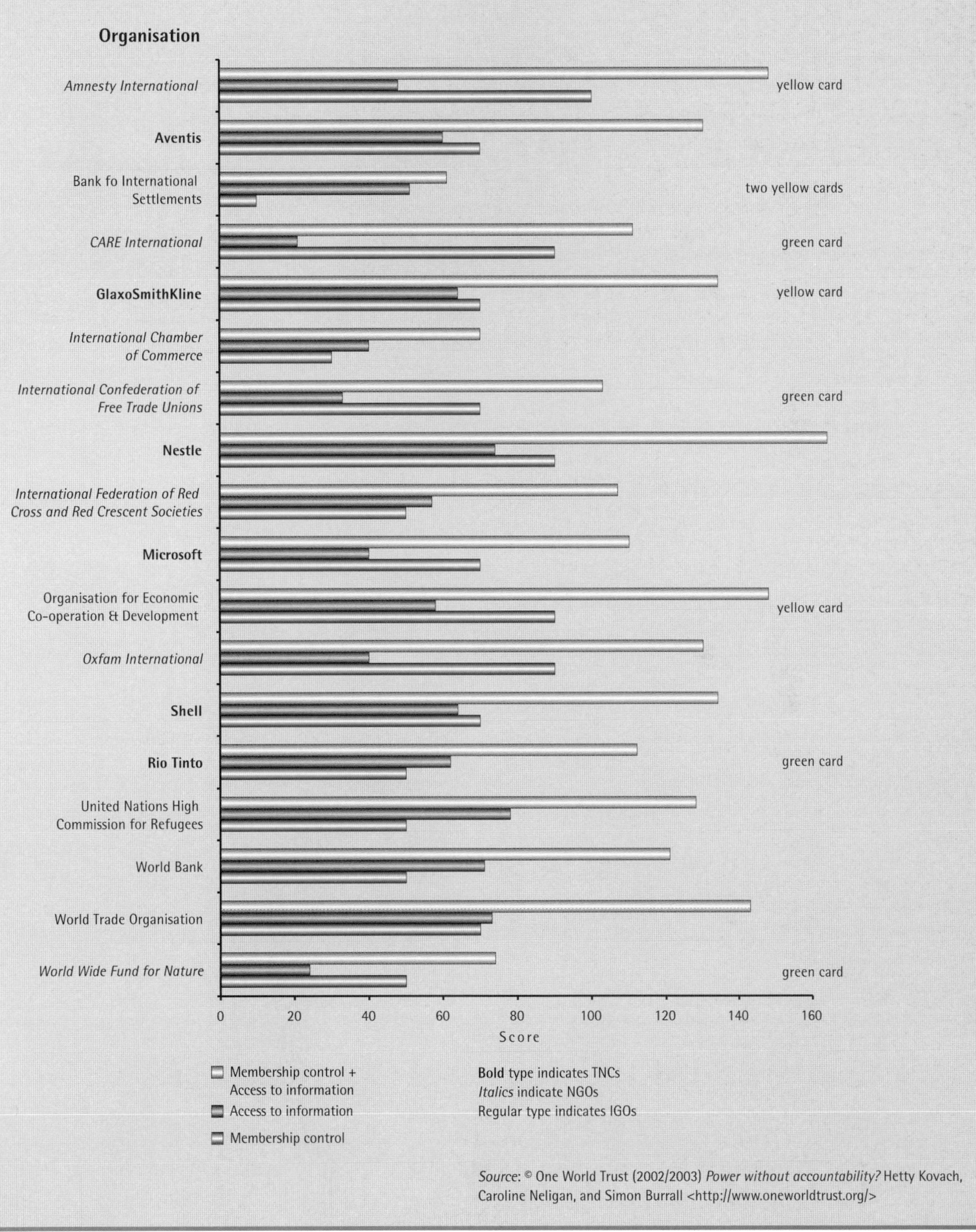

Source: © One World Trust (2002/2003) *Power without accountability?* Hetty Kovach, Caroline Neligan, and Simon Burrall <http://www.oneworldtrust.org/>

Record 8 Ratification of treaties

Global civil society is both dependent on the international rule of law and one of the main actors pushing for the adoption and enforcement of international law. The table indicates which countries have ratified the major human rights, humanitarian, disarmament, and environmental treaties, and in which years, up to 28 February 2003. It also shows how many countries have ratified each particular treaty, and how many of the listed treaties each country has ratified.

ICESCR – International Covenant on Economic, Social and Cultural Rights

ICCPR – International Convenant on Civil and Political Rights

ICCPR-OP1 – Optional Protocol to the International Convenant on Civil and Political Rights

ICCPR-OP2 – Second Optional Protocol to the International Convenant on Civil and Political Rights

CERD – International Convention on the Elimination of all forms of Racial Discrimination

CEDAW – Convention on the Elimination of All Forms of Discrimination Against Women

CAT – Convention against Torture and Other Cruel, Inhuman or Degrading Treatment or Punishment

Gen – Convention on the Prevention and Punishment of the Crime of the Genocide

ILO 87 – Freedom of Association and Protection of the Right to Organise Convention

CSR – Convention relating to the Status of Refugees

ICC – Rome Statute on the International Criminal Court

CWC Chemical Weapons Convention

BWC – Biological Weapons Convention

BC – Basel Convention on the Control of Transboundary Movements of Hazardous Wastes and Their Disposal

CBD – Convention on Biological Diversity

UNFCCC – United Nations Framework Convention on Climate Change

KP – Kyoto Protocol to United Nations Framework Convention on Climate Change

LMC – Convention on the Prohibition of the Use, Stockpiling, Production and Transfer of Anti-Personnel Mines and on their Destruction

VCPOL – Vienna Convention for the Protection of the Ozone Layer

Gen – Convention on the Prevention and Punishment of the Crime of the Genocide

Geneva – Geneva Conventions

Prot 1 – First Additional to the Geneva Conventions

Prot 2 – Second Additional Protocol to the Geneva Conventions

	Human Rights											Humanitarian Law						Environmental Law					
Country	ICESCR	ICCPR	CCPR-OP1	CCPR-OP2	CERD	CEDAW	CAT	Gen	ILO 87	CSR	ICC	CWC	BWC	LMC	Geneva	Prot 1	Prot2	BC	CBD	UNFCCC	KP	VCPOL	Total
East Asia & Pacific																							
Low income economies																							
Cambodia	92	92			83	92	92	50	99	92			83	99	58	98	98	01	95	95	02	01	18
Indonesia & East Timor					99	84	98		98			98	92		58			93	94	94		92	11
Korea, Dem. Rep.	81	81				01		89					87		57	88			94	94		95	10
Laos					74	81		50				97	73		56	80	80		96	95		98	11
Mongolia	74	74	91		69	81	02	67	69			95	72		58	95	95	97	93	93	99	96	18
Myanmar						97		56	55						92				94	94		93	7
Papua New Guinea					82	95		82	00	86		94	80		76			95	93	93	02	92	12
Solomon Islands	82				82	02				95			81	99	81	88	88		95	94		93	11
Vietnam	82	82			82	82		81				98	80		57	81		95	94	94	02	94	14
Middle income economies																							
China & Tibet	01				81	80	88	83		82		97	84		56	83	83	91	93	93		89	15
Fiji					73	95		73	02	72	99	93	73	98	71				93	93	98	89	13
Malaysia						95		94				00	91	99	62			93	94	94	02	89	10
Philippines	74	86	89		67	81	86	50	53	81		96	73	00	52		86	93	93	94		91	18
Samoa						92				88		02		98	84	84	84	02	94	94	00	92	10
Thailand	99	96				85						03	75	98	54			97		94	02	89	9
Tonga					72			72					76		78	03	03		98	98		98	9
Vanuatu						95							90		82	85	85		93	93	01	94	9
High income economies																							
Australia	75	80	91	90	75	83	89	49	73	54		94	77	99	58	91	91	92	93	92		87	20

Record 8 continued

Country	ICESCR	ICCPR	CCPR-OP1	CCPR-OP2	CERD	CEDAW	CAT	Gen	ILO 87	CSR	ICC	CWC	BWC	LMC	Geneva	Prot 1	Prot2	BC	CBD	UNFCCC	KP	VCPOL	Total
	Human Rights											**Humanitarian Law**						**Environmental Law**					
Brunei												97	91		91	91	91	02				90	6
Korea, Rep.	90	90	90		78	84	95	50		92		97	87		66	82	82	94	94	93	02	92	17
Japan	79	79			95	85	99		65	81		95	82	98	53			93	93	93		88	15
New Zealand	78	78	89	90	72	85	89	78		60	00	96	72	99	59	88	88	94	93	93	02	87	20
Singapore						95		95				97	75		73			96	95	97		89	9
Europe & Central Asia																							
Low income economies																							
Armenia	93	93	93		93	93	93	93		93		94	94		93	93	93	99	93	94		99	17
Azerbaijan	92	92	01	99	96	95	96	96	92	93		00			93			01	00	95	00	96	17
Georgia	94	94	94	99	99	94	94	93	99	99		95	96		93	93	93	99	94	94	99	96	20
Kyrgyzstan	94	94	95		97	97	97	97	92	96					92	92	92	96	96	00		00	16
Moldova	93	93			93	94	95	93	96	02		96		00	93	93	93	98	95	95		96	16
Tajikistan	99	99	99		95	93	95		93	93	00	95		99	93	93	93		97	98		96	17
Ukraine	73	73	91		69	81	87	54	56			98	75		54	90	90	99	95	97		86	17
Uzbekistan	95	95	95		95	95	95	99				96	96		93	93	93	96	95	93	99	93	17
Middle income economies																							
Albania	91	91			94	94	94	55		92		94	92	00	57	93	93	99	94	94		99	17
Belarus	73	73	92		69	81	87	54	56			96	75		54	89	89	99	93	00		86	17
Bosnia & Herzegovina	92	93	95	01	93	93	93	92	93	93		97	94	98	92	92	92	01	02	00		92	19
Bulgaria	70	70	92	99	66	82	86	50	59	93		94	72	98	54	89	89	96	96	95	02	90	20
Croatia	91	92	95	95	92	92	92	92	91	92	01	95	93	98	92	92	92	94	96	96		91	21
Czech Republic	93	93	93		93	93	93	93	93	93		96	93	99	93	93	93	93	93	93	01	93	20
Estonia	91	91	91		91	91	91	91	94	97		99	93		93	93	93	92	94	94	02	96	18
Hungary	74	74	88	94	67	80	87	52	57	89		96	72	98	54	89	89	90	94	94	02	88	20
Kazakhstan					98	98	98	98	00	99		00			92	92	92		94	95		98	13
Latvia	92	92	94		92	92	92	92	92	97		96	97		91	91	91	92	95	95	02	95	18
Lithuania	91	91	91	02	98	94	96	96	94	97		98	98		96	00	00	99	96	95	03	95	18
Macedonia	94	94	94	95	94	94	94	94	91	94		97	96	98	93	93	93	97	97	98		94	20
Poland	77	77	91		68	80	89	50	57	91		95	73		54	91	91	92	96	99	02	90	18
Romania	74	74	93	91	70	82	90	50	57	91		95	79	00	54	90	90	91	94	94	01	93	21
Russian Federation	73	73	91		69	81	87	54	56	93		97	75		54	89	89	95	95	94		86	18
Serbia & Montenegro	01	01	01	01	01	82	01	01	00	01		00			01	01	01	00	02	97		92	17
Slovakia	93	93	93	99	93	93	93	93	93	93		95	93	99	93	93	93	93	94	94	02	93	20
Slovenia	92	92	93	94	92	92	93	92	92	92		97	92	98	92	92	92	93	96	95	02	92	20
Turkey					02	85	88	50	93	62		97	74		54			94	97			91	11
Turkmenistan	97	97	97	00	94	97	99		97	98		94	96	98	92	92	92	96	96	95	00	93	20
High income economies																							
Austria	78	78	87	93	72	82	87	58	50	54	00	95	73	98	53	82	82	93	94	94	02	87	21
Belgium	83	83	94	98	75	85	99	51	51	53	00	97	79	98	52	86	86	93	96	96	02	88	21
Cyprus	69	69	92	99	67	85	91	82	66	63		98	73	03	62	79	96	92	96	97	99	92	20
Denmark	72	72	72	94	71	83	87	51	51	52	01	95	73	98	51	82	82	94	93	93	02	88	21
Finland	75	75	75	91	70	86	89	59	50	68	00	95	74		55	80	80	91	94	94	02	86	20
France	80	80	84		71	83	86	50	51	54	00	95	84	98	51	01	84	91	94	94		87	20
Germany	73	73	93	92	69	85	90	54	57	53	00	94	72	98	54	91	91	95	93	93	02	88	21
Greece	85	97	97	97	70	83	88	54	62	60		94	75		56	89	93	94	94	94	02	88	19
Iceland	79	79	79	91	67	85	96	49	50	55	00	97	73	99	65	87	87	95	94	93	02	89	21
Ireland	89	89	89	93	00	85		76	55	56		96	72	97	62	99	99	94	96	94	02	88	19
Italy	78	78	78	95	76	85	89	52	58	54	99	95	75	99	51	86	86	94	94	94	02	88	21

Record 8 continued	Human Rights											Humanitarian Law						Environmental Law					
Country	ICESCR	ICCPR	CCPR-OP1	CCPR-OP2	CERD	CEDAW	CAT	Gen	ILO 87	CSR	ICC	CWC	BWC	LMC	Geneva	Prot 1	Prot2	BC	CBD	UNFCCC	KP	VCPOL	Total
Luxembourg	83	83	83	92	78	89	87	81	58	53	00	97	76	99	53	89	89	94	94	94	02	88	21
Netherlands	78	78	78	91	71	91	88	66	50	56	01	95	81	99	54	87	87	93	94	93	02	88	21
Norway	72	72	72	91	70	81	86	49	49	53	00	94	73	98	51	81	81	90	93	93	02	86	21
Portugal	78	78	83	90	82	80	89	99	77	60		96	75	99	61	92	92	94	93	93		88	20
Spain	77	77	85	91	68	84	87	68	77	78	00	94	79	99	52	89	89	94	93	93	02	88	21
Sweden	71	71	71	90	71	80	86	52	49	54	01	93	76	98	53	79	79	91	93	93	02	86	21
Switzerland	92	92		94	94	97	86	00	75	55		95	76	98	50	82	82	90	94	93		87	19
United Kingdom	76	76		99	69	86	88	70	49	54		96	75	98	57	98	98	94	94	93	02	87	19
Latin America & Caribbean																							
Low income countries																							
Haiti		91			72	81		50	79	84					57				96	96		00	10
Nicaragua	80	80	80		78	81		52	67	80		99	75	98	53	99	99	97	95	95	99	93	18
Middle income countries																							
Argentina	86	86	86		68	85	86	56	60	61	01	95	79	99	56	86	86	91	94	93	01	90	21
Barbados	73	73	73		72	80		80	67				73	99	68	90	90	95	93	94	00	92	17
Belize		96			01	90	86	98	83	90	00		86	98	84	84	84	97	93	94		97	17
Bolivia	82	82	82		70	90	99		65	82		98	75	98	76	83	83	96	94	94	99	94	19
Brazil	92	92			68	84	89	52		60		96	73	99	57	92	92	92	94	94	02	90	17
Chile	72	72	92		71	89	88	53	99	72		96	80	01	50	91	91	92	94	94	02	90	19
Colombia	69	69	69	97	81	82	87	59	76	61		00	83	00	61	93	95	96	94	95	01	90	21
Costa Rica	68	68	68	98	67	86	93	50	60	78	01	96	93	99	69	83	83	95	94	94	02	91	21
Cuba					72	80	95	53	52			97	76		54	82	99	94	94	94	02	92	14
Dominican Republic	78	78	78		83	82			56	78			73	00	58	94	94	00	96	98	02	93	16
Ecuador	69	69	69	93	66	81	88	49	67	55		95	75	99	54	79	79	93	93	93	00	90	21
El Salvador	79	79	95		79	81	96	50		83		95	91	99	53	78	78	91	94	95	98	92	19
Guatemala	88	92	00		83	82	90	50	52	83			73	99	52	87	87	95	95	95	99	87	19
Guyana	77	77	93		77	80	88		67			97			68	88	88	01	94	94		93	15
Honduras	81	97			02	83	96	52	56	92			79	98	65	95	95	95	95	95	00	93	17
Jamaica	75	75			71	84		68	62	64		00	75	98	64	86	86		95	94	99	93	17
Mexico	81	81	02		75	81	86	52	61	00		94	74	98	52	83		91	93	93	00	87	18
Panama	77	77	77	93	67	81	87	50	58	78		98	74	98	56	95	95	91	95	95	99	89	21
Paraguay	92	92	95			87	90	01	62	70	01	96	76	98	61	90	90	95	94	94	99	92	20
Peru	78	78	80		71	82	88	60	60	64		95	85	98	56	89	89	93	93	93	02	89	19
St. Lucia					90	82			80			97	86	99	81	82	82	93	93	93		93	13
St. Vincent & the Grenadines	81	81	81		81	81	01	81	01	93		02	99	01	81	83	83	96	96	96		96	18
Suriname	76	76	76		84	93			76	78		97	93		76	85	85		96	97		97	15
Trinidad & Tobago	78	78			73	90			63	00	99	97		98	63	01	01	94	96	94	99	89	17
Uruguay	70	70	70	93	68	81	86	67	54	70		94	81	01	69	85	85	91	93	94	01	89	21
Venezuela	78	78	78	93	67	83	91	60	82		00	97	78	99	56	98	98	98	94	94		88	20
High income countries																							
Bahamas					75	93		75	01	93			86	98	75	80	80	92	93	94	99	93	15
Middle East & North Africa																							
Low income countries																							
Yemen	87	87			72	84	91	87	76	80		00	79	98	70	90	90	96	96	96		96	18
Middle income countries																							
Algeria	89	89	89		72	96	89	63	62	63		95	01	01	62	89	89	98	95	93		92	19

Record 8 continued

Country	ICESCR	ICCPR	CCPR-OP1	CCPR-OP2	CERD	CEDAW	CAT	Gen	ILO 87	CSR	ICC	CWC	BWC	LMC	Geneva	Prot 1	Prot2	BC	CBD	UNFCCC	KP	VCPOL	Total
	Human Rights											**Humanitarian Law**						**Environmental Law**					
Djibouti	02	02	02	02		98	02		78	77				98	78	91	91		94	95	02	99	11
Egypt	82	82			67	81	86	52	57	81					52	92	92	93	94	94		88	15
Iran	75	75			68			56		76		97	73		57			93	96	96		90	12
Iraq	71	71			70	86		59					91		56								7
Jordan	75	75			74	92	91	50				97	75	98	51	79	79	89	93	93		89	16
Lebanon	72	72			71	97	00	53					75		51	97	97	94	94	94		93	14
Libya	70	70	89		68	89	89	89	00				82		56	78	78	01	01	99		90	16
Malta	90	90	90	94	71	91	90		65	71		97	75	01	68	89	89	00	00	94	01	88	20
Morocco & Western Sahara	79	79			70	93	93	58		56		95	02		56			95	95	95	02	95	13
Oman												95	92		74	84	84	95	95	95		99	9
Saudi Arabia					97	00	97	50				96	72		63	87		90		94		93	11
Syria	69	69			69			55	60						53	83		92	96	96		89	11
Tunisia	69	69			67	85	88	56	57	57		97	73	99	57	79	79	95	93	93		89	18
High income countries																							
Bahrain					90	02	98	90				97	88		71	86	86	92	96	94		90	12
Israel & Occupied Territiories	91	91			79	91	91	50	57	54					51			94	95	96		92	13
Kuwait	96	96			68	94	96	95	61			97	72		67	85	85	93	02	94		92	15
Qatar					76		00					97	75	98	75	88		95	96	96		96	11
United Arab Emirates					74							00			72	83	83	92	00	95		89	9
North America																							
High income countries																							
Canada	76	76	76		70	81	87	52	72	69	00	95	72	97	65	90	90	92	92	92	02	86	20
United States		92			94		94	88				97	75		55					92		86	9
South Asia																							
Low income countries																							
Afganistan	83	83			83		87	56	57				75	02	56				02	02			8
Bangladesh	98	00			79	84	98	98	72			97	85	00	72	80	80	93	94	94	01	90	18
Bhutan						81							78		91			02	95	95	02		5
India	79	79			68	93		59				96	74		50			92	94	93	02	91	12
Nepal	91	91	91	98	71	91	91	69				97			64			96	93	94		94	14
Pakistan					66	96		57	51			97	74		51			94	94	94		92	11
Middle income countries																							
Maldives					84	93		84				94	93	00	91	91	91	92	92	92	98	88	14
Sri Lanka	80	80	97		82	81	94	50	95			94	86		59			92	94	93	02	89	15
Sub-Saharan Africa																							
Low income countries																							
Angola	92	92	92			86			01	81				02	84	84			98	00		00	9
Benin	92	92	92			92	92		60	62		98	75	98	61	86	86	97	94	94		93	17
Burkina Faso	99	99	99		74	87	99	65	60	80		97	91	98	61	87	87	99	93	93		89	19
Burundi	90	90			77	92	93	97	93	63		98			71	93	93	97	97	97	01	97	17
Cameroon	84	84	84		71	94	86		60	61		96		02	63	84	84	01	94	94	02	89	16
Central African Republic	81	81	81		71	91			60	62				02	66	84	84		95	95		93	13
Chad	95	95	95		77	95	95		60	81				99	70	97	97		94	94		89	15
Comoros						94			78					02	85	85	85	94	94	94		94	9
Congo, Rep.	83	83	83		88	82			60	62			78	01	67	83	83		96			94	14

Record 8 continued

Country	Human Rights										Humanitarian Law							Environmental Law					
	ICESCR	ICCPR	CCPR-OP1	CCPR-OP2	CERD	CEDAW	CAT	Gen	ILO 87	CSR	ICC	CWC	BWC	LMC	Geneva	Prot 1	Prot2	BC	CBD	UNFCCC	KP	VCPOL	Total
Congo, Dem. Rep.	76	76	76		76	86	96	62	01	65			75	02	61	82	02	94	94	95		94	16
Côte d'Ivoire	92	92	97		73	95	95	95	60	61		95		00	61	89	89	94	94	94		93	18
Equatorial Guinea	87	87	87		02	84			01	86		97	89	98	86	86	86		94	00	00	88	16
Eritrea	01	02			01	95			00			00		01	00				96	95			9
Ethiopia	93	93			76	81	94	49	63	69		96	75		69	94	94	00	94	94		94	17
Gambia	78	79	88		78	93		78	00	66		98	91	02	66	89	89	97	94	94	01	90	18
Ghana	00	00	00		66	86	00	58	65	63	99	97	75	00	58	78	78		94	95		89	19
Guinea	78	78	93		77	82	89	00	59	65		97		98	84	84	84	95	93	93	00	92	19
Guinea-Bissau	92					85				76			76	01	74	86	86		95	95		02	10
Kenya	72	72			01	84	97			66		97	76	01	66	99	99	00	94	94		88	16
Lesotho	92	92	00		71	95	01	74	66	81	00	94	77	98	68	94	94	00	95	95	00	94	21
Liberia					76	84		50	62	64				99	54	88	88		00	02	02	96	11
Madagascar	71	71	71		69	89			60	67				99	63	92	92	99	96	99		96	15
Malawi	93	93	96		96	87	96		99	87		98		98	68	91	91	94	94	94	01	91	18
Mali	74	74	01		74	85	99	74	60	73	00	97		98	65	89	89	00	95	94	02	94	19
Mozambique		93		93	83	97	99	83	96	83		00		98	83	83	02	97	95	95		94	16
Niger	86	86	86		67	99	98		61	61		97	72	99	64	79	79	98	95	95		92	18
Nigeria	93	93			67	85	01		60	67		99	73	01	61	88	88	91	94	94		88	17
Rwanda	75	75			75	81		75	88	80			75	00	64	84	84		96	98		01	15
Sao Tome & Principe									92	78			79		76	96	96		99	99		01	9
Senegal	78	78	78		72	85	86	83	60	63	99	98	75	98	63	85	85	92	94	94	01	93	21
Sierra Leone	96	96	96		67	88	01		61	81	00		76	01	65	86	86		94	95		01	17
Somalia	90	90	90		75		90			78					62							01	8
Sudan	86	76			77					74		99			57				95	93		93	9
Tanzania	76	76			72	85		84	00	64		98		00	62	83	83	93	96	96	02	93	16
Togo	84	84	88		72	83	87	84	60	62		97	76	00	62	84	84		95	95		91	18
Uganda	87	95	95		80	85	86	95		76		01	92	99	64	91	91	99	93	93	02	88	18
Zambia	84	84	84		72	85	98		96	69		01		01	66	95	95	94	93	93		90	17
Zimbabwe	91	91			91	91		91		81		97	90	98	83	92	92		94	92		92	15
Middle income countries																							
Botswana		00			74	96	00		97	69	00	98	92	00	68	79	79	98	95	94		91	17
Cape Verde	93	93	00	00	79	80	92		99				77	01	84	95	95	99	95	95		01	17
Gabon	83	83			80	83	00	83	60	64	00	00		00	65	80	80		97	98		94	17
Mauritius	73	73	73		72	84	92					93	72	97	70	82	82	92	92	92	01	92	17
Namibia	94	94	94	94	82	92	94	94	95	95		95		98	91	94	94	95	97	95		93	19
South Africa		98	02	02	98	95	98	98	96	96	00	95	75	98	52	95	95	94	95	97	02	90	18
Swaziland					69				78			96	91	98	73	95	95		94	96		92	11
Total States Parties*	146	149	104	49	165	170	132	133	142	140	89	151	165	132	190	161	156	156	187	188	106	185	

* Total States Parties refers to the total number of ratifications for each treaty, including from those countries with populations of less than one hundred thousand that are not included in this table.

Sources: Office of the UN High Commissioner for Human Rights, http://www.unhchr.ch/html/intlinst.htm; Coalition for the International Criminal Court, http://www.iccnow.org/countryinfo/worldsigsandratifications.html; Organisation for the Prohibition of Chemical Weapons, http://www.opcw.org/html/global/profiles_frameset.html; SIPRI, http://projects.sipri.se/cbw/docs/bw-btwc-sig.html; Secretariat, Basel Convention on the Control of Transboundary Movements of Hazardous Wastes and Their Disposal, http://www.basel.int/ratif/ratif.html; Secretariat, United Nations Framework Convention on Climate Change, http://unfccc.int/resource/conv/ratlist.pdf; International Committee of the Red Cross, http://www.icrc.org/eng/party_gc and http://www.icrc.org/eng/party_cmines; Convention on Biological Diversity, http://www.biodiv.org/world/parties.asp; Kyoto Protocol, http://unfccc.int/resource/kpstats.pdf; UNEP, The Ozone Secretariat, http://www.unep.org/ozone/ratif.shtml; ILO, http://webfusion.ilo.org/public/db/standards/normes/appl/appl-byconv.cfm?conv=C087&lang=EN&hdroff=1; Genocide Convention, http://www.unhchr.ch/html/menu3/b/treaty1gen.htm; Convention relating to the Status of Refugees, http://www.unhchr.ch/html/menu3/b/treaty2ref.htm.

Record 9 Human rights violations

Global civil society is instrumental in exposing human rights violations. At the same time, human rights violations form one of the main threats to the survival of local civil societies. While Record 8 shows the extent to which states have committed themselves to abide by international law, this table shows the extent to which they actually respect international human rights law. The table displays information on human rights abuses by country, covering extrajudicial executions and disappearances, arbitrary detentions, torture, freedom of expression, and the situation of minorities, using the latest information available from three different sources: Amnesty International (report of 2001), Human Rights Watch and the US State Department (reports of 2002). The information offers an indication of whether certain basic human rights have been violated, but it does not quantify the number of violations in each country. Blank spaces in the table indicate either no violation or no data available, and so must be interpreted with some caution.

	Disappearances & extrajudicial executions			Arbitrary detentions			Torture			Discrimination against minorities			Freedom of expression & association		
Country	AI	HRW	SD	AI	HRW	SD	AI	HRW	SD	AI	HRW	SD	AI	HRW	SD
East Asia & Pacific															
Low income economies															
Cambodia						yes		yes	yes					no	no
Indonesia	yes	yes	yes	yes		yes	yes	yes	yes						
Korea, Dem. Rep.			yes			yes			yes			yes			no
Laos						yes	yes		yes				no		no
Mongolia						yes									
Myanmar	yes	yes	yes			yes		yes	yes			yes		no	no
Papua New Guinea															no
Solomon Islands									yes						
Vietnam									yes						
Middle income economies															
China & Tibet				yes		yes	yes		yes			yes	no	no	no
Fiji															
Malaysia									yes				no	no	no
Philippines	yes		yes	yes		yes	yes		yes						
Samoa												yes			
Thailand	yes						yes					yes			
Tonga															
Vanuatu															
High income economies															
Australia															
Brunei								yes				yes	no		no
Korea, Rep.												yes	no		
Japan															
New Zealand															
Singapore													no		no
Europe & Central Asia															
Low income economies															
Armenia						yes	yes	yes			yes			no	
Azerbaijan						yes	yes					yes		no	no
Georgia							yes	yes	yes						no
Kyrgyzstan											yes	yes		no	no
Moldova			yes	yes			yes					yes			
Tajikistan			yes			yes	yes	yes							no

Record 9 continued	Disappearances & extrajudicial executions			Arbitrary detentions			Torture			Discrimination against minorities			Freedom of expression & association		
Country	AI	HRW	SD	AI	HRW	SD	AI	HRW	SD	AI	HRW	SD	AI	HRW	SD
Ukraine						yes	yes		yes			yes	no		no
Uzbekistan					yes	yes	yes	yes	yes		yes	yes		no	no
Middle income economies															
Albania						yes	yes		yes		yes	yes			
Belarus						yes	yes					yes	no	no	no
Bosnia & Herzegovina				yes							yes	yes			
Bulgaria		yes			yes	yes	yes	yes			yes	yes	no	no	
Croatia											yes	yes			
Czech Republic				yes						yes	yes	yes			
Estonia															
Hungary											yes	yes			
Kazakhstan						yes	yes		yes			yes		no	no
Latvia			yes				yes								
Lithuania							yes								
Macedonia	yes		yes			yes	yes		yes		yes	yes		no	no
Poland												yes			
Romania							yes				yes	yes			
Russian Federation	yes	yes	yes	yes	yes	yes	yes	yes	yes			yes	no	no	no
Serbia & Montenegro					yes			yes			yes	yes	no	no	
Slovakia					yes		yes	yes			yes	yes		no	
Slovenia															
Turkey	yes		yes			yes	yes	yes	yes			yes	no	no	no
Turkmenistan						yes	yes			yes	yes	yes		no	no
High income economies															
Austria															
Belgium															
Cyprus											yes				
Denmark															
Finland															
France															
Germany															
Greece											yes	yes			
Iceland															
Ireland															
Italy							yes								
Luxembourg															
Netherlands															
Norway															
Portugal															
Spain							yes								
Sweden															
Switzerland															
United Kingdom															
Latin America & Caribbean															
Low income countries															
Haiti			yes		yes	yes			yes				no	no	
Nicaragua						yes									

Record 9 continued	Disappearances & extrajudicial executions			Arbitrary detentions			Torture			Discrimination against minorities			Freedom of expression & association		
Country	**AI**	**HRW**	**SD**	**AI**	**HRW**	**SD**	**AI**	**HRW**	**SD**	**AI**	**HRW**	**SD**	**AI**	**HRW**	**SD**
Middle income countries															
Argentina						yes	yes	yes	yes						
Barbados															
Belize							yes								
Bolivia						yes						yes			
Brazil	yes	yes	yes			yes	yes	yes	yes		yes	yes		no	
Chile														no	
Colombia	yes		yes			yes	yes		yes			yes			
Costa Rica															
Cuba					yes	yes						yes	no	no	no
Dominican Republic	yes		yes			yes	yes		yes			yes			
Ecuador	yes		yes			yes	yes		yes			yes			
El Salvador															
Guatemala			yes			yes			yes						
Guyana			yes				yes								
Honduras			yes												
Jamaica	yes		yes				yes		yes						
Mexico	yes		yes	yes		yes	yes		yes					no	
Panama												yes			no
Paraguay			yes			yes	yes		yes			yes			
Peru						yes	yes	yes	yes			yes			
St. Lucia															
Suriname															
Trinidad & Tobago							yes								
Uruguay															
Venezuela	yes		yes			yes	yes		yes				no	no	
High income countries															
Bahamas						yes									
Middle East & North Africa															
Low income countries															
Yemen		yes			yes	yes	yes	yes	yes			yes	no	no	no
Middle income countries															
Algeria		yes	yes		yes	yes	yes	yes	yes		yes		no	no	no
Djibouti						yes	yes		yes	yes		yes	no		no
Egypt			yes		yes	yes	yes	yes	yes		yes	yes	no	no	no
Iran						yes	yes		yes		yes	yes	no	no	no
Iraq		yes	yes	yes	yes	yes	yes	yes	yes		yes	yes		no	no
Jordan						yes	yes					yes			no
Lebanon						yes	yes		yes				no		no
Libya						yes	yes		yes			yes	no		no
Malta															
Morocco & Western Sahara						yes			yes				no	no	no
Oman															no
Saudi Arabia						yes		yes	yes			yes	no	no	no
Syria						yes	yes		yes					no	no
Tunisia						yes	yes	yes	yes					no	no

Record 9 continued	Disappearances & extrajudicial executions			Arbitrary detentions			Torture			Discrimination against minorities			Freedom of expression & association		
Country	AI	HRW	SD	AI	HRW	SD	AI	HRW	SD	AI	HRW	SD	AI	HRW	SD
High income countries															
Bahrain					yes		yes						no		no
Israel & Occupied Territories			yes			yes	yes	yes	yes	yes		yes	yes		
Kuwait												yes			no
Qatar												yes	no		no
United Arab Emirates							yes					yes	no		no
North America															
High income countries															
Canada															
United States							yes	yes							
South Asia															
Low income countries															
Afghanistan			yes			yes	yes		yes	yes		yes			
Bangladesh			yes			yes	yes		yes			yes			no
Bhutan						yes						yes			no
India			yes			yes	yes		yes	yes	yes	yes		no	
Nepal	yes		yes	yes			yes		yes			yes			no
Pakistan			yes			yes	yes		yes		yes	yes	no	no	no
Middle income countries															
Maldives															no
Sri Lanka	yes			yes	yes		yes	yes	yes		yes				
Sub-Saharan Africa															
Low income countries															
Angola	yes		yes	yes		yes	yes		yes				no		no
Benin	yes			yes		yes			yes						
Burkina Faso	yes		yes		yes	yes		yes	yes					no	no
Burundi	yes	yes	yes	yes		yes	yes	yes	yes			yes		no	no
Cameroon	yes		yes	yes		yes			yes			yes			no
Central African Republic	yes		yes	yes		yes	yes		yes			yes	no		no
Chad	yes		yes	yes		yes	yes		yes			yes	no		no
Comoros						yes									
Congo, Dem Rep.	yes	yes	yes	yes		yes	yes	yes	yes					no	no
Congo, Rep.			yes	yes		yes			yes				no		
Côte d'Ivoire			yes	yes		yes	yes		yes						no
Equatorial Guinea			yes			yes			yes			yes	no		no
Eritrea				yes	yes	yes		yes					no	no	no
Ethiopia	yes		yes	yes	yes	yes	yes	yes					no	no	no
Gambia				yes		yes	yes						no		no
Ghana			yes			yes			yes						no
Guinea			yes	yes		yes	yes		yes						no
Guinea-Bissau				yes		yes			yes				no		no
Kenya	yes		yes			yes	yes		yes			yes	no	no	no
Lesotho							yes								
Liberia	yes	yes	yes	yes	yes	yes	yes	yes	yes		yes	yes	no	no	no
Madagascar			yes			yes			yes						no

Record 9 continued	Disappearances & extrajudicial executions			Arbitrary detentions			Torture			Discrimination against minorities			Freedom of expression & association		
Country	**AI**	**HRW**	**SD**	**AI**	**HRW**	**SD**	**AI**	**HRW**	**SD**	**AI**	**HRW**	**SD**	**AI**	**HRW**	**SD**
Malawi							yes						no		
Mali						yes									
Mauritania						yes			yes			yes			no
Mozambique		yes				yes		yes	yes						
Niger				yes		yes			yes			yes	no		
Nigeria	yes	yes	yes		yes	yes			yes						
Rwanda	yes	yes		yes		yes	yes			yes			no	no	no
Sao Tome & Principe															
Senegal			yes			yes			yes				yes		
Sierra Leone	yes				yes	yes	yes					yes			
Somalia						yes			yes			yes	no		no
Sudan	yes		yes	yes		yes	yes	yes	yes			yes	no	no	no
Tanzania			yes			yes	yes		yes			yes	no		no
Togo						yes	yes					yes	no		no
Uganda			yes	yes	yes	yes	yes	yes	yes			yes			no
Zambia		yes	yes	yes		yes	yes	yes					no	no	
Zimbabwe			yes	yes		yes	yes		yes			yes	no		no
Middle income countries															
Botswana															
Cape Verde															
Gabon						yes			yes			yes			
Mauritius							yes								
Namibia	yes		yes			yes	yes		yes				no		
South Africa							yes		yes						
Swaziland				yes			yes		yes			yes	no		no

Absence of data indicates that either no violations have been recorded or that no data are available.

In the first four categories, 'yes' denotes a violation, whereas in the final category, 'no' denotes a violation.

Sources: Human Rights Watch World Report 2003, http://www.hrw.org/wr2k3/; Amnesty International Report 2002, http://web.amnesty.org/web/ar2002.nsf/home/home?OpenDocument; U.S. State Department 2002 Country Reports on Human Rights Practices http://www.state.gov/g/drl/rls/hrrpt/2002/index.htm.

Record 10 Social justice

This record illustrates another element of the spread of the international rule of law, namely, the realisation of social and economic rights, or social justice. This record thus contains indicators of poverty, inequality, and social exclusion. Growing inequality appears to be one of the characteristics of globalisation. It can be seen as inhibiting the emergence of global civil society, but it is also one of global civil society's major causes. Figures are given for 1990 and 2001 unless otherwise indicated. The Human Development Index (HDI) is the first indicator listed. It is a composite index of three separate indicators measuring GDP per capita, educational attainment, and life expectancy at birth. Higher numbers suggest higher levels of development. As further measures of social justice, the table includes adult literacy, the extent of income inequality using the Gini coefficient, with higher numbers indicating greater inequality, and the percentage of women in secondary education.

The map shows that HDI has increased for most countries over the period 1990–2000.

	Human Development Index (HDI)			GDP per capita, PPP in current international $			Infant mortality rate (% live births)			Life expectancy at birth (years)			Adult illiteracy (% adult population)			Income inequality (Gini Index)*	Net enrolment in secondary education (% of women)
Country	value 1990	value 2000	% change 1990–2000	1990	2001	% change 1990–2001	1990	2000	% change 1990–2000	1990	2000	% change 1990–2000	1990	2001	% change 1990–2001	see note below	1999
East Asia & Pacific																	
Low income economies																	
Cambodia	0.501	0.543	8	980	1,521	55	9.5	8.8	-7	50	54	7	38.3	31.5	-18	40.4	11
Indonesia	0.623	0.684	10	1,952	3,059	57	6.0	4.1	-32	65	69	7	20.4	12.6	-38	31.7	46
Korea, Dem. Rep.							4.5	5.4	21	70	73	4					
Laos	0.404	0.485	20	900	1,662	85	10.6	9.2	-14	69	70	2	63.8	50.0	-22	37	25
Mongolia	0.657	0.655	0	1,804	1,829	1	7.3	5.6	-23	63	67	6	1.8	1.0	-44	33.2	92
Myanmar		0.552					10.0	8.9	-11	58	47	-18	19.3	15.0	-22		
Papua New Guinea	0.479	0.535	12	1,580	2,257	43	8.3	5.6	-33	68	70	3	43.4	35.4	-18	50.9	
Solomon Islands		0.622		1,801	1,680	-7	3.0	2.2	-26	64	69	6				19.5	
Vietnam	0.605	0.688	14		2,130		4.0	2.8	-31	65	69	7	9.5	6.4	-33	36.1	
Middle income economies																	
China & Tibet**	0.625	0.726	16	1,394	4,329	211	3.8	3.2	-16	69	70	2	23.1	15.3	-34	40.3	
Fiji	0.723	0.758	5	3,804	5,069	33	3.5	1.4	-61	67	69	4	11.4	6.8	-41		96
Malaysia	0.722	0.782	8	4,739	8,424	78	1.6	0.8	-50	62	68	11	19.2	12.1	-37	49.2	
Philippines	0.716	0.754	5	3,332	4,113	23	3.7	3.1	-17	71	73	3	7.6	4.5	-41	46.2	
Samoa	0.666	0.715	7	4,325	5,499	27	2.7	2.2	-20	66	69	4	24.8	19.3	-22		22
Thailand	0.713	0.762	7	3,835	6,630	73	3.7	2.8	-25	69	69	0	7.6	4.3	-43	41.4	
Tonga***							2.5	2.0	-20	68.8	71.0	3					72
Vanuatu		0.542		2,445	2,778	14	4.6	3.0	-34	64	68	6					
High income economies																	
Australia	0.888	0.939	6	17,271	26,552	54	0.8	0.5	-34	77	79	3				35.2	88
Brunei		0.856		14,727			0.9	0.7	-28	74	76	3	14.5	8.4	-42		
Korea, Rep.	0.815	0.882	8	8,880	18,149	104	1.2	0.8	-33	75	77	2	4.1	2.1	-48	31.6	94
Japan	0.909	0.933	3	20,183	27,101	34	0.5	0.4	-17	68	72	4				24.8	101
New Zealand	0.875	0.917	5	14,190	20,725	46	0.8	0.6	-29	64	69	7					59
Singapore	0.818	0.885	8	12,783			0.7	0.3	-57	74	78	4	11.1	7.4	-33		

Record 10 continued	Human Development Index (HDI)			GDP per capita, PPP in current international $			Infant mortality rate (% live births)			Life expectancy at birth (years)			Adult illiteracy (% adult population)			Income inequality (Gini Index)*	Net enrolment in secondary education (% of women)
Country	value 1990	value 2000	% change 1990–2000	1990	2001	% change 1990–2001	1990	2000	% change 1990–2000	1990	2000	% change 1990–2000	1990	2001	% change 1990–2001	see note below	1999
Europe & Central Asia																	
Low income economies																	
Armenia	0.759	0.754	-1	3,565	2,808	-21	1.9	1.5	-22	72	74	3	2.5	1.5	-41	44.4	
Azerbaijan		0.741		4,591	3,226	-30	2.3	1.3	-44	71	72	1				36	
Georgia		0.748		9,101	2,839	-69	1.6	1.7	9	72	73	1				37.1	88
Kyrgyzstan		0.712		3,608	2,823	-22	3.0	2.3	-23	50	54	8				34.6	
Moldova	0.759	0.701	-8	5,216	2,351	-55	3.9	3.1	-20	63	67	7	2.5	1.0	-59	40.6	40
Tajikistan	0.74	0.667	-10	2,796	1,207	-57	4.1	2.1	-49	69	69	-1	1.8	0.8	-59	34.7	
Ukraine	0.795	0.748	-6	6,694	4,224	-37	1.3	1.3	-1	70	68	-3	0.6	0.4	-35	29	21
Uzbekistan	0.731	0.727	-1		2,516		3.5	2.2	-38	69	70	1	1.4	0.8	-44	44.6	
Middle income economies																	
Albania	0.702	0.733	4	2,843	3,743	32	2.8	2.0	-29	71	74	4	23.0	14.7	-36		73
Belarus	0.809	0.788	-3	7,031	8,076	15	1.2	1.1	-5	71	68	-4	0.7	0.4	-43	21.7	
Bosnia & Herzegovina							1.5	1.3	-16	71	73	3					
Bulgaria	0.786	0.779	-1	5,797	6,182	7	1.5	1.3	-10	71	72	0	2.8	1.5	-46	26.4	85
Croatia	0.797	0.809	2	7,133	8,414	18	1.1	0.8	-30	72	73	2	3.1	1.6	-48	29	80
Czech Republic	0.835	0.849	2		14,885		1.1	0.4	-63	72	75	4				25.4	85
Estonia		0.826		7,957	10,380	30	1.2	0.8	-32	69	71	2		0.2		37.6	
Hungary	0.804	0.835	4	9,447	12,941	37	1.5	0.9	-38	78	80	2	0.9	0.7	-30	24.4	88
Kazakhstan		0.75		6,095	6,727	10	2.6	2.1	-20	57	47	-18				35.4	
Latvia	0.804	0.8	0	8,487	7,750	-9	1.4	1.0	-28	68	70	4	0.2	0.2	-1	32.4	85
Lithuania	0.816	0.808	-1	8,534	7,764	-9	1.0	0.9	-17	75	77	2	0.7	0.4	-38	32.4	85
Macedonia		0.772		5,011	4,941	-1	3.2	1.4	-55	53	55	4					33
Poland	0.792	0.833	5	5,684	9,327	64	1.9	0.9	-55	74	76	3	0.4	0.3	-37	31.6	
Romania	0.777	0.775	0	6,219	7,036	13	2.7	1.9	-30	70	70	0	3.0	1.8	-39	31.1	
Russian Federation	0.824	0.781	-5	10,079	8,948	-11	1.7	1.6	-7	69	65	-5	0.8	0.4	-43	48.7	
Serbia & Montenegro								2.3	1.3	-43	72	72	1				
Slovakia	0.82	0.835	2	9,028	11,739	30	1.2	0.8	-31	71	73	3				62.9	92
Slovenia	0.845	0.879	4	11,345	18,233	61	0.8	0.5	-45	73	75	3	0.4	0.4	-19		
Turkey	0.686	0.742	8	4,834	6,716	39	5.8	3.5	-41	66	70	5	22.1	14.4	-35	41.5	72
Turkmenistan		0.741		5,962	4,584	-23	4.5	2.7	-40	66	66	0				40.8	81
High income economies																	
Austria	0.89	0.926	4	18,664	27,518	47	0.8	0.5	-38	76	78	3				31	89
Belgium	0.896	0.939	5	19,411	27,912	44	0.8	0.5	-33	76	78	3				28.7	96
Cyprus	0.845	0.883	4	12,784			1.1	0.6	-45	77	78	2	5.7	2.7	-52		80
Denmark	0.891	0.926	4	19,513	28,342	45	0.8	0.4	-43	75	76	2				24.7	91
Finland	0.896	0.93	4	17,797	25,611	44	0.6	0.4	-25	75	77	3				25.6	94
France	0.897	0.928	3	17,966	25,074	40	0.7	0.4	-40	77	79	3				32.7	
Germany	0.885	0.925	5	18,224	25,715	41	0.7	0.5	-36	75	77	3				30	
Greece	0.859	0.885	3	11,464	17,482	52	1.0	0.5	-44	77	78	1	5.1	2.7	-47	32.7	

Record 10 continued Country	Human Development Index (HDI) value 1990	value 2000	% change 1990–2000	GDP per capita, PPP in current international $ 1990	2001	% change 1990–2001	Infant mortality rate (% live births) 1990	2000	% change 1990–2000	Life expectancy at birth (years) 1990	2000	% change 1990–2000	Adult illiteracy (% adult population) 1990	2001	% change 1990–2001	Income inequality (Gini Index)* see note below	Net enrolment in secondary education (% of women) 1999
Iceland	0.913	0.936	3	21,343	30,725	44	0.6	0.3	-47	59	63	6					78
Ireland	0.87	0.925	6	12,687	32,133	153	0.8	0.6	-28	76	78	3				35.9	102
Italy	0.879	0.913	4	17,438	24,510	41	0.8	0.5	-34	73	75	3	2.3	1.5	-35	27.3	86
Luxembourg	0.884	0.925	5	21,363	52,936	148	0.7	0.5	-32	72	73	2				26.9	
Netherlands	0.902	0.935	4	17,407	26,242	51	0.7	0.5	-31	75	78	4				32.6	
Norway	0.901	0.942	5	19,527	30,727	57	0.7	0.4	-43	69	74	7				25.8	46
Portugal	0.819	0.88	7	11,176	17,571	57	1.1	0.6	-50	75	76	2	12.7	7.4	-42	35.6	73
Spain	0.876	0.913	4	12,848	20,374	59	0.8	0.4	-49	77	78	2	3.7	2.3	-39		
Sweden	0.894	0.941	5	18,284	24,978	37	0.6	0.3	-43	78	80	3				25	
Switzerland	0.905	0.928	3	24,154	29,587	22	0.7	0.4	-46	77	80	3				33.1	67
United Kingdom	0.878	0.928	6	16,706	24,421	46	0.8	0.6	-29	76	77	2				36.8	58
Latin America & Caribbean																	
Low income countries																	
Haiti	0.447	0.471	5	1,638	1,444	-12	10.2	7.3	-29	65	66	2	60.3	49.2	-18		92
Nicaragua	0.592	0.635	7	1,721			5.1	3.3	-35	45	46	2	37.2	33.1	-11	60.3	
High income countries																	
Argentina	0.808	0.844	4	7,721	12,098	57	2.5	1.7	-31	72	74	3	4.3	3.1	-28		79
Barbados		0.871		11,252			1.2	1.7	43	75	75	1					71
Belize	0.75	0.784	5	3,633	5,900	62	3.5	3.1	-11	72	74	2	10.9	6.6	-40		40
Bolivia	0.597	0.653	9	1,826	2,439	34	8.0	5.7	-29	58	63	7	21.8	13.9	-36	44.7	
Brazil	0.713	0.757	6	5,562	7,759	39	4.8	3.2	-34	66	68	4	19.1	14.4	-25	60.7	71
Chile	0.782	0.831	6	4,981	9,754	96	1.6	1.0	-37	74	76	3	5.9	4.1	-31	56.6	73
Colombia	0.724	0.772	7	7,195	6,202	-14	3.0	2.0	-36	68	72	5	11.5	8.0	-30	57.1	57
Costa Rica	0.787	0.82	4	5,288	8,490	61	1.5	1.0	-31	75	77	3	6.1	4.3	-30	45.9	46
Cuba		0.795					1.1	0.6	-41	75	76	2	4.8	3.2	-34		81
Dominican Republic	0.677	0.727	7	3,361	6,198	84	5.0	3.9	-23	66	67	2	20.6	16.0	-22	47.4	45
Ecuador	0.705	0.732	4	2,781	3,295	18	4.5	2.8	-39	67	70	4	12.3	8.1	-34	43.7	77
El Salvador	0.644	0.706	10	2,969	4,603	55	4.6	2.9	-36	66	70	7	27.5	20.8	-25	52.2	
Guatemala	0.579	0.631	9	2,824	3,879	37	5.6	3.9	-31	44	46	6	38.9	30.7	-21	55.8	
Guyana	0.68	0.708	4	2,858	4,105	44	5.9	5.4	-9	53	53	0	2.8	1.4	-50	40.2	
Honduras	0.615	0.638	4	2,074	2,505	21	5.0	3.5	-31	78	80	3	31.5	24.9	-21	56.3	
Jamaica	0.72	0.742	3	3,261	3,890	19	2.5	2.0	-22	79	81	2	17.9	12.8	-29	37.9	76
Mexico	0.761	0.796	5	6,383	8,969	41	3.6	2.9	-20	68	68	-1	12.1	8.3	-31	53.1	65
Panama	0.747	0.787	5	3,871	5,986	55	2.6	2.0	-24	55	59	6	11.0	7.9	-28	48.5	91
Paraguay	0.717	0.74	3	3,922	4,379	12	3.1	2.3	-26	66	69	5	9.7	6.5	-33	57.7	
Peru	0.704	0.747	6	3,251	4,797	48	5.4	3.2	-41	66	69	6	14.5	9.8	-33	46.2	77
St Lucia		0.772		4,360	5,537	27	1.9	1.3	-30	71	71	0				34.4	86
Suriname		0.756		2,508	3,677	47	3.4	2.7	-22	69	70	2					57
Trinidad & Tobago	0.781	0.805	3	6,035	10,018	66	1.8	1.6	-10	71	73	2	8.6	6.0	-30	40.3	95
Uruguay	0.801	0.831	4	6,177	8,781	42	2.1	1.4	-35	73	74	2	3.4	2.2	-36	42.3	
Venezuela	0.757	0.77	2	5,050	5,966	18	2.5	1.9	-21	71	73	3	11.0	7.1	-35	49.5	40

Record 10 continued	Human Development Index (HDI)			GDP per capita, PPP in current international $			Infant mortality rate (% live births)			Life expectancy at birth (years)			Adult illiteracy (% adult population)			Income inequality (Gini Index)*	Net enrolment in secondary education (% of women)
Country	value 1990	value 2000	% change 1990–2000	1990	2001	% change 1990–2001	1990	2000	% change 1990–2000	1990	2000	% change 1990–2000	1990	2001	% change 1990–2001	see note below	1999
High income countries																	
Bahamas	0.822	0.826	0	14,521			2.8	1.8	-37	69	69	0	5.6	4.5	-19		
Middle East & North Africa																	
Low income countries																	
Yemen	0.399	0.479	20	567	812	43	11.0	7.6	-31	52	56	8	67.3	52.4	-22	33.4	
Middle income countries																	
Algeria	0.639	0.697	9	4,502	5,319	18	4.6	3.3	-28	67	71	5	47.4	32.2	-32	35.3	60
Djibouti***		0.445			2,077		12.1	11.5	-5	47.8	45.8	-4	47.0	34.5	-27		
Egypt	0.574	0.642	12	2,509	3,750	49	6.8	4.2	-38	63	67	7	52.9	43.9	-17	28.9	
Iran	0.645	0.721	12	3,878	6,128	58	5.4	3.3	-39	61	61	0	36.5	22.7	-38		
Iraq							4.0	9.3	133	75	76	2	54.7	43.1	-21		26
Jordan	0.677	0.717	6	3,304	4,080	23	3.0	2.5	-16	68	65	-4	19.0	9.8	-48	36.4	78
Lebanon	0.68	0.755	11	1,870	4,391	135	3.6	2.6	-30	58	44	-24	19.7	13.5	-31		24
Libya		0.773					3.3	2.6	-20	71	73	2	31.9	19.2	-40		
Malta	0.826	0.875	6	8,742			0.9	0.6	-33	49	52	5	11.5	7.7	-34		
Morocco & Western Sahara	0.54	0.602	11	2,888	3,787	31	6.6	4.7	-29	43	42	-2	61.3	50.2	-18	39.5	68
Oman		0.751					2.2	1.7	-24	59	63	7	45.3	27.0	-40		
Saudi Arabia	0.706	0.759	8	9,401			3.2	1.8	-43	69	73	5	33.7	22.9	-32		
Syria	0.634	0.691	9	2,215	3,626	64	3.9	2.4	-38	66	70	5	35.2	24.7	-30		70
Tunisia	0.646	0.722	12	3,900	6,769	74	3.7	2.6	-31	70	72	3	40.9	27.9	-32	41.7	88
High income countries																	
Bahrain		0.831		12,088			2.3	0.7	-68	71	73	2	17.8	12.1	-32		87
Israel	0.855	0.896	5	13,450			1.0	0.6	-44	77	79	2	9.2	5.2	-44	38.1	89
Kuwait		0.813		9,952			1.4	0.9	-31	68	67	-1	23.3	17.5	-25		
Qatar		0.803					2.1	1.4	-34	72	75	4	23.0	18.3	-20		
United Arab Emirates		0.812		20,204			2.0	0.8	-63	74	75	2	28.8	23.2	-19		55
North America																	
High income countries																	
Canada	0.926	0.94	2	20,122	28,611	42	0.7	0.5	-24	77	79	2				31.5	98
United States	0.914	0.939	3	23,447	34,888	49	0.9	0.7	-24	75	77	2				40.8	
South Asia																	
Low income countries																	
Afghanistan***							16.9	16.3	-4	41.5	43.0	3					
Bangladesh	0.416	0.478	15	1,004	1,644	64	9.1	6.0	-34	55	61	12	65.0	58.0	-11	33.6	
Bhutan		0.494		882	1,490	69		5.8			62						
India	0.511	0.577	13	1,400	2,464	76	8.0	6.9	-14	62	66	7	50.7	42.0	-17	37.8	
Nepal	0.416	0.49	18	883	1,389	57	10.1	7.4	-27	77	78	1	69.5	57.1	-18	36.7	
Pakistan	0.442	0.499	13	1,394	1,990	43	11.0	8.3	-25	72	75	3	64.6	55.9	-13	31.2	

Record 10 continued	Human Development Index (HDI)			GDP per capita, PPP in current international $			Infant mortality rate (% live births)			Life expectancy at birth (years)			Adult illiteracy (% adult population)			Income inequality (Gini Index)*	Net enrolment in secondary education (% of women)
Country	value 1990	value 2000	% change 1990–2000	1990	2001	% change 1990–2001	1990	2000	% change 1990–2000	1990	2000	% change 1990–2000	1990	2001	% change 1990–2001	see note below	1999
Middle income countries																	
Maldives	0.676	0.743	10	3,611	4,780	32	6.0	2.8	-54	45	42	-6	5.5	3.1	-43		
Sri Lanka	0.697	0.741	6	2,036	3,634	78	1.9	1.5	-19	70	73	4	11.3	8.1	-28	59.3	
Sub-Saharan Africa																	
Low income countries																	
Angola		0.403		1,581	1,866	18	13.0	12.8	-2	45	47	2					
Benin	0.358	0.42	17	706	1,041	47	10.4	8.7	-16	52	53	2	73.6	61.4	-17		11
Burkina Faso	0.29	0.325	12	636	1,025	61	11.1	10.4	-6	45	44	-3	83.6	75.2	-10	55.1	7
Burundi	0.344	0.313	-9	722	598	-17	11.9	10.2	-14	44	42	-4	63.0	50.8	-19	42.5	
Cameroon	0.513	0.512	0	1,561	1,772	13	8.1	7.6	-6	54	50	-8	37.5	23.1	-38	47.7	
Central African Republic	0.372	0.375	1	1,060	1,184	12	10.2	9.6	-6	48	43	-9	66.7	51.8	-22	61.3	
Chad	0.322	0.365	13	766	938	22	11.8	10.1	-14	46	48	5	72.3	55.8	-23		4
Comoros	0.502	0.511	2	1,716	1,607	-6	8.4	6.0	-29	56	61	9	46.2	44.0	-5		
Congo, Dem. Rep.		0.431		1,290			8.4	6.0	-29	52	46	-11	52.5	37.3	-29		
Congo, Rep.	0.51	0.512	0	760	767	1	8.2	6.8	-16	51	51	0	32.9	18.2	-45		
Côte d'Ivoire	0.415	0.428	3	1,552	1,568	1	9.5	11.1	17	50	46	-8	66.7	51.8	-22	36.7	
Equatorial Guinea	0.553	0.679	23	1,052	22,901	2,077	12.1	10.2	-16	47	51	8	26.7	15.8	-41		20
Eritrea		0.421			803		8.1	6.0	-27	49	52	6	53.6	43.3	-19		93
Ethiopia	0.297	0.327	10	486	717	47	13.1	9.8	-25	45	42	-6	71.3	59.7	-16	40	90
Gambia		0.405		1,488	1,730	16	10.9	7.3	-33	49	53	8	74.4	62.2	-16	50.2	56
Ghana	0.506	0.548	8	1,368	2,054	50	6.6	5.8	-12	57	57	-1	41.6	27.4	-34	40.7	88
Guinea		0.414		1,520	2,052	35	12.1	9.5	-21	42	45	6				40.3	
Guinea-Bissau	0.304	0.349	15	686	771	12	14.5	12.6	-13	64	63	-1	72.8	60.3	-17	56.2	
Kenya	0.533	0.513	-4	977	1,032	6	6.2	7.8	26	66	61	-7	29.2	16.7	-43	44.9	
Lesotho	0.574	0.535	-7	1,087	2,093	93	10.2	9.1	-10	45	47	5	22.1	16.2	-27	56	17
Liberia							16.8	11.1	-34	68	71	4	60.6	44.7	-26		
Madagascar	0.434	0.469	8	818	889	9	10.3	8.8	-15	45	39	-13	42.0	32.7	-22	38.1	
Malawi	0.362	0.4	10	445	631	42	12.8	10.3	-20	71	73	3	48.2	39.0	-19		
Mali	0.312	0.386	24	582	935	61	13.6	12.0	-11	75	78	3	74.4	56.9	-24	50.5	74
Mauritania	0.39	0.438	12	1,167	1,783	53	11.2	10.1	-10	70	72	3	65.2	59.3	-9	37.3	
Mozambique	0.31	0.322	4	521	1,110	113	15.0	12.9	-14	55	56	3	66.5	54.8	-18	39.6	
Niger	0.256	0.277	8	738	776	5	15.0	11.4	-24	49	47	-5	88.6	83.5	-6	50.5	
Nigeria	0.425	0.462	9	764	898	18	8.6	8.4	-2	77	79	3	51.4	34.7	-32	50.6	64
Rwanda	0.346	0.403	16	952	1,007	6	13.2	12.3	-7	40	40	-1	46.7	32.0	-31	28.9	
Sao Tome & Principe		0.632					6.1	4.6	-25	62	65	5				42.6	
Senegal	0.38	0.431	13	1,199	1,583	32	7.4	6.0	-19	50	52	6	71.7	61.7	-14		
Sierra Leone		0.275		894	474	-47	19.0	15.4	-19	35	39	11				41.3	
Somalia							15.2	11.7	-23	42	48	16				28.4	80
Sudan	0.419	0.499	19	803	1,878	134	9.8	8.1	-17	52	56	8	54.0	41.1	-24		5

Record 10 continued	Human Development Index (HDI)			GDP per capita, PPP in current international $			Infant mortality rate (% live births)			Life expectancy at birth (years)			Adult illiteracy (% adult population)			Income inequality (Gini Index)*	Net enrolment in secondary education (% of women)
Country	value 1990	value 2000	% change 1990–2000	1990	2001	% change 1990–2001	1990	2000	% change 1990–2000	1990	2000	% change 1990–2000	1990	2001	% change 1990–2001	see note below	1999
Tanzania	0.422	0.44	4	453	545	20	11.5	9.3	-19	50	44	-11	37.0	23.9	-35	38.2	
Togo	0.465	0.493	6	1,400	1,449	3	8.1	7.5	-7	50	49	-2	55.7	41.6	-25		
Uganda	0.388	0.444	14	746	1,255	68	10.4	8.3	-20	47	42	-10	43.9	32.0	-27	37.4	
Zambia	0.468	0.433	-7	837	820	-2	10.7	11.5	7	49	38	-23	31.9	21.0	-34	52.6	
Zimbabwe	0.597	0.551	-8	2,336	2,406	3	5.2	6.9	33	56	40	-29	19.3	10.7	-45	50.1	
Middle income countries																	
Botswana	0.653	0.572	-12	4,911	8,196	67	5.5	5.8	6	57	39	-31	31.9	21.9	-31		63
Cape Verde	0.626	0.715	14	2,926	4,902	68	6.4	3.7	-42	65	69	5	36.2	25.1	-31		
Gabon		0.637		5,241	6,310	20	7.2	5.8	-19	52	53	2					
Mauritius	0.723	0.772	7	5,597	10,400	86	2.0	1.6	-24	71	73	3	20.1	15.1	-25		
Namibia		0.61		4,411	6,650	51	6.4	6.3	-2	54	59	10	25.1	17.3	-31		
South Africa	0.714	0.695	-3	8,282	9,565	15	5.5	6.3	14	62	48	-23	18.8	14.4	-23		
Swaziland	0.615	0.577	-6	3,630	4,586	26	7.9	8.9	13	57	46	-19	28.4	19.7	-31	60.9	

	Human Development Index (HDI)	GDP per capita PPP in current international $	Infant mortality rate (percentage live births)	Life expectancy at birth (years)
Region	value 2000	2001	2000	2000
Low income	0.554	2,084	7.6	59
Middle income	0.747	5,817	3.1	70
Low & middle income:				
East Asia & the Pacific	0.726	4,103	3.5	69
Europe & Central Asia	0.783	7,147	2.0	69
Latin America & Caribbean	0.767	7,310	2.9	70
Middle East & North Africa	0.653	*5,296*	4.3	68
South Asia	0.570	2,317	7.3	62
Sub-Saharan Africa	0.471	1,689	9.1	47
High income	0.930	27,695	0.6	78
World	0.722	7,629	5.4	66

*Survey data for Gini index varies by country. 0 represents perfect equality, 100 represents perfect inequality.

**Data for China do not include Hong Kong

Figures in italics indicate data from 2000 due to data from 2001 being unavailable.

Sources (***denoting data, except for HDI index, from WDI): World Bank, World Development Indicators 2002 (WDI-Online); United Nations Development Programme, Human Development Report 2002: Deepening democracy in a Fragmented World (New York: Oxford University Press)

R10 Social Justice: Human Development Index

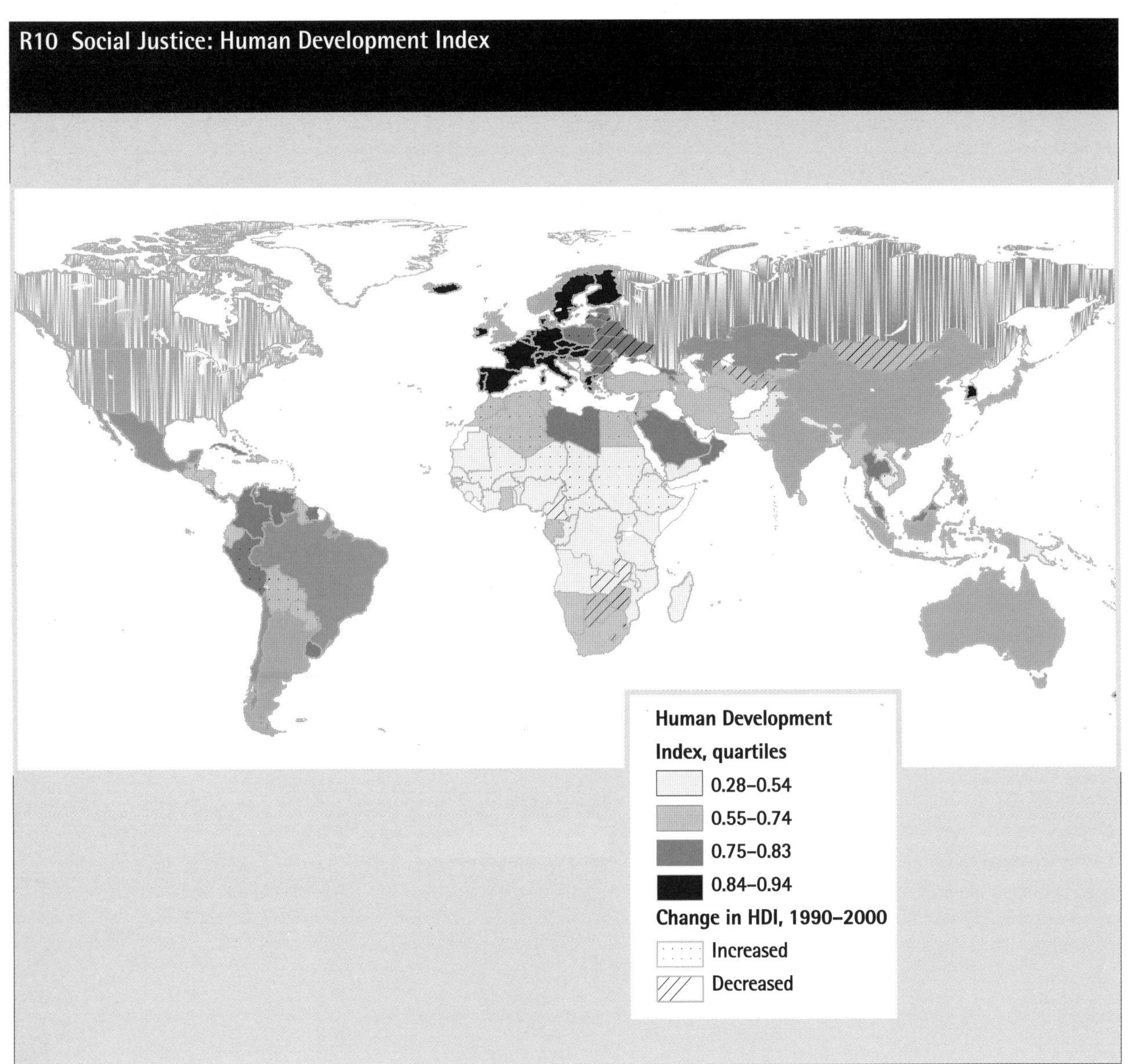

Record 11 Corruption

This record examines the state of the rule of law through the prism of corruption. Corruption not only hinders economic development, it inhibits the formation of trust and social capital. It is therefore likely to be an obstacle to the growth of civil society generally as well as a focus of civil society activism, both locally and globally. The table presents three kinds of indicators of corruption: the Corruption Perceptions Index by Transparency International, and the Institute for Management Development's Bribing and Corruption and Transparency of Government indices. Since these are relatively new measures, we compare 2000 with 2002. Scores range between 10, indicating high transparency and the absence of bribery and corruption, and 0, indicating lack of transparency and high levels of perceived corruption and bribery.

	Corruption Perception Index		Bribing and Corruption		Transparency of Government	
Country	2000	2002	2000	2002	2000	2002
East Asia & Pacific						
Low income economies						
Indonesia	1.7	1.9	1.3	1.0	5.0	2.4
Vietnam	2.5	2.4				
Mongolia						
Middle income economies						
China	3.1	3.5	2.2	2.6	6.3	4.7
Malaysia	4.8	4.9	3.2	4.5	6.4	5.0
Philippines	2.8	2.6	1.6	1.5	3.3	3.9
Thailand	3.2	3.2	2.0	2.8	4.3	4.4
High income economies						
Australia	8.3	8.6	8.2	8.0	6.9	7.0
Korea, Rep.	4.0	4.5	2.6	3.7	3.7	4.0
Japan	6.4	7.1	5.3	5.2	3.7	3.4
New Zealand	9.4	9.5	8.8	9.0	6.6	6.9
Singapore	9.1	9.3	8.7	8.8	8.4	7.3
Europe & Central Asia						
Low income economies						
Armenia	2.5					
Azerbaijan	1.5	2.0				
Georgia		2.4				
Kyrgyzstan						
Moldova	2.6	2.1				
Ukraine	1.5	2.4				
Uzbekistan	2.4	2.9				
Middle income economies						
Albania		2.5				
Belarus	4.1	4.8				
Bulgaria	3.5	4.0				
Croatia	3.7	3.8				
Czech Republic	4.3	3.7	1.8	2.6	3.2	4.4
Estonia	5.7	5.6		4.9		5.5
Hungary	5.2	4.9	3.3	2.7	5.2	3.4
Kazakhstan	3.0	2.3				
Latvia	3.4	3.7				
Lithuania	4.1	4.8				
Macedonia						
Poland	4.1	4.0	2.9	1.5	3.4	3.2
Romania	2.9	2.6				

R11 continued	Corruption Perception Index		Bribing and corruption		Transparency of government	
Country	2000	2002	2000	2002	2000	2002
Russian Federation	2.1	2.7	1.9	1.6	2.5	4.1
Serbia & Montenegro	1.3					
Slovakia	3.5	3.7		1.5		4.3
Slovenia	5.5	6.0	3.7	3.7	3.1	3.8
Turkey	3.8	3.2	2.6	2.3	6.0	3.4
High income economies						
Austria	7.7	7.8	6.7	7.5	5.3	6.5
Belgium	6.1	7.1	5.0	5.3	5.9	4.5
Denmark	9.8	9.5	9.2	9.3	5.5	7.7
Finland	10.0	9.7	9.5	9.5	7.6	8.1
France	6.7	6.3	5.0	5.1	5.8	4.4
Germany	7.6	7.3	5.4	6.6	4.5	5.8
Greece	4.9	4.2	2.4	2.5	5.5	3.8
Iceland	9.1	9.4	8.5	8.4	6.8	6.4
Ireland	7.2	6.9	6.5	6.1	7.5	6.2
Italy	4.6	5.2	2.8	3.3	3.8	4.4
Luxembourg	8.6	9.0	7.2	7.4	6.9	6.9
Netherlands	8.9	9.0	7.8	7.4	7.3	6.9
Norway	9.1	8.5	8.3	8.0	5.3	6.8
Portugal	6.4	6.3	4.3	3.9	5.4	3.1
Spain	7.0	7.1	5.3	5.3	6.9	5.9
Sweden	9.4	9.3	8.4	8.6	4.2	6.5
Switzerland	8.6	8.5	7.5	7.7	6.1	7.4
United Kingdom	8.7	8.7	7.6	7.1	5.8	5.6
Latin America & Caribbean						
Low income countries						
Haiti		2.2				
Nicaragua		2.5				
Middle income countries						
Argentina	3.5	2.8	1.5	0.7	5.2	0.7
Bolivia	2.7	2.2				
Brazil	3.9	4.0	2.6	2.9	5.3	5.7
Chile	7.4	7.5	6.3	7.0	5.6	6.4
Colombia	3.2	3.6	1.6	1.9	5.0	3.5
Costa Rica	5.4	4.5				
Dominican Republic		3.5				
Ecuador	2.6	2.2				
El Salvador	4.1	3.4				
Guatemala		2.5				
Honduras		2.7				
Jamaica		4.0				
Mexico	3.3	3.6	2.1	2.2	5.5	5.1
Panama		3.0				
Paraguay		1.7				
Peru	4.4	4.0				
Trinidad & Tobago		4.9				
Uruguay		5.1				
Venezuela	2.7	2.5	1.4	1.0	2.4	0.8

R11 continued	Corruption Perception Index		Bribing and corruption		Transparency of government	
Country	**2000**	**2002**	**2000**	**2002**	**2000**	**2002**
Middle East & North Africa						
Middle income countries						
Egypt	3.1	3.4				
Jordan	4.6	4.5				
Morocco	4.7	3.7				
Tunisia	5.2	4.8				
High income countries						
Israel	6.6	7.3	6.0	6.6	5.5	4.7
North America						
High income countries						
Canada	9.2	9.0	8.3	7.5	6.9	6.1
United States	7.8	7.7	6.8	7.0	6.2	6.6
South Asia						
Low income countries						
Bangladesh		1.2				
India	2.8	2.7	1.5	1.5	5.0	3.7
Pakistan		2.6				
Middle income countries						
Sri Lanka		3.7				
Sub-Saharan Africa						
Low income countries						
Angola	1.7	1.7				
Burkina Faso	3					
Cameroon	2.0	2.2				
Côte d'Ivoire	2.7	2.7				
Ethiopia	3.2	3.5				
Ghana	3.5	3.9				
Kenya	2.1	1.9				
Madagascar		1.7				
Malawi	4.1	2.9				
Mozambique	2.2					
Nigeria	1.2	1.6				
Senegal	3.5	3.1				
Tanzania	2.5	2.7				
Uganda	2.3	2.1				
Zambia	3.4	2.6				
Zimbabwe	3.0	2.7				
Middle income countries						
Botswana	6.0	6.4				
Mauritius	4.7	4.5				
Namibia	5.4	5.7				
South Africa	5.0	4.8	2.7	2.8	6.0	6.0

Sources: Transparency International, 2000 Corruption Perceptions Index available at http://www.transparency.org/cpi/2000/cpi2000.html; Transparency International, 2002 Corruption Perceptions Index available at http://www.transparency.org/cpi/2002/cpi2002.en.html; International Institute for Management Development (2000), Tables 3.30 'Transparency' and 3.36 'Bribing and Corruption', The World Competitiveness Yearbook 1999, Institute for Management Development, Lausanne, Switzerland; International Institute for Management Development (2002), Tables 2.3.14 'Transparency' and 2.3.17 'Bribing and Corruption', The World Competitiveness Yearbook 2002, Institute for Management Development, Lausanne, Switzerland.

Record 12 Refugee populations and flows

This record shows two dimensions of the refugee problem: if a country 'generates' many refugees or internally displaced persons (IDP)s, it can be assumed that there is little respect for the rule of law in that country. On the other hand, countries that host many refugees can be considered as extending international hospitality and bearing the associated financial burden. The table presents data on refugee populations, both in total counts and per 1,000 inhabitants for 1991 and 2001. In addition, the table provides information on inflows and outflows of refugees during 2001, as well as estimates of IDPs. Negative inflow for a country indicates that there are fewer refugees in that country at the end of the year than at the beginning, while negative outflow indicates that the number of refugees originating from that country decreased over the year.

The map shows numbers of refugees per thousand of population, for each country, at the end of 2001.

	Refugee populations						IDPs	Refugee flows		IDP flows
	Total			per thousand inhabitants				Inflow	Outflow	
Country of asylum	1991	2001*	% change	1991	2001	% change	2001	2001	2001	2001
East Asia & Pacific										
Low income economies										
Cambodia		50						16	-2,120	
Indonesia & East Timor	18,700	73,551	293	0.1	0.3	234		-49,067	-49,325	
Laos					0.0				-3,285	
Myanmar					0.0				8,909	
Papua New Guinea	6,100	4,941	-19	1.5	0.9	-37		-922		
Solomon Islands					0.0					
Vietnam	20,100	15,945	-21	0.3	0.2	-33		0	-17,423	
Middle income economies										
China & Tibet	288,900	295,325	2	0.3	0.2	-8		1,215	6,561	
Fiji					0.0				334	
Malaysia	13,900	50,466	263	0.7	2.1	185		-21		
Philippines	20,000	136	-99	0.3	0.0	-99		-39	-5	
Thailand	88,200	110,711	26	1.6	1.8	16		5,746	-48	
High income economies										
Australia	32,400	55,146	70	1.9	2.8	52		-2,646		
Korea, Rep.	200	7	-97	0.0	0.0	-97		1		
Japan	9,100	3,200	-65	0.1	0.0	-66		-552		
New Zealand	16,800	5,264	-69	4.8	1.4	-72		321		
Singapore	200	2	-99	0.1	0.0	-99		2		
Europe & Central Asia										
Low income economies										
Armenia		264,337			69.4			-16,254	1,609	
Azerbaijan		367			0.0		572,955	80	-15,476	
Georgia		7,901			1.6		264,221	281	-4,284	-7,880
Kyrgyzstan		9,296			1.9			-1,313	-55	
Moldova		159			0.0		1,000	91	1,085	
Tajikistan		15,346			2.5			-18	-3,515	
Ukraine		2,983			0.1			22	7,368	
Uzbekistan		39,579			1.6			1,229	-114	
Middle income economies										
Albania		292			0.1			-231	840	
Belarus		584			0.1			126	1,226	
Bosnia & Herzegovina		32,745			8.1		438,253	-5,407	-53,108	-79,999

Record 12 continued	Refugee populations							Refugee flows		
	Total			per thousand inhabitants			IDPs	Inflow	Outflow	IDP flows
Country of asylum	1991	2001*	% change	1991	2001	% change	2001	2001	2001	2001
Bulgaria		3,004			0.4			1,530	-353	
Croatia		21,875			5.0		23,402	-562	-42,006	-10,732
Czech Republic		1,216			0.1			30	147	
Estonia		11			0.0			7	149	
Hungary	73,800	4,710	-94	7.1	0.5	-94		-353	441	
Kazakhstan		19,531			1.3			-1,043	295	
Latvia		8			0.0			1	143	
Lithuania		287			0.1			232	68	
Macedonia		4,363			2.1		16,371	-4,687	10,302	16,371
Poland	200	1,311	556	0.0	0.0	549		291	754	
Romania	700	1,805	158	0.0	0.1	167		120	-2,041	
Russian Federation		17,970			0.1		443,288	-8,295	5,416	-47,362
Serbia & Montenegro	500	400,304	79,961	0.0	37.6	78,842	263,600	-84,087	-1,322	-3,900
Slovakia		472			0.1			16	22	
Slovenia		2,415			1.2			-401	-2,489	
Turkey	29,400	3,472	-88	0.5	0.1	-90		369	-258	
Turkmenistan		14,005			2.6			-183	68	
High income economies										
Austria	18,700	14,390	-23	2.4	1.8	-26		-2,702		
Belgium	24,100	12,265	-49	2.4	1.2	-50		-6,567		
Cyprus		83			0.1			7		
Denmark	44,000	73,284	67	8.5	13.7	60		2,250		
Finland	7,700	12,728	65	1.5	2.5	60		-548		
France	170,000	131,601	-23	3.0	2.2	-25		-907		
Germany	383,900	903,000	135	4.8	11.0	129		-3,000	-63	
Greece	9,000	6,948	-23	0.9	0.7	-25		295	-22	
Iceland	100	213	113	0.4	0.8	94		-31		
Ireland	300	3,598	1,099	0.1	0.9	1,003		1,055		
Italy	12,200	8,571	-30	0.2	0.1	-31		1,722		
Luxembourg	700	1,201	72	1.8	2.7	50		442		
Netherlands	21,300	152,338	615	1.4	9.5	572		6,158		
Norway	29,100	50,128	72	6.8	11.1	62		2,475		
Portugal	1,000	449	-55	0.1	0.0	-57		16		
Spain	9,200	6,806	-26	0.2	0.2	-27		-181		
Sweden	238,400	146,491	-39	27.7	16.5	-40		-10,726		
Switzerland	27,600	58,494	112	4.1	8.1	100		841		
United Kingdom	100,000	148,550	49	1.7	2.5	43		27,275	-1	
Latin America & Caribbean										
Low income countries										
Haiti					0.0				171	
Nicaragua	14,900	325	-98	3.8	0.1	-98		-7	-641	
Middle income countries										
Argentina	11,500	2,396	-79	0.3	0.1	-82		0	74	
Belize	19,400	1,129	-94	99.8	4.6	-95		-121		
Bolivia	300	347	16	0.0	0.0	-9		-4	75	
Brazil	5,400	2,884	-47	0.0	0.0	-53		162	34	
Chile	100	389	289	0.0	0.0	237		25	10	

Record 12 continued	Refugee populations							Refugee flows		
	Total			per thousand inhabitants			IDPs	Inflow	Outflow	IDP flows
Country of asylum	1991	2001*	% change	1991	2001	% change	2001	2001	2001	2001
Colombia	500	210	-58	0.0	0.0	-65	720,000	-29	8,699	195,000
Costa Rica	117,500	8,104	-93	37.5	2.1	-94		2,585		
Cuba		1,036			0.1			82	-1,066	
Dominican Republic	1,600		-100	0.2	0.0	-100				
Ecuador	300	1,957	552	0.0	0.2	432		355	74	
El Salvador	20,100	69	-100	3.9	0.0	-100		10	-1,200	
Guatemala	223,200	729	-100	24.9	0.1	-100		9	-3,909	
Honduras	102,000	20	-100	20.3	0.0	-100		8	-114	
Mexico	354,500	15,455	-96	4.2	0.2	-96		-2,996	305	
Panama	900	1,474	64	0.4	0.5	38		163		
Paraguay	100	21	-79	0.0	0.0	-84		0		
Peru	700	683	-2	0.0	0.0	-18		-4	-467	
Suriname					0.0				-100	
Uruguay	100	90	-10	0.0	0.0	-16		11		
Venezuela	1,700	59	-97	0.1	0.0	-97		-73	57	
Middle East & North Africa										
Low income countries										
Yemen	30,000	69,468	132	2.2	3.9	73		8,923	-108	
Middle income countries										
Algeria	169,100	169,422	0	6.6	5.5	-17		-234	473	
Djibouti	96,100	23,176	-76	190.4	36.0	-81		-67	-1,412	
Egypt	2,200	7,230	229	0.0	0.1	170		390	965	
Iran	4,405,000	1,868,000	-58	79.7	28.9	-64		0	3,725	
Iraq	88,000	128,142	46	4.7	5.4	14		384	4,141	
Jordan	400	1,067	167	0.1	0.2	88		-5	-3	
Lebanon	5,200	2,815	-46	1.4	0.6	-54		143	-1,422	
Libya		11,664			2.2			123	277	
Malta		190			0.5			0		
Morocco	300	2,091	597	0.0	0.1	486		-14	47	
Saudi Arabia	33,100	245,268	641	2.0	11.5	464		239,959		
Syria	4,200	3,351	-20	0.3	0.2	-40		-112	-1,052	
Tunisia	100	97	-3	0.0	0.0	-17		-339	284	
High income countries										
Bahrain		1			0.0			0		
Israel		4,168			0.7			90	25	
Kuwait	125,000	1,255	-99	91.7	0.6	-99		-1,521	25	
Qatar		67			0.1			36		
United Arab Emirates		556			0.2			-6		
North America										
High income countries										
Canada	538,100	129,224	-76	19.1	4.2	-78		2,233		
United States	482,000	515,853	7	1.9	1.8	-5		9,731	60	
South Asia										
Low income countries										
Afghanistan		6			0.0		1,200,000	6	222,793	511,000
Bangladesh	40,300	22,173	-45	0.4	0.2	-54		546	130	

Record 12 continued

Country of asylum	Refugee populations Total 1991	2001*	% change	per thousand inhabitants 1991	2001	% change	IDPs 2001	Refugee flows Inflow 2001	Outflow 2001	IDP flows 2001
Bhutan					0.0				1,906	
India	210,600	169,549	-19	0.2	0.2	-32		-1,392	319	
Nepal	9,600	130,945	1,264	0.5	5.6	974		1,708	77	
Pakistan	3,099,900	2,198,797	-29	28.0	15.5	-44		197,331	2,381	
Middle income countries										
Sri Lanka		17			0.0		683,286	1	-1,415	-23,228
Sub-Saharan Africa										
Low income countries										
Angola	11,000	12,250	11	1.1	0.9	-18	202,000	164	37,017	504
Benin	500	4,799	860	0.1	0.7	625		503		
Burkina Faso	300	457	52	0.0	0.0	20		-239		
Burundi	270,100	27,896	-90	48.2	4.0	-92	20,000	760	-14,439	-36,000
Cameroon	45,200	41,186	-9	3.8	2.7	-28		-2,494	664	
Central African Republic	12,200	49,239	304	4.1	13.1	221		-6,422	28,557	
Chad		12,950			1.6			-4,742	-8,511	
Comoros		13			0.0			2		
Congo, Dem. Rep.	483,000	362,012	-25	12.6	6.9	-45	3,458	29,762	19,551	458
Congo, Rep.	3,400	119,147	3,404	1.5	38.4	2,495		-4,043	-3,301	
Côte d'Ivoire	230,300	126,239	-45	18.9	7.7	-59		5,548	117	
Equatorial Guinea				0	0				29	
Eritrea		2,272			0.5			288	-43,399	
Ethiopia		152,554			2.3			-45,405	-7,444	
Gambia	200	8,133	3,967	0.2	6.1	2,837		-3,883	0	
Ghana	8,100	11,792	46	0.5	0.6	16		-928	9	
Guinea	548,000	178,444	-67	92.5	23.5	-75		-248,761	524	
Guinea-Bissau	4,600	7,332	59	4.7	6.0	27		-255	36	
Kenya	120,200	239,221	99	5.0	7.8	56		33,115	286	
Lesotho	200	39	-81	0.1	0.0	-84		39		
Liberia		54,760			17.0		196,116	-14,555	-22,323	85,430
Madagascar		34			0.0			-16		
Malawi	981,800	6,200	-99	113.6	0.6	-99		2,300		
Mali	13,100	8,439	-36	1.5	0.8	-50		27	6	
Mauritania	35,200	365	-99	17.2	0.1	-99		15	116	
Mozambique	400	207	-48	0.0	0.0	-59		0		
Niger	1,400	83	-94	0.2	0.0	-96		24	-8	
Nigeria	3,600	7,200	100	0.0	0.1	52		-70	376	
Rwanda	34,000	34,786	2	4.8	4.0	-16		4,708	-13,217	
Senegal	71,900	20,707	-71	9.6	2.1	-78		-59	-2,519	
Sierra Leone	28,000	10,501	-62	6.8	2.0	-70		3,955	-223,745	-300,000
Somalia		589			0.1			31	-35,495	-18,000
Sudan	729,200	349,209	-52	28.8	11.0	-62		-65,719	-4,363	
Tanzania	288,100	668,107	132	11.0	19.4	77		-12,755	107	
Togo	3,400	12,257	261	1.0	2.6	174		34	362	
Uganda	162,500	199,736	23	9.6	8.8	-9		-36,886	7,724	
Zambia	140,700	284,173	102	17.5	27.6	58		33,263	170	
Zimbabwe	197,600	8,706	-96	18.8	0.7	-96		4,579	170	

Record 12 continued

Country of asylum	Refugee populations: Total 1991	Total 2001*	Total % change	per thousand inhabitants 1991	per thousand inhabitants 2001	per thousand inhabitants % change	IDPs 2001	Refugee flows: Inflow 2001	Outflow 2001	IDP flows 2001
Middle income countries										
Botswana	900	3,581	298	0.7	2.2	224		30		
Gabon	200	15,581	7,691	0.2	12.4	5,854		-2,401		
Mauritius		14			0.0			14		
Namibia		30,885			17.2			3,622	-41	
South Africa		18,605			0.4			3,542	16	
Swaziland	49,600	690	-99	62.4	0.6	-99		27		

Region	Refugee populations: Total 1991	Total 2001	% change	Total IDPs 2001	Refugee flows: Total inflow 2001	Total outflow 2001	Refugee populations per 1000 2001	Refugee flows per 1000 inhabitants: Inflow 2001	Outflow 2000	IDP flows 2000
East Asia & Pacific	514,600	614,744	19		-45946	-56,402	0.337	-0.025	-0.031	
Europe & Central Asia	1,201,900	2,601,486	116	2,023,090	-100535	-95,174	5.459	-0.211	-0.200	-0.280
Latin America & Caribbean	874,800	37,377	-96	720,000	176	2,002	0.072	0.000	0.004	0.375
Middle East & North Africa	4,958,700	2,538,028	-49		247750	5,965	8.528	0.832	0.020	
North America	1,020,100	645,077	-37		11964	60	2.048	0.038	0.000	
South Asia	3,360,400	2,521,487	-25	1,883,286	198200	226,191	1.827	0.144	0.164	0.353
Sub-Saharan Africa	4,478,900	3,091,390	-31	421,574	-323281	-282,968	4.588	-0.480	-0.420	-0.397

Empty cells indicate that the value is below 100, zero or not available.

* The figures for refugee populations are as of end 2001.
** Figures for inflow and outflow of refugees were obtained by netting the populations of refugees reported in the beginning of 2001 and at the end of 2001 for the country of asylum in the case of inflow and for the country of origin in the case of outflow. In yearbook 2001, the figures for inflow and outflow were computed differently by aggregating the number of refugees seeking asylum in a particular country for inflow and the number of refugees fleeing a particular country for outflow.

Inflows and outflows based on primae facie arrivals and and individually recognised refugees. IDPs refer to internally displaced persons of concern to/assisted by UNHCR at end of 2000.

Sources: UNHCHR, The State of the World's Refugees 1993: The Challenge of Protection, Annex I.1, (Penguin), World Bank, UNHCR, 2001 Population Statistics (provisional) http://www.unhcr.org, World Development Indicators 2002 (WDI-Online)

R12 Refugee populations, 2001

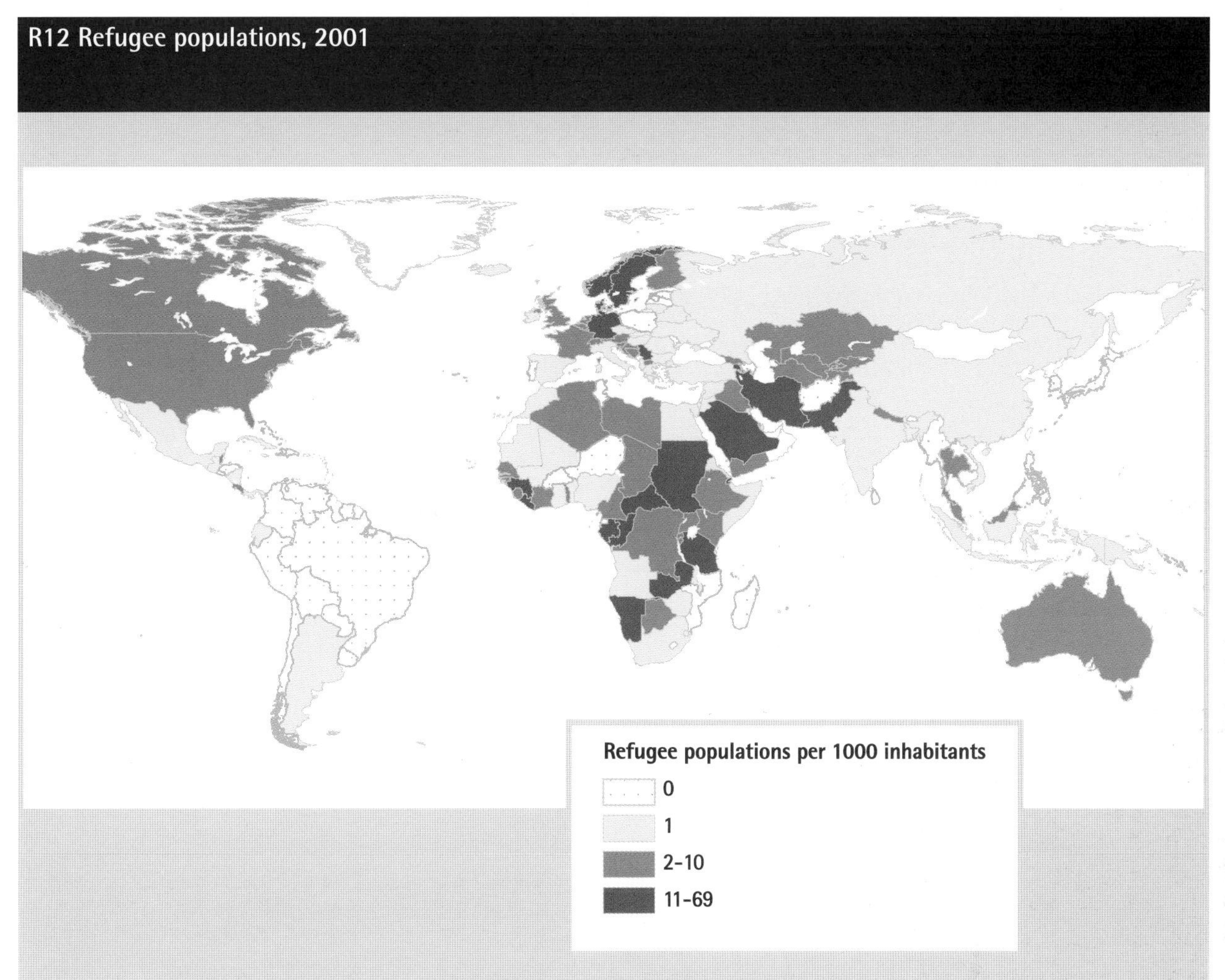

Record 13 Peacekeeping

A country's preparedness to contribute part of its armed forces to United Nations peacekeeping duties in foreign conflicts can be seen as a commitment to the international rule of law. This record reports the ratio of peacekeeping forces to total military personnel, comparing numbers of military personnel (for 1999, the latest available data) with the total number of forces per country committed to peacekeeping (as of 31 January 2003).

Country	Total military personnel 1999 (1998)	Peace-keeping forces as of 31 Jan 2003*	Peacekeeping forces per 1000 military personnel
East Asia & Pacific			
Low income economies			
Cambodia	*60,000*		
Indonesia & East Timor	281,000	33	0.1
Korea, Dem. Rep.	*1,100,000*		
Laos	*50,000*		
Mongolia	*20,000*	4	0.2
Myanmar	*322,000*		
Papua New Guinea	*5,000*		
Vietnam	*650,000*		
Middle income economies			
China & Tibet	*2,600,000*	54	0.0
Fiji	*4,000*	198	49.5
Malaysia	104,500	77	0.7
Philippines	107,000	62	0.6
Thailand	290,000	525	1.8
High income economies			
Australia	*65,000*	859	13.2
Brunei	*5,000*		
Korea, Rep.	*670,000*	473	0.7
Japan	*250,000*	680	2.7
New Zealand	*10,000*	19	1.9
Singapore	55,500	232	4.2
Europe & Central Asia			
Low income economies			
Armenia	*60,000*		
Azerbaijan	*75,000*		
Georgia	*11,000*		
Kyrgyzstan	*14,000*	2	0.1
Moldova	*11,000*		
Tajikistan	*10,000*		
Ukraine	310,000	948	3.1
Uzbekistan	*65,000*		
Middle income economies			
Albania	*52,000*	3	0.1
Belarus	*65,000*		
Bosnia & Herzegovina	*40,000*	14	0.4
Bulgaria	*80,000*	8	0.1
Croatia	*58,000*	19	0.3
Czech Republic	55,000	18	0.3
Estonia	*7,000*	1	0.1
Hungary	*50,000*	136	2.7
Kazakhstan	*34,000*		
Latvia	*5,000*		
Lithuania	*12,000*		
Macedonia	*15,000*		
Poland	*230,000*	617	2.7
Romania	*200,000*	42	0.2
Russian Federation	1,200,000	210	0.2
Serbia & Montenegro	*115,000*	3	0.0
Slovakia	44,000	610	13.9
Slovenia	*10,000*	3	0.3
Turkey	716,600	14	0.0
Turkmenistan	*21,000*		
High income economies			
Austria	*48,000*	391	8.1
Belgium	*46,000*	14	0.3
Cyprus	*10,000*		
Denmark	*29,000*	40	1.4
Finland	*35,000*	44	1.3
France	*475,000*	257	0.5
Germany	*335,000*	37	0.1
Greece	*206,000*	13	0.1
Ireland	*17,000*	257	15.1
Italy	*419,000*	142	0.3
Luxembourg	*1,000*		
Netherlands	*57,000*	13	0.2
Norway	*33,000*	23	0.7
Portugal	*72,000*	654	9.1
Spain	*107,000*	9	0.1
Sweden	*60,000*	38	0.6
Switzerland	*39,000*	21	0.5
United Kingdom	*218,000*	467	2.1
Latin America & Caribbean			
Low income countries			
Nicaragua	14,000		
Middle income countries			
Argentina	98,100	474	4.8
Belize	*1,000*		
Bolivia	*33,000*	216	6.5
Brazil	204,700	71	0.3
Chile	87,500	11	0.1

Record 13 continued

Country	Total military personnel 1999 (1998)	Peace-keeping forces as of 31 Jan 2003*	Peacekeeping forces per 1000 military personnel
Colombia	260,086		
Costa Rica	*10,000*		
Cuba	*55,000*		
Dominican Republic	*22,000*		
Ecuador	*58,000*		
El Salvador	15,000	5	0.3
Guatemala	30,000		
Guyana	*2,000*		
Honduras	11,244	5	0.4
Jamaica	*3,000*		
Mexico	*250,000*		
Panama	*12,000*		
Paraguay	*16,000*	22	1.4
Peru	122,000	5	0.0
Suriname	*2,000*		
Trinidad & Tobago	*2,000*		
Uruguay	*25,000*	1,662	66.5
Venezuela	*75,000*	3	0.0
Middle East & North Africa			
Low income countries			
Yemen	*69,000*		
Middle income countries			
Algeria	*124,000*	20	0.2
Djibouti	*8,000*		
Egypt	400,000	60	0.2
Iran	*575,000*	2	0.0
Iraq	*400,000*		
Jordan	*102,000*	1,139	11.2
Lebanon	*57,000*		
Libya	*70,000*		
Malta	*2,000*		
Morocco & Western Sahara	205,000	658	3.2
Oman	*38,000*		
Saudi Arabia	191,500		
Syria	*320,000*		
Tunisia	*35,000*	286	8.2
High income countries			
Bahrain	*9,000*		
Israel & Occupied Territories	173,000		
Kuwait	25,420		
Qatar	*11,000*		
United Arab Emirates	*60,000*		
North America			
High income countries			
Canada	*61,000*	218	3.6
United States	*1,530,000*	25	0.0

Country	Total military personnel 1999 (1998)	Peace-keeping forces as of 31 Jan 2003*	Peacekeeping forces per 1000 military personnel
South Asia			
Low income countries			
Afganistan			
Bangladesh	*110,000*	4,115	37.4
Bhutan	*8,000*		
India	1,140,000	2,246	2.0
Nepal	*35,000*	845	24.1
Pakistan	610,000	4,073	6.7
Middle income countries			
Maldives			
Sri Lanka	*110,000*	4	0.0
Sub-Saharan Africa			
Low income countries			
Angola	*95,000*		
Benin	*8,000*	22	2.8
Burkina Faso	*9,000*	12	1.3
Burundi	*35,000*		
Cameroon	*13,000*	2	0.2
Central African Republic	*5,000*		
Chad	*35,000*		
Congo, Rep.	*10,000*		
Côte d'Ivoire	*15,000*		
Equatorial Guinea	*1,000*		
Eritrea	200,000		
Ethiopia	300,000		
Gambia	*1,000*	17	17.0
Ghana	7,000	1,976	282.3
Guinea	*12,000*	793	66.1
Guinea-Bissau	*7,000*		
Kenya	27,000	1,726	63.9
Lesotho	*2,000*		
Liberia	*21,000*		
Madagascar	*8,000*	18	2.3
Malawi	*10,000*	34	3.4
Mali	*11,000*		
Mozambique	*14,000*	4	0.3
Niger	*5,000*	14	2.8
Nigeria	76,000	3,215	42.3
Rwanda	*40,000*		
Sao Tome & Principe	*1,000*		
Senegal	*14,000*	492	35.1
Sierra Leone	*5,000*		
Sudan	*105,000*		
Tanzania	*35,000*	20	0.6
Togo	*12,000*		
Uganda	*50,000*		
Zambia	*21,000*	861	41.0
Zimbabwe	40,000		

Record 13 continued Country	Total military personnel 1999 (1998)	Peace-keeping forces as of 31 Jan 2003	Peacekeeping forces per 1000 military personnel
Middle income countries			
Botswana	*8,000*		
Cape Verde	*1,000*		
Gabon	*10,000*		
Mauritius	*1,000*		
Namibia	*8,000*	2	0.3
South Africa	*75,000*	158	2.1
Swaziland	*3,000*		
Total	*21,665,150*	33,815	

Country of mission	Name of mission
Democratic Republic of Congo	MONUC
East Timor	UNTAET
India/Pakistan	UNMOGIP
Bosnia and Herzegovina	UNMIBIH
Cyprus	UNFICIP
Georgia	UNIMIG
Kosovo	UNMIK
Golan Heights	UNDOF
Iraq/Kuwait	UNOKOM
Lebanon	UNIFIL
Middle East	UNTSO

Data in italics are from 1998.

* Peacekeeping forces here comprise military observers and troops

Sources: U.S. Department of State, Bureau of Arms Control, World Military Expenditures and Arms Transfers 1998; U.S. Department of State, Annual Report on Military Expenditures, 1999; United Nations, Department of Peacekeeping Operations, http://www.un.org/Depts/dpko/dpko/contributors/index.htm

Record 14 Environment

This record gives an indication of the extent to which countries protect or harm the global environment, using the latest data available. It is now generally agreed that carbon dioxide emission is a major contributor to the problem of global warming: a large volume of emissions can therefore be considered as an infringement of the environmental element of the international rule of law. It is difficult to evaluate emissions indicators at the country level, since per capita figures may favour populous countries, while per unit of income measures may favour high-income countries. We therefore present both in the table, for comparison purposes. The map shows emissions levels in units of income.

Energy consumption may be taken as another indicator of environmental responsibility, although of course one also related to levels of development. This measure, given in thousand tons of oil equivalent, is calculated as the total amount of primary energy consumed from all energy sources, including losses through transportation, friction, heat, and other inefficiencies.

The final two columns of the table give the numbers of companies that have received International Standards Organisation (ISO) 14000 certification, as of the ends of 1995 and 2000. The ISO is comprised of national standards institutes from individual countries, which as a group have developed a number of voluntary environmental standards for business operations. Further details of ISO certification may be found in the Glossary. While the coverage of this indicator is not as broad as some of the more established environmental measures, it is illuminating in showing the shift over time towards greater environmental accountability for corporations, in terms of shared standards and practices.

	Carbon dioxide emissions						Energy consumption per capita (1000 metric tons of oil equivalent)			Number of certified ISO 14000 companies	
	metric tons per capita		% change	kg per PPP $ of GDP		% change			% change		
Country	1990	1998	1990-1998	1990	1998	1990-1998	1990	1999	1990-1999	1995	2000
East Asia & Pacific											
Low income economies											
Cambodia	0.0	0.1	17	0.1	0.0	-13					
Indonesia	0.9	1.1	24	0.5	0.4	-14	0.5	0.7	30		77
Korea, Dem. Rep.	12.3	10.3	-16				1.8	2.7	48		26
Laos	0.1	0.1	33	0.1	0.1	-14					
Mongolia	4.7	3.3	-31	2.6	2.0	-24					
Myanmar	0.1	0.2	71				0.3	0.3	-9		
Papua New Guinea	0.6	0.5	-21	0.4	0.2	-44					
Solomon Islands	0.5	0.4	-24	0.3	0.2	-34					
Vietnam	0.3	0.6	69		0.3		0.4	0.5	14		9
Middle income economies											
China	2.1	2.5	18	1.5	0.7	-51	0.7	0.9	23		616
Fiji	1.1	0.9	-17	0.3	0.2	-36					616
Malaysia	3.0	5.4	79	0.6	0.7	10	1.3	2.0	51		174
Philippines	0.7	1.0	44	0.2	0.3	30	0.5	0.5	10		46
Samoa	0.8	0.8	1	0.2	0.2	3					
Thailand	1.7	3.2	87	0.4	0.6	23	0.8	1.1	42		310
Tonga	0.8	1.2	48								
Vanuatu	0.4	0.3	-25	0.2	0.1	-41					
High income economies											
Australia	15.6	17.7	13	0.9	0.7	-17	5.2	5.7	10	1	1,049
Brunei	22.6	17.1	-25	1.5	1.0	-34	5.7	4.4	-22		2
Korea, Rep.	5.6	7.8	39	0.6	0.6	-13	2.1	3.9	86	19	544
Japan	8.7	9.0	3	0.4	0.4	-16	3.6	4.1	13	4	5,556
New Zealand	6.9	7.9	16	0.5	0.4	-10	4.2	4.9	15		63
Singapore	13.8	21.0	52	1.1	1.1	0	4.4	5.8	32		100

Record 14 continued	Carbon dioxide emissions						Energy consumption per capita (1000 metric tons of oil equivalent)			Number of certified ISO 14000 companies	
	metric tons per capita		% change	kg per PPP $ of GDP		% change			% change		
Country	1990	1998	1990-1998	1990	1998	1990-1998	1990	1999	1990-1999	1995	2000
Europe & Central Asia											
Low income economies											
Armenia		0.9			0.4		2.2	0.5	-78		
Azerbaijan		4.9			2.2		3.2	1.6	-51		
Georgia		1.0			0.4		1.9	0.5	-74		
Kyrgyztan		1.3			0.6		0.4	0.5	26		
Moldova		2.2			1.1		2.3	0.7	-72		
Tajikistan		0.8			0.9		0.6	0.6	-8		
Ukraine		7.0			2.1		4.9	3.0	-39		
Uzbekistan		4.5			2.1		2.1	2.0	-4		
Middle income economies											
Albania	2.2	0.5	-79	0.8	0.2	-80	0.8	0.3	-58		
Belarus		6.0			0.9		4.2	2.3	-44		
Bosnia & Herzegovina		1.2					0.2	0.5	161		
Bulgaria	8.6	5.7	-34	1.5	1.2	-22	3.1	2.3	-27		
Croatia		4.5			0.6		0.7	1.8	150		8
Czech Republic		11.5			0.9		4.4	3.8	-15		116
Estonia		12.1			1.4		6.5	3.2	-50		18
Hungary	5.6	5.7	2	0.6	0.5	-10	2.8	2.5	-10		164
Kazakhstan		8.2			1.7		6.3	2.2	-65		
Latvia		3.2			0.5		1.2	1.6	31		4
Lithuania		4.4			0.6		4.6	2.1	-54		10
Macedonia		6.1			1.4		1.6	1.5	-5		
Poland	9.1	8.3	-9	1.6	1.0	-35	2.6	2.4	-7		66
Romania	6.7	4.1	-39	1.1	0.7	-39	2.6	1.6	-38		5
Russian Federation		9.8			1.4		6.1	4.1	-32		3
Serbia & Montenegro	12.4						1.7	1.3	-26		2
Slovakia		7.1			0.7		4.1	3.3	-19		36
Slovenia		7.4			0.5		2.7	3.3	21		88
Turkey	2.6	3.2	24	0.5	0.5	-10	0.9	1.1	19	3	91
Turkmenistan		5.7			2.1		5.2	2.9	-43		
High income economies											
Austria	7.4	7.9	6	0.4	0.3	-18	3.3	3.5	7	11	203
Belgium	10.1	9.9	-2	0.5	0.4	-22	4.9	5.7	17		130
Cyprus	6.8	7.9	16	0.5	0.4	-19	2.3	3.0	29		4
Denmark	9.9	10.1	2	0.5	0.4	-21	3.6	3.8	5	21	580
Finland	10.6	10.3	-2	0.6	0.5	-21	5.8	6.5	11	10	508
France	6.3	6.3	1	0.4	0.3	-18	4.0	4.3	8	3	710
Germany		10.1			0.4		4.5	4.1	-9	35	1,260
Greece	7.1	8.1	14	0.6	0.6	-11	2.2	2.5	15		42
Iceland	7.9	7.6	-4	0.4	0.3	-22	8.2	11.5	40		2
Ireland	8.5	10.3	21	0.7	0.5	-33	3.0	3.7	24	3	163
Italy	7.0	7.2	2	0.4	0.3	-18	2.7	2.9	9		521
Luxembourg	25.9	18.0	-31	1.2	0.5	-62	9.4	8.1	-14		9
Netherlands	10.0	10.4	4	0.6	0.5	-22	4.5	4.7	4	74	784
Norway	7.5	7.6	1	0.4	0.3	-29	5.1	6.0	17	3	227

Record 14 continued

Country	Carbon dioxide emissions: metric tons per capita 1990	metric tons per capita 1998	% change 1990-1998	kg per PPP $ of GDP 1990	kg per PPP $ of GDP 1998	% change 1990-1998	Energy consumption per capita (1000 metric tons of oil equivalent) 1990	1999	% change 1990-1999	Number of certified ISO 14000 companies 1995	2000
Portugal	4.3	5.5	28	0.4	0.4	-8	1.7	2.4	39		47
Spain	5.5	6.3	15	0.4	0.4	-14	2.3	3.0	29		600
Sweden	5.7	5.5	-3	0.3	0.3	-18	5.6	5.8	3	2	1,370
Switzerland	6.4	5.9	-8	0.3	0.2	-15	3.7	3.7	1		690
United Kingdom	9.9	9.2	-7	0.6	0.4	-27	3.7	3.9	5	61	2,534
Latin America & Caribbean											
Low income countries											
Haiti	0.2	0.2	8	0.1	0.1	25	0.2	0.3	29		
Nicaragua	0.7	0.7	5	0.4	0.3	-16	0.6	0.5	-10		
Middle income countries											
Argentina	3.4	3.8	12	0.4	0.3	-31	1.3	1.7	33	1	114
Barbados	4.2	5.9	42	0.4	0.4	14					3
Belize	1.6	1.8	8	0.5	0.4	-19					
Bolivia	0.8	1.5	82	0.5	0.6	42	0.4	0.6	40		1
Brazil	1.4	1.8	32	0.2	0.3	5	0.9	1.1	19	2	330
Chile	2.7	4.1	51	0.5	0.5	-15	1.1	1.7	53		11
Colombia	1.6	1.7	4	0.3	0.3	-16	0.8	0.7	-15		21
Costa Rica	1.0	1.4	45	0.2	0.2	3	0.7	0.8	11		20
Cuba	3.0	2.2	-26				1.6	1.1	-30		
Dominican Republic	1.3	2.5	87	0.4	0.5	22	0.6	0.9	51		1
Ecuador	1.6	2.2	34	0.6	0.7	14	0.6	0.7	17		1
El Salvador	0.5	1.0	96	0.2	0.2	38	0.5	0.7	30		
Guatemala	0.6	0.9	54	0.2	0.2	22	0.5	0.5	10		2
Guyana	1.5	2.2	41	0.5	0.6	7					
Honduras	0.5	0.8	58	0.3	0.3	34	0.5	0.5	4		2
Jamaica	3.3	4.3	29	1.0	1.2	20	1.3	1.6	25		
Mexico	3.7	3.9	7	0.6	0.5	-15	1.5	1.5	2		159
Panama	1.3	2.1	61	0.3	0.4	11	0.6	0.8	39		
Paraguay	0.5	0.9	63	0.1	0.2	43	0.7	0.8	10		1
Peru	1.0	1.1	12	0.3	0.2	-20	0.5	0.5	4		13
St. Lucia	1.2	1.3	8	0.3	0.2	-13					2
Suriname	4.5	5.2	15	1.8	1.4	-24					
Trinidad & Tobago	13.9	17.4	25	2.3	2.3	-1	4.7	6.2	32		1
Uruguay	1.3	1.8	41	0.2	0.2	-4	0.7	1.0	39		22
Venezuela	5.8	6.7	15	1.2	1.1	-4	2.1	2.3	7		7
High income countries											
Bahamas	7.6	6.1	-20	0.5	0.4	-25					
Middle East & North Africa											
Low income countries											
Yemen		0.9			1.2		0.2	0.2	-11		
Middle income countries											
Algeria	3.2	3.6	12	0.7	0.7	3	1.0	1.0	-5		
Djibouti	0.7	0.6	-19		0.3						
Egypt	1.4	1.7	19	0.6	0.5	-7	0.6	0.7	11		78
Iran	3.9	4.7	20	1.0	0.9	-14	1.3	1.5	15		12
Iraq	2.7	3.7	35				1.2	1.3	7		

Record 14 continued

Country	Carbon dioxide emissions: metric tons per capita 1990	metric tons per capita 1998	% change 1990-1998	kg per PPP $ of GDP 1990	kg per PPP $ of GDP 1998	% change 1990-1998	Energy consumption per capita (1000 metric tons of oil equivalent) 1990	1999	% change 1990-1999	Number of certified ISO 14000 companies 1995	2000
Jordan	3.2	3.0	-6	1.0	0.8	-18	0.8	1.0	27		16
Lebanon	2.5	3.9	55	1.3	0.9	-31	0.9	1.6	77		5
Libya	8.8	7.2	-18				2.7	2.4	-12		
Malta	4.6	4.7	2	0.5	0.3	-41	2.2	2.5	16		2
Morocco	1.0	1.2	18	0.3	0.3	-2	0.3	0.3	13		4
Oman	7.1	8.8	24				2.4	3.4	44		2
Saudi Arabia	11.3	14.4	28	1.2	1.3	11	3.9	4.3	11		6
Syria	3.0	3.3	11	1.3	0.9	-29	1.0	1.1	14		3
Tunisia	1.6	2.4	47	0.4	0.4	3	0.7	0.8	17		3
High income countries											
Bahrain	23.3	29.1	25	1.9	2.0	5	11.3	9.6	-15		2
Israel	7.4	10.1	36	0.6	0.6	0	2.6	3.1	20		60
Kuwait	19.9	26.3	32		1.7		6.1	9.4	53		
Qatar	28.2	85.7	204				11.9	28.8	142		1
United Arab Emirates	33.0	32.4	-2	1.6	1.8	10	11.2	11.0	-2		48
North America											
High income countries											
Canada	15.4	15.4	0	0.8	0.6	-19	7.6	7.9	4		475
United States	19.3	19.8	3	0.8	0.6	-21	7.6	8.1	7	1	1,042
South Asia											
Low income countries											
Afghanistan	0.1	0.0	-72								4
Bangladesh	0.1	0.2	32	0.1	0.1	-7	0.2	0.1	-33		
Bhutan	0.2	0.5	138	0.2	0.4	67					
India	0.8	1.1	36	0.6	0.5	-9	0.4	0.5	21	1	257
Nepal	0.0	0.1	300	0.0	0.1	191	0.3	0.4	19		
Pakistan	0.6	0.7	17	0.5	0.4	-9	0.4	0.4	9		4
Middle income countries											
Maldives	0.7	1.3	74	0.2	0.2	0					
Sri Lanka	0.2	0.4	91	0.1	0.1	24	0.3	0.4	37		2
Sub-Saharan Africa											
Low income countries											
Angola	0.5	0.5	-2	0.2	0.3	14	0.6	0.6	-1		
Benin	0.1	0.1	3	0.2	0.1	-19	0.4	0.3	-19		
Burkina Faso	0.1	0.1	-16	0.2	0.1	-41					
Burundi	0.0	0.0	-1	0.0	0.1	23					
Cameroon	0.1	0.1	-4	0.1	0.1	-2	0.4	0.4	5		
Central African Republic	0.1	0.1	3	0.1	0.1	-1					
Chad	0.0	0.0	-39	0.0	0.0	-46					
Comoros	0.2	0.1	-14	0.1	0.1	-7					
Congo, Rep.	0.1	0.1	-54				0.5	0.2	-51		
Congo, Dem. Rep.	0.9	0.6	-30	1.2	0.8	-31	0.3	0.3	-2		
Côte d'Ivoire	1.0	0.9	-13	0.6	0.5	-17	0.4	0.4	-4		
Equatorial Guinea	0.3	0.6	75	0.3	0.2	-52					
Ethiopia	0.1	0.0	-44	0.1	0.1	-54	0.3	0.3	-1		

Record 14 continued

Country	Carbon dioxide emissions: metric tons per capita 1990	metric tons per capita 1998	% change 1990-1998	kg per PPP $ of GDP 1990	kg per PPP $ of GDP 1998	% change 1990-1998	Energy consumption per capita (1000 metric tons of oil equivalent) 1990	1999	% change 1990-1999	Number of certified ISO 14000 companies 1995	2000
Gambia	0.2	0.2	-10	0.1	0.1	-9					
Ghana	0.2	0.2	1	0.2	0.1	-23	0.4	0.4	-6		
Guinea	0.2	0.2	-2	0.1	0.1	-21					
Guinea-Bissau	0.8			1.2							
Kenya	0.2	0.3	28	0.3	0.3	23	0.5	0.5	-2		2
Liberia	0.2	0.1	-38								
Madagascar	0.1	0.1	5	0.1	0.1	11					
Malawi	0.1	0.1	7	0.2	0.1	-18					
Mali	0.0	0.0	-5	0.1	0.1	-28					
Mauritania	1.3	1.2	-12	1.1	0.7	-35					
Mozambique	0.1	0.1	12	0.1	0.1	-25	0.5	0.4	-22		
Niger	0.1	0.1	-20	0.2	0.1	-23					
Nigeria	0.9	0.6	-30	1.2	0.8	-36	0.8	0.8	-2		1
Rwanda	0.1	0.1	-17	0.1	0.1	-6					
Sao Tome & Principe	0.6	0.5	-5								
Senegal	0.4	0.4	-8	0.3	0.3	-19	0.3	0.3	7		
Sierra Leone	0.1	0.1	30	0.1	0.2	100					
Somalia	0.0	0.0	-100								
Sudan	0.1	0.1	-14	0.2	0.1	-57	0.4	0.5	26		
Tanzania	0.1	0.1	-22	0.2	0.1	-27	0.5	0.4	-12		
Togo	0.2	0.2	4	0.1	0.1	1					
Uganda	0.0	0.1	22	0.1	0.1	-17					
Zambia	0.3	0.2	-49	0.4	0.2	-43	0.7	0.6	-13		2
Zimbabwe	1.6	1.2	-29	0.7	0.4	-42	0.9	0.8	-9		4
Middle income countries											
Botswana	1.7	2.4	42	0.3	0.4	18					
Cape Verde	0.2	0.3	18	0.1	0.1	-18					
Gabon	7.1	2.4	-66	1.4	0.4	-72	1.4	1.3	-4		
Mauritius	1.1	1.5	37	0.2	0.2	-13					4
Namibia		0.0			0.0						4
South Africa	8.3	8.3	0	1.0	0.9	-6	2.7	2.6	-5		126
Swaziland	0.6	0.4	-27	0.2	0.1	-39					

Sources: World Development Indicators 2002, WDI Online; World Resources Institute 2003. EarthTrends: The Environmental Information Portal. Available at http://earthtrends.wri.org. Washington DC: World Resources Institute; International Energy Agency (IEA), Energy Balances of Organization for Economic Cooperation and Development (OECD) Countries, 1960-1997 on diskette (OECD, Paris, 1999) and Energy Balances on OECD Countries, 1960-1997 on diskette (OECD, Paris, 1999); International Standards Organization (ISO) 2001. The ISO Survey of ISO 9000 and ISO 14000 Certificates. Available on-line at http://www.iso.ch/iso/en/iso9000-14000/pdf/survey10thcycle.pdf Geneva: ISO

R14 continued

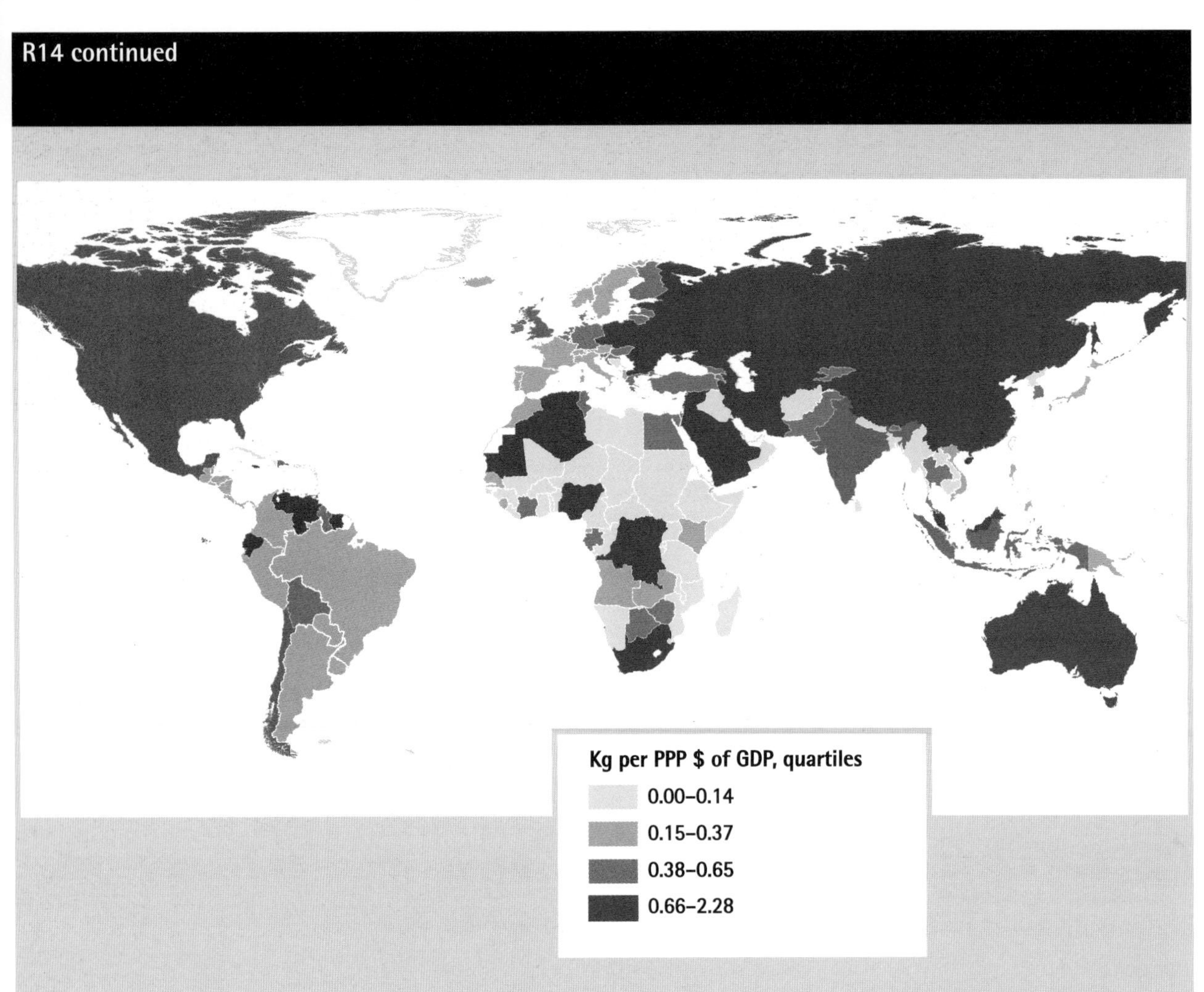

Record 15 Numbers of NGOs in countries and cities

The first table gives the total number of secretariats (headquarters) of international non-governmental organisations (INGOs) and internationally oriented NGOs in a given country for 1992 and 2002. These are the principal secretariats (headquarters or main office) of the organisation. Secondary (including regional) secretariats are not included. The table also indicates the number of secretariats per one million of population, that is, 'organisational density', and the expansion or contraction in the number of secretariats by country over the time period.

The second part of the record shows in which cities the secretariats are primarily based, for 2001 and 2002.

Country	1992 Number of secretariats	1992 Organisational density per million of population	2002 Number of secretariats	2002 Organisational density per million of population	Absolute growth % 1992–2002	Density growth % 1992–2002
MEast Asia & Pacific						
Low income economies						
Cambodia	0	0.0	5	0.4		
Indonesia	35	0.2	34	0.1	-3	-18
Korea, Dem. Rep.	0	0.0	1	0.0		
Laos	0	0.0	1	0.2		
Mongolia	2	0.9	3	1.1	50	30
Myanmar	0	0.0	1	0.0		
Papua New Guinea	2	0.5	6	1.2	200	133
Solomon Islands	1	2.8	0	0.0		
Vietnam	1	0.0	4	0.0	300	244
Middle income economies						
China & Tibet*	28	0.0	105	0.0		
Fiji	15	20.0	28	32.7	87	64
Malaysia	54	2.9	75	3.3	39	12
Philippines	97	1.4	99	1.2	2	-17
Samoa	0	0.0	3	16.8		
Thailand	56	1.0	101	1.6	80	61
Vanuatu	3	18.6	1	5.1	-67	-73
High income economies						
Australia	168	9.6	359	18.4	114	91
Brunei	1	3.7	4	11.4	300	212
Korea, Rep.	45	1.0	51	1.1	13	3
Japan	173	1.4	263	2.1	52	49
New Zealand	27	7.9	48	12.3	78	56
Singapore	45	14.2	81	18.2	80	29
Europe & Central Asia						
Low income economies						
Armenia	0	0.0	1	0.3		
Azerbaijan	0	0.0	2	0.3		
Georgia	0	0.0	4	0.8		
Kyrgyzstan	0	0.0	2	0.4		
Moldova	0	0.0	2	0.5		
Tajikistan	0	0.0	0	0.0		
Ukraine	1	0.0	21	0.4	2,000	2,154
Uzbekistan	0	0.0	2	0.1		

Record 15 continued Country	Number of secretariats 1992	Organisational density per million of population 1992	Number of secretariats 2002	Organisational density per million of population 2002	Absolute growth % 1992–2002	Density growth % 1992–2002
Middle income economies						
Albania	1	0.3	1	0.3	0	-10
Belarus	2	0.2	4	0.4	100	99
Bosnia & Herzegovina	1	0.2	1	0.3	0	12
Bulgaria	30	3.5	32	4.2	7	21
Croatia	8	1.8	13	3.0	63	64
Czech Republic			44	4.3		
Estonia	0	0.0	5	3.5		
Hungary	40	3.9	58	5.8	45	49
Kazakhstan	0	0.0	3	0.2		
Latvia	0	0.0	10	4.2		
Lithuania	1	0.3	10	2.8	900	929
Macedonia	0	0.0	2	1.0		
Poland	28	0.7	48	1.2	71	70
Romania	10	0.4	14	0.6	40	43
Russian Federation	30	0.2	85	0.6	183	190
Serbia & Montenegro	13	1.3	9	0.8	-31	-34
Slovakia			11	2.0		
Slovenia	7	3.7	17	8.8	143	138
Turkey	10	0.2	39	0.6	290	237
Turkmenistan	0	0.0	0	0.0		
High income economies						
Austria	139	17.6	263	32.2	89	83
Belgium	1419	141.3	1865	181.5	31	28
Cyprus	4	5.7	17	22.2	325	292
Denmark	209	40.4	238	44.3	14	10
Finland	105	20.8	129	24.9	23	19
France	1342	23.4	1423	23.7	6	2
Germany	630	7.8	955	11.6	52	48
Greece	35	3.4	97	9.1	177	170
Iceland	11	42.5	15	53.7	36	26
Ireland	50	14.1	67	17.3	34	23
Italy	391	6.9	545	9.4	39	37
Luxembourg	47	120.1	42	93.6	-11	-22
Netherlands	502	33.1	801	49.9	60	51
Norway	124	28.9	173	38.2	40	32
Portugal	28	2.8	61	6.0	118	114
Spain	125	3.2	315	7.8	152	148
Sweden	255	29.4	321	36.2	26	23
Switzerland	592	84.6	690	94.5	17	12
United Kingdom	1177	20.3	1841	30.7	56	51
Latin America & Caribbean						
Low income countries						
Haiti	2	0.3	0	0.0		
Nicaragua	12	3.0	14	2.8	17	-8
Middle income countries						
Argentina	93	2.7	125	3.3	34	19

Record 15 continued Country	Number of secretariats 1992	Organisational density per million of population 1992	Number of secretariats 2002	Organisational density per million of population 2002	Absolute growth % 1992–2002	Density growth % 1992–2002
Barbados	28	105.7	21	76.0	-25	-28
Belize	1	5.0	1	3.8	0	-23
Bolivia	3	0.4	10	1.2	233	172
Brazil	66	0.4	91	0.5	38	20
Chile	63	4.6	49	3.2	-22	-32
Colombia	47	1.4	46	1.1	-2	-18
Costa Rica	47	14.8	74	19.3	57	30
Cuba	20	1.9	30	2.7	50	43
Dominican Republic	6	0.8	5	0.6	-17	-29
Ecuador	20	1.8	29	2.2	45	17
El Salvador	10	1.9	10	1.6	0	-17
Guatemala	14	1.4	13	1.0	-7	-30
Guyana	6	8.2	11	15.7	83	92
Honduras	1	0.2	12	1.8	1,100	823
Jamaica	19	7.6	17	6.3	-11	-16
Mexico	70	0.8	116	1.1	66	40
Panama	15	6.0	19	6.5	27	8
Paraguay	7	1.6	4	0.7	-43	-56
Peru	53	2.3	46	1.6	-13	-29
Saint Lucia	3	21.1	3	18.7	0	-11
Saint Vincent & the Grenadines	2	18.5	4	34.4	100	86
Suriname	0	0.0	0	0.0		
Trinidad & Tobago	21	17.7	43	38.7	105	118
Uruguay	38	12.1	45	13.3	18	10
Venezuela	65	3.2	61	2.5	-6	-22
High income countries						
Bahamas	1	3.8	5	16.9	400	347
Middle East & North Africa						
Low income countries						
Yemen	0	0.0	0	0.0		
Middle income countries						
Algeria	13	0.5	10	0.3	-23	-37
Djibouti	0	0.0	0	0.0		
Egypt	57	1.0	64	0.9	12	-9
Iran	1	0.0	7	0.1	600	530
Iraq	36	2.0	10	0.4	-72	-79
Jordan	18	4.7	24	4.5	33	-3
Lebanon	14	4.3	29	7.9	107	81
Libya	16	3.7	7	1.3	-56	-64
Malta	13	35.5	22	55.3	69	56
Morocco & Western Sahara	17	0.7	16	0.5	-6	-22
Oman	1	0.5	2	0.7	100	41
Saudi Arabia	22	1.3	20	0.9	-9	-35
Syria	20	1.5	9	0.5	-55	-65
Tunisia	27	3.2	29	3.0	7	-7
High income countries						
Bahrain	3	5.7	6	9.1	100	61

Record 15 continued Country	Number of secretariats 1992	Organisational density per million of population 1992	Number of secretariats 2002	Organisational density per million of population 2002	Absolute growth % 1992–2002	Density growth % 1992–2002
Israel & Occupied Territories*	73	10.4	96	10.2	32	-2
Kuwait	9	6.3	6	2.8	-33	-55
Qatar	2	3.8	0	0.0	-100	-100
United Arab Emirates	2	1.0	6	2.5	200	151
North America						
High income countries						
Canada	321	11.3	448	14.0	40	25
United States	1964	7.6	3259	11.3	66	48
South Asia						
Low income countries						
Afghanistan	0	0.0	0	0.0		
Bangladesh	13	0.1	23	0.2	77	48
Bhutan	0	0.0	0	0.0		
India	124	0.1	175	0.2	41	19
Nepal	7	0.3	20	0.8	186	124
Pakistan	27	0.2	28	0.2	4	-16
Middle income countries						
Maldives	0	0.0	0	0.0		
Sri Lanka	17	1.0	17	0.9	0	-10
Sub-Saharan Africa						
Low income countries						
Angola	1	0.1	1	0.1	0	-20
Benin	11	2.2	21	3.1	91	39
Burkina Faso	15	1.5	19	1.5	27	-5
Burundi	0	0.0	1	0.2		
Cameroon	17	1.4	22	1.4	29	3
Central African Republic	3	1.0	0	0.0	-100	-100
Chad	0	0.0	0	0.0		
Comoros	0	0.0	0	0.0		
Congo, Rep.	11	4.7	1	0.3	-91	-93
Congo, Dem. Rep.	14	0.3	5	0.1	-64	-74
Cote d'Ivoire	28	2.2	26	1.6	-7	-29
Equatorial Guinea	0	0.0	0	0.0		
Eritrea	0	0.0	0	0.0		
Ethiopia	20	0.4	19	0.3	-5	-25
Gambia	2	1.9	4	2.7	100	42
Ghana	31	1.9	36	1.8	16	-6
Guinea	0	0.0	2	0.2		
Guinea-Bissau	0	0.0	0	0.0		
Kenya	102	4.0	113	3.6	11	-9
Lesotho	3	1.7	3	1.6	0	-6
Liberia	0	0.0	0	0.0		
Madagascar	2	0.2	1	0.1	-50	-63
Malawi	3	0.3	3	0.3	0	-13
Mali	5	0.6	6	0.5	20	-9
Mauritania	2	0.9	3	1.1	50	12

Record 15 continued Country	Number of secretariats (1992)	Organisational density per million of population (1992)	Number of secretariats (2002)	Organisational density per million of population (2002)	Absolute growth % 1992–2002	Density growth % 1992–2002
Mozambique	1	0.1	3	0.2	200	128
Niger	5	0.6	2	0.2	-60	-70
Nigeria	58	0.6	56	0.4	-3	-27
Rwanda	2	0.3	3	0.4	50	43
Senegal	53	6.8	55	5.3	4	-21
Sierra Leone	5	1.2	2	0.4	-60	-69
Somalia	0	0.0	0	0.0		
Sudan	10	0.4	9	0.2	-10	-32
Tanzania	15	0.6	16	0.5	7	-18
Togo	5	1.3	18	3.4	260	170
Uganda	6	0.3	19	0.8	217	135
Zambia	12	1.5	10	1.0	-17	-32
Zimbabwe	24	2.2	41	3.3	71	47
Middle income countries						
Botswana	3	2.2	7	4.4	133	104
Cape Verde	0	0.0	0	0.0		
Gabon	3	3.0	3	2.3	0	-23
Mauritius	7	6.4	15	12.5	114	96
Namibia	0	0.0	2	1.1		
South Africa	21	0.5	142	3.3	576	512
Swaziland	3	3.1	2	1.7	-33	-44
Total	12,173		17,428			

Country	Number of secretariats (1992)	Organisational density per million of population (1992)	Number of secretariats (2002)	Organisational density per million of population (2002)	Absolute growth % 1992–2002	Density growth % 1992–2002
Low income	693	0.3	869	0.3	27	5
Middle income	1,461	0.6	2,069	0.8	42	27
Low & middle income	2,154	0.5	2,938	0.6	37	18
East Asia & the Pacific	294	0.2	396	0.2	35	20
Europe & Central Asia	182	0.4	440	0.9	142	139
Latin America & Caribbean	732	1.6	899	1.7	24	6
Middle East & North Africa	255	1.0	249	0.8	-2	-21
South Asia	188	0.2	263	0.2	40	17
Sub-Saharan Africa	503	0.9	691	1.0	37	8
High income	10,019	11.5	14,490	15.6	45	35
World	12,173	2.3	17,428	2.8	43	25

* The number of secretariats have been given as for China & Tibet and Israel & Occupied Territories as geographical units. There are however no secretariats in either Tibet or the Occupied Territories. Since the 2002 figures for China include Hong Kong and Macao, 1992 and 2002 figures are not strictly comparable. Hence, no growth figures are given.

Readers cross-referring to Record 16a in the 2002 Yearbook will notice an apparent decline in numbers of secretariats between 2001 and 2002. It is unlikely that this downturn is statistically significant; it is probably mostly attributable to increasing numbers of internationally-oriented NGOs that do not maintain their records with the UIA following initial registration.

Source: © Union of International Associations, Yearbook of International Organizations: Guide to Civil Society Networks, 1992 and 2002

Source of population: U.S. Bureau of the Census International Data Base. (October 10, 2002). United States Department of Commerce. IDB Data Access – Spreadsheet. <http://www.census.gov/ipc/www/idbsprd.html>

Secretariats in cities

City	Country	Number of secretariats 2001	2002	% Change 2001-2002
Amsterdam	Netherlands	162	152	-6
Antwerp	Belgium	49	52	6
Athens	Greece	64	60	-6
Bangkok	Thailand	75	80	7
Barcelona	Spain	71	73	3
Berlin	Germany	101	113	12
Bonn	Germany	81	78	-4
Brussels	Belgium	1,407	1,420	1
Buenos Aires	Argentina	110	110	0
Cairo	Egypt	62	51	-18
Caracas	Venezuela	56	48	-14
Copenhagen	Denmark	108	114	6
Dakar	Senegal	58	53	-9
Frankfurt Main	Germany	51	57	12
Geneva	Switzerland	272	276	1
Helsinki	Finland	65	62	-5
Jerusalem	Israel	50	46	-8
Lausanne	Switzerland	67	68	1
Leiden	Netherlands	52	51	-2
London	United Kingdom	807	781	-3
Los Angeles	USA	50	46	-8
Leuven	Belgium	50	48	-4
Madrid	Spain	140	143	2
Mexico	Mexico	87	78	-10
Milan	Italy	82	82	0
Montreal	Canada	86	86	0
Moscow	Russia	61	70	15
Munich	Germany	61	61	0
Nairobi	Kenya	100	110	10
New Delhi	India	65	74	14
New York	USA	390	355	-9
Oslo	Norway	95	96	1
Ottawa	Canada	68	65	-4
Oxford	United Kingdom	52	46	-12
Paris	France	729	706	-3
Rome	Italy	228	210	-8
San Francisco	USA	61	63	3
San Jose	Costa Rica	56	58	4
Singapore	Singapore	79	80	1
Stockholm	Sweden	133	135	2
Strasbourg	France	65	59	-9
The Hague	Netherlands	97	98	1
Tokyo	Japan	174	160	-8
Toronto	Canada	70	70	0
Utrecht	Netherlands	80	83	4
Vienna	Austria	190	194	2
Washington DC	USA	487	461	-5
Zurich	Switzerland	79	77	-3

This table lists all cities with 50 or more NGO headquarters

Source: © Union of International Associations, Yearbook of International Organizations: Guide to Civil Society Networks, 2001 and 2002 (presenting data collected in 2000 and 2001, respectively). Data have been restructured from more comprehensive country and organisation coverage in the Yearbook of International Organizations.

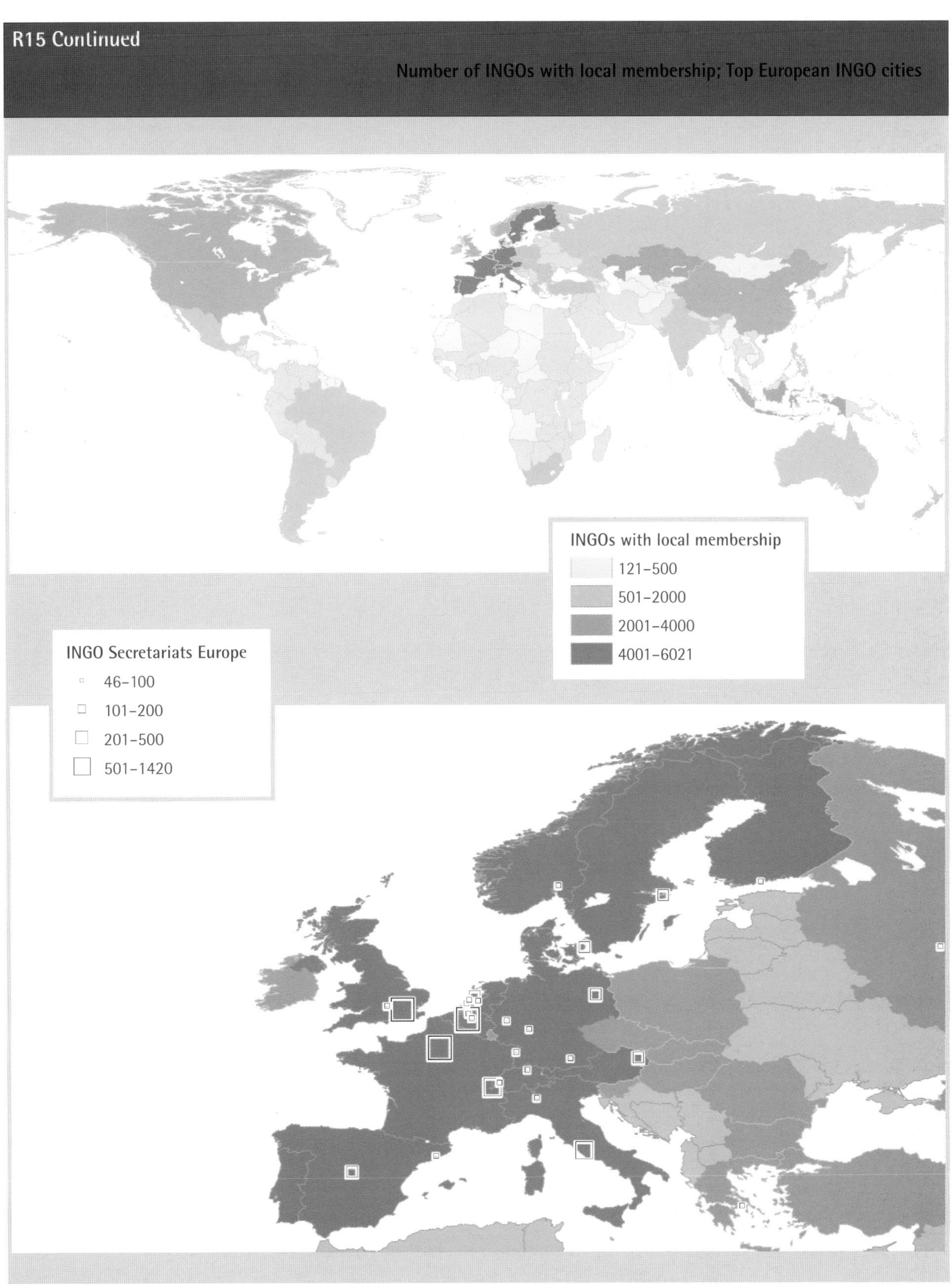
R15 Continued
Number of INGOs with local membership; Top European INGO cities
INGOs with local membership
121–500
501–2000
2001–4000
4001–6021
INGO Secretariats Europe
46–100
101–200
201–500
501–1420

Record 16 Country participation in INGOs

This record indicates the extent to which organisations and individuals in each country are members of International NGOs (INGOs), for 1992 and 2002. Data are for INGOs only; no information is available for internationally oriented NGOs. 'Membership' has a specific meaning here: whether an INGO has a million members or a single member in a given country, this is counted as one membership. So a count of 100 for a country means that 100 INGOs each have at least one member or member organisation in that country. The table also offers data on membership density for each country, expressed as the number of memberships in INGOs per 1 million of the population, for the same years, and presents the percentage growth during the decade.

The map combines information from Records 15 and 16; countries are shaded according to numbers of organisation memberships in 2002, while the inset shows numbers of secretariats in European cities.

Country	Number of organisation memberships 1992	Membership density per million of population 1992	Number of organisation memberships 2002	Membership density per million of population 2002	Absolute growth % 1992–2002	Density growth % 1992–2002
East Asia & Pacific						
Low income economies						
Cambodia	93	9.2	366	28.4	294	207
Indonesia	1,278	6.6	1,891	8.2	48	25
Korea, Dem. Rep.	203	9.8	261	11.7	29	20
Laos	104	23.3	251	43.4	141	86
Mongolia	148	64.0	429	160.4	190	151
Maynmar	276	7.1	405	9.6	47	36
Papua New Guinea	533	132.5	701	135.5	32	2
Solomon Islands	192	535.2	271	547.7	41	2
Vietnam	337	4.9	878	10.9	161	124
Middle income economies						
China & Tibet	1,251	1.1	4,312	3.4	245	213
Fiji	455	606.5	635	741.5	40	22
Malaysia	1,316	71.8	1,965	86.7	49	21
Philippines	1,456	21.7	2,036	24.5	40	13
Samoa	208	1,195.3	313	1,752.2	50	47
Thailand	1,269	22.4	1,915	30.1	51	34
Vanuatu	163	1,009.9	273	1,391.6	67	38
High income economies						
Australia	2,575	147.3	3,889	199.0	51	35
Brunei	214	781.9	333	949.0	56	21
Korea, Rep.	1,357	31.0	2,241	46.7	65	51
Japan	2,548	20.5	3,751	29.5	47	44
New Zealand	1,744	507.3	2,610	667.9	50	32
Singapore	1,163	365.8	1,844	414.1	59	13
Europe & Central Asia						
Low income economies						
Armenia	10	2.9	525	157.7	5,150	5,336
Azerbaijan	2	0.3	412	52.8	20,500	19,483
Georgia	13	2.4	684	137.9	5,162	5,698
Kyrgyzstan	2	0.4	279	57.9	13,850	13,010
Moldova	2	0.4	512	115.5	25,500	25,578
Tajikistan	1	0.2	197	29.3	19,600	16,320
Ukraine	24	0.5	1,626	33.6	6,675	7,172

Record 16 continued Country	Number of organisation memberships	Membership density per million of population 1992	Number of organisation memberships	Membership density per million of population 2002	Absolute growth % 1992–2002	Density growth % 1992–2002
Uzbekistan	2	0.1	385	15.1	19,150	16,176
Middle income economies						
Albania	121	38.1	792	223.4	555	486
Belarus	11	1.1	780	75.5	6,991	6,971
Bosnia & Herzegovina			613	154.6		
Bulgaria	1,157	133.6	2,156	282.9	86	112
Croatia	19	4.3	1,957	445.7	10,200	10,297
Czech Republic			3,319	323.6		
Estonia	106	68.6	1,573	1,111.1	1,384	1,520
Hungary	1,909	184.5	3,530	350.4	85	90
Kazakhstan	1	0.1	516	30.8	51,500	52,251
Latvia	78	29.6	1,353	571.7	1,635	1,828
Lithuania	92	24.8	1,494	414.9	1,524	1,571
Macedonia			700	340.7		
Poland	2,002	52.2	3,643	94.3	82	81
Romania	1,111	48.7	2,431	108.9	119	124
Russian Federation	1,560	10.5	3,130	21.6	101	106
Serbia & Montenegro	1,762	172.2	1,656	155.4	-6	-10
Slovakia			2,117	390.4		
Slovenia	24	12.7	2,036	1,053.3	8,383	8,202
Turkey	1,375	23.6	2,394	35.6	74	50
Turkmenistan	1	0.3	159	33.9	15,800	12,950
High income economies						
Austria	2,976	376.3	4,581	560.7	54	49
Belgium	4,008	399.0	5,740	558.7	43	40
Cyprus	768	1,085.8	1,345	1,752.9	75	61
Denmark	3,517	680.1	4,881	909.1	39	34
Finland	2,918	578.8	4,592	885.9	57	53
France	4,517	78.7	5,892	98.3	30	25
Germany	4,416	54.8	6,021	73.1	36	33
Greece	2,403	232.0	3,729	350.3	55	51
Iceland	1,156	4,463.1	1,746	6,249.5	51	40
Ireland	2,357	662.6	3,671	945.4	56	43
Italy	4,064	71.5	5,921	102.2	46	43
Luxembourg	1,597	4,080.7	2,123	4,732.8	33	16
Netherlands	4,011	264.3	5,855	364.4	46	38
Norway	2,949	688.0	4,371	965.9	48	40
Portugal	2,660	268.3	4,075	404.1	53	51
Spain	3,721	94.1	5,621	140.0	51	49
Sweden	3,417	393.9	5,267	757.6	54	92
Switzerland	3,518	502.5	5,234	716.8	49	43
United Kingdom	4,223	73.0	6,010	100.3	42	37
Latin America & Caribbean						
Low income countries						
Haiti	470	74.9	598	80.8	27	8
Nicaragua	582	147.4	775	154.3	33	5

Record 16 continued Country	Number of organisation memberships	Membership density per million of population 1992	Number of organisation memberships	Membership density per million of population 2002	Absolute growth % 1992–2002	Density growth % 1992–2002
Middle income countries						
Argentina	2,041	60.1	2,918	76.1	43	27
Barbados	496	1,872.2	640	2,317.3	29	24
Belize	278	1,385.5	390	1,500.3	40	8
Bolivia	874	126.8	1,189	140.8	36	11
Brazil	2,263	14.5	3,232	18.0	43	24
Chile	1,522	112.1	2,162	139.5	42	24
Colombia	1,423	41.6	1,984	48.4	39	16
Costa Rica	1,046	329.6	1,391	362.7	33	10
Cuba	666	62.1	1,069	95.2	61	53
Dominican Republic	737	100.3	938	109.1	27	9
Ecuador	978	90.4	1,321	98.2	35	9
El Salvador	607	115.1	861	135.5	42	18
Guatemala	813	79.6	1,065	78.6	31	-1
Guyana	424	579.0	491	701.9	16	21
Honduras	610	121.8	809	124.2	33	2
Jamaica	751	299.7	889	331.7	18	11
Mexico	1,970	22.5	2,797	27.1	42	20
Panama	852	343.6	1,041	356.5	22	4
Paraguay	696	155.2	945	160.6	36	3
Peru	1,319	57.3	1,765	63.1	34	10
Saint Lucia	261	1,832.9	345	2,154.3	32	18
Saint Vincent & the Grenadines	200	1,850.2	275	2,362.7	38	28
Suriname	277	687.4	337	777.1	22	13
Trinidad & Tobago	656	554.0	815	733.2	24	32
Uruguay	1,150	365.2	1,550	457.7	35	25
Venezuela	1,445	71.3	1,867	76.9	29	8
High income countries						
Bahamas	407	1,541.2	512	1,734.8	26	13
Middle East & North Africa						
Low income countries						
Yemen	238	17.8	335	17.9	41	1
Middle income countries						
Algeria	798	30.0	1,062	32.9	33	10
Djibouti	170	442.5	218	487.2	28	10
Egypt	1,399	23.6	1,963	26.8	40	14
Iran	676	11.1	966	14.3	43	29
Iraq	545	30.5	518	21.6	-5	-29
Jordan	653	168.8	941	177.3	44	5
Lebanon	710	220.5	1,030	280.1	45	27
Libya	373	85.5	452	84.2	21	-1
Malta	655	1,790.1	1,174	2,953.5	79	65
Morocco & Western Sahara	1,003	38.6	1,358	43.2	35	12
Oman	230	120.1	394	145.2	71	21
Saudi Arabia	710	42.5	1,082	46.0	52	8
Syria	471	35.6	592	34.5	26	-3

Record 16 continued

Country	Number of organisation memberships 1992	Membership density per million of population 1992	Number of organisation memberships 2002	Membership density per million of population 2002	Absolute growth % 1992–2002	Density growth % 1992–2002
Tunisia	918	107.7	1,228	125.1	34	16
High income countries						
Bahrain	328	619.5	484	737.4	48	19
Israel & Occupied Territories	2,043	290.1	3,348	355.4	64	23
Kuwait	602	424.5	767	363.2	27	-14
Qatar	220	415.6	350	441.2	59	6
United Arab Emirates	399	194.7	750	306.6	88	57
North America						
High income countries						
Canada	2,937	103.0	4,295	134.6	46	31
United States	3,328	13.0	5,054	17.6	52	36
South Asia						
Low income countries						
Afghanistan	141	8.5	159	5.7	13	-33
Bangladesh	772	6.8	1,163	8.6	51	26
Bhutan	85	50.8	135	64.5	59	27
India	2,193	2.5	3,130	3.0	43	21
Nepal	482	23.7	834	32.2	73	36
Pakistan	1,057	8.9	1,561	10.6	48	19
Middle income countries						
Maldives	81	349.1	158	493.5	95	41
Sri Lanka	1,011	57.5	1,332	68.0	32	18
Sub-Saharan Africa						
Low income countries						
Angola	297	35.1	452	42.8	52	22
Benin	441	88.6	708	103.6	61	17
Burkina Faso	451	46.5	691	53.6	53	15
Burundi	321	58.6	481	80.6	50	38
Cameroon	704	57.1	1,049	68.0	49	19
Central African Republic	288	97.2	394	108.7	37	12
Chad	254	39.4	403	44.9	59	14
Comoros	113	248.7	166	270.2	47	9
Congo, Rep.	425	180.4	864	15.7	103	-91
Congo, Dem. Rep.	733	18.1	547	188.1	-25	940
Côte d'Ivoire	727	56.9	982	59.2	35	4
Equatorial Guinea	110	283.7	162	325.2	47	15
Eritrea	5	1.4	175	40.6	3,400	2,825
Ethiopia	549	10.6	764	11.7	39	10
Gambia	350	337.7	477	327.6	36	-3
Ghana	891	54.7	1,217	60.4	37	10
Guinea	303	43.4	489	55.5	61	28
Guinea-Bissau	144	137.0	240	180.0	67	31
Kenya	1,171	45.9	1,618	51.8	38	13
Lesotho	373	214.4	487	262.1	31	22
Liberia	428	215.6	426	130.6	0	-39
Madagascar	536	43.9	687	41.7	28	-5

Record 16 continued

Country	Number of organisation memberships 1992	Membership density per million of population 1992	Number of organisation memberships 2002	Membership density per million of population 2002	Absolute growth % 1992–2002	Density growth % 1992–2002
Malawi	448	45.4	640	56.2	43	24
Mali	419	48.9	626	55.4	49	13
Mauritania	291	137.3	419	148.1	44	8
Mozambique	342	26.0	619	35.7	81	37
Niger	336	41.6	487	45.3	45	9
Nigeria	1,280	13.0	1,629	12.5	27	-4
Rwanda	365	49.8	518	67.6	42	36
Sao Tome & Principe	69	548.0	121	710.2	75	30
Senegal	860	110.0	1,088	105.5	27	-4
Sierra Leone	512	119.9	605	108.7	18	-9
Somalia	251	41.1	222	28.6	-12	-30
Sudan	635	22.5	739	19.9	16	-11
Tanzania	774	28.5	1,087	30.8	40	8
Togo	495	124.6	672	126.8	36	2
Uganda	639	34.5	990	39.8	55	15
Zambia	714	86.4	929	91.5	30	6
Zimbabwe	937	87.3	1,314	105.4	40	21
Middle income countries						
Botswana	425	307.0	663	419.8	56	37
Cape Verde	126	348.4	234	572.5	86	64
Gabon	371	375.9	485	376.5	31	0
Mauritius	600	547.3	793	660.7	32	21
Namibia	256	171.7	639	336.9	150	96
South Africa	1,496	38.7	2,828	66.2	89	71
Swaziland	333	345.9	461	400.8	38	16

Region	Number of organisation memberships 1992	Membership density per million of population 1992	Number of organisation memberships 2002	Membership density per million of population 2002	Absolute growth % 1992–2002	Density growth % 1992–2002
Low income	28,221	13.4	44,947	17.6	59	32
Middle income	55,812	23.0	101,455	37.4	82	60
Low & middle income:	84,033	18.5	146,402	27.8	74	50
East Asia & the Pacific	9,282	5.6	16,902	9.1	82	63
Europe & Central Asia	11,385	24.1	40,969	85.7	260	255
Latin America & Caribbean	25,407	56.0	34,459	64.7	36	16
Middle East & North Africa	9,549	37.2	13,313	42.2	39	13
South Asia	5,822	5.0	8,472	6.1	46	21
Sub-Saharan Africa	22,588	42.1	32,287	47.1	43	12
High income	79,061	90.8	116,903	125.6	48	38
World	163,094	30.2	263,305	42.5	61	41

Sources: © Union of International Associations, Yearbook of International Organisations: Guide to Civil Society Networks, Brussels 1992 and 2002.

Source of population: U.S. Bureau of the Census International Data Base. (October 10, 2002). United States Department of Commerce. IDB Data Access – Spreadsheet. <http://www.census.gov/ipc/www/idbsprd.html>

Record 17 Links between international organisations

This record indicates different aspects of the inter-organisational networks that link international and internationally oriented NGOs to each other and to international governmental organisations (IGOs). It indicates the number of citations, or references , made by either NGOs or IGOs to any other international organisation (whether NGO or IGO). Examples of citations would be (1) '. . . founded under the auspices of "X"' . . , (2) '. . . financed by annual subventions from "X", "Y" and "Z" . . ', (3) ' . . . consultative relations with "X"'. The number of links is shown for 1992 and 2002, in addition to a percentage growth figure.

Citations from NGO to IGO and NGO; Citations from IGO to IGO and NGO

Paragraph	1992	2002	% change	
Founded				
NGOs	3,013	4,957	65	The citing organisation cites another organisation as having had some role in its founding or establishment.
IGOs	2,230	3,411	53	
Total	**5,243**	**8,368**	**60**	
Structure				
NGOs	897	1,690	88	The citing organisation has a structural link with another organisation, for instance as sister organisations or parent and subsidiary organisation.
IGOs	1,210	1,971	63	
Total	**2,107**	**3,661**	**74**	
Staff				
NGOs	0	4		The citing organisation shares key staff with, or is provided with key staff from, the other organisation it cites.
IGOs	73	122	67	
Total	**73**	**126**	**73**	
Finances				
NGOs	743	2,965	299	There is a financial link between the citing organisation and another organisation.
IGOs	233	554	138	
Total	**976**	**3,519**	**261**	
Activities				
NGOs	2,190	2,591	18	The citing organisation cites another organisation as having a role in its activities, for instance joint activities, or activities aimed at the cited organisation.
IGOs	2,217	4,090	84	
Total	**4,407**	**6,681**	**52**	
Publications				
NGOs	7	19	171	The citing organisation cites another organisation as having a role in its publications, for instance joint publications, or publications about the cited organisation.
IGOs	27	33	22	
Total	**34**	**52**	**53**	
Members				
NGOs	5,652	13,061	131	There is a membership link between the citing organisation and another organisation, for instance because one of them is a federation of organisations, or coordinating body of which the other is a member.
IGOs	547	1,173	114	
Total	**6,199**	**14,234**	**130**	
Consultative Status				
NGOs	3,112	3,305	6	The citing organisation has consultative status with another organisation. This mainly concerns NGOs having such a status with IGOs.
IGOs	7	6	-14	
Total	**3,119**	**3,311**	**6**	

Record 17 continued

Citations from NGO to IGO and NGO; Citations from IGO to IGO and NGO

Paragraph	1992	2002	% change	
Other IGO Relations				
NGOs	7,750	15,014	94	The citing organisation has some other form of relation with an IGO.
IGOs	10,901	15,117	39	
Total	**18,651**	**30,131**	**62**	
Other NGO Relations				
NGOs	23,754	45,669	92	The citing organisation has some other form of relation with an NGO.
IGOs	10,845	12,974	20	
Total	**34,599**	**58,643**	**69**	
Total number of organisations cited				
NGOs	12,457	18,067	45	
IGOs	1,690	1,859	10	
Total	**14,147**	**19,926**	**41**	
Total number of citations				
NGOs	47,124	89,275	89	
IGOs	28,296	39,451	39	
Total	**75,420**	**128,726**	**71**	
Average number of citations				
NGOs	3.8	4.9	31	
IGOs	16.7	21.2	27	
Total	**5.3**	**6.5**	**21**	

Source: © Union of International Associations, Yearbook of International Organizations: Guide to Civil Society Networks, 1992 and 2002 (presenting data collected in 1991 and 2001, respectively). Data have been restructured from more comprehensive country and organisation coverage in the Yearbook of International Organizations.

Record 18 Meetings of NGOs

Following the International Classification of Nonprofit Organisations, this record presents data on international meetings according to the country in which events were held, and their purposes. These include meetings organised by INGOs, internationally oriented NGOs and IGOs, and other significant international meetings recorded by the Union of International Associations. Most meetings are recorded as having several purposes. In the first table, the number of meetings held in each country in 2002 is shown in absolute figures and as a percentage of all meetings recorded as being held in that year. The absolute figures are also displayed in the map. The second table shows the number of meetings ('hits' in the meetings database) held for a particular purpose in each country in 2002, as a percentage of the total number of meetings for that purpose. In the map, countries are shaded according to the number of meetings in each country. While most meetings still take place in developed countries, large developing countries like Brazil, China and South Africa are also popular.

Country	2002 no. of meetings	2002 % of total meetings
East Asia & Pacific		
Low income economies		
Cambodia	12	0.1
Indonesia	49	0.5
Laos	11	0.1
Myanmar	8	0.1
Vietnam	15	0.2
Middle income economies		
China & Tibet*	122	1.3
Fiji	13	0.1
Malaysia	69	0.7
Philippines	35	0.4
Samoa	3	0.0
Thailand	100	1.1
High income economies		
Australia	238	2.5
Brunei	17	0.2
Korea, Rep.	156	1.7
Japan	259	2.7
New Zealand	42	0.4
Singapore	182	1.9
Europe & Central Asia		
Low income economies		
Azerbaijan	3	0.0
Georgia	4	0.0
Kyrgyzstan	3	0.0
Moldova	2	0.0
Ukraine	16	0.2
Uzbekistan	5	0.1
Middle income economies		
Belarus	1	0.0
Bosnia & Herzegovina	2	0.0
Bulgaria	21	0.2
Croatia	42	0.4
Czech Republic	88	0.9
Estonia	8	0.1
Hungary	102	1.1
Kazakhstan	5	0.1
Latvia	13	0.1
Lithuania	18	0.2
Macedonia	5	0.1
Poland	92	1.0
Romania	27	0.3
Russian Federation	101	1.1
Slovakia	32	0.3
Slovenia	39	0.4
Turkey	73	0.8
High income economies		
Austria	274	2.9
Belgium	299	3.2
Cyprus	19	0.2
Denmark	232	2.5
Finland	195	2.1
France	660	7.0
Germany	485	5.1
Greece	120	1.3
Iceland	30	0.3
Ireland	50	0.5
Italy	387	4.1
Luxembourg	18	0.2
Netherlands	265	2.8
Norway	121	1.3
Portugal	123	1.3
Spain	415	4.4
Sweden	178	1.9
Switzerland	322	3.4
United Kingdom	455	4.8
Latin America & Caribbean		
Low income countries		
Nicaragua	2	0.0
Middle income countries		
Argentina	52	0.6
Barbados	4	0.0
Belize	2	0.0

Record 18 continued

Country	2002 no. of meetings	2002 % of total meetings
Bolivia	9	0.1
Brazil	105	1.1
Chile	37	0.4
Colombia	16	0.2
Costa Rica	19	0.2
Cuba	56	0.6
Dominican Republic	13	0.1
Ecuador	15	0.2
El Salvador	2	0.0
Guatemala	4	0.0
Guyana	4	0.0
Honduras	3	0.0
Jamaica	4	0.0
Mexico	104	1.1
Panama	5	0.1
Peru	18	0.2
St Lucia	4	0.0
Trinidad & Tobago	5	0.1
Uruguay	12	0.1
Venezuela	18	0.2
High income countries		
Bahamas	5	0.1
Middle East & North Africa		
Middle income countries		
Algeria	7	0.1
Egypt	59	0.6
Iran	9	0.1
Iraq	1	0.0
Jordan	9	0.1
Lebanon	17	0.2
Libya	3	0.0
Malta	14	0.1
Morocco & Western Sahara	40	0.4
Oman	2	0.0
Saudi Arabia	3	0.0
Syria	6	0.1
Tunisia	21	0.2
High income countries		
Bahrain	6	0.1
Israel & Occupied Territories	39	0.4
Kuwait	6	0.1
Qatar	1	0.0
United Arab Emirates	13	0.1
North America		
High income countries		
Canada	321	3.4
United States	1,131	12.0

Country	2002 no. of meetings	2002 % of total meetings
South Asia		
Low income countries		
Bangladesh	9	0.1
India	91	1.0
Nepal	21	0.2
Pakistan	9	0.1
High income countries		
Sri Lanka	15	0.2
Sub-Saharan Africa		
Low income countries		
Angola	3	0.0
Benin	2	0.0
Burkina Faso	4	0.0
Cameroon	7	0.1
Ethiopia	5	0.1
Gambia	1	0.0
Ghana	12	0.1
Guinea	2	0.0
Kenya	20	0.2
Lesotho	1	0.0
Madagascar	1	0.0
Malawi	2	0.0
Mali	5	0.1
Mozambique	2	0.0
Nigeria	14	0.1
Senegal	11	0.1
Sudan	5	0.1
Tanzania	16	0.2
Togo	2	0.0
Uganda	9	0.1
Zambia	4	0.0
Zimbabwe	1	0.0
High income countries		
Botswana	3	0.0
Gabon	1	0.0
Mauritius	3	0.0
Namibia	5	0.1
South Africa	113	1.2
Swaziland	2	0.0
Total meetings in sample	**9,308**	**100.0**

*Does not include Hong Kong

Source: © Union of International Associations,Yearbook of International Organizations: Guide to Civil Society Networks, Brussels 2002.

Purposes of meetings for selected countries*

2002 Country % of hits per purpose	Culture & recreation	Education	Research	Health	Social development	Environment	Economic development	Law, policy & advocacy	Religion	Defence	Politics	Hits per country**	country % of all hits for year
East Asia & Pacific													
Low income economies													
Cambodia	1.7	0.7	0.6			1.0	1.0	1.1			1.2	295	0.8
Indonesia	3.0	1.9	1.4	0.2	0.2	2.2	2.2	2.3	0.7		2.3	661	1.9
Laos	1.3	0.7	0.6	0.1	0.1	1.1	0.9	1.0			1.0	265	0.8
Middle income economies													
China & Tibet	2.0	1.1	1.7	0.6	1.1	3.1	1.5	0.8	0.5	0.9	1.1	555	1.6
Malaysia	3.3	1.7	1.2	0.6	0.9	1.8	1.8	1.5	0.2		1.4	554	1.6
Philippines	0.7	0.7	0.6	0.1	0.3	2.0	0.8	0.8	2.0		0.7	272	0.8
Thailand	3.3	2.1	1.7	1.6	1.4	2.0	2.2	2.7	1.1	0.4	2.3	789	2.2
High income economies													
Australia	4.7	2.7	2.6	2.8	1.9	1.7	1.7	1.5	1.1	1.8	0.9	824	2.3
Brunei	1.2	0.6	0.5		0.0	0.7	0.9	0.9			1.2	256	0.7
Korea, Rep.	4.8	1.5	1.4	0.9	1.2	1.8	1.6	1.4	0.7	1.8	1.2	595	1.7
Japan	3.1	1.1	3.3	3.3	1.7	2.1	2.2	1.1	0.5	2.2	1.4	925	2.6
New Zealand	1.7	0.9	0.4	0.4	0.4	0.5	0.3	0.4			0.2	150	0.4
Singapore	3.1	1.5	1.7	1.1	0.9	0.7	1.9	0.8	0.7	1.3	1.4	600	1.7
Europe & Central Asia													
Middle income economies													
Croatia		1.0	0.3	0.3	0.3	0.1	0.3	0.3		1.3	0.4	125	0.4
Czech Republic		1.0	0.9	1.0	0.7	0.5	0.9	0.6	1.6	0.4	0.3	321	0.9
Hungary		1.4	1.0	2.1	1.0	1.0	1.0	0.8	1.1	0.4	0.7	399	1.1
Poland		1.6	1.1	0.6	0.8	1.1	0.6	0.8	0.9	0.9	0.7	335	1.0
Romania		0.3	0.4	0.3	0.4	0.4	0.4	0.4	1.5	0.4	0.4	151	0.4
Russian Federation		1.3	1.5	0.3	1.0	0.7	1.0	0.7	0.2	2.2	2.0	451	1.3
Turkey		0.6	0.8	0.8	0.8	0.7	0.9	0.9	0.4	0.4	1.2	334	0.9
High income economies													
Austria		4.3	2.5	3.5	2.9	1.8	2.8	3.3	2.9	5.8	3.7	1,141	3.2
Belgium		3.2	2.2	2.9	4.1	3.4	3.4	3.3	4.2	3.6	4.0	1,202	3.4
Denmark		2.7	1.5	2.7	1.8	1.8	1.8	2.7	1.3	2.2	2.8	763	2.2
Finland		2.7	1.5	2.1	1.8	2.2	1.8	1.8	0.2	0.4	1.8	679	1.9
France		6.5	6.5	6.2	8.6	6.1	6.0	8.4	3.5	6.2	7.9	2,650	7.5
Germany		5.2	5.1	4.9	4.3	4.6	4.4	3.3	4.2	5.3	3.3	1,760	5.0
Greece		1.6	1.4	0.6	0.9	0.7	1.1	1.0	1.5		1.1	451	0.2
Ireland		0.8	0.2	0.8	0.5	0.6	0.5	0.3	0.2	1.3	0.2	160	0.5
Italy		3.3	4.3	4.9	3.8	4.4	3.6	3.6	3.3	4.4	3.4	1,533	4.3
Netherlands		3.3	2.5	3.4	3.1	1.5	3.0	2.6	2.0	2.7	2.0	1,060	3.0
Norway		1.1	1.2	2.0	1.0	1.0	0.9	0.6	0.4	0.9	0.4	380	1.1
Portugal		1.1	0.9	1.8	1.5	0.4	1.3	1.0	0.7	1.8	0.6	431	1.2
Spain		3.5	4.2	6.2	4.0	3.8	4.1	3.9	3.8	3.1	3.7	1,609	4.6
Sweden		1.0	1.4	2.5	1.7	1.2	1.5	0.9		1.8	1.4	547	1.6
Switzerland		1.4	3.0	4.4	7.5	3.9	4.6	7.4	12.2	7.6	4.2	1,795	5.1
United Kingdom		5.7	4.3	3.9	4.2	4.4	4.0	3.1	8.5	3.6	2.8	1,592	4.5

2002 Country % of hits per purpose	Culture & recreation	Education	Research	Health	Social development	Environment	Economic development	Law, policy & advocacy	Religion	Defence	Politics	Hits per country**	country % of all hits for year
Latin America & Caribbean													
Middle income countries													
Argentina	1.3	0.3	0.3	0.2	0.4	0.4	0.4	0.4	0.2		0.2	142	0.4
Brazil	4.4	1.2	1.3	1.2	1.2	1.0	1.0	0.9	0.7	0.9	1.1	468	1.3
Cuba	1.3	0.9	0.5	1.7	1.1	1.1	0.6	1.0	0.2	0.4	0.5	298	0.8
Mexico	2.5	0.6	1.2	0.7	1.2	1.8	1.3	1.4	1.8	2.2	1.5	506	1.4
Middle East & North Africa													
Middle income countries													
Egypt	2.0	0.3	0.6	0.4	1.0	1.4	1.0	1.3	0.4	0.9	0.8	341	1.0
Iran	0.4	0.1	0.1		0.1	0.2		0.1	1.8		0.2	47	0.1
Lebanon	0.8	0.1	0.1	0.1	0.1	0.1	0.4	0.2	1.3		0.5	96	0.3
Morocco	2.0	1.0	0.6	0.7	1.0	1.3	0.9	1.0	0.4	0.4	1.1	349	1.0
Tunisia	1.2	0.3	0.3	0.9	0.4	0.5	0.2	0.2			0.2	119	0.3
High income countries													
Israel & Occupied Territories***	0.4	0.5	0.5	0.6	0.3	0.2	0.1	0.3	1.6		0.1	130	0.4
North America													
High income countries													
Canada	14.9	2.4	3.5	2.4	3.6	3.7	2.2	2.1	5.3	2.2	1.6	1,213	3.4
United States	17.2	6.3	13.3	9.8	10.1	7.8	10.3	8.3	8.2	14.2	8.6	4,302	12.2
South Asia													
Low income countries													
India	1.3	1.0	1.2	1.8	1.5	1.2	1.0	1.3	3.1		0.9	483	1.4
Sub-Saharan Africa													
Middle income countries													
South Africa	2.3	1.9	1.1	0.8	1.6	1.5	1.3	1.4	1.1	1.8	1.6	535	1.5

* Covers only countries that had 1% of all international meetings in at least one of the categories. Empty cells indicate that the share of meetings was below 0.05%.

** One 'hit' is recorded for each meeting purpose: multi-purpose meetings may therefore generate several hits.

***All hits recorded here are for Israel; total for the Occupied Territories is zero.

Source: © Union of International Associations,Yearbook of International Organizations: Guide to Civil Society Networks, 2002.

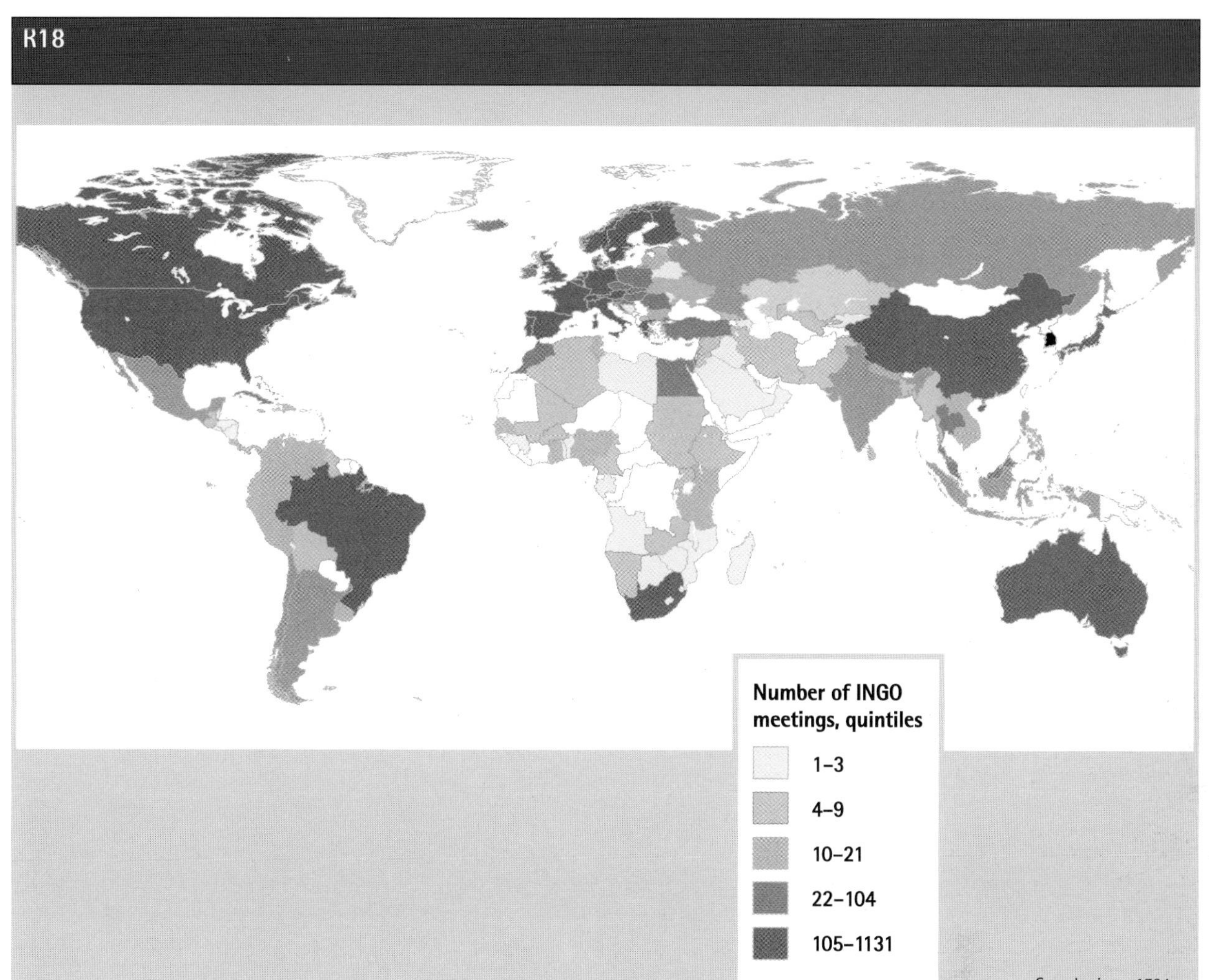
R18
Number of INGO meetings, quintiles
1–3
4–9
10–21
22–104
105–1131
Sample size = 1724

Record 19 NGOs by purpose

Following the International Classification of Nonprofit Organisations, this record presents data on the purposes of activities of international and internationally oriented NGOs by country. The classification does not report actual activities or expenditures but is based on statements of intent. The first column gives the percentage of each purpose type in relation to the total number of NGOs in that country for 2002. The second column gives the percentage change from 2001 to 2002. The summary table shows the overall rate of growth or decline for each purpose over the last year.

	Culture & Recreation		Education		Research		Health		Social development	
Country	% country total 2002	% change 2001-2002	% country total 2002	% change 2001-2002	% country total 2002	% change 2001-2002	% country total 2002	% change 2001-2002	% country total 2002	% change 2001-2002
East Asia & Pacific										
Middle income economies										
China & Tibet	5.2	0.0	8.0	33.0	21.8	22.0	6.9	20.0	8.7	18.8
Malaysia	6.8	60.0	2.1	120.0	21.6	40.0	6.4	7.1	10.6	31.8
Philippines	1.1	-42.9	6.2	37.5	15.3	39.6	4.3	5.3	14.5	37.8
Thailand	0.9	600.0	5.0	146.7	22.5	74.3	5.3	29.4	14.1	102.9
High income economies										
Australia	6.7	6.6	5.9	-3.2	29.7	8.7	6.2	0.0	9.9	9.9
Japan	6.1	0.0	5.3	18.9	24.0	18.7	4.0	30.4	9.0	14.3
Singapore	7.1	20.0	9.4	29.4	29.5	23.6	10.3	0.0	7.6	-5.6
Europe & Central Asia										
Middle income economies										
Czech Republic	3.8	50.0	5.1	-11.1	28.2	15.0	8.3	18.2	15.4	0.0
Hungary	12.4	-13.8	6.0	0.0	30.3	14.8	2.5	66.7	5.0	10.0
Poland	11.6	-6.3	2.3	-57.1	34.9	33.3	3.1	-33.3	8.5	62.5
Romania	11.9	-25.0	21.4	75.0	21.4	-72.7	14.3	0.0	4.8	-60.0
Russian Federation	4.8	650.0	10.0	133.3	24.7	154.5	1.5	33.3	8.9	68.8
Turkey	0.9	500.0	5.3	33.3	34.5	42.5	5.3	0.0	6.2	-8.3
High income economies										
Austria	7.0	-11.3	5.6	20.0	25.4	23.8	3.0	43.5	9.6	42.5
Belgium	4.4	3.2	4.5	0.0	17.7	5.2	4.6	-0.7	11.7	14.6
Denmark	6.9	19.2	5.6	13.6	25.7	14.4	8.2	9.5	11.0	23.8
Finland	6.0	23.8	8.8	2.9	28.3	27.2	8.8	5.4	10.0	24.4
France	9.3	6.8	5.3	1.0	21.4	13.5	4.1	4.7	10.4	10.0
Germany	7.2	2.8	5.2	6.6	22.0	10.8	5.9	0.0	9.4	9.4
Greece	11.5	-3.1	5.9	42.9	21.9	25.4	5.9	-11.1	7.8	38.1
Ireland	4.3	14.3	6.5	-7.7	16.3	0.0	10.9	23.5	17.4	9.7
Italy	6.6	6.0	4.7	5.5	23.5	20.2	5.0	29.4	10.0	17.6
Luxembourg	11.5	-6.7	4.9	200.0	10.7	107.1	4.1	0.0	13.9	13.6
Netherlands	7.1	-5.8	6.4	-1.7	22.9	4.0	5.9	-1.8	10.3	3.9
Norway	6.3	22.2	6.9	-2.9	25.1	13.3	5.1	23.8	9.0	25.6
Portugal	12.9	25.0	7.9	28.6	20.3	65.4	4.5	83.3	10.4	76.5
Spain	7.8	5.2	5.7	3.5	22.4	11.0	6.0	33.3	11.2	24.2
Sweden	6.9	11.1	5.4	40.0	24.3	5.5	6.5	-1.4	11.0	10.6
Switzerland	8.4	6.0	4.0	7.8	16.3	40.1	4.7	22.6	12.4	33.3

Environment		Economic development infrastructure		Law, policy and advocacy		Religion		Defence		Politics	
% country total 2002	% change 2001-2002	% country total 2002	% change 2001-2002	% country total 2002	% change 2001-2002	% country total 2002	% change 2001-2002	% country total 2002	% change 2001-2002	% country total 2002	% change 2001-2002
1.7	0.0	21.8	95.0	12.5	66.7	8.0	27.8	0.3	0.0	5.2	
4.7	30.0	29.2	44.3	11.9	31.8	4.2	0.0	0.0		2.5	60.0
6.7	50.0	26.5	10.1	15.3	17.6	5.1	-17.4	0.3	0.0	4.8	5.9
7.2	113.6	18.8	121.1	17.2	41.2	4.7	66.7	0.0		4.4	46.2
3.1	25.9	20.7	0.5	9.6	4.4	2.9	-15.2	0.3	0.0	5.0	2.0
4.2	24.1	23.8	6.9	11.9	3.4	2.8	5.0	0.7	-44.4	8.4	-1.4
1.8	300.0	20.1	20.5	7.1	17.6	4.5	-33.3	0.0	-100.0	2.7	200.0
2.6	0.0	14.7	8.7	11.5	0.0	3.8	-25.0	0.0		6.4	0.0
3.0	14.3	19.9	27.0	8.5	13.3	3.0	0.0	0.5	0.0	9.0	12.5
3.1		23.3	36.7	6.2	71.4	0.0	-100.0	0.0	-100.0	7.0	0.0
0.0		4.8	-68.8	11.9	-46.2	0.0		0.0		9.5	-71.4
4.4	71.4	16.2	462.5	14.8	100.0	3.0	33.3	1.1	33.3	10.7	466.7
1.8	150.0	24.8	11.1	8.8	0.0	5.3	42.9	0.0		7.1	18.2
1.6	30.8	24.4	26.7	12.2	37.6	1.7	15.4	0.8	142.9	8.6	47.0
2.8	5.3	36.8	7.5	10.5	11.6	2.6	-6.3	0.6	142.4	3.8	35.4
3.3	52.2	24.4	35.3	8.3	25.8	2.7	-4.8	0.3	-25.0	3.5	110.7
2.5	7.7	20.0	17.9	9.5	40.6	3.8	-6.3	0.0		2.5	-18.8
2.8	21.8	27.6	7.8	10.8	13.6	3.2	10.3	0.6	21.9	4.4	27.6
2.5	5.0	26.4	6.9	10.8	10.6	4.3	0.8	0.8	47.6	5.3	9.7
4.4	36.4	14.1	23.3	13.3	30.3	4.1	0.0	2.2	0.0	8.9	-4.0
3.3	50.0	21.7	2.0	12.5	0.0	1.6	200.0	0.5		4.9	11.1
2.4	158.1	22.4	37.2	11.5	20.1	8.9	-0.6	0.6	36.4	4.5	45.3
2.5	0.0	29.5	75.0	9.0	133.3	5.7	16.7	0.8	200.0	7.4	250.0
3.5	0.0	26.1	1.0	10.8	3.8	2.6	-9.0	0.8	31.8	3.5	0.0
3.7	26.3	22.2	15.2	12.4	14.3	2.9	-6.7	0.8	-20.0	5.7	25.0
2.0	100.0	24.3	126.9	7.4	88.9	4.0	60.0	0.0		6.4	350.0
3.2	17.9	25.0	6.3	10.9	6.4	1.3	0.0	0.8	57.1	5.7	6.8
3.0	45.8	25.8	17.2	9.5	18.8	2.5	0.0	1.2	9.1	3.9	24.3
2.0	49.1	27.0	31.6	13.1	31.3	6.6	0.6	0.6	46.7	5.0	37.6

Record 19 continued

Country	Culture & Recreation		Education		Research		Health		Social Services	
	% country total 2002	% change 2001-2002	% country total 2002	% change 2001-2002	% country total 2002	% change 2001-2002	% country total 2002	% change 2001-2002	% country total 2002	% change 2001-2002
United Kingdom	5.2	-3.0	4.5	1.8	21.8	4.1	5.3	4.4	11.7	6.8
Latin America & Caribbean										
Middle income countries										
Argentina	4.3	0.0	4.5	-5.3	23.2	34.7	6.3	18.2	11.9	11.1
Brazil	5.2	0.0	5.2	7.7	27.4	42.6	5.2	-11.1	11.5	66.7
Chile	1.2	0.0	4.3	50.0	23.6	47.4	4.3	60.0	18.0	24.0
Colombia	2.7	16.7	12.3	31.3	20.5	16.1	6.2	12.5	10.3	0.0
Costa Rica	1.0	200.0	9.7	33.3	16.8	25.6	1.0	-33.3	15.3	48.0
Ecuador	0.0	600.0	6.0	0.0	16.2	105.3	1.7	50.0	12.0	33.3
Mexico	5.8	0.0	9.1	21.4	23.1	20.8	7.9	17.4	9.6	25.0
Peru	5.0	0.0	6.3	25.0	17.0	83.3	3.1	28.6	9.4	53.3
Uruguay	5.2	50.0	3.9	120.0	30.3	40.0	4.5	42.9	11.6	10.5
Venezuela	6.8	63.6	8.7	25.0	21.4	25.0	4.4	80.0	17.5	8.3
Middle East & North Africa										
Middle income countries										
Egypt	7.6	-39.3	4.3	180.0	13.3	111.5	4.3	128.6	14.3	113.6
Saudi Arabia	6.3	300.0	3.1	500.0	9.4	100.0	6.3		6.8	1200.0
Israel	6.7	18.8	2.8	14.3	13.1	0.0	1.8	25.0	5.7	-10.0
North America										
High income countries										
Canada	7.1	13.4	6.1	0.0	20.6	14.7	5.3	1.3	11.3	8.0
United States	4.8	-3.1	5.1	-6.2	21.5	7.4	5.0	4.4	11.1	7.5
South Asia										
Low income countries										
India	3.1	133.3	5.6	24.1	21.9	30.4	4.7	10.7	10.5	11.9
Sub-Saharan Africa										
Low income countries										
Côte d'Ivoire	13.5	-29.0	11.2	0.0	16.9	60.0	3.4	-25.0	6.7	-11.0
Ghana	8.2	71.4	8.2	0.0	9.8	69.2	3.3	50.0	13.1	21.4
Kenya	0.9	25.0	6.4	11.1	25.8	47.2	3.1	54.5	12.4	36.5
Nigeria	6.1	128.6	8.0	72.7	23.1	85.7	8.0	30.8	9.0	40.0
Senegal	6.1	54.5	5.6	171.4	17.4	92.9	0.9	300.0	10.8	13.0
Zimbabwe	4.5	20.0	7.5	11.1	14.9	61.1	3.7	40.0	14.9	15.0
Middle income countries										
South Africa	7.7	30.4	4.1	45.5	22.1	21.9	5.4	16.7	8.2	22.2

Environment		Economic development infrastructure		Law, policy and advocacy		Religion		Defence		Politics	
% country total 2002	% change 2001-2002	% country total 2002	% change 2001-2002	% country total 2002	% change 2001-2002	% country total 2002	% change 2001-2002	% country total 2002	% change 2001-2002	% country total 2002	% change 2001-2002
3.1	6.2	26.8	4.7	11.2	3.3	5.0	3.0	1.2	1.4	4.1	4.7
1.8	100.0	25.8	27.6	11.6	2.0	4.5	28.6	0.0		6.1	75.0
2.6	28.6	20.4	22.2	11.9	22.2	3.7	0.0	0.0		7.0	41.2
6.2	112.5	24.2	29.5	10.6	60.0	3.7	100.0	1.2	0.0	2.5	50.0
2.1	0.0	23.3	35.1	9.6	31.3	8.2	-25.0	0.0		4.8	57.1
5.1	70.0	27.6	44.9	15.8	40.0	1.0	-50.0	0.0		6.6	72.7
2.6	60.0	23.9	28.1	19.7	36.4	6.0	-22.2	1.7	0.0	10.3	0.0
4.4	12.5	21.3	12.3	9.6	31.0	1.8	20.0	0.0		7.3	12.5
6.9	77.8	29.6	65.0	16.4	66.7	0.0		0.0		6.3	30.8
5.2	22.2	18.1	57.1	16.1	56.5	1.9	-25.0	0.0		3.2	400.0
1.0	33.3	23.3	43.8	10.7	-22.6	1.5	0.0	0.5	0.0	4.4	62.5
5.2	100.0	25.7	106.3	14.8	2.5	5.2	30.0	0.0	-100.0	5.2	100.0
2.6	0.0	30.2	152.0	13.5	136.0	14.6	2700.0	0.5	0.0	6.8	550.0
1.1	0.0	16.3	11.4	23.3	17.2	18.7	0.0	0.7	33.3	9.9	14.8
2.9	26.8	21.4	-1.5	13.4	5.3	4.3	-10.0	0.7	66.7	7.0	10.3
2.9	11.2	22.5	7.5	12.3	9.6	7.5	1.1	0.8	54.3	6.7	21.6
2.6	5.9	22.7	35.7	17.8	29.2	6.3	-2.5	0.0		5.0	24.0
2.2	-20.0	25.8	106.0	11.2	64.0	7.9	0.0	0.0		1.1	200.0
2.5	150.0	22.1	60.0	13.1	13.3	13.9	-26.1	0.0		5.7	33.3
7.9	75.9	24.1	72.7	8.2	31.4	9.7	7.3	0.0		1.5	533.3
5.7	85.7	18.4	114.3	12.7	75.0	4.7	-9.1	0.9	50.0	3.3	66.7
3.8	83.3	34.3	53.2	16.4	85.7	1.4	50.0	0.5	0.0	2.8	250.0
3.7	33.3	24.6	51.6	13.4	-14.3	8.2	-15.4	0.0		4.5	0.0
3.8	-20.0	25.9	32.9	6.4	40.0	12.8	47.1	0.0		3.6	13.3

Source: © Union of International Associations, Yearbook of International Organizations: Guide to Civil Society Networks, 2002. Data have been restructured from more comprehensive country and organisation coverage in the Yearbook of International Organisations.

Record 19 continued

Overall growth rate of number of NGOs by purpose*

Purpose	2001	2002	% change 2001–2002
Culture and recreation	5,511	5,481	-0.5
Education	4,420	4,319	-2.3
Research	18,985	19,079	0.5
Health	3,935	3,918	-0.4
Social development	9,944	10,001	0.6
Environment	3,077	3,111	1.1
Economic development, infrastructure	25,013	24,766	-1.0
Law, policy and advocacy	10,039	10,171	1.3
Religion	4,387	4,302	-1.9
Defence	904	953	5.4
Politics	5,048	5,075	0.5
Totals	91,263	91,176	-0.1

*This table is not directly comparable to Record 20b from Yearbook 2002, due to the data having been compiled using a different method.

Source: © Union of International Associations, Yearbook of International Organizations: Guide to Civil Society Networks, 2002. Data have been restructured from more comprehensive country and organisation coverage in the Yearbook of International Organisations.

Record 20 International organisation leaders

This record presents information on the characteristics of the leaders of both international NGOs and intergovernmental organisations (IGOs). The first table gives information on the distribution of leading people in international non-profit organisations of all types. These are people who occupy prominent positions, whether elected, voluntary, or salaried; they have titles such as 'Secretary-General', 'President', Director', Chief Executive Officer', 'Chairman', Secretary', Coordinator', 'General Manager', 'Commissioner', 'Head' etc. It shows numbers of leaders as absolute figures and percentages of the total number of leaders in the database. It also shows numbers of organisation memberships ('membership' in the sense defined in Record 16) held by those leaders as absolute figures and percentages of total number of memberships. Data are given for leaders classified by their country of citizenship, for 1996 and 2002 and corresponding changes over that time period. The last two columns in the table represent this information for 2002 in terms of density of leadership within the home country populations of leaders. Numbers of leaders and organisational memberships are expressed here per million of the populations of the leaders' home countries.

The subsequent tables and charts present information on the characteristics of executives of international NGOs and IGOs. Data on gender for the period 1992–2002 suggest that male dominance of organisation leadership is on the decline.

Leaders of international organisations tend to be highly proficient in languages, as shown by the next chart—the majority speak more than two languages. The overwhelming majority speak English, as shown by the next chart.

Leaders also tend to have high levels of formal education, with the average leader holding more than two degrees, as shown in the next table. It appears that the proportion of leaders with postgraduate degrees has fallen between 1996 and 2002, whereas the proportion with multiple graduate degrees has increased. Such degrees are obtained from institutions in a variety of places, as illustrated by the last table in this record, which shows the cities where leaders have most commonly studied.

A note of caution: the most serious flaw in the data, according to the editors of the Who's Who in International Organisations, is the limited amount of information included in most of the biographical entries. There are several reasons for this. (1) The structure of many organisations works against the collection and establishment of a list of its officers. Many organisations elect or appoint new officers annually or biannually, still others at irregular and sometimes unannounced intervals (so that some people in Who's Who no longer hold significant positions in the organisation to which they are associated in the publication). (2) Some organisations are publicly represented by individuals who do not hold the most significant positions in terms of the development and operation of the organisation. It is not always possible to gather information on anyone other than the known representative, usually the person with the 'most elevated' title.

Distribution of leaders of international organisations

Country	Leaders Number 1996	Leaders % 1996	Organisation memberships Number 1996	Organisation memberships % 1996	Leaders Number 2002	Leaders % 2002	Organisation memberships Number 2002	Organisation memberships % 2002	Change in % of leaders * 1996-2002	Change in organisation memberships* in % 1996-2002	Leaders per mill. of population 2002	Organisation membership per mill. of population 2002
East Asia & Pacific												
Low income economies												
Cambodia	0	0.0	0	0.0							0.00	0.00
Indonesia	10	0.3	20	0.3	6	0.2	11	0.2	-24	-37	0.03	0.05
Korea, Dem. Rep.	7	0.2	14	0.2	9	0.3	16	0.3	63	32	0.41	0.72
Laos	0	0.0	0	0.0							0.00	0.00
Mongolia	1	0.0	1	0.0	1	0.0	3	0.1	27	246	0.37	1.12
Myanmar	1	0.0	1	0.0							0.00	0.00
Papua New Guinea	0	0.0	0	0.0	1	0.0	4	0.1			0.19	0.77
Solomon Islands	0	0.0	0	0.0							0.00	0.00
Vietnam	0	0.0	0	0.0							0.00	0.00

Record 20 continued

Country	Leaders Number 1996	Leaders % 1996	Organisation memberships Number 1996	Organisation memberships % 1996	Leaders Number 2002	Leaders % 2002	Organisation memberships Number 2002	Organisation memberships % 2002	Change in % of leaders * 1996-2002	Change in organisation memberships* in % 1996-2002	Leaders per mill. 2002	Organisation membership of population 2002
Middle income economies												
China & Tibet	12	0.4	24	0.4	12	0.5	16	0.3	27	-23	0.01	0.01
Fiji	3	0.1	5	0.1	4	0.2	11	0.2	69	154	4.67	12.85
Malaysia	17	0.5	33	0.6	16	0.6	31	0.6	19	8	0.71	1.37
Philippines	28	0.8	65	1.1	25	0.9	59	1.1	13	5	0.30	0.71
Samoa	0	0.0	0	0.0							0.00	0.00
Thailand	10	0.3	18	0.3	9	0.3	19	0.4	14	22	0.14	0.30
Tonga	2	0.1	4	0.1	1	0.0	2	0.0	-37	-42	9.42	18.84
Vanuatu	0	0.0	0	0.0							0.00	0.00
High income economies												
Australia	56	1.7	100	1.7	54	2.0	90	1.8	22	4	2.76	4.60
Brunei	0	0.0	0	0.0							0.00	0.00
Korea, Rep.	0	0.0	0	0.0							0.00	0.00
Japan	41	1.2	71	1.2	28	1.1	41	0.8	-14	-33	0.22	0.32
New Zealand	18	0.5	27	0.5	20	0.8	36	0.7	41	54	5.12	9.21
Singapore	11	0.3	17	0.3	13	0.5	22	0.4	50	49	2.92	4.94
Europe & Central Asia												
Low income economies												
Armenia	0	0.0	0	0.0							0.00	0.00
Azerbaijan	0	0.0	0	0.0	1	0.0	1	0.0			0.13	0.13
Georgia	0	0.0	0	0.0	1	0.0	1	0.0			0.20	0.20
Kyrgyzstan	0	0.0	0	0.0	2	0.1	5	0.1			0.41	1.04
Moldova	0	0.0	0	0.0	1	0.0	1	0.0			0.23	0.23
Tajikistan	0	0.0	0	0.0	2	0.1	3	0.1			0.30	0.45
Ukraine	0	0.0	0	0.0	2	0.1	4	0.1			0.04	0.08
Uzbekistan	0	0.0	0	0.0							0.00	0.00
Middle income economies												
Albania	0	0.0	0	0.0	1	0.0	1	0.0			0.28	0.28
Belarus	1	0.0	1	0.0	1	0.0	1	0.0	27	15	0.10	0.10
Bosnia & Herzegovina	0	0.0	0	0.0							0.00	0.00
Bulgaria	5	0.1	9	0.2	6	0.2	17	0.3	52	118	0.79	2.23
Croatia	4	0.1	10	0.2	6	0.2	19	0.4	90	119	1.37	4.33
Czech Republic	9	0.3	21	0.4	9	0.3	18	0.4	27	-1	0.88	1.75
Estonia	3	0.1	7	0.1	1	0.0	1	0.0	-58	-84	0.71	0.71
Hungary	21	0.6	35	0.6	11	0.4	23	0.4	-34	-24	1.09	2.28
Kazakhstan	0	0.0	0	0.0							0.00	0.00
Latvia	1	0.0	1	0.0	1	0.0	1	0.0	27	15	0.42	0.42
Lithuania	1	0.0	1	0.0	1	0.0	1	0.0	27	15	0.28	0.28
Macedonia	0	0.0	0	0.0	1	0.0	1	0.0			0.49	0.49
Poland	18	0.5	34	0.6	10	0.4	21	0.4	-30	-29	0.26	0.54
Romania	4	0.1	10	0.2	2	0.1	3	0.1	-37	-65	0.09	0.13
Russian Federation	15	0.4	34	0.6	18	0.7	46	0.9	52	56	0.12	0.32
Serbia & Montenegro	1	0.0	1	0.0	1	0.0	1	0.0	27	15	0.09	0.09
Slovakia	3	0.1	3	0.1	4	0.2	4	0.1	69	54	0.74	0.74
Slovenia	3	0.1	5	0.1	5	0.2	8	0.2	111	85	2.59	4.14
Turkey	8	0.2	19	0.3	9	0.3	18	0.4	42	9	0.13	0.27
Turkmenistan	0	0.0	0	0.0	0	0.0	0	0.0			0.00	0.00

Record 20 continued

Country	Leaders Number 1996	Leaders % 1996	Organisation memberships Number 1996	Organisation memberships % 1996	Leaders Number 2002	Leaders % 2002	Organisation memberships Number 2002	Organisation memberships % 2002	Change in % of leaders * 1996-2002	Change in organisation memberships* in % 1996-2002	Leaders per mill. 2002	Organisation membership of population 2002
High income economies												
Austria	32	1.0	46	0.8	35	1.3	54	1.1	38	35	4.28	6.61
Belgium	283	8.5	502	8.5	210	8.0	403	7.8	-6	-7	20.44	39.22
Cyprus	4	0.1	5	0.1	2	0.1	4	0.1	-37	-8	2.61	5.21
Denmark	61	1.8	94	1.6	48	1.8	94	1.8	0	15	8.94	17.51
Finland	41	1.2	97	1.6	41	1.6	98	1.9	27	17	7.91	18.91
France	321	9.6	517	8.7	231	8.8	412	8.0	-9	-8	3.85	6.88
Germany	214	6.4	345	5.8	150	5.7	275	5.4	-11	-8	1.82	3.34
Greece	17	0.5	39	0.7	18	0.7	40	0.8	34	18	1.69	3.76
Iceland	7	0.2	15	0.3	4	0.2	12	0.2	-28	-8	14.32	42.95
Ireland	23	0.7	41	0.7	15	0.6	23	0.4	-17	-35	3.86	5.92
Italy	97	2.9	176	3.0	85	3.2	179	3.5	11	17	1.47	3.09
Luxembourg	18	0.5	23	0.4	10	0.4	15	0.3	-30	-25	22.29	33.44
Netherlands	151	4.5	254	4.3	120	4.6	209	4.1	1	-5	7.47	13.01
Norway	40	1.2	63	1.1	26	1.0	36	0.7	-18	-34	5.75	7.96
Portugal	8	0.2	9	0.2	9	0.3	12	0.2	42	54	0.89	1.19
Spain	45	1.3	94	1.6	35	1.3	75	1.5	-2	-8	0.87	1.87
Sweden	72	2.2	122	2.1	56	2.1	101	2.0	-2	-4	6.31	11.38
Switzerland	93	2.8	160	2.7	76	2.9	144	2.8	3	4	10.41	19.72
United Kingdom	455	13.6	721	12.2	326	12.4	577	11.2	-9	-8	5.44	9.63
Latin America & Caribbean												
Low income countries												
Haiti	2	0.1	2	0.0							0.00	0.00
Nicaragua	1	0.0	2	0.0	2	0.1	3	0.1	153	73	0.40	0.60
High income countries												
Argentina	23	0.7	44	0.7	25	0.9	48	0.9	38	26	0.65	1.25
Barbados	7	0.2	14	0.2	8	0.3	15	0.3	45	24	28.97	54.31
Belize	0	0.0	0	0.0	2	0.1	6	0.1			7.69	23.08
Bolivia	3	0.1	5	0.1	3	0.1	6	0.1	27	38	0.36	0.71
Brazil	16	0.5	29	0.5	21	0.8	38	0.7	66	51	0.12	0.21
Chile	11	0.3	20	0.3	9	0.3	23	0.4	4	33	0.58	1.48
Colombia	12	0.4	23	0.4	8	0.3	17	0.3	-16	-15	0.20	0.41
Costa Rica	7	0.2	11	0.2	4	0.2	8	0.2	-28	-16	1.04	2.09
Cuba	5	0.1	6	0.1	6	0.2	12	0.2	52	131	0.53	1.07
Dominican Republic	3	0.1	5	0.1	2	0.1	3	0.1	-16	-31	0.23	0.35
Ecuador	5	0.1	9	0.2	5	0.2	12	0.2	27	54	0.37	0.89
El Salvador	0	0.0	0	0.0							0.00	0.00
Guatemala	4	0.1	6	0.1	1	0.0	2	0.0	-68	-62	0.07	0.15
Guyana	5	0.1	26	0.4	3	0.1	19	0.4	-24	-16	4.29	27.16
Honduras	1	0.0	1	0.0							0.00	0.00
Jamaica	6	0.2	9	0.2	1	0.0	2	0.0	-79	-74	0.37	0.75
Mexico	20	0.6	29	0.5	12	0.5	18	0.4	-24	-28	0.12	0.17
Panama	2	0.1	3	0.1	1	0.0	2	0.0	-37	-23	0.34	0.68
Paraguay	0	0.0	0	0.0							0.00	0.00
Peru	9	0.3	14	0.2	5	0.2	10	0.2	-30	-18	0.18	0.36

Record 20 continued

Country	Leaders Number 1996	Leaders % 1996	Organisation memberships Number 1996	Organisation memberships % 1996	Leaders Number 2002	Leaders % 2002	Organisation memberships Number 2002	Organisation memberships % 2002	Change in % of leaders* 1996-2002	Change in organisation memberships* in % 1996-2002	Leaders per mill. 2002	Organisation membership of population 2002
Saint Lucia	0	0.0	0	0.0							0.00	0.00
Suriname	0	0.0	0	0.0							0.00	0.00
Trinidad & Tobago	1	0.0	2	0.0	3	0.1	8	0.2	280	362	2.70	7.20
Uruguay	12	0.4	30	0.5	10	0.4	25	0.5	5	-4	2.95	7.38
Venezuela	10	0.3	20	0.3	10	0.4	22	0.4	27	27	0.41	0.91
High income countries												
Bahamas	0	0.0	0	0.0							0.00	0.00
Middle East & North Africa												
Low income countries												
Yemen	0	0.0	0	0.0							0.00	0.00
High income countries												
Algeria	8	0.2	16	0.3	8	0.3	19	0.4	27	37	0.25	0.59
Djibouti	0	0.0	0	0.0							0.00	0.00
Egypt	21	0.6	52	0.9	21	0.8	57	1.1	27	26	0.29	0.78
Iran	5	0.1	11	0.2	3	0.1	7	0.1	-24	-27	0.04	0.10
Iraq	12	0.4	20	0.3	7	0.3	12	0.2	-26	-31	0.29	0.50
Jordan	10	0.3	23	0.4	5	0.2	10	0.2	-37	-50	0.94	1.88
Lebanon	6	0.2	13	0.2	6	0.2	11	0.2	27	-2	1.63	2.99
Libya	5	0.1	11	0.2	3	0.1	3	0.1	-24	-69	0.56	0.56
Malta	4	0.1	5	0.1	4	0.2	4	0.1	27	-8	10.06	10.06
Morocco & Western Sahara	3	0.1	4	0.1	4	0.2	5	0.1	69	44	0.13	0.16
Oman	0	0.0	0	0.0							0.00	0.00
Saudi Arabia	16	0.5	59	1.0	18	0.7	54	1.1	42	6	0.77	2.30
Syria	2	0.1	3	0.1	2	0.1	6	0.1	27	131	0.12	0.35
Tunisia	11	0.3	21	0.4	10	0.4	18	0.4	15	-1	1.02	1.83
High income countries												
Bahrain	0	0.0	0	0.0							0.00	0.00
Israel & Occupied Territories	14	0.4	23	0.4	14	0.5	27	0.5	27	35	1.49	2.87
Kuwait	2	0.1	3	0.1	4	0.2	9	0.2	153	246	1.89	4.26
Qatar	0	0.0	0	0.0							0.00	0.00
United Arab Emirates	0	0.0	0	0.0							0.00	0.00
North America												
High income countries												
Canada	100	3.0	185	3.1	93	3.5	192	3.7	18	20	2.92	6.02
United States	378	11.3	667	11.3	276	10.5	553	10.8	-8	-4	0.96	1.92
South Asia												
Low income countries												
Afghanistan	0	0.0	0	0.0	1	0.0	1	0.0			0.04	0.04
Bangladesh	7	0.2	14	0.2	7	0.3	13	0.3	27	7	0.05	0.10
Bhutan	0	0.0	0	0.0	1	0.0	2	0.0			0.48	0.96
India	61	1.8	132	2.2	41	1.6	91	1.8	-15	-20	0.04	0.09
Nepal	4	0.1	8	0.1	2	0.1	4	0.1	-37	-42	0.08	0.15
Pakistan	15	0.4	30	0.5	12	0.5	29	0.6	1	12	0.08	0.20

Record 20 continued

Country	Leaders Number 1996	Leaders % 1996	Organisation memberships Number 1996	Organisation memberships % 1996	Leaders Number 2002	Leaders % 2002	Organisation memberships Number 2002	Organisation memberships % 2002	Change in % of leaders * 1996-2002	Change in organisation memberships* in % 1996-2002	Leaders per mill. 2002	Organisation membership of population 2002
High income countries												
Maldives	0	0.0	0	0.0							0.00	0.00
Sri Lanka	18	0.5	31	0.5	13	0.5	33	0.6	-9	23	0.66	1.69
Sub-Saharan Africa												
Low income countries												
Angola	1	0.0	1	0.0	1	0.0	2	0.0	27	131	0.09	0.19
Benin	2	0.1	12	0.2	2	0.1	10	0.2	27	-4	0.29	1.46
Burkina Faso	2	0.1	4	0.1							0.00	0.00
Burundi	0	0.0	0	0.0							0.00	0.00
Cameroon	7	0.2	14	0.2	6	0.2	8	0.2	8	-34	0.39	0.52
Central African Republic	0	0.0	0	0.0							0.00	0.00
Chad	0	0.0	0	0.0							0.00	0.00
Comoros	0	0.0	0	0.0							0.00	0.00
Congo, Dem. Rep.	5	0.1	7	0.1	4	0.2	7	0.1	1	15	0.34	0.69
Congo, Rep.	3	0.1	5	0.1	1	0.0	2	0.0	-58	-54	0.07	0.13
Côte d'Ivoire	7	0.2	10	0.2	8	0.3	13	0.3	45	50	0.48	0.78
Equatorial Guinea	0	0.0	0	0.0							0.00	0.00
Eritrea	0	0.0	0	0.0	1	0.0	1	0.0			0.23	0.23
Ethiopia	7	0.2	16	0.3	3	0.1	8	0.2	-46	-42	0.05	0.12
Gambia	3	0.1	11	0.2	3	0.1	15	0.3	27	57	2.06	10.30
Ghana	15	0.4	27	0.5	11	0.4	22	0.4	-7	-6	0.55	1.09
Guinea	2	0.1	3	0.1							0.00	0.00
Guinea-Bissau	0	0.0	0	0.0							0.00	0.00
Kenya	12	0.4	23	0.4	12	0.5	23	0.4	27	15	0.38	0.74
Lesotho	1	0.0	8	0.1	1	0.0	7	0.1	27	1	0.54	3.77
Liberia	1	0.0	3	0.1	1	0.0	3	0.1	27	15	0.31	0.92
Madagascar	1	0.0	3	0.1	1	0.0	3	0.1	27	15	0.06	0.18
Malawi	1	0.0	6	0.1	1	0.0	5	0.1	27	-4	0.09	0.44
Mali	4	0.1	5	0.1	2	0.1	6	0.1	-37	38	0.18	0.53
Mauritania	3	0.1	5	0.1	4	0.2	6	0.1	69	38	1.41	2.12
Mozambique	0	0.0	0	0.0	1	0.0	2	0.0			0.06	0.12
Niger	1	0.0	3	0.1	2	0.1	3	0.1	153	15	0.19	0.28
Nigeria	30	0.9	83	1.4	28	1.1	92	1.8	18	28	0.21	0.70
Rwanda	0	0.0	0	0.0	1	0.0	1	0.0			0.13	0.13
Sao Tome & Principe	0	0.0	0	0.0							0.00	0.00
Senegal	11	0.3	26	0.4	10	0.4	26	0.5	15	15	0.97	2.52
Sierra Leone	2	0.1	4	0.1	2	0.1	2	0.0	27	-42	0.36	0.36
Somalia	0	0.0	0	0.0							0.00	0.00
Sudan	8	0.2	20	0.3	6	0.2	19	0.4	-5	10	0.16	0.51
Tanzania	7	0.2	8	0.1	6	0.2	10	0.2	8	44	0.17	0.28
Togo	5	0.1	8	0.1	4	0.2	6	0.1	1	-13	0.75	1.13
Uganda	7	0.2	15	0.3	5	0.2	9	0.2	-10	-31	0.20	0.36
Zambia	4	0.1	8	0.1							0.00	0.00
Zimbabwe	5	0.1	9	0.2	7	0.3	17	0.3	77	118	0.56	1.36

Record 20 continued

Country	Leaders Number 1996	Leaders % 1996	Organisation memberships Number 1996	Organisation memberships % 1996	Leaders Number 2002	Leaders % 2002	Organisation memberships Number 2002	Organisation memberships % 2002	Change in % of leaders * 1996-2002	Change in organisation memberships* in % 1996-2002	Leaders per mill. 2002	Organisation membership of population 2002
High income countries												
Botswana	2	0.1	3	0.1	1	0.0	1	0.0	-37	-62	0.63	0.63
Cape Verde	0	0.0	0	0.0	1	0.0	2	0.0			2.45	4.89
Gabon	0	0.0	0	0.0							0.00	0.00
Mauritius	5	0.1	7	0.1	5	0.2	6	0.1	27	-1	4.17	5.00
Namibia	0	0.0	0	0.0	1	0.0	1	0.0			0.53	0.53
South Africa	9	0.3	14	0.2	5	0.2	10	0.2	-30	-18	0.12	0.23
Swaziland	0	0.0	0	0.0	1	0.0	6	0.1			0.87	5.22
Total	3336	100.0	5926	100.0	2636	100.0	5136	100.0				

* adjusted for sample size: sample sizes are slightly larger that the number of people in the sample because of dual citizenships.

Sample sizes:

1996: 3346 citizenships (=3275 individuals + 71 (individuals with dual nationality), 5942 organisations

2002: 2646 citizenships (= 2584 individuals + 62 (individuals with dual nationality), 5150 organisations

Sources: International organisation secretariats: Union of International Organizations, Yearbook of International Associations: Guide to Civil Society Networks, 1990 and 2002 (presenting data collected in 1995 and 2001, respectively (see detailed note), International organisation people: Union of International Organizations, Who's Who in International Organizations, 1996 and 2002 (presenting data collected in 1995, 1999 and 2001, respectively).

Gender of international organisation leaders

	Number 1992	Percentage 1992	Number 1996	Percentage 1996	Number 2000	Percentage 2000	Number 2002	Percentage 2002
Male	4,096	87.5	4,100	82.8	3,343	71.3	9,947	74.0
Female	584	12.5	854	17.2	1,347	28.7	3,501	26.0
Total	4,680	100	4,954	100	4,690	100	13,448	100

Source: © Union of International Associations, Who's Who in International Organizations, 1992, 1996, 2000 and 2002 (presenting data collected in 1991, 1995, 1999 and 2001 respectively). Data have been restructured from more comprehensive coverage in the Who's Who.

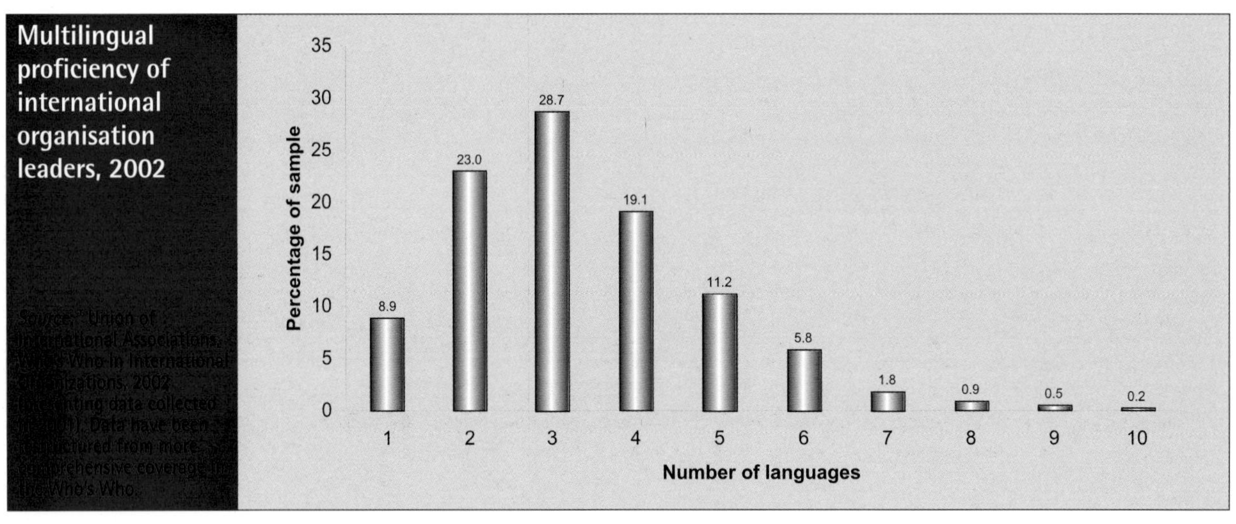

Multilingual proficiency of international organisation leaders, 2002

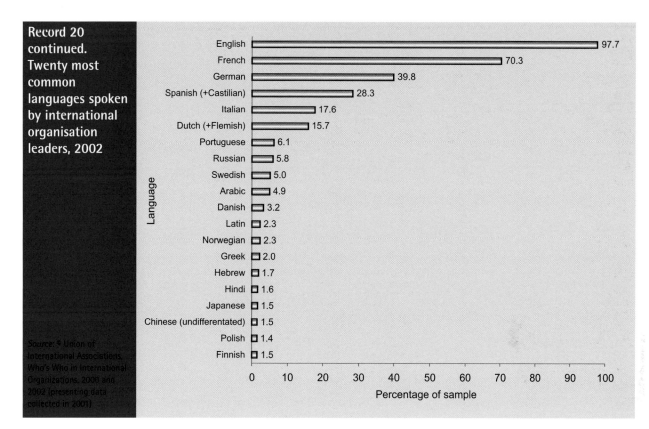

Record 20 continued. Twenty most common languages spoken by international organisation leaders, 2002

Source: © Union of International Associations, Who's Who in International Organizations, 2000 and 2002 (presenting data collected in 2001)

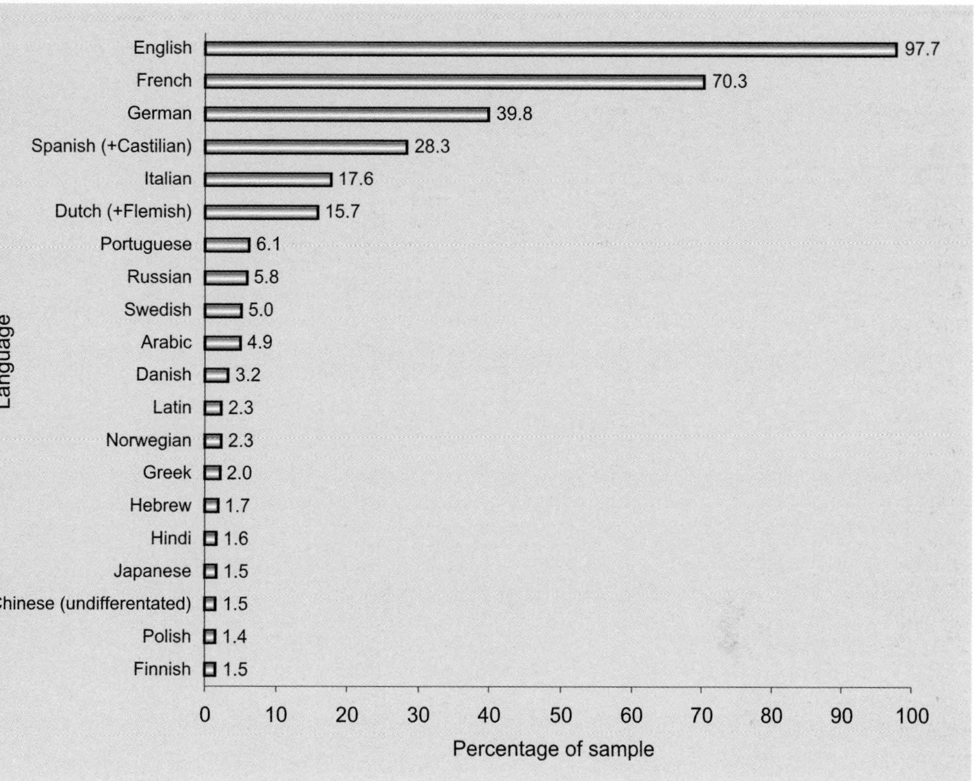

Formal higher educational qualifications of international organisation leaders

Qualifications	Number of degrees within sample of leaders (1996)	Percentage of sample with that qualification (if single*) (1996)	Number of degrees within sample of leaders (2000)	Percentage of sample with that qualification (if single*) (2000)	Number of degrees within sample of leaders (2002)	Percentage of sample with that qualification (if single*) (2002)	Change in percentage (1996–2002)
Ordinary or basic degrees							
Bachelor, Candidate, Diploma or other basic graduate qualification	2,962	77.2	2,400	103.9	4,943	173.8	96.6
Postgraduate and higher degrees							
Master (MS, MA, MBA equivalent)	2,619	68.2	2,113	91.4	1,509	53.1	-15.2
Doctorate (PhD or MD equivalent)	2,263	59.0	1,759	76.1	1,546	54.4	-4.6
Average number of degrees held per person	2.0		2.7		2.8		
Sample size	3,838		2,311		2,844		

NB figures for 1996 and 2000 are not strictly comparable with those presented in *2001 Global Civil Society*. Totals are not additive, since more than one degree may be held by each person.

*Assuming each person had only one degree of each kind, which is clearly not the case. Figures above 100% indicate more than one degree per person.

Data have been restructured from more comprehensive coverage in the Who's Who.

Record 20 continued

Locations of institutions of higher education attended by international organisation leaders

City/region	Country	Percentage of sample 1996	2000	2002
Amsterdam	Netherlands	2.9	1.3	1.8
Berlin	Germany	1.0	1.8	1.3
Birmingham	United Kingdom	2.8	2.4	1.4
Bonn	Germany	1.0	1.9	2.8
Brussels	Belgium	7.2	3.8	3.8
Cairo	Egypt	2.8		1.4
California	United States	1.8	7.0	4.1
Cambridge	United Kingdom	1.3		3.3
Chicago	United States	1.0	2.0	1.3
Copenhagen	Denmark	2.7	3.4	1.9
Cornell	United States	2.2	1.7	0.8
Geneva	Switzerland	1.0	2.8	1.8
Ghent	Belgium	1.0	2.2	2.3
Hamburg	Germany	1.8	1.1	1.1
Harvard	United States	2.5	2.6	5.1
Helsinki	Finland	1.1	1.3	1.9
Lausanne	Switzerland	1.7	1.3	0.9
Leiden	Netherlands	1.4	1.5	1.7
Leuven	Belgium	1.0	2.6	1.7
London	United Kingdom	6.7	4.1	10.6
Louvain	Belgium	2.5	4.8	2.8
Madrid	Spain	2.2		1.6
Manchester	United Kingdom	1.4	2.5	1.2
Michigan	United States	3.5	3.0	1.7
Milan	Italy	2.1	1.1	1.2
Montreal	Canada	4.8	3.5	1.1
Moscow	Russia	2.0		1.7
New York	United States	8.6	7.9	3.2
Oxford	United Kingdom	1.0	1.5	4.7
Paris	France	11.5	8.6	14.5
Pennsylvania	United States	1.0	2.4	1.4
Philippines (all)	Philippines	1.0	1.7	1.6
Stockholm	Sweden	2.1	1.1	1.1
Tokyo	Japan	1.1	2.4	1.3
Toronto	Canada	1.6	1.8	0.9
Vienna	Austria	2.2		1.4
Washington	United States	2.7	1.8	1.8
Yale	United States	1.2	3.0	2.3
York	United Kingdom	2.8		3.4
Total		**100.0**	**100.0**	**100.0**
Sample size		**921**	**847**	**1798**

Locations included in this list are limited to those attended by 10 or more leaders included in Who's Who. Many of the locations listed in the last table cover more than one institution of higher education; for example, the total for "London" includes leaders who have attended the University of London, the London School of Economics, the London School of Oriental Studies, etc. The totals given are not exclusive: a leader who has attended institutions of higher education in different locations will have been included in the totals for each location.

Blank cells indicate <10, estimated on basis of trend evident in subsequent years except where improbable.

Source: © Union of International Associations, Who's Who in International Organizations, 1996, 2000 and 2002 (presenting data collected in 1995, 1999 and 2001 respectively).

Data have been restructured from more comprehensive coverage in the Who's Who.

Record 21 Employment, volunteering and revenue of NGOs

For a selected number of countries that participated in the Johns Hopkins Comparative Nonprofit Sector Project, this record presents employment and volunteering figures (first table), and revenue structure (second table), for non-profit organisations operating primarily at the international level. These include prominently international humanitarian and relief organisations as well as INGOs active in supporting development. They also include associations promoting international understanding, exchange, and friendship. The first part of the revenue table shows the percentages in terms of cash flow, while the second accounts for the financial value of volunteer input.

Employment and Volunteering

1995/1996	INGOs		Total non-profit sector		INGOs as % of total nonprofit sector	
Country	number of paid FTE workers	number of FTE volunteers	number of paid FTE workers	number of FTE volunteers	In % of paid employment	In % of paid employment and volunteers
Argentina	5,201	7	464,214	391,043	1.1	0.0
Australia	919	1,227	415,651	218,352	0.2	0.6
Austria	1,110		150,425	40,686	0.7	0.0
Belgium	594	1,018	358,853	100,686	0.2	1.0
Brazil	4,182		1,128,387	335,098	0.4	0.0
Colombia	181	22	286,861	90,756	0.1	0.0
Czech Rep.	814	816	78,200	45,400	1.0	1.8
Egypt			611,888	17,335	0.0	0.0
Finland	160	367	66,043	77,030	0.2	0.5
France	17,403	30,986	974,867	1,114,816	1.8	2.8
Germany	9,750	28,510	1,480,850	1,211,474	0.7	2.4
Hungary	342	226	45,101	10,187	0.8	2.2
Ireland	370	234	125,584	33,690	0.3	0.7
Israel	98		147,166	32,405	0.1	0.0
Italy	1,400	4,625	580,109	430,130	0.2	1.1
Japan	7,693	37,785	2,287,993	850,264	0.3	4.4
Kenya			177,075	113,873	0.0	0.0
Korea, Rep.			513,820	188,703	0.0	0.0
Mexico			93,809	47,215	0.0	0.0
Morocco			74,514	83,364	0.0	0.0
Netherlands	3,860	8,644	669,122	425,554	0.6	2.0
Norway	1,066	3,635	66,243	115,229	1.6	3.2
Pakistan			264,251	212,324	0.0	0.0
Peru	3		129,826	80,144	0.0	0.0
Philippines	1,259	593	207,025	337,694	0.6	0.2
Poland	884	637	122,944	33,126	0.7	1.9
Romania	485	2,828	37,974	49,417	1.3	5.7
Slovakia	138	68	18,888	7,233	0.7	0.9
South Africa	113	149	328,327	316,995	0.0	0.0
Spain	9,380	9,794	475,179	253,599	2.0	3.9
Sweden	2,224	5,625	82,559	260,300	2.7	2.2
Tanzania	3,534	9,236	82,192	249,381	4.3	3.7
Uganda	7,522	146	111,634	132,496	6.7	0.1
United Kingdom	53,726	7,298	1,473,443	1,664,003	3.6	0.4
United States		45,026	8,555,980	7,246,856	0.0	0.6

Source: Johns Hopkins Comparative Nonprofit Sector Project

Revenue structure of INGOs 1995/1996/1997	Cash Revenue Only			Cash and volunteer input		
Country	Public sector payments %	Private giving %	Private fees and charges %	Public sector payments %	Private giving %	Private fees and charges %
Argentina	100			100	0	
Australia	30	70		26	74	
Austria	40	55	5			
Belgium	33	58	9	28	64	8
Brazil			100			100
Colombia		99	1		99	1
Czech Rep.	37	52	11	23	70	7
Finland	30	8	61	14	58	28
France	43	40	17	16	78	6
Germany	51	41	8	15	83	2
Hungary	66	14	20	64	17	19
Ireland	24	76		22	78	
Israel	23	51	26	23	51	26
Italy	35	35	30			
Japan	19	27	54	5	82	14
Netherlands	45	35	20	35	50	15
Norway	35	24	41	25	46	29
Peru		3	97		3	97
Poland	19	36	45	19	38	44
Romania	47	31	22	8	88	4
Slovakia	22	21	57	22	24	55
Spain	56	36	8	32	63	5
Sweden	49	37	14			
Tanzania	31	22	48			
United Kingdom	40	33	27	38	36	26

Source: Johns Hopkins Comparative Nonprofit Sector Project

Record 22 Value attached to democracy

This record shows the extent to which people in different countries believe in democracy, using the latest available data from the European and World Values Surveys. The surveys ask respondents whether they agree or disagree more or less with the following statements about democracy:

- Democracy may have problems but it's better than any other form of government.
- In a democracy, the economic system runs badly.
- Democracies are indecisive and have too much squabbling.
- Democracies aren't good at maintaining order.

The average level of agreement is given for each country, on a 1–10 scale, where 1 indicates strong disagreement with the item and 10 indicates strong agreement.

in average agreement score per country Country	Best despite problems	Bad for economy	Indecisive/ squabbling	Not good at order
		2000		
East Asia & Pacific				
Low income economies				
Indonesia	6.3	4.3	4.5	4.4
Vietnam	6.7	4.4	4.7	4.6
Middle income economies				
China	7.0	4.8	5.0	4.4
Philippines	7.0	5.7	5.9	5.7
High income economies				
Australia	*7.6*	*4.8*	*5.5*	*4.8*
Korea, Rep.	7.3	4.2	5.0	4.3
Japan	7.2	4.3	5.2	4.2
New Zealand	*7.5*	*4.5*	*5.3*	*4.5*
Europe & Central Asia				
Low income economies				
Armenia	*6.5*	*5.4*	*6.0*	*5.6*
Azerbaijan	*7.5*	*4.3*	*4.1*	*4.1*
Georgia	*7.4*	*4.7*	*5.4*	*5.3*
Moldova	6.7	5.3	5.2	5.2
Ukraine	7.1	5.1	5.8	5.6
Middle income economies				
Albania	8.5	4.1	4.2	4.3
Belarus	7.5	4.7	5.0	5.1
Bosnia & Herzegovina	7.8	4.4	5.2	4.0
Bulgaria	7.7	5.1	5.2	4.8
Croatia	8.2	4.5	4.3	3.8
Czech Republic	8.0	5.0	5.6	5.7
Estonia	7.3	4.9	5.4	4.8
Hungary	7.1	5.0	6.1	5.0
Latvia	7.3	5.5	6.3	5.3
Lithuania	7.3	5.2	6.2	5.6
Macedonia	7.3	5.6	5.3	5.3
Poland	7.4	5.5	7.0	6.5

Record 22 continued

Country (in average agreement score per country)	Best despite problems	Bad for economy	Indecisive/ squabbling	Not good at order
		2000		
Romania	7.2	5.8	6.8	5.5
Russian Federation	6.1	5.8	6.7	6.4
Serbia & Montenegro	7.8	4.5	5.3	4.6
Slovakia	7.4	5.5	5.9	5.1
Slovenia	7.4	5.5	6.5	5.4
Turkey	7.8	4.6	5.7	4.6
High income economies				
Austria	8.7	3.6	4.9	3.2
Belgium	8.5	4.6	6.2	4.8
Denmark	9.1	3.8	5.0	3.8
Finland	7.8	4.4	5.4	4.2
France	8.6	5.5	6.8	5.8
Germany	8.7	3.4	4.4	3.4
Greece	8.7	5.9	5.7	5.5
Iceland	8.5	3.8	3.9	3.5
Ireland	7.9	4.3	5.0	4.4
Italy	8.1	4.9	5.7	4.2
Luxembourg	8.7	3.8	5.4	3.7
Netherlands	8.3	3.7	5.2	4.5
Norway	*9.0*	*4.2*	*5.7*	*4.3*
Portugal	8.0	5.1	6.0	5.3
Spain	8.0	4.7	5.1	3.9
Sweden	8.3	3.7	5.4	3.8
Switzerland	*8.0*	*4.4*	*6.5*	*4.5*
United Kingdom	7.3	4.1	4.9	4.3
Latin America & Caribbean				
High income countries				
Argentina	8.0	5.3	6.1	4.9
Brazil	*7.8*	*6.8*	*8.0*	*5.8*
Chile	7.6	4.8	5.2	4.7
Dominican Republic	*8.5*	*4.4*	*5.0*	*4.8*
Mexico	7.1	5.5	5.9	5.3
Peru	7.5	5.8	5.8	5.5
Uruguay	*8.2*	*4.4*	*5.2*	*4.4*
Venezuela	8.8	4.9	5.6	4.6
Middle East & North Africa				
High income countries				
Algeria	8.0	4.8	6.1	4.8
Malta	8.2	4.0	4.3	3.9
Morocco	9.1	4.9	6.8	5.2
North America				
High income countries				
Canada	7.7	4.8	5.6	4.9
United States	7.8	4.4	5.1	4.4

Record 22 continued

Country	Best despite problems	Bad for economy	Indecisive/ squabbling	Not good at order
		2000		
South Asia				
Low income countries				
Bangladesh	9.0	3.9	4.1	4.0
India	8.1	5.4	6.3	5.2
Pakistan	7.5	5.1	4.4	5.8
Sub-Saharan Africa				
Low income countries				
Nigeria	5.4	5.0	5.8	5.4
Tanzania	8.5	4.3	5.4	3.8
Uganda	8.1	4.1	5.0	4.2
Zimbabwe	7.5	4.6	4.9	4.7
High income countries				
South Africa	7.4	5.3	5.6	5.2
Average	7.8	4.8	5.5	4.8

Information restructured from original 1-4 scale to facilitate comparisons. Values in italics indicate that 1995-1997 data have been used.

Sources: © European Values Survey, WORC, Tilburg University, Netherlands, 1999-2000, by permission; © World Values Survey, Institute for Social Research, University of Michigan, by permission..

Record 23 Attitudes towards globalisation

This record presents the views of four different groups of people in relation to globalisation: the general public, global civil society organisations, 'global stakeholders' (including business, government, and civil society leaders), and global business executives.

The first three charts summarise responses to a public opinion poll commissioned by the World Social Forum and carried out by Environics International in a number of countries. In the majority of these countries, respondents show a high level of concern regarding poverty. The first chart shows the percentages of respondents who say that they would pay higher taxes in order to improve the lives of those in need. When asked for their views on the consequences of globalisation for their families, a variety of positions are taken—for most countries (barring Argentina and Turkey), optimism about globalisation outweighs pessimism. In terms of the effects of globalisation on their country's economy, respondents hold somewhat varying views. In Argentina, France, Indonesia, Japan, and South Africa, pessimists outnumber optimists. In other countries, overall feelings are positive.

The next two charts present some results from the survey of global civil society organisations carried out by Pianta and Silva (2003) (see the Parallel Summits section for further details). In the first item, respondents are asked to identify the broad vision of their organisation or group on the issue of globalisation. The chart shows that some 60% of respondents would like to see civil society and human beings at the centre of globalisation. By contrast, only 11% emphasise the need for governance and just 4% declare themselves to be anti-globalisation. At the same time, however, one-sixth of respondents state their focus to be on the national/local dimension, playing down the importance of globalisation to their organisation's identity. These responses suggest that the long-abused term 'anti-globalisation' is an inappropriate label for social movements that are active on global issues. The second chart shows the distribution of responses to question, 'What is the best definition of the attitude and approach of your organisation/group towards economic globalisation?' These data similarly illustrate the emphasis which civil society organisations place on their autonomy in working on global issues. They also show the presence of different political strategies—both reformist and radical—in global social movements, and suggest that purely rejectionist stances towards economic globalisation are relatively rare in the world of civil society.

The next two tables summarise the opinions of the sample of leaders of NGOs, governments, and companies included in the first 2020 Global Stakeholders Panel. In the first set of items, respondents are asked the extent to which they agree or disagree with some statements on various aspects of globalisation. The table shows that they tend to agree that increasing globalisation is inevitable and that the benefits of economic globalisation are unequally distributed. They remain optimistic that a 'better world' can be achieved, though perhaps not solely through the efforts of existing multilateral agencies. In the second set of items, respondents select priority areas of action for achieving sustainable development globally. Although all areas suggested are given considerable importance, more weight is given to meeting basic needs than to matters of policy and infrastructure.

This topic is presented from another angle in the last table, which summarises the views of a cross-section of top- and middle-management leaders from the international business community. The results from two contrasting questions are juxtaposed; leaders are asked to what extent globalisation is threatening to their country's economy, and also to what extent they consider general attitudes towards globalisation to be positive in their country. Scores are given on a scale of 0–10, where 0 represents a pessimistic outlook with regard to globalisation (globalisation is threatening, attitudes generally are negative) and 10 represents an optimistic position (globalisation is not threatening, attitudes generally are positive).

Views held by the public: Willingness to pay 1% more in taxes to help the world's poor

Percentages of respondents agreeing or strongly agreeing that they would support 1% higher taxes if they were sure it would improve the lives of the world's poor.

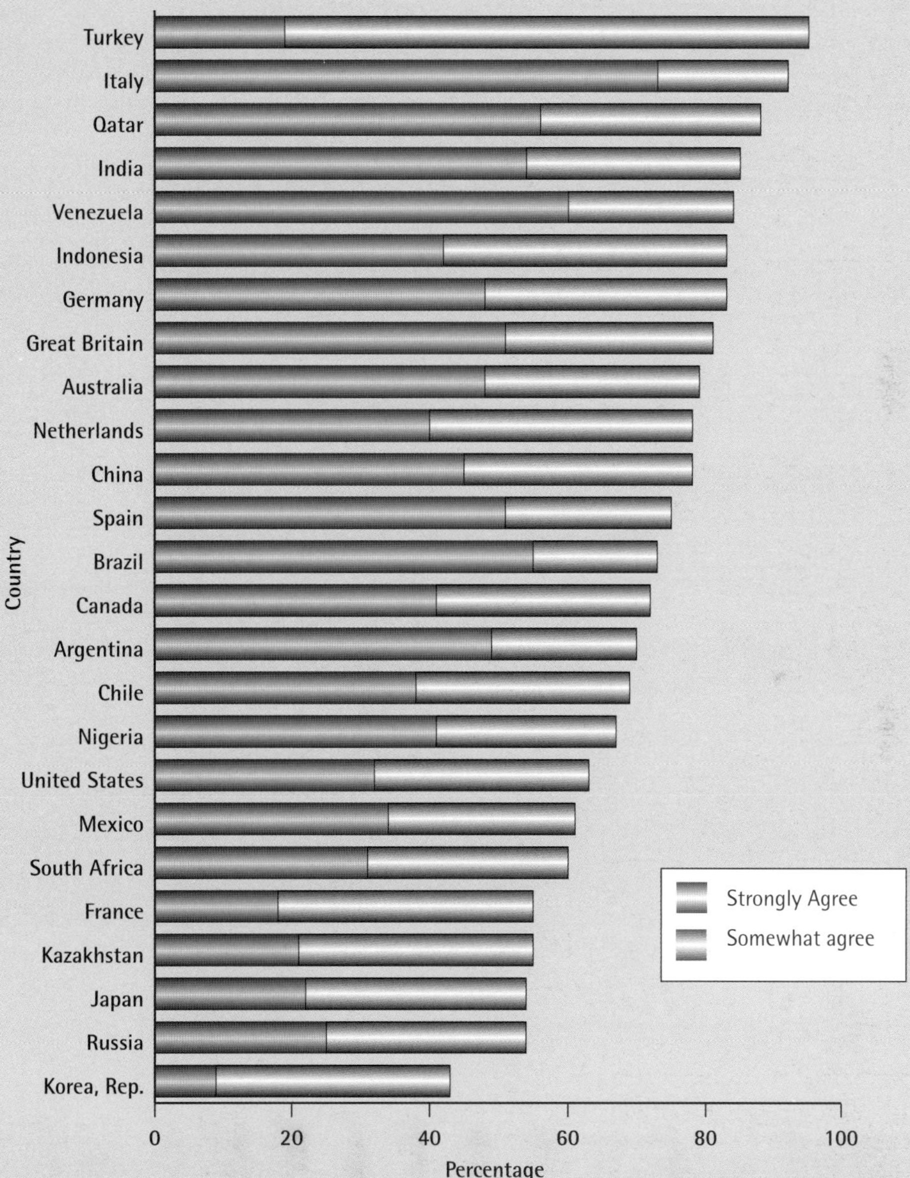

Source: © Environics International World Economic Forum Poll: Global Public Opinion on Globalisation, February 2002, http://www.environicsinternational.com/brochures/WEF_Poll_Brief.pdf

Record 23 Continued. Views held by the public: consequences of globalisation for families

Netherlands
Venezuela
India
Qatar
Germany
United States
Korea, Rep.
China
Canada
Indonesia
Great Britain
Nigeria
Mexico
Brazil
Italy
South Africa
Australia
Chile
Kazakhstan
Argentina
France
Spain
Russia
Japan
Turkey

Country

0 20 40 60 80 100

Percentage

Positive
Negative

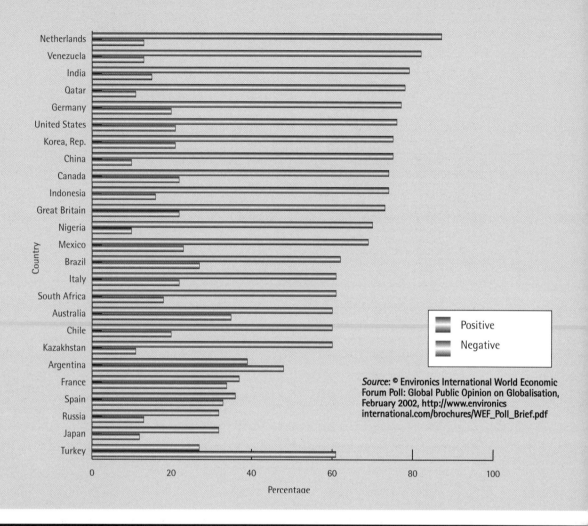

Source: © Environics International World Economic Forum Poll: Global Public Opinion on Globalisation, February 2002, http://www.environics international.com/brochures/WEF_Poll_Brief.pdf

Views of global civil society activists: vision of globalisation

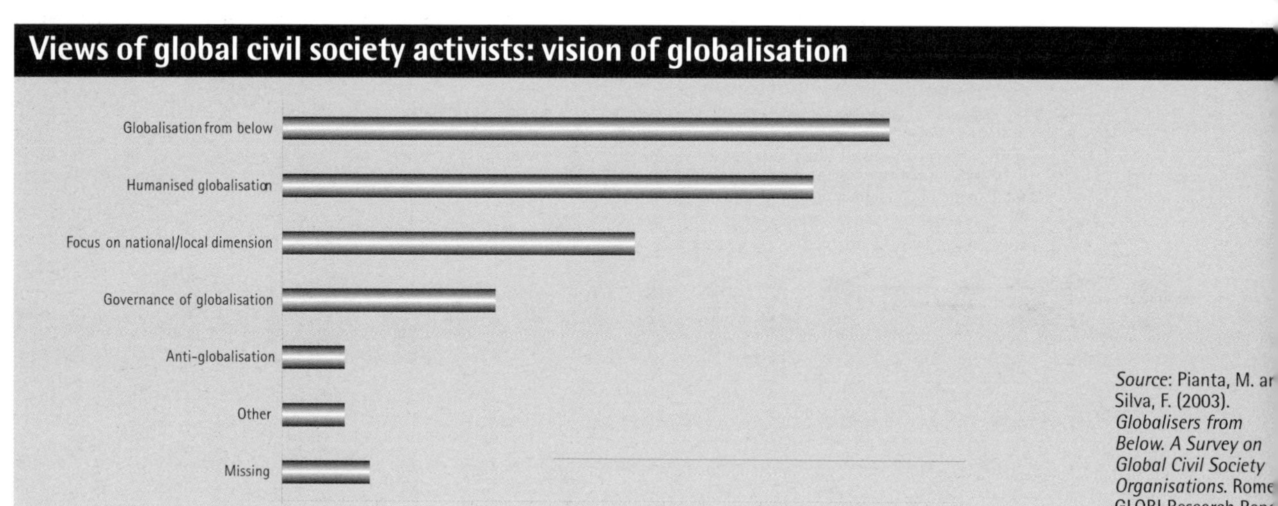

Source: Pianta, M. ar Silva, F. (2003). *Globalisers from Below. A Survey on Global Civil Society Organisations.* Rome GLOBI Research Repo

Views held by the public: effect of globalisation for country

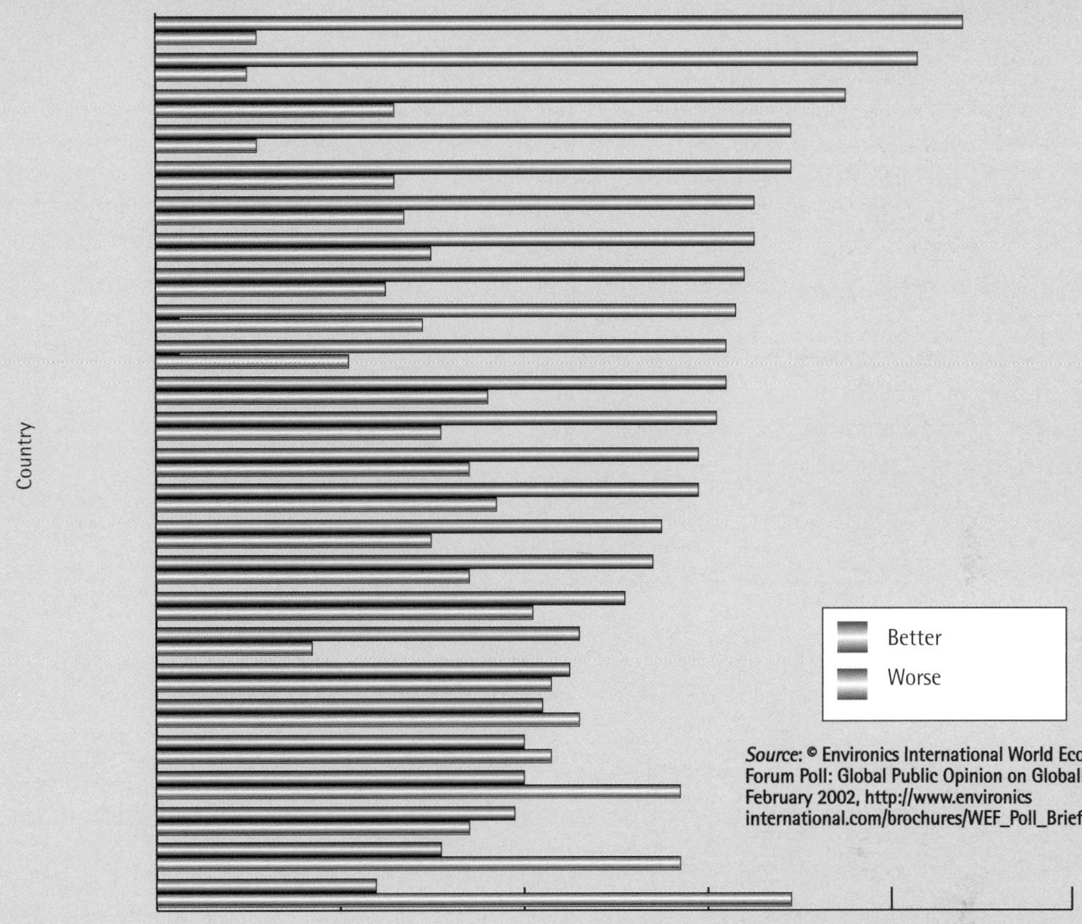

Country

Better

Worse

Source: © Environics International World Economic Forum Poll: Global Public Opinion on Globalisation, February 2002, http://www.environics international.com/brochures/WEF_Poll_Brief.pdf

Views of global civil society activists: attitudes to economic globalisation

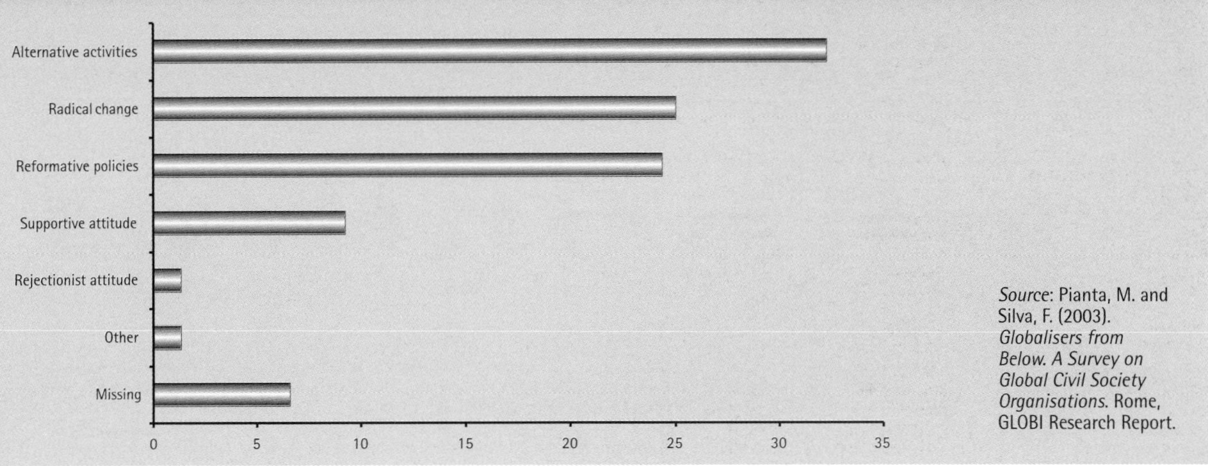

Source: Pianta, M. and Silva, F. (2003). *Globalisers from Below. A Survey on Global Civil Society Organisations*. Rome, GLOBI Research Report.

Record 23 continued

Views of 'global stakeholders'

Do you strongly disagree, somewhat disagree, somewhat agree, or strongly agree with each of the following statements?

On a 4-point scale, where 1 = 'strongly disagree' and 4 = 'strongly agree'. If you neither agree nor disagree with a statement, please leave blank.

	Mean rating score
I support people who take part in peaceful demonstrations against globalisation because they are supporting my interests.	2.94
Violence is sometimes a legitimate form of protest against globalisation.	1.60
Increasing globalisation is inevitable.	3.11
Developing countries benefit as much as rich countries from free trade and globalisation.	1.91
When it comes to globalisation, there is too much focus on increasing trade and investment, and not enough on protecting things like human rights and the environment.	3.56
The free enterprise system and free market economy is the best system on which to base the future of the world.	2.36
The free enterprise system and free market economy work best in society's interests when accompanied by strong government regulations.	3.08
National governments are becoming less and less relevant in the world.	2.78
Major industrialised countries tend to act to protect their interests in world affairs, thereby playing a major role in keeping developing countries poor.	3.34
A fundamentally better world – one that works for all life – is both possible and achievable.	3.57
The United Nations system together with existing multilateral agencies are capable of dealing with current world challenges.	2.49

Please rate the importance of each of the following action areas for speeding progress towards sustainable development globally.

On a 5-point scale, where 1 = 'not important' and 5 = 'very important.

	Mean rating score
Producing and using cleaner energy.	4.65
Ensuring the quality and supply of fresh water.	4.76
Producing enough quality food without damaging the environment.	4.55
Protecting long-term human health.	4.37
Protecting the variety (and health) of plants and animals.	4.31
Substantively addressing poverty.	4.61
Changing unsustainable patterns of consumption and production.	4.52
Developing a more effective institutional framework for sustainable development globally.	4.22
Making globalisation equitable, environmentally sustainable, inclusive and responsive to the needs of developing countries and the poor.	4.47
Getting acceptance of the principle of "common but differentiated responsibilities" in implementing sustainable development, where developing countries' obligations would be different from those of industralised countries.	4.13

Sample size for this wave of the survey = 258.

Source: 2020 Fund, Towards the Future We Want for Our Children: Report of the first survey of the 2020 global stakeholder panel, available at http://www.2020fund.org/downloads/GSP_wave1.pdf

Views of leading business executives

Country	Globalisation is threatening/not threatening to your economy	Attitudes towards globalisation are generally negative/positive in your country
	(score 0–10 scale)	
Argentina	4.60	3.57
Australia	6.31	5.27
Austria	6.88	5.92
Belgium	5.92	5.94
Brazil	5.29	5.57
Canada	6.96	6.52
Chile	6.98	7.24
China*	4.46	5.92
Colombia	4.68	4.45
Czech Republic	6.56	6.06
Denmark	7.66	6.62
Estonia	6.75	6.55
Finland	8.23	7.43
France	5.98	3.58
Germany	6.51	5.74
Greece	5.05	4.22
Hungary	6.19	5.04
Iceland	7.95	6.93
India	4.76	4.64
Indonesia	2.83	4.57
Ireland	7.05	6.86
Israel	6.41	7.32
Italy	6.15	5.29
Japan	4.51	6.15
Korea	5.67	6.47
Luxembourg	6.23	6.88
Malaysia	5.29	6.00
Mexico	5.23	5.50
Netherlands	7.90	7.97
New Zealand	6.12	5.96
Norway	6.45	5.52
Philippines	3.71	4.45
Poland	4.85	4.03
Portugal	4.42	5.42
Russia	5.03	4.16
Singapore	6.64	7.91
Slovakia	5.62	5.33
Slovenia	5.12	4.61
South Africa	4.85	5.11
Spain	6.36	5.94
Sweden	7.50	6.53
Switzerland	7.14	5.87
Thailand	3.49	5.44
Turkey	5.53	6.41
United Kingdom	5.86	5.35
United States	8.08	7.20
Venezuela	4.84	2.53

*does not include Hong Kong

Source: The World Competitiveness Yearbook 2002, published by the International Institute for Management Development (IMD), Lausanne, Switzerland, http://www01.imd.ch/wcy/

Record 24 Confidence in institutions

This record shows findings from the European and World Values Surveys regarding the extent to which people in different countries have confidence in civil society institutions such as the church, trade unions, and the press, as well as state institutions such as parliament and government, and how their confidence in these institutions has evolved over the period 1990–2000. For 2000, it also illustrates faith in the main global governance institution, the United Nations. The average figure is given for each country on a scale of 1–10, where the higher the number, the greater the degree of confidence in the institution in question. Note that the average scores given at the end of the table are based on different collections of countries, so are not comparable.

	1990–1993						2000						
Country (in average agreement score per country)	Church	Press	Trade unions	Companies	Parliament	Government	Church	Press	Trade unions	Companies	Parliament	Government	United Nations
East Asia & Pacific													
Low income economies													
Indonesia							9.1	5.8	5.1	5.4	5.2	5.7	5.4
Vietnam							4.2	7.5	7.3	5.6	9.2	9.2	6.2
Middle income economies													
China								6.3	6.3	5.6	7.8	8.1	6.2
Philippines							8.6	6.6	5.9	6.0	6.2	5.6	7.0
High income economies													
Australia							5.3	3.9	4.2	5.8	4.6	4.2	5.5
Korea, Rep.	5.9	6.2	6.1	4.5	4.6		5.6	6.1	5.5	4.5	3.2	4.6	5.9
Japan	3.3	5.7	4.5	4.6	4.6		2.8	6.4	5.1	4.5	4.1	4.3	5.9
New Zealand							5.1	4.7	3.9	5.1	3.7	3.7	5.7
Europe & Central Asia													
Low income economies													
Armenia							6.5	4.5	3.5	5.2	3.8	4.7	6.3
Azerbaijan							6.5	4.2	4.4	4.8	6.8	7.9	4.1
Georgia							7.3	5.7	3.8	5.4	4.6	5.1	5.7
Moldova							7.6	5.2	4.3	5.3	4.4	4.5	6.6
Ukraine							6.4	5.2	4.6	3.6	3.9		5.5
Middle income economies													
Albania							6.5	4.6	4.2	5.1	5.0	5.9	7.5
Belarus	5.9	4.5	4.1	4.9	4.5	4.0	6.5	4.9	4.3	5.8	4.6		5.4
Bosnia & Herzegovina							5.6	4.4	4.3	4.8	4.0	4.5	4.9
Bulgaria	4.1	4.8	4.5	4.7	5.4	4.3	4.6	4.3	3.4		4.2		4.9
Croatia							6.2	3.8	4.3	4.1	4.0		4.9
Czech Rep							3.6	5.0	3.9		3.5	6.4	5.4
Estonia	5.7	6.1	4.3	3.6	6.4	3.1	5.1	5.0	4.5		4.3		5.0
Hungary	5.8	4.8	4.2	4.5	4.8		5.2	4.3	3.7		4.5		5.7
Latvia	6.1	6.1	4.0	3.0	6.9	3.2	6.4	5.2	4.3		4.1		5.1
Lithuania	6.6	6.1	4.4	3.7	6.1	3.3	6.6	6.4	5.1	3.9	3.5		5.1
Macedonia							5.5	4.0	3.3	3.9	2.5	2.8	4.6
Poland	8.0	5.5	3.7	6.8	7.1	2.2	6.9	5.4	4.6		4.6		5.9
Romania	7.2	4.3	4.4	4.7	3.7		7.8	5.0	4.4		3.5		5.0
Russian Federation*	6.3	5.2	5.1	5.1	5.2	5.1	6.0	4.2	4.1	3.3	3.4		3.7
Serbia & Montenegro							5.6	4.3	3.8	4.4	3.9	4.3	3.2

Record 24 continued *in average agreement score per country* Country	1990–1993 Church	Press	Trade unions	Companies	Parliament	Government	2000 Church	Press	Trade unions	Companies	Parliament	Government	United Nations
Slovakia	5.4	4.8	4.0	4.4	4.6	4.6	6.6	5.3	4.9		4.8		5.2
Slovenia	4.9	5.5	4.2	4.7	4.8		4.6	6.1	4.5		4.3		5.4
Turkey	6.8	5.2	5.0	4.4	6.0	5.3	6.5	4.2	5.3	5.2	4.8	4.8	4.9
High income economies													
Austria	5.6	4.0	4.7	5.1	5.1		5.0	4.7	4.5	5.1	5.2		5.0
Belgium	5.4	5.0	4.7	5.4	5.0		4.9	4.7	4.6		4.7		5.1
Denmark	5.4	4.6	5.2	5.0	5.1		5.8	4.7	5.4		5.4		6.0
Finland	4.6	5.0	4.7	5.0	4.7		5.9	4.9	5.6	5.1	5.2		5.2
France	5.1	4.6	4.2	6.0	5.1		4.8	4.4	4.4	5.1	4.6		5.4
Germany	5.1	4.5	4.6	5.0	5.3		4.8	4.8	5.0	4.8	4.7	6.3	5.5
Greece							6.4	4.4	3.4	3.4	4.1		3.1
Iceland	6.5	4.1	5.6	4.9	5.6		6.2	5.0	5.5	5.0	6.5		6.5
Ireland	7.2	4.8	5.2	5.6	5.6		5.9	4.9	5.4		4.6		6.1
Italy	6.2	4.8	4.5	5.9	4.4		6.6	4.8	4.3	5.3	4.7		6.4
Luxembourg							5.3	5.2	5.5	4.8	5.9		6.2
Netherlands	4.4	4.7	5.3	5.2	5.5		4.5	5.7	5.7		5.7		5.7
Norway	5.3	5.3	5.8	5.6	5.9		5.7	4.8	6.0	5.8	6.2	6.1	6.5
Portugal	6.4	4.9	4.5	5.3	4.7		7.3	6.1	5.2	5.4	5.2		6.3
Spain	5.5	5.4	4.9	5.2	4.7	3.9	5.0	5.0	4.3	4.6	5.3		4.9
Sweden	4.7	4.6	4.9	5.6	5.3		5.3	5.3	5.1		5.5		6.5
Switzerland							4.9	4.2	4.7	5.1	5.1	5.4	5.0
United Kingdom	5.9	3.7	4.3	5.4	5.3		4.8	3.5	4.2		4.7	4.2	5.9
Latin America & Caribbean													
High income countries													
Argentina	5.5	4.3	2.6	3.9	3.4		6.4	5.0	3.0	4.0	3.1	3.5	4.9
Brazil	7.2	5.6	5.2	5.8	3.4		6.9	5.8	5.3	6.2	3.8	4.8	6.4
Chile	7.7	5.5	5.7	6.0	6.5	5.7	7.6	5.2	5.1	5.5	4.5	5.7	6.0
Colombia							7.8	5.1	4.4	5.8	3.7	4.5	
Dominican Republic							7.5	4.9	4.0	5.5	3.5	3.4	5.3
El Salvador							6.7	5.4	3.0	4.9	4.2	4.9	5.7
Mexico	7.4	5.3	4.6	5.1	4.4	3.9	7.8	5.0	4.0	5.1	3.6	4.5	5.2
Peru							7.3	4.5	4.3	4.6	3.5	4.2	5.4
Uruguay							5.9	5.8	4.5	4.9	4.7	4.7	5.6
Venezuela							7.6	6.3	3.4	6.2	4.3	5.7	5.3
Middle East & North Africa													
High income countries													
Algeria							8.4	5.2	3.8	4.9	4.1	5.4	2.8
Malta							7.9	4.6	5.3		5.4		5.9
Morocco							9.6	4.6	3.3	4.6	3.3	5.9	2.5
North America													
High income countries													
Canada	6.4	5.3	4.7	5.5	5.0	4.9							
United States	7.3	5.6	4.8	5.6	5.2	5.8	7.2	4.4	5.0	5.7	4.9	4.9	5.9
South Asia													
Low income countries													
Bangladesh							9.7	7.7	6.4	7.8	8.0	7.8	8.4

Record 24 continued	1990-1993						2000						
Country (in average agreement score per country)	Church	Press	Trade unions	Companies	Parliament	Government	Church	Press	Trade unions	Companies	Parliament	Government	United Nations
India	8.2	6.4	5.5	6.0	6.3	5.6	8.2	6.7	5.4	5.1	5.7	5.8	5.7
Pakistan							8.7	6.0	4.4	4.8	7.1	4.8	3.5
Sub-Saharan Africa													
Low income countries													
Nigeria	8.8	7.2	7.0	7.6	5.9	4.9	9.3	6.6	6.6	7.0	5.2	5.4	6.9
Tanzania							8.7	7.3	6.9	6.6	7.7	8.0	7.7
Uganda							8.4	6.7	6.1	6.9	7.3	7.5	8.1
Zimbabwe							8.3	6.0	6.3	7.1	5.5	5.7	6.5
High income countries													
South Africa	7.8	5.6	5.3	6.9	6.4	6.0	8.0	5.8	5.1	6.7	5.4	5.6	6.1
Average	6.1	5.1	4.8	5.2	5.2	4.5	6.5	5.2	4.7	5.2	4.8	5.4	5.5

Information restructured to 1-10 scale from original 1-4 scale to facilitate comparisons. Values in italics indicate that 1995-1997 data have been used.

*Russian Federation figures for 1990 are for USSR

Sources: © European Values Survey, WORC, Tilburg University, Netherlands, 1999-2000, by permission; © World Values Survey, Institute for Social Research, University of Michigan, by permission; Inglehart, R., Basañez, M., and Moreno, A., Human Values and Beliefs: A Cross-Cultural Sourcebook: Political, Religious, Sexual, and Economic Norms in 43 Societies: Findings from the 1990-1993 World Values Survey, The University of Michigan Press, Ann Arbor, 1998.

Record 25 Tolerance

This record presents the idea of tolerance as part of a general value system in the population. It shows percentages of survey respondents who mention 'tolerance' in answer to the following question: 'Here is a list of qualities which children can be encouraged to learn at home. Which, if any, do you consider to be especially important? (Multiple responses possible.)

- Tolerance and respect for other people
- Independence
- Responsibility
- Obedience
- Unselfishness.'

Figures are given for two waves of the European and World Values Surveys: 1990–93 and 2000. Figures for 2000 are also provided in map form. The overall average figures given in the table for 1990–93 and 2000 cannot be compared with each other as they refer to different sets of countries. The last figure in the table gives the average change for those countries surveyed both in 1990–1993 and in 2000.

in % all respondents per country Country	**Mentioned** 1990-1993	**Mentioned** 2000	**% change** 1990-2000
East Asia & Pacific			
Low income economies			
Indonesia		62.9	
Korea, Dem. Rep.	55.4	46.9	-15
Vietnam		67.9	
Middle income economies			
China & Tibet		72.6	
Philippines		60.2	
High income economies			
Australia		*80.9*	
Korea, Rep.	55.4	64.7	17
Japan	59.5	71.2	20
Singapore		69.0	
Europe & Central Asia			
Low income economies			
Armenia		*48.5*	
Azerbaijan		*59.1*	
Georgia		*57.0*	
Moldova		77.7	
Ukraine		65.0	
Middle income economies			
Albania		85.5	
Belarus	79.8	71.8	-10
Bosnia & Herzegovina		71.7	
Bulgaria	51.5	58.9	14
Croatia		64.6	
Czech Republic	66.1	62.9	-5
Estonia	70.2	70.9	1
Hungary	61.6	64.7	5
Latvia	69.7	69.5	0
Lithuania	56.7	56.5	0

Record 25 continued **in % all respondents per country** Country	**Mentioned** 1990-1993	**Mentioned** 2000	**% change** 1990-2000
Macedonia		75.2	
Poland		79.6	
Romania	56.0	55.6	-1
Russian Federation**	70.2	66.9	-5
Serbia & Montenegro		64.1	
Slovakia	55.0	57.0	4
Slovenia	74.5	70.1	-6
Turkey	69.1	64.0	-7
High income economies			
Austria	65.7	71.4	9
Belgium	67.2	83.5	24
Denmark	80.5	87.0	8
Finland	78.9	82.6	5
France	78.0	84.4	8
Germany*	75.8	72.5	-4
Greece		55.9	
Iceland	93.0	84.1	-10
Ireland	76.4	75.0	-2
Italy	66.9	74.7	12
Luxembourg		78.0	
Netherlands	87.1	90.4	4
Norway	63.7	*65.9*	3
Portugal	67.1	65.3	-3
Spain	73.3	82.1	12
Sweden	90.8	92.5	2
Switzerland	77.4	*78.6*	2
United Kingdom***	79.6	82.8	4
Latin America & Caribbean			
Middle income countries			
Argentina	77.6	70.2	-10
Brazil	65.7	*59.4*	-10
Chile	79.0	76.0	-4
Colombia		*68.5*	
Dominican Republic		*67.9*	
El Salvador		58.8	
Mexico	64.3	71.8	12
Peru		72.6	
Uruguay		*71.1*	
Venezuela		79.6	
Middle East & North Africa			
Middle income countries			
Algeria		59.9	
Malta		61.0	
Morocco & Western Sahara		64.7	
High income countries			
Israel		84.1	

Record 25 continued

in % all respondents per country Country	**Mentioned** 1990-1993	**Mentioned** 2000	**% change** 1990-2000
North America			
High income countries			
Canada	80.2	81.6	2
United States	72.4	79.8	10
South Asia			
Low income countries			
Bangladesh		98.4	
India	59.2	63.2	7
Pakistan		53.8	
Sub-Saharan Africa			
Low income countries			
Nigeria	75.0	59.1	-21
Tanzania		83.4	
Uganda		56.6	
Zimbabwe		76.7	
Middle income countries			
South Africa	58.6	73.6	26
Average:	70.1	70.4	2

Values in italics indicate that 1995-1997 data have been used

*West Germany only for 1990-93

** Russian Federation figures for 1990-93 are for USSR

***UK excluding Northern Ireland for 1990-1993

Sources: © European Values Survey, WORC, Tilburg University, Netherlands, 1999-2000, by permission; © World Values Survey, Institute for Social Research, University of Michigan, by permission; Inglehart, R., Basañez, M., and Moreno, A., Human Values and Beliefs: A Cross-Cultural Sourcebook: Political, Religious, Sexual, and Economic Norms in 43 Societies: Findings from the 1990-1993 World Values Survey, The University of Michigan Press, Ann Arbor, 1998.

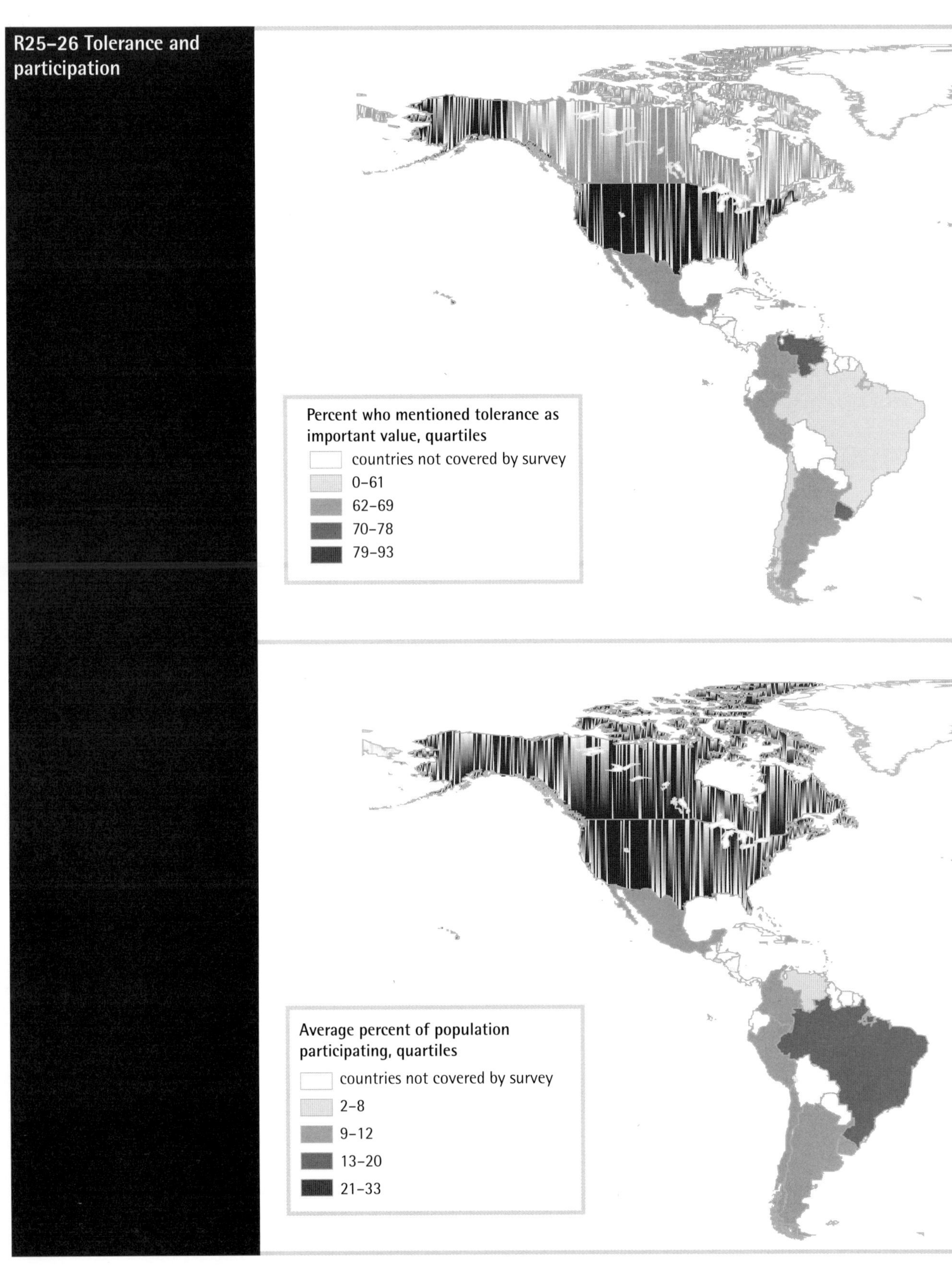
R25–26 Tolerance and participation
Percent who mentioned tolerance as important value, quartiles
countries not covered by survey
0–61
62–69
70–78
79–93
Average percent of population participating, quartiles
countries not covered by survey
2–8
9–12
13–20
21–33

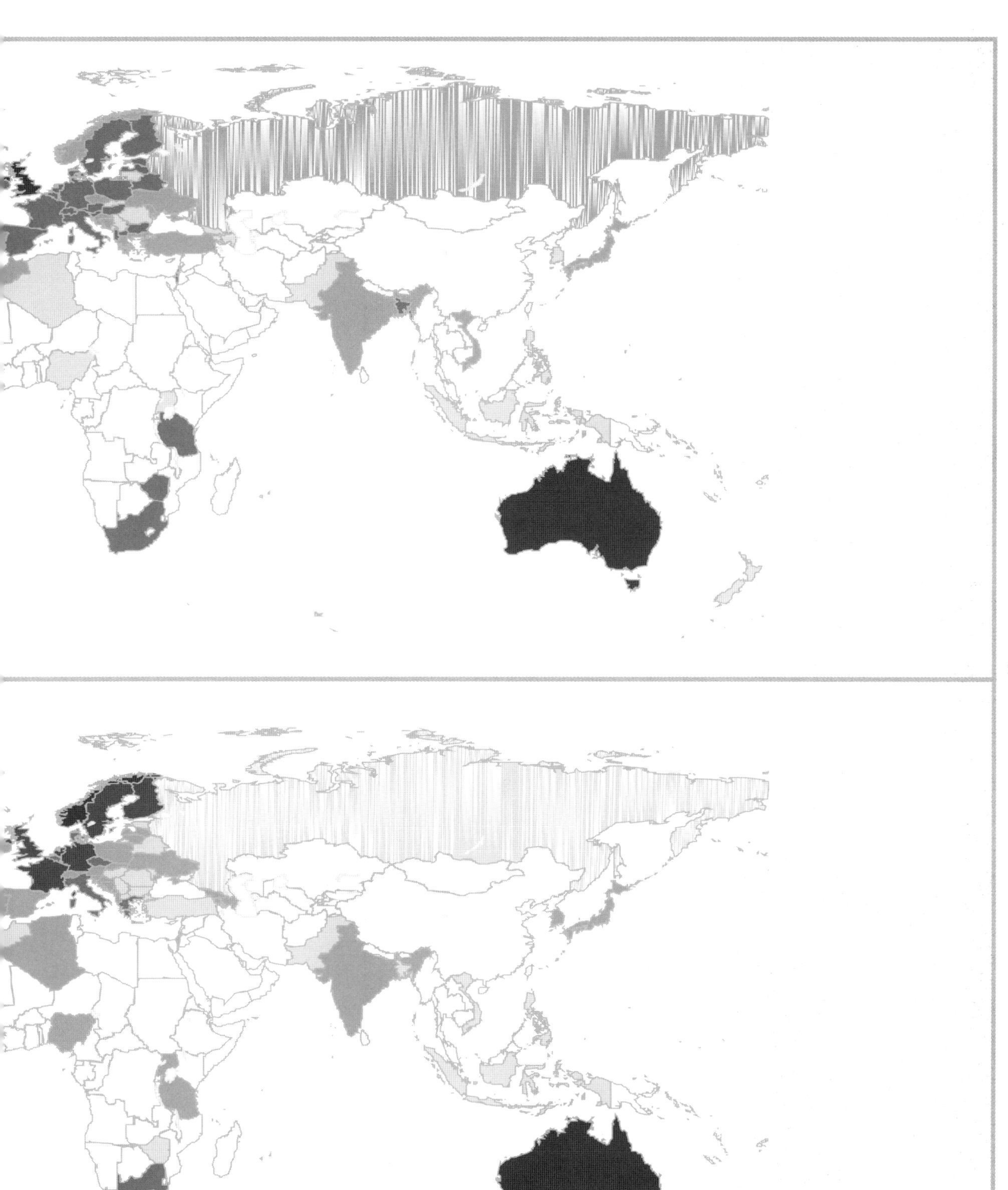

Record 26 Participation in political action

The extent to which people are prepared to take political action for or against a particular cause can be considered as a general indicator of political mobilisation. This record, based on the latest European and World Values Surveys, shows the percentages of respondents who say they have taken part in specific actions (signing a petition, joining a boycott, attending a lawful demonstration, joining an unofficial strike, or occupying a building) for or against a particular cause. The responses on 'lawful demonstrations' for the former Eastern bloc countries, which are high, may be skewed by past participation in the quasi-obligatory manifestations of the old regime. Data are given for 1990–93 and 2000. The overall average figures given in the table for 1990–93 and 2000 cannot be compared with each other as they refer to different sets of countries. Taking the average score for each country on the five types of political action, using data from the 2000 wave, the map shows in which countries respondents have been most politically active.

Country (in % of all respondents per country)	1990–1993					2000				
	Sign petition	Join boycott	Attend lawful demonstration	Join unofficial strike	Occupy building	Sign petition	Join boycott	Attend lawful demonstration	Join unofficial strike	Occupy building
East Asia & Pacific										
Low income economies										
Indonesia						5.4	2.9	11.4	2.0	4.0
Vietnam						5.6	0.6	1.9	0.3	1.2
Middle income economies										
Philippines						10.6	5.1	6.8	2.3	0.8
High income economies										
Australia						*78.4*	*21.5*	*17.8*	*8.1*	*2.0*
Korea, Rep.	42.0	11.3	19.8		10.7	52.3	10.1	22.7	9.5	*2.3*
Japan	61.5	3.8	13.2	3.0	0.4	63.2	8.4	12.9	2.7	0.1
New Zealand						*90.6*	*19.1*	*21.4*	*5.2*	*1.2*
Singapore						8.8	1.7	1.9		
Europe & Central Asia										
Low income economies										
Armenia						*17.8*	*12.1*	*28.2*	*15.0*	*1.2*
Azerbaijan						*10.1*	*2.6*	*20.5*	*9.0*	*0.2*
Georgia						*14.0*	*5.8*	*19.3*	*9.8*	*0.8*
Moldova						18.1	4.1	18.1	12.9	2.0
Ukraine						14.2	5.0	18.9	2.7	0.9
Middle income economies										
Albania						22.4	5.6	24.6	2.1	0.5
Belarus	27.0	4.6	18.1	2.3	0.8	8.8	4.1	16.3	1.1	0.6
Bosnia & Herzegovina						22.0	6.7	9.2	3.6	0.5
Bulgaria	21.6	3.4	14.5	3.2	1.5	11.2	3.6	14.8	4.9	3.1
Croatia						37.4	8.0	7.7	3.2	1.2
Czech Republic						58.7	9.2	27.8	10.2	1.0
Estonia	39.0	3.3	25.9	4.2	0.8	20.7	2.9	11.1	1.3	0.1
Hungary	18.0	2.2	4.4	2.9	0.1	14.7	2.8	4.5	0.8	0.5
Latvia	64.6	4.1	35.6	6.1	1.1	19.1	4.0	25.1	1.1	0.3
Lithuania	58.3	7.3	34.0	2.6	0.2	27.3	4.6	11.5	2.2	1.4
Macedonia						26.5	13.6	17.8	5.0	1.1
Poland	14.0	5.8	11.7	6.2	3.8	22.6	4.2	10.0	4.7	2.9

Record 26 continued

Country (in % of all respondents per country)	Sign petition	Join boycott	Attend lawful demonstration	Join unofficial strike	Occupy building	Sign petition	Join boycott	Attend lawful demonstration	Join unofficial strike	Occupy building
Romania						10.7	1.9	14.8	1.2	0.5
Russian Federation**	27.1	4.2	34.5	2.4	0.7	11.6	2.6	23.3	1.6	0.7
Serbia & Montenegro						28.5	19.0	23.8	7.3	2.0
Slovakia						59.3	4.3	14.3	2.3	0.9
Slovenia	27.6	8.0	10.1	1.5	0.8	32.4	8.2	9.8	3.6	1.6
Turkey	13.6	5.6	5.7	1.5	1.2	15.5	6.4	7.6	2.2	0.7
High income economies										
Austria	47.7	5.2	10.4	1.1	0.7	56.7	9.8	16.7	2.2	0.7
Belgium	50.2	10.2	25.4	7.2	4.3	71.4	12.0	39.6	8.9	6.0
Denmark	51.0	10.7	27.6	17.4	2.0	56.8	24.9	29.3	22.2	2.8
Finland	40.7	13.5	14.2	8.1	1.6	49.5	19.9	19.8	9.6	6.8
France	53.7	12.5	32.7	10.1	7.9	68.3	13.2	39.7	12.6	9.0
Germany*	56.5	10.0	20.5	2.3	1.1	50.8	10.1	27.5	1.9	0.7
Greece						33.7	3.8	38.7	6.8	18.8
Iceland	47.3	21.4	23.7	5.0	1.3	53.0	17.8	20.7	3.4	0.7
Ireland	42.1	7.4	16.4	3.5	1.7	59.5	9.0	20.9	6.3	2.3
Italy	48.1	10.9	36.0	6.1	7.6	54.6	10.3	34.8	5.4	8.0
Luxembourg						53.2	8.9	28.3	6.5	1.6
Netherlands	50.8	7.8	25.3	1.9	3.0	61.3	23.4	34.1	4.6	5.5
Norway	61.1	12.0	19.5	24.4	1.0				*5.1*	*1.8*
Portugal	29.1	4.7	24.8	3.6	1.4	22.6	4.6	14.9	3.0	1.2
Spain	20.4	5.6	23.5	6.9	2.9	28.6	5.6	26.9	8.7	3.1
Sweden	71.7	16.5	22.6	3.1	0.2	87.4	33.0	35.2	4.6	2.6
Switzerland	62.9		15.4	2.1		*63.6*	*12.2*	*16.9*	*1.9*	*1.1*
United Kingdom***	75.4	14.7	13.6	8.5	2.3	78.9	16.6	13.6	9.7	2.2
Latin America & Caribbean										
Middle income countries										
Argentina	22.4	3.4	15.0	7.3	2.7	22.8	2.0	13.3	5.2	1.9
Brazil	50.8	10.5	17.9	7.9	1.9	*47.1*	*6.4*	*24.8*	*6.5*	*2.7*
Chile	22.9	4.0	30.1	8.2	4.2	19.5	5.0	15.7	8.7	4.2
Colombia						*18.9*	*7.7*	*11.5*	*4.9*	*1.3*
Dominican Republic						*14.9*	*5.6*	*26.5*	*8.4*	*4.6*
El Salvador						19.3		5.0	1.5	0.7
Mexico	34.7	6.9	22.0	7.4	5.2	19.1	2.4	4.2	2.5	2.1
Peru						22.4	7.7	17.0	4.0	1.7
Uruguay						*35.5*	*4.0*	*5.0*	*10.2*	*7.6*
Venezuela						14.9	1.6	7.8	2.5	1.7
Middle East & North Africa										
Middle income countries										
Algeria						15.1	7.9	20.0	8.7	1.6
Malta						33.1	10.6	25.5	4.6	1.2
Morocco						15.4	7.0	11.6	1.6	0.4
High income countries										
Israel						39.0	7.8	24.6	7.1	1.0

Record 26 continued

Country (in % of all respondents per country)	Sign petition	Join boycott	Attend lawful demonstration	Join unofficial strike	Occupy building	Sign petition	Join boycott	Attend lawful demonstration	Join unofficial strike	Occupy building
North America										
High income countries										
Canada	76.8	22.3	20.8	7.0	3.0	74.1	19.0	19.7	7.4	2.8
United States	70.9	17.9	15.5	4.4	2.0	81.1	24.7	20.0	5.4	3.8
South Asia										
Low income countries										
Bangladesh						14.4	6.1	7.2	3.6	1.3
India						28.9	13.3	22.9	9.9	4.5
Pakistan						4.6	5.6	6.9	0.9	0.5
Sub-Saharan Africa										
Low income countries										
Nigeria	7.2	13.1	20.2	5.5	2.3	6.7	7.6	17.3	6.7	9.1
Tanzania						10.5	4.7	28.6	1.8	1.8
Uganda						20.9	12.7	14.9	6.8	9.9
Zimbabwe						4.5	4.8	4.9	1.4	0.2
Middle income countries										
South Africa	24.2	21.5	18.8	8.5	2.5	0.0	0.0	10.4	*3.7*	*2.4*
Average:	41.7	8.4	21.9	6.2	2.6	32.1	9.0	17.5	5.2	2.5

Values in italics indicate that 1995-1997 data have been used.

*West-Germany only for 1990

**Russian Federation figures for 1990 are for USSR

***UK excluding Northern Ireland for 1990

Sources: © European Values Survey, WORC, Tilburg University, Netherlands, 1999-2000, by permission; © World Values Survey, Institute for Social Research, University of Michigan, by permission; Inglehart, R., Basañez, M., and Moreno, A., Human Values and Beliefs: A Cross-Cultural Sourcebook: Political, Religious, Sexual, and Economic Norms in 43 Societies: Findings from the 1990–1993 World Values Survey, The University of Michigan Press, Ann Arbor, 1998

Record 27 Membership and volunteering

This record, using the latest available data from the European and World Values Surveys, shows percentages of respondents who are members of community action groups or organisations concerned variously with the environment, third world development and human rights, and peace. The table also includes percentages of respondents who volunteer for these types of associations. The following question was asked: 'Look carefully at the following list of voluntary organisations and activities and say...

a) Which, if any, do you belong to?
b) Which, if any, are you currently doing unpaid work for?

- Community action on issues like poverty, employment, housing, racial equality
- Third world development and human rights
- Environment, conservation, ecology
- Peace movement'

Data are given for 1990–93 and 2000. The average figures for the complete data sets in 1990–93 and 2000 cannot be compared with each other as they refer to different sets of countries.

in % of respondents per country who are members of or volunteers in organisations, by type	1990–1993								2000							
	Membership				Volunteering (unpaid)				Membership				Volunteering (unpaid)			
Country	Community action	Third world/human rights	Environment	Peace	Community action	Third world/human rights	Environment	Peace	Community action	Third world/human rights	Environment	Peace	Community action	Third world/human rights	Environment	Peace
East Asia & Pacific																
Low income economies																
Vietnam									26.2	1.5	7.6	9.2	25.8	1.3	7.9	6.8
Middle income economies																
China	0.5	0.2	0.8	0.3	3.9	0.1	1.5	0.5	1.5	0.4	1.2	0.9	14.2	4.6	27.9	15.1
Philippines									7.2	5.0	8.2	11.8	6.5	5.7	9.0	11.2
High income economies																
Korea, Rep.	12.5	2.4	2	2	3.4	1.8	2.4	2.1	6.9	2.3	6.2	1.8	6.9	1.3	4.5	1.8
Japan	0.2	0.2	1.1	0.6	0.5	0.2	1.2	0.8	1.2	1.7	3.2	2.0	0.4	0.3	1.2	0.7
Singapore									2.1	0.7	1.1	1.2	2.1	0.7	1.3	1.1
Europe & Central Asia																
Low income economies																
Moldova									2.6	2.4	4.7	2.4	3.1	2.4	4.4	2.1
Ukraine									1.9	0.6	0.6	0.1	1.0	0.2	0.3	0.4
Middle income economies																
Albania									11.6	6.4	10.4	7.2	7.7	2.4	7	3.4
Belarus									0.1	0.5	0.9	0.1	0.9	0.7	2.2	0.6
Bosnia & Herzegovina									1.1	0.3	1.9	0.3	1.3	0.3	1.5	0.2
Bulgaria	2	1.5	3.8	1.1	1.7	1.4	3.4	0.9	1.1	0.4	1.5	0.7	0.8	0.3	1.5	0.8
Croatia									1.3	0.5	3.0	1.0	0.7	0.4	2.1	1.4
Czech Republic									3.2	0.8	6.6	1.4	1.9	0.4	3.0	1.1
Estonia	4.5	0.6	2.7	1.3	4	0.9	2	0.9	1.8	0.1	1.7	0.2	1.8	0.3	1.2	1.4

Record 27 continued

Country (in % of respondents per country who are members of or volunteers in organisations, by type)	1990–1993 Membership: Community action	Third world/human rights	Environment	Peace	1990–1993 Volunteering (unpaid): Community action	Third world/human rights	Environment	Peace	2000 Membership: Community action	Third world/human rights	Environment	Peace	2000 Volunteering (unpaid): Community action	Third world/human rights	Environment	Peace
Hungary	1.4	0.2	1.4	0.5	1.5	0.3	1.3	0.2	1.2	0.4	1.9	0.3	1.1	0.2	1.9	0.2
Latvia	5.4	1.3	4.3	1.2	8.4	4	4.9	0.9	0.7	0.6	0.7	0.2	1.7	0.3	0.5	0.3
Lithuania	2.1	1	2.1	0.6	1.5	0.9	1.8	0.8	0.7	0.4	0.8	0.2	0.7	0.3	0.6	0.3
Macedonia									5.5	3.3	4.9	5.5	3.3	2	3.1	2.8
Poland		0.1	1.5	0.2		0.5	1.6	0.1	1.9	0.3	1.4	0.4	1.3	0.2	0.7	0.5
Romania	1.1	0.2	1	0.2	0.6	0.1	0.9	0.1	0.9	0.6	1.0	0.1	0.6	0.4	0.6	0.3
Russian Federation**	2.5	0.3	1.6	1.1	1.7	0.3	1.3	0.8	0.9	0.1	0.7	0.1	0.6	0.0	0.4	0.3
Serbia & Montenegro									0.6	0.5	1.0	0.0	0.3	0.2	0.4	0.0
Slovakia		0.4	5.8	1.6		0.2	3	0.1	8.3	0.2	2.6	0.3	6.8	0.2	2.0	4.7
Slovenia	5.8	0.1	1.7	0.1	2.7	0.5	1.4	0.3	9.2	0.8	3.3	0.8	5.8	0.4	2.9	1.3
High income economies																
Austria	2.2	1.6	2.9	0.8	1.4	0.7	1.4	0.3	3.0	3.2	9.6	1.2	1.3	0.8	2.3	2.7
Belgium	4.6	6.5	7.7	2.2	2.9	3.3	2.6	1	5.0	9.9	10.5	2.4	2.7	5.0	3.3	2.9
Denmark	5.2	2.8	12.5	2.1	1.9	0.9	0.9	0.2	6.2	4.1	13.2	0.8	3.1	1.2	2.3	0.8
Finland	3.2	5.9	5.5	1.7	2.9	2.9	4.3	1.2	2.6	5.9	4.8	1.3	1.5	3.3	2.1	1.8
France	3.3	2.6	2.3	0.5	2.9	1.4	1.5	0.5	2.5	1.2	2.1	0.4	1.7	0.6	0.9	0.1
Germany*	1.7	2.1	4.5	2	1	0.8	1.4	1	0.8	0.6	2.7	0.2	0.4	0.2	1.0	0.1
Greece									4.3	5.0	11.0	4.1	6.7	5.7	9.5	3.0
Iceland	2	3.4	4.8	1.4	0.6	0.4	2	0.3	2.5	7.5	4.6	1.1	0.7	1.3	1.3	2.3
Ireland	3.3	1.6	2.2	0.6	2.8	1.3	0.6	0.2	5.8	3.0	3.2	1.5	3.4	2.0	1.3	2.8
Italy	2.5	1.1	2.9	1.1	2	0.7	1.4	0.6	2.4	2.9	3.8	1.4	1.8	1.9	1.8	0.4
Luxembourg									5.1	9.7	9.7	2.2	2.8	5.0	4.1	2.3
Netherlands	5	14.1	23.3	2.9	2.5	3	2.9	1.3	6.9	24.4	45.1	2.8	4.0	4.1	2.4	0.5
Portugal	1.7	0.6	1.5	0.5	0.8	0.6	0.7	0.2	1.5	1.0	0.9	0.9	1.1	0.8	0.6	0.1
Spain	1.2	1	1.4	0.7	0.4	0.8	1	0.5	2.1	2.7	2.0	1.1	1.7	1.4	1.1	0.8
Sweden	2.2	9.3	10.6	3.1	1	3.2	2.5	1.5	9.4	15.0	35.3	1.5	5.5	4.5	3.8	0.4
United Kingdom***	3.5	2.3	5.9	1.3	1	1.1	1.8	0.6	3.8	2.6	1.5	0.6	1.6	4.2	6.3	3.6
Latin America & Caribbean																
High income countries																
Argentina	1.3	0.4	0.2	0.2	1.1	0.2	0.1	0.1	3.2	0.5	2.2		2.6	0.3	1.4	0.7
Chile	4.1	1.3	1.6	0.8	3.3	0.9	0.9	0.5	4.9	2.0	3.1	1.7	3.8	1.7	2.2	2.2
Mexico	4.3	0.9	2.8	1.4	2.7	0.6	2.4	0.7	5.0	2.5	4.7	2.8	4.2	1.4	3.4	3.0
Peru									6.5	2.4	3.1	0.9	4.2	1.6	2.2	0.4
Venezuela									10.3	8.9	11.9	5.8				
Middle East & North Africa																
High income countries																
Algeria									0	3.3	4.4	0	0	5.5	6	
Malta									2.8	0.3	2.0	0.2	3.9	1.6	1.9	1.7
Morocco									1	0.2	0.6	0.6	0	0	0	

Record 27 continued

Country (in % of respondents per country who are members of or volunteers in organisations, by type)	1990–1993 Membership: Community action	Third world/human rights	Environment	Peace	1990–1993 Volunteering (unpaid): Community action	Third world/human rights	Environment	Peace	2000 Membership: Community action	Third world/human rights	Environment	Peace	2000 Volunteering (unpaid): Community action	Third world/human rights	Environment	Peace
North America																
High income countries																
Canada	5.1	4.6	7.5	2	4	2.7	3.5	1.6	7.3	4.5	8.1	1.8	4.6	2.4	3.9	1.1
United States	4.6	1.7	8.5	2	3	0.9	3.5	0.7	12.9	5.5	15.9	4.3	7.3	2.9	8.8	2.1
South Asia																
Low income countries																
Bangladesh									25.9	10.9	20.3	23.0	27.0	12.0	21.6	30.1
India									6.0	2.8	7.0	4.8	5.3	2.2	5.3	4.0
Sub-Saharan Africa																
Low income countries																
Tanzania									23.8	18.8	20.1	5	23.3	19.6	21.1	4.3
Uganda									10.5	4.9	9.7	10.3	6.2	2.9	6.9	6.3
Zimbabwe									4.8	1.6	2.6	2.9	2.1	0.5	1.4	1.2
Middle income countries																
South Africa									6.6	2.2	3.8	4.1	4.5	1.3	1.8	2.5
Average	3.3	2.3	4.3	1.2	2.3	1.2	1.9	0.7	5.2	3.5	6.3	2.5	4.2	2.2	3.9	2.7

*1990-1993 data West-Germany only

** Russian Federation figures for 1990 are for USSR

***UK excluding Northern Ireland for 1990-1993 data

Sources: © European Values Survey, WORC, Tilburg University, Netherlands, 1999-2000, by permission; © World Values Survey, Institute for Social Research, University of Michigan, by permission; Inglehart, R., Basañez, M., and Moreno, A., Human Values and Beliefs: A Cross-Cultural Sourcebook: Political, Religious, Sexual, and Economic Norms in 43 Societies: Findings from the 1990–1993 World Values Survey, The University of Michigan Press, Ann Arbor, 1998.

Glossary of Terms in Data Programme

Arbitrary detention. Deprivation of liberty imposed arbitrarily, that is, where no final decision has been taken by domestic courts in conformity with domestic law and with the relevant international standards set forth in the Universal Declaration of Human Rights and with the relevant international instruments accepted by the states concerned.

Bribing and corruption. This indicator is taken from the survey of business executives which forms part of the Institute for Management Development's World Competitiveness Yearbook. Respondents are asked to what extent bribing and corruption exist in the economy.

Corruption Perceptions Index (CPI). Measures corruption in the public sector and defines corruption as the abuse of public office for private gain. The CPI makes no effort to reflect private sector fraud. The index is based on surveys compiled by Transparency International from other organisations which tend to ask questions about the misuse of public power for private benefits, with a focus, for example, on bribing of public officials, taking kickbacks in public procurement, or embezzling public funds, etc. Surveys consulted:

- Economist Intelligence Unit (Country Risk Service and Country Forecasts);
- Gallup International (50th Anniversary Survey);
- Institute for Management Development (World Competitiveness Yearbook);
- Political & Economic Risk Consultancy (Asian Intelligence Issue);
- Political Risk Services (International Country Risk Guide);
- World Development Report (private sector survey by the World Bank); and
- World Economic Forum & Harvard Institute for International Development (Global Competitiveness Survey).

Daily newspapers. The number of newspapers published at least four times a week per 1,000 people. Newspapers are periodic publications intended for the general public and mainly designed to be a primary source of written information on current events connected with public affairs, international questions, politics, etc. Although according to UNESCO definitions newspapers and periodicals are to be distinguished by content rather than frequency of publication, a few countries, including some demographically important ones, classify any periodic publication as a daily or a non-daily simply according to the frequency of appearance. Circulation figures should include the number of copies (a) sold directly, (b) sold by subscription, and (c) mainly distributed free of charge both inside the country and abroad.

Discrimination. Any distinction, exclusion, restriction, or preference based on any ground such as race, colour, sex, language, religion, political or other opinion, national or social origin, property, birth, or other status which has the purpose or effect of nullifying or impairing the recognition, enjoyment, or exercise, on an equal footing, of human rights and fundamental freedoms in the political, economic, social, cultural, or any other field of public life.

Emissions. Emissions refer to the release of greenhouse gases and/or their precursors and aerosols into the atmosphere over a specified area and period of time.

Energy consumption per capita. Energy consumption is the amount of energy consumed by each country, divided by its population estimate. Energy consumption means the total amount of primary energy consumed from all energy sources, including losses through transportation, friction, heat loss, and other inefficiencies. Specifically, consumption equals indigenous production plus imports minus exports plus stock changes minus international marine bunkers. The values presented are calculated by the International Energy Agency (IEA) using an energy balance methodology based on the calorific content of energy commodities. The IEA calls this category Total Primary Energy Supply (TPES).

Enforced disappearances. Enforced disappearances occur when persons are arrested, detained, or abducted against their will or otherwise deprived of their liberty by officials of different branches or levels of government, or by organized groups or private individuals acting on behalf of, or with the support, direct or indirect, consent, or acquiescence of the government, followed by a refusal to disclose the fate or whereabouts of the persons concerned or a refusal to acknowledge the deprivation of their liberty, which places such persons outside the protection of the law.

Extrajudicial executions. Full expression 'extrajudicial, summary, or arbitrary executions': all acts and omissions of state representatives that constitute a violation of the general recognition of the right to life embodied in the Universal Declaration of Human Rights and the International Covenant on Civil and Political Rights.

Foreign direct investment (FDI). Investment to acquire a lasting management interest (10 per cent or more of voting stock) in an enterprise operating in an economy other than that of the investor. It is the sum of equity capital, reinvestment of earnings, other long-term capital, and short-term capital as shown in the balance of payments. FDI stock is the value of the share of capital and reserves (including retained profits) attributable to enterprises based outside the domestic economy, plus the net indebtedness of domestic affiliates to the parent enterprise. UNCTAD FDI stock data are frequently estimated by accumulating FDI *flows* over a period of time or adding flows to an FDI *stock* that has been obtained for a particular year.

Freedom of association. The right to establish and, subject only to the rules of the organisation concerned, to join organisations of one's own choosing without prior authorisation.

Freedom of expression. Freedom to hold opinions without interference and to seek, receive, and impart information and ideas through any media and regardless of frontiers.

Full-time equivalent employment. Indicates total employment in terms of full-time jobs. Part-time employment is converted into full-time jobs and added to the number of full-time jobs, based on country-specific conventions.

Gross domestic product (GDP). Total domestic expenditure of a country, minus imports, plus exports of goods and services.

GDP per capita, PPP. GDP per capita based on purchasing power parity (PPP). GDP PPP is gross domestic product converted to international dollars using purchasing power parity rates. An international dollar has the same purchasing power over GDP as the US dollar in the United States. Data are in current international dollars.

Gini index. Measures the extent to which the distribution of income (or, in some cases, consumption expenditures) among individuals or households within an economy deviates from a perfectly equal distribution. A Lorenz curve plots the cumulative percentages of total income received against the cumulative number of recipients, starting with the poorest individual or household. The Gini index measures the area between the Lorenz curve and a hypothetical line of absolute equality, expressed as a percentage of the maximum area under the line. Thus, a Gini index of zero represents perfect equality, while an index of 100 implies perfect inequality.

Gross national income (GNI). Formerly known as gross national product or GNP. The sum of value added by all resident producers plus any product taxes (less subsidies) not included in the valuation of output plus net receipts of primary income (compensation of employees and property income) from abroad.

Human Development Index (HDI). A composite index based on three indicators: longevity, as measured by life expectancy at birth; educational attainment, as measured by a combination of adult literacy (two-thirds weight) and the combined gross primary, secondary, and tertiary enrolment ratio (one-third weight); and standard of living, as measured by GDP per capita (PPP US$).

Illiteracy rate. Calculated as 100 minus the adult literacy rate, which refers to the people aged 15 and above who can, with understanding, both read and write a short, simple statement on their everyday lives.

Imputed value for volunteers. Calculated by converting the total volunteer hours into full-time equivalent employment, multiplied by the average wage for the group, industry, or the economy as a whole.

Infant mortality rate. The probability of dying between birth and exactly one year of age times 1,000.

Internally displaced persons (IDPs). Individuals or groups of people who have been forced to flee their homes to escape armed conflict, generalised violence, human rights abuses, or natural or man-made disasters, *and* have remained within the borders of their home country.

International NGOs. These are currently active, autonomous non-profit making organisations with operations or activities in at least three countries, or members with voting rights in at least three countries, a formal structure with election of governing officers from several member countries and some continuity of activities. Notably excluded are obviously national or bilateral organisations, informal social movements and ad hoc bodies, and international business enterprises, investment houses or cartels and other obvious profit making bodies. Irrelevant are size, importance, degree of activity, financial strength, political or ideological position, field of interest or activity, location of headquarters and language.

Internationally oriented NGOs. These are national, currently active, autonomous, non-profit making organisations with various forms of international activity or concern such as research, peace, development or relief. They may also include national bodies which have relations with international organisations, where these international organisations list them in conjunction with truly international bodies. They may also be organisations which appear from their titles to be international. This criterion includes organisations having consultative status with United Nations and other intergovernmental organisations.

ISO 14000 certification. This was designed to provide any type of public or private organisation with environmental management systems standards. Companies adhering to the ISO 14000 implement environmental management systems, conduct environmental audits, and evaluate their environmental performance with guidance from the International Standards Organisation (ISO). Their products adhere to environmental labelling standards, and waste streams are managed through life-cycle assessment of all products. See <http://www.iso.ch/iso/en/iso9000-14000/pdf/iso14000.pdf>.

Meetings. These are meetings organised or sponsored by 'international organisations' (INGOs, internationally oriented NGOs and IGOs) that appear in the Union of International Associations' *Yearbook of International Organizations*, and other meetings of significant international character. Excluded are purely national meetings, as well as those of an essentially religious, didactic, political, commercial or sporting nature and meetings with strictly limited participation, such as those of subsidiary (internal) statutory bodies, committees, groups of experts etc., and corporate and incentive meetings.

Merchandise trade. Includes all trade in goods. Trade in services is excluded.

Network. Interpersonal or inter-organisational ties that reflect structural or legal relations, information flows and other exchanges. Network analysis seeks to identify patterns in complex networks.

Official development assistance (ODA). Official development assistance and net official aid record the actual international transfer by the donor of financial resources or of goods or services valued at the cost to the donor, minus any repayments of loan principal during the same period. ODA data are comprised of disbursements of loans made on concessional terms (net of repayments of principal) and grants by official agencies of the members of the Development Assistance Committee (DAC) of the OECD, by multilateral institutions, and by certain Arab countries to promote economic development and welfare in recipient economies listed as 'developing' by DAC. Loans with a grant element of at least 25 per cent are included in ODA, as are technical cooperation and assistance.

Passengers carried. Air passengers carried include both domestic and international aircraft passengers.

Peacekeeping forces. Military personnel and civilian police serving in United Nations peacekeeping missions.

Public sector or government. All branches of the government, including the executive, judicial, and administrative and regulatory activities of federal, Statestate, local, or regional political entities; the terms 'government' and 'public sector' are used synonymously.

Public sector payments. Include grants and contracts, i.e. direct contributions by the government to the organisation in support of specific activities and programmes; statutory transfers, i.e. contributions by the government, as mandated by law, to provide general support to an organisation in carrying out its public programmes, and third-party payments, i.e. indirect government payments reimbursing an organisation for services rendered to individuals (e.g. health insurance, 'vouchers', or payments for day care).

Private giving. Includes foundation giving, including grants from grant-making foundations, operating foundations, and community foundations; business or corporate donations, which includes giving directly by businesses or giving by business or corporate foundations; and individual giving, i.e. direct contributions by individuals and contributions through 'federated fund-raising' campaigns.

Private fees and charges (or 'programme fees'). These include four types of business or commercial income: fees for service, dues (e.g. membership charges), proceeds from sales of products, and investment income.

Refugee. As defined by the UN High Commissioner for Refugees, a person is a refugee if she/he qualifies under the Arrangements of 12 May 1926 and 30 June 1928 or under the Conventions of 28 October 1933 and 10 February 1938, the Protocol of 14 September 1939 or the Constitution of the International Refugee Organisation. See <http://www.unhcr.ch> for further information.

Telephone mainlines. Telephone lines connecting a customer's equipment to the public switched telephone network.

Transnationality Index (TNI). The average of three ratios: a corporation's foreign assets to total assets, foreign sales to total sales, and foreign employment to total employment.

Transparency of government. This indicator is taken from the survey of business executives which forms part of the Institute for Management Development's World Competitiveness Yearbook. Respondents are asked to what extent their government communicates its policy intentions clearly and publicly.

Torture. Any act by which severe pain or suffering, whether physical or mental, is intentionally inflicted on a person for such purposes as obtaining from him or a third person information or a confession, punishing him for an act he or a third person has committed or is suspected of having committed, or intimidating or coercing him or a third person, or for any reason based on discrimination of any kind, when such pain or suffering is inflicted by or at the instigation of or with the consent or acquiescence of a public official or other person acting in an official capacity. It does not include pain or suffering arising only from, inherent in, or incidental to lawful sanctions.

Total military personnel. Active duty military personnel, including paramilitary forces if those forces resemble regular units in their organisation, equipment, training, or mission.

Total trade. The sum of the market value of imports and exports of goods and services.

Tourists. Visitors who travel to a country other than that where they have their usual residence for a period not exceeding 12 months and whose main purpose in visiting is other than an activity remunerated from within the country visited.

PARALLEL SUMMITS OF GLOBAL CIVIL SOCIETY: AN UPDATE

Mario Pianta and Federico Silva

No longer parallel

Introduction

Global activities of civil society are growing very fast. In 2002 and in the first three months of 2003, growth of international meetings has been exponential. 33 major events took place, accounting for more than 30 per cent of all 108 recorded parallel summits since 1988. Many were part of the process started in 2001 with the first World Social Forum in Porto Alegre, Brasil, which has now spread in all continents, asserting the autonomy of global initiatives of civil society: 58% of all events are now civil society meetings with no corresponding 'official summit' (the share was 40% in last year's Yearbook).

A symbol of this transition has been February 15, 2003, perhaps the first truly global day of civil society action, in protest for peace and against the war on Iraq that was being prepared by the United States and the United Kingdom. Hundreds of cities all over the world hosted record demonstrations. While no single 'world event' took place, this was the start of a new generation of global civil society actions, advancing a common political agenda in most countries of the world and reflecting – according to all available polls – the consensus of a majority of world public opinion, what *The New York Times* described as the birth of a 'second superpower' (Tyler, 2003). This year, we also present some findings from our survey of global civil society organisations.

Parallel summits and global civil society meetings

The records presented here extend the analysis of the chapter on Parallel Summits of Global Civil Society, published in the 2001 edition of this Yearbook (Pianta, 2001), and of the update in the 2002 edition (Pianta, 2002a). We have followed the same procedure for collecting and organising information on global civil society events; the main sources this time were websites, newspapers and magazines which now devote extensive attention to such gatherings. The 33 cases identified for 2002 and the first three months of 2003 are considered representative of the range of events, topics and locations.

As they move from 'parallel summits' organised in coincidence with meetings of governments or international organisations, to independent global civil society gatherings, such events are becoming larger (55% had more than 10,000 participants, and 8 events had demonstrations with more than 50,000 people), more coordinated across the globe, and with a bigger political agenda, increasingly integrating economic and development issues with demands for democracy and peace. The objectives tend to be more outwardlooking; while networking among global civil society organisations was, in last year's data, still the most important aim of the gatherings, now proposal of alternatives and public opinion work have become the top objectives.

The survey on global civil society organisations

This year, the findings on global civil society meetings and parallel summits are integrated with the results of a survey on global civil society organisations, where the focus of the analysis was the individual organisation active on global issues (Record 29; see also Record 22 on attitudes to globalisation). A questionnaire was prepared in order to gather data on the profile of global civil society organisations, their activities, priorities and views on policy proposals. The questionnaire was circulated among the international participants at the Genoa Social Forum in July 2001 in Genoa, at the 4th Assembly of the Peoples' United Nations in Perugia in October 2001, and at the Second World Social Forum in Porto Alegre in January 2002. It was e-mailed to hundreds of civil society organisations drawn from a variety of accessible sources (such as UN NGO lists, Civicus and others). The selected records shown below are drawn from a broader study, carried out by the GLOBI project

(Pianta and Silva, 2003; help from Lunaria, a civil society research centre in Rome and from the Peace Roundtable, the organiser of the Assemblies of the Peoples' United Nations in Perugia is gratefully acknowledged).

The results presented here are based on 152 respondents, representative of all continents, types of organisations and fields of action. Twenty per cent of the respondents were international NGOs, 45% were national associations or NGOs, 18% international or national networks or campaigns, the rest mainly include trade unions, local groups and research centres; they are mainly active on development, economic policies, peace, human rights, environmental and democracy issues.

Respondents to the questionnaire were civil society organisations active on global issues whose national base was for 35% in Europe, 24% in Asia and the Middle East, 22% in Africa, 6% in North America and 14% in Latin America. Such a geographical distribution assures a balanced perspective from all continents and confirms the growing presence of civil society groups in the countries of the South. Moreover, it may be noted that the share of organisations based in the North (41%) is not different from the share of global civil society events taking place in the North (44%) over the period in which the questionnaire was compiled.

The group of respondents cover all size classes in terms of members of civil society organisations (about 10% are not membership organisations). More than a quarter of respondents are large associations with more than 1,000 members; the rest is equally spread between very small units (up to 20 members), small groups (21-100 members) and medium-sized organisations (101-1,000 members). Such a composition makes sure that a diversity of experiences and perspectives is represented in the results.

Networking is a crucial aspect in the global activities of such organisations. Two thirds of respondents belong to an international network or campaign, and the responses from networks show that they tend to be large coalitions, in half of the cases coordinating more than 26 groups.

Record 28 Parallel summits

Growth of parallel summits

Parallel summits and global civil society meetings are increasing rapidly. In 2002 and in the first three months of 2003 one-third of all gatherings of global civil society since 1988 took place, 50% more than in 2001, while in 2000 the same number of parallel summits were recorded as in the four previous years. There is a clear exponential growth in the number of events, which always include an international conference and, in most cases, a street demonstration, in addition to several fringe and media-oriented initiatives.

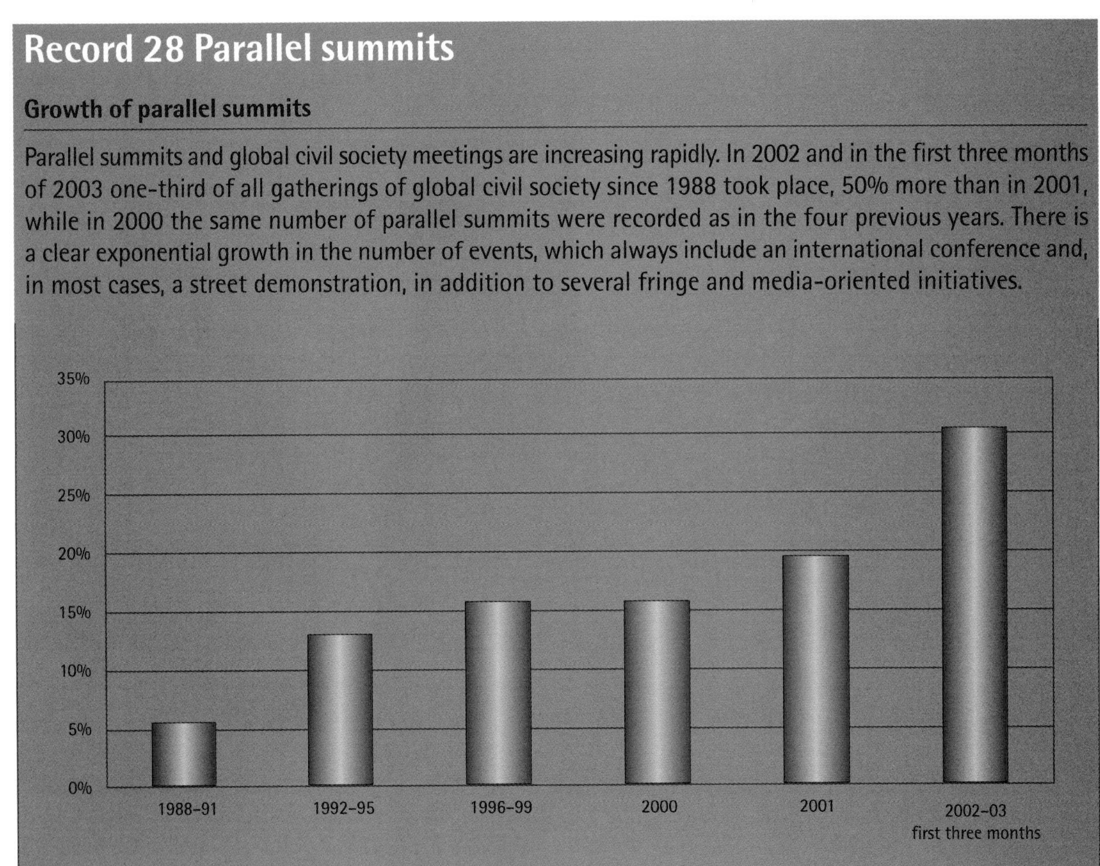

Record 28 continued. Location of parallel summits

Parallel summits are no longer an affair of rich countries: the majority of global civil society meetings now takes place in the South. In the events recorded from 1988 to 2001, Europe and North America had more than three quarters of cases; now their share is 44%. A major driver behind the growth of Latin American meetings has been the Porto Alegre (Brazil) model of Social Forums, which has been replicated at the national and regional level with events in Argentina, Colombia, Uruguay, while major meetings have addressed Pan-Amazonian issues and the contested project of the Free Trade Areas of the Americas.

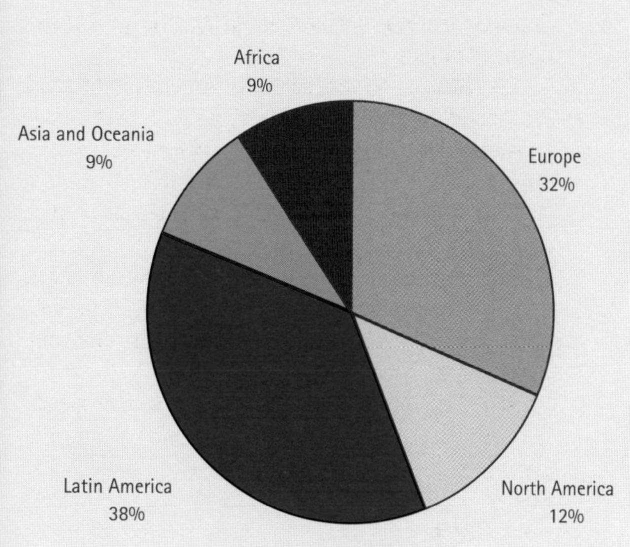

Types of parallel summits

Parallel summits, shadowing official meetings of governments, have now given way to independent global civil society meetings. 58% of all events have no corresponding 'official summit' (the share was 40% in last year's Yearbook and 10% between 1988 and 2000). 12% of parallel summits deal with regional conferences (European Union, American or Asian government meetings) and 21% concern summits of the United Nations, G8, IMF, World Bank or WTO. From 1988 to 2001 these events accounted for almost two thirds of all cases.

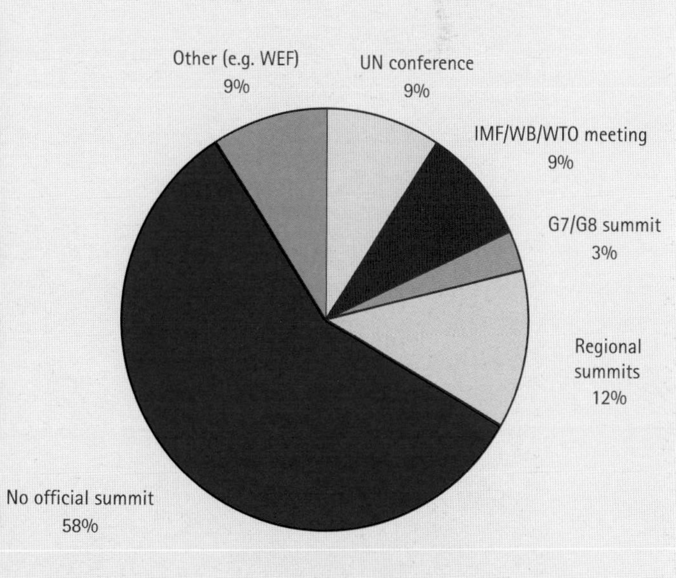

Record 28 continued. Number of participants

Global civil society meetings are becoming larger. Since January 2002, 55% of events have had more than 10.000 participants; of these, half had demonstrations with more than 50,000 people and an additional 25% have had between 1,000 and 10,000 people. In last year's Yearbook events with more than 10,000 people accounted for 33% of all cases. The increase in the number of events goes hand in hand with their growing size, as they move from being the reserve of small groups of specialists - between 1988 and 2001 40% of events had less than 1,000 people – to becoming a widespread experience with mass participation.

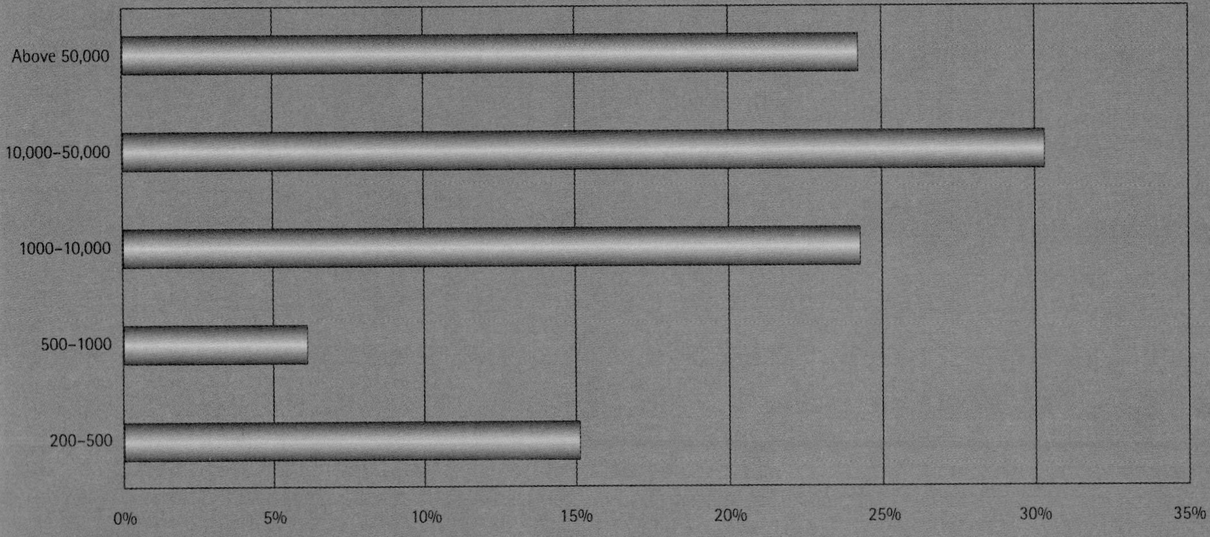

Fields of activity of the organisations involved

What are the themes on which the organisations involved in global events work? As in the past, two-thirds of events (multiple responses are possible here) have resulted from the work of civil society organisations active in development and economic issues (trade, finance, debt, etc.). As in last year's data, groups working on democracy issues are active in close to a half of global event; peace organisations are also stable with a presence in 25% of parallel summits. Human rights issues lose importance to one-fifth of events, while environmental organisation recover their historically large presence in one third of events. There is an increase in the presence of trade unions and labour organisations, which are found in close to a quarter of all events, and of groups active on migrations and refugees issues (6% of cases).

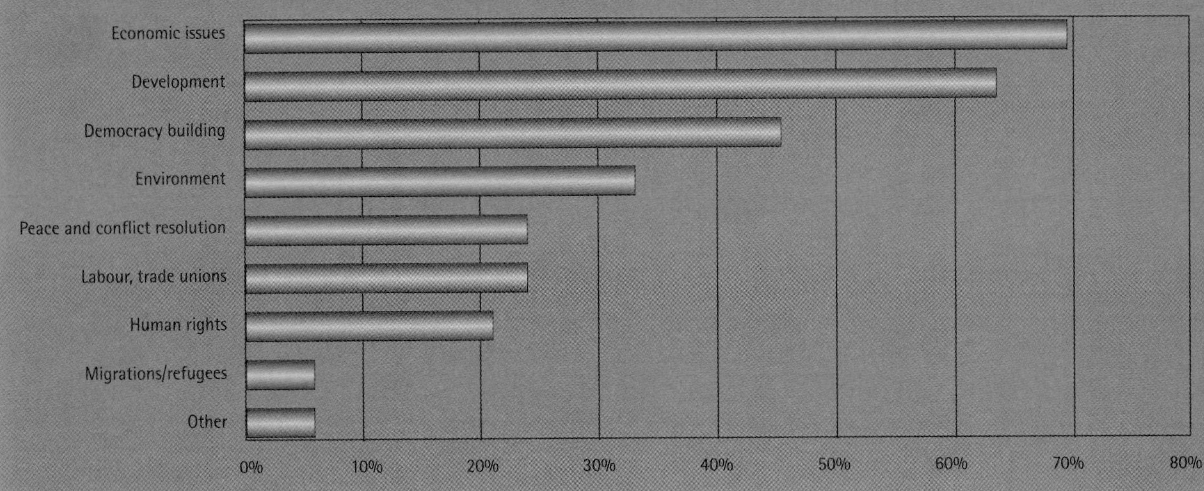

Record 28 continued. **Assessments of the results**

Do global civil society events have an impact? This evaluation, based on the judgement of organisers, participants or from media reports, clearly has to be treated with great caution. As in the past, the strongest impact is on civil society itself, where 40% of events is judged to have a strong or very strong effect, a big increase compared to the 25% of 2001. Another 40% of events has a medium impact. By all evidence, parallel summits and global meetings have indeed changed the face of global civil society organisations. On the basis of available documentation, their impact is rapidly increasing also on public opinion and the international media, where a medium or strong effect may be identified in the majority of events. Little or no impact can be detected on international policies and on official summits.

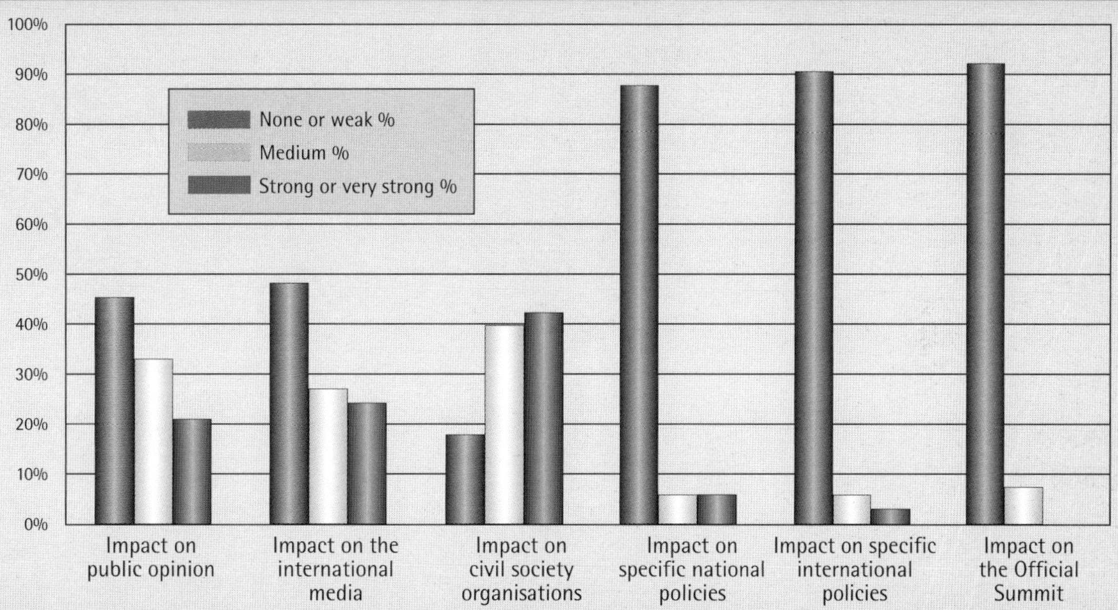

Record 28e **Objectives of parallel summits**

What are the purposes of global civil society meetings? Since January 2002, in more than four-fifths of cases (multiple responses are possible) the objectives were disseminating public information, proposing alternative policies, and networking among civil society organisations. The latter has maintained its past relevance, associated to the need for building the internal strengths of global civil society. The outreach to a wider public and the pressure on policy makers have increased in importance as global movements are increasingly able to develop alternative policies to those carried out by governments and international organisations.

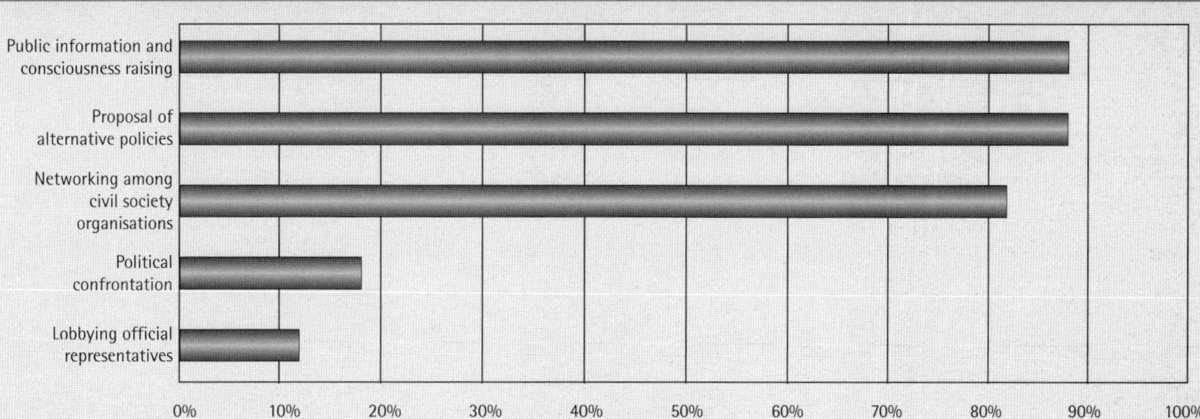

Record 29 Survey of global civil society organisations

Attitude towards official summits

The survey on global civil society organisations included a specific question on parallel and official summits: *'What is the main attitude of your organisation/group versus official summits?'* More than half of respondents chose *Active dialogue*, one quarter *Criticism of policies*, 11% *Integration in the official summit*, and 7% *Strong conflict*. These answers are a useful complement to the data provided above on Parallel Summits, as they emphasise the search for dialogue which emerges from civil society groups (with little reciprocity so far from governments and international institutions). Within organisations active on global issues we may therefore identify a large group of dialogue seekers, a substantial group of radical critics, a small group prepared to be integrated in official activities and a very small (and probably under-represented in the survey) group with rejectionist positions.

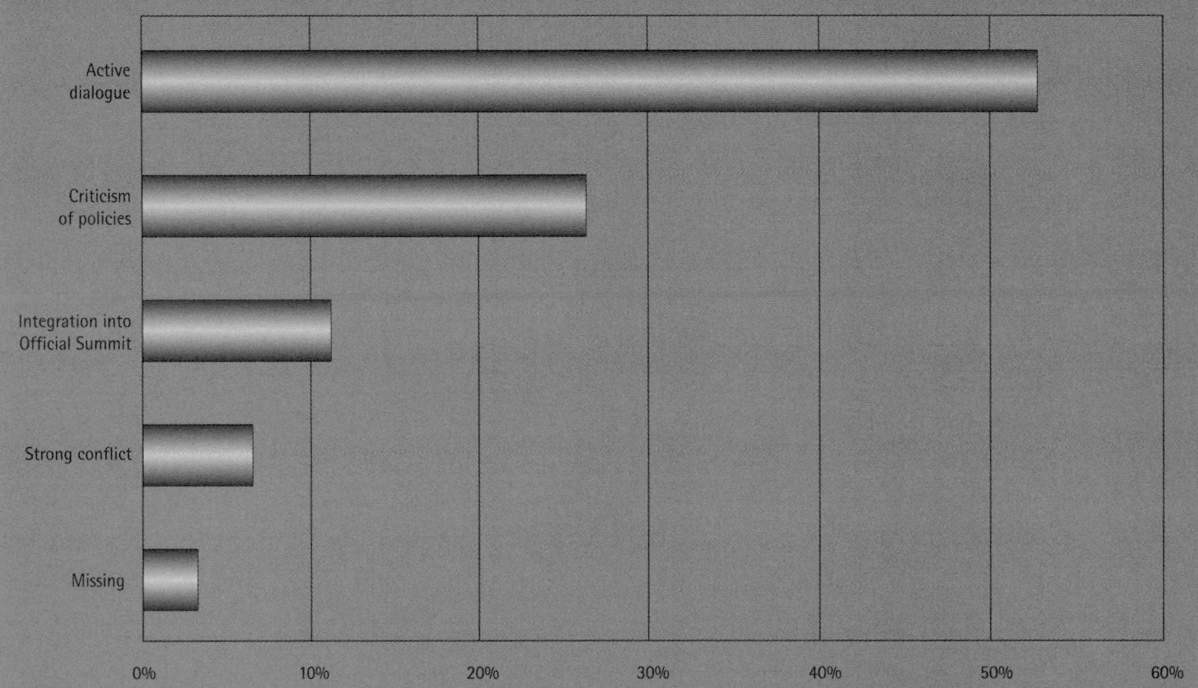

Record 29 continued. **Ways to democratise global civil society events**

'How could global civil society events be made more democratic and effective?'. The problems of internal democracy are important as the global reach of civil society becomes wider and more diverse. More than 40% of respondents (which could provide up to three answers) recommended to extend the number of organisations and countries involved in global events; a better balance between North and South organisations; building a broader common agenda on different issues. The emphasis is therefore on the inclusive capacity of global civil society events to integrate more experiences and more issues. A second group of recommendations, with 20 to 27% of preferences, deals with the practicalities of global meetings and the search for effectiveness, including the need for more inclusive discussion of the agenda and documents of meetings, for more information, for building a network of networks, and for more work on common policy proposals. Insisting on gender/racial balance is demanded by 18% of respondents, while only 14% argue for introducing voting in civil society meetings. In the search for greater internal democracy and external effectiveness, the emphasis is put on the need to broaden the base of civil society groups active on global issues and stimulate their participation and involvement. The strong interest in building a common agenda and common proposals shows that there is more interest in democratising the content of civil society actions, through consensus building, than in the procedures (such as voting), which may become important in formally established institutions.

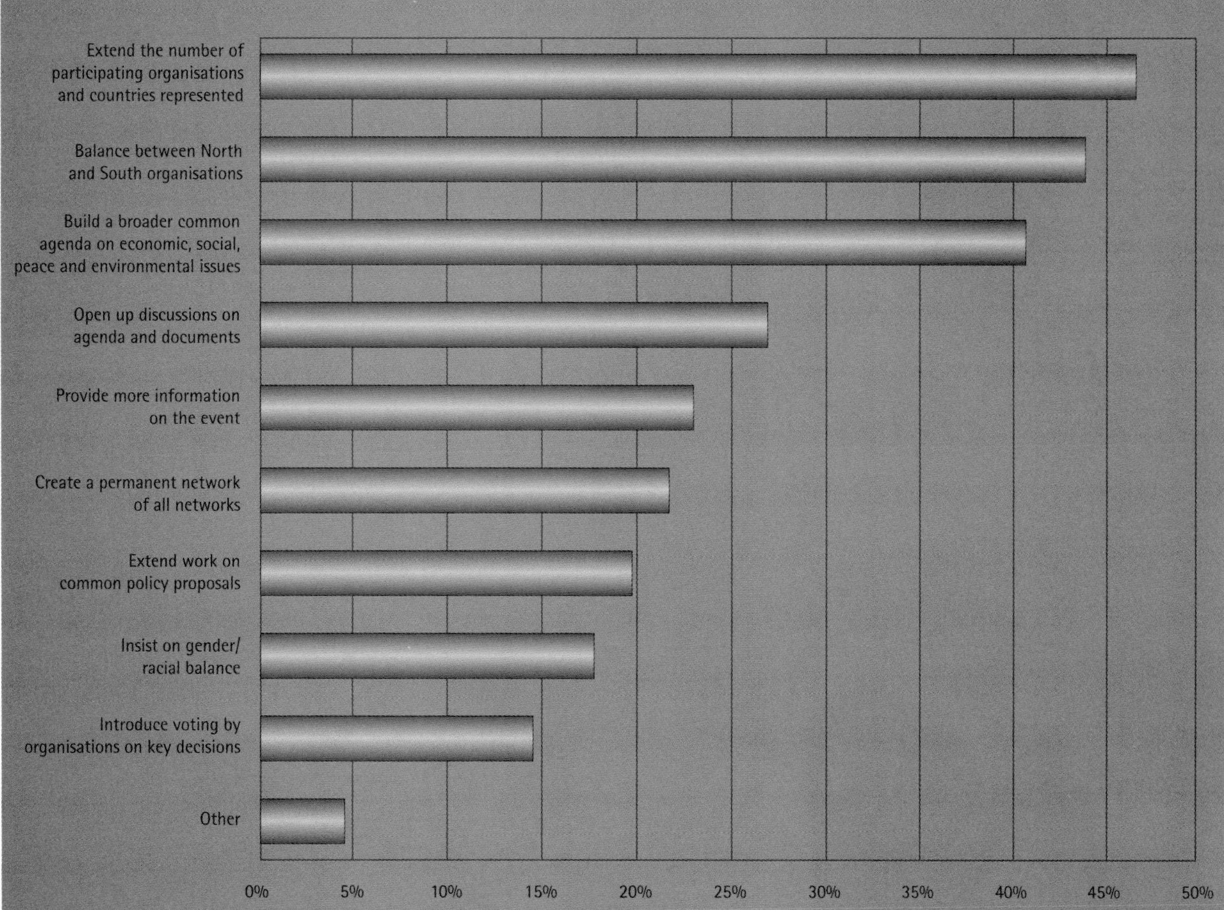

Record 29 continued. Alternative policy proposals of global civil society organisations

'How do you judge the relevance of the following policy proposals for global civil society activities?' A variety of proposals circulating among global civil society groups were listed, concerning different issues and topics. Make global civil society visible and established is the most popular objective, including the creation of a permanent Global Civil Society Assembly modelled on the World Social Forum. Make development possible is the demand behind support for the cancellation of Third World debt, greater flows of development aid, a greater role of NGOs and support to fair trade and ethical finance. Assure peace and justice is a need associated to nuclear disarmament and the International Criminal Court. Balance global capital and labour is the aim of demands for labour rights and limits on corporations. Democratise international institutions is a call addressed to the UN, IMF, World Bank and WTO. Control global finance is the demand receiving the least attention among economic issues. Protect the environment and Grant rights to immigrants are issues with the lowest priorities.

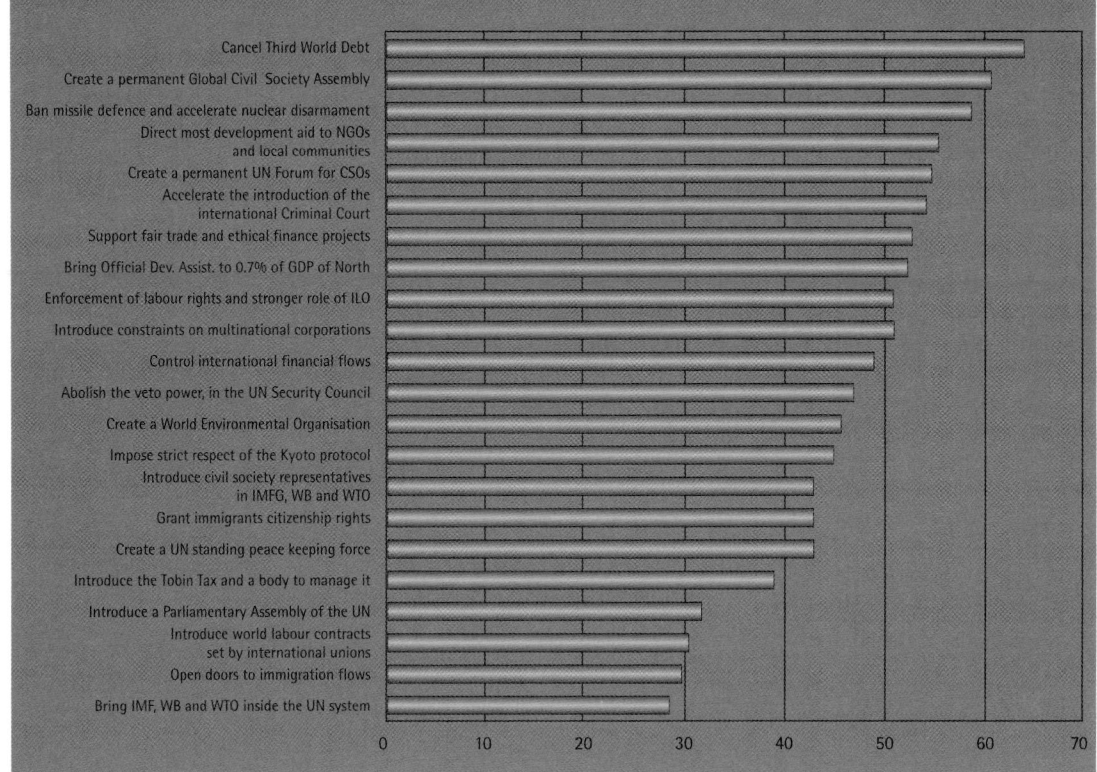

References

Pianta, M. (2001), 'Parallel Summits of Global Civil Society', in H. Anheier, M. Glasius and M. Kaldor (eds), *Global Civil Society 2001*, Oxford University Press, Oxford, 2001, pp. 169-194.

Pianta, M. (2002), 'Parallel Summits of Global Civil Society: an Update', in M. Glasius, M. Kaldor and H. Anheier (eds), *Global Civil Society 2002*, Oxford University Press, Oxford, 2002, pp. 371-377.

Pianta, M. (2003), 'Democracy vs. Globalisation. The Growth of Parallel Summits and Global Movements'. In D. Archibugi (ed.) *Debating Cosmopolitics*, Verso, London, pp.232-256.

Pianta, M. and Silva, F. (2003), *Globalisers from below. A survey on global civil society organisations*, GLOBI Research Report, Rome.

Tyler, P. E. (2003), 'Suddenly, it's U.S. and Rest of the World'. *The New York Times*, 17 February 2003.

Chronology of Global Civil Society Events

Compiled by Jill Timms

With contributions from Yeshaiahu Ben Aharon, Mustapha Kamel Al-Sayyid, Mulya Amri, Brian Appelbe, Reine Borja, Joabe Cavalcanti, Hyo-Je Cho, James Deane, Bernard Dreano, Mary Fischer, Louise Fraser, Nihad Gohar, Habib Guiza, Anil Gupta, Vicky Holland, Hagai Katz, Zafarullah Khan, Svetlana Kuts, Silke Lechner, Natalia Leshchenko, Maritza Lopez-Quintana, Maite San Miguel, Nuria Molina, Alejandro Natal, Beatriz Martín Nieto, Mario Pianta, Thomas Ruddy, Yahia Said, Trilochan Sastry, Mukul Sinha, Robert Sommers, Toralf Staud, Elena Tonkacheva, Kate Townsend, Eduard Vallory, Caroline Walker.

Note on the Chronology

The aim of this chronology is to provide an account of global civil society events that took place in 2002. We seek to be as comprehensive as possible in covering the major events of the year and to offer an insight into the diversity and depth of civil society activities that have had global significance in terms of theme, participants, or resonance. This chronology offers a space for exploring and acknowledging the variety of activities and groups which can be described as part of civil society in the broadest understanding of the concept. It therefore differs from the usual end-of-year reviews in several significant ways. Our chronology does not focus on the events that have come to the attention of the world through mainstream media, and preference is not given to reports from Northern or Western countries. Our aim is to include the activities of all forms of civil society groups in all parts of the world, when they have significance beyond the local and national.

Thus, the Chronology of Global Civil Society Events contributes to the records section of the Yearbook as it offers a method of including events and actions without reducing the richness and diversity of the information we have to mere statistics. In the 2002 chronology we have been able to include civil society actions from over 70 countries.

To achieve this alternative chronology, we work with a team of global correspondents made up of activists, journalists, academics, students, and interested parties around the world who report to us on global civil society events. The chronology is not intended to be a complete list of all actions in all places, thankfully, that would be impossible! However, we are continually building up our team of correspondents to ensure that we cover all events with a global significance and hope you will consider joining us (please see the details below). As this team expands and as each chronology is written, our criterion of what constitutes a global civil society event is refined. Broadly, it includes civil society events which have implications beyond the confines of one nation or country. When deemed relevant, a number of other events, such as court rulings or election results, are included, when civil society is directly affected or has had an influence on bringing them about. We do not systematically list all local Social Forums; however, these are detailed as comprehensively as possible in the table on our website: www.lse.ac.uk/depts/global/yearbook. As the years go by, our criterion is repeatedly challenged by the growing number, diversity, and creativity of civil society events that come to our attention. We hope and expect this will continue.

Your opportunity to contribute to the Global Civil Society Yearbook

This chronology has been possible only through the contributions of our global correspondents, acknowledged above. We are very grateful to them all for their help, and we invite you to become a member of the team. The Global Civil Society Yearbook is a project that aims to reflect on and contribute to global civil society. As such, it is designed as an interactive initiative, a space for encouraging debate and understanding of civil society activity in a global context. As well as the chapters contributed by international academics and activists, we aim to include inputs from as many other groups and individuals as possible through a variety of means. Central to this is our team of Global Civil Society correspondents, who play a vital role in helping us to record the events that have a global significance.

What does being a Yearbook correspondent involve? Correspondents are required to monitor and describe major civil society events in various fields in their country or region. This usually means writing only a few entries, unless it has been a particularly eventful year in your part of the world. At regular intervals the Yearbook team will be in contact with you for a report of these events, including for each details of date and place, description of what happened and how it has global significance, and, where possible, a reference to further information, such as a web site.

If you would like to become a correspondent, or know someone who might, or have any questions or any comments about this year's chronology, we would be very pleased to hear from you. Details of how to contact us can be found at <www.lse.ac.uk/Depts/global/Yearbook>. All correspondents, as part of the Yearbook team, are officially acknowledged as contributors to the book and receive a complimentary copy of the Yearbook annually, as well as our thanks.

Global Civil Society Events of 2002

January

1 January Mass demonstrations greet the announcement of Eduardo Duhalde as Argentina's fifth new president in the two weeks since citizen protests forced Fernando de la Rua to resign on 20 December. When it is also announced that full elections will not be held until December 2003, protesters go onto the streets banging pots and pans to demand immediate elections. In the capital, a force of 45,000 police and soldiers use tear gas and rubber bullets to disperse the crowd, whilst Mr Duhalde pledges to work with businesses, unions, and NGOs to solve Argentina's serious difficulties arising from its foreign debt of $132 billion, which the government has already said cannot be repaid.

15 January A peace organisation in the Middle East called 'Green Line – Students Set the Border' pitch a tent at the site of an Israeli settlement. It names the tent 'Ma'aleh Miyus', a pun on a typical settlement name as it translates as 'Upper Disgust'. This is to protest against, and draw attention to, the dangers of extremist settlers dominating the political discourse regarding occupations.

15 January Argentina experiences further demonstrations across the country, initiated by increasingly radical groups protesting against continuing economic hardships. Banks are targeted and smashed as citizens rebel against strict banking restrictions, which include the freezing of savings accounts and limits on cash withdrawals. The new president, Eduardo Duhalde, warns that if planned new economic measures do not work the country will fall into anarchy.

19 January The former head of the Ukraine President's office and current Ukraine parliamentary speaker, Mr Lytwyn, publishes the first governmental assessment of civil society in the Ukraine. The negative conclusion—that civil society could be dangerous for the country—triggers a nationwide public discussion on the state and role of civil society in the Ukraine, resulting in the publication of more than 30 articles, the majority of which counter the government's scepticism.

23 January In Venezuela, the biggest demonstrations in the country's history commemorate the end of Marcos Pérez Jiménez's dictatorship in 1958, which marked the beginning of Venezuelan democracy. Political parties, civil society groups, and trades unions join two rival marches, one supporting and one opposing the current president, Hugo Chávez.

Late January Under pressure from protesters, the Hong Kong government withdraws its proposed 15–20 per cent wage cut for Filipino maids, which it claimed would help ease the economic crisis. The proposed cut has been denounced by the Asian Migrant Coalition, the Coalition for Migrants' Rights, and other migrant and local labour advocates as being anti-migrant as well as constituting both racial and class discrimination as the cut targets only foreign domestic workers. This successful outcome results from protests by domestic workers from the Philippines, Indonesia,

Thailand, and Nepal, who also lobbied their respective governments; and formal appeals were made by Hong Kong-based diplomats.

30 January–5 February In Porto Alegre, Brazil, the second World Social Forum (WSF) is held, with 68,000 participants. Delegates travel from 131 countries and represent more than 5,000 associations. The forum aims to provide a space for the development of alternatives to the current form of globalisation and the neo-liberal policies that lead to it, as well as aiming to share ideas for protesting against and resisting current economic and social policies. In the forum's final statement, which is agreed by many of the associations, the activists describe themselves as a 'global movement for social justice and solidarity'. It is also decided that a range of regional and themed forums will be held before the WSF meets again in 2003.

31 January–4 February During the World Economic Forum (WEF), approximately 10,000 join protests against the policies of the WEF, the International Monetary Fund (IMF) and the World Bank. For the first time in 31 years the event is not held in Davos, Switzerland. Organisers claim New York was chosen for security reasons and to show solidarity with the city since the 11 September terrorist attacks, but activists say it is an attempt to discourage them. Alternative forums are also held, such as the Counter Summit organised by Students for Social Justice. Protest organisers claim they are not an anti-globalisation movement but a global justice movement.

February

1 February In Munich, Germany, thousands of anti-war demonstrators hold a protest while 400 defence experts, representing most NATO countries, attend a major NATO defence summit there. Activists clash with police as authorities have obtained a city-wide ban on demonstrations for the duration of the summit.

2 February Citizens in Argentina who claim that the freeze on their savings imposed by the government is illegal have their case upheld by the Supreme Court, which rules that the measure is unconstitutional. The government immediately announces a two-day bank holiday, closing banks and foreign exchange houses, to prevent a run on bank deposits.

3 February The first international meeting of ATTAC takes place, facilitated by the WSF in Porto Alegre. Members from 40 countries are able to join the meeting, coming together for the first time to discuss issues of identity and to plan campaigns for the promotion of the 'Tobin tax'.

4 February Civil society activity in Venezuela continues to increase, as the country marks the tenth anniversary of the attempted coup d'état staged by Hugo Chávez, who later became the elected president. His supporters, Chavistas, celebrate the occasion, while his opponents, Antichavistas, resort to 'active mourning' by covering their houses, cars, and themselves in black.

17–24 February A civilian protection mission travels to Palestine, co-organised by the Association of Maghrebian Workers in France and the French Jewish Union for Peace. This is one of many groups of international peace activists who travel to the areas affected by the Israeli Defence Force incursions into Palestinian cities and refugee camps. The activists aim to offer support and protection to the Palestinians there and to provide them with necessities such as food, water, and medicines.

19 February In Amsterdam, the Netherlands, activists hold a protest at the opening of the Eye-for-Energy conference on carbon emission trading. The protesters are armed with water pistols, blue wigs, and 'farting gas' to emphasise that carbon trading 'stinks' and that the endless pursuit of profits by corporations will never solve the problem of global climate change. The activists demand an immediate 60 per cent reduction in the emission of greenhouse gases, which is in line with UN scientists' recommendations.

20 February In Luanda, the capital of Angola, civil society organisations meet to discuss the continuing violence of the 26-year civil war. These groups, who represent non-political civic interests and include priests, academics, humanitarian officers, and traditional chiefs, call for an immediate ceasefire. In criticising the UN

Security Council's handling of the peace process, the coalition requests that a delegation of civil society organisations be allowed to address the Security Council so they can have an input in the process. Although civil society groups have been active in Angola for a number of years, the agreement on a unified position is described as a breakthrough.

27 February In Israel, 200,000 join a mass peace march in Tel Aviv. This is organised by the Peace Coalition, which brings together civil society groups from Israel, Palestine, and European countries, such as Peace Now, Women for Peace, and Ta'ayush et Gush Shalom. The aim is to strengthen and draw attention to the coalition's campaign against Israeli occupation of the Palestinian Territories and to support Israeli reserve officers who signed a declaration refusing to serve there.

27 February–6 March In Gujarat, India, Hindu volunteers returning from the disputed holy site of Ayodhyaya are killed in a train near Godhra station. Many are burnt alive, trapped in carriages allegedly set alight by bystanders. This is followed by days of large-scale violence between Hindus and Muslims. More than 2,000 people, mainly Muslims, are killed and many flee to relief camps. It is the worst communal violence in the country for over ten years. Religious, peace, and human rights groups begin to mobilise aid and, throughout the crisis, lobby the government to act. On 3 March students and faculty members from the Indian Institute of Management, the Physics Research Laboratory, and Gujarat Institute of Development appeal for peace through a sit-in and fast, while others organise a petition appealing for peace. The protests culminate in a mass peace rally on 6 March, organised by senior Gandhians and NGOs.

March

Early March Bahraini human rights activists receive official authorisation to establish the Bahrain Human Rights Association, the first independent human rights monitoring group in the country. This is accomplished with the support and encouragement of international human rights groups.

1–2 March The second meeting of the World Forum of Civil Society Networks (UBUNTU) is held in Barcelona, Spain, with approximately 70 people attending. Diverse global civil society actors, such as Nobel Peace Prize Laureates, global civil society networks, academics, and representatives of global alternative media, gather at the Parliament of Catalonia, in Barcelona. One of the main outcomes is an agreement to set up a process leading to the launching of a World Campaign to Reform International Institutions.

1 March–May A march by 3,000 former Daqing Oil workers to the company's headquarters in China marks the start of three months of protests in the north-eastern Chinese cities of Liaoyang, Daqing, and Fushun. These bring unprecedented numbers of unemployed and disaffected workers on to the streets. The first protest is a reaction to changes to pension premiums and an announcement that the company will no longer pay heating allowances. The campaign soon grows to involve wider employment issues, including non-payment of wages and pensions, insufficient severance pay, manoeuvres intended to bypass elected workers congresses, and unfulfilled government promises to help the unemployed. Demonstrations involve over 50,000 workers from many factories and mines, and last longer than any protest since the violent suppression of the 1989 Democracy Movement. Between 7,000 and 8,000 protest daily at Iron Man Square in Daqing, despite police roadblocks. To prevent copycat protests a total domestic media blackout is ordered. The campaign successfully attracts international attention and support on 4 March, as 20,000 activists block the path of a train heading for Russia. When organisers of the campaign are regularly arrested for such actions, the number of daily protesters increases correspondingly, and on some occasions only the elderly and retired demonstrate as they are less likely to be arrested.

8 March Women's groups use International Women's Day to highlight the specific difficulties of women around the world and to celebrate their achievements through a variety of activities. The UN declares a special focus on women in Afghanistan. In Bangladesh, a male-led march is organised to show solidarity with women who are disfigured by acid attacks, often thrown out of jealousy by spurned admirers or husbands. The demonstrators call for tougher laws and punishments to stop the rising number of acid attacks in the country. The Colombian government imposes a six-hour curfew for men in the capital Bogotá, to allow women access to events organised by women's groups there. In Russia, the police let women off motoring offences, instead giving them gifts of perfume and flowers.

14–16 March A three-day demonstration is held in Barcelona, Spain, initially called by the Confederation of European Trade Unions, with representatives from the 15 EU countries. Protesters call for full employment and social rights. This coincides with the EU summit that marks the end of the Spanish EU Presidency. The event is also used by anti-capitalists and different civil society organisations both to protest at the policies of the EU and to hold a counter-conference to discuss alternatives. In preparation, the city launches its biggest security operation ever, with NATO AWACS surveillance planes patrolling the skies and jet fighters on alert. The Spanish authorities also temporarily suspend the free movement of EU citizens by bringing in passport checks that were made unnecessary by the Schengen Agreement of 1995. Despite this, it is estimated that 300,000 join the protests.

15 March The dramatic entry of 25 North Korean asylum seekers into the Spanish Embassy in China is found to be the result of months of collaboration between South Korean and overseas NGOs. The attempt was first proposed by a South Korean NGO based in China, and then supported by various domestic, Japanese, and European NGOs.

18–22 March In Monterrey, Mexico, the International Conference on Financing for Development is held, called by the UN. Simultaneously, peasants, indigenous organisations, and other civil society activists gather at the parallel summit, 'Social Assembly Another World is Possible', sponsored by the Foro Social Mexicano. They denounce the pauperisation of rural communities caused by policies of liberalisation and free trade, and emphasise their opposition to the Puebla-Panama Plan, which would convert southern Mexico and the whole of Central America into a free trade zone.

23 March In Rome, Italy, a mass demonstration and march with over one million workers takes place. Protesters travel to Rome from all over Italy on hired transport including 9,000 buses, 60 trains, 3 ships, and 2 planes. This is organised by trade unionists to defend labour rights, as the government plans to scrap legislation protecting employees from unfair dismissal.

24 March In Tel Aviv, a conference is held to bring together peace activists from a variety of groups. The theme is 'Israel in a Time of National Crisis'.

31 March In Ramallah, in the Palestinian Territories, an international civil society mission to support the Palestinian Authority Office under siege by Israeli troops is joined by a group of civil society activists including Jose Bové, the French peasant leader, members of the Genoa Social Forum, and a number of overseas activists. A group of these remain in the compound throughout the siege.

Late March–May In Azerbaijan, NGOs and international civil society groups working there learn by chance that parliament has passed a bill requiring organisations to register all grants with the central government before using the money. This has significant implications for the work of civil society and raises fears of government corruption and control. As the president has 54 days to sign the bill, the Eurasia Foundation organises a coordinated campaign with international organisations and the largest Azerbaijani NGO association. Major international donors, humanitarian NGOs, diplomatic representatives, oil companies, and local NGOs unanimously agree to fight the bill. As a result of protests held in the capital Baku and other regions of Azerbaijan, and the support demonstrated in Washington, London, Paris, and in European institutions in Strasbourg and Vienna, the bill remains unsigned.

April

6 April The Italian Consortium of Solidarity and a coalition of European civil society groups bring 400 people from the rest of Europe and the head of the EU Commission, Romano Prodi, to Bosnia to discuss integration and cooperation in the Balkans. The event is held under the banner 'Europe From Below in Sarajevo'.

6 April In Johannesburg, South Africa, a march to the home of Johannesburg's mayor takes place to protest against the privatisation of the state-owned electricity company, Eskom. Protesters claim that, to attract foreign investors, Eskom is disconnecting poor people who cannot afford the increase in bills while providing the 'cheapest electricity in the world' to minerals mega-corporations in South Africa, which produce vast carbon and sulphur dioxide emissions. As the protest reaches the mayor's house, a bodyguard shoots eight live rounds into the peaceful crowd, injuring two Sowetans. A total of 87 protesters face charges of 'public violence', a serious crime in South Africa, with 40 of those charged being elderly or children. Those charged later become known as the 'Kensington 87' and are the focus of an international justice campaign.

11 April In Cairo, 217 Egyptian NGOs representing 10 million citizens address a plea to global civil society to defend the Palestinian right to life. They address a message to American President George Bush, the EU, the UN Secretary General, and the Arab League Secretary General, as well as to human rights organisations.

11 April In Caracas, Venezuela, the federation of employers' associations, Fedecámaras, and the confederation of trade union workers, Confederación de Trabajadores de Venezuela, join forces to organise an Antichavista protest march to call for the resignation of Hugo Chávez. When marchers arrive at the presidential palace, 18 people die and 160 people are injured as a result of sniper fire. A government investigation into the incident remains open. A 24-hour coup d'état follows the march, led by the president of Fedecámaras Pedro Carmona and several military officers. All constitutional rights are suspended. However, due to international pressure and national mass demonstrations, President Hugo Chávez is returned to power, but approximately 40–60 protesters are killed during the events.

13 April Approximately 5,000 Arab and Israeli peace activists join a convoy organised by 'Ta'ayush: Arab-Jewish Partnership' to bring humanitarian aid to the devastated town of Jenin.

15–19 April In Washington DC representatives of rural workers from Brazil, Bolivia, Colombia, El Salvador, England, Germany, Guatemala, Honduras, Mexico, South Africa, Switzerland, Thailand, USA, and Zimbabwe attend a forum on 'The Negative Impact of World Bank Land Policies'. The objective is to promote an encounter of international civil society organisations, NGOs, social and popular movements, and universities to reinforce the discussion of agrarian reform and the market proposals of the World Bank.

17 April On the Worldwide Peasant Struggle Day, civil society organisations of farmers, rural workers, and peasants from around the world take part in a variety of activities to mark an international day of farmers' struggle. Co-ordinators of the campaign request that actions focus on the themes of seeds, the problem of patents, and the freeing of partners who are being persecuted or jailed. Actions include a Resistance is Fertile campaign in the Netherlands, involving the planting of eco-potatoes in GM test fields and the erection of DNA scarecrows, and land is taken by activists in Brazil and Guatemala. Other activities take place in Austria, Belgium, Canada, Honduras, India, Italy, Spain, and the USA.

21 April–5 May The shock victory of the far-right National Front leader, Jean-Marie Le Pen, in the first round of the French presidential elections sparks protests across Europe. These go on daily until he is defeated in the second round on 5 May. The largest protest is on 1 May, when 2 million demonstrate across France.

24 April In London, a protest is held outside the Royal Albert Hall where Henry Kissinger, the former US Secretary of State, is to address the Institute of Directors. Protesters claim he is a war criminal and should be tried for his involvement in past US foreign activities. Attempts to make a citizen's arrest fail, but judges in France and Spain make inquiries to Interpol about the visit as they wish to question him. The protests are part of an international campaign called Kissinger Watch, organised by the International Campaign against Impunity, working to highlight alleged war crimes of high-status figures.

Late April The founding conference of the Arab NGO Network is held in Beirut, Lebanon. The network aims to contribute to the enhancement of relations of cooperation between national and international associations active in sustainable development, and international and regional funding organisations, and also to promote civil society involvement in efforts aimed at achieving sustainable development.

May

1 May Around the world, Labour Day is celebrated by demonstrations for employment rights and economic and social justice. In Australia, the main theme is the government's immigration policy. In Cambodia, rival protests are held. Members of the largest union demonstrate in the capital, Phnom Penh, to demand better working conditions, while another group describing itself as the parents of workers, though allegedly organised by the government, drives through the city on open trucks claiming the union leaders are trouble-makers. In China, the continuing protests by laid-off and disaffected workers in the north-eastern cities of Liaoyang, Daqing, and Fushun are highlighted. In France, 2 million protest in more than 70 towns and cities to oppose the far-right presidential candidate Jean-Marie Le Pen. In Berlin, Germany, activists clash with police as 10,000 protesters hold a street party. A general strike is held in Greece to mark the day, and activists march to both the US and Israeli embassies to call for an end to attacks on Palestinians. 3,000 sex workers from India, Bangladesh, and Nepal hold a demonstration in Calcutta, India, to demand the right to legal status and social security. In the Philippines, a rally of 40,000 anti-government demonstrators takes place. Naga City stages the largest protest ever outside the capital, Manila, as peasants, public employees, labourers, and transport workers fill the main streets carrying red flags and placards. Most protesters call for the resignation of President Gloria Macapagal-Arroyo amid greater poverty brought about by liberal economic policies and increasing militarisation of the countryside. In Russia, rallies are held in 500 towns and cities. In the capital Moscow 140,000 trade unionists gather, and in a separate rally 100,000 communists meet in Karl Marx Square. Arrests are made in Singapore as civil rights activists attempt to stage a demonstration that does not have the approval of the authorities. In the UK, 15,000 march through the streets of London, for what is a peaceful protest after police intolerance dominated the event the previous year.

13 May Grass-roots-owned radio stations join together to form the Indonesian Community Radios Network in Jakarta, to defy the Government's planned new broadcasting law that would ban community media. After resistance also from corporate-owned radio and television stations, the government finally passes a new broadcasting law that acknowledges the community's right to broadcast.

20 May A Middle East peace conference takes place in Shefaram, Israel, 'Towards New Strategic Partnership Between Jews and Arabs in Israel', involving civil society peace organisations from a number of nations.

21 May In Argentina, tens of thousands of protesters take to the streets across the country to demand the free distribution of food and medicine to those who cannot now afford them. The high levels of unemployment and growing poverty are seen to be the result of the government's economic policies, which the demonstrators demand should be abandoned. This is followed by a 12-hour national strike.

26–27 May In Quito, Ecuador, civil society organisations from across Central and South America meet to participate in the Continental Campaign Against the Free Trade Agreement of the Americans (FTAA). Together they demonstrate their opposition to the creation of a hemispheric free trade area in the Americas.

27 May The Egyptian Shura Advisory Council, the Upper Chamber of the Egyptian Parliament, approves an NGO draft law which puts restrictions on the foreign funding of human rights organisations by requiring the prior authorisation of the Ministry of Social Affairs.

29 May A protest is called by trade union federations and civil society organisations representing the unemployed, students, and pensioners in Argentina. Tens of thousands join the protest, blocking all access roads into the capital Buenos Aires, striking from schools and hospitals, and setting up other roadblocks throughout the country. Some activists wave Argentine flags while burning American ones. They claim that the government's deal with the IMF only brings more unemployment, poverty, and hunger to the people.

30 May An international campaign to promote migrant workers' rights in Japan and South Korea is launched to coincide with the FIFA World Cup 2002, to bring attention to the initiative. The campaigners claim that war and neo-liberal globalisation have caused an increase in exploitative international migration, and that current policies are anti-migrant and racist.

June

5 June International NGOs such as Friends of the Earth, Greenpeace, and the World Wildlife Fund join thousands of protesters at the Indonesia People's Forum in Bali, Indonesia. This is a parallel summit to challenge the Fourth Preparatory Committee Meeting for the World Summit on Sustainable Development. The coalition rejects the results of the official meeting, claiming they are biased in favour of Northern countries' interests and do not accommodate peripheral voices from the civil society sector.

8 June It is announced that the World Alliance for Citizen Participation (Civicus) is to form a strategic partnership with OneWorld.net, an online network and portal of organisations working in human rights and sustainable development worldwide. Both organisations aim to strengthen civil society worldwide and to bring news of the sector to broader audiences.

9–13 June An NGO/Civil Society Organisation Forum on Food Sovereignty is held in Rome, Italy. This aims to set an Agenda for Action on Food Sovereignty, to be presented to the UN Food and Agricultural Organisation's World Food Summit to be held in Rome on 13 June.

20–22 June To coincide with the EU summit being held in Seville, Seville Social Forum organises two days of conferences, seminars, and grass-roots discussions on issues relating to immigration, social exclusion, and the casualisation of labour. The opening day is marked by a general strike organised by Spanish trade unions, with reports of up to 85 per cent support. The counter-conference ends with a 200,000-strong demonstration. During this, 300 international activists and immigrants lock themselves into Salvador University to protest against the anti-immigrant initiatives of the EU.

21 June In Israel, a demonstration named 'A Time for Peace in Jerusalem' is held with 1,000 European peace activists taking part. A planned human chain across the border between Israel and Palestine is banned by the Israeli authorities.

21–26 June A People's Summit is held is Calgary as an alternative to the G8 Summit in Kananaskis, Canada. It is named the 'G6B' to reflect a focus on the needs of the entire global population of 6 billion. The small mountain resort of Kananaskis has been chosen as the site of the official summit as it is difficult to access. Organisers of the demonstrations call for an end to costly 'summit-hopping' and instead protests occur in different cities, the biggest in Calgary. Nearly 5,000 police are involved in the security operation, with the city purchasing two RG-12 armoured vehicles at a cost of $1.1 million.

24 June The Annual World Bank Conference on Development Economics in Europe takes place in Oslo, Norway, and is paralleled by the counter-conference 'South Meets North'. This is organised by the civil society network Oslo2002, with the final demonstration of the event drawing 15,000 protesters.

25–28 June In Siby, Mali, in West Africa, the first counter-summit to the G8 to be organised by Africans takes place to protest against the dominant neo-liberal policies of international financial institutions and the agricultural policies of the World Bank. Participants include organisations of teachers, women, farmers, journalists, youths, and religious leaders, who have travelled from the rest of Mali, Burkina Faso, Niger, the Ivory Coast, and Senegal. The main themes of the summit are strategies for the reduction of poverty in Africa and the New Partnership Agreement for Africa's Development (NEPAD), both of which are also key issues at the official G8 summit. However, the summits differ in most other ways as the participants in Africa are the ones suffering from poverty as well as discussing it. The choice of venue is significant since, in contrast to the luxury of the G8 leaders in Kananaskis, Siby has no transportation system, no clean drinking water, and no access to telephones. The meetings and workshops take place in the open air and in the classrooms of a local school.

26 June During a protest in Argentina against the economic crisis, two demonstrators are killed as police try to stop over 2,000 poor and unemployed demonstrators from blocking access to a bridge into the capital Buenos Aires. Others are seriously injured when the police use batons and tear gas to disperse them. The demonstration is part of a larger campaign against the problems faced by the increasing numbers of poor and unemployed. Since the forced resignation of the government in December, demonstrations have been held on a nearly daily basis.

28–29 June In Xalapa, Mexico, civil society organisations from Central America meet under the slogan 'Because People are First: No to the Puebla-Panama Plan'. The activists demonstrate against the plan to integrate Mexico and Central America to create a huge free trade zone.

July

1 July The world's first International Criminal Court (ICC) comes into existence in The Hague, empowered to prosecute individuals anywhere in the world (with the provision that the country has ratified the treaty) for genocide, war crimes, and crimes against humanity. Civil society organisations, including women's groups, religious and human rights organisations, and peace activists, were seen to be instrumental in the drafting of the treaty, and their involvement has been seen as a significant success for global civil society. By this date, 74 countries have ratified the treaty; campaigners continue to put pressure on countries such as the USA, Russia, China, and Israel, which are refusing to do so.

1–5 July The first Preparatory Committee Meeting (PrepCom 1) of the World Summit on the Information Society (WSIS) is held in Geneva hosted by the UN, with a total of 969 participants from state bodies, international agencies, businesses, and civil society organisations. This culminates in a broad agreement that the stakeholders must coordinate and consolidate their efforts to ensure that information and communication technologies benefit all the inhabitants of the world. Preparations for the WSIS, which will take place in December 2003, are deemed vital, as representatives of civil society claim it will be the first time the UN allows civil society to participate in the negotiations themselves.

2 July In Syria, the founding meeting of the Independent Human Rights Society is held. The organisation aims to promote and monitor human rights in the country and to liaise with international human rights NGOs.

7 July After recent elections in Hungary, protests take place calling for a recount of the ballot papers, which are about to be destroyed as required by Hungarian law 90 days after the vote. The capital, Budapest, sees the first major civil disobedience action for ten years, bringing the centre to a standstill and blocking bridges. This leads to the court considering the demand for a recount due to allegations of election fraud and corruption.

9 July Activists call for Independence Day in Argentina to become 'A Day of Rage', with tens of thousands of protesters rallying on the streets of the country's cities to protest against the government's policies for dealing with the economic crisis. The groups involved include the unemployed, trade unions, students, and human rights activists.

14–19 July Geneva-based Mandat International convenes the World Civil Society Forum to promote cooperation among civil society organisations across the world, and to facilitate cooperation between organisations of civil society and the UN. A thousand participants attend, representing over 500 organisations from 70 countries, including many developing ones.

18–28 July The first Europe-wide 'no border camp' is initiated by the Noborder Network, organised by social movements from several European countries.

The camp consists of ten days of workshops and discussions around the central demand for 'Freedom of Movement and Settlement for Everyone'. Strasbourg is chosen because it is home to the central headquarters of the Schengen Information Systems (SIS), the database used to store details of immigrants, terrorists, political protestors, and 'anti-globalisation' protestors. About 2,000 people take part in the camp; and a sit-in of 1,000 protesters outside the European Court of Human Rights is organised under the slogan 'No border! No nation! Stop deportation!'.

20 July To commemorate the anniversary of the death of Carlo Giuliani, who was killed by police during the anti-G8 summit protests in Genoa in 2001, a week of activities culminates in a march of 150,000 people. In the port of Genoa, at exactly the time Carlo was killed, dockers sound their horns, hundreds of balloons are released in Piazza Alimonda, 'illegal immigrants' from Pakistan, Senegal, and Morocco landing at the sea front are welcomed with a brass band and fruit, and activists occupying the Diaz school, which was the site of violent police raids the previous year, unfurl banners stating 'This time, please knock before entering!'

26–28 July The Tunisian Foundation Mohamed Ali for Workers' Culture, an NGO working on the education of workers and the study of labour conditions, holds a forum on labour and economic changes and their impact on the labour market. The event is attended by European and Northern African trade unions and NGOs.

28 July In South Korea, the US military's apology for the deaths of two girls struck by a military vehicle is rebuked by NGO activists locally and internationally. In response a major protest is held in central Seoul demanding justice.

August

15 August A further hearing of the case against the Kensington 87, those arrested as a result of the march in Johannesburg on 6 April, takes place amidst strong protests in Johannesburg and around the world. The Jeppe Regional Courthouse in Johannesburg is surrounded by activists and human rights groups, and in London a demonstration is held outside South Africa House in support of those accused and to protest against the South African government's handling of the case.

22–24 August The Argentina Thematic Social Forum, which was planned at the WSF, opens in Buenos Aires with a march of 10,000 people. The themes of the forum are the campaign against the FTAA and neo-liberal policies, and alliance-building to help those in Argentina suffering from the country's economic crisis.

26 August–4 September The World Summit on Sustainable Development (WSSD) is held in Johannesburg, South Africa, and a counter-summit and protests held simultaneously by civil society organisations. Critics of the main summit, which is the follow-up to the 1992 Rio Summit on Climate Change, describe it as a failure and corporate washout, on the grounds that many aspects of the summit have been sponsored by multinationals and the outcomes benefit big business rather than the environment. NGOs use the opportunity to give 'greenwash' awards to those corporations which spend most on promoting their image of being socially responsible and environmentally friendly but which are allegedly guilty of major unethical practices.

31 August Coinciding with the summit in Johannesburg, a Global Day of Action Against a Corporate UN is marked around the world. In Croatia, groups distribute pamphlets on corporate greenwash and the global day of action. In Copenhagen, Nature and Youth, together with other groups, organise demonstrations in front of the parliament and in the main square. In Germany, a test field of Novartis and Agrevo genetically engineered plants is destroyed by environmental activists. In Amsterdam, a UN-Masquerade Parade with puppets, banners, samba band and dancers, as well as bicycle-powered music, attracts many activists. In Portugal, a group of activists attempt to wash the front of the offices of Monsanto, which they claim to be a 'greenwasher'. In Romania, a Food Not Bombs action is held, where information is also distributed on the corporate co-option of the UN and the WSSD. In Johannesburg, the World

Campaign for In-depth Reform of the System of International Institutions is launched, organised by the World Forum of Civil Society Networks (UBUNTU). In Barcelona, a protest takes place at the central office of the multinational Gas Natural and later at the local Greenpeace office, because the director of Greenpeace appeared in public together with the president of the World Business Council for Sustainable Development. The protesters argue that these kinds of partnerships legitimise business. In Sweden, activists from Fältbiologerna, Friends of The Earth, Green Youth, Loesje, ATTAC, and other organisations take part in a demonstration marching backwards to symbolise the direction in which the Johannesburg summit is taking the environment. Protesters also dress as business-people to kick an inflatable planet around. A Reclaim the Streets party is held in the financial centre of Switzerland in Zurich. In the UK, London Solidarity holds a protest at the headquarters of Anglo American.

31 August In Ireland, campaigners occupy the Carrickmines Castle Site in County Dublin to prevent the construction of a controversial motorway. This is the culmination of a month of protests by environmentalist groups, joined by international activists who aim to protect the medieval archaeological site in the path of the planned motorway. The site is a significant find, containing approximately 80,000 artefacts. Campaigners successfully block further construction in a court case which reveals government corruption. The campaign is destined to continue for the remainder of the year, employing tactics from international environmentalists developed during previous campaigns.

Late August and September The Syrian government initiates a series of arrests of civil society actors who liaise with international human rights organisations. Those arrested include Habib Issa and Wahid al Bunni, who attended the founding meeting of the Independent Human Rights Society in Syria on 2 July, and Kamal Labwani, member of the Administrative Council of the Committees for the Defence of Human Rights. International agencies condemn the arrests and work to free them.

September

6 September In Mexico, a group of native communities have their legal challenge to constitution reforms rejected. The challengers were protesting over the changes made to the original package of rights they were promised by the government. The original package was offered as a result of pressure from sustained campaigns by Zapatistas and civil society groups working for the rights of indigenous peoples. These included native rights to have authority over their own land and to own the land collectively rather than only individually. However, before the reforms were approved, amendments were made which significantly reduced the Indian rights offered by the package. The failure of this court case challenging the changes results in the amended version being implemented.

7 September Social movements in the Americas mobilise for the annual Cry of the Excluded protest, a huge grass-roots demonstration originally started in Brazil to highlight and condemn social exclusion. The protests this year take on a special meaning as the day is used to focus attention on the Continental Campaign Against the FTAA. Rallies and protest marches are organised throughout the countries of the Americas.

9 September A statement is released by 230 civil society organisations in South Korea, supported by international groups, calling for a withdrawal of the new migrant policy. They claim the policy's real aim is to expel 260,000 illegal foreign workers by March 2003, after which the government will reinforce the 'industrial trainee system'. Activists describe this system as modern-day slavery. Activists have been staging sit-ins since the measure was announced in July, religious organisations held a nine-day hunger strike, and the National Human Rights Commission drew up a policy resolution to abolish the trainee system as it systematically violates the human rights of migrant workers.

11 September Commemorative events are held across the USA and the world to remember the terrorist attacks of last year. The organisation, September Eleventh Family Members for Peaceful Tomorrows, which has become an active peace organisation, writes an open letter to President Bush to express its concerns about a possible war in Iraq.

14 September Under the banner 'Another World is Possible', a day of action and a protest march is held by 40,000 protesters in Cologne, Germany, to protest against process of neo-liberal globalisation and against a possible war in Iraq. The action is organised by youth trade union movements, ATTAC Germany, and peace organisations.

16 September In Colombia, 125,000 people, mainly belonging to associations of farmers, farm workers, and peasants, meet to protest and to discuss a Global Campaign for Agrarian Reform. The event is considered a success, as it takes place despite attempts to prevent their protest against neo-liberalism and the FTAA. The activists call for agrarian reform and the rights to life, to land, to work, and to organise. The mobilised farmers come under attack from public authorities, and two Spanish delegates are deported.

22 September The Countryside Alliance mobilises farmers and rural civil society organisations from across the UK for a march in London to highlight the problems faced by rural communities. An estimated 400,000 people take part as a result of much coordinated planning by concerned groups. A major theme is the protest against the proposed banning of hunting with dogs, although a spectrum of causes relating to rural life are represented. A counter-protest is also held by anti-hunt lobbyists.

25 September The citizens of Argentina turn out lights across the country in a mass protest against privatisation and the resulting rises in their utility bills. From 8 p.m. local time, protesters turn off lights inside and outside their homes for half an hour, and activists take to the streets with drums.

27 September Women's groups claim a victory in North Africa as 35 women gain seats in the 325-member Moroccan Parliament. In this first parliamentary election in the country since King Mohammed VI acceded to the throne in 1999, it had been determined that women would be guaranteed 10 per cent of the seats.

27–28 September In Washington DC, thousands of activists hold a two-day protest against international trading policies while the IMF and the World Bank hold their annual meeting. The event is also used as an anti-war platform, with thousands protesting outside the White House against the threat of military action in Iraq. Confrontations occur with the police, who are out in force in the capital, and mass arrests take place.

28 September One of Europe's largest anti-war protests in recent years takes place as approximately 400,000 demonstrators march through the streets of London. The anti-war protesters, from many different groups and individuals from all walks of life, come to demonstrate their opposition to the threatened military action in Iraq.

October

October In Bahrain, women's groups hold demonstrations in response to a new personal status law. This law establishes the minimum age for marriage as 16 for girls and 18 for boys, and requires men to provide support for divorced wives and minor children. However, as different versions will be enforced for different groups, demonstrators demand a unified law, rejecting the separate versions for Shi'ites and Sunnis.

5 October In Italy, a protest of one hundred cities against a possible war in Iraq draws 1.5 million protesters in a wave of local mobilisations.

5–12 October A week of actions against the militarisation of space takes places worldwide under the banner 'Keep Space for Peace'. This begins with 1,117 non-violent activists being arrested during a protest at the NATO nuclear base of Kleine Brogel, in north-east Belgium, thought to be the largest number of arrests during a single action in the country. Groups travel from the Netherlands, Germany, Italy, Sweden, Britain, France, and Finland to protest, numbering 2,000. A further example is a demonstration at Lakenheath airbase, UK, the biggest demonstration at the base since the 1980s.

8 October In Belarus, human rights organisations and other NGOs meet to coordinate their campaign against 'political disappearances' in the country. Several prominent politicians, civil servants, business people, and a journalist have disappeared in Belarus since 2000. This is attributed to the actions of an alleged death squad under presidential command.

Criminal investigations remain inconclusive, and protesters claim the government is not confronting the issue.

10 October In Pakistan, general elections are held for the first time in three years of military rule, partly as a result of sustained campaigns by civil society groups such as Human Rights Commission of Pakistan and Liberal Forum Pakistan, which campaigned with international support for the restoration of democracy. The new civilian prime minister is Zafarullah Khan Jamali. However, international democracy organisations claim this is only a minor success as President Pervez Musharraf, who came to power through a military coup in 1999, retains overall power and still has the authority to dissolve parliament and sack the prime minister.

12 October On Columbus Day, celebrated in the USA as the day the explorer 'discovered' America, civil society organisations across Central America protest against what they claim is a new wave of colonisation in the form of the FTAA and the Puebla-Panama Plan. In El Salvador, activists successfully bring the nation to a standstill, halting commerce and blocking most major highways and border crossings, with 23,000 demonstrators in at least 14 locations. Actions also take place in Brazil, the Dominican Republic, Mexico, and Nicaragua.

22 October In Los Cabos, Baja California, Mexico, leaders from the countries that constitute Asia-Pacific Economic Cooperation (APEC) meet. Meanwhile, trade unions demand the creation of a Labour Forum, and NGOs from the countries of the region participate in several parallel forums. The economic ministers in the region participate in a colloquium with NGOs and civil society leaders.

25 October–1 November In Ecuador, a Continental Encounter of Organisations of the Field brings together farmers groups, trade unions, and civil society groups working on land reform from around South America. The focus of the conference is the struggle for agrarian reform in the continent, and it aims to share experiences and develop a global campaign of actions for agrarian reform.

26 October The biggest anti-war demonstrations since the Vietnam War takes place in the USA, as 200,000 people march in Washington DC, 100,000 in San Francisco, and tens of thousands in other cities around the US. They announce the creation of a new anti-war movement to stop President George W. Bush's plans to wage war against Iraq.

27 October Many civil society groups worldwide welcome the announcement of Luis Inacio Lula da Silva's victory in the Brazilian presidential elections. Popularly known as Lula of the Workers Party, Partido dos Trabalhadores (PT), he has a strong civil society background, particularly through trade unions, and has been involved in the promotion of the WSF in Porto Alegre. He offers encouragement to civil society organisations by vowing to continue to promote civil society activity in the country and to help strengthen links internationally, as he supports much of the criticism made by many social movements against dominant neo-liberal economic policies.

29–30 October In Cairo, Egypt, a forum is held by trade unions, NGOs working on democracy and workers' rights, employers, and universities, with participants from Egypt, Syria, the Palestinian Territories, Cyprus, Tunisia, Spain, France, Greece, and Italy. It is sponsored by the European Commission, with topics including Euro-Mediterranean partnership and the participation of civil society, the right of association of trade unions and employers, the consultative role of social agents as a means to developing and strengthening democracy, and social dialogue in Spain, Egypt, Syria, Palestinian Territories, Cyprus, Tunisia, and at European Union level.

31 October Anti-war demonstrators in the UK use Hallowe'en to coordinate a day of protest against a possible war in Iraq. A major feature is an effort coordinated by university and college students to demonstrate via 'teach-ins', occupying lecture halls, and substituting normal teaching with debate on the war and protest methods. Marches, roadblocks, and cycle rides are held throughout the country, including a major transport bridge blockade in Wales, marches throughout cities in Scotland, Southampton's biggest ever protest in the form of a human roadblock, and the largest rally of the day in Parliament Square in London.

November

Early November Civil society organisations working for women's rights and equality in the Middle East claim a victory in Jordan. Legislation is passed enabling female citizens married to foreigners to pass on Jordanian citizenship to their offspring, and also allowing women to acquire passports without written permission from their husbands.

4 November Organisations making up the Anti-chavista movement in Venezuela hand over 1.5 million signatures to the National Electoral Council, demanding a consultative referendum to establish the extent of Chávez' support.

6–10 November As one of the regional forums planned at the WSF, the European Social Forum is held in Florence, Italy. This is seen to be one of the most successful events of global civil society so far in terms of the capacity to attract public attention and massive participation, and to make substantive proposals. The exact figure of participants is not known, since at 60,000 registration badges run out. Seminars and workshops focus on the three major themes of liberalism, war, and rights. The event culminates in a mass anti-war march through the city, with a record 1 million protesters estimated to have taken part. Despite security fears due to the problems met in Genoa last year, the event is described as peaceful.

14 November In Belarus, both chambers of parliament endorse a bill on charitable activity, which is the first law to be introduced to the parliament by the public. Furthermore, it overrules presidential versions of the bill. Civil society groups campaigned for the law because current legislation does not provide mechanisms for the work of NGOs, and the conditions for charitable activity are extremely harsh as there are no tax breaks on charitable donations and aid from abroad is subjected to 30 per cent tax. However, the bill has still to be signed by the president before it can become law.

14 November In Sydney, Australia, protests are held as trade ministers from 20 countries arrive for informal trade talks. The demonstrators, who include trade unionists, anti-capitalists, peace activists, and refugee advocates, march to the US consulate and the offices of the company responsible for asylum-seeker detention centres.

15–18 November The Uruguay Social Forum is held in the country's capital, Montevideo. The event starts with a march against the FTAA from the Plaza Libertad to the Esplanade of the University in Montevideo. During the three days, more than 100 hundreds events, including workshops, debates, and cultural events, take place.

19–22 November Volunteers from across Spain and Europe travel to Galicia, Spain, to help limit the devastating environmental damage caused by the sinking of the Prestige oil tanker. Civil organisations, including trade unions and ecologists, and individuals constitute the 'Nunca Mas Platform' to coordinate emergency recovery actions in Galicia and together call for tougher national and international legal measures to prevent this type of ecological disaster being repeated. Civil society groups are seen to be key to the coordination of immediate action and their successful mobilisation of volunteers is seen to counter the lack of immediate action by the Spanish government.

20 November This date marks the 13th anniversary of the adoption of the Convention on the Rights of the Child by the United Nations. However, leading NGOs working on children's rights make scathing attacks on the UN for using the occasion to promote the alliance between UNICEF and McDonald's, one of its major sponsors. An action alert is put out by the Alliance for a Corporate-Free UN, and the ensuing campaign results in UNICEF declaring that it intends to review its relationship with McDonald's in the coming year.

20 November In Katowice, southern Poland, 10,000 protesters march to demonstrate against the government closure of seven coal mines. Steelworkers and nurses join the miners in their protest as they also call for higher wages. Marching to the provincial governor's office, the protesters chant 'thieves' and then erect seven wooden crosses to represent the seven closures and the 35,000 miners that will be out of work as a result.

20–21 November A NATO summit in the Czech Republic is marked by a week of actions and demonstrations organised by anti-war protesters.

The main demonstration draws 4,000 activists to a march around the conference centre in Prague where the summit is being held.

23 November Irish peace activist Caoimhe Butterly is shot by Israeli forces in Jenin refugee camp as she tries to protect Palestinian children. This occurs during the same incursion as that in which UN worker Iain Hook is killed. Caoimhe Butterly is part of a peace group called Voices in the Wilderness, founded by Mary Kelly, an Irish American.

25 November The global trade union, the International Transport Workers Federation (ITF), Greenpeace International, and the conservation organisation, the World Wildlife Fund (WWF), take the unusual step of joining forces to appeal to UN Secretary General Kofi Anan for fundamental reform of the vast worldwide shipping industry.

30 November Australia's largest anti-war demonstration in recent years is held as 15,000 protesters march through Sydney, and further rallies occur simultaneously in the capital Canberra, Adelaide, and Melbourne. The demonstrators call for diplomacy not military intervention in Iraq, after Prime Minister John Howard has already committed Australian troops to support any American-led campaign.

December

2 December The fourth general strike starts in Venezuela, this time of indeterminate duration. Small, medium-sized, and large companies participate, as well as managers of the PDVSA oil company at the centre of the original dispute. Eventually banks, custom officers, and airports join the strike to bring the country to a virtual standstill.

2 December An anti-war protest in central London brings traffic in Whitehall to a standstill as demonstrators lie down in the road to represent the possible civilian victims of a war in Iraq. Many are wrapped in bandages daubed with red paint to represent the blood that could be shed.

7 December The Miss World beauty contest takes place in London despite protests from women's groups. The contest arrives from Nigeria after being forced to decamp when 200 Nigerians died in riots following a controversial newspaper article about the event. Some contestants had previously resigned from the contest in protest over conditions for women in Nigeria, and in particular over the case of a women sentenced to death by stoning for adultery in northern Nigeria, where shariah law is practised. The organisers of the event come under strong criticism for not taking into account the religious context and the human rights record of the host country.

9–13 December The Asian Civil Society Forum is held in Bangkok, Thailand. This aims to promote cooperation and solidarity among NGOs in Asia engaged in advocacy activities with the UN. Around 200 organisations from Asia and, to a lesser extent, from other parts of the world are represented.

10 December Around the world, International Human Rights Day is used to highlight human-rights abuses and the campaigns of international human rights organisations. During a protest march in Indian-administered Kashmir, the leading human rights activist and chairman of the state's Human Rights Forum, Mohammad Ahsan Untoo, sets himself on fire to protest against alleged human rights abuses by the armed forces and police. He is not seriously injured. Peace activists in America initiate a Day of Human Rights Action and hold mass protests against possible war in Iraq and also against the conditions for prisoners held at Guantanamo Bay. Demonstrations and marches are held in over 100 towns and cities in the US. In the UK, the occasion is used to highlight the plight of journalists imprisoned worldwide. Prisoners in Belarus, Burma, China, Cuba, Eritrea, Nepal, Russia, Tunisia, and Uzbekistan are the focus of the campaign.

12 December Demonstrations are held across Italy to protest against the arrest of 20 Italian activists who were centrally involved in the organisation of the European Social Forum in Florence in November. Several of the charges brought against them were made under laws enacted during Fascist rule of the 1920s and never repealed. 100,000 people demonstrate in Cosenza and 20,000 in Florence to call for the charges to be dropped.

12–15 December During the EU summit in Copenhagen, an alternative civil society forum is organised by 59 NGOs. The parallel summit includes numerous lectures, discussions, and demonstrations against attacks on the welfare state throughout Europe, the economic and social consequences of EU plans for eastward expansion, and the process of growing militarism, as well as EU policies on migration. The forum ends with a 10,000-strong Our World is Not for Sale demonstration outside Christianborg, the castle housing the Danish government. Fifteen activists are arrested, mainly for wearing masks, which is illegal in Denmark. It is later discovered that one of those arrested is an undercover police officer.

18 December International Migrants Day is celebrated around the world on or around this date by civil society organisations working for labour and migrant rights. A major theme of events is the need to ratify the UN Convention of 1990 for the Protection of the Rights of All Migrant Workers and Members of their Families. Demonstrations to pressure governments into ratifying this are held in Bangladesh, Belgium, Chile, Ireland, Japan, and Indonesia. Forums and conferences are organised to promote awareness of this issue and others concerning worker's rights in Canada, Israel, Italy, Malaysia, Nepal, Sri Lanka, and the USA. Many of these activities and others are highlighted and supported by the web-based portal for the promotion and protection of the rights of migrants, December18.net.

19–20 December Two days of protests take place in Argentina to mark the anniversary of the deaths during street protests one year ago which led to the downfall of President Fernando de la Rua. Protesters use the opportunity to show their displeasure at the current government's handling of the economy, as they burn effigies of politicians and throw paint at the stock exchange.

20–21 December A Global Day of Disobedience is organised in solidarity with the people of Argentina and to protest against consumerist culture, on the retailers' busiest day of the year. In London's Oxford Street, The Wombles with other groups organise a Free Shop where books, CDs, toys, and clothes can be 'bought' for free, a mobile kitchen gives away free vegetarian burgers and other food, and free dancing lessons are offered. Similar actions are organised by Disobbedienti in Italy, JNM in Belgium, Yomango in Spain, Black Revolution in Switzerland, and other groups in Jordan, Finland, the US, and Germany.

20–22 December The Moroccan Social Forum takes place in Bouznika, northern Morocco. Participants are from a diverse range of civil society groups, and workshops are held under the banner Another Morocco is Possible.

26 December In Shefaram, Israel, A Day of Civil Hearing is held, which brings together peace activists from Palestine, Israel, and a number of other countries to discuss the current conflict.

27–30 December The Thematic Social Forum Palestine, which was planned at the World Social Forum, is held in Ramallah, the Palestinian city under siege by Israel. This is jointly organised by Israeli and Palestinian groups. A total of 750 activists take part, 500 from Palestine and 250 from around the world. Delegates have problems getting to the venue, with some Belgians, Spaniards, and Filipinos being sent home on their arrival at Tel Aviv airport. The forum's main aim is to integrate the problems of the Middle East into the agenda of global civil society.

31 December In Australia, protests are held at refugee asylums in Sydney and the remote centre of Woomera in the South Australian desert. Detained refugees and human rights and immigrant advocacy organisations call on the Australian government to end mandatory detention of all asylum seekers, including children. They also call for an end to the policy of diverting all refugee boats, which mainly contain Afghan and Middle Eastern asylum seekers, to the Pacific Islands. These policies have brought criticism from international refugee organisations as well as from the United Nations.

Global Civil Society: A Text without a Context

Update on Chapter 2, 2002

Neera Chandhoke

We live in a world where capital marches across the borders of the countries of the South as if they were simply not there. We live in a world where armies of major powers march across the borders of the countries of the South as if these borders were just irrelevant. But we also live in a world where people have come together in massive demonstrations to protest against both these developments. At the end of 1999 for instance, protests involving some 700 organisations and about 40,000 students, workers, NGOs, religious groups, and representatives of business and finance brought the third ministerial meeting of the World Trade Organisation (WTO) at Seattle to a halt. The WTO was to set in motion a new multilateral round of trade negotiations. Collective anger at the relocation of industries to the Third World, at the unsafe and abusive work conditions in the sweatshops found there, at environmental degradation, and at the wide spread exploitation of working people, exploded in a series of angry demonstrations. Though large-scale protests against the WTO, the International Monetary Fund, and the World Bank were not new, what was new was both the scale of mobilisation and the intensity of protest. Demonstrations by students, unions, environmentalists or 'tree huggers', economic and xenophobic nationalists, church groups, anarchists, protectionists, consumer groups, NGOs, and even business and financial groups, were hailed by some scholars as 'globalisation from below', or as heralding a new internationalism. The space where all this took place is global civil society.

Ever since the latter part of 2002 when it became clear that the US was preparing to invade Iraq for its own purposes, we were to once again witness a major mobilisation, this time against the war. Mammoth demonstrations in most large and many small cities of the world exhibited both ire and revulsion at the idea of the US invading a sovereign country without any substantive reason and without the sanction of the UN. The scale of the protest against the war was truly impressive. Political activists were connecting via the Internet, the Security Council of the UN was bombarded with anxious e-mails, major rallies protesting against the war dotted landscapes from Spain to Washington to London, and politically committed observers authored impassioned pieces on why the Bush government should not subject the innocent people of Iraq to more suffering. The space where all this took place is global civil society.

Political commentators compare incensed demonstrations in cities across the world with the anti-War protests in the late 1960s against American intervention in Vietnam. Yet we find a major difference between the two protests. For the anti-Vietnam war movement was to have some kind of impact upon the American government, even as it forced the government to withdraw from its determination to fight Communism in a third world country. Further, allied as it was to other protest movements—the civil liberties movement of the Afro-Americans, the women's movement, the sexual liberation movement, the anti-nuclear movement, and the labour movement—the anti-Vietnam movement marked a turning point in American politics. Most of the progressive legislation in American politics can in fact be traced to the social upheavals of the late 1960s. Today the American and the British people have, along with people in other parts of the world, launched a virtual tirade against the war in Iraq. But this has had little impact upon the determination of George Bush and Tony Blair to make the world safe for their own projects. Why is this so? Why did the anti-Vietnam war protests make history, and why have the current demonstrations failed to speak back to the making of history in an imperialist mode?

The difference perhaps does not lie in the text; it lies in the context. Recollect for instance that protests against American involvement in Vietnam were to take place in an era of virulent anti-imperialism, in an era of politicisation. When we look back upon the first three-quarters of the twentieth century, the one thing that strikes us is the way ordinary people across the world had been politicised through processes of sustained mass struggle. People became aware of what it was that they were fighting for; they become conscious of what was possible and probable; what was politically desirable, and what was not, what has to be fought against, and what has to be fought for. In short ordinary people became supremely conscious of both the constraints and the opportunities of history, and indeed aware that ordinary people have the capacity to speak back to histories of oppression.

Remember in this connection how people, forsaking the ordinariness of their daily lives, were to participate in the major political events of the twentieth century—the Bolshevik revolution, the Chinese revolution, the Vietnamese revolution, or the revolution in the small undistinguished colony of Guinea Bissau. The last managed to overturn the regime in the capital of the colonial power Portugal. Above all people were politicised all over the continents of Asia and Africa in the cause of anti-imperialism. In the course of these struggles, people were inspired by the grand visions that Marx, that Mao, that Gandhi, that Ho Chi Min, that Frantz Fanon, and that Amilcar Cabral had fashioned for human emancipation. Not all these protests succeeded in the long run, many of them failed, but that is not the point. The point is that ordinary people garnered the courage to speak back to history, to participate in the making of history.

But history can be made only if people have both the vocabulary and the vision of an alternative world to struggle for. This vision was given by the vocabularies of the twentieth century: imperialism, anti-colonialism, oppression, power, struggle, emancipation, and swaraj. It was in this context that the struggle against American involvement in Vietnam was waged. It was waged in the midst of political imaginations that resonated with anti-imperialism, with the determination to roll back any kind of muscle-flexing.

By the last two decades of the twentieth century however a gigantic process was set in motion—a process of taming unruly and recalcitrant civil societies; a process of de-politicisation of people who had once been made aware of the possibilities of history. Witness the political languages that have erupted recently onto the political scene: globalisation instead of imperialism, governance instead of politics, social capital and trust instead of struggle, community instead of class, civil society instead of the revolutionary imaginaries, and NGOs instead of popular mobilisation. These vocabularies are so trite that they seem banal, our political visions are so ordinary that they seem commonplace.

No longer do we find any idea of struggle and emancipation in these political vocabularies, only ideas of resignation. In the middle of these political languages that call for social capital and for building networks of trust—vocabularies that conjure away the fact of political, social, and economic oppression through semantic engineering—anti-war protests and also the anti-globalisation protests stand alone. And we all know what happens to political struggles when they stand alone and bereft of support from attendant ideas of solidarity against anti-imperialism, they become isolated.

If global civil society has to make any headway in its self-appointed task of bringing states driven by imperatives of power back to civility, its members will have to bring back the revolutionary imaginary. They will have to sharpen political sensibilities and generate new visions of what is a desirable world. Global civil society will at some point have to begin to think of contexts instead of isolated texts.

Media and Empowerment in Developing Countries

Update on Chapter 7, 2002

James Deane

The chapter entitled 'The Other Information Revolution: Media and Empowerment in Developing Countries', in *Global Civil Society 2002*, made three main claims:

First, that a major liberalisation and commercialisation of media over the last decade had led at once to a much more democratic, dynamic, crowded, complex media landscape - which particularly in the field of radio was opening up new spaces for public debate and civic engagement; and to a more commercial, advertising driven media in which information and power divisions within developing countries between rich and poor, urban and rural were growing.

Second, that increased concentration of media ownership—at the global, regional and national levels—was squeezing out independent media players and threatening to replace an earlier government controlled concentration of media power with a commercial and political one.

Third, that developing countries were increasingly, not decreasingly, reliant on powerful Northern news providers (BBC, Reuters, CNN etc) for their international news and information, particularly on global stories of globalisation, trade and international politics; and that, in newly democratic countries in the South, and particularly within civil society, there is a renewed and growing frustration at the Southern media's dependence on what are perceived to be partial, biased or at least fundamentally western centric news organisations for international coverage and the setting of news agendas.

Of these three trends, the most substantial changes over the last year have related to the final one. They are exemplified by two main stories - the Iraqi war and the revelation that more than 3 million people have died in the Congo as a consequence of an almost invisible and unreported war.

The dominant global media stories since *Global Civil Society 2002* was written—the Afghan conflict, the hunt for Al Qaeda and the prelude, implementation and aftermath of the war against Iraq—have catalysed major new challenges to the Western media domination of international news coverage.

The challenge of Al Jazeera and other Arabic satellite channels to the global western based news networks - already highlighted in the last Yearbook - has intensified. Vilified by western political leaders and much of the mainstream western media for its sensational and graphic coverage of the Iraqi war, Al Jazeera in particular has established itself as the media most trusted by publics in the Arabic world. For the first time, the Arab world has a news source which it regards as credible, accurate and reasonably free of political control, and which above all is rooted in and reflects the values of the region. Targeted, according to some commentators, by US forces in their bombing of its offices and the killing of a journalist, and by hackers disabling the English language website, it has also been the subject of the most visible and intensive, if probably uncoordinated, attack on freedom of expression to emerge from Western countries targeted at a southern news operation in recent years.

This raises the question of whether the emergence of Al Jazeera is indicative of a broader trend in the developing world, and whether it is possible to discern a new generation of developing country or non western transnational media capable of establishing a credible, independent, professional—if highly contentious—news sources which reflect the priorities of their publics. The probable answer is that Al Jazeera is unique and no such wider trend is discernible. No similar news based service of comparable independence, credibility and penetration has emerged in South Asia, for example, or in Africa.

Nor have these events challenged the capacity of the western media to set media agendas for the rest of the world. Issues of debt, globalisation, terms of trade and other issues of concern to the vast majority of people on the planet continue to be highlighted and placed on global media agendas only in relation to their interest to the media in the West; media in most developing countries, with declining resources for their own international news coverage, continue to reflect these global news stories. Some hopes were expressed after the appalling attacks of September 11 that a new interest and curiosity about global affairs and the poorer nations of the world would emerge in the US and elsewhere in the West. Arguably, the opposite has happened and the media are providing less context, less diversity of perspectives, less insight, and more uniformity of coverage than before the attacks, and providing less information for their audiences to make sense of the world than before.

The 2002 Yearbook pointed to the Internet and the emergence of civil society and southern based news networks and services as a key potential way of countering these trends. However, where internet news sites have mattered and had an impact they have often been attacked, and even the best independent sites have faced difficulties. Tehelka.com, the Indian internet site whose investigative journalism triggered a major scandal over defence procurement and led to the resignation of defence minister, George Fernandes, has been subject to an extraordinarily intensive establishment onslaught, with its staff now reduced from 120 people to three, and having incurred substantial debts (it has recently launched a recovery plan and plans for a new newspaper). Mediachannel.org, which probably provides the best analysis and tracking of public interest media issues anywhere, is struggling financially because of the death of a key investor. The story is repeated among several other leading alternative internet sites.

For the vast majority of people on the planet, and particularly the more than 2.7 billion people living on less than two dollars a day, the international media—with important exceptions such as the BBC World Service—have shown themselves largely uninterested and incapable of reflecting their realities. The revelation by the New York based International Rescue Committee that more than 3 million people have died in the Democratic Republic of Congo as a consequence of war in the country since 1998 – more people than any other conflict since World War II, is shocking in itself. The fact that the war has been almost universally ignored internationally makes it inexcusable.

The picture painted in the 2002 Yearbook was a mixed one, but its principal analysis argued that little progress towards greater equity or development could be achieved unless the concerns of those most excluded from national and international affairs were reflected through public interest media. The final analysis was a grim one. That analysis has been mostly reinforced since.

Towards a Working International Criminal Court

Update on Chapter 6, 2002

Marlies Glasius

The judges for the International Criminal Court (ICC) were elected in March 2002, and the new Prosecutor, Luis Moreno Ocampo, started work on 16 June 2003. The ICC is ready to begin hearing cases in the coming year.

Global civil society, which played such a major part in the drafting and adoption of the Court Statute (see chapter 6 in Global Civil Society 2002) has continued to follow and help shape the establishment of the Court. The large number of female judges elected (seven out of eighteen, despite a disappointing number of female candidates), can be attributed to the efforts of the organisations forming the Coalition for an International Criminal Court (www.iccnow.org) in general, and the Women's Caucus in particular. Luis Moreno Ocampo, the Argentine lawyer who successfully prosecuted members of the Argentine junta for human rights violations directly after the transition to democracy, is civil society's dream candidate for prosecutor.

The work of civil society organisations with respect to the ICC now focuses on obtaining ratifications and supporting the adoption of implementing legislation. At the time of writing, ninety countries had ratified the Statute. While there is great enthusiasm for the Court in Africa, Europe and Latin-America, ratifications in Asia continue to lag. In many countries, civil society organisations are actively consulted in the ratification process and adoption of implementing legislation; in the Democratic Republic of Congo the legislation was actually finalised in a series of seminars in which both government officials and civil society experts participated. The Coalition for an International Criminal Court has been decentralised, and now has offices in Africa, Asia and Latin-America, as well as New York and The Hague. In many countries, local organisations have formed national coalitions, too.

The United States continues to oppose the ICC with all its might. It uses carrot and stick tactics concerning military and development aid to push other countries, especially poor and small states, into concluding so-called immunity (or according to civil society organisations: impunity) agreements for US citizens stationed in these countries. At the time of writing it had concluded thirty-four such agreements, however, many of these were with micro-states and less than half were states parties to the Court. Meanwhile, thirty non-governmental organisations in the U.S. have founded AMICC (www.amicc.org), a coalition committed to achieving full United States support for the ICC. They hope that in the long run, the US will give up its opposition and become a party to the ICC.

While U.S. opposition will not prevent the Court from assuming its case load, it does block the possibility of making use of the Court in some of the most appropriate cases. Security Council resolutions would make it possible for the prosecutor to investigate both alleged Al-Qaeda members captured in Afghanistan and members of Saddam Hussein's regime for war crimes and crimes against humanity. The US would, of course, veto any attempt to adopt such resolutions.

Who's Minding the Store? Global Civil Society and Corporate Responsibility

Update on Chapter 4, 2002

Melanie Beth Oliviero and Adele Simmons

In our chapter in *Global Civil Society 2002* we mapped the tactical advances that civil society organisations (CSOs) have made in pressing for corporate social responsibility (CSR). We ended with the question: 'Are these CSOs "making a difference?"' CSOs are still assuming a role that governments should be undertaking. At the same time, there is growing recognition that countries that are competing for foreign direct investment (FDI) are not likely to be leaders in setting high standards for corporate investors. Governments facing this tension between attracting FDI and setting high standards are still more likely to sacrifice the latter for the former.

While incremental progress has been made in developing incentives for companies to take the social good into account, mandates abound without enforcement, especially in the home countries of large multinational corporations. When nations are preoccupied with foreign policy crises, the attention paid to domestic matters wanes. This phenomenon affects CSOs, as well. While civil society mobilisation exhibited dramatic global convergence in early 2003, the shift to organising anti-war activities distracted from the focus on corporate practice.

Among the new initiatives is the legislative proposal of the US Office of the Trade Representative to make the 'Kimberley Process' for certifying diamonds a legitimate human rights component of trade agreements. Such national legislation will ban non-certified diamonds. Designating an exemption to trade rules for human rights purposes in this case is a development that could create a precedent and reorder priorities, placing human life above economic gain.

A broader extraction industry approach is being directed at Western nations in the form of the Publish What You Pay Initiative (PWYP) of George Soros and the Open Society Institute announced in June 2002 which calls for new standards of transparency. Modelled on the success of OECD and US anti-bribery conventions, PWYP calls for regulations that require companies headquartered in G8 countries to disclose all payments to foreign governments. The goal is to generate information that local CSOs can use to 'follow the money' and hold their governments accountable. The British international NGO, Global Witness, has been designated to lead the campaign.

There are indications that the voluntary corporate social responsibility (CSR) code approach is having an impact on government policy in less developed countries. Contrary to the trend of attracting FDI, Vietnam is positioning itself to be the socially responsible alternative in Asia for retailers in search of cheap labour. The government, along with factory managers, trade unions, and international retailers, is working with the Corporate Social Responsibility Practice unit of the World Bank to develop standards that meet the International Labour Organization (ILO) and human rights conventions' requirements. It is not yet clear that the supply chain of global manufacturing can be reinvented through a governmental policy framework. Notwithstanding this overt strategy of the Vietnamese government, low wages and less accountable workplaces elsewhere may still win out.

As reported in our 2002 chapter, CSOs in the United States have applied a 1789 statute, the Alien Tort Claims Act (ATCA), to hold private companies accountable for human rights abuses wherever they do business. The first of these cases achieved a major breakthrough. After years of procedural motions in both the federal and state of California courts, the cases filed on behalf of Burmese villagers enslaved and forced to work in violation of their human rights on a UNOCAL pipeline project are finally scheduled to be heard on their merits. Federal judges meeting *en banc* will now decide what UNOCAL knew and did not know about the abuses inflicted on workers. At the same time, members of the US Congress are being lobbied by oil companies named in these suits through the US Chamber of Commerce and an association of like-minded corporate interests to pass legislation overturning the ATCA.

Corporate opposition to civil society efforts continues. For example, the sugar industry has attacked the World Health Organization (WHO) for its guidelines recommending on health grounds that sugar intake be limited to 10 per cent of total daily consumption. The companies are lobbying the US Congress to withhold the entire US funding allocation for WHO, and misrepresenting research data from independent sources.

On the positive side, new cooperative agreements were also reached. The 2002 agreement between the COLISBA federation of Central American banana worker unions and the Chiquita corporation that secures workers' rights has become the platform for further CSR advances. Third-party evaluators (such as COVERCO) have been engaged to monitor the agreement. As the economic strains on the industry continue to squeeze producers, Chiquita has focused its cost-cutting efforts on sustainable agriculture practices and logistical reforms rather than workforce reduction. (US/LEAP (url); Silver, 2002)

CSO evolution

As approaches to CSR evolve, so does the capacity of civil society organisations. CSOs are demonstrating greater awareness of their own effectiveness and need for accountability. To that end, groups are becoming more transparent and seeking to work with one another, minimising duplication and sharing learning experiences. For example, a consortium of labour and women's groups has formed the Central American/Caribbean 'Regional Initiative for Social Responsibility and Jobs with Dignity' to increase the capacity of Southern CSOs to hold multinational companies accountable. And the Fair Labor Association now posts reports of monitors on its web-site.

Direct action continues to be necessary and effective. As the 2002 Yearbook was going to press, the middle-aged wives and mothers of the Niger Delta were taking matters into their own hands and occupying the Chevron Nigeria Ltd. oil facilities. They deliberately chose not to inform the traditional (male) leaders and organised themselves independently. Alarmed at the environmental degradation, economic exploitation of their communities, and government failure to respond, the women confronted the company directly. As a result, company officials have entered into a Memorandum of Understanding with the women and agreed to regular job offers for community members, increased support for schools fees, and a credit program to aid local business development in ten communities.

The investor owners of pension funds, which represent the largest holders of equity securities worldwide – more than half of the US$ 7.5 trillion total – are also increasing pressure on companies. Voting of proxies and submission of shareholder resolutions have increased in 2003. Exercising their ownership responsibilities, these shareholders have forced companies to measure performance with regard to global warming, global labour standards, the AIDS pandemic, and sustainability reporting, among other social and environmental imperatives.

Future directions

Many in the civil society and business sectors are also thinking beyond the codes of conduct and monitoring approaches. The profusion and incompatibility of codes and standards has frustrated many in civil society, government, and the private sector. The Global Reporting Initiative, the UN Global Compact, and the International Standards Organization (ISO) are collaborating on something akin to the International Accounting Standards Board to align the different standards and codes of conduct.

Other groups are focusing on more systemic changes, such as strengthening worker representation in the factory. Inspections and monitoring are still important, but effective communication within a factory can promote a culture of accountability that is more pervasive. The worker health and safety committees in China that were highlighted in the 2002 chapter continue to expand in the direction of this goal. Secret-ballot elections for self-selected union candidates were recently held for the first time in two Chinese factories (owned by Taiwanese and Hong Kong firms). The union is the state-sponsored All China Federation of Trade Unions, but this is the first time rank and file members have been permitted to serve as representatives. Reebok has been widely credited with facilitating this process. As the major contractor to these two factories, it leveraged its clout to provide an impetus for the management to cooperate with the labour rights organisations Chinese Working Women's Network, Hong Kong Christian Industrial Committee and the Asia Monitor Resource Centre (Maitland, 2002; Reebok, 2003, 25).

Conclusion

Civil society groups remain focused on reducing harmful consequences of irresponsible corporate practice through direct action, research, and collaborative strategies. Companies in various sectors have continued to respond, and in some cases, take the lead in instituting reforms. And governments have considered, and to a lesser degree, enacted, policies that encourage socially responsible corporate behavior though trade and tax incentives, and stepped up enforcement of disincentives.

While there are signs of progress, there are also areas characterised by persistent inertia and even opportunistic attempts to backslide while attention is diverted elsewhere. Civil society must remain vigilant. Opportunism works both ways. The 2008 Olympics in China present a strategic lever in advancing corporate accountability. The evidence remains clear that neither government nor the private sector is going to take the lead. More watchdogs, more research, more challenging questions such as whether disclosure requirements actually free markets to respond to civil society pressures need to be tested. Ultimately it is to civil society that corporations must be accountable.

References

Maitland, Alison (2002). 'Inside Track: Sewing a Seam of Worker Democracy in China'. *Financial Times.* 12 December 2002.

Reebok International Ltd. (2003). *Our Commitment to Human Rights.* http://www.reebok.com/x/us/humanRights/pdf/ReebokHR_OurCommitment.pdf

Silver, Sara (2002). 'Inside Track: The Banana Giant that Found Its Gentle Side'. *Financial Times.* 2 December 2002.

US/LEAP (US Labor Education in the Americas Project (url). www.usleap.org.

Funding Global Civil Society Organisations

Update on Chapter 8, 2001

Frances Pinter

This update should be read in conjunction with Chapter Eight of the first edition of the Global Civil Society Yearbook (2001). There the main argument is made that the bulk of the funding for global civil society organisations (CSOs) comes from development initiatives of one form or another. At the turn of the millennium about $7 billion flowed from the multilateral and bilateral agencies into the civil society sector. The second largest source of CSO funding came from Western (primarily US) foundations, of which something in the order of 16 per cent of the total $2 billion given in 2000 went to international/cross-border programmes.

Within these overall figures certain trends should be noted; first the backdrop of the nineties. Although funding for development in general decreased, the amount directed towards and through CSOs grew. Money poured into private foundations as wealth appeared to be magically created on the stock markets. CSOs were becoming more professional and successful at raising funds. The Internet made it easier to access funding sources. The politics of funding was such that money was beginning to be directed at Southern/Eastern NGOs, increasingly bypassing the established Northern/Western organisations.

The World Bank, while still working with CSOs, has moved on from its first flush of enthusiasm to a more reserved position as both sides vacillate between optimism and skepticism about the cost and efficiency of collaboration. The link between development and security which followed from the attacks of 11 September has entered a new phase as a result of the war in Iraq and at the time of writing the precise positioning of CSOs from various sectors in a post-war situation is unclear.

The decline in the global equity market has adversely affected the assets of many private foundations. And while giving levels remained static between 2001 and 2002, a drop in 2003 is anticipated. To put this into perspective, this follows a period of six years in which growth was always measured in double digits. While the assets of the larger foundations have fallen in value by an average of 10-12 per cent the number of new foundations has increased, registered foundations in the US alone rose by 9.2 per cent in 2001 and a further increase is expected for 2002 (final figures not available yet.) However, international giving fell to 14.9 per cent of the total in 2002 from a high of 16.3 per cent in 2001. The amounts ear-marked for international causes that were channelled through US NGOs rather than directly to recipient country NGOs has increased from $1.5 billion to $1.7 billion, reversing the trend mentioned earlier.

At the same time some positive initiatives to make giving easier are bearing fruit. Guidestar UK followed in the footsteps of Guidestar in the US, greatly facilitating on-line giving, thus enabling greater numbers of people to support civil society causes. The International Gift Planning Alliance is an instance of consolidation that pulls together national and regional bodies (in this case the National Committee on Planned Giving in the USA, the European Association for Planned Giving and the Canadian Association of Gift Planners) to improve the skills and opportunities of philanthropists worldwide.

Global Cities and Diasporic Networks

Update on Chapter 9, 2002

Saskia Sassen

This chapter focused on disadvantaged sectors in global cities: a variety of groupings and organisations with limited resources, limited or no power, often without proper documentation, often invisible to national politics and national civil society, and unrecognised as politico/civic actors or unauthorised to be such by the formal political system.

The effort was to understand whether and how such disadvantaged sectors can be part of and contribute to constituting global civil society. In this regard the chapter was a critical response to a common assumption that global civil society is fundamentally a kind of cosmopolitanism. It showed that types of groups and organisations that are basically place-bound and concerned with localised struggles can nonetheless become part of global networks and horizontal forms of globality. This opens up the conceptual framework for detecting conditions for and modes of participation in global civil society. It makes legible the existence of non-cosmopolitan forms of global practice and consciousness.

The key spaces where these dynamics were identified are of two types. One is the concrete space of the city, particularly the global city, as a space for politico-civic activities (as distinct from the highly formalised space of national politics and national civil society); the global city is also a strategic space for the command functions of global corporate capital. The other space is that of partly de-territorialised global networks; this is a space at least partly constituted via the new digital media, especially the public-access Internet in the case of to the disadvantaged, and the high-performance private digital networks in the case of global corporate capital.

The key issues I focused on were of five types: a) the forms of politico-civic engagement that are made possible for the disadvantaged in global cities (at least partly enabled by globalisation and the human rights regime and its consequences for older hierarchies of formalised power); b) the extent to which the presence of immigrant communities produces specific transnational forms of engagement and to what extent it enables immigrant groups to begin to think of themselves as global Diasporas, rather than expatriates; c) the extent to which access to the new media, specifically the Internet, allows/induces other types of groups to transnationalise their efforts (e.g. poor women's organisations such as SPARC); d) the types of engagement made possible in the global city between the disadvantaged and global corporate power; e) the extent to which these multiple activities and engagements contribute to denationalise the global city and thereby enable more global forms of consciousness and notions of membership/belonging.

The chapter showed how these types of actors and spaces produce a concrete social infrastructure for some of the components of global civil society. So the question then becomes how the post-September 11 2001 events have affected this social infrastructure. In terms of the types of issues discussed in the chapter, one of the most significant developments is the sharpened war on terrorism, including the bombing of Afghanistan and the war on Iraq. It has had two contradictory effects.

On the one hand, the war on terrorism has produced new kinds of fractures in the global civic web and sharpened old or latent conflicts. But it has also contributed to strengthen cross-border networks and solidarities precisely among groups in countries whose leaderships were or came to be in conflict. This was perhaps most evident in the movement opposing the war on Iraq; in the major European countries the network of global cities became a space for shared politics, with significant numbers of residents bypassing the politics of their leaders. Even though the intensity of the experience is inevitably short-lived it set a new standard for cross-border solidarities, regardless of formal politics. There was a similar though more diluted effect at the global scale, with a sharp recognition that over 600 cities worldwide had seen anti-war demonstrations, in this case bypassing the Christian-Muslim divide so present in formal political discourse.

On the other hand, the increasingly decentralised and world-spanning networks of global civil society described in the chapter are today increasingly paralleled by those of organised terrorism. This is creating a distinctive triangulation: the war on terrorism partly plays out in the network of cities. What this might signal is not clear at this point. There are disturbing elements that put some of the infrastructure for global civil society at risk. This would be the opposite effect of the strengthening of political geographies that bypass the formal political landscape.

Among these disturbing signals are the data in the Annual Report on Patterns of Global Terrorism of the U.S. Department of State (2001; 2002) showing the growing importance of cities in these attacks. The Report provides detailed listings of incidents and places for terrorist acts. Already in the 2000 report issued on April 30 2001, that is before the September 11 attacks, the evidence is there showing the increase in urban targets over the decade. Using the Department of State data, Savitch and Ardashev (2001) report that from 1993 to 2000, cities accounted for 94% of the injuries resulting from all terrorist attacks, and for 61% of the deaths. Secondly, in the last decade the number of incidents doubled, rising especially sharply after 1998. In contrast, in the 1980s hijacked airplanes accounted for a larger share of terrorist deaths and destruction than they did in the 1990s.

A crucial issue here is that these types of threats and data should not be deployed to terrorise civilians into vigilantism or to paralise their daily lives. Rather, this type of information should be used to understand to what extent cities in both the global North and South may pay a very high price for military operations aimed at terrorists. The Bush Administration regularly alerts the US people to the certainty of a major attack inside the US. But this was and is used as an argument to justify the war on Iraq. There is another possible logical sequence here that the Bush Administration never raises in public: this type of war will tend to raise the likelihood of such attacks, and these attacks in turn make civilians, not the military, more vulnerable. The Bush team does not address the fact that US military escalation could result in increased civilian deaths in cities both in the US and abroad. A search for a statement of this sort in major newspapers from September 2001 onwards did not produce a single mention of this likelihood, supported by the government's own data, in the hundreds of articles dealing with the September terrorist attacks. The dyad of military against military, with civilian losses as collateral damage, now becomes a triangulation with the insertion of civilian populations as a key target and hence an increase in such targeting with increased military attacks.

There are a handful of cities which have particular symbolic value due to a mix of historical, political and sometimes economic conditions: New York, London and Paris as global cities, strategic to the world economy, but also with specific political histories. Then there are cities such as Athens, Istanbul, Jerusalem, Berlin and Rome. These cities are key nodes in a variety of specific cross-border regional networks and in that sense targets of international terrorism. Each of these cities is a highly visible and important site for communicating a message to a large audience, often a specific audience rather than the world. In each there are different reasons for the attacks. In New York, it was the economic and military power of the US that was being hit, not New York per se. The city is then, a concentrated site with communicative capabilities rather than the enemy as such.

A large question coming out of these conditions is whether the sharpened challenge to global civil society coming out of the war on terrorism might actually strengthen the commitment of global civic actors.

References

Savitch H. V. and Ardashev G. (2001). 'Does Terror Have an Urban Future?' *Urban Studies*. December. 38/13: 2515-2533.

U.S. Department of State (2001). *Patterns of Global Terrorism*. 30 April.

U.S. Department of State (2002). *Patterns of Global Terrorism*. 21 May.

HIV/AIDs, Global Civil Society and People's Politics

Update on Chapter 5, 2002

Hakan Seckinelgin

In the absence of treatment, global actors are prioritising care and behavioural change in the developing world. However, both are being undermined by lack of input from infected and affected people, and a failure to take into account society and culture. Take the voluntary counselling and testing (VCT) method to initiate behaviour change in most of sub-Saharan Africa. The assumption behind interventions is that once you know your status you can take control of your life and decide to abandon risky behaviour. This assumption is based on a society where there are various medical and social choices for people with HIV positive status. It also suggests that people are free to choose options which may alienate them from the community which is the primary locus of meaning in their lives. Such conditions do not exist for many people in the region. Furthermore, behavioural change needs to be supported by communities so that it can be sustained. This suggests that behaviour change needs to address the state of communities' reaction and the possibilities available within them.

Although VCT might be an important tool, without social and economic support in communities for those tested it can have negative effects. Knowing one's status does not necessarily lead to non-risky lifes-styles as many do not have social or economic options to rethink their lives. Therefore, having thousands of people tested to achieve funding guidelines will not produce the expected results, unless funders also target improving general living standards.

There are exceptional interventions which are using this understanding such as Thandizani Community Based HIV/AIDS Care and Prevention Project, Lundazi District, Zambia. Initiated by the community and supported by Zambia Integrated Health Programme (ZIHP), Thandizani presents an innovative approach. The project is based on the idea that everyone is involved in problems faced by people with HIV/AIDS, and that it is the problem of the community. Therefore, the intervention tools are located within the socio-cultural systems, and the mechanisms of change within them include using existing hierarchies of chiefs, healers and others. Rather than imposing change on community, the community is internally stimulated towards change. Thus, the VCT process has become sustainable in the community structures and that in itself has removed sources of stigma. As a result 'the HIV rate among women in Thadizani areas as of May 2001 was 16.9 per cent compared to 25.4 per cent in women from non-Thadizani areas' (Mutonyi 2003).

The failure to take gender into account is also undermining efforts to deal with the pandemic. Many programs refer to the importance of gender, but seem to target only women. The difficulty of drawing men into discussions of behaviour change, and the short time scales within which projects need to show results, make gender concerns one-sided. This means that most interventions miss the most important component of change: men. The result: men ignore the disease in their everyday lives, in many cases even after they suspect they have contracted it. The interventions are not engaging with the social contexts and communities which enable men to change behaviour; instead they deal with individuals as if they lived in empty space. Therefore, interventions also ignore the *hidden stigma* which often persists despite the assumed openness about the disease. Although much has been said about how the stigma has been dealt with, social norms still single out people infected and affected. Stigma is reinforced by many campaigns which continue to implicitly moralise against the sexual behaviour of HIV positive persons. It is clear that most policies have no understanding of how people and communities change behaviour in urban, rural, traditional, industrial, military, and school contexts, or in different age groups. They assume a standard behaviour change for individuals who are exposed to particular information, and fail to understand why, despite being given relevant information, people do not change their behaviour.

An important example of this is the behaviour of youth in Botswana where most of the services are not designed to address their concerns and needs. Condom promotion has not helped the youth, as they feel unable to talk about their sexual needs or obtain condoms openly due to the existing social norms. These norms consider talking about sex among various gender and age groups unacceptable. To deal with the situation several groups are bringing communities of infected and affected people into the discussion, for example Bawani Mutshewa of Anti-AIDS Parents Project in Botswana is working with parents to educate them, while Botswana Network for PLWHA (BONEPWA) is developing a community care system. In these schemes, the patient is not taken to be an abstract individual, but a member of a community which also needs help. It relocates people back into their communities.

Another issue is the promotion of abstention. This issue will increase in importance as it will be the main focus of US official aid. So far it has been a questionable strategy for sexually active youth. Many projects that focus on abstention do not provide strategies for abstention (See poster). Public campaigns designed to promote such ideas remain ambiguous without suggesting options to facilitate abstention. Many billboard and poster campaigns costing millions of dollars have fallen on deaf ears as they have provided no other option than no sex at all!

Despite the participation of many community activists in policy interventions, the influence of people infected and affected presents a negligible part of civil society action. The disproportionate reliance on international aid and actors presents a major challenge. As the funding is by and large external, the sustainability of many policy interventions is questionable. In most cases even successful projects are considered to be one-off events and banished to the reports. Funding for their replication is precarious.

Much civil society activity is stimulated by international NGOs. This raises problems about both funding priorities and mechanisms. Prioritising aims such as behaviour change is often attached to methods of intervention mandated by the funders, that establishes what civil society actors can and cannot do. For example the increased VCT activity and condomisation of sub-Saharan Africa seem to be working through such arrangements.

The focus of international policy-makers on civil society actors is insufficient. It is difficult to create a coherent policy framework through civil society without central coordination. Often, the messages carried in many civil society projects contradict each other and create indifference among the target groups. The disease requires engagement on the multiple fronts of health, education and economy. In the absence of basic structures creating an enabling environment for civil society actors in these fields, the impact of their work is bound to be limited. Also, the situation degenerates into a state of dependency where people can deal with their own problem *only* if they have international funding and support. Therefore, there needs to be a shift in understanding the role of governments in dealing with HIV/AIDS.

This is also linked to the need for investment in capacity building within countries. Although many civil society groups would claim that they have engaged in capacity building in their work, the sustainability of this sort of capacity is questionable. Employment of local people in international projects is hardly creating sustainable local capacity. Many key roles are filled by international staff, many of whom are working as volunteers to NGOs, governments and international groups. Although international volunteers are demonstrating solidarity with people and trying to help, this system is unsustainable and unhealthy. Volunteering seems to help at precise moments in time but does not add much in the long run, as high turnover rates make it difficult to institutionalise the experiences of volunteers working in the field. The impact of the volunteers work is not carried into future as there is no local capacity to maintain the level of engagement by providing overall policy frameworks.

All these problems require a change in the way international policy makers consider their roles, and a need to clarify why they are engaging in the field. Funding for HIV/AIDS needs to be based on social needs on the ground, not on funders' aspirations. The problems presented by HIV/AIDS cannot be solved through the conventional aid structures aimed at reducing the role of the state in a society by supporting civil society groups. HIV/AIDS requires societal interventions grounded on the capacities of state structures that can support civil society in the long term. The funding is required, but it has to be building capacity for enabling policy environments that would support the work of existing actors in the long term. It is clear that the needs of people infected and affected are urgent. However, to reduce the problem to an emergency has its own problems. Dealing with HIV/AIDS urgently needs long term thinking and attempting to understand how what is done today can influence and change tomorrow, rather than creating yet another emergency in the future.

I would like to thank Shirley Baker, Prisca B. Chitomfuna, Alison Cook, Michaela Durrant, Margaret Kalane, Andrew Kiptoo, Miyanda Kuunda, Mariola Mierzejewska, Valencia Mogegeh, Malebogo,

Poster: The message of abstention among the young is intended to delay sexual relations. However, these campaigns tend to focus on the idea of abstention while neglecting strategies which would enable people to abstain. The poster 'Masturbation Do It Yourself' produced by the Youth Health Organization (YOHO) in Botswana shows there is an alternative path. Designed by youth for the youth, the poster is clear and direct. Rather than stigmatising sex it develops alternatives. This gives it a strength over several other campaigns in the region. It should be considered as a starting point for a behaviour change campaign in which young could articulate a series of life strategies for young people to support their behavioural change. In this way the idea of abstention would become meaningful for people's lives and young people could engage with the debate through thinking about choices they have rather than put into a position of choosing between abstention or sex.

Monguakekse, Karabo Mongwaketse, David Mugo, David Mukuyamba, Kennedy Mupeli, Bawani Mutshewa, Simon Mutonyi, David Chizao Ngele, Vuyisele Otukile, Divya Rajaraman, Michelle Marian Schaan, Exhilda Siakanomba, Tumie Thahane, Walter Otis Tamfumaneyi, and Maryla Wiesniewski.

References

Mutonyi , Simon (2003) *Thandizani Community Based HIV/AIDS Care and Prevention Project*, Lundazi District, PIR Report. Zambia Integrated Health Programme.

INDEX